WINGED FAITH

WINGED FAITH

Rethinking Globalization and Religious Pluralism
Through the Sathya Sai Movement

Tulasi Srinivas

Columbia University Press   New York

Columbia University Press

Publishers Since 1893

New York Chichester, West Sussex

Library of Congress Cataloging-in-Publication Data

Srinivas, Tulasi.

   Winged faith: rethinking globalization and
religious pluralism through the Sathya Sai
movement / Tulasi Srinivas.

      p. cm.

  Includes bibliographical references and index.

   ISBN 978-0-231-14932-7 (cloth)—

   ISBN 978-0-231-14933-4 (pbk.)

   1. Sathya Sai Baba, 1926—Cult.

2. Globalization —Religious aspects.

3. Religious pluralism.   I. Title.

   BP605.S14S75 2010

   294.5092—dc22   2009043266

In memory of my father, M. N. Srinivas,
with affection, respect, and gratitude

Contents

Acknowledgments   ix
Note on Translation   xiii
List of Abbreviations   xv

Introduction: Toward Cultural Understanding   1

1. Becoming God: The Story of Sathya Sai Baba   50

2. *Deus Loci:* Economies of Faith, Sacred Travel, and the Building of a Moral Architecture   93

3. Illusion, Play, and Work in a Moral Community: Divine Darshan and the Practices of Transnational Devotion   156

4. Renegotiating the Body: Muscular Morality, Truancy, and the Satisfaction of Desire   201

5. Secrecy, Ambiguity, Truth, and Power: The Global Sai Organization and the Anti-Sai Network   232

6. Out of God's Hands: Reframing Material Worlds   282

   In Lieu of a Conclusion: Some Thoughts on Cultural Translation and Engaged Cosmopolitanism   323

Appendix   343
Notes   347
References   381
Index   413

Acknowledgments

This research was supported in part by the Pew Charitable Trust and by postdoctoral fellowships at the Center for the Study of World Religions, Harvard University, and the Berkley Center for Religion, Peace, and World Affairs at Georgetown University. I thank Peter L. Berger, director, Institute on Culture, Religion, and World Affairs, Boston University, for his ongoing support of my interest in the transnational Sathya Sai movement and his valued counsel. I also thank Tom Banchoff, director, the Berkley Center for Religion, Peace, and World Affairs, Georgetown University, for giving me time to think, and my colleagues at Georgetown University for their support during my fellowship year there.

At Boston University, thanks are due to Robert Weller and Charles Lindholm for laughs, inspiration, and for being generous enough to take the time to read unedited drafts and make supportive noises, in spite of their busy schedules, and to Robert Hefner, Merry White, Frank Korom, and Nazli Kibria, who have provided intellectual inspiration. I would also like to thank Wendy Doniger, who (whether she knows it or not) talked me out of a writing block over lunch in her house on Cape Cod, and Kirin Narayan who kindly shared her expertise, homemade pizza, and thoughts when I was intellectually lost.

Portions of this work have been presented at the American Anthropological Association meetings in 2004 and 2005, the South Asia meetings at Madison, Wisconsin in 2004, the Society for Psychological Anthropology meetings in 2005, the American Academy of Arts and Sciences, the Institute for Religion and Culture at the University of Virginia, and the Institute for Human Sciences (IWM), Vienna, in 2001. I thank my colleagues James Davison Hunter, Yunxiang Yuan, Michael Hsiao, Tamotsu Aoki, Hansfried Kellner, and Hans Soeffner, János Kovác, Ann Bernstein, Arturo Talavera, Ergun Özbudun, and E. Fuat Keyman for their helpful comments when I began this study. I have also been fortunate to have discussions with Hyun Kim and Bruce Owens at Wheaton College during the course of working on this volume.

In Bangalore I would like to thank Krishna and Aruna Chidambi, for hilarious and illuminating conversations about faith around their dining table, and Mr. and Mrs. Venkatachar, whose unstinting support of this endeavor made it workable. Thanks to the Venkatachar family in general for their love and support even though they often wondered what I was doing. Thanks to to Ravi Parthasarathy for going out of his way to share his pictures of the Sathya Sai center in Singapore. And particular thanks to Mr. Kekie Mistry, photographer to Sathya Sai Baba, and his wife Sheru who shared their knowledge of Sai devotional ways, his many photographs, and cooking tips with generosity.

My colleagues in Bangalore, Dr. V. Vijayalakshmi, who assisted me initially to collect data, and Professor G. K. Karanth of the Institute of Social and Economic Change, both helped me as I conceived of this study. The National Institute of Advanced Studies, Bangalore, provided me with a home during fieldwork. I would like to thank the then director, Dr. Roddam Narasimha, for his support and friendship. I would like to acknowledge other colleagues in Bangalore, Sundar Sarukkai, Hamsa Kalyani, Dhanvantri Nayak, for their faith and encouragement and their help at various stages of this study, either accompanying me to the Sai ashram or through endless critiques of globalization and religion in and of India.

I am indebted to my friends in Boston and other parts of America: Sarah Lamb, Isabelle Clark-Deces, and Pauline Kolenda, who also read unedited sections of this manuscript or listened to me give often incoherent talks as I worked through the data; Nicole Newendorp, Hanna Kim, and Elizabeth Bucar, who patiently read the work in its entirety many times and pushed me uphill and whose input has certainly made the book more theoretically sound and more readable; and Julia Huang, Keith McNeal, Michael Hill, and Paulo Pinto, who all had conversations with me that helped clarify my thoughts. Thanks to Rebecca Sachs Norris, Deepa Reddy,

John Zavos, Paula Richman, and Vasudha Narayanan, all of whom gave me opportunities to talk about the Sai movement at various conferences over the past several years. Most important, I have benefited enormously from continuous and wide-ranging academic discussions about contemporary India and global culture with my colleague and sister Lakshmi Srinivas, who has served as support system, inspiration, and friend all rolled into one.

I mention a few friends and colleagues who have studied the Sai movement and from whose work I draw inspiration: first and foremost Alan Babb, who gave me unstinting support and invited me to Amherst to give a talk on Sai artifacts; Chad Baumann and Norris Palmer, who have been very helpful both in sharing their written work and thoughts; and Smriti Srinivas and Alexandra Kent, who, though I never met them, gave me much to chew on.

Most recently, my colleagues at Emerson College have been very supportive in making time for me to continue with my research. My friends Donald Halstead and Helen Snively ruthlessly cut the manuscript down to a readable size and my editor Stacy Lathrop helped me enormously in making it accessible. Wendy Lochner, my editor at Columbia University Press, was supportive of this work from the beginning and her colleagues, particularly Christine Mortlock and Susan Pensak, were both professional and friendly, and it has been a wonderful and stress-free experience to work with them from my end. I also would like to thank the book design and production team at Columbia University press for accommodating my many suggestions. The anonymous reviewers who read and commented on the manuscript so generously helped make the book far more sound. Any errors in the book are solely attributable to me.

Particular thanks are due the many devotees of Sathya Sai Baba who spent their valuable time talking to me and corresponding with me about their faith. Particular acknowledgment is extended to Shanti, Leela, Anna, Trudy, Alistair, Stephen, Mr. Murthy, Mr. Iyer, Venkat and Professor S. S. Sivakumar for their unstinting support. I would also like to thank the former devotees, who sent me inordinate amounts of information, particularly Brian Steel and Barry Pittard, for sharing their thoughts, their collected material, and their networks of friends and supporters who talked to me, directed me to sources, and exchanged e-mails over many months.

Last, I would like to thank my mother, Rukmini Srinivas, who brewed me endless cups of tea, was forgiving of the time this manuscript took from her life as well as mine, saw me through the many emotional ups and downs of writing this book, and was kind and thoughtful, though I often failed to recognize her gestures at the time; my sister, Lakshmi Srinivas, for much hilarity, belief in me, and for being there when I needed her the most. And, to my spouse, Popsi Narasimhan, I owe many thanks for cheerfully resurrecting my ancient computer whenever it broke down and listening patiently to my fieldwork anecdotes and my grumbling for nine long years.

Note on Translation

Since this book deals with a transnational religious movement and the fieldwork is located in numerous countries, I have not used the scholarly system of diacritical marks and transliteration for Sanskrit, Hindi, Tamil Kannada, Urdu, or any other South Asian language terms that may appear in the text. Rather I have used popular recognizable English forms of spelling reflecting the common usage by Sai devotees and others. I generally italicize the words in the text when they derive from a South Asian language such as *avatar* (incarnation) or *bhajan* (devotional song/hymn) when they are introduced and then remove them as per the humanities style guidelines . I do not italicize sacred texts such as the Ramayana or the Rg Veda. Nor do I italicize words that are familiar to English speakers and readers such as *guru*, but it is italicized here as word qua word. When indicating a plural form I simplify and add an *s* to the end of the South Asian language term (for example, gurus). When referring to texts of the Sathya Sai movement, I generally use the spelling preferred by the author rather than the transliterated term (for example, *sanathana* rather than *sanatana*). However, the literature produced by the Sathya Sai Book and Publications Trust does not have a standard system of transliteration, so variations may occur.

List of Abbreviations

EHV	Education in Human Values Program
NRM	New Religious Movement
SCT	Sai Central Trust
SS	*Sanathana Sarathi*
SSB	*Summer Showers in Brindavan*
SSS	*Sathya Sai Speaks*
SSSIHMS	Sri Sathya Sai Institute of Higher Medical Studies

WINGED FAITH

This story is true. Of course, there are many lies therein and most of it did not happen, but it's all true. In that sense it is deeply religious, perhaps even biblical.
 —Craig Ferguson, comedian, author of Between the Bridge and the River

Truth is One and for all time, Truth is Truth. Whatever changes, know that as Untruth. —Sathya Sai Baba

Introduction
Toward Cultural Understanding

Meeting Anna and Finding a New Direction

When I arrived in my hometown of Bangalore, on a warm February night in 1998, my intention was to study the economic forces of globalization and their impact on Indian religion, particularly temple Hinduism. Globalization was at that time seen by theorists as the dominance of the culture of the West (Euro-America) upon the rest of the world (Appadurai 1996; Berger 1997), the "center upon the periphery" (Hannerz 1990: i–x) as cultural flows were thought to move from the hegemonic West to the peripheral rest of the world. India had tentatively opened its economy to global market forces in 1989, and over the following several years the Indian government hesitantly dismantled some of the archaic protectionist laws that restricted full economic participation. Nearly a decade into the process there was active debate in India, especially among the Indian middle class, about what this opening of the Indian marketplace meant for Indian society and culture, particularly in terms of morality and values. Conservative parents wrung their hands in newspaper op-ed pieces over the growing lewdness of Indian youth and blamed it on Western popular culture, as nationalist politicians echoed this worry as a drumbeat in their speeches. On the other hand, in the business section of the same newspaper, market enthusiasts salivated over an emergent middle class with the purchasing power and desire for global products. Banking, knowledge, and economic sectors pointed with pride to the growing information technology boom of India and spin doctors for politicians pushed the vision of a "fully global," "shining" India.[1] As I began my research I was filled with questions that I expected to answer: How do Indians deal with the subtle and not so subtle forces of globalization? How does it affect "Indian" "culture," particularly religion? Did many culturally "alien" ways of being enter India, as the conservative parents suggested? Was India, as a nation, overall, interested in a debate about multiculturalism?[2] If so, what form would the debate take?

But, while in Bangalore, I became lead investigator for an international university-sponsored comparative two-year project on cultural globalization. One day I was returning to Bangalore from Delhi after a fieldwork trip to study a new controversial entrant to India, the McDonalds Corporation , when I had an encounter that propelled me to examine globalization and its complex links with culture—more specifically with religion—with new eyes. I enclose the entry from my field diary for that day.

November 10, 1998. 8.00 A.M. Delhi's Palam airport. Waiting for the fog to clear. I saw a group of people all dressed in white wearing the medallions of the Sathya Sai movement that held pictures of the global guru and godman Sri [honorific] Sathya Sai Baba. A rather large woman with her hair in a bun sat down next to me. She must have been in her late sixties. She wore a white *salwar khameez* (long trousers and a tunic) and sported a beribboned medallion of Sai Baba. I stared at her beribboned chest and she caught me looking at her. I knew the "correct" way to greet Sathya Sai devotees was "Sai Ram." Her face split into a smile, "Sai Ram, Sai Ram" she said cheerfully. She then waved over her copilgrims (about twenty of them all in white) who came and surrounded us. "My name is Anna, we come from Torino," she announced. "We are here for Swami's [the Lord's] birthday. You will go for the birthday *darshan* (sacred viewing and witnessing of divinity)?" she inquired. I told her that I was not planning to participate. "There is World Congress of Religion meeting. Thousands of people come to Puttaparthi. . . . We stay for one month. After Swami's birthday we go back to Torino for Christmas. You *must* come," she continued. I felt, in spite of our short acquaintance that I was somehow letting her down by not going to the celebration, and I resented her for these unwelcome expectations for my spiritual self. So I shifted the conversation to her journey and how she had gotten to Delhi. She explained to me that they were on a package pilgrimage tour led by a long-term Sai devotee.

The fog lifted, and our flight was called. I found I was seated in the midst of the Turin devotee group. They were ecstatic, singing Hindi and Italian *bhajans* (devotional songs) to Sai Baba from takeoff to landing. Anna sat next to me. "Sing," she commanded me. I replied that I did not know the words, but it was a *bhajan* that I could easily have picked up, as the Hindu god's name to whom it was dedicated was replaced directly with Sai Baba's name, and the tune was simple and repetitive. But she accommodated my reluctance to sing, "Clap." As we clapped, she told me the story of her "coming to Swami" [the lord, i.e., Sai Baba]. "I was very sick. I woke up in the night and Swami was there. He came in my dream . . . and He said, 'Anna it will be alright. You come to me. Trust me.'" She was moved by the memory, and her eyes filled with tears. "Next week I went to church. When I came out of church I see His picture in travel agents' shop. I went in and said 'Who is that?' and the lady, she said, 'That is Swami Sathya Sai Baba from India.' I went home and told my husband, 'I am going to India.' So I came. Now when I am in Torino I go to church; when in India, I go for darshan of Swami."

I bid Anna goodbye at the Bangalore airport as she and her group joyously boarded a silver bus with saffron wing panels that read "Sathya Sai Travels." As I did so, I realized that I had been immersed in the dialogue of typical global cultural institutions (with their economic roots in Western-style capitalism), such as the McDonalds Corporation, which moved *to* India, but the Sathya Sai movement was an example of an Indian religiocultural movement that had people from different regions of the globe gravitating *toward it*. Watching Anna and her group, it seemed clear that the "global ecumene" was shifting, and it was incumbent upon social scientists like me to explore these shifting dynamics (Hannerz 1990) against the plethora of emerging and established theories of globalization and culture.

Let me clarify that, though I deal in the main with religion in the global sphere, I speak here of the broader rubric of culture for two reasons—first, because religion is subsumed under the broader expanse of culture and, second, because the scholarly literature focuses largely upon culture and globalization. So while I seek specifically to rethink religion and its complex links with globalization, defaulting to discussing culture will be inevitable when referencing theories and unpacking processes of "cultural globalization" in order to set the Sathya Sai movement against the current theories of cultural globalization and to demonstrate the lacunae in the literature when discussing the complexities of religion. It is only by understanding where the lacunae lie that we can move forward to understand how religion can, as I suggest, provide the basis for a new civil dialogue on identity in the global era. So in the following pages we will move between more general discussions of cultural globalization and more specific examinations of religion in a global era.

But, to return to my encounter with Anna; I was beset by questions . . . what did Anna's presence in Bangalore mean for the ten international project teams studying cultural globalization? What did her story and presence mean for the theoretical assumptions made by cultural globalization literature? Anna had aroused my curiosity about the seemingly successful globalization of the Sathya Sai religious movement. What was the Sathya Sai movement, and was it truly a global religious phenomenon? If so, how did people like Anna comprehend the esoteric Hindu understandings of darshan and other rituals? How did the Sathya Sai movement become global? How did it translate rituals, cultural norms, and values, rooted in Hinduism or in the syncretic Hindu-Islamic culture of the subcontinent, for the wider world? What about the identity of individuals within the movement? How did they adapt? And so on.

These questions, and many more, fed into a nine-year-long ethnographic study that detailed the existence and growth of the transnational Sathya Sai movement as a "religion" in the transglobal economies of capital spirituality, affect and cultural identity. Let me state that I use the term "movement" reservedly to describe the loose compilation of practices, behaviors, organizational armatures, strategies, structures, spaces and memories that originate from and surround Sathya Sai Baba, since, as Csordas notes, the term *movement* is questionable to apply to any charismatic religious phenomenon (1997:42–43). Charles White (1972:866) situates Sathya Sai Baba in the tradition he refers to as the Sathya Sai movement, which has roots in the syncretic Hindu-Muslim culture of saints and mystics. Recent scholars working on the Sathya Sai movement have argued that it is in fact a separate "sect" within Hinduism, though it has not been historically linked, as sects traditionally have, to caste-based and local identity constructs in India. The Sathya Sai movement has also been called a "revitalization movement within Hinduism," a "neo-Hindu" movement with links to Indian nationalist enterprises, and a "new religious movement" that is transnational. I suggest, as does sociologist Smriti Srinivas, who also notes her problems with the term *movement* in her recent work on Sai Baba (2008:17), that we must be nuanced in our articulation of boundaries between the nomenclature since the Sathya Sai movement appears to fit many of the criteria: it is global (in the sense that it is based on practices and ideas spawned in one culture that have moved to another culture and been translated), universalizing (as it seeks to go beyond one single religious tradition and culture), international in its organizational structure (as it straddles several time zones, locales, and countries), and postmodern (as it imbricates postcolonial histories and trajectories), and it invents new logics, hermeneutics, and praxes of faith (Palmer 2005:97, 100). However, from an insider's perspective, devotees themselves do not call their community of faith a movement. If they use the term, it refers to a lifestyle of faith (*sampradaya*) or a movement "of the spirit," indicating that it is a personal relationship between Sathya Sai Baba and the individual devotee. In this sense the sociocultural aspect of the movement is subordinated to the spiritual. So although using the term *movement* best describes the collective of Sai faithful, this work also problematizes the term as it questions the cohesiveness of devotional behavior, the construction of meaning through social dynamics of the devotees, the phenomena of Sai devotion as seen as evocative of Indian and Hindu culture, and the role of transformation of selfhood within the religious phenomenon.

But while I examine the problematic intersections between globalization and religion with the specific focus of rethinking both, when speaking specifically of the Sathya Sai movement, I recognize it to be a religious movement in the main I will also occasionally, when dealing with theoretical constructs describe it as a religiocultural movement, and my theorizing will move between *religion* (when I am being specific) to the broader *culture* (as a general frame). This terminology may be troubling to some, and I recognize it as such, but it is expedient.

But Anna's presence in Delhi raised for me the issue around which the Indian debate about globalization and culture (in which religion played a prominent part) revolved—of the politics of cultural reinvention and cultural transmission—the unequal playing field created by the history of colonization, racial and national inequalities, and the structure of capitalism that weighted the process toward the West across cultural divides.

This issue is at the core of problematizing the process of cultural global-ization. Questioning these politics cuts to the center of the debate on glo-balization and religion: the need for a non Euro-American-centered defi-nition of a cosmopolitan culture and imagination suited to living in an increasingly plural world (Appiah 2006; Nussbaum 2007; Sen 2006; Hannerz 1990). Such a focus leads naturally to a larger examination of the relationship between subjects, objects, and power in the global frame. It suggests that a sophisticated understanding of our contemporary world implies a reconstruction and reorientation of complex subject positions through a reevaluation of process, language, space, embodiment, emo-tion, and gesture.

A more complex picture of the reality of the tensions of plural societies raises the discussion of what it takes to share public life in a plural na-tion. As Prime Minister Jawaharlal Nehru said, some sixty years ago on the eve of India's independence, "all nations and peoples are too closely knit together today for any one of them to imagine they can live apart." I suggest that, as it globalizes, the achievement of imagination of the Sathya Sai movement is the creation of a metatext of meaning: what I shall call a "matrix of possible meanings" that is rooted in the plural, the ambiguous, the plastic, and the layered, which devotees can differentially interpret to create what Sandhya Shukla has epigrammatically termed a "grammar of diversity" (2008). This grammar can be productive toward the construction of a possible language of what I call, for lack of a better term, *engaged cosmopolitanism*. Rather than the domestication of other-ness, which has been the modus operandi for plural societies located in the Euro-American center, I suggest that engaged cosmopolitanism lo-cated both in a lucrative strategic ambiguity and in an alternate under-standing of plurality enables the Sathya Sai movement, and perhaps other religiocultural movements that emerge out of the periphery, to better navi-gate the opportunities and dangers of the multiculturalist societies of the future, a destination that, I suggest, the processes of globalization brings inexorably closer.

I argue that through a study of the Sathya Sai Baba case—an Indic, civil, charismatic religiocultural movement—we come to the rather more general understanding of the two established dialogues within popular and scholarly understandings of globalization and religion, that is, be-tween the opposing forces of equality, tolerance, and respect leading to a language of cosmopolitanism and the twinned policy of multicultural-ism and, oppositionally, an ethnic, linguistic, or religious homogeneity achieved through dominance often associated with fundamentalist agendas.[3] The contemporary understanding of diversity is *the* question of our age. But it is often politically muddied and distorted through well-meaning maneuvers and is therefore the subject of much contestation. It is imperative, I humbly suggest, that we create a theoretical language to speak of the challenges of pluralism and its legal twin multiculturalism.

But I contend that, in order to engage the transformative language of engaged cosmopolitanism, it is necessary to look not at the *why* of globalization, as scholars have done thus far, but at the *how* of globalization, the processes and subprocesses that fuel the transformation of cultural globalization and cultural transmission. A focus on the processual in cultural globalization toward constructing a schema of how cultural globalization works will move us in the direction of more productive theorizing. I contend that an examination of the example of the transnational Sathya Sai movement may offer a starting point for the creation of such a language, and, in so doing, the reclamation of religion for a liberal dialogue on globalization may not be such an impossible task as it currently appears.

To make a persuasive argument I must, I realize, 1. demonstrate that the transformation is located in the mundane and widespread that it is transmissible, 2. demonstrate that the mundane is made into the meaningful, 3. that the transformed meanings are mobile, global, and reflect new ways of seeing the world (Csordas 1994a, b), and 4. that numbers of people are affected by these changes. Through an examination of the everyday lives of Sathya Sai devotees—embodiment issues, proxemics and mobility, institutional architectures, political space, aesthetics, emotions, narratives, commodities, and selfhood—this transformation of meaning and the politics of knowledge and interpretation challenges that accompany the cultural and spatial logics of a modern global religiosity are discussed in the following pages.

Watching Anna and her group that November morning, I realized that globalization was no longer, and perhaps never was, a movement of goods, ideologies, and ways of being solely from "West to rest." In the following pages I argue that the Sathya Sai movement reverses the *usually perceived* flow of such transglobal economies and emits to the global ecumene rather than simply receiving. I do not aim to suggest that the Sathya Sai movement is unique in emitting into the global network, nor am I the first to suggest global culture flows in many directions, but the exploration of the Sathya Sai movement under this rubric of analysis

leads to some other interesting questions regarding how deeply culturally embedded theaters, performance, embodiments, values, notions of
moral stakeholding and institutional structures are translated to allow
them to "go global." Through an in-depth, focused analysis of the Sathya
Sai movement, I seek a conceptual mapping of the project of cultural
globalization by focusing on two main processes: *flows and translations*.

A secondary concern in this work is with positioning the Sathya Sai
movement within two ideas that I see as similar but not identical: a kind
of postmodern condition that characterizes contemporary ways of being
and the condition of globalization. I follow Baudrillard and Heelas and
Woodhead to tease out an imbrication of the postmodern and the global
and the confusing links and oppositions that these ideas suggest as they
interweave through the Sathya Sai movement. It appears, as Kent notes
(2005), that the Sathya Sai movement is seen as an antidote to the negative conditions of late modern culture (consumption, hedonism, loss of
identity, loss of metanarratives of transcendence, etc.) as are many religious and spiritual faith groups, while, at the same time, it is a product of
modernity, particularly late modernity (Weiss 2005). This dual existence
leads to conundrums and paradoxes within which interpretative issues
emerge that need to be solved on a daily ad hoc basis by devotees and organization alike. The study suggests that plurality must be supported by
a comfort with paradox and questions the application of current understandings of cosmopolitanism emergent from European philosophic
roots to the anthropological enterprise.

Introducing the Sathya Sai Movement

The Sathya Sai movement is sixty-five years old and has a single
identifiable charismatic leader—Shri (honorific) Sathya Sai Baba (b.
1926). His personal prefix, *Sathya* (truth), refers both to his given name
of Sathyanarayana as well as to the quality his devotees believe him to
embody. Sathya Sai Baba's birth in a rural, dominant-caste peasant family on November 23, 1926, in the remote village of Puttaparthi in the
Rayalseema district (boundaries of kings) of the South Indian state of
Andhra Pradesh, was, according to apostolic texts, accompanied by divine signs heralding the birth of a great soul.[4] His compassion, intelligence, musical skill, his magical materializations of food and sweets and
his healing abilities were all seen as signs of future greatness (Bauman

2007:1–2). After suffering a series of seizures and falling into trances, he declared his greatness at the age of thirteen and proclaimed that he was Sai Baba, a reincarnation of Shirdi Sai Baba, a Muslim saint from Maharashtra who had died in 1918. Many (including his family) were suspicious of his claims and recommended exorcism or institutionalization, but he reportedly substantiated his claims with miraculous acts. For example, Sathya Sai Baba, as he had come to be known, regularly materialized healing *vibhuti*, sacred ash which devotees imbibe and/or apply to their foreheads. These materializations established Sathya Sai Baba's connection to Shirdi Sai Baba, who had also materialized *vibhuti* for his followers (Bauman 2007:1–2; Srinivas 2008:40–42, 76–77).

In 1963 Sai Baba suffered another seizure, which left him unconscious and unable to communicate. After a few days he appeared before his followers in a hemiplegic state and stated that he had taken on the sickness of a devotee in order to save his life. He took water into his right hand and sprinkled it on his paralyzed left, thereby effecting a cure. He then announced that he was not only Shirdi Sai Baba reincarnated but also Shiva and Shakti (Shiva's consort, embodied divine feminine power). Accordingly, Sathya Sai Baba is most frequently associated, iconographically and in bhajans, with Shiva. However, drawing from the widespread Hindu belief that all gods and goddesses are but manifestations of one divine principle, Sai Baba and his followers claim that all names creatively include many other divine and semidivine figures, as we will see in the following pages. So the Sathya Sai movement draws seamlessly from several great strands of religion in the subcontinent—Sufi mysticism and popular Hinduism in its Vedanta form, contemporary Christian teachings and indigenous healing rituals—to weave a constantly evolving Indic urban syncretism in which the problems of dogma, creed, and literature appear to magically fade into the background as also problems of divisions of caste, class, nationality, and religion.[5] Bharathi argues against such simplification of complex Hindu thought: "Antagonism toward scholastic, tradition and primary-source oriented Hinduism goes so far that non-Hindu religious idioms are frequently preferred to orthodox parlance. Simplistic statements about the love of Christ, the renunciation of Jesus, or Sufi-Islamic mystics occur rather more frequently in Renaissance talk than references to the Brahmin masters of the commentary" (1962:285). But devotees abide by what Sai Baba says in his sermons and talks, and it is his articulation of any intention, problem, or solution that is important in the devotee's mind.

So Sathya Sai Baba is thought by some to be a charismatic guru (teacher) and by others to be a reincarnated Muslim seer (*faqir*), a saint, or an *avatar* (incarnation) of God. He[6] is called *Bhagawan* (God) by devotees, or, fondly, *Baba* or *Swami* (Lord).[7] He, in turn, addresses them as *bangaru* (Telugu = the golden ones). In his discourses, which number tens of thousands, he has divided his life into four phases, each of sixteen years: during the first sixteen he engaged in mischief and playful pranks (*balalilas*), during the second he performed miracles (*mahimas*), for the third sixteen-year segment he dedicated himself to general teaching (*upadesh*), while still performing miracles, and in the last segment (which would have begun around 1984) he has dedicated his life to teaching select devotees his spiritual discipline (*sadhana*). He has predicted his own death at the age of ninety-six, but his body, it is said, will remain young until then (Bauman 2007:5–6).[8] Apostolic and apologetic accounts of Sathya Sai Baba's life make riveting reading woven through with magical interludes, self-proclaimed revelations of divinity, and dramatic contestations and confessions (Srinivas 2008:67–75).

Chapter 1 focuses upon Sathya Sai Baba's life story the politics and translation of his sacred personhood. The chapter consists of two interlocking parts that are easily apprehended: first, the transformation of Sathya Sai Baba's divinity from local guru to global godman, which is a complex articulation spanning the logics of Hindu divinity and postmodern individuality to construct a universally mobile charisma, and, second, an anxious transformation in the selfhood of the devotee through the listening and absorbing of the life story of Sathya Sai Baba. I am concerned with how, through his life story, the possibility of transformation is introduced and how the fourfold paradigm of his sacred humanity is interpreted by devotees to envision possibilities of transformation within their own lives where Indic categories of religious personhood are used to extend into new cultural realms through the creation of what I call "nomadic charisma." The politics of interpretation of a culturally embedded understanding of an intersection of sacredness and personhood is at issue. An illuminating translation failure occurs, for example, when devotees attempt to equate Sathya Sai Baba with Jesus Christ.

Between 1940–1950 Sathya Sai Baba's following grew slowly within India from south to the north, creating a pan-Indian movement. By 1950 the movement had garnered enough support and some wealthy devotees to fund the building of an ashram called Prasanthi Nilayam (abode of supreme peace) in Sai Baba's hometown of Puttaparthi in the arid Rayalseema (boundaries of kings) district in rural Andhra Pradesh state. The ashram grew rather rapidly into an international movement, primarily through the efforts of a few individuals from California who were brought to Puttaparthi by Indira Devi, an entrepreneurial devotee. The American counterculture movement of the 1960s, fueled by an international cultural need to find in Indian spirituality an opposition to Western rationality and greed, led to a spiritual seeking in India as an expression of the zeitgeist. Hundreds if not thousands of young Americans and Europeans came to India to find *their* guru. A few became devotees of Sai Baba in the mid 1970s and wrote the first devotional books that soon became a flood of devotional literature that introduced Sai Baba to the larger world. This effort was matched by the now functional Sai organization comprised of many subsidiary institutions that issued collected translations of Sathya Sai Baba's many discourses, creating a newsletter called *Santhana Sarathi* (the way of the charioteer; an analogy to the Mahabharata's divine charioteer Krishna), several journals as well as other keepsakes. The bookshops stocking devotional literature run by the Sai movement became central to the globalizing efforts of the early movement, and they remain integral to the institutional structure of the movement even today. This unorganized proselytization effort was also enabled by devotees' assertion that Sai Baba had "called" them to him, and many devotees arrived in Puttaparthi claiming they had been summoned to his side. Today devotees claim that Web sites and material objects act as portals to call devotees to Sai Baba. When I visited Puttaparthi, I saw several thousand devotees present everyday for darshan coming from South Africa, the Netherlands, Chile, Germany, Australia, Taiwan, Japan, Spain, and more.[9]

Chapter 2 begins with an examination of the nature of contemporary "spiritual travel" to the Sathya Sai ashram in Puttaparthi where the metaphor of the journey and the figure of the stranger, combined with the increasingly universal experience of displacement, are at the center of the examination. Sathya Sai Baba lives in the remote village of Puttaparthi in the Anantapur district of southwestern rural Andhra Pradesh, one of the driest regions of India, about 150 kilometers (110 miles) from the city of Bangalore, and does not leave the ashram, so devotees have to travel to the ashram to experience darshan and be close to him. I expand the investigation, looking at the physical journey that devotees take to Puttaparthi, to explore the contemporary aesthetic practices of travel and the vision of spiritual surfeit they represent. Further, the architecture of the ashram and of Puttaparthi city is unique, and devotees who travel there often say they find it "beautiful" and "awe inspiring." The architecture are, as S. Srinivas notes, metonymical of his charisma and provide insights for an understanding of sacred scapes and urban hermeneutics (2008; Orsi 1999): the relationship between religious mythical imagery and the production of urban space, understandings of affect or memory, of mobility and charisma. I look at the buildings, particularly the gateways of the city, and the spaces of Puttaparthi, the schools, colleges, dormitories, and the recently built Chaitanya Jyothi Museum, over time as an apparatus of devotion and as a destination both real and imagined. The central devotional space of Puttaparthi and the network of Sai transnational spaces of devotion and worship—devotees' altars in Bethesda, Boston, Bangalore, and London, Sai centers in Tokyo, Singapore, Wimbledon, and Hollywood, Sai bookstores in Tustin and Puttaparthi, Sai temples in Toronto, , and Mumbai, Sai schools in Puttaparthi and Guadalajara—link together in a network of postmodern devotional enspacement. These spaces are central texts to explore the hermeneutics of devotion through spatial production and usage. The chapter focuses upon the mobility of these exemplar architectures of devotion to remote destinations and examines the complexity of cultural and spatial transformation. My concern is with the broader patterns of belonging, the construction of devotional narratives of "being and becoming" part of the Sai community motivated by the need to outline the processes of individual transformation toward a communitarian ideal set against the backdrop of cultural translation and I look at how the architecture symbolizes this transformation for devotees and acts persuasively to enable it.

Estimates vary widely and depend at least in part on definitions, but Sai Baba is said to have somewhere between 5 and 50 million followers worldwide, with perhaps one half to one third of those followers located in India and the rest elsewhere. The Sathya Sai movement—which, according to self-reporting, has between 6,000 and 8,000 centers[10] and 50 million devotees all over the globe—is rapidly growing in the West and East Asia.[11] Some sources within the movement provided a figure of 3,050[12] centers in approximately 167 countries all over the world in 2001.[13] A likely figure of devotional strength suggested by the news magazine *India Today* is 20 million in 137 countries. The Sathya Sai movement is known to be the largest faith-based foreign exchange earner for India, earning approximately Indian Rs 881.8 million (approximately $5 million) for the year 2002–2003, [14] and their net worth is approximately $6 billion.[15] The Sai international following is not confined to the Indian, primarily Hindu diaspora (Klass 1991; Babb 1986), though they form a significant part of the devotional base, but has expanded to include the middle classes of many different countries and cultures (T. Srinivas 2002). During the first half of the movement's life (approximately between 1950–1975) the devotees appeared to be largely lower middle class and rural, with a smattering of very wealthy urban devotees, but in the past three decades the devotional base has become largely middle class and urban, though one can still see in Puttaparthi vestigial groups of lower-middle-class and rural devotees. The devotees—professional, techno-cratic, "Westernized" (Kent 2004, 2005), or what sociologist Smriti Srinivas calls an "urban following" (2008)—are characterized by their mobility, their affluence, and their focus on creating a healthy union be-tween body, spirit, and mind (Heelas and Woodhead 2005:75–79) and Sai Baba is what Weiss aptly calls "a prophet of the jet-set more than he is a guru of peasants" (2005:7). Socially, they strive for a "better society" defined as less poverty, cruelty, inequality, and other forms of repression. Politically, they are relatively inactive, but their beliefs appear to include a politically liberal, feminist, environmentally conscious viewpoint. The mission of the Sai movement is the "establishment of Dharma (righ-teousness)" on earth (Sandweiss 1975:89). But there is no formal doctrine for the movement, though thousands of books are published detailing Sai Baba's many discourses and established and recommended practices to encourage dharmic behavior. So, while Babb describes the Sai doc-trine deprecatingly as having "relatively little to dwell upon, or at least nothing very distinctive philosophical views are simplistic, eclectic and entirely unoriginal (1983:117), in actuality, as Knet suggests, the "lack of doctrinal originality" allows for the contention that Sai faith "rekindles awareness of eternal truths not to invent new ones" (2005:57). Their sim-plicity makes them accessible to a broad audience and their eclecticism makes them appealing to people of many cultures.

Twice a day, every day, at dawn and nearing dusk, Sathya Sai Baba gives darshan (witnessing of divinity/sacred viewing) of himself to devo-tees who come from all over the world to gather in the ornate Sai Kulwant Darshan Hall at Prasanthi Nilayam. Devotees witness his *anubhava* (di-vine grace), as he walks through the crowds of devotees gathered, and a few "lucky" ones receive his blessings or communicate their hopes to him through letters, whilst the rest wait in hope for another day. For this darshan devotees spend the better part of the day queuing around the ashram to obtain "good" seats close to where Sai Baba may sit or walk, and yet they claim that the places they receive in the audience chamber are all due to Sathya Sai Baba's *leela* (divine play) and therefore cannot be predicted by lowly mortals. This twice-daily darshan accommodates roughly five to nine thousand devotees everyday And part of the ritual includes magical materializations for devotees of sacred gifts such as images of Sathya Sai Baba, sacred healing *vibhuti* (ash), which devotees consume, and healings of devotees by Sai Baba's touch. Devotees may often wait many months in order to interact with Sai Baba and see this wait, with its daily emotions of expectation and rejection, as part of the work of becoming a good Sai devotee. They construct a discourse of oppositions between the Sai leela and the work of devotion where "true" devotion is rewarded by Sai Baba's attention, which in turn is believed to arouse a need for self-transformation in the devotee that is harnessed for communitarian ideals.

Chapter 3 thus focuses upon the magical encounter of darshan, the centerpoint of a devotee's desire: the need to see Sathya Sai Baba and be seen by him. The chapter is concerned with the relationship between illusion, transformation, and democracy for the moral discourse of the Sai communities in various locations. The performance of sacred spectating is analyzed, in concordance with the dominant Indic theological discourse of divine play and illusion, to unearth the embedded Indic concept of magicality and the logics of unveiling of divinity. Sacred spectating is seen as translated from this magicality to a global therapeutic paradigm in which devotees "find themselves" in a self-defined moment of transformation when converted by Sathya Sai Baba, the Sathya Sai Organization, and devotees, which is then translated to an overt attempt at transforming the habitus through moral stakeholdership and civic participation that rests on a therapeutic rhetoric of building a "better world." The translation of the idea of the healing of self to healing of the world through a strategic shift is at the center of this chapter. It examines what is proper public discursive space for civic religious discourse, arguing that Sai Baba changes both the audience for public theology as well as the parameters of good citizenry. My concern in this chapter is to evaluate the efficacy of magical thinking in constructing a politics of exemplar devotion to aid development. The transformation from postmodern understandings of individual good to common good problematizes the complex links between moral citizenship, public responsibility, and cosmopolitanism toward a conceptualization of the role for public, civic, engaged belief in the contemporary world.

An early emblem of the Sathya Sai Organization consisted of a five-petaled lotus flower displaying on its petals symbols from five "world" religions (Hinduism, Christianity, Islam, , Zoroastrianism, and Buddhism) and at its center the lamp of knowledge. More recently, Jewish devotees asked for their religious symbol to be included and so in some cases the Zoroastrian fire is replaced by the Star of David. The symbol of the ecumenism of the Sai faith (the *Sarva Dharma* image) is found on all official communiqués of the Sathya Sai movement and in iconic form in every Sai center in the world. Doctrinally, as well, the Sai faith is ecumenical, drawing ideas from all major world religions. In 1995 to that emblem was added another, also with five petals , on which are written the Sai faith's five central values: truth, nonviolence, love, peace, and right conduct, and the two symbols are used interchangeably. The universalism of Sai faith and its enactment through an institutional edifice that links hundreds of Sai centers all over the globe is central to any analysis of a successful global religious movement .

Sai Baba's followers have created an international institutional edifice, which is managed by the Shri Sathya Sai Central Trust (also called the Sai Central Trust or known by the acronym SCT), and active through various branches of the International Sai Organization (or International Sathya Sai Baba Organization). The International Sai Organization (ISO) is involved in service to humanity—distributing aid to the poor (especially those in wartorn or natural disaster zones; Palmer 2005:117), providing potable water to communities in need, establishing educational institutions and supporting medical facilities, homeless shelters, food banks, clothing drives, festival dinners, hospital visits, free clinics, and other participatory social services. The Sathya Sai charitable work is understood by most to be the least controversial and most laudable aspect of the worldwide mission. Some, though not all,of this activity takes place in India concentrated around Prasanthi Nilayam, where the ISO runs top-notch schools and universities and manages state-of-the-art medical facilities staffed by doctors from all over the world who provide health care free of charge. Devotees spend considerable time doing *seva* (charitable work) as part of their mission to heal the world of contemporary problems and to transform themselves into better people. In contemporary understandings, faith-based stakeholdership and citizenship are seen as mutually exclusive. Using the Sathya Sai example, we can examine how religious actors operate in the social realm within plural democracies, their activities, valorizations, and objectives, and the consequences of their involvement.

The ISO also projects Sai's mission abroad, largely through a network of Sai Baba Centers all over the world. The Sathya Sai Baba Central Council of America's Web site (www.sathyasai.org) includes information on nearly two hundred U.S. Sai centers in forty-three states (Bauman 2007:5–9). Organizationally the devotees are divided into three wings by the transnational Sathya Sai Seva Organization (SSSO)—the service wing, the education wing, and the devotion wing based on their interest and aptitude and are assigned to various zones based on their country of origin.[16] Each zone may consist of various nations—for example, zone 1 consists of the United States and Canada—and regions with local chapters. The local chapters and centers emphasize education in the Sai faith's five central values: truth (*sathya*), right conduct (*dharma*), nonviolence (*ahimsa*), love for God and God's creatures (*prema*), and peace (*shanti*). Education in these and other human values is central to the mission of Sai Baba Centers, and indeed to the guru's entire organization, which has established schools around the globe for their perpetuation, as well as a curriculum in human values for use in Bal Vikas (children's spiritual education) classes. This curriculum, now called Sathya Sai Educare, was, until recently, called Sathya Sai Education in Human Values. Each chapter invariably has a meeting place in either a temple or a devotees' home. Thus devotees are linked hierarchically through the organization to Sathya Sai Baba, the charismatic head of the spiritual movement (Srinivas 2008:1–2). The global Sai organization did not have a dramatic history for the first thirty years of the movement (between 1940–1970), but in the past two decades it has undergone moments of crisis, with ideological and leadership struggles linked to scandals within the ashram.

The most recent and significant crisis was the death of four youth in the Sai ashram in 1993, which brought in its wake allegations of "sexual healing" popularly understood to be sexual misconduct with minor boys against the Sai organization and Sathya Sai Baba himself (Bharathi 1962:284).[17] The most talked about controversy was Sathya Sai Baba's magical materializations, filmed and aired in a BBC documentary in 2004, in which it was suggested that the materializations were nothing more than skillful prestidigitation, which angered devotees worldwide (Weiss 2005). The materializations have historically been seen as problematic by rationalist and skeptic organizations within India since the 1970s and formed the basis for early anti-Sai rhetoric, but in the past decade the sexual healing controversy has overtaken the materialization debate, and anti-Sai activism has organized itself globally around it (Palmer

2005:119–121). Allegations of corruption,[18] fiscal mismanagement, conspiracy, abuse,[19] and even murder by a significant though small global
anti-Sai movement, comprised primarily of former devotees, has en-
sued.[20] Despite his critics' claims of malfeasance, Sai Baba has never been
accused (much less convicted) of wrongdoing in an Indian court of law
(Bauman 2007:5). Most devotees consider the various accusations untrue,
a side effect of Sai Baba's international fame and popularity, and we will
examine the politics of difference that concealed knowledge—seen to be
a necessity by the Sai organization, given the many accusations made
against it—and the opposing yet matching force of transparency, a stri-
dent call made by the "former devotees " of Sai Baba, creates and substan-
tiates between stranger and insider, between the magical and mundane.
Concealed knowledge is an essential part of the global world through
copyright protection and intellectual property rights. Transparency is also
an accepted part of the lexicon of the postcolonial world through calls for
transparent practices of government and "open" democratic procedures.
What is hidden, therefore, has as much bearing—perhaps more—on cultural translation as knowledge of that which is accessible and the precise
nexus between ineffable knowledge and the politics of knowledge is the
key problem that I will try to unpack through a consideration of the prob-
lematics of secrecy, the assumptions of acceptable structures of "truth,"
and the imbricated construction of new meanings that question contemporary understandings of truth, and its complex relationship to trust, in a
globalized world.

So Chapter 4 is concerned with the important relationship between democracy, transparency, and theology toward a discussion of the "appropriate" paradigm for knowledge construction and interpretation in global organizations and social voluntary movements. It focuses on the global Sai
organization, which did not have a dramatic history for the first forty years
of the movement (between 1940 and 1980) but in the past two decades has
had moments of crisis and conflicting ideological and leadership struggles.
Discussing the allegations of "sexual healing" unearths a series of new
issues that potentially act as roadblocks on the path of cultural globalization: the translatability of the culturally embedded concept of Indic asceticism as a necessary construct of divinity; the various understandings of
"sexual healing"; the discussion of the hermeneutics of certain acts and the
different conceptions of morality encased within; and, finally, the problems
of power and control that these issues raise for a transnational movement. I
examine the allegations as a way of penetrating the "habit of concealment"

and the "strategies of secrecy" that pervade the many complex levels of the Sathya Sai Organization, which informs the problem of penetration of the opacity of everyday life through social contestation of what are considered basic values. The potential denouement of Sathya Sai Baba over the issue of sexual healing brings into question the different cultural valorizations and contestatory meanings of a single act; a moral collision. I examine the relationship between "truth" and perception, arguing that it provides an exciting moment where the processes and structure of cultural translation are put to the test.

Within the ashram, encoded bodily ascetic prescriptions, including powerful daily liturgical practices of recitation of prayers, naming and remembering of the Sai divinity (*namasmarana*), of attending darshan, of dressing modestly, eating a *sattvic* (pure) diet, singing devotional bhajans, reading sacred texts (such as Sai Baba's discourses), engaging in Sai worship, and prayer dominate the everyday experience of devotees. The "everyday" or De Certeauist mundane, repetitive, and almost unthinking daily praxes of eating, sitting, praying, singing, dreaming, working, and other unnamed sensory, extrasensory, somatic, kinetic, tactile, and aural receptors and prophylactics become ritualized as embodied hermeneutic pathways for devotees, creating "new ways of being" and erasing the self through discipline, a central ingredient of self-transformation (Comaroff and Comaroff 1991, 1992, 1993). Codification of these transformative rituals enables them to be made mobile, which is crucial for their spread through the network of cultural globalization. In the following pages I am concerned with the metonymical relationship between the body and self for Sai devotees and the differing cultural valorizations of embodiment, liberty, and selfhood engaged in the transnational milieu.

The study focuses on the spaces of the globalized devotional body, what Csordas refers to as "the indeterminate field defined by perceptual experience and mode of presence and engagement with the world" (Csordas 1994:12). Using the work of Turner (1982), Csordas (1994, 1997), and Douglas (1989 [1966]), embodied social, charismatic, emotional, and devotional orderings, including phenomenological understandings, spatial orientations, and the politics of resistance are explored by focusing upon the microgeographies of daily spiritual life, questioning the categories of "language"(semiotics) and "experience" (phenomenology) constructed by Ricoeur (1991a, b).

Chapter 5 examines encoded bodily ascetic prescriptions, including powerful daily liturgical practices of prayer, *namasmarana*, darshan, dressing modestly, pure diet, bhajans, and sacred texts such as Sai Baba's discourses-. I argue that these contextualized practices—ritual radicalized and yet made quotidian—creates an orderly world of the senses—what S. Srinivas has called a "somatic" embodied regime inhabited by the devotee. First of all, the chapter reflects on a politics of knowledge that shapes conceptions of devotion and desire through an analysis of the transnational Sathya Sai movement's conception of somatic experiences and the varying emotional and moral values inherent in and assigned to these conceptions. I argue that the codification of these transformative rituals enable them to be made mobile, crucial for their spread through the network of cultural globalization. But the data suggests that the Sai religious self is thought to be deliberately reconstructed through cognitive, corporeal, and emotional building blocks of ascetic experience, what Bourdieu calls the "socially informed body" (Bourdieu 1977), which, in turn, provide the language for the larger symbolic world of Sai devotion. So, secondly, this chapter will examine the bodily rules within the ashram, their implementation by the transnational Sathya Sai Seva organization, and the problems this implementation creates for Sai devotees from different cultures at the central Sathya Sai ashram in Puttaparthi in South India. The failure of certain devotees to abide by the ashram rules illuminates differential understandings of embodiment, salvation, desire, and discipline that speak to problems in the process of cultural translation. I am concerned in this chapter with the relationship between the body and self for Sai devotees, as I question the differing cultural valorizations of embodiment, liberty, and selfhood located in contradictory culturally embedded understandings of desire and self-control. Needless to say, Sathya Sai Baba's image is instantly recognizable by cognoscenti, lower to upper middle class, all over the world, but his image is distinctive even to nondevotees. His long saffron robe, which some scholars have labeled "effeminate" (Bowen 1988:149–151), his graceful gliding walk, his smile, and his electrically charged jet black hair (which Americans refer to as an afro or fro) are unforgettable.[21] Devotees know by rote byte-sized popular, often rhythmic, sayings attributed to Sathya Sai Baba. Calligraphic graffiti of these sayings and his image adorn all sorts of unexpected places, signifying a devotional space that others of the faith recognize. I found one of his sayings, "Love all, serve all," etched behind the cash register at the Hard Rock Café, in central London,[22] and another, "Help ever, hurt never," adorning the plastic tops on Seven Stars yogurt containers from the biodynamic dairy farm in Pennsylvania.[23] They adorn the backs of autorickshaws (three-wheel vehicles) in India and are popular on electronic greeting cards that devotees send one another (Srinivas 2008:5–7). I found the Satya Sai Nag Champa incense (said to be Sathya Sai Baba's favorite incense) in a new age shop in Burlington, Vermont;[24] DVDs feature various bands that dedicate their songs to him, including the controversially named "Lightstorm,"[25] are available in airport bookshops all over India and the Middle East; and small pictures of him can be seen in homes and commercial establishments from Manchester to Tokyo.

The proliferation of his image, and through them the extension and growth of his power, is enabled through these many networked portals— Internet, music, radio, books and television. His presence proliferates in every kind of media (Feike 2007). Web sites constructed by technophile devotees feature photographs of him, both historical and contemporary, music, events at centers around the world, maps, useful tips about traveling to India, books, merchandise and links to other sites that deal with his life and work. His audio sermons play endlessly on a global radio channel owned by the Sai Central Trust (Sai Global Harmony), as a "news" bulletin and commentary on the Internet (Heart 2 Heart), and in videos, news items, documentary movies (both pro and anti) (Feike 2007:48– 60,). He has recently created a Monopoly-style board game about spiritual life and the everyday, appropriately titled Life Is a Game, Play It!" and is the central character in a comic book, *Sai Baba for Beginners*.[26] His image graces a huge array of items, from jewelry gifted by him to devotees, sculptures and life-size photographs worshipped by devotees, to kitsch such as calendars, snowglobes, incense boxes, and cushions that are eagerly purchased in Puttaparthi and Sai centers all over the world. The growing cultural and religious self-awareness of Sai devotees as consumers of religious objects transforms their markets, distribution strategies, and their consumer behavior. I find Sai religious consumer culture of interest as an example of an intersection between a global consumer culture and faith. Though studies very often acknowledge or include the interdisciplinary character of non-Abrahamic religious consumer culture, there is still a need for a comprehensive analysis of its many aspects.

Chapter 6 demonstrates how the devotional politics of belonging get interpreted in the consumption of religious objects and religious media. The chapter describes the Sai sacred objects and the "ideal" method of acquisition of the object- through a personal gift from Sathya Sai Baba to the devotee. However, not all devotees can receive these gifts, and so the chapter explores the multiple networks of trade, transaction, and distribution Sai sacred objects that are not gifted directly to devotees travel and inhabit. Offering multiple ethnographies of the Sai objects as they pass through many hands—Sathya Sai Baba, devotees, traders, and members of the Sai organization—the chapter demonstrates how globalization shapes and reshapes these sacred objects through a continuous, often oppositional, and largely unacknowledged dialogue between the various parties. I examine how the Sai sacred objects are seen to legitimate Sai Baba's long-distance charismatic authority for the transnational devotee base through innovative strategies of affiliation, both visual and narrative; how devotees interpret the "value" of these commodities based on their mode of acquisition, allocating them into two groups, the gifted sacra and the purchased ephemera; and how the traders who deal in nongifted objects see the transaction and their (often contentious) relationship to the Sai organization and the space of the ashram. The analysis illuminates the motivating forces and differential effects of globalization and demonstrates that attention to transformations in the material world of devotion problematizes. So this is not merely a book about Sai Baba, his devotees or former devotees, though he and they are of central interest, but of the processes of social constructions of reality, of cultural transmission and the often difficult and as yet understudied processes of cultural translation, that have untold effects on cross-cultural discourse. I argue that the questions raised by this study are a springboard from which one can fashion a different approach to understanding culture and cosmopolitanist imperative. I hope to better understand religion in an era of globalization, which demands that we describe worlds located in different epistemic roots if the description of difference is to be a constructive one. In the conclusion I suggest a *tentative* and *preliminary* schema of dynamic cultural translation and flows, comprised of dyadic pairings of processes, that charts the movement of cultural goods and ideologies. The schema is merely conceived as a starting point to focus an examination of how the project of cultural globalization can be reframed to better study religiocultural movements and institutions.

But it is clear to me, even in attempting this exercise, that it requires us to question received understandings of religion in the postmodern world and problematize their subjectivities, describe worlds located in different epistemic roots and the networks of their connectedness, and map a way forward to engage a dialogue between cultures in order to productively engage the politics of knowledge and meaning (Hannerz 1990:9–10) toward a better understanding of cultural globalization. I begin with a reexamination of *cultural flows and cultural translations*—the two processes that are essential units of cultural globalization.

Of Flows and Translation: Confronting the Theoretical Legacy of Cultural Globalization

Returning to academia in Boston in early 2000, I read a significant number of theoretical works on globalization and culture, but little of my reading seemed to fit the data I had gathered. It was some time before I realized that the unique moment represented by the Sathya Sai movement provided a sophisticated critique of the theories I had been reading. This was brought home to me when I heard a renowned academic describe cultural globalization metaphorically as a train. The train, according to the scholar, was powered by neoliberal, Western capitalism and ran on a linear track, driven by an "engine master" who knew both the route and the mechanics of driving the train. The train invariably ran on time, or, if it didn't, passengers could expect to be updated as to delays. Those who could, boarded the train, and those who did not, or could not, were left behind. The train model suggested that globalization was a deracinated and decultural project—that it was not emplaced in any one space—and, therefore, any nation-state or people could become globalized, provided they had the will. The implication of the visual image of the train was one of orderliness and progress.

And, yet, when I examined the data on the Sathya Sai movement, the orderly train of progress was nowhere in evidence. The metaphor that seemed most appropriate to the processes of globalization that I witnessed was that of a bus on a complex and incomplete system of Indian roads. As anyone who has ridden an Indian bus will attest, the journey is both exhilarating and tortuous. The roads that are indicated on the map are often impassable for various reasons, and these uncertainties force the riders/drivers to figure out innovative and alternate routes to reach the destination (culture is process). Those riders who are comfortable with uncertainty and paradox invariably fare better in the processes of cultural globalization (culture is contextual knowledge rooted in iterative cycles of praxis). Furthermore, sometimes the destination is unclear, since decisions are taken by democratic process; there are many people on the bus who have different ideas of where it should stop and when, based on their contestatory subject positions, and it is not always the most obvious or seemingly powerful group of passengers that win (culture is knowledge based on subject positions). The bus is driven primarily by people with a lot of practice in capitalist markets and political organization (primarily the West), but in recent times newcomers have gotten on (such as China and India). These newcomers have different ideological maps (culture is linked to ethnic groups, language base, and territory; a tribal or caste understanding of cultural identity). Alarmingly, for those who liked riding the train, this bus is picking up speed. Looking out of the dust-streaked windows of the cultural globalization bus, it is clear that what is outside the windows will influence what happens on the bus. The economic engagement or disenfranchisement of millions of people, cultural shifts, political change, and other complex forces that cannot be appropriately quantified or predicted will all influence how the bus performs and, indeed, where it ends up (cultural dialogue both within and across nations, whether violent or pacifist, has unexpected results). Still the bus moves on and reaches unplanned and often exciting destinations, reinventing the journey (the processes of cultural flow and translation) and the destination (cultural understanding) along the way.

But it is the "unintended consequences" of cultural globalization—the messiness of globalization forces and the complexity of their interlinking combined with the popular acceptance that religion could not be the basis for any civil cosmopolitanist ideology that was often echoed in scholarly work—that made the study of the Sathya Sai movement, focused on the goal of finding a language of cosmopolitanism, compelling to me. But I realized that I had to revisit existent theories and descriptions of cultural globalization first to understand our inherited legacy of thought, which directed theories sharply away from the processes of flows and translations that I found so imperative and so illuminating.

John Tomlinson, states that "globalization lies at the heart of modern culture and cultural practices lie at the heart of globalization," and the huge transformative processes that globalization has engaged, he suggests, are best understood through "the vocabularies of culture" (1999:1–2, 5–7). But both globalization and culture are contested intellectual territory. I do not aim to create an exhaustive account of either, but to examine the links between the two with a view to a working definition of cultural globalization that will enable us to proceed with our study of the Sathya Sai movement as a religiocultural one.

For the purposes of this study, culture can be defined as both the process of creating meaning and the end product of that process. To study culture is to study "ideas, experiences, feelings and the external forms that such internalities take as they are made public, available to the senses and thus truly social" (Hannerz 1990:1). Culture encompasses praxis and product—material, symbolic and social worlds—in which people create and engage meaning, what Geertz refers to as "semiotic webs" (1973a and 1973b:3) Within an understanding of globalization, culture is no longer merely an intellectual product but "an intellectual maneuver against the background of social political and intellectual context" (Trouillot, in Fox and King 2002:40–44). Anthropologists have long been discontent with the traditional understandings of culture (Abu-Lughod 1991; Bourdieu 1977 [1972]; Ortner 1984, to name but a few), and there have been several attempts to rework culture. This is one of them. But in going down this well-trodden path of "rethinking culture," I would like to veer away from the accepted wisdom of cultural theorists and turn in a different direction: toward globalization.

Let us begin with anthropologists Inda and Rosaldo's comprehensive description of the globalized world:

> It is a world of motion, of complex interconnections . . . capital traverses frontiers almost effortlessly, drawing more and more places into dense networks of financial interconnectedness: people readily (although certainly not freely and without difficulty) cut across national boundaries . . . various cultures converge, clash and struggle with each other: commodities drift briskly from one locality to another, becoming primary mediators in the encounter between culturally distant others; images flicker quickly from screen to screen providing people with resources from which to fashion new ways of being in the world; and ideologies circulate rapidly through ever expanding circuits, furnishing fodder for struggles couched in terms of cultural authenticity versus foreign influence. The pictures thus describe a world in which a myriad of processes, operating on a global scale, ceaselessly cut across national boundaries, integrating and connecting cultures and communities in new space time combinations.
>
> (2001:3–4)

Inda and Rosaldo's description speaks of a breathlessly changing world that creates the cutting edge of new economic and political structures, as it engages technological innovation, media power, and communications to allow goods, ideologies, and people to flow across the world in new interconnected ways. Compressing various important theoretical stances on globalization, David Held et al. (1999) list the characteristics of globalization as the speeding up of flows of capital, ideology, knowledge, people, and goods across an increasingly networked world, which results in quicker processes and distancing interactions, the intensification, multiplication, and rationalization of connections and networks, the expansion of the modern over traditional horizons, and exposure to new ways of being in the world where local activities have global implications and vice versa. It is in this sense, to describe a contemporary phenomenon, that globalization is most often used in this text.

As is evident from any brief review of the literature, "anthropologists are not the only ones interested in globalization" (Inda and Rosaldo 2001:4). Definitions of globalization have emerged from fields as varied as economics, anthropology, biogenetics, business, political science and agricultural science. Contemporary globalization research focuses on a variety of themes: labor markets, international economics (Bhagwati 2004); industrial and social organizations (Ohmae 1988); transformations in the role of the state and citizen (Rosenau 2003; Tilly 2007); international migration and diasporic cultures (Berger 2002; Giddens 1991, 2003; Sassen 2007; Stiglitz 2003); urban governance (Brenner 1999a, 1999b, 2003) and political development; global political policy and civil society (Huntington 1996); religion and the public sphere (Barber1995; Friedman 2000, 2007); democracy (Fukuyama 1992) and nationalism; ethnic and state violence and concordant disenfranchisement (Nandy 2001; Sen 2006); politicocultural worlds and shifting identities; cosmopolitanism, cultural dialogue, and valorizations of morality (Nussbaum 2007; Appiah 2006); and transnational space and multiple cultures. The purpose of this introduction is not to summarize the diverse views and studies of globalization, but we should be alert, as we engage its processes from various perspectives, that globalization means many different things to many different people, which leads to a definitional ambiguity over the concept and the processes it enfolds.

When one examines a few of these descriptions of globalization, they expose the complex and paradoxical relationship between modernity and cultural difference (Kurasawa 2004:2) where the theoretical tension between the universalism of globalization, or "the transhistorical and transcultural applicability" of modern culture (Kurasawa 2004:2–3)—"a

false universalism" and the spatial and temporal embeddedness of contextual theorizing, "a radical particularism"—arises. Contemporary theorists have inherited complete watertight theories of modernity and Westernization that encompass a whole range of poorly understood ontological
processes. As Kurasawa notes, the assumed structural overlap in modernity theory between society, culture, and nation-state has led to theoretical reflection on discrete, contained, homogenous structures that overlap
nation, territory, culture, and society, and so theories of modernity have
drawn on a narrow range of experiences located in a single site, which
have been presumed to be easily universalizable (Kurasawa 2004:4–6), a
deeply flawed exercise as evidenced in the Boston scholar's antiseptic metaphor of the train. In this sense, then, though globalization draws primarily
from modernity, there are also elements of the postmodern woven through:
in its critique of modernity, its multivalent voices, and its turning of the
categories of modernity on their head.

To return to our inherited legacy of thought: I see three significant
inherited theoretical problematic foci that have dominated discussions of
cultural globalization and led to certain assumptions that limit the understanding of the processes and outcomes of cultural globalization: 1.
the possible (in)commensurability of cultures leading to discussions of
cultural homogeneity or heterogenity, 2. the understanding of the direc-
tionality of cultural flows and the power vested in them leading to analysis of cultural hybridization models, 3. the interpretive agency that peoples of different cultures bring to bear in the politics of identity leading to
discussions of fundamentalist agendas or debates about the significance
of diasporic religions. I suggest that, while these various foci and their
accompanying discussions have all undoubtedly led us forward, they
have also led us into theoretical and linguistic cul de sacs, by which we
bring to bear outdated language and thought to new problems.

The first inherited problematic focus is the 1970s representation of difference being posed in *contemporary cultural globalization theories as
a problem of the semiosis of cultures.* From Samuel Huntington (1996) to
Martha Nussbaum (2007) and Amartya Sen (2006), the question of
cultural interaction and therefore of transmission has revolved around
whether *two (or more) cultures are commensurable* or incommensurable
and, whether the values, norms, and ways of being and believing of one
culture can be mapped onto another. The answer has always been that
some can and some cannot. For example, Samuel Huntington's political
argument on "the clash of civilizations," as early as 1993, focused com-

pletely on non-Western culture/religion, primarily Islam, as problematic to align with Western-style capitalism and democracy. His polemical vision where "ideologies circulate rapidly through ever expanding circuits furnishing fodder for struggles couched in terms of cultural authenticity versus foreign influence" (Inda and Rosaldo 2002:11–12) is a natural outcome of this view. The "bloody borders of Islam," according to Huntington, are proof positive of this cultural incommensurability. This focus upon fears of religious "fundamentalisms" (Barber 1996; Huntington 1996) that pitted one culture against another, both between nations and within them, was profoundly influential and has dominated discourses on religion ever since. The long-standing debate on nationalism/fundamentalism in the Indian context (Madan 1991; van der Veer 1994; Nandy 2003) that locates Hinduism and Indic culture within politicized nationalist debates is derivative but nonetheless influential and powerful.

As globalization was understood to rest on an apparatus of hypercapitalism, politico-economic arguments were frequently brought to bear on cultural commensurability; in 1996 Thomas L. Friedman, a market economist, argued that a "golden arches theory of conflict prevention" reigned whereby no two societies with a McDonalds burger restaurant franchise would ever go to war with each other because they merely wanted to do "business as usual," a model that favored economic globalization as a possible point of commensurability. Economic globalization was seen as the fin de siècle emancipating dialogue, and so, in all these Toynbee-like challenge-response models, culture was either seen as irrelevant or an obstacle to neoliberal democracy and hypercapitalism.

In contrast to Huntington and Nussbaum, I argue, based on the data in the following pages, that the commensurability or incommensurability of cultures is merely a historical and not a structural condition (as reflected in the works of Subramanyam, Asad, Nandy, and Dalrymple). I suggest that cross-cultural analysis is less about finding sui generis forms of alterity or universality and more about studying multiple frames of beliefs, practices, norms, and values in different levels of analysis, from the local, the global, the regional to the ethnic and the cultural simultaneously, which leads to the natural conclusion that efficient translation is the key to cultural interaction. I will return to explore this idea.

But, in these earlier models of cultural globalization, processes, societies, and cultures were classified primarily in relationship to the West, which implied, mutatis mutandis, that the West, i.e., Euro-America, had the "primacy model of globalization"[27] which was Western-style capitalism combined with a secular worldview, a view derived from modernity theory of the 1960s (Berger and Luckmann 1966). As John Tomlinson states, this model involved "the installation worldwide of Western versions of basic socio-cultural reality; the West's epistemological and ontological theories, its values, ethical systems, approaches to rationality, technical scientific worldview, political culture and so on" (1999:144), a *political model of cultural hegemony* in which the end product is a global homogenized, largely rational, secular culture (Nederveen-Pieterse 2003:46–51).

The idea that the West had penetrated developing countries like India culturally through economic globalization was a powerful one (both for the West and for Indians) that allowed a populist resistance to build in India through a theoretical and affect-ridden coupling of globalization with the colonialism India had suffered (under the British and various other foreign rulers) until 1947. So globalization came to symbolize, for many developing countries, including India, a neocolonial push that must be resisted, imported with caution, or mastered (de Soto 2000). Indeed this push was understood to encapsulate all that was wrong with contemporary global culture—excessive consumption, ungodliness, hedonism, a focus on rationality, hubris, and loss of rooted identity.

By the late 1990s the public conversation on globalization in and of India had dealt in the main with a center-to-periphery understanding of cultural flows—Western-based neoliberal capitalist processes and their impact on the culture and society of India. This led to the populist understanding of globalization as analogous to Westernization that many Indians felt must be resisted as a corrupting and homogenizing influence. In this center-periphery approach it was assumed that peripheral cultures would "step by step assimilate more and more of the imported meanings and forms, becoming gradually indistinguishable from the center" (Hannerz 1990:122). Those cultural mores that did not fit the development agenda would be shed, and those cultural traits that fit and encouraged a "progressive" agenda would remain (Nandy 2003:1), leading to an elimination of difference and, finally, it was hoped, to the delight of some and dismay of others, to a culturally homogeneous world resting on a global politico-economic structure that linked neoliberal capitalism and "liberal" democracy.

This response/resistance gave credence to an inherited lexicon, leading to shallow conceptualizations, which I will problematize in the following pages. The terms *local* and *global* or *center* and *periphery*. which were first instituted by anthropologists to aid the analysis of the field of globalization as comprising of "cultural flows" from one sphere to another (Appadurai 1996; Hannerz 1990), rapidly became the lingua franca of globalization in the late 1990s as the recognition of the mobility of cultures and their resultant reinvention became common understanding. *Local* and *indigenous* cultures were set in opposition to the bland and homogeneous uniformity of the *global*. This stifling dialectic became a doorstop to critical thinking as the multidimensionality of the local was seen, not unfairly, as being eroded by the homogeneity of the global. So contemporary scholars (including myself) yielded to the temptation to use the terms politically with power-laden connotations (if it is local then it is worthy of cultural survival) or as acts of categorization (is it local or is it global?), thus simplifying the inherent complexity of these initial categories.

Whereas globalization was incontrovertibly dominated by Western economic and ideological structures, in actuality the data suggested that India had "emitted" cultural goods, ideologies, and ways of being regularly into the network (T. Srinivas 2002)—that cultural goods, services, and ideas flowed *out* of India—though little attention was paid to analyzing how cultural ideologies and forms *from* India *engaged* and *affected* the global network (T. Srinivas 2002).

However, this understanding of globalization as "West to rest" was based on a misunderstanding arising out of a conflation of two opposing analytical streams of thought: anthropological theorists of globalization understood the center as acting on the periphery, but, in their nuanced work, the center and the periphery were constantly shifting (Hannerz 1990). Many of the anthropologists who made the center-periphery argument (inspired by Wallerstein 1974, 1984, 1991) had in fact understood the West to be in decline, so globalization became a shifting force with its locus in limbo over time. This was quite different than the single flow of culture from West to rest that economists and labor analysts argued and that was embraced by the popular understanding. The simplistic idea that globalization—specifically cultural globalization—was a movement of goods, services, and ideas, from West to rest, stuck.

But if one assumed that cultural globalization processes were not binary and center and periphery were shifting (Kurasawa 2004:1–9), as anthropologists had originally suggested, cultural flows could be seen to be multidirectional, which examples like the Sai movement, yoga, and Ayurveda proved. So one key question that we will examine in these pages is what does a multidirectional understanding of the network of cultural globalization imply in terms of process and outcome? This question is central to evaluating how cultural globalization forces affect our lives and ways of being and thinking. The evaluation of "the extent to which forces of globalization have altered or will alter . . . regional, national or inter- and transnational flows of people, material, ideas, power and the like" (see Bestor 2001; cf. Waters 1995; Hannerz 1990) is the critical issue of our times.

By 2000 the theory of cultural globalization was being revised, *and the second focus of theory had switched to attempting to comprehend cultural flows in their contemporary incarnation.*[28] In the face of the reality of violence, increasing nationalism, inequality, and exclusion, and the economic and political rise of Asia, Fukuyama had recast his polemical debate of the "end of history," resulting in universal liberal democracy for all mankind,[29] to focus on the causal relationships between multiculturalism and identity politics in modern liberal, primarily Western, democracies. Understanding culture, particularly religion, became the new cause célèbre. The developed countries of the West, for whom the link between religion and development had been effectively broken through modernization (Berger and Luckmann 1966), were surprised by the rise of religion, both in its fundamentalist form (which they see as inexorably linked to the rise of fundamentalist Islam) along with its more "peaceful" variants such as Buddhism in America during the 1990s. But Berger, one of the key architects of the secularization modernity thesis, bravely revised his initial argument and stated, "The assumption that we live in a secularized world is false . . . the world is as furiously religious as it ever was." As early as 1999, sociologist Eisenstadt had argued that globalization comprised a series of "alternate" or "multiple" modernities (Hefner 1998), alternatives to the Western secular concept of modernity, that enable a combination of a deeply religious attitude with a modern consciousness (Berger 2002; Weller 1999). Furthermore an unexpected conjunction of economics and labor occurred, which shifted the locus of economic theorizing to India. So Friedman's 2005 new treatise, *The World Is Flat,* found him on the golf course in Bangalore, India, describing the potential economic growth of Asia through technological "flattening" in which India emitted culture, capital, and power into the network, where Nandan Nilekani, an Indian CEO, explained to him the "mysteries" of postmodern capitalism in a "flattened" world.

Scholars of India saw this second phase of globalization theory as India's cultural "strength" (Huntington 1996), as its redemption or its nemesis, depending upon one's political position. Writers chronicled how

India had managed the unexpected leap onto the global stage, but they also examined the inherent problems that India faced as a closed economy that had suddenly and rapidly globalized. The questions that emerged concerned the identity of Indians in relationship to global culture and posited as another dialectic, this time between cosmopolitan identities (often seen as the worldly alternative) and the local parochial identities that were often seen as inextricably meshed with fundamentalist programs. Indian scholars, such as Ashish Nandy (1983, 1995, 2001), and journalists, such as Gurcharan Das (2001, 2002), focused on the Indian emission of cultural fragments, capital, labor, knowledge, and power. Anthropologists and sociologists had long argued that mutual imbrication between cultures was the case, and the result was a cultural hybridization in which religion played a significant role in the construction of identity.

Often called *melange* (Nederveen-Pieterse 2001) and *creolization* (Hannerz 1990) or syncretism, cultural hybridization points to the increasing complexity of the world and the complex crossings and countercrossings of culture that occur. Hybridization has enabled people to deal with the reality of globalization and cultural transmission; that of living in multicultural spaces where others' lifestyles and choices are as relevant and meaningful as one's own.[30] However, for some scholars cultural hybridity was merely seen as reactive. A central concept of this paradigm (called McDonaldization or global localization) argues that "the principles of the fast food restaurant are coming to dominate more and more sectors of American society as well as the rest of the world" (Ritzer 1993:19), where cultural diffusion is based on a response model. So indigenes face an imported text and frequently do not absorb its values, ideologies, and lifestyle positions, but they interpret it according to their own embedded cultural codifications. Still the processes of cultural globalization were seen in response to the West.

The second focus did deal in some way with process, but it too failed at the task of conveying the complexity, paradoxes, and randomness that was endemic to cultural globalization. For example, critical geographer David Harvey has suggested that globalization creates a "time-space compression" (1989:141–172). The challenge of globalization is thus to "learn (ing) to cope with an overwhelming sense of compression of our spatial and temporal worlds" (Harvey 1989:240, in Low and Lawrence-Zúñiga 2003:8–9). On the other hand, Anthony Giddens argues for a time-space distantiation, that is, "remote encounters are made possible through increased technology where larger and larger numbers of people live in circumstances in which disembedded institutions linking local practices with globalized social relations organize major aspects of day-to-day life" (1991:79). Compression and distantiation of space are countercurrents that flow through globalization. But, as anthropologists have pointed out (Hannerz 1990), the processes of globalization have simultaneously caused culture to become separated from place. This "deterritorialization of culture" is a world where cultural forms "are unhinged from particular localities" and "erode the natural isomorphism between culture and place" (Inda and Rosaldo 2002:11).

But for every deterritorialization move, there is a reterritorialization as cultural forms reinscribe culture with new context-based time-space meanings (Inda and Rosaldo 2002:12); an "interpretative double movement" that Bivins describes when discussing the Zen Buddhist community in San Francisco during the time of the charismatic and troubled leadership of Baker Roshi (2007:57–58). This interpretive double movement "captures the ways in which those in search of an alternative to religious culture impose (their) own idiosyncratic values onto another religious tradition, all the while remaining paradoxically within the interpretive confines of the culture they hope to "escape"" through extracting the dynamics and tropes of the processes of cultural translation and highlighting the many interpretive lacunae.

The problem that itinerant culture raises is that of cultural congress and interaction, the asymmetry and efficacy of the process, and its outcome as cultures influence each other and reinvent themselves in the process. Scholars engaged in conceptual and linguistic (naming and framing) calisthenics to account for simultaneous divergent and convergent interpretive processes within cultural hybridization: *glocalization,* indicating that which lies between local and global (Robertson 1992); *fragmagration,* coined from fragmentation and integration (Rosenau 2006), to demonstrate the concordant fragmenting and integrating pulls of globalization; *third space* (Fischer 2004), reminiscent of Edward Soja's "third space" of urbanism (1996) that is both real and imagined, and neither lies in the global or the local; and the *push downwards pull upwards* theory of Giddens to denote the counterforces of cultural globalization (1991, 2003). What we must understand is that, in trying to describe the converging and diverging simultaneous processes of cultural globalization, it is necessary to reclaim the intellectual initiative away from political imperatives and their power-laden structures toward a recovery of meaning. An awareness and understanding of the shifts and convergences, divergences, intersections, and erasures that occur as part of the cultural interaction process are necessary to plot both the emergence of complexity and the various domains of complexity complicit in the reinvention (from what ought to be to what is). Therefore the process of interpretation is privileged and complicated and the production of knowledge is made relational between cultures. But I think the theoretical takeaway is important: cultural materials do not transfer unilaterally and will not lead to a global monoculture since they are received differently.

The third focus that emerged in recent studies of globalization is identity. Identity and the politics of it seemed to cut through the problems of mobility: it became the watchword of scholars who discussed religious fundamentalism in India and abroad (Nussbaum 2007; Vanaik, Bidwai, and Mukhia 1996; Van der Veer 1994) as well as a watchword in studies of the diaspora particularly those who studied diasporic religion. Emergent at that time but oppositional in tone to the study of religious fundamentalism discourse was the "challenge of pluralism" (Eck 2006; Ammerman 2006; Levitt 2007) approach (arising out of immigration studies and diasporic studies of religion), which was more sophisticated and sliced the problem somewhat differently, focusing on the politics of religious identity. This school argued that the incorporation of religious difference into the predominantly Judeo-Christian tradition of the West and the appearance, or lack thereof, of tolerance and acceptance was the issue.[31] While this theory recognized that globalization had to be understood as a "process of mutual imbrication" (Inda and Rosaldo 2001:22) between cultures, where the problem of grappling with strangeness was implicit and expected, the exploration of the South Asian diaspora (Punzo-Waghorne 2004; Vertovec 1999; Biju and Prasad 2000) often remained site specific and context based, focusing on the problematic incorporation of non-Western religious faiths into Western plural societies.

Examining the nature of contemporary plural societies, European sociologist Hervieu-Léger (2001) argued that the construction of identity and the politics that surrounded it—ethnic caste based, class based, religious—would be *the* central question of the late modern era. Anthony Giddens appears to agree with Hervieu-Léger when he states that, in the posttraditional global order, identity is not inherited nor is it static, rather, it becomes a reflexive project—an endeavor that is continuously worked and reflected upon to create a better narrative of self. These scholars have drawn heavily from the prolific and pathbreaking work on identity by scholars of modernity, chief among them Peter Berger, whose formulation of the theory of "the homeless mind"—where identities, consciousness, and social relationships are linked through a systemic destabilization of the religious point of view—was seminal in describing a shift from a religious worldview in modern Europe to a secular worldview. Thus as more parts of the abstract world were removed from the religious sphere—including science, art, philosophy, and literature—it became imperative, in Berger's view, to construct ones' own identity through negotiation with the world. Identity was, for the moderns, no longer "taken for granted," but rather an individual "project." In the old world of overarching meaning, identity was a given, but in the modern world one could, in a sense, design and redesign oneself, within the social situations in which one found oneself or that one sought out. So identity could be expansive and freeing, but simultaneously was the product of rootlessness and anomie. Thus, for modernity theorists, identity is not a set of observable characteristics of a moment, but an account of a person's life where individuality is important in self-construction and this theoretical preoccupation with self-construction and identity carries through (almost as an underlying assumption) into the literature on globalization. Giddens writes (1991:54) that "a person's identity is not to be found in behaviour, nor—important though this is—in the reactions of others, but in the capacity to keep a particular narrative going. The individual's biography, if she is to maintain regular interaction with others in the day-to-day world, cannot be wholly fictive. It must continually integrate events which occur in the external world, and sort them into the ongoing 'story' about the self." For cultural globalization scholars, identity, and the politics of it, are one of *the* key constructs of the late modern, global era.

Berger, Berger, and Kellner (1973) argue that we live in a framework of symbols and these convey meaning, and their pattern conveys overall meaning. In other words, the individual mind interacts with society on a symbolic interface. Thus interpretation of symbols must be privileged. Paraphrasing Meili Steele (1996), an influential critical theorist, I suggest that the politics of interpretation of religion in South Asia has been held hostage by the postmodern theoretical concept of power. Power and its effects dominate explanation, constructions of selfhood, achievements and hermeneutics (Foucault and Derrida) in which accounts of self-explanation, while lauded, are redescribed without due explanation of their embedded logic or coherence. While I use postmodern theory and language, I also argue for a sensitivity to the limitations of the theory, as a stifling theoretical narrowness cannot hope to adequately describe such complex and interrelated data as the phenomena of the Sai movement offer. I argue that postmodern power theories alone are inadequate to explain the increasingly interwoven interfaces of culture and the iterative processes in which the forces of globalization work contrapuntally and counterintuitively. Berger has argued that in the modern world a plurality of meanings replaces one general meaning, and these often compete. But, as Hannerz has noted, the problem of postmodernist thought as opposed to modern thought is that plurality is taken for granted in this worldview and, while it emphasizes diversity and is wary of totalitarian thought, it has itself "frequently been on the verge of becoming an all-encompassing formula" (1993:35) .

However, as Judith Butler informs us, the articulation of the critique of our intellectual legacy (in which we have just engaged) does not remove us from the influence of inherited thinking; "Critique always takes place . . . immanent to the regime of discourse /power whose claims it seeks to adjudicate, which is to say the practice of the critique is implicated in the very power relations it seeks to adjudicate. There is no pure place . . ." (cited in Benhabib 1996:134–135). The larger hermeneutic challenge that follows the reframing of the critical project of cultural globalization is to be able to provide a method that enables us to examine subjects not as victims or agents but as interactors and interlocutors who reinvent their everyday culture through engaging efficacious cultural translation as they experience varied cultural and, more particularly, religious forms that flow through the network.

Methods for Cross-Cultural Comparisons: Metrics and Vectors

So it is clear that the methodological issue facing a scholar of cultural globalization is comparison across cultures. Wendy Doniger sees this problem of comparison as the "third side" of any comparative triangle.[32] I suggest we must reframe the problem through the data and find metrics of analysis from within that allow us to look at it both from the meta and micro perspectives, taking into account the complexity of cultural flows across the network, the interaction between cultures as subjects, institutions, and objects engage in myriad ways, as well as the dynamics of cultural translation including interpretive, affiliative, and valorizing processes.

One metric of analysis for the dynamics of cultural globalization that emerged in this study was how *relations between subjects* (for example, Sai devotees and Sathya Sai Baba, Sai officials and devotees, Sai devotees in California and those in Japan) expanded and became complex. Complex relationships bear a causal relationship to cultural mobility, often the more mobile cultural fragments are and the more intercultural congress occurs, the more complex they become. But complexity can also be a unit of analysis. "Complexity," as Hannerz notes, is endemic to understanding culture. It refers to interpretation—the many ways in which meanings are read and understood—in which the various perspectives that subjects engage are valued. For example, we found that embodied discipline at Puttaparthi, which included dietary restrictions, was understood variously by devotees as salvation focused or therapeutic depending upon their originary culture. Kessing has argued that the study of culture includes an understanding of the sociology of knowledge, of subject positions—of how meanings and knowledge are "distributed and controlled" and "cultures as texts . . . are differently read" (Kessing 1987:161, in Hannerz 1990:13). So complexity is this acknowledgment of varied subject positions and perspectives, which is enhanced through the increase in social relations that globalization demands and the interweaving and layering of symbolic processes, logics, epistemologies, and hermeneutics that occur in iterative cycles of knowledge building. I will argue that the Sathya Sai ovement creates plastic "matrices of possible meanings" (such as images, texts, and embodied ways of being) and these plastic forms allow people from various cultures to affiliate with them through their semiotic flexibility.

Considering subject positions leads to an understanding of the second metric of relations between subjects (for example, between Sai devotees and Sathya Sai Baba, between Sai officials and devotees, between Sai devotees in California and those in Japan), relationality. *Relationality* is used to describe the connections between cultures brought about because of the cultural interactions that occur in the network of cultural globalization. De Certeau states that "analysis always shows that a relation (always social) determines its terms" (1984: xi). Relationality is interactionist; "people shape social structures and meanings in their contacts with one another . . . and societies and cultures emerge and cohere as results of the accumulation and aggregation of these activities" (14), and so employing the analytical tool of relationality enables us to shift the conversation from mere abstract explanation of the forces of cultural globalization upon one another to a critical examination of iteration and mobility, of the complex relationships and perceptual shifts that provide what Paul Virilio calls the "trajective" movement that underpins the broad horizons of this book.

The third metric one can apply would be *affectivity*. It was apparent to me that my conversation with Anna was rooted in the emotional. I felt that such an examination of narratives of affect, of how people feel, is an essential component that is missing in our understanding of cultural globalization. In her pathbreaking study of the globalization of Indian cinema, Lakshmi Srinivas suggests that Bombay films "convey sensual and emotional experiences—the most immediate and embodied effects of globalization," through what she terms "feeling rules." She suggests that the films act as "a medium of translation," through "a structure of feeling" (2005). Affectivity as an analytical tool enables us to explore the frameworks and dynamics of cultural translation. I consider grammars, economies, and nuanced understandings of the power of affect (Munn 1986; Kapferer 1972) and their transformation and their codification (Obeyesekere 1988).This work follows the pathways of affectivity toward interpretation through a bicameral examination of the interpretative ethos established by the scholars of religion and globalization and the strategies that architects of the Sathya Sai movement employed to shape this complicated tradition specifically for an urban-educated practitioner seeking an experiential path beyond their middle-class backgrounds.

This exploration naturally leads not only to an understanding of interpretation but of valorization as well. What do Sathya Sai devotees value and why? How is valorization arrived at? How is this value codified? Part of the project here, in light of this articulation, is to offer an account of the novel and flexible forms of relationality that the Sathya Sai movement engages, to examine the politics of cultural ownership, of knowledge, and of interpretation.

The "Culture of Complaint" as a Symptom of Something Larger: Developing a Method for the Study of Cultural Globalization

But I was still stymied by how to go about understanding the phenomena that I was studying . . . or indeed how to study it at all. The initial interactions with Anna and her group and my ruminations on them led me to four continents, to speak in four languages (Hindi,

English, Tamil, and Kannada), to dozens of devotees, practitioners, officials, former devotees, and others. I started by casually visiting the Sathya Sai ashram in the small town of Puttaparthi in the Rayalseema (boundaries of kings) district of rural southern Andhra Pradesh, some three hours from Bangalore city, and his summer ashram in the town of Whitefield, some twelve miles outside Bangalore. In common with Alexandra Kent's fieldwork (2005) on the Sai movement, initially there was no real method to my work, as I was just curious, and I moved through a rolling sample, meeting one devotee after another individually as each devotee introduced me to the next; some were affluent, some lower middle class; some had been devotees their entire lives and some had just started on a life of devotion. Although I always introduced myself as an anthropologist who planned to study the movement, for the devotees it was obvious that Sathya Sai Baba had "called" me to be a devotee. Initially, I "lurked,"[33] relying more on observation than participation, but soon the discomfort of the unknown gave way to familiarity as I made friends among the devotees. As Alexandra Kent observes in her study of Sathya Sai devotees in Malaysia, in time, through certain sponsors and friends, one could become a full participant in the movement (2005:xvi). I became a full participant; I attended darshan of Sri Sathya Sai Baba at dawn in the Sai ashram, visited the Sathya Sai temple in Indiranagar, an affluent suburb of Bangalore for the bhajan sessions, distributed clothes and food to homeless people as seva in Framingham, and sat in endless study circles deciphering the discourses of Sathya Sai Baba. Since Sai devotees gather socially as family to build devotional communities, with activities for genders and generations, I got to know whole families of devotees (Kent 2005:xvi–xvii), many of them spread all over the world. I had teas, lunches and dinners at devotee's homes, attended weddings, baby naming ceremonies, festivals, and other kin-based celebrations. Through my enlarging circle of contacts, I could access a few Sai officials of the SSSO who ran parts of the global faith organization.

The profound devotion of all the people I met impressed me. With a colleague at the Institute of Social and Economic Change I did a circumscribed study as part of the cultural globalization project which I had undertaken.[34] The study was completed in early 1999, and the resulting book chapter written in 2001. But there were many questions left unanswered for me, so I continued research on my own through my tenure in India from 1999 and into 2000.

As I got more comfortable with devotees, and them with me (Luhrmann 1996:vii) I found that despite their assertions that they were "*all*" "devotees of Swami," they were extremely critical of other devotees, often spending a great deal of time grumbling about "them." I found, and I generalize here, that these querulous complaints were often distinguished by "stereotypical" assumptions about cultural identity and power relations, and they were split along nationalist/regional lines. South Asians complained about Western devotees and their inability to "be mentally disciplined" and their "lack of understanding" of, and "impatience" with, sophisticated, abstract, spiritual philosophy; the northern Europeans (Germans and Swedes) complained about Indians "ignoring their environment" and being "very corrupt"; the Singaporean Indians and Chinese (not Malays) thought that the unruly behavior of the Indians from India and the Americans when queuing for activities was "upsetting"; the Americans complained about Indians being "cheats," and the Japanese complained that the Americans were "aggressive." All the devotees unanimously complained vigorously about the lower and mid-range officials and volunteers who kept order at the ashram, labeling them "bullies," "tyrants" and "big headed" with power.[35]

I became increasingly uncomfortable at these interviews for this reason. In fact I am still uncomfortable writing these thoughts down as they seem to essentialize devotees into cultural and national groups. So I would try vainly to divert the discussion. There was something wrong in their quarreling I thought, rather naively. After all, the Sathya Sai Movement purported to be global, and in all the texts and discourses the Sathya Sai devotees stated they were one community and all devotees were equal. Furthermore, since they had chosen to devote themselves to Sathya Sai Baba did this not imply a shared set of values, activities and agency through their choice of devotion? Did devotees see this, to me,visible "culture of complaint" (Weeks 2003), I wondered?

As I returned to the field in 2001, 2002, 2003, 2005, and 2006 for short bursts of fieldwork, I began to understand that in reality these criticisms were symptomatic of a small regional and then national movement stretching itself to adjust to a global reality that was far different than the one devotees were used to. I saw the complaints in a new light; as articulated difficulties of the process of reconstruction and reorientation that these new "colliding worlds" (Boot and Dunne 2002) created. But this cultural movement was not alone in complaining, pointing to the fact that globalization was not a perfect process anywhere, and many cultural ideas were "lost in translation" in the congress of two or more cultures, a point that this work emphasizes.

In 2000 I returned to Boston and contacted Sathya Sai devotional groups. Through my friends and informants in New England, I met Sathya Sai devotees and officials of the international SSSO from Toronto, Hamburg, Cincinnati, and California. I looked for variations between the non-Indian devotees and the Indian devotees in their attitudes, representations, and opinions, as I investigated the doctrinal aspects of the Sathya Sai "religion" and the Sathya Sai discourses in greater detail. It seemed to me that the Sathya Sai devotees outside India were struggling with a different kind of globalization problem, that of a politics of practice intermeshed indivisibly with a politics of identity. They dealt with the complex creation of meaning and value, set against a dominant, usually highly capitalist, alien culture, through rhetorical and discursive positionings and repositionings that wove through their everyday mundane practice as devotees. Consequently, they constantly discussed the "meaning of life" and looked for a "re-enchantment of the world" (Berman 1981) that enabled them to recreate a certain basic social trust. If the processes of globalization encouraged the mobility of cultural forms and ideas and their travel to new host cultures through the network of globalization,[36] processes of cultural congress and cultural reinvention, the individuals I met were struggling to create a language of cultural reinvention that spoke to itinerancy.

During this second half of my fieldwork, I also happened to travel to a few international academic conferences. Wherever I went I met Sathya Sai devotees: on a thirty-seater bi-plane in South Africa; in a Buddhist restaurant in New York city; at breakfast at a resort in Kerala, South India; at Wheaton College, in the rural community of Norton, Massachusetts; in an upscale boutique hotel in La Jolla, California. I realized that the image of a global class of devotees that I had in Puttaparthi was merely the tip of the iceberg. In reality, the devotional base was much larger, more invisible, and spread further than I imagined, and part of my mandate was to examine the multisitedness of these cultural forms. Did the Sathya Sai narrative change based on the positionality within the network? How did they define value in various settings? What were the cultural positionings that they undertook in the practice of the everyday in various sites?

By 2003 my work had attracted the attention of some ex-devotees of Sathya Sai Baba. I contacted them and they rebuffed me initially, confusing me with another scholar whom they claimed had ties to the movement. Ultimately we developed a dialogue largely fueled by phone conversations and Internet exchanges. I found that the opposition to Sathya Sai Baba in the form of the anti-Sai network was scattered over Australia, Russia, the UK, Europe, India, and the United States, which were also the strongest sites of devotion. The anti-Sai activists, who preferred to be called former devotees, were able to discuss their previous devotion and their retreat from the movement with candor and reflexivity. But their presence raised other questions of translation, interpretation, and valorization. How did they fit into the dialogue of globalization? Was the former devotees' opposition similar to the political resistance to globalization? Was it resistance to hegemonic cultural codings? Or an alternate cultural understanding of religion and therefore of morality? And, last, my interaction with the former devotees of Sathya Sai Baba brought the contentious nature of the construction of religious identity and belief to the forefront. The fierce devotion of anti–Sathya Sai activists to the exposing of Sathya Sai Baba, and the equally fierce devotion of devotees to him, underlined that "belief" and "devotional loyalty" are in themselves highly contentious and emotionally charged categories because they point to the paradoxes of crafting a cultural identity in a globalizing world where engagement with other cultures can lead to a shifting of the boundaries of morality. How do cultural assumptions affect Sai devotees' understandings of self and other? How do devotees craft a moral and spiritual identity? Is there fear of moral relativism with increased engagement with the culture of the Other?

The outcomes of this disorganized yet serendipitous fieldwork were surprising. It was brought home to me the obvious facts that the Sathya Sai devotees were a varied group and had different understandings of devotion that ranged from slightly skeptical to deeply unquestioning. They came from different nation-states, cultures, regions, linguistic areas, castes, classes, and religious and tribal groups. Based on their subject positions, these groups engaged the global network very differently; often there was Bakhtinian contestation over "proper" ways to engage globalization. These conflicts were symptomatic of differing interpretations and representations of a movement that was dealing with sudden enormous change. I became interested in the Sathya Sai development of a faith-based language to enable mass customization of culturally embedded liturgical concepts. How were strategic ambiguities, hermeneutic intersections, and erasures embedded within this language? In short, how did the Sathya

Sai create a language of devotion that accounted for the diversity of their potential congregation?

I found I had no tools with which to begin to answer such questions. Through this work I document the finding or forging of anthropological tools and methods to study religious mobility and cultural interaction on a global scale, to recast the inherited dialectical opposition built into studies of cultural globalization into a productive incommensurability that engages the politics of knowledge and interpretation to explore the dynamics of cultural translation. From my initial encounters with Sathya Sai devotees, I elicited two obvious analytical spaces to begin—*interaction and distribution*—within which the processes of cultural translation occur. The importance of these two analytical spaces was emphasized in my fieldwork: interaction through discourses and praxis—in the theaters, embodiments, articulations, spaces, rituals, objects, journeys and scandals—that enabled me to unearth the many-sided narrative embedded within, which illuminated distribution—how they were interpreted differently, by various groups, as well as reflexively, the unexplored multidirectionality of the network of cultural translation. Meshed together, these two analytical spaces of interaction and distribution, combined with the regimes of discourse and praxes, straddle structuralist genealogies (mapping out processes, rules, and coda by which cultural units are recombined) and poststructuralist vocabularies (experiential explanations of subjects) to overcome the incommensurability of situating a critique both within and without. Combining them enables the productive tension between the two to yield to discuss the field of cross-cultural dialogue. As we engage these spaces and regimes in different theaters of transformation, the reader will see that they themselves model and interpret translation differently.

The ethnographic pitfalls I frequently encountered in this study led me to an unintended, enforced analysis of my ethnographic method, where I analyzed my familiar problems as samples of inherited ethnographic praxis. Better understanding the provenance of method, I can now point to the need for a new method of analysis that I locate in critical hermeneutics and an emergent paradigm of praxis, which I articulate through three constructs: multisited studies, networked optics, and mobile description. I contend that a combination of these three kinds of praxis will enable ethnographers to construct a more accurate and data driven picture of cultural globalization, diversity, and the diaspora. But, while I want to suggest that ethnography needs a new method to study "mobile" culture, I am sensitive to the ways in which "historical, geo-graphic, political, cultural and discursive peculiarities of a subject"(Bucar 2007) are pertinent to constructing a method of study relevant to the subject. So I begin by exploring the validity of contemporary ethno-graphic methods for the kind of comparative focus necessary for this analysis.

Charles Simonyi, the successful code writer for Microsoft,[37] suggests that all problems of analysis can be solved by going above or beyond—what he calls "going meta"—because most problems arise when one is too close to the subject of study. But anthropologists, unlike their billionaire soft-ware writing counterparts, need to be both close and distant—both micro-scopic and telescopic at once (Doniger 1998)—close enough to understand the "fabric of the lives" of informants and subjects, yet meta enough to see overarching patterns of code formation, what some anthropologists have called "zooming in and zooming out," in an analogy to a camera lens. I have attempted to undertake this bifocal methodology here and in so doing I engage both the decoding of existing structures and systems of making meaning—a method rooted in critical hermeneutics. I suggest that critical hermeneutics is an appropriate method for studies of cultural globaliza-tion because it can be understood as an attempt to reconcile the activities of interpretation (Habermas) and critical thinking (Gadamer) with a quest of meaning. It raises the act of interpretation to a seminal position in the so-cial sciences, but does not limit it to the constitution of monologically driven enterprises. It also enables both a distantiation and a closeness to the subject. Where the hermeneutical tradition strives to achieve a proxim-ity to the subject and empathy with her worldview, critical theory works conversely to create and engage distances to nurture critique. So both "in-volvement" with and "detachment" from (Elias 2000 [1939]) processes oc-cur concordantly in a cross-cultural situation. Comprehending that under-standing is construed intersubjectively and through dialogue, critical hermeneutics engages in both the decoding of existing systems of mean-ing making as well as in constructing new ones. For these reasons, critical hermeneutics seems to better allow for a humanistic exploration of sense-making strategies from the structural position while still making room for individual agency.

But contemporary studies in anthropology, even studies of cultural globalization and global religion, are still based on what Trouillot defines as a "reified ethnographic trilogy: one observer, one time, one place" (Trouillot 2003:104, in Fox and King 2002:44). I speak to the "one observer, one place and one time" mantra in the globalization context, with particular reference to studies that focus on the globalization of and in South Asia. Anthropologists have called increasingly for "multi-sited studies" to counteract this problem (Marcus 1998). It is abundantly clear that a single field site can no longer be adequate for understanding global communities, but this call has been interpreted (far too easily) as a reinvention of type, not of method, and we fall back into studies with varying metrics and watertight locales (for example, in a recent study of religious citizenship in India, Trinidad, and South Africa, the author addressed different problems in each location), making it difficult to trace the data back and forth across the global network, leaving us with an incommensurable set of pictures. As we have seen, transnational phenomena, such as the Sai movement, engage with many field sites as subjects and imaginaires move from place to place. So "multi-sited" ethnographies must become the norm (Abu Lughod 1997:4) for globalization studies. The comparison of the same phenomena in many sites that I try to achieve in the following pages will enable us to discuss the varying dynamics that influence the phenomena with different perspectives in mind.

Such multisited ethnography opens us up to alterity—to different ways of being in this world and different ways of comprehending along with the creative disorientation that it provides. Alterity, Csordas reminds us, "is the phenomenological kernel of religion, and insofar as alterity is part of the structure of being-in-the-world, religion is an inevitable feature of human existence" (2004:4502). So religion and alterity are inevitably linked. Furthermore, as Taussig notes, alterity, or how we distance ourselves from the other, also says something about its opposite, mimesis, or how we come to adopt another's culture (1993), leading us to understand that our conception of alterity links religion and cultural transmission in central ways. The decentering of self that alterity implies toward engaging multiplicity is central to understanding transnationalism and pluralism as it enables multiple reference points (Kurasawa 2004:29). We need to grasp different understandings of personhood, of morality of embodiment, of belief, of space, of time, and other constituents of meaning making inherent and embedded in the Sai movement that come to light as they globalize. As I engaged in this study, the repeated disorientation I felt, began to feel familiar. As I came to grips with how Singaporean Sai devotees understood the movement, I knew that a Russian Sai devotee would blow my carefully constructed house of cards into disarray. Of course, one of the pitfalls of this method, as many of my friends and colleagues have argued, with validity, is that multisited ethnography will lead to terrible generalizations and destroy the authenticity of any study. But I suggest that we must explore new methods for new problems and simultaneously take into account their lacunae.

Moreover, my work underlined the fact that the processes of globalization have made both the subject and the anthropologist mobile; but, as Jeffrey Sachs has argued, social science has not given us the tools to comprehend mobility. I attempted to maintain contact with devotees and former devotees through travel, phone conversations, e-mail connections, digital mailing of photographs and videos, and so on, but as I did so I saw that mobility posed unique problems and hazards for the fieldworker. The most elemental was how to study a population that is on the move. What is their relationship to "their" place? How is "their culture" defined? What do cultural forms mean when they are seen in relation to another culture? I realized that the problem of the convoluted symbolism of the mirrored Geertzian wink (an essay that every anthropologist has read and admired) takes on new dimensions in contemporary cultural translation as the wink and other forms of nonverbal and symbolic communication engage cross-cultural boundaries. Anthropological method needs to account for the mobility of the subject.

I am not alone in pointing out this problem. Several anthropologists have done so in recent years, and, from their collective writings, it appears that a central problem is the nature and spread of the field. We are ill-equipped to deal with "translocal" phenomena (Cvetovich and Kellner 1997). The answer perhaps lies in *mobile description,* based on "thick description" à la Geertz, that "demonstrates the power of the scientific imagination to bring us into touch with the lives of strangers" and extends it to a mobile community.

Dynamic ethnography, the culmination of mobile description and multisited studies, will hopefully enable us to resist the pitfalls of "radical particularism" (Kurasawa 2004:31) in which cultures are seen as incommensurable and static. It engages both a widening and deepening of the ethnographic enterprise and allows one to "investigate how particular human societies differ from one another" and "how human societies resemble one another": both questions are inseparable (Elias 1978:104). Accepting dynamic ethnography opens us up to the obvious possibility (evident from the data) of mediation and common frameworks of understanding that might lead to a dialogue between cultures. While I may not have achieved the simultaneous broadening and deepening that this enterprise ideally involves, I argue that dynamic ethnography embraces rather than resolves dialectical tensions between similar cultures and distant cultures. Following John Tomlinson's idea that globalization implies a flooding of different perspectives, my work suggests that most societies are complex and flawed and cultural understanding is difficult. While the legacy of thought that we inherit through the prevalent theories of globalization trap us even more firmly in misunderstanding and power struggles, cultural movements like the Sathya Sai movement can show us alternate pathways of understanding.

Notes on Studying a Religious Movement . . .

But it is disingenuous to suggest that I went to India to study the Sathya Sai movement to define my own position on religion and culture. My epiphanous encounter with Anna highlighted an important problem: it disclosed the ignorance that characterized my initial approach to my subject matter and the prejudice I felt towards the subject. Despite being Indian and Hindu, my middle class upbringing combined with the fact that both my parents were academics had led me to appreciate Hinduism's more abstract philosophies and the embedded framework for knowledge and abstraction, not its grassroots, quotidian formulations. And so I had my own knowledge lacunae and prejudices to overcome.

My interactions with current and former devotees made me think about myself as a student of religion, which, I discovered, has changed in the course of the study. As I moved further into the study I could feel empathy with many of my informants from both within and without the Sathya Sai movement. I realized that my own "objectivity" and inclinations toward analysis formed a barrier to immersing myself in the world of former and current Sai devotees completely. My identification of the "Other" led to a barrier in identifying with the "Other" a feeling that I have come to understand many anthropologists have shared.

The Sathya Sai movement had categories to incorporate people as "potential devotees," but, as an Indian and as someone who did not become a devotee, I was not Other enough. Therefore for me as an Indian Hindu and an academic the problem was, as Luhrmann notes for her study of the Parsis (1996), not a question of going far, but not going far enough. This empathetic siting of the anthropological subject in studies of religious belief is a problem that many anthropologists of religion face. If one defines the sect as the devotee does, then one is accused of being an apologist. However, if one ruthlessly negates the essential construct of belief in the sect, one is left questioning the nature of empathy with the subject and informant. This "epistemological break" (Ardener 1985, in Rappaport and Overing 2000) for me was at the core of the problem of studying the Sathya Sai movement. As Rita M. Gross (2004:113) argues about the place of the scholar of religion: "A common prejudice in the discipline of religious studies is that the best scholars are 'objective,' detached from and uninvolved with their subject matter. . . . However, because objectivity is impossible, it is important to rethink conventional assumptions regarding the relationship between religious identity and teaching or doing research on religion."Gross concludes that "the closest semblance to neutrality we can achieve is to be aware of and self-conscious concerning the identities that influence our teaching and scholarship"(115). Recent studies of the Sathya Sai movement (Kent 2004, 2005; Srinivas 2008) focus on what Lawrence Babb has evocatively dubbed "the anthropology of credibility" (1983:116) approach, in understanding how religious believers "inhabit, understand or coproduce" the realms of belief (Srinivas 2008:21), and they only explore the devotee's perspective. I suggest that this approach, though giving us a great deal of information on devotees, has led to a unique lacunae in our understanding of the conflict-ridden discourse between devotees and anti-Sai activists who call themselves "former devotees." While protagonists on both sides of the debate have created their own narratives of devotion and disaffection, which give them reason and meaning, they also attempt to delegitimize claims by their antagonists, sometimes accusing each other of mendacity, appropriations, and stealing. To understand the construction of identity in this world of conflict, having as its the larger purpose the understanding of cultural globalization with a view to encouraging cosmopolitanism, we cannot afford to disinclude any particular voice in measuring the locus of disagreements and rival claims. This study goes against this prior approach to include the views of "former devotees," introducing the "hermeneutics of suspicion" where all data supplied by believers is suspect (Ricoeur 1970:33), first because, although they are a small group, they are an increasingly vocal, influential, and global lobby and, second, to suggest a more nuanced and meaningful discussion of faith in which dissension, doubt, and accusations are all part of what many believers contend with everyday. I aim to set an understanding of faith against the complexities of interpretation and the messiness of cultural translation during globalization, where conflicting ideas flow in many directions at once (Hannerz 1990; Appadurai 1996). For, as Gross elegantly argues, "Identification as a scholar is critical. Whatever other identities we may have, this one cannot be absent" (2004:117). While some scholars have argued that this allows for a devotee insider position, or an "affinity with Sai Baba" does not cloud their data,[38] my own feeling is that this delicate balance is difficult though not impossible.

But my interest lies not only in questioning my objectivity as an ethnographer but also in discussing what constitutes normalcy. During my eight-year study, aspects of the Sai movement became very familiar to me. My knowledge has grown cumulatively, and what I previously may have thought of as strange has become familiar and normal. It is ironic that I began by thinking many things I encountered in the movement strange and now find their presence and their logic strangely comforting because of their familiarity.

Some Sathya Sai devotees might not like this book. A few of the devotees, if they read it, might be angry and embarrassed, and some might say it is not true. Criticisms of the community have been voiced on many levels by the literati of India, by journalists, by former devotees, by Christian right-wing movements and others, and devotees might resign themselves to what they see as yet another misapprehension of the Sathya Sai phenomenon. But a few friends and devotees who have read my pre-published work told me it was necessary I write this book telling the "truth"—to them echoed in Sathya (truth) Sai Baba's name—as it would be what He himself would have wanted. It may be that a few former devotees will also not like this book, but for other reasons. They have been ignored by most of the literature on the Sathya Sai movement and have established a significant (and, to devotees, annoying) Internet presence. They might be irritated by this work, since I question their claims through a critique of their methods. However, a few former devotees also expressed their support of this work, stating that it was the lack of transparency in the Sai movement that they objected to and they themselves should not be opaque to any critique.

Throughout this introduction I have contended that in an era of globalization religious pluralism presents a fascinating and long-awaited critical challenge. The current theoretical impasse is a point at which we can look both backward, and assess the intellectual legacy of modernization, and forward to a cross-cultural, yet grounded, critical hermeneutic study of religious globalization. My hope is to resist the polarizing debates and dead-ends that questions of cultural alterity inevitably birth by clothing the liens of globalization theory with the rich messiness of field data, to enable us to question our language, our discursive practices, our unexamined assumptions, and our understandings of contemporary culture.

It is only with the heart that one can see rightly; what is essential is invisible to the eye.
                                                            —*Antoine de Saint-Exupéry*

I am the Self (Atma) seated in the hearts of all creatures. I am beginning, the middle, and the end.
                                                            —*Sathya Sai Baba*

1   Becoming God
     The Story of Sathya Sai Baba

Ashes to Power: Transformations and Translations

August 14, 1999. 11.00 A.M. Brindavan, Whitefield ashram. Gokulam canteen dining hall. Shanti (forty-three) from Bombay, Teresa (sixty-two) from London, and Joule (fifty-five) from Amsterdam, all devotees of over twenty years, are shelling beans in the dining room in preparation for the evening meal for the many thousands of devotees in residence. Usually this activity is completed in meditative silence or with whispered bouts of conversation, as per the rules of the ashram, but they are known as devout, so they can talk to me as they work. We talk about the miracles attendant to Shri Sathya Sai Baba's life and the announcement of his divinity, a favorite topic among devotees.

Shanti: "See, when Swami was a small boy in the town of Uravakonda near Puttaparthi, a big black scorpion stung Him. There was a belief in Uravakonda that no one will survive a scorpion sting in that place, they searched and searched to kill the scorpion, but no scorpion was discovered! They were all scared that Swami would die. But he lapsed in and out of coma, and when he was not in coma he gave lectures on philosophy and God which they could not understand. They were . . ."

Joule interrupts: "Swami's family thought some bad spirit had possessed him, and they took him to a devil doctor who did terrible things like putting acid in Swami's eyes. But Swami still continued to talk about Hindu philosophy. Then Swami told everyone that he was Shirdi Baba reincarnated."

Shanti nods assent and continued,

> You should read Sathyam Shivam Sundaram, Narayan Kasturi's book. It is a great book. . . . Swami himself told Kasturi all the stories and Kasturi recorded them. What I mean to say is . . . Swami has said, later, that He Himself initiated the process. . . . He could not wait any longer, playing about as a mere boy, with "brother" and "sister." He wanted to demonstrate, as He said, that He was beyond both Visha (life world) and vishaya (poison), unaffected by poison or the objective world. There was no scorpion that could sting Him. Swami is omniscient, omnipotent, and omnipresent. He is avatar (divine incarnation). . . . He knows everything. . . . He has wisdom, and we should listen. He has come here to help us, to teach us.

Her eyes filled with tears.

Teresa pulls out a book marked with yellow Post-it notes and many handwritten entries. She reads out a much marked passage: "I always remember this passage . . . 'For the bird in mid-ocean flying over the dark deep blue waters, the only resting place is the mast of a ship that sails across. In the same way, the Lord is the only refuge for man who is swept by storms over a restless sea. However far the bird may fly, it knows where it can rest; that knowledge gives it confidence. It has the picture of that mast steady in its mind; its form is fixed in the eye. The Name of the Lord is the mast for you; remember it ever.'[1] I was at the beach when I read this passage about the lost bird. I was at a very bad point in my life and I could see the seagulls circling about. . . I thought *I am* like a lost bird. I cried and cried. He changed my life . . . He saved me . . . I know that now. I did the *namasmarana* chanting (chanting of the names of the divine) the next day and I felt like a weight had been lifted from me. From my personal experience, the constant invocation of His name places me in a state of happiness."

How did an obscure peasant boy from an arid village in a remote corner of rural South India become a globally recognized and revered spiritual leader? And what does this paradigmatic life story mean for devotees' self understanding of happiness and its pursuit? There are two transformations of import in this chapter—first, the transformation of Sathya Sai Baba's divinity from local guru to global godman, which is a complex articulation spanning the logics of Hindu divinity and postmodern individuality to construct a universally mobile "nomadic" charisma and, second, its slide into an anxious transformation in the selfhood of the devotee while listening to and absorbing the life story of Sathya Sai Baba. In the introductory conversation with Teresa, Shanti, and Joule, this focus emerged naturally (as it did quite frequently in other interviews) when the conversation shifted from the transformation in the life story of Sathya Sai Baba to devotees' empathetic understandings of it and their concomitant ideal of self transformation. The shifting/sliding is emblematic of the interaction between Sathya Sai Baba and his devotees and is echoed in the structure of this chapter: the first section of the chapter deals with Sathya Sai Baba's life narrative and the strategic construction of sacred personhood inscribed within through "moments of transformation," which is a temporal, epistemological maneuver; and the second section deals with devotees' hermeneutic tactics of devotion, the telling and retelling of the mythic life story, repetitive singing and chanting, that enable this narrative of sacred personhood to be made mobile, a spatial maneuver that has affective resonances for the individual and is crucial to the growth of a transnational religious movement. The shift represents a tension between the understanding of religion as an individual, the interactive act of faith between divinity and devotee, and the need of the movement to recognize the global, social, and cultural processes of religion as being subject to possible manipulation in an effort to enlarge the devotee base.

The Sathya Sai Life Story

The Sathya Sai Baba's biography is shrouded in mystery, as is common with many charismatic sacred leaders, but devotee accounts construct a complete and complex mythic biography for him that replaces lost incidents in his life.[2] The *katha* or *purana* (story/ divine story), as this account is known to devotees, is familiar in its contours and is endlessly reproduced in texts and visual and aural form. Sai stories are translated into thirty-odd languages, and a running translation of his discourses occurs as he speaks. Radio Sai, a radio station owned by the global Sathya Sai Seva Organization, broadcasts segments from Sathya Sai Baba's life as parables, as does the "official" Sathya Sai Web page and thousands of unofficial Internet portals; cassettes are sold with stories of Sai Baba's life and poems and songs sung by devotees; pictures, paintings, and collaged photographs point to miraculous incidents and affiliated religious figures in his life and beyond; and newsletters of the SSSO celebrate episodes from his life (Srinivas 2008:2–4, 190–207).

Lawrence Babb, in his work on Sai Baba, raises the embedded problem of viewing Sai Baba "objectively" (1987:170), and this is a problem that haunts this study as well. "The first thing that must be said about Sathya Sai Baba is that the man himself is nearly impossible to find. . . . Submerged somewhere in the hubbub and symbolic paraphernalis of his cult is a person that we as outside observers would call the 'real man.' But whoever this real Sathya Sai Baba is, he is inaccessible." Babb continues (1987:161–162): "The strict facts of his personal biography and manner of his life are buried beneath layer upon layer of hagiography. . . . No objective account of Sathya Sai Baba's life has been written by anyone close to him. . . . It is unlikely that anyone who is allowed into his inner circle would want to write in such a vein. . . . No supposedly 'real' can be any more real than an imagined character in fiction."Sathya Sai Baba has been the subject of a number of biographies (at last count 342)[3] written by devotees,[4] of which three—written by Kasturi, Hislop, and Padmanaban[5]—are deemed official by devotees and seen as apostolic literature. In all the biographies, Sathya Sai Baba is constructed as suprahuman—as omnipresent, omniscient, and omnipotent —and they include hagiographical material that enables this construction. Norris Palmer (in Forsthoefel and Humes 2005:100–104) suggests that for devotees Sai Baba's omnipresence and omniscience are in fact part of divine "portfolio." However, as Spurr notes in his thorough and scholarly examination of the avatar concept in the Sathya Sai movement, Sathya Sai Baba himself acknowledges that his biography as written by devotees might appear as a "fairy tale," and he is believed to have told Kasturi, his "official" biographer, that readers may doubt his, i.e., Kasturi's sanity (Spurr 2007:33) after reading his work. But as Babb notes, the real Sai Baba is not of interest, rather, "the most interesting and in some senses, the most real too, is the one worshipped by devotees . . . at this level the extravangances of hagiography are not an impediment but an important aid to discovery" (1986:162). So, while many of Sathya Sai Baba's life stories are aggrandized, they are in some senses the closest to a life history of a charismatic religious leader that it is possible to obtain.

Devotees usually tell the story of Sai Baba both in texts and orally, focusing on three "moments of revelation" where the sacred person of Sathya Sai Baba reveals his "true" divine self to the world.[6] First, he announces that he is the reincarnation of the popular Indian Sufi mystical saint Shirdi Sai Baba. Second, he elevates himself to a pan-Indian Hindu guru by healing people, producing magical materializations, and giving darshan of himself as a divine figure. Third, he pronounces he is the second of three divine forms of Shiva-Shakti (male-female) divinity reincarnated on earth with a past and future incarnation. For Hindus these moments of "revelation" of the true self of divinity is, to quote Bakhtin, a "chronotrope" of divinity within which all space and time is subsumed.[7] These three transformations, from local peasant boy to magical guru to national spiritual leader and finally to international divine, are different strategic constructions of Sai Baba's global sacred personhood, where specific, non-Western indigenous Indic concepts of sacred personhood are engaged and transformed into a globally accessible narrative of sacred personhood.

From Peasant Boy to Local Guru

Sathya Sai Baba, or Sathyanarayana Raju, as he was then known, was born to a peasant family in the arid village of Puttaparthi (Telugu = *putta* = an anthill in which snakes live, *parthi* = multiplied) in Anantapur district in southern Andhra Pradesh on November 23, 1926. His family members were small peasant landowners of the Bhat Raju caste (of the Ratnakaram claim to chiefly status and as bards in princely courts), known for "interpreting and popularizing sacred literature" (Padmanaban 2000:11).[8] The mythic reconstruction of Sai Baba's life has included giving the Rajus a higher social status, not only through a higher caste affiliation but also through examples of their "Sanskritic" (Srinivas 1952) piety and devotion (Spurr 2007:100–104, quoting Thurston and Rangachari 2001 [1909], 1:223–224). For example, Kasturi, devotee and author, in his exhaustive work chronicling the life of Sri Sathya Sai Baba, claims that "the Raju family itself was noted for its piety since the days of the renowned sage, Venkavadhootha. . . . The pious Sri Ratnakaram Kondama Raju (grandfather of Sathya Sai Baba) dedicated a temple to Sathyabhama" (1962:3–4). Besides caste ambiguity, there also seems to be debate between chroniclers of Sai Baba's life as to whether his family were poor or wealthy. Some accounts state that his family was desperately poor,[9] others describe his grandfather as a wealthy landowner.[10] Sai Baba himself told Dr. John Hislop, an ardent devotee and biographer, that he was very poor when he was young. Hislop recounts the travails of this poverty in Sathya Sai Baba's own words: "I used to attend classes everyday wearing the same shirt, for I did not have a second. Some of the boys who discovered this fact started laughing at me. They teased me on the way to school, pulling at my worn-out shirt; they tore it. As I had no pin to even keep it together, I was forced to use a cactus thorn plucked from the fence of my neighbor's field to serve the purpose" (Hislop 1978:130).

In the apostolic literature, Sathya Sai Baba's birth in 1925 is "miraculous." Eashwaramma (Sathya Sai Baba's mother)[11] observed several *Satyanarayana pujas*[12] (wish fulfillment worship to the god Satynarayana) and "miraculously" conceived a child (Kasturi 1962:7–8). The story emphasizes Hindu mythic signs of the birth of the impending great soul that parallel the birth of prescient divine figures: miraculous music where no one plays the instruments, a cobra that refuses to harm the child, and divine light entering the womb of the mother (Kasturi 1962:8–9, 10–11). On November 23, 2003,[13] Sathya Sai Baba himself told a story where he recast his mother Eashwaramma as an exemplary woman-mother of God (*Theotókos*). "A light enter(ed) her stomach" (parallels with the idea of a virgin birth) before his own birth. Often we find, as Spurr notes (2007:37), that the "extravagances of hagiography" are either instigated or emphasized by Sathya Sai Baba. Sathya Sai Baba, through the initial telling of his life story and later insertions and retellings in discourses, has often provided material that has found its way into the official biography or supported it through what Spurr calls "autohagiographical" anecdotes (2007:37), and in this he is an unusually active participant in the creation and maintenance of his life story.

When Sathyanarayana was eleven or so, his elder brother became a teacher in the neighboring village of Uravakonda (Telugu = *urava* = serpent, *kunda* = hill). Sathyanarayana went with him to Uravakonda for schooling, and stories suggest, as Smriti Srinivas notes, that he seems to have been intuitive, magical, and entrepreneurial (2008:52–54).[14] The town of Uravakonda is geographically and experientially sacred in the Sai *katha* because it is where Sai Baba first declared his divinity. The declaration was a long drawn-out affair, occurring over a year, in four distinct episodes of revelation. On the evening of the March 8, 1940 in Uravakonda, Sathya Sai Baba was apparently stung by a scorpion (Kasturi 1962:37). He fell unconscious and remained that way for several days.[15] When he awoke, he appeared to be a different person, weeping, or catatonic, spouting Vedanta philosophy, singing songs in Sanskrit, and describing faraway places and images of deities that his family had never seen (Kasturi 1962:38–40; Murphet 1971:55). Worried that their son had been possessed by demon spirits, his parents took him to a renowned exorcist (whom Kasturi calls "a torture specialist") in the neighboring town of Kadiri who nearly rendered him blind. Regarding this experience, Sai Baba is believed to have told Dr. Hislop:

> Baba underwent torture at the hands of the village doctors when he first allowed His divine powers to manifest on a fairly large scale. This was around the age of ten. The doctors drilled holes in his head, and stuck in hot irons, cut open his skin and poured in burning fluids, buried him in a trench in sand up to his neck and iron bars to keep him fixed in one position. But he would move and be free. He smiled and felt no pain. . . . When Baba was born he knew his divinity and that he was God himself.   (1978:113)

After this, Sathya Sai Baba remained in his home village of Puttaparthi until May 23, 1940, when he magically materialized some sugar candy and milk (luxury goods in rural India at the time) and gave them to the villagers.[16] When his father was told that his son was performing *leela* (play or miracles), he went home shouting; "Who are you? Are you a ghost or a madcap?" In response, the thirteen year old is said to have replied calmly, but with great emphasis; "I am Sai Baba," clarifying further, "I am Sai, I belong to *Apasthamba Suthra* (the Brahma Sutras); I am of the *Bharadwaja gothra* (lineal descent from the Hindu sage Bharadwaja; a genealogical referent); I am Sai Baba; I have come to ward off all your troubles and to keep your houses clean and pure" (Kasturi 1962:39–40; Srinivas 2008:52–53).[17] According to some of the recent biographers, this announcement was met with incomprehension since no one in the village had heard of a "Sai Baba" at the time.[18] Shirdi Sai Baba (the Muslim Sufi *faqir* of the town of Shirdi in Maharashtra), with whom Sathya Sai Baba was claiming this extraordinary affiliation, was supposedly unknown in South India at the time.[19] Spurr suggests that Sathya Sai Baba might have been "in the throes of an identity crisis" (2007:105), but Swallow (1982:120) argues that Sathya Sai Baba's claim is typical of a renouncer who "rejects the world and breaks ties with family, caste and village."

Spurr notes (2007:51) in this regard that Sathya Sai Baba was often "inconsistent and/or inaccurate," in his telling of his life story, suggesting that to Sathya Sai Baba the moral of the story, rather than the historical detail, is important. However, the plethora of works on Sai Baba underscore the assumption that his "official" biography is "the story of the Lord come in human form" (Kasturi 1962:1).

At this point in the narration, devotees invariably stopped to assert that the "revelations" of Sathya Sai Baba's "true self" were not arbitrary in their timing.[20] According to them, it was divine determination that Sathyanarayana had decided to reveal himself as the magical reincarnation of the revered southern Indian saint and Maharashtrian Muslim faqir, Shirdi Sai Baba, who died in 1918.[21] This version of the story is corroborated by Sai Baba himself, who spoke some twenty years later to Kasturi about "the reveal." Sathya Sai Baba told Kasturi that, at the time, he had been "impatient" to reveal his "true self" to the world.[22] He said that as Shirdi Sai Baba of Shirdi (his previous incarnation)[23] he had known he would be reborn in the body of Sathya Sai Baba and had predicted it.[24] Devotees freely admit that the revelations were in fact no accident, suggesting that they were strategic, though they do not claim the strategic focus was attracting a wider devotee base. Palmer notes that the biography of Sathya Sai Baba underscores his ability to transcend time and space yet simultaneously be incarnate within them (in Forsthoefel and Humes 2005:101), creating the God-man: "the infinite deity who preaches a contextual message."

After the second episode, Sathyanarayana demanded that people refer to him as Sathya Sai,[25] linking him irrevocably in the popular imagination with the Muslim mystical Sufi faqir tradition of Shirdi Sai Baba. On October 20, 1940, Sathya Sai Baba completed the final step in his metamorphosis from ordinary schoolboy to religious mystic. He left school (the institution) and left his family (society) and told his family with finality, "I am going: I don't belong to you: Maya [illusion] is gone: My Bhaktas (devotees) are calling Me: I have My work: I can't stay any longer" (Kasturi 1962:44). According to Kasturi, on that day a divine halo appeared around his head. Sathya Sai Baba left home for three days to stay in the garden of the local excise inspector, and after that he never returned, moving to the home of a Brahmin woman named Subamma who was his first devotee (Padmanaban 2000:140–141, 161–171). This decisive step was a first moment of transformation for Sathya Sai Baba.

Sai Baba's (re)construction of himself as the reincarnation of the Muslim saint Shirdi Sai Baba a faqir and mystic, who was often compared to

Kabir[26] and who at time of his death had a significant local following among both Muslims and Hindus,[27] marks him as a Sufi religious scholar and poet (Rigolopoulos 1993; Shepherd 1985) of the Nanapanthi order (White 1972; Ernst 2005:20–23). As S. Srinivas notes (2008:29, 36, 40, the worship sequence at Shirdi, a major center of pilgrimage in India, is supposed to derive from the Vaishnavite devotional center at Pandarpur and have connections with the popular Krishna bhakti (devotional) tradition of the region. This open declaration of affiliation with Shirdi Sai Baba and inscribed subtle declaration of affiliation to Krishna was, and is, a recurrent theme in the Sathya Sai Baba's discourses, from the 1940s to the 1960s, and then again from the 1990's to the present.[28]

Devotees are familiar with the link to Shirdi Sai Baba because of the apologetic literature, and images of Shirdi Sai Baba are prominently displayed around Puttaparthi and the ashram.[29] Religious images of Sathya Sai Baba show him dressed as a Muslim faqir, wearing a *kafni* (robe made of gerua, an ochre-colored homespun cloth) and head cloth,[30] in a posture that is reminiscent of Shirdi Sai Baba. But Sathya Sai Baba does not claim that Shirdi Sai Baba was his *satguru* (true spiritual teacher); rather he claims to be Shirdi Sai Baba reincarnated in a new age, for a new purpose (Srinivas 2008:69). He suggests that the spirit that links them is one that is continuous, though their forms/bodies may be discontinuous (Rao 1995:44–45). Sathya Sai Baba often refers to Shirdi Sai Baba as "the previous body" in his discourses, underlining the legitimacy of his reincarnation, as in, "Let me tell you an incident which happened while in the previous body at Shirdi . . ." (SSS 2, 270). Recently a teleserial titled *Shirdi Sai Parthi Sai Divyakatha* (The divine story of Shirdi Sai and [putta] Parthi Sai) referenced this unfication visually.However, while some scholars have suggested that the Sai Baba movement is one phenomenon (Srinivas 2008:23–49),not all Shirdi devotees feel that Sathya Sai Baba is in fact the reincarnated form of the mystical Sufi faqir, and they repudiate Sathya Sai Baba's claim. This is the source of tension and hostility between some Shirdi Sai groups and Sathya Sai devotees and has led to confusion among prospective devotees and scholars that is often resolved by an appeal to their visual differences. In fact when I tell scholars of South Asian origin that I study Sathya Sai Baba,their first question will be, "Is he the one with the hair or without?"

Sathya Sai Baba follows the ideal Indic template for self-realization. In the life stories of many Indic spiritual leaders, the announcement of purpose followed by separation from the bonds of society in pursuit of

FIGURE 1.1. Sathya Sai Baba as a young man. Postcard image. *Collection of Tulasi Srinivas*

transformation is a central episode: the Buddha left his palace to seek enlightenment, Jain laity who wish to become monks have an elaborate ritual in which they sever their bonds with home and family (Cort 2001:333–335, 2002:719–742), and so on. Photographs of Sai Baba from this period show him wearing the *lungi* or *dhoti* (lower cloth tied at the waist covering the legs), and a long shirt, as most young men of rural small towns would dress. He appears distinctly charismatic,[31] often seated on a hard wooden chair, wearing long garlands of flowers, and staring fixedly though unsmilingly, at the camera. The transformation of the rural peasant boy into the local guru was complete. The mobility across dichotomies—from poor to rich, from unaware to aware, from peasant to charismatic leader—are all forerunners of cultural mobility.

From Local Guru to National Spiritual Leader

After his two revelations, Sai Baba began to demonstrate magical and healing powers, and people flocked to him (Kasturi 1962:45–70) from the neighboring villages to be healed and to get darshan. By 1946, important and wealthy devotees from all over South India were making the trip to Puttaparthi: Mrs. Sakamma, a rich coffee planter's wife from Coorg in southwestern Mysore state; Mr. Thirumal Rao of Bangalore, who dealt in transportation; the *raja* (chieftain) of Venkatagiri, a kingdom in the state of Andhra Pradesh; the *rani* (princess) of Chincholi, and the rich Ursus, an erstwhile princely family of Mysore (Srinivas 2008:54–57). These wealthy devotees contributed in large part to the development of the physical and institutional infrastructure of the early Sai movement (Kasturi 1962:77–82). In 1945 a shrine was built for Sai Baba—now referred to as the Old Mandir (temple) (Kasturi 1962:59–60). Sathya Sai Baba regularly worshipped an image of Shirdi Sai Baba at the temple and led the assembled devotees in singing bhajans (Padmanaban 2000:259–263) to him.

Between 1945 and 1947 Sathya Sai Baba's ministry began to expand in earnest, and he traveled extensively all over South India (Padmanaban 2000:182–220; Kasturi 1962:45–67), attending sacred meetings, song sessions, and performing charismatic healings (Padmanaban 2000:289, 307). Until the late 1940s, Sai Baba materializations were accompanied by private interaction with each devotee. But, as the movement began to grow, this became increasingly difficult, and public interaction became the norm. The shift from patrimony with intense personal interaction to beauracratic "public" interface, where the ocular vision was more important than the spoken word, was not initially received well by devotees. Despite this, the movement grew, as did the popularity of Sathya Sai Baba. His first public discourse occurred in the small town of Karur in Karnataka state on October 26, 1947 (Padmanaban 2000:391), where he addressed a group of devotees. The discourse was so popular among devotees that it became a feature of the Sai evening darshan as well as a platform where Sathya Sai Baba would announce changes in the mission, structure, and form of the organization, where he frequently discussed the expanding central concepts of the Sai doctrine.[32]

As the devotee following grew, Sathya Sai Baba established certain Sai "traditions": Sathya Sai Baba's birthday was celebrated as a public festival for the first time in 1946, as was the Hindu festival of Dussehra (the nine nights of victory) and Deepavali (festival of lights). On February 2, 1955, on Mahashivarathri (night dedicated to the worship of the Hindu god Shiva) Sathya Sai Baba is reported to have materialized a *lingam* (sphere representing the sexual/powerful form of Shiva) from within his body (Padmanaban 2000:323–345; Srinivas 2008:55), another feature that became institutionalized as part of the festivities.[33]

Coinciding with this growth of his ministry and the creation of unique festival traditions, Sathya Sai Baba is believed to have performed many important miracles that form the core of the Sai katha. His abilities, according to devotee accounts, ranged from simple healings with or without sacred ash, magical materializations of fruit, sweets, ash, pictures, watches, all "mobile material vehicles of his power" (Babb 1987:178), but soon extended to include teleportation, telekinesis, mind reading, appearance in dreams to give guidance, speaking many languages, and resurrecting people from the dead.[34] Because of miracle stories, the village of Puttaparthi became an encampment as the curious gathered in large numbers to bear witness. But, despite their increasing numbers, Sathya Sai Baba seemed reluctant to start a new religion of his own, exhorting people to stay in their "traditional" religions: "I will never force you to take up a particular name or Form of the Lord. . . . The Lord has a million Names and a million Forms and He wants that faith and attachment should be evoked in you by them as you recite the Names and contemplate the Forms" (SSS 1:218).

Despite the bloody partition of the Indian subcontinent into the two nation-states of secular India and Muslim Pakistan in August 1947, and the social and political chaos that both preceded and succeeded it, Sathya Sai Baba's devotional strength grew all over the subcontinent (Khilnani 1999; Bose and Jalal 1998). He built a new ashram (sacred residence, hermitage), Prasanthi Nilayam, in 1950 on the southwestern outskirts of his village of Puttaparthi on land donated to the movement by his rich devotees. Subsequently, two new ashrams, one on the outskirts of Bangalore called Brindavan (symbolic of the Hindu deity Krishna's pastoral paradise) and another summer residence in the hill station of Kodaikanal were acquired or built, as were subsidiary ashrams in Chennai, Hyderabad, and Mumbai.

Paralleling the physical growth of his ministry, Sathya Sai Baba's own legitimacy as a respected spiritual guide and teacher grew within India (Palmer in Forstoefhel and Humes 2005:103–104), as he was often seen in the company of highly respected Hindu saints such as Swami Satchitananda and Swami Sivananda (Srinivas 2008:57–59). On July 22, 1957, Sai Baba spoke of the need for the transformation of the self using the generic name of divinity in Hindu thought (*Bhagawan*) as a titular endowment specific to himself; " 'Bha' means creation. 'Ga' means protection and 'Va' means change or transformation; "Bha-ga-van (the lord) is capable of all three. That is My secret," he announced.

In July 1957 he echoed this self-ascribed ascension to divine realms when he traveled to the sacred city of Rishikesh in the Himalayas, Delhi, and Mathura, Brindavan—the sacred *pithas* or seats of Vishnavite Hinduism—to receive legitimacy and cement his position as a new and rising guru (Kasturi 1962:101–121) with an emergent urban syncretic Hindu-Muslim religious message. He made a pathbreaking speech in which he declared himself a guru-avatar,[35] identifying himself as both an "avatar for the ages" and human guru (collapsing into one what were previously two separate categories)—a significant second transformation. In the discourse he laid out the central principles of the mission of *seva* (work for those less fortunate), the idea of *siddhi* (self-control), and of *prema, prema, prema* (universal love). He welcomed "people of all types into the ashram" and swore that "there was only one religion; the religion of love" (Kasturi 1962:210–216). In practice, of course, the speech was ingenuous. Any organization on the national scale must rationalize its bureaucracy to some extent to address problems of running the institution and leadership succession. Nevertheless, the statement captured the movement's "self-presentation as a group organized by love rather than rational calculation, and by charisma rather than bureaucracy" (Huang and Weller 2007).

This self-defining speech was recorded in the first volume of *Sanathana Sarathi* (the way of the charioteer),[36] which was to become a devotee newsletter documenting discourses, the growth of the ministry, devotees' activities, and news of the movement. N. Kasturi, the original editor and apparent originator of the project, in 1958 created the newsletter to enclose transcripts of speeches given by Sathya Sai Baba for devotees to read.[37] In 1962, alongside his travels, his legend grew with the publication of the first volume of Kasturi's biography, *Sathyam Shivam Sundaram* (Kasturi 1968:19). At the same time Sathya Sai Baba installed a Vedic studies and Sanskrit studies academy in Puttaparthi, developing the infrastructure of the city as a center of religious life (Kasturi 1968:41, 53, in Srinivas 2008:60).

Throughout the 1960s, as more and more Indians flooded into the ashram, Sathya Sai Baba articulated his main claim to being an avatar of the Hindu tradition linking himself with the other two *poorna avatar* (complete incarnations) of the Hindu Vaishnavite tradition; Krishna and Rama.[38] "This is a human form in which every Divine entity, every Divine principle, that is to say, all the names and forms ascribed by man to God, are manifest. . . . You are very fortunate that you have the chance to experiences the bliss of the vision of the form, which is the form of all gods, now, in this life itself" (SSS 8:99f).Kasturi, Sai Baba's chronicler, gives many examples of the Krishna-Rama frame of affiliation, linking them backward in a textual "flashback" to earlier times. He states: "In 1945 . . . Sai Baba had gone to Masulipatam (a coastal town). One day while on the sands of Masulipatam Baba walked straight into the sea! . . . the devotees looked towards the sea and they saw a vision of the Lord (Vishnu) on the serpent Sesha reclining on the waves!" (Kasturi 1968:70) and, "On December 15th 1958 during Baba's Kerala tour. He went to Kovalam beach. . . . During this prayer session Baba 'took' from the sands a bewitching sandalwood image of lord Krishna playing the flute" (1968:103). Kasturi has hundreds of such anecdotes of the Sai Vishnu connection in his records. Sathya Sai Baba himself underlined his direct descent: "Rama and Krishna and Sai Baba appear different because of the dress each has donned, but it is the Self-same Entity, believe Me" (SSS 2, 18:92). He declared repeatedly, in speech after speech, that his task was the task of his incarnation (avatar) and the reestablishment of righteousness in the *kali yuga* (the age of modern evil). As Kent notes in her work, the internationalization of the Sai movement coincided with a recession of the Islamic influences in Sathya Sai Baba's discourses, but whether this was planned, as Kent suggests, or spontaneous, is unknown (2005:39).

Between 1963 and 1965, Sathya Sai Baba visited several sacred shrines all over India establishing himself as a sacred guru-avatar who combined (within himself and the movement) the syncretic principles of Indic religion and theology, merging together, as Spurr so evocatively demonstrates (2007), the influence of the Brahmanas, the Upanishads, the Bhagavad Gita, yoga, and earlier Vedic sacrifical traditions with the philosophies of the Dvaita, Advaita, and Samkhya traditions.

Photographs from this period show him dressed in an orange or white silk robe covering most of his body from neck to feet. The ordinary peasant dress of dhoti and shirt are gone. His hair appears as a halo around his head. The garlands are gone, as is the intense expression, and he appears more relaxed, often smiling into the camera. Most often he is photographed seated on a golden throne or a silver swing, his feet on a velvet cushion, surrounded by adoring devotees. Through the photographs the evolution from a rural peasant boy to charismatic divine figure emerges. Both his initial assertion of his reincarnated links with Shirdi Sai Baba and his later recasting of himself as a Hindu guru-avatar were unique

FIGURE 1.2. Sathya Sai Baba seated on a throne. *Photo courtesy Kekie Mistry*

transformative strategies that created a paradigmatic Indic postcolonial charismatic figure.

From National Guru to International Divinity

On July 6, 1963 (Gurupoornima Day—the festival honoring the guru), Sai Baba is recorded as having suffered paralysis on his left side. As he recovered, he made his most publicized and extensive claim—and a third reinventive transformation, perhaps the most important in terms of cultural translation and global reach. In his discourse he stated that he was the incarnation of the Hindu god Shiva and his consort Shakti (the female principle). They had made a promise to the divine sage Bharadwaja[39] that they would take a human form and be born thrice in Bharadwaja's lineage on earth (Kasturi 1968:84–85): Shiva alone would be born first in the form of Shirdi Sai Baba, both Shiva and Shakti together would then be born again as Sathya Sai Baba, and Shakti alone would be born finally as Sai Baba's final form, called Prema Sai.[40] He stated: "I am Siva-Sakti born in the Gothra of Bharadwaja according to a boon won by the sage from Siva and Sakti. Sakti herself was born in the Gothra of the sage, as Sai Baba of Shirdi; Siva and Sakti have incarnated as myself in this gothra now, Siva alone will incarnate as the third Sai in the same gothra in Mysore state" (Gokak 1983: 305; SSS 3:22). Sai Baba claimed that he was the middle incarnation and that he therefore combined the roles of both male and female, of both mother (*sai*) and father (*baba*), to his devotees (SSS 3:5, 1).[41] The twist of *Sai* being equated to mother is contested, as some scholars argue that the etymological relationship with *sai'h*, the Persian word for saint, is not very clear (Babb 1986:170–172). Brian Steel, a former devotee,[42] suggests that Sathya Sai Baba's "boldly imaginative extensions" in etymology are not restricted to this naming but weave through his discourses. Michael Spurr argues that the "episteme of resemblance" links all the avatars, and that the ideas of "enumeration" and "categorization" that he attributes to "early yogis and philosophical viewpoints" suggest that Sathya Sai Baba is a neo-Hindu religious leader (2007:19) who uses the avataric concept to widen his reach.

This historic-prophetic claim, of being the middle incarnation of three incarnations of Shiva and Shakti, allowed Sathya Sai Baba the furthest access, theologically and socially. He could claim Brahminic status (through Bharadwaja), within the Hindu Shaivite tradition (as an incarnation of Shiva),[43] an appeal to female devotees (through the female

Shakti principle), Islamic Sufi sainthood (through the "flashback" of his previous incarnation as Shirdi Sai Baba), the potential to prophesy his future divinity as Prema Sai (the savior of the universe in an immoral age), and the Hindu concept of divine androgyny (as he declared himself to be the unification of male and female principles of the universe). Divine androgyny has a long and revered history in South Asia and rests most specifically in the Shiva-Shakti yin and yang configuration. The Hindu deities Shiva and Shakti are masculine and feminine aspects of both the deity and the universe simultaneously. According to Babb, "they represent the absolute" (1987:13). So Sai Baba's claim to represent them both in one avatar gives him tremendous attributable divine power. As Babb thoughtfully notes (1987:174), Sai Baba resists any and all attempts at categorization, enabling a "theology of transcendance" through his very person (Spurr 2007:47): "In his identity as Shiva and Shakti, Sathya Sai Baba's persona opens out into transcendental inclusiveness and ambiguity. He is beyond all limiting categories. All time and space are one to him. His character also transcends gender, for he is male and female in one body." The bisexuality and androgyny of Sathya Sai Baba's dual claim has historic and philosophical parallels in Tantric (White 2003), Vedic (Doniger 1981, 1982), yogic (Alter 1994), and popular (Goldberg 2002) religious literature, but was unique to him. Goldberg states: "(androgynes are) . . . a paradigm of sacred human knowledge—a symbolic cultural landscape, formulating, regulating and legitimizing religious and ideological presuppositions including gender, on the one hand, while also providing a diagnostic paradigm for mapping the transformations of human consciousness through the subtle conjunction of the male and female form" (2002:19–23), "act (ing) as an encoded cultural motif both in terms of cosmogenesis and human processes." The innovative engaging of divine androgyny enabled Sathya Sai Baba to get beyond traditional categorizations of divinity and humanity, and male and female, by engaging a religiously embedded idea. The announcement of this androgynous divinity enabled Sai Baba to reach beyond India, "beyond Bharath," for his devotees (Palmer in Forstoefhel and Humes 2005:106–107). Palmer indicates that Sai Baba promotes the unity of one religions through his own divinity as the one God and that this does not seem to devotees that Sai Baba "cribbed" from any other religion but rather that he is "represent(ing) in one context what he taught in another" (2005:107). But Palmer suggests that the religion Sai Baba promotes as "universal"is in fact rooted in Hinduism and Sai Baba feels no need to mention that his stories, ideas, and myths are rooted in Hinduism because "the heart of his audience has historically been Hindu" (2005:105). According to Palmer, for Sai Baba, then, "Hindu" and "Indian" are "coterminous" realities leading to a conflation of Indian and Hindu identity, an idea that is echoed in Alexandra Kent's study of Sai devotees in Kuala Lumpur, Malaysia, where she suggests through what she terms "organizing ambivalence," the SSSO packages the Sai credo as an "Asian morality" where "in the intra communal arena Hinduism is portrayed as generative, encompassing all other religious forms" (2005:93–94). I will return to this idea of whether the Sai movement is a revitalizing movement within Hinduism or a generative force encompassing other religions later.

Sathya Sai Baba also envisioned the future of the movement through the imagined embodiment of his future sacred form—Prema Sai Baba.[44] Delighted devotees fastened onto this prophesy of reincarnated divinity. Sheela Thakur (sixty-eight) from Bombay, a Sathya Sai devotee for over thirty years, told me: "We have heard often that Prema Sai will be born eight years after the passing of Sathya Sai Baba, which will take place when Sathya Sai Baba is ninety-six years old." In *The Sai Trinity*, (2000 [1994]), author Dr. S. P. Ruhela writes that Sathya Sai Baba has been disclosing small amounts of information to close devotees from time to time and states that Sai Baba has predicted that Prema Sai will be born in Karnataka about eight years after he "leaves this body." Sai Baba is believed to have told John Hislop, "This body will live to age 96, and will remain young," and other myths state that Sathya Sai Baba has claimed that he would not become old or infirm.

John Hislop writes about Swami materializing a ring for him with an image of Prema Sai on it: "The stone was a cameo of Prema Sai, the loving Lord of Creation, destined to appear on Earth *a few years after the death of the Sathya Sai body*. It was a noble head with shoulder-length hair, moustache, and beard; the head resting on, or emerging from, a lotus flower. His countenance was tranquil, peaceful, majestic. Baba said, "He is only now in the process of birth, so I cannot show more of him. This is the first time he is shown to the world" (1985:55–56) Images of Prema Sai materialized for devotees are considered very valuable, since they represent a glimpse into the future of the movement. Devotees develop Sathya Sai Baba's assertion of a future form. For example, Shakuntala Balu writes, "Sri Sathya Sai Baba has said that there will be one more Sai Avatara called Prema Sai. The third Sai will be born in Gunaparthi, a village in the Mandya district of Karnataka. Thus, Sathya Sai Baba refers not only to his past, but also to the future form he will assume as Prema Sai" (1981:16), what author and devotee Rao refers to succinctly as the "three-in-one" phenomenon (Rao 1995:35–37). But despite the strategic turn toward the future face of the movement through the figure of Prema Sai, there seemed to be some ambivalence about the shift, both within the devotee population and Sathya Sai Baba himself. In August 1963, following Sai Baba's July declaration of his reincarnated tripartite divinity, the news-letter *Sanathana Sarathi*'s cover showed a picture of Sathya Sai Baba with Shirdi Sai Baba and with Krishna. It linked the rural peasant Hindu tradi-tion with the mystical folk Sufi tradition and portrayed Sai Baba as a syn-cretic, universalist religious figure striding many paradigms—rural/ urban, Sufi/ Hindu, and past and future divinity—but as markedly an In-dic divinity (Rao 1995:22–29).

But by the late 1960s the hostility toward global growth appears to have been resolved and Sathya Sai Baba began making repeated refer-ences to Jesus Christ both in his discourses and his private interviews with Western devotees, though he never claimed Jesus as one of his many divine forms. For example, Sathya Sai Baba said with reference to Jesus Christ, "Call me by any name—Krishna, Allah, Christ. Can't you recognize Me in any Form? Continue your worship of your chosen God along the lines familiar to you and you'll find you are coming near to Me, for all Names and Forms are Mine."[45] It is through this "three-in-one" fluid phenomenon that Sathya Sai Baba hopes to overcome the Hindu orthodoxy that threatens to haunt the movement by postulating the three-in-one avatar idea as a gateway to affiliation with other di-vine and semidivine beings. In fact, though the Hindu right wing has sought Sathya Sai Baba's support, he has never openly given it (Srinivas 2008:60).

Having established himself as an avatar on earth to educate human beings, he then established a connection to divine beings from other faiths. For example, he said; "God sends sages, saints and prophets to unveil the Truth and Himself appears as an *Avatar* to awaken and liber-ate mankind. Two thousand years ago, when narrow pride and ignorance defiled mankind, Jesus came as the embodiment of Love and Compas-sion and lived among men, holding forth the highest ideals of life." Christmas discourses were instituted in 1968 and in 1970. Sathya Sai Baba stated; "This Day marks the beginning of the Christian Era, the year of Christ. Christ sacrificed his life for the sake of those who put their faith in him. He propagated the truth that service is God, that sacrifice is God" (SSS 10:264). In 1971 Sai Baba hinted at a relationship between Christ and himself: "This birth has been undertaken by you for this very mission: the mission of crucifying the ego on the cross of compassion" (SSS 11:30). The images at Puttaparthi begin to include photographs and sculptures of Jesus Christ in a white or blue robe. In 1972, according to devotee accounts, Sathya Sai Baba claimed to be "the cosmic Christ" in the Christmas discourse. In January 1980, devotees Ron Laing and Peggy Maison record their ecstasy when Sathya Sai Baba answers their question about Christ: " 'Does this omission in the Bible mean it was you who sent Jesus of Nazareth into incarnation?' 'Yes,' he replied. Ron Laing continues, 'In that case, are you what Western Christians call the Cosmic Christ?' 'Yes,' he replied. So Sathya Sai Baba was the one whom Jesus called the Father, the Christ indeed, the Cosmic Christ. The second coming had come, had lived for forty-four years on earth and perhaps only a handful of Christians were aware of it.' "[46] Devotees who believe in the Jesus avatar give further proof:

> On April 20, 1972 while seated among a small group of American devotees Sai Baba reportedly performed a miracle which more than words could points out the connection between Christ, Shiva and himself. The devotees said that by a wave of his hand he materialized this small medallion picturing Jesus on its surface. The tiny medallion was passed from person to person through the group of devotees for everyone to examine. Taking it back into his hand, Baba blew on it twice transforming the image on the surface, according to those present, to that of Lord Shiva.[47]

Brian Steel, states on his Web site: "It (the references to Jesus Christ) marked the fusion of the initial Hindu Mission with a massive ecumenical global outreach phase which began in the late 1960s. . . . In the last few years that Christmas Discourse has been prominently displayed by Sathya Sai Baba's Organization on one of its official websites as one of his four most important Discourses. The bold title added to the Discourse is, 'He whom Christ Announced.' " The avatar of Jesus Christ is still one of Sathya Sai Baba's most controversial affiliations.

In 1968 at the World Conference of Sai Organizations held at Dharmakshetra, Mumbai, Sathya Sai Baba extended his avatarhood to include other divinities previously excluded. He said, "Continue your worship of your chosen God along the lines already familiar to you. Then you will find you are coming nearer and nearer to Me for all the names are Mine and all the forms are Mine. . . . I will succeed in warding off a crisis that has come upon humanity" (Sathya Sai Baba 1976a:23–29). Sathya Sai Baba extended his divinity to an umbrella concept of sacred personhood that included other religious divine and semidivine figures. In 1974 the cover of *Sanathana Sarathi* became thoroughly internationalized, incorporating the new ecumenical logo of the Sai movement—a lotus with the symbols of the crescent and the star (Islam), the cross (Christianity), the Om (Hinduism), the fire (Zoroastrianism), and the wheel (Buddhism). Some thirty years later in 2002 the cover of *Sanathana Sarathi* represents a global movement. The image is that of a Puttaparthi transformed into a fertile valley, an imagined Elysium, where it is accepted that "the global Sai family" (*Sanathana Sarathi* November 2002:320), with photographs of different racial and ethnic devotee groups to convey the pluralism of the Sai devotional base, is the societal and devotional norm (Srinivas 2008:200–204).

Guru, Sant, Avatar, Future: The Fourfold Complexity of Sai Baba's Divine Personhood[48]

As S. Srinivas rightly notes (2008:67–75) the divine humanity of Sai Baba, as described by himself and his devotees, falls into three broad representational categories—guru, sant, avatar—to which I would add a fourth, a future.[49] The Sathya Sai religious persona draws pieces of the Sai *katha* from the sant-guru-avatar combination, each of which has distinct meanings and value, drawn from historical and religious contexts on the subcontinent, and subtly creates a universally appealing charismatic figure who transcends the human-divine chasm to create a future. These representational categories help construct a new language and tradition within the movement.

The term *guru* (teacher) has had a cachet in the United States since the counterculture 1960s (see Srinivas 2008). But the term *guru* (Sanskrit = big/weighty) is an ancient one in Hinduism (translated as "one who shows the path"), and in South Asia it can be traced to Upanishadic texts (ca. 600 BC). The guru tradition is Sanskritic (Srinivas 1952) and Brahminical (Gold 1987:49), and while this tradition is deeply rooted in Hindu mythopoetics it is somewhat paralleled in Jewish traditions of

respect for rabbinical learning and miracle working recorded in the Tal-
mud and the Bible, which recurs as a motif into the present day. Starting
with the North Indian poet-saints (often of Muslim or Sikh origin) of the
fifteenth and sixteenth centuries (Schomer 1987:2–4), the *sant* tradition
(Sanskrit = *sat* = truth) is an Indic folk tradition that refers to saints and
holy persons, keepers of mystical knowledge (often of poetry/music, sacred texts, and indigenous healing) and revolutionary charismatics. Lineages that were chosen by mystical figures that crossed sectarian and religious boundaries, drawing syncretically from Sufi mystical and Vaishnavite
Hindu *sampradaya* (traditions) were encouraged in the sant trandition. Indeed, the worship of sants as divine beings is of fairly recent origin where
the sant-guru is higher "than rituals or god" (Gold 1987:3; Srinivas 2008,
Jugensmeyer 1987, 1991).

While the guru and the sant are mortals that have a suprahuman component of enlightenment through faith and knowledge, the avatar is divinity incarnate on earth. The Sanskrit word *avatar* literally means "descent"
and usually implies a deliberate descent into lower realms of existence for
special purposes: a human god or what Raymond Williams calls "the human face of God." The avatar is a post-Vedic concept that is best articulated
in the Bhagavad Gita (song of the Lord), the *locus classicus* of Indian philosophy (ca. 1000 BC),[50] though it appears in the Mahabharata and the Ramayana, the two epics of Hinduism, as well. Avatars are believed to reappear time and time again on earth to rescue humanity when *satya* (truth)
and *dharma* (duty) are in peril, and the exemplar is the avatar of Vishnu,
Krishna, who in the mythic epic Mahabharatha war is quoted: "whenever
there is decay of dharma (righteousness) and the rise of *adharma* (evil)
I embody myself O Bharatha" (Bhagavad Gita, chapter 4, verse 8; Spurr
2007).[51] Krishna is a *poorna avatar*, in which all the full flowering (fourteen attributes) of the Godhead are expressed. Avatars supposedly descend
to earth to cleanse it of evil. The evils of the fourth and final stage of this
world—the kali yuga "black age"—which we are currently believed to be
in, calls for a new avataric savior (Spurr 2007:144) who delinates new
tasks, many of which Sathya Sai Baba "adopts or adapts." Indeed, Spurr
(196–197) suggests that Sathya Sai Baba is "said to have changed the second half of the Bhagavad Gita stanza in which Krishna describes his re-
birth in avatar form, from *sambhavami yuge yuge* (I incarnate from age to
age) to *sambhavami pade pade* (I incarnate from time to time)" harnessing
himself, Spurr suggests, to the mythological figure of Kalki the Hindu
savior in the final dark age, as he attributes to himself the three moral

characteristics of avatar: *shrishti, sthithi,* and *laya* (creation, preservation, and destruction).

The affiliation with the two important Vaishnavite avatars—Rama and Krishna—presents devotees with a popular understanding of the epistemological link between the philosophies of Upanishadic Hinduism[52] and the problems of self-knowledge in the various strains of Vedanta philosophy,[53] which focuses on the complex links between the self (*atman*) and the supreme godhead (*Brahman*), which we will address later in this work. Avatars rarely, if ever, confirm their divinity to humans or define themselves; "they are, in Hindu philosophical terms, the uncategorizable"—*neti neti neti*—(not this, not this, not this) (Spurr 2007:239). Part of the appeal of avatars is their secrecy in unveiling their "real" selves to humans on earth. The avatar concept is one that has been employed to great effect to argue that divinity emerges in many forms on earth and that human purpose is the recognition of divinity within that form; a sacred guessing game. As an intellectual strategy, therefore, the avatar enables the sacred divinity (the godhead) to be separated conceptually from the form or body of that person. Sacred embodiment thus becomes a twinned puzzle of carnal knowledge and unveiling of divinity in popular Hindu myth, a theme that will reappear in subsequent chapters. The Hindu cycle of creation, evolution, and destruction contains the essence of the idea of avatars[54] and presumes equal opportunity salvation, since God manifests in a form that can be appreciated by the true believer, even if he is not intellectually sophisticated.[55]

Norris Palmer, in his study of Sathya Sai Baba, suggests that in essence Sathya Sai Baba's story is calling "for a return to Vedic Religion" (Palmer in Forsthoefel and Humes 2005:105), that his teachings are "drawn from Hindu texts and traditions," but that he uses "Indian" instead of "Hindu" when discussing the origin and content of the Sai faith. Palmer argues that for Sai Baba Indian and Hindu are "coterminous realities" and that by conflating the two he calls for a resurgent Hindu identity. Palmer suggests that Baba's "teachings center on reappropriating and reenergizing Indian/Hindu culture and traditions to such a degree that Hindu nationalists count him as one of their own" (in Forsthoefel and Humes 2005:106). However, Sai Baba has argued, to the contrary, that he is no Hindu nationalist and does not expect his devotees to "convert" to Hinduism, but to retain the faith of their birth.

It is clear that Sathya Sai Baba's life story draws on all three categories of the Hindu cycle in the construction of his charisma. The shift from guru to sant to avatar to future sacred person is governed by the logic of evolution. The collapsing of guru-sant-avatar-future into a single model of divine humanity enables two distinct strategies that stretch Sathya Sai Baba's sacred personhood—the strategy of extended affiliation (whereby Sathya Sai Baba extends his reach to devotees of other religions) and the strategy of future memory (where the life story enables a projection into the future). Both strategies are located in the temporal-historical domain. The strategy of extended affiliation enables the divinity of Sai Baba to engage and engulf what may be seen as "oppositional figures" of divinity across time and to incorporate them within his own divinity.[56] The avatar concept enables an extension of Sai divinity into the uncharted future—a strategy of future memory—that devotees can hold onto as a trajectory. The creation of a tripartite Sai chain of reincarnation where the future holds greater things ingeniously solves the Weberian puzzle of the evolution from charismatic authority to legal-rational, but retains the nascent power of charisma in the affective relationality between devotee and charismatic leader. The image of Prema Sai ensures the charismatic succession and institutionalization of the Sai Baba figure and the creation of a "triadic typology" (Rigolopoulos 1993:251) ensures the continuation of the global Sai movement long after Sathya Sai Baba's death. Aspects of this avatar descent crafted by Sai Baba are an "interpretation of Hindu tradition" that falls into line with "preconceived philosophical ideas," moving it from mere inclusion to active synthesis (Spurr 2007: 243).

As we see, the sacred personhood constructs charisma through a narrative of unity in multiplicity that collapses several ontological and epistemological frames upon one another through clever etymological play with linguistic, morphological, and syntactical forms familiar to the scholars of theological discourses of the subcontinent (from medieval commentary on the Vedic sacred texts to contemporary popular culture). This collapsing of many divine forms removes the problem of perfidy from devotee's minds, allowing them to see Theosophy, Christanity, the Sai movement, and Islamic Sufism as various "spiritualisms"(see Rao 1998:27–29) that are interwoven within the sacred charismatic form of Sathya Sai Baba. But, for these two temporal strategies to work, the logic of amanesis (of the multiple returning to the one) must hold good, where Sathya Sai Baba can claim that all these divine forms lead back to one unifying sacred entity, his *true* self (a logic that encompasses cosmological understandings of space-time). Palmer argues that this true self is essentially Hindu, i.e., while Baba professes a universality of religious truth, in reality he "offers a form of acceptance that subsumes difference and particularity into the fold of an ever absorbent Hindu tradition" (in Forsthoefel and Humes 2005:107). Palmer appears to argue that religious unity as evidenced in Hinduism is enabled by the logic that Sai Baba is the one true God, which makes it easier for him to promote the idea of one faith. This concept of the "absorbent Hindu tradition" and how it is read by devotees and critics is at the basis of the problems of cultural translation of what are seen as "Hindu" ideals and values during globalization.

For example, the devotee's perspective about Baba's "true self" is revealed in a story told in the 1980s by John Hislop, a longtime devotee and author who accompanied Sai Baba on a road journey Sai Baba revealed his "true self"to Hislop beyond any incarnation:

at some point in the journey, perhaps about halfway, Baba was talking and I turned to look. My breathing stopped and I was transfixed! What transfixed my movements and stopped my breathing now, was his face—the Baba I knew was not there! Instead there was a face of extraordinary beauty—quite different in shape and cast of features of our beloved Sai. Never in my life . . . have I seen a face of such exquisite beauty. It was beyond imagination and concept, beyond experience. And his colour was blue . . . deep blue, like velvet blue that sometimes can be seen in a dark sky, like blue that I have at times seen from the deck of a ship thousands of miles from shore on the Pacific Ocean. "Swami what was that blue color?" He replied, "Oh! That? Whenever there is something of unfathomable depth it appears to be deep blue."   (Hislop 1985:38)

In this story Sai Baba's "true self" is revealed as beyond limitation, "unfathomable," like the depths of the ocean or the breadth of the sky, a formless form that encompasses many different points within it. Thomas told me after reading Hislop's description of Sai Baba's "true divinity" (Rao 1995:29): "You know because we cannot understand how limitless God is, he gives us something to help us to understand." In this way he straddles the human-divine schism. The operational core of the guru-sant-avatar-future fourfold narrative is the modality of strategic ambiguity; that there are several different points of view about divine identity, many of which are either unknown or indescribable, and the various plastic forms articulated by Sathya Sai Baba cover the various possibilities. This modality of strategic ambiguity located in temporal stretching enables Sathya Sai Baba to transform himself from local guru to global godman.

Sathya Sai Baba deliberately constructs a sacred personhood he inhabits, which slides between an Indic, culturally embedded, evolutionary understanding of human divinity (guru-sant-avatar) to one that is Western, global, and mobile (constructed charisma) with a view toward articulating the complexity of representation of sacred personhood and the interlinking allegorical and metaphorical meaning between representations. Whereas, in the Western understanding, God and man are two different categories, the meaning of God in the Indic understanding is split between the personality of the God itself and the interactive process of propitiation through praxis: the relationship between divinity and devotee. Act, intent, and reconstruction of selfhood are all combined within this cultural configuration, which enables multicultural access because of its innate fluidity. Note, however, that Sathya Sai Baba acknowledges there may be conflict in the devotees' mind over Christ as an Abrahamic monotheistic God and the Hindu concept of avatar, but he argues that in fact there is no tension since

Every Avatar is an amazing phenomenon. But, it is also amazing not to recognise him.

FIGURE 1.3. Sathya Sai Baba and images of many avatars. Postcard image. *Collection of Tulasi Srinivas*

the avatar is a meta-understanding of divinity. The task therefore, as articulated by Sathya Sai Baba, is transformative; an unearthing of the "true
divine self" within.

Constructed Charisma and Global Guruhood

But what is this "true self," this validated sacred personhood?
Anthropology today is very concerned with the questioning of the language of the construction of personhood through gender, nationality,
ethnicity, embodiment, and agency (Douglas and Ney 1998; Desjarlais
1999; Lamb 2000; Glucklich 2001; Rasmussen 1995; and Delvecchio-
Good 1992). Relationality between people and what they perceive as "transcendant" experiences is largely ignored in the scholarly literature. And yet
the term *person* in the West, as author Kenneth L. Schmitz, informs us,
"exhibits a close association with the manifest and the hidden, and with
representation and communication" (*pro-, ops-, on*: to see and be seen), so
that the encounter with the Numen (the sacred being) was historically
privileged. But, at some point in the development, the open transcendence
no longer appealed in public discourse. So, in our contemporary postmodern understanding of personhood, all the elements or aspects remain (the
manifest and hidden, the communicability, the distinctiveness, and the
intimacy), but they take on a new configuration where autonomous power,
now seen as "free will," assumes new importance. In postmodern thinking, free will, rather than the sacred, is seen as the ultimate transformative
agent.

Edward Bailey, in *The Encyclopaedia of Religion and Society*, defines
the sacred as possessing four distinct properties: "In experience it is
special even unique, in value it is important, in consciousness it is fundamental even primordial; in communication, it is dynamic yet ineffable. . . . All these characteristics issue a single consequence that is
easily described but is less a separate quality than an aspect or by product of all of them." Simply put, the "sacred person" is the intersection
of secrecy and openness, of dynamic communication with unique experience, and signifies both the particular as well as the all encompassing. Charisma is one facet of sacred personhood that applies, but it
is limiting in its very humanness. Devotees of Sathya Sai Baba would
not consider him a "mere" charismatic leader, but a consideration of
charisma as an etic concept provides a useful starting point for the

investigation of the understanding of the Sai understandings of divine personhood.

Charisma, literally meaning "gift of grace" (Weber 1968:216), is an extraordinary yet undefinable quality that defines leaders, legitimates their authority, and elevates the individual who is charismatic beyond the ordinary realm. Weber defines charisma as "an extraordinary quality of a person, regardless of whether this quality is actual, alleged, or presumed. 'Charismatic authority,' hence, shall refer to a rule over men, whether predominantly external or predominantly internal, to which the governed submit because of their belief in the extraordinary quality of the specific person" (Weber 1968:295).[57] Weber stresses that the charismatic figure rises up ex nihilo to lead his "charismatic community" (Gemeinde)—"an organized group subject to the charismatic authority" (Weber 1968:243), governing by virtue of personal appeal, "every charismatic authority would have to subscribe to the proposition, 'It is written . . . but I say unto you'" (Weber 1968:243). Weber comments that charisma and its manifestation are strongly linked to "emotional states of being."[58] Thomas Dow argues that devotees "(are) moved to complete personal devotion," because they see, in the leader, "forces" that exist within themselves, that are being freed by the "being and action of the leader": a mimetic understanding of charisma. Accordingly, Dow argues, the follower obtains freedom from the mundane by surrendering to the initiatives of the leader (1968:83–84), presupposing Charles Lindholm's idea that emotion (the cultivation of its display and release) is the interactional "bridge" created between charismatics and their followers: "They (the charismatics) are marked by a unique and innate capacity to display highly colored emotions, of whatever kind. . . . The intense emotional state of the charismatic is transmitted spontaneously to onlookers, infecting them with enthusiasm and a feeling of vitality" (1993 [1990]:173–175). In Lindholm's unique conceptualization of charisma as a mode of embodied emotion, the charismatic figure is a natural-born performer of heightened emotional expressivity.[59] Ruth Willner argues that these emotional states are brought about by the projected personal qualities of a charismatic leader: "insofar as charisma can be seen to be the quality of an individual it lies in his capacity to project successfully the image of himself as an extraordinary leader," but by discussing the "projection" of the charismatic "image" she subtly shifts the locus of questioning from the personality of the charismatic to the devotee's perception of the charismatic and the possible manipulation of this perception (1984:3–3) through storytelling. Willner suggests that, while the charismatic properties are attributed to the leader, the "perceptions" of these properties by the devotees/followers build on the charisma (1984:6–9). Sathya Sai devotees recognize some element of manipulation in the construction of the Sathya Sai divine image, though they denied it when I questioned them. The understanding of perception changes the intent and the positionality of the emotional act of charisma locating it in the interaction between leader and follower.

Devotional Hermeneutics and the Transformative Tactics of Devotion

March 12, 2005. Hollywood, California, Sathya Sai temple. The Sathya Sai temple in Hollywood, California is situated five blocks east of Highland Avenue where the flat grid of Los Angeles meets the Hollywood Hills. The neighborhood here consists of three-story apartment buildings with barred windows and small office buildings. It is far from the trendy nightclubs and the boutiques of Melrose Avenue three blocks to the south. The temple is a small building on Wilcox Avenue, and inside the heat and glare of city fade away. Orderly rows of cushions with bhajan books placed on them face the altar with a lifesize framed and garlanded photograph of Sathya Sai Baba and an empty throne. The altar has offerings of fresh flowers, incense, and fruit and pictures of Jesus, the Virgin Mary, and Krishna. Thomas Wright (forty-eight), a Sai devotee of twelve years, was leading a particularly long-suffering "study circle." In a typical study circle, devotees read out philosophical passages from Sai Baba's many discourses and discuss them (Roof 1994:1–7). As Wright began a discussion on the concept of *anugraha* (divine grace) by reading out Sai Baba's many quotations, one of the assembled devotees (who was clearly a newcomer, as indicated by his demeanor) stopped and asked, "Is Swami Jesus reincarnated?"

Thomas replied patiently: "Swami has addressed this before." He went out returned with a sheaf of printed papers from which he read:

"God cannot be identified with one Name and one Form. He is all Names and all Forms. All Names are His; all Forms are His. Your Names too are His, you are His Forms. . . . When you clarify and sanctify your vision and look at them through the Atmic eye (the eye that penetrates behind the physical), then you will see the Supreme sovereign person. . . . Strive to win that vision and to saturate your-self with that bliss." This is from the *Sathya Sai Speaks* collection of discourses by Bhagawan. For those of you interested, it is volume 9, chapter 41, called "The Middle Path" (pages 212–213). But, I tell you, you can find peace not by questioning his forms, you can find peace only by repeating the names of Swami . . . namasmarana. This re-membering of his names with adoration will lead you to the right path.

The tactic of repetition is institutionalized in the rituals of the Sai movement. As Teresa stated, the tactic of memorial naming of Sathya Sai Baba is encouraged by the Sathya Sai Organization and the movement as a whole. The ritual called namasmarana is part of the structured ritual sequence at the Sai ashram in Puttaparthi and in Sai Centers all over the world and is encouraged by Sathya Sai Baba himself: "The constant re-cital of the Name of God—any of the million Names by which He is identified by human imagination or intelligence—is the best means of correcting and cleansing the mind of man" (SSS 6:133–134). Sathya Sai Baba emphasizes the spiritual gain in the practice of memorial repeti-tion: "The Name of the God, if recited with love and faith, has the power to bring upon the eager aspirant the grace of God. The Name . . . can award unimagined strength and courage. . . . The name has so much ef-ficacy. . . . The tongue must be sanctified by the repetition of the Name. Select some Name and Form for this all pervasive immanent God and keep it in your tongue and before your mental eye" (SSS 7:377–388). Or again; "To evoke the Divine in you, there is no better method than na-masmarana" (SSS 2:195). In many discourses Sathya Sai Baba exhorts the devotees to engage in the namasmarana every day by drawing out the practical and philosophical merits of the ritual praxis and the engender-ing equality that the ritual provides.[60]

The tactic of memorial repetition extends into singing repetitious songs and chants throughout the city in procession as well, called *naga-rasankeertana* (music spanning the city) which contains the entire aural spectrum: chanting, singing, and saying. All three are supposed to be-come one meditative act of sound in which the devotee is immersed. By surrounding him/herself with these auspicious sounds the devotee "comes closer to God."[61] Devotees extolled the virtues of *namasmarana*

and *nagarsakeertana* to me. As S. Srinivas notes in her work (2008:78–
85), listening to these sounds of the divine name are believed to imbue
the reciter and the listener with moral qualities and "correct" emotions,
what Turner has identified as "a set of evocative devices for rousing,
channeling and domesticating powerful emotions" (1995 [1969]:42–43).
Sathya Sai Baba encourages the domestication of emotions through the
repetition, arguing: "Words have tremendous power; they can arouse
emotions and they can calm them. They direct, they infuriate, they reveal, they confuse; they are potent forces that bring up great reserves of
strength and wisdom. Therefore have faith in the Name and repeat it
whenever you get the chance" (SSS 4:184).

The affective connections generated in the interaction between divinity and the devotee is categorized into four different expressions (*bhava*)
of emotion in Hinduism; 1. *madhura-bhava* (sweet love for the divine), as
in faqir Kabir's Bhakti poetry; 2. *vatsalya-bhava* (love between a mother
and child), where the recitation brings up the love between mother and
child recording parallels between the mythic Yasoda, the foster mother
of Krishna, and Krishna the divine child himself; 3. *anuraga-bhava* (love
for a lover), exemplified in the mythic stories of the many lovers of the
god Krishna; 4. *sakhya-bhava* (love between friends), as that of Arjuna
and Krishna; and finally 5. *dasya-bhava* (servant-master fealty), a normative form that exhorts devotees to serve divinity, as Hanuman (the monkey king) did Rama in the Ramayana epic. Categorization of emotions
between divinity and the devotee demonstrates that feeling emotional
connections is critical to the transformation of the devotee. Devotees'
agency lies in picking the form of divinity that best enables a deep and
compelling relationship to develop.

The affective power of the repetition is considered to be its transformative efficacy, its inherent power to call up divinity, in times of need,
and has the added benefit of arousing or controlling emotions. The sacred presence of Sathya Sai Baba is believed to respond both to the telling
of his life story and the rhythmic chanting. Devotees believe that the
chanting induces his presence and his blessings upon them. Believing
the episodes from his life story, devotees see Sai Baba as someone who
overcame all manner of adversity—poverty, ill-health, disbelief, and location—to live for his cause, and so they trust Sai Baba in a unique way.
The repetition of his name encourages the creation and maintenance of
this bond of trust in the hope of being transformed toward divinity.
Sathya Sai devotees equate this trust with the eternal love (*prema*) of

Sathya Sai Baba, the core emotion devotees are "supposed" to feel, and often do feel, toward Sathya Sai Baba. His discourses conflate the praxis of namasmarana and the enhancement of this exemplary prema. "Namasmarana can grant full happiness to all people, in all places and at all times. The names Rama, Hari, Hara, Sai, Baba, Krishna—having each two syllables are all derived from the word *prema*, which is the essence and core of the Atma. Namasmarana must be done with emphasis on tone, tune and timing, attitude and attachment and the attainment of highest good. It is not singing for singing's sake. This will certainly liberate the individual and transform the community and the world" (SSS 11:245–249).

Sai Baba himself stresses remembering the name of God, listening to Him and remembering the form of God as paths of devotion. Sai Baba states that the name of God is "sweet" and is as necessary as "air for your lungs" (SSS 1:214); it is like "water" that washes away the "dirt" of egoism (SSS 1:19); it is "food" that gives spiritual energy (SSS 2:11); it is the "rock" that makes the devotional self into "clay" (SSS 2: 184); it is the "medicine" that is the "balm" to the hurt soul; and it encourages the "seedling" of devotion to grow into an enormous "tree" of "virtue, sacrifice and love" (SSS 2:11). The chant of remembrance of the name of God (namasmarana) is part of the darshan ritual sequence; it is considered to be healing and necessary as breathing for the devotional self (Srinivas 2008:85–91).

In Kirin Narayan's evocative work on devotional belief in the Hindu tradition, storytelling is considered central to constructing devotion (1989). The stories and the storytellers suggest that telling (and retelling) these worn narratives creates a moral context (Narayan 1989, 1997) within which devotees begin to operate, offering them as parables of action or as telling examples of the fruits of inaction. In Indic religious traditions, oral storytelling of the myths and exploits of divine beings is a recognizable part of the embedded folk tradition. The story is a cultural mechanism to create familiarity and devotion to divinity.

Devotees tell each other important episodes from the life story, and they read and reread certain devotee authors' accounts of Sathya Sai Baba's story, creating a milieu of memorialization. The stories of Sai divinity and the repeated retelling of the Sai life story by devotees not only strengthens ties between devotees and Sathya Sai Baba but also form a "remembered" narratable body of happenings—a story—that they can all relate to and from which they gain spiritual instruction (Narayan 1989).[62] For example, Shanti told me: "I like Narayana Kasturi's book best. He is Baba's first, best *bhakta* (devotee). So nicely he writes about the Swami's childhood years and different miracles. When Swami was young boy he used to make sweets and *vibhuti* (sacred ash) and *amritham* (nectar) for all the people who came for darshan (sacred sighting) on the banks of the Chitravathi River. He even made a *kalpatharu* (tree bearing all fruits) out of an ordinary tamarind tree" (See Kasturi 1962; Padman-aban 2000). Stephen said; "I have Howard Murphet's book, *Sai Baba: Man of Miracles.* I found it to be good because it describes the time when Bhagawan brought Mr. Radhakrishna to life after he died in front of Elsie and Walter Cowan. Stories of healing are important to me because I am a healer myself . . . I do Reiki and Buddhist healing techniques. I also like some of the questions in Sam Sandweiss the psychoanalyst's book, when he came to meet Bhagawan." Aki said; "I like the story of Swami making food for everyone" (Kasturi 1962,1972, 1980).

I found many of the newer devotees reading various "official" apostolic versions of the life story while queuing for various events at the ashram. They are aided by the fact that all Sathya Sai Baba's stories and discourses are translated into languages including Swahili, Russian, and Japanese, and published by the Sri Sathya Sai Books and Publications Trust at Put-taparthi, sold in Sai bookshops all over the world. Former devotees such as Brian Steel argue that the translations of Sai Baba's discourses often editorilaize Sai Baba's words to make them seem more profound, logical, and informed than they actually are.[63] His oral discourses on his birthday and other festival days are simultaneously translated into English and Hindi. Sathya Sai Baba has always had a translator, usually drawn from the many core devotees. His current translator, Mr. Anil Kumar, who should be inured to his discourses, purports to be "astonished" at Sathya Sai Baba's teachings: "Sometimes I even forget to translate and instead I say, 'Abba!What a statement Swami!'" (Spurr 2007:80). In his individual interactions with devotees, Sai Baba is believed not to need a translator since devotees claim he is adept at speaking to them in every language, a form of mind reading they claim he specializes in, which makes him in-stantly comprehensible. Thus devotees are very familiar with the elabo-rate contours of his words and his stories.

Devotees would often correct me if I got certain dates or places wrong since they were anxious to demonstrate their understanding of Sai Baba's unique place in the world to other devotees. They also wanted me to have the "correct" facts as they knew them. For example, on November 10, 2003, while I was in Puttaparthi, a young woman devotee named Kate told me in passing while we sat in a queue for darshan: "You know the story of Bhagawan and the gold coin that he produced for a devotee? Well I heard from the daughter of a devotee who was there that it was solid gold and it had the American eagle stamped on it, since he was American!" As we were talking, Aki, the Japanese woman devotee, joined in: "Aaah! That I did not know." Former devotees also suffer from this devotional failing. When I discussed the intricacies of Sathya Sai Baba's life with them, if they felt I had "facts" wrong, they immediately corrected me, citing innumerable devotee texts.[64] Many new devotees like Aki also told me that they had learned a great deal about him through discussing apostolic accounts. The familiarity with the details of the Sai katha demonstrates closeness to Sathya Sai Baba and his divine revelation to other devotees. Devotees are constantly telling and retelling these stories to one another and commenting on small, intimate details. Devotees tell each other the stories of the five moments of reinvention constantly, and they read about these moments in apostolic accounts.

An embedded tactic in the telling of stories of mythic kings and gods is that of unveiling. Devotees often expressed to me, that despite the evocative stories that were told to them, or that they told themselves, it was the poverty of their human imagination that they could not imagine Sai Baba to be these multiple forms of divinity at once. But, for Sai devotees like Sarah, the transcendent as represented by Sai Baba is real and close. Devotees follow the logic of the avatar to its logical conclusion where the body (shariram) of the avatar houses the residing divinity rather like a masquerade that, unlike Doniger's theory of masquerade, is beyond sexuality, though as we will see that sex nonetheless causes problems both for the avatar and for the devotees (Doniger 2005). Helene (forty-eight) from Marseille described an "unveiling" story in an interview: "When I came to Puttaparthi, first day in 1989, I meet one lady from the town of Lille in north of France, and, she and I, we got call for 'interview.' We go inside the room and Swami, He say to her, 'Why you do not know me? You owe me money.' She is scared . . . 'Why He ask me this?' Then Swami said with smile on his face: 'You remember three years ago in the marketplace your son fall down and he became sick . . . and a lady came and gave you help?' She said, 'Aah, yes, I remember.' Then Swami said, 'I am that lady!'" Dominating devotees' conversations are insider discussions of Sai Baba's divine qualities and abilities, where unveiling Sai Baba's divinity or "seeing through the human masquerade" is the dominant quest. Being able to see the "true" divinity within the human form is believed to be a divinely ordained moment of transformation akin to Arjuna's viewing of the Purna avatar of Vishnu when looking at Krishna during the Mahabharatha war. In fact, devotees constantly brought up this Hindu myth of viewing the ultimate divinity as the "ideal" viewing situation where "god is revealed in all his glory" to the mesmerized devotee.

But, in the context of oral descriptions of viewing, it is necessary to also discuss the linguistic conventions of interaction with Sathya Sai Baba. While Sathya Sai Baba speaks and lectures primarily in Telugu, with a few English and Sanskrit words and phrases thrown in, his live speeches are often simultaneously translated into English and Hindi and when recorded are often transated into other languages such as Russian, Italian, French, etc., to enable devotees from all over the world to read them. However, devotees believe that understanding Sai Baba in interaction is a litmus test of belief. In fact many of my informants (who did not know Telugu) claimed that when they met him he spoke to them in their "native" language and they could understand him "perfectly." When I asked if he spoke their language or they heard a language they understood when he spoke, one of them replied, "I don't know what he did, but he was speaking, and I could understand it as though it was English or French so it did not matter if he spoke Mandarin or Sanskrit. I could understand him." Thus the literal translation of Sathya Sai Baba's words, while helpful, is not considered necessary for devotion.

As important as linguistic mores are for devotees in interaction with Sathya Sai Baba, it is the fact that devotees are not perturbed by the human-divine nexus that Sai Baba represents that is central to the growth of the movement. Rather than see it as an intellectual mystery to be unraveled and categorized within a hierarchy—a Judeo-Christian understanding of divinity where the theistic premise is that God and man are separate and often oppositional—devotees view their interaction with Sai Baba as affective, where an emotional connection to the mystery of divinity is forged and interpreted, an essential Hindu understanding of divinity and humanity as fluid categories. Hayley (1980) and and Das (1983), writing on sacrifice in the Hindu context, illuminate the Hindu understanding of divinity as an extension of humanity. Das, writing on Vedic sacrifice, notes that, for the sacrifice to work, God's submission to man is necessary (1983:460) in Hindu thought. Hayley comments on the fluidity between the concepts of God and man in Assamese Vaishnavism (1980:18–112, in Samantha 1994:785).

Devotees presented the concept of avatarhood as they saw it, as divinity encased in a mortal frame, in interesting and thought-provoking ways. Shudipto said when interviewed, "The problem about Baba is that he is god but he is man also. He is *poorna avatara*. This makes him have human feelings and ego and all our faults, but that is just his body, you know what I mean? He himself is God and he is above all that. But sometimes he hides himself to test us. Then we do not know who he is, and that is the test . . . how we behave to everyone whether they are a sweeper or God or both!" Anna, from Turin, told me, "See, we cannot understand how it is for Baba. He is god, he is Christ, he is everyone, but, like Christ, he is also like us. So he feels our pain, you know?" Through the devotees' discursive practices, we see that devotees often slide one divine frame into another. Devotees believe that the *avatar* is a universal divinity that takes different "bodies" on earth, in the reality of the everyday, to construct a modality of empathy between divinity and humanity. The modality of empathy is operationalized through the tactic of agency: devotees pick among the many forms of divinity of Sai Baba as their favorite form, based on an individual choice (*ishta devata* = god of choice). Devotees may see Krishna as an avatara of Sai Baba and vice versa. They pick either Krishna or Jesus or Prema Sai as variants of Sai Baba's divine form, and this choice is based on individual feelings of affiliation with one divinity or another. This understanding of individual choice of divine form is not unique to the Sai movement but exists in traditional Hinduism as well. When I asked Sai devotees which form of Sathya Sai Baba they "liked," they all hastened to assure me "that they were all the same," but, when pressed, Teresa said, "My favorite form of Swami is as the Prema Sai. He is so handsome and wonderful. I see the future in Him." Stephen said, "You know, I think of Shirdi Sai Baba when I see Bhagawan. I don't know why. . . . That is the image that stays with me. I have a picture of Swami and Shirdi Baba in my altar at home in Wimbledon." But while devotees have strong emotional links to the avatar of their choice, they still recognize them as "representations." For Sai devotees, the many incarnations and forms of Sai Baba are the emotional lenses through which to make affective and interactive connections to abstract divinity, which enables their own transformation to a higher spiritual plane.

Through the tactics listed—repetition, naming, unveiling, and agency—devotees come to a new modality of empathy by which to see Sathya Sai Baba as the embodiment of their ultimate concerns, that is, as the exemplar of a sacred lifestyle, the font of divine truth, or, as Christians put it, God incarnate. This process of interpretation is further compli- cated by the fact that, in the globalizing world, the communication of sacred personhood becomes a negotiation of the tension between man- ufactured charisma through discursive, mobile, transparent tactics by devotees and the retention of the power of the *mysterium tremendum* through strategies of charismatic regeneration. Part of the deconstruc- tion of sacred personhood involves an examination of the nature of charismatic leadership in the postcolonial world, which I will come to later in this chapter.

Translation Failures

Despite the success of Sathya Sai Baba in enfolding divinities from other faiths into his own, and the hermeneutic tactics of devotees that makes his sacred personhood mobile, there are some divinities that are difficult to enfold. For Western scholars, perhaps the strangest char- ismatic affiliation that Sai devotees claim is that of Jesus Christ. This ava- tar form can be traced back to the late 1970s, when John Hislop claimed he was privy to a specific Christian Sai miracle (*mahima*) of the crucifix that could turn fair skies stormy. Devotees cite the *yesu mahima* of the crucifix given to Hislop as evidence of Sai Baba's ability to emerge as an avatar that crosses religions. Christian devotees make the affiliation be- tween Christ and Baba, often collapsing the two into one divine, prophy- lactic, benevolent figure. While Hislop is one of the few devotees linking Sai Baba and Jesus Christ in the 1970s, in the 1990s the Christ link has become stronger in the movement, as Sai Baba has produced images of, variously, the risen Christ, the shroud of Turin, Christ on the cross, and, last, pictures of himself with Jesus. For example, one devotee's Web site has this story to offer: "In 1985, Barbara had gone to Puttaparthi with a friend from New Zealand. Barbara was spell-bound as, with a lift and a wave of his hand, Sai Baba drew from that photograph of the Turin Shroud, the black and white image of Christ."[65] The claim of a divine link with Christ is warranted by the Internet sites dedicated to Sai Baba, many run by Indian Christian devotees of Sathya Sai Baba, that repeatedly cite the miracle of the Hislop crucifix and other stories conflating the two divine figures.

I never found direct textual and aural evidence that Sathya Sai Baba had ever claimed to be Christ reincarnated, but there were always subtle claims and linking devices to the divinity of Jesus Christ. In Murphet's book: "Divine incarnation is not an exclusively Indian doctrine. Christianity teaches that Jesus the carpenter of Nazareth was an incarnation of the triune godhead, but it states that this was the only divine incarnation" (1971:202–203). Joule said to me: "Jesus was the son of God and an incarnation of the father and holy ghost, but in Christianity it says He was the only one. I don't think that is true. I think there were many prophets and gods. Swami is an incarnation of the supreme divinity." This confusion over Sathya Sai Baba's relationship to Jesus Christ is compounded by Sathya Sai Baba's usage of Christlike sayings in his discourses. For example, where the Bible states: "Do not think that I have come to do away with the Law of Moses and the teachings of the prophets. I have not come to do away with them, but to make their teachings come true," Sai Baba has stated: "I have not come on any mission of publicity for any sect, creed or cause; nor have I come to collect followers for any doctrine. I have come to tell you of this universal unitary faith, this atmic principle, this path of love."

Abrahamic traditions outside India are uneasy with this ecumenism between divine figures of various religious traditions in India. Alexandra Kent describes the case of Aunty Elizabeth in Malaysia, a charismatic healer who believes she is channeling Sai Baba's mystical healing power. She explains this, as Kent notes, by "filtering Sai's healing power through a Christian scheme" (2005:140–142) where Jesus and Sai Baba are "subsumed on mutual terms." It turns out that Auntie Elizabeth is herself Hindu, but her husband and children are Catholic, and Auntie believes that as Catholics they are clean and therefore do not require protection from the spirits, which both refuses any notion of Hindu supremacy and, simultaneously, as Kent suggests, "opens the way for considerable maneuverability" where Christianity is intriguingly understood from within a Hindu framework but the framework is not necessarily more powerful or overarching (2005:140). This open syncreticism is peculiar to the people of the subcontinent and is often the source of much dissent in societies in which paradox is seen as untenable and resistance to any hegemony comes with rigid social and political consequence.

For orthodox Christians outside India, Christ is the only son of God, and to suggest otherwise is heresy, since the Bible states: "Jesus saith unto him, I am the way, the truth, and the life: *no man cometh unto the Father, but by me*" (John 14:6; my emphasis). In fact, a Web site run by conservative Christians (former devotees of Sathya Sai Baba) suggests that Sathya Sai Baba is the anti-Christ for his claims of Christlike divinity.[66] Devotees counter that he is a yuga avatar (avatar for the age). The translation "confusion" over avatar and descent, a seemingly irrelevant and innocent confusion to Sathya Sai Baba and the Sai organization, is a sign to the watching Western world of hubris. This cultural collision lends itself to defensive semiotics on both sides.

How do we read this cultural collision? The most important consequence seems to me to be that of power politics, in which the assertion of yugavatara (avatar of the ages) by Sathya Sai Baba is seen as a challenge to Jesus Christ's supremacy. Scholars of religion specializing in Christianity asked me repeatedly: "Is he saying he is bigger than Christ? Is he saying he came before? Is he saying that he is the Father from whom Christ descended?" whereupon Sathya Sai Baba is forced to adopt a debate over his rightful place as sacred person. These "problems" of translation, of which this is but one example, indicate different answers with different values to a single moral dilemma, a characteristic of a plural culture.

Charisma and Belief

For Sai devotees, the Sai katha becomes more than "historical facts or lived experiences" (Kim 2001:279). It also emphasizes the compassion and grace of God to come down to earth in a human form to engage with humans and help them comprehend their larger purpose in life. The Sai narrative enables some devotees to see, in perspective, "the illusory fetters of the human body" (Kim 2001:279). Thus the link with Sai Baba enables the devotee to see the limited existence of her/his being. The finding of this true self is warranted in the devotee's worldview by a philosophical hermeneutics of suffering that has been expanded globally in the postmodern lived experience. According to devotees like Hislop, reality is marked by a struggle for salvation, and lived experience is one of pain and suffering. Since these realities ground devotees' understandings of life, they are interested in incarnations as encountering different realities and creating paths to salvation and self-understanding. But the Sai narratives also underline the supreme power of the human divinity and the ability to control the uncontrollable and, in that sense, are in keeping with postmodern, hopeful, therapeutic understandings of self as malleable and reinventable. In a strangely ironic twist, some devotees extend this logic backward to interpret the life story of Sathya Sai Baba through the interventionist lens of individual self-will: as a Horatio Algier story of self determination and reinvention. They see this story as evidence of an ability to reinvent themselves in their own lives. As Stephen, the British devotee whom I met in Heathrow Airport said to me, excitedly; "It's self-contouring of the spirit for a new world!"[67]

Cultural perceptions of religious phenomena (including the transformation of self and habitus through the life story and devotional praxis) are properly understood as accretions of meaning applied both strategically and tactically over time and space—an ongoing transformation of meaning—that support many voices. Csordas, who studied the Charismatic Christian community, argues that charisma is a transformative act (an ongoing shift in the way people see their being in the world in relation to the charismatic leader) that is host to many perspectives, described by Weber variously as "the incarnation within man of the Supernatural being," "self deification," "where the primary ungodlike factors were actually the average habitus of the human body and the everyday world" (Weber, in Csordas 1997:135–139). This transformation extends from the self of the divine leader to the self and habitus of the devotee. Charisma in this reading is a "product of the rhetorical apparatus in use of which the leader and the follower alike convinced themselves that the world is constituted in a certain way," that is, a product of interaction (Csordas 1997:139–140) between leader and follower that reshapes meaning and value for the devotee. Interestingly, this is posited only as a moment of transformation for the devotee, not for the guru, though it is in reality a highly interactive model. In his famous novel *The Guide*, world-renowned author R. K. Narayan describes the career arc of protagonist Raju from railway vendor, tourist guide, impresario, dance manager, convict, and finally spiritual guide. In tracing this story, Narayan posits Raju as a reluctant guru, one who is thrust into the role of leader rather than a voluntary saint to a village of God-fearing people. Raju finds in himself the ability to "be" the guru. In a rare moment of revelation, he thinks to himself, "The essence of sainthood seems to be in the ability to utter mystifying statements" (1958:57). William Walsh describes Raju as devoid of character and therefore capable of taking on the character of others: the true engagement for which charismatics are known (1983:117). Some scholars have interpreted this as being morally persuadable, but this connection is not automatic. What is, of course, of greater import to this chapter is the fact that Raju's reflections on being a reluctant guru to the villagers sheds much needed light on the guru in a postmodern world where scepticism is an essential part of the imagination. Raju is in fact shaped by his interactions with the world around him, and its expectations of him as a saint, as much as it is shaped by his pronouncements. Robert Bellah comments that this relational aspect of charisma is evidenced best in a group where social order is manifest (1976:7–8). Clifford Geertz sees charisma as evidence of an "involvement, even oppositional involvement, with such arenas and with the momentous events that occur in them. . . . It is a sign, not of popular appeal or inventive craziness, but of being near the heart of things" (Geertz 1983:123). For Geertz, the definition charisma includes both power and value.

The valorization of different meanings into a hierarchy, where some are more valuable than others, is a central problem of cultural translation that will reappear throughout the following pages. The predicament, both for devotees and for scholarship, is parsing through the varying values of charisma. And they solve this puzzle by threading through a common motif in the various readings—the concept of the multiple as one. Whereas Sathya Sai Baba's story may raise feelings of ambivalence or attachment for devotees, it brings with it a comfort with multiplicity and plural forms, which will prove significant later on.

Transforming Sacred Personhood and Agency: Toward a Nomadic Charisma

This chapter has explored two perspectives of the life story of Sathya Sai Baba—one that he constructs temporally through his life story and the other that devotees construct through a spatialization of the praxis of devotion—aimed at forming how the interaction between Sathya Sai Baba and the devotees creates and distributes an ideology of personhood. He is seen as the guru; a reincarnated spiritual teacher derived from various religious traditions within India and abroad; a *sant* or holy man, a mystic with magical powers; and as a cosmic divine avatar (incarnation) of God, a mythological divine figure who removes darkness in a terrible age of evil (kali yuga) to bring back a "golden age of righteousness" (Srinivas 2001). As we have seen, Sathya Sai Baba's divine persona shows some elements of Weber's charismatic prophet, a mystagogue—one "who can

perform magical acts that contain the boon of salvation" (1968:54)—
he is a Parsonian ideal type, an agent of escape from rationalization.
As an avatar, he acts as an exemplary divine person who also fuses
the ideal of the teacher/guru "mingling human and divine" in one (Spurr
2007:373).

Thus we learn the Hindu sacred person is, more than a distinct person, a concept and experienced as transcendant and immanent at the
same time (Samantha 1994:786), both aniconic and anthropomorphic.
The onus therefore lies on the interpreter to understand the context and
interaction, to fix the sacred personhood and remove the inherent
ambiguity.

The transformative Sathya Sai Baba katha leads to an understanding of
divine representations (Spurr 2007). The affectivity the forms of divinity
encapsulate for devotees is the basis for the construction of a successful
transnational sacred personhood. Sathya Sai Baba and his devotees rear-
range and reconceptualize components of different philosophical traditions of divinity. The components of these understandings; the life story
located in the temporal and the hermeneutic practices located in the spatialization of discourse, are used as building blocks to construct a new
understanding of sacred personhood. They are not mythophilosophic or
argumentative, but rather transformative of the tradition, which leads to
an active redefinition located in the emotional interaction between Sathya
Sai Baba and his devotees.

No longer rooted in traditional Hinduism, the new sacred person of
Sai Baba is disembedded from the religiocultural milieu and is free to
travel across the global network. The portability of divinity is enabled
through the three logical instruments that weave through this chapter:
the reinvention of Sathya Sai Baba as he transforms himself from obscure peasant boy to global guru and godhead through his life story—a
temporal move; the creation and performance of the discursive tactics
that enables anyone to become a devotee of Sathya Sai Baba provided the
tactics proscribed are rigidly adhered to, increasing the reach of the
movement and therefore its transnational reach—a spatializing move;
and the creation of a "structure of affect" (Srinivas 2005), an affective
logos within which the Sai devotees operate, enabling the different
cultures within the transnational movement to cohere—an interactive
move. By way of the interaction between the strategies of Sathya Sai Baba
and the tactics of devotion a mobile charisma—nomadic charisma—is
formed. The creation of nomadic charisma is the mobile condition that

includes the possibility of a new sacred personhood through a range of mutually reinforcing meanings and behaviors. Nomadic charisma brings together temporal, spatial, and interactive frames into a coherent whole, engaging the possibility of travel as well as the possibility of becoming grounded in one place simultaneously.

You have two birth places. You have the place where you were really born and the place of predilection where you wake up to reality.
　　　　　　　　　　　　　　　　—Lawrence Durrell, Blue Thirst

No invitation has ever been distributed at Puttaparthi. Love, the invitation of the heart, draws people here.　　　*—Sathya Sai Baba*, Sathya Sai Speaks

2　*Deus Loci*

Economies of Faith, Cultures of Travel, and the Building of a Moral Architecture

An Economy of Faith on the Margins of the Sacred

Boston. December 17, 2004. Frederyck (forty-nine) a Polish devotee currently living in Paris.

India, I always wanted to go there. It was like a dream, a fantasy. One day I went to the Sai temple in Singapore. There was a sign, "A trip to Puttaparthi, India, is being organized from 8 to 16 Dec 1997. For trip details contact Brother Manoj" and a phone number. I was thinking of calling but I didn't. That night I dreamt of Sai Baba. He was in front of me calling me by name. He said, "Frederyck, you must come to 'Parthi." When I woke up, I called the number.

On the trip most were Indians, a few families from Singapore, China, few Malay families, three Americans and myself. Most of them had been before. The Tamil family began singing bhajans (devotional songs). I even remember they sang *Ganesha sharanam Sai sharanam* (I surrender to Ganesha, I surrender to Sai). Every hour or so we discussed how much more time before we see *Bhagawan*. When we saw the first gate with the lotus on top saying we were entering Sathya Sai Taluk (district) everyone said a heartfelt "Sai Ram."

The American woman, Linda, started crying and Mrs. Lim (she's from Singapore) took out several hundred pages on which she had written Sai Baba's name ten thousand times and threw them. She said it was a vow. As we came closer to town, we left our seats to look out. We saw the street signs in five different languages, and so many different people on the streets. I was amazed at the beautiful buildings . . . the architecture, gold domes and beautiful columns. I had seen some Indian temples in Singapore but nothing like this! We passed under a huge gate painted a blue and pink and gold saying in English "Welcome to Puttaparthi." I knew then that this trip was a life-changing experience for me.

We waited for darshan. On the dais in the center was an empty solid silver throne waiting for Him. But when Sai Baba came in, He walked directly up to me and said, "You have come! I have been waiting." I told Him how happy and proud I was to be in His home. He said in a serene voice that He was happy to see me in His home, but His real home was in the hearts of His devotees, *in my heart where He lives.* . . . I have never forgotten that amazing first trip!"[1]

As this field interview suggests, for devotees, one of the central acts that marks Sai devotees is travel to the Sai ashram in Puttaparthi. Since Sathya Sai Baba has only left India once, residing most of the year at his ashram Prasanthi Nilayam, in Puttaparthi, devotees and spiritual tourists make the journey to see him, witness his miracles, and be close to him. Every year over four million Sai devotees from around the world, backpackers, spiritual sojourners, and elite tourists, from countries as diverse as Italy, the United States, Japan, Singapore, China, South Africa, Brazil, and Fiji make their way to the remote town of Puttaparthi to experience life and worship at the ashram. The literature on pilgrimage and identity argues that different sets of pilgrims seek different identities: they may be tribal, as in the case of Berber pilgrims in Morocco (Rabinow 1977) or rooted in newer nationalist concerns, as is the case with Hindu pilgrims in India (Eck 1988); the pilgrimage may construct an aspired civilizational identity or legitimize existing social inequalities, located in class, caste, age, and power, within the larger social system, determining who can go on pilgrimage, and where they can go. Pilgrimage must be read multivocally as a text that contains many voices, encasing a "pluralism of symbols and connections" (Eade and Sallnow 1991; Werbner 1996; Morinis 1984), particularly in the case of Sai pilgrimage, since devotees come to Puttaparthi from 137 different cultures and countries. As spiritual sojourners, they experience both the space of the journey and the stay at the ashram as deeply transformative, and they move conceptually during the sojourn toward a cartography of religious affect that enables the expression of a globally inclusive economy of faith.

In dealing with Puttaparthi, travelers unwittingly "enact" and "contest" (White 2000:52) the established role of space in constructing, contesting and legitimizing collective sentiments as they engage the "built forms and spatial transformations . . . produced by the economy of late capitalism" (Low and Lawrence-Zúñiga 2003:25). The city of Puttaparthi becomes *the* crucible where Sai devotional identity is forged and emplaced, where the matrix of possible meanings is visibly interpreted, and where "social actors forge connections between localities across national borders that increasingly sustain new modes of politics, economics and culture" (Smith 2005:5). Examining the town of Puttaparthi's spaces of devotion allows us to capture "emergent social relations which are situated in particular places yet operate across geographical distances" (Smith 2005:6) and to move us toward an understanding of Sai faith. So Puttaparthi is an iconic site to unearth the "different life worlds" (Glover 2006:xix) of a city within a universalizing narrative of globalization. How this difference is encompassed within the material form of the South Asian city is the central question in many recent works on urban history. In one scenario, the city is seen by non-natives to be opaque, and the difficulty lies in mastering its texture—the olfactory, auditory, visual, and other matrices—and turning them to an advantage to make the city accessible (Chattopadhyay 2005), a problem that we see some travelers to Puttaparthi encounter. But others see Indian cities as "hybrid" sites that are not "purely Indian or purely Western creations," but display "the irregular, the uneven, and the unexpected" through material juxtapositions of varied elements across space and time (Hosagrahar 2005 in Glover 2006:xix) in which the difficulty lies in interpreting the hybridity. But in both inquiries urban society can be "recursively shaped by and through material objects and arrangements of space " (Glover 2006:xx–xxi) with deep implications for how we might formulate the project of inclusivity, through the emotions and sentiments engendered by the built form. Since Henri Lefebvre argues that space is "not a thing but rather a set of [social] relations," the city of Puttaparthi is both an evocation of Sai society as it is as well as a built form of the ideal society it wishes to be, as such subject both to the politics of space as well as the politics of being and becoming in a period of globalization. Claire Rasmussen warns readers about a glib comprehension of complex modern urbanity and the push-pull forces inherent within the metropolis: "I do not want to exaggerate the power and achievements of these emerging . . . struggles over the spatial specificities and structures of privilege in the metropolis, but neither should they be buried under the Edenic visions of urban boosterism or the apocalyptic predictions of a cynical Left withdrawing from the conditions of postmodernity."[2] So Puttaparthi and its image as a sacred city acts as a lens to unearth what Jameson has appropriately called "the cultural logic of late capitalism," an *economy of faith*, as it were.

The key point here is that interventions in the city directly depend upon the way it is imagined, memorialized, conceptualized, and drawn into the discourse of global devotion. This harnessing of the spatial imagination toward increased devotion though the construction and manipulation of desired sentiments rests on the Taylorean concept of the social imaginary where large groups of people imagine their world, how they fit together with others, how expectations are normally met, and the deeper normative notions and images that underlie these expectations. Consequently, societies produce a complete spatial imagination within which their own distinctive synthesis of subjective and objective assessments and observations occur. But, during globalization, as this chapter demonstrates, the plural representations within the spatial imagination move across space and time engaging the concepts of transcendence and permanence, of exclusion and inclusion, and of historicity and future simultaneously, to create sentimental connections between the inhabitants and the spaces themselves.

The literature on globalization and culture has been dominated by the dialogic paradigm of the local and the global with regard to space and its traversing—the local is the indigenous, the enspaced, and the territorial, while the global is the new and the translocal—and this dialectic is seen to be true of both the reality as well as the imagination. While such analysis is important, it does not help to conceptualize spaces like the sacred city of Puttaparthi as emergent, transnational places of sacredness in which "social actors forge connections between localities across national borders that increasingly sustain new modes of politics, economics and culture," nor to capture "emergent social relations which are situated in particular places yet operate across geographical distances"(Smith 2005:5–6). So to find a way to study the Sathya Sai ashram I took my cue from Venkat (thirty-five), a biotechnologist and former student of the Sathya Sai Institute of Higher Studies, who said, "Actually, the space of the ashram says a lot about what was happening inside. It is like Disneyland for spiritual tourists" (Grimshaw 2001). Following Venkat's analogy, my focus on the Sai ashram and the spaces it enfolds leads me to ask the the question of the Sai ashram that Rayner Banham first asked in 1971 when viewing Disneyland, what is the relationship between what happens inside the gates to what happens in the world outside,[3] so as to unearth the links between urban space, global religion, and the economies of faith embedded in the travel to this sacred center.

In engaging this question, I analyze travel writing and visual material culture to discuss how travel is carried out, apprehended, and memorialized by Sathya Sai devotees and spiritual tourists. Travel is usually associated with leisure and tourism activities (Bruner 1986; Clifford and Marcus 1986; Gupta and Ferguson 1997), but I examine how the spiritual journey (Turner and Turner 1995 [1978]) becomes a "trope" for identity construction and can be considered a lens for examining the culture of belief: how the particular site at Puttaparthi becomes reflective of a narrative of self and how this narrative of self intersects and is juxtaposed against larger structures of colonialism and power. I try to present a panoramic view of travel through the employment of various lenses. First, the global mobility of Sathya Sai devotees and the cultures of their spiritual travel as they make their way to the city of Puttaparthi, including their *narratives of transformation* from "spiritual seekers" to "devotee pilgrims" as they go to Puttaparthi and the *antinarrative of prodigality* as they move away from Puttaparthi. Second, the singular space of the town of Puttaparthi and travel within it as an evocation of a universal spiritual "home" that devotees memorialize and the corresponding *narrative of exile* they manufacture and engage. Third, the holy spaces of Puttaparthi as built metaphors of Sathya Sai Baba's nomadic charisma, which manufactures a "retro-future aesthetic" the Sathya Sai movement locates, engages, and manipulates through "self-constructed" tours of "sites of memory." And, finally, the spaces of the virtual world through which devotees see and touch one another, creating *narratives of accessibility,* which are a requirement of any global ideological movement. I suggest that all these narratives collapse into an overarching *narrative of redemption:* the devotee's rationale for traveling to and inhabiting these sacred spaces.

Spiritual Travel and Sojourns of Seeking

The journey to Puttaparthi appears to be one of the distinct rites de passage marking the point when a spiritual tourist becomes a Sai devotee.[4] In interviews I found that over 43 percent of devotees I interviewed had been looking for a guru or spiritual leader for at least five years prior to finding Sathya Sai Baba; some were spiritual seekers for a decade or more. Reed (thirty-nine) of Portland, and Jitsu (forty-three) of Tokyo, told me in Brindavan on July 14, 1998:

> Reed: "I wandered all over the place looking for a guru. I went to Tibet and then I went to Indonesia. I tried four different trips before someone in Modesto [California] told me that the *avatara* of God was in Puttaparthi in India. So when I first came here I just sort of thought it would be another one of those trips, you know . . .

> Jitsu: I also traveled all over Asia looking for an enlightened master. I traveled to Taiwan to see a Buddhist monk, you know? And to Nepal for time in a monastery and then back to Japan. Then I meet Manohar in shop, and he tells me that Sai Baba is the master, and I come here to Prasanthi Nilayam. Then I see for myself, and I feel so light. So I come back.

"Spiritual tourists" (Brown 1998) like Jitsu and Reed traveled the globe looking for a teacher, picking and choosing among traditions to construct a religious selfhood that is unique. For example, Colin (fifty-six) described his friend Sarah's quest for a guru:

"She went to Pune," Colin said. "To the Rajneesh ashram?" I ask. He nods yes. "Then she went to Rishikesh and found a guru there," he adds, "and then she tried Swami Muktananda Paramahamsa's siddha yoga practice. She went to Ganeshpuri to his Gurudev siddha peeth and then went to South Fallsburg to the ashram, but she said she was unhappy. She was looking everywhere. She was on a collision course with her own inner self. Then I told her about Bhagawan. And she resisted me at first. Then she came with me to a *satsang* (singing and worship group) in London. . . . She said she had never felt such peace. So that's how she became a Sai bhakta."

Spiritual tourists have usually lost their traditional faith and are looking for something that will replace it. They seek across a variety of religious traditions, choosing among many to find what they are looking for: a "good fit," as one devotee put it. Many Sai devotees claimed they had looked elsewhere before finding their "true guru" in Sathya Sai Baba. I have no numbers of those who tested the Sathya Sai movement for "fit" and moved on, but I am sure that some potential devotees found a better fit with other gurus such as the Ma Amritanandayamayi movement, the Art of Living Foundation of Shri Ravi Shankar, Sufi mystical sects, Deepak Chopra, or even some sects within the Christian evangelical movement.[5]

Often, while searching, prospective devotees might attend a satsang or a bhajan session at the local Sai chapter or temple. In the Singapore temple, a senior devotee, Brother Manoj, told me that often there would be some devotees who came for "some time and did not come again." Heelas suggests that this "spiritual searching" is emblematic of postmodern religiosity and is marked by dedifferentiation. This dedifferentiation is "a refusal to regard positivistic rationalistic instrumental criteria as the sole or exclusive standard of worthwhile knowledge; a willingness to combine symbols from disparate codes or frameworks of meaning even at the cost of disjunctions and eclecticism; a celebration of spontaneity, fragmentation, superficiality, irony and playfulness; and a willingness to abandon the search for overarching or triumphalist myths, narratives or frameworks of meaning" (Heelas and Woodhead 2005:4, quoting Beckford 1986:19). These dedifferentiating processes allow for an "equality cum diversity" that leads to a "spiritual revolution" in which alternate narratives of devotion and new ways of being religious are manufactured and employed.

But Mr. Iyer, a core devotee and official within the Sai Central Trust (SCT), was impatient with my distinction between spiritual tourists and pilgrims. He said: "They are not tourists. . . . They are looking for Swami. Once they find Him, they dissolve into Him like sugar into milk." Mr. Iyer's statement argues that the pilgrimage is a *rit des passage* (van Gennep 1960 [1909]) in which Sai prospective pilgrims moved from "lost" seekers to found pilgrims, forming a collective faith-based identity located in Sai devotion (Turner and Turner 1995 [1978]). As Eade and Sallnow note in their pathbreaking work on pilgrimage, "Pilgrimage, to the degree that it strips actors of their social personae and restores their essential individuality, is the ritual context par excellence in which a world religion strives to realize its defining transcultural universalism; for to reach the individual is to reach the universal" (Eade and Sallnow 1991:4). I will use the term *prospective pilgrim* to identify travelers before and during the sacred journey and *pilgrim* to indicate those who have made the journey and become devotees and those who are returnees.

Traversing the Globe to Save Yourself: Narratives of Redemption

The sacred journey consists of many steps. Initially, prospective pilgrims believe that Sathya Sai Baba "calls them" to him, and the call is the beginning of self-transformation. Frederyck mentioned the personal call in the form of a dream from Sai Baba in his opening narrative. Simon (fifty-seven) told me that he, too, was "called" by Sai Baba in a dream when he fell asleep one rainy afternoon in the Bodleian Library at Oxford University. Leela was also "called," though she was awake during a bhajan session in her hometown. Anna felt she had been called by Sathya Sai Baba since he had shown her the way to reach him when she was ill. Susanna (sixty-three), an herbalist from Germany whom I met in Heathrow Airport (who had changed her name to Jyothi, "light," because "she felt full of light after meeting Swami"),[6] told me that she too had been called when the Sai Baba ring she had bought in the Sathya Sai bookstore in Tustin came alive and spoke to her, "commanding" her to "come home." Finally, a former devotee, who did not want to be identified, told me that when he was drowning he heard and saw Sai Baba lift him out of the ocean to the shore and call him by name, whereupon he "resolved to go to Puttaparthi and meet him." Devotees feel this holy invitation to be central to their journey, the beginning of redemptive transformation.

This *narrative of redemption* invests the whole of the sacred journey. As prospective pilgrims move through the process of the sacred journey, they see it as a spiritual sojourn in which they move from seeking a path to finding it, thereby "being saved." As Huang and Weller (2007) note, the travel to the sacred center is reconstructed not merely as a journey but as a journey of higher meaning—a moral narrative—to create a new history for the devotee. This is in keeping with what Carr argues is the nature of the narrative form (2006:120–121). "Human acts and experiences plans and projects already has the narrative form in which hiostorical writing is largely cast . . . this form is found below the level of explicit storytelling and is characteristic of the way in which Time is experienced and structured." Thus, the more difficult it becomes, the more worthwhile it is in the minds of the prospective pilgrim. The official Sathya Sai Web page draws parallels between the arduous journey to Puttaparthi and the journey of life. "Life is a pilgrimage where man drags his feet along the rough and thorny road, With the Name of God on his lips, he will have no thirst, with the Form of God in his heart, he will feel no exhaustion. The company of the holy will inspire him to travel in hope and faith."[7] The journey is seen as transforming and redemptive in many spheres, both mundane and sacred, which interweave together. When prospective pilgrims and pilgrims concentrated their storytelling on the problems of the mundane, as they often did, they ended with what they had learned; a significant spiritual takeaway. Pilgrims acknowledged that their fears were transformed after the journey into "moments of personal growth," as my informant Alistair described them.

When I attended two prepilgrimage information briefing sessions—one in Los Angeles, California (2003) and the other in Framingham, Massachusetts (2004, 2005)—some devotees told me that they were afraid of going to India. Prospective pilgrims told me that they had looked up the U.S. State Department Web site, which indicated India was "not OK." They feared "not being able to communicate," "being cheated," "catching a disease," "things not going as planned," "losing luggage," "not getting medication," "not finding edible food," "getting lost," "sharing bathrooms," and "terrorists." Bruce (sixty-eight), from Pasadena, told me in an initial interview that he expected India to look, "you know, like a National Geographic special or like the tsunami coverage" (referencing the South Asian tsunami of January 2005). Upon his return, he told me over the phone, "It was so different from what I imagined. I've started reading. I came back with a suitcase full of heavy books, history, philosophy and all that stuff. I've even signed on for an Indian cooking class. I want know about India more, and its history. . . . I felt at home there. It was weird. It was so accepting. I felt, I am home. I can let go! So I knew at that moment in India, through India, I will find myself."

But prospective pilgrims had differential understandings of India, which was made clear from an interview with Claire (fifty-four), who believed she had a great deal of knowledge about India before she came to the session: "I have worked with this Christian ecumenical group that helps the women squatters of Mumbai. So I know a lot about India. I've read many books. . . . Everyone who has been there has told me not to drink or eat anything fresh and not to drink the water!" Upon her return she said:

In the beginning I was just scared. Everything was so big and people, people everywhere . . . the mobs coming at you! I always carried my pepper spray in my handbag to be safe. But then I got to the ashram and listened to people, and saw how friendly they were . . . And one guy—he didn't even know me—helped me to buy a bed and carry it! I think India changed me. I found who I really was . . . or maybe that's being egotistical. *Ahamkara* (ego)! I, I, I . . . !! But let me say I found my path with Bhagawan and it will help me be a better person. Not to be so locked down in fear.

But Claire was not alone. Prospective pilgrims, both Indian and non-Indian, often commented about the cities they traveled through. Hui said: "I liked Bangalore. Such a nice city . . . so open. Everyone is welcome there. I liked the streets and the restaurants and the beautiful ladies wearing silk saris. I saw a monkey eating a banana in a temple in Bangalore . . . first time I saw this monkey!" Sneha (forty-six) said: "Coming from Bombay (Mumbai) Bangalore is so cool and green. Still not as polluted as Bombay but I know it is getting worse. Too many people. But still such a pretty city with the gardens and even the new apartment blocks are quite nice with big trees and nice flowers. It reminds me of Bombay when I first went there in the 1950s when I got married."

Laura (thirty-eight), from Goa, said of the destination of Puttaparthi:

When I first came to Puttaparthi ten years ago it was so small like our villages in Goa but now it has become a big city! For us it does not take us long to get to 'Parthi . . . but for some people who come from England or America it takes one/two days. My sister-in-law from England comes to Bombay and then she comes to Goa by flight or train, and we both take the train to Bangalore and then we go by bus to 'Parthi. It is a nice journey if you go with family and friends. Of course you can only go if Swami calls you. First time I went from Panjim (the capital of Goa), I had tried for three years to go but I couldn't. Something or other would come in the way. Then one day, early in the morning, my brother came and said, "I am going to Puttaparthi, if you want to come you must get ready in one hour." I got ready and just left. Like that (she snapped her fingers).

These detailed accounts of the cities and travel that devotees go through to get to Puttaparthi speak both to what is familiar as well as to what is unfamiliar, depending upon the perspective of the devotee and they give us some sense of how travel texts construct the other through the voices of both pilgrim and stranger. They comment on difference and familiarity and in so doing create an ethnographic register of distance and familiarity, themes that pursue devotees throughout their stay and their life.

Some devotees felt afraid of the expected quality of the living arrangements in the ashram. I read passages they had marked in two handbooks in the information session, one of an American devotee which said (italics demonstrate one devotee's margin notes and comments): "On arrival at the Ashram, the first stop is the Public Relations office where the travel documents are registered, then the Accomodation Office where lodgings are assigned. According to availability, rooms with *bathroom will be given to be shared with 4 or 5 people of the same sex or family.* Of course, preference is given to the ill, aged, and families with children." This next commentary on the handbook appeared in the book of an Indian devotee in Delhi: "When rooms are no longer available, lodgings are provided in communal buildings (sheds) divided for: men, women, and families. *The bathrooms here are communal and there are no wall dividers.* Lodgings are usually without mattresses, pillows, sheets, and *mosquito nets (remember to buy mosquito coil!)* which can all be bought at very cheap prices. The camp beds can be rented for a few rupees a week." A Singaporean devotee had these comments: "It is *not allowed to use radios, tape-recorders or sing* bhajans at any time of the day in the rooms or sheds in respect for others *(ask about iPod).* Authorised personnel (porters and laundry staff) have special identity tags *and all number should be noted each time they are given something. (what?!)* It is not allowed to *walk around the ashram after 9 PM which is when lights in the rooms and sheds are turned off."* The "lack of comfort" encountered by the sojourners, the Sathya Sai Web site argued, was part of the process of redemption.

> In foreign countries, while you are able to have a comfortable life, while you are able to command the material comforts, you feel that you are lacking peace of mind. And, with great hopes that you will be able to get that peace of mind, you spend a lot of money, and at great personal expense and inconvenience you come all the way to this place. . . . One should ask oneself: "What is it that we are taking back with us? . . . Why is it that we have come here?" This kind of questioning and inquiry, each one should make for oneself every day.

The process of rationalization was not limited to the Sathya Sai Organization, but was undertaken by the travelers themselves after the journey. Susan (fifty-three), who was "freaking out" about sharing bathrooms, said, "I haven't done that since college," as did Jyotsna (twenty-eight) from Mumbai, during the prepilgrimage information session. On her return from Puttapathi, Susan told me:

> Sharing wasn't such a big deal. Learning to share is so important. There were three frogs in my bathroom, and I shared the bathwater with them too. I will miss them in my bathroom here. I found such pleasure there in doing simple things; saving water, saving energy. . . . We can all learn that . . . We save our planet and we save ourselves and our children. We live in such luxury in this country and we waste such a lot. I saw this guy hosing down his car when I got back. He used enough water for ten people to have baths in the ashram. It gives you perspective.

Nirmala (thirty-four), from Chennai, said: "The bathroom was OK. Nothing luxurious, but very clean and neat. But, after all, we are not going there to be sitting in the bathroom. Once you are there everything goes away. The only thought in your head and heart is for Baba." As we see, prospective pilgrims often start the journey in fear, but in the process of sojourning are moved to a need for understanding, which they saw as self-transformatory and often redemptive. The process of self-transformation led to extended rationalization of their situations upon return.

What is more, the narrative of redemption extended into intercultural communication as well. Prospective pilgrims who had lived in Puttaparthi or at the ashram for about a month became lyrical about other devotees and their kindness and generosity. Jim said:

> Once you get to know people, it's different. I found this guy Abbas . . . he was so great. He was from Madras and he was such a great Sai bhakta. He would come everyday to my room with hot coffee and never charge me. Why should he do that? He took me to meet his family. . . . Three little kids. Reminded me of my grandkids. It's funny, I know he is Muslim, but we connected. That's what Swami says, you know. Abbas made me see that the only thing preventing me from reaching my full potential is my fear of failure.

Prospective pilgrims built personal connections of trust and friendship across traditional lines of separation such as nationality, class, and religion.

Besides the personal connections of trust and friendship that they built across intercultural lines, the prospective pilgrims spoke about the change in affect they experienced during their tenure in the ashram: a third moment of redemption. A devotees' Web site stated;

> Before you can reach Lord Sai Baba, you will be "shacked, drained, tired, emptied, etc." But don't worry, this is part and parcel of the spiritual journey home. Once you arrived in that tattered condition, you will be in a better condition to receive. Call this initial phase, a psychological preparation of the mind. But there is no need to worry too much or fear. Lord Sai has always said, nobody comes to Me unless I will it. And those whom He has called, He will clear the path of obstacles, and make sure you arrive safely and in one peace.[8]

Prospective pilgrims felt that they often began emptied, drained, and fearful and moved into joy, delight, and pleasure. Leela said: "When I first came here I was so worried . . . about so many things. But I first came only for the day but I stayed one week. In that week the *bhari bhoj* (heavy burden) was lifted from my head! I felt that I was at peace! Shanti said, I was very sick when I first came, sick in my heart and mind. After one month at Prasanthi I was cured! I left it all to Bhagawan. He had called me. . . . He will make sure it is all OK!" Stephen, in his home in London after returning from his tenth trip to Puttaparthi: "Each time I go there tired and empty, and each time I come back full of life and love!" Jill from San Francisco, California said: "I have a diary. This was before blogs and I recorded all my feelings when I went to 'Parthi the first time. (Reading from the dairy) Day 1: I don't know what I am doing here. Am I crazy? What makes me think this is going to solve all my problems? Day 10: I feel better, lighter! I got up at 4.30 A.M. . . . me! I went for early morning prayers at the ashram. The sun was rising by the time we were through. The peace was glorious! Day 15: I know I have changed. I believe it is Him . . . His Glory, His grace. I feel full of energy and love. Day 22 (last day): The days have slipped past. I wish I could stay here forever. I feel such peace here."

The Sathya Sai Web site emphasizes Jill's emotional journey as the ideal one where the true self as devotee is found at the end of the journey.

> Remember that with every step, you are nearing God, and God too, when you take one step towards Him, takes ten towards you. There is no stopping place in this pilgrimage, it is one continuous journey, through day and night, through valley and desert, through tears and smile, through death and birth, through tomb and womb. When the road ends and the Goal is gained the pilgrim finds that he has traveled only from himself to himself, that the way was long and lonesome, but, that the God whom he reached was all the while in him, around him, with him, and besides him.[9]

Prospective pilgrims moved during the course of the sojourn from fear of the unknown to a deep confidence in their chosen paths as devotees. Alistair, a devotee from London said, "When I first came here I wasn't ready. But after ten days, I noticed a change in myself. I knew I had to come back. I knew I was on the right path." Aki from Japan said, "When I see Bhagawan and look into his eyes I know that this is the true path." Shanti said, "Swami helps us to find the proper way to *atma gyana* (self-knowledge). I know He will lead me in the right direction." The travel is transformative and the "right path" of devotion, which was obscured before, is found at the end of the travel, with Sathya Sai Baba's aid. Devotees argue that they find an authentic self that is redemptive either in the travel to Puttaparthi or during their stay.

The dislocation inherent in travel and mobility is the lens that enables this transformation toward redemption. Regarding prospective pilgrims' ideas of the dislocation inherent to sojourning and the finding of the self, Jim said, "Have you watched the movie *The Wizard of Oz?* At the end of the trip, Dorothy [the lead protagonist] finds what she was looking for all the while at home.[10] That is like every devotee of Sathya Sai Baba . . . what we find is a deep faith that we had all along, only we are blind to it because of the kind of world we live in. It takes this journey to lift the curtains from our eyes!"

So the journey to Puttaparthi is seen as redemptive and focused toward the finding of the real self. Prospective pilgrims equate their dislocated mobility across countries and cultures as a spiritual sojourn in which they move from seeking to finding devotion and finding themselves as pilgrims and devotees. Dislocation is reconstructed as a template for rethinking their identities as they make the move from prospective pilgrim to devotee. But, equally important, the excerpts from the travel diaries suggest that all polities are essentially the same regardless of their seeming differences. The travel texts create both a strategy for ethnographizing as well as a strategy for devotionalizing: two registers that become increasingly relevant to create a *grammar of devotion* based in a *matrix of possible meanings*, located in meaningful symbols and strategies, which enable a project of inclusivity that global religious movements require to spread worldwide.

The Sai "Home" and Narratives of Exile and Prodigality

The focus of Sai pilgrimage is toward the goal of residence in the holy city of Puttaparthi, close to the sacred person of Sathya Sai Baba. Today most overseas devotees come to Puttaparthi as part of a structured spiritual tour from Sathya Sai centers overseas.[11] Indian devotees may come as part of a package tour or in small kin groups, depending upon a variety of factors including length of stay, whether it is a first visit, how many people in the party, among others. The local Sai temple/satsang group acts as a hub for the organization of the travel. Tickets are booked through travel agents in large lots so that pilgrims travel as a group. These groups are organized on locality or region. Anna told me that she had been to Puttaparthi six times in six years as part of the annual tour from the Turin Sai Center.[12] In 2002/2003 the Sai Center in Turin ran six tours to Puttaparthi each with fifty to sixty devotees.

In many Sai centers and gatherings, four Thursdays before the departure of the pilgrims, potlucks cum information sessions followed the usual bhajan sessions where an "experienced" pilgrim would speak and take prospective pilgrims on a "visual journey" to Puttaparthi through slides, home movies, and pictures. The feasts were both a bonding and marking experience. Often I found devotees made friendships during these initial potlucks that lasted through the duration of the pilgrimage.

The pilgrims were also led by unofficial tour guides. Mrs. Shashi Sinha (fifty-eight) was a tour guide for a group from the northeast of the United States. She said of her guide work, "I am free now. My children are all grown up, married, so I have nothing to do. I have been Baba's bhakta for twenty-eight years now. I go to Puttaparthi for three weeks twice a year and take these people. I help people to meet Bhagawan."[13] The pilgrims traveled to Bombay or Bangalore, where they usually spent a couple of days before leaving for Puttaparthi. Once in Puttaparthi they spent several days (even a month or so) in spiritual contemplation, worship, and darshan of Sathya Sai Baba before preparing to go home during the last couple of days. Of the nineteen people I interviewed, fifteen said they felt very unhappy by the prospect of going home; many of them said they cried for days before their departure.

On the Thursday after their return, a "homecoming" party was held to allow pilgrims to formally share their experiences. Returnees were given an exalted place in the circle of devotees, and this is the way they were introduced to me: "This is Jim. He just got back from Puttaparthi," or "This is Jane. She spent three months at Prasanthi Nilayam,"or "This is Shyam, he also just got back from 'Parthy,"and so on. The trip to the ashram gave them higher status in the eyes of the devotees "back home." Often I noticed that the returnees, like Jane, Shyam, and Jim, in the first few days of their return, reminisced about their impressions of India, the ashram, and Baba. As time went on, and the experience became more distant, these snippets were woven together to become full-fledged stories of devotion and praise of Sai Baba.

Devotees told me that, on returning home, they felt they were returning to an alien world, frightened and disoriented. Jim (fifty-seven) said how "bored" he felt in the first couple of days and how he had gotten used to "the hustle and bustle of the ashram." Returnees often felt alienation and anxiety about their lives. Jane (forty-four) said: "We were so close in the ashram, and people would tell us, 'time to go for darshan' or 'time to get to lunch' and so on. Now it is my own life, and I feel weird about it. Nobody to tell me what to do." Shyam, who is also called "Sam" (thirty-four), said: "I walked into my house and I thought . . . "this can't be *my* home. It isn't you know, not my 'true *Home.*'" Chitra said: "Where Bhagawan is, is my home. Not anyone else, not even my husband, children . . . I would say."

A *narrative of prodigality,* where the lost child returns home to the loving and forgiving arms of the parent (i.e., Sathya Sai Baba), is constantly invoked in interviews with devotees. The sojourn is not only a finding of a space without, but reflexively aids in finding a redemptive space within. The rest of life is portrayed as a dry and exiled existence in perdition. Sai devotees suggest emphatically that Puttaparthi is their true "spiritual home" where they are "at peace" and their everyday lives, away from Puttaparthi, are "lives of exile."[14] Anna said: "This is our real home . . . where Bhagawan is near to us. We think it is Torino or Roma, but that is only the home of our body. Our home of the spirit is here with Swami (the Lord). We always want to come back and back."[15]

The overarching affect effect for devotees is that their everyday life is "away" from their spiritual center. They articulate a loss of something precious and an overwhelming desire to return to the place of meaning. Stephen said; "This is my true Home. The place where I feel alive! Yes, I exist in London but here I live, fully and completely." Shanti said: " 'Parthy is like *swarga* (heaven) when you are there. It is like living in heaven. Everything gets done by Swami's will there. I feel like I have gone to my mother's home. In your mother-in-law's house you will be careful, scared, but in your mother's house you can enjoy, like that it is." Puttaparthi is posited as the *True Home* of the soul, as opposed to the devotees' real home in which they live lives of "spiritual exile." Jim said; "When I am back in Buffalo, it's like being in exile. It's like *being in the desert*." The *narrative of exile* is frequently invoked, accompanied by biblical images of deserts and fears of an uncertain future. The narrative of exile is a powerful one, arguing that devotees feel like outcasts in their home societies, though they are neither marginal nor powerless. Devotees see living away from Sai Baba as an involuntary banishment from their "home" and the pilgrimage as a difficult journey of return to their rightful place. Therefore, though prospective pilgrims were making the journey for the first time to Puttaparthi, they talked about "returning." Shyam said:" I felt so much at home in 'Parthy, even though it was my first time there." Selva (sixty-seven) said, "When Sita (my wife) went there first and said she felt peace, I told her, "you must be joking, la," but when I went there, Tulasi, I felt like so strange . . . easy, so nice, like being home, but without any worry."

Mr. Vishwanathan, a lecturer in the Sathya Sai College, echoed these understandings of devotees by involving the mythic logics of the famous epic story of the Hindu God King Rama to explain devotees' sense of exile: "You know Lord Rama took *vana vasa* for fourteen years because the Queen Kaikeyi banished him from the palace. When he came home he became king. That was a homecoming. Like that, these people are lost in the forest [*kadu*] of their lives, and they came to the town [*uru*] that is Puttaparthi and to their home [*veedu*] near Swami." The evocations of "uncivilized" spaces of desert and forest in devotees' narratives, as opposed to the civilized spaces of town and the central, comforting spaces of home, argues that devotees *do* see their everyday lives as lives of exile in uncivilized spaces even when they are surrounded by the relative luxury of living

accommodations in the developed or urban world.[16] Exile encases a disenfranchisement and separation from the nation and culture that one resides
in, and a link to a distant promised land of spiritual fulfillment at Sai Baba's feet; all of which the devotees appear to feel.

The Sathya Sai life story encourages this view of closeness to Sai Baba
as a "spiritual destination." For example, biographer Kasturi states: "Sai
Baba is not enamored by tours to see places or admire scenery nor has he
the urge to go on pilgrimages since he is the goal of all pilgrimages!"
(Kasturi 1968:124). By articulating their journey as a movement from the
chaotic edges toward the comfort of the home center, devotees construct
a *narrative of prodigality* in which the dialectical spaces of exile and home
are the two endpoints. However, most transnational devotees visit Puttaparthi at most once or twice a year, and Indian devotees a maximum of
five to ten times a year. The space of Puttaparthi becomes one of the
imagination where a "longing to return" is invested.

Devotees spatialize this narrative of prodigality and read the city of Puttaparthi and the district of Rayalseema where it is located as hinged on a
spatial hierarchy based on a central principle of calibration of proximity to
the spiritual center of the movement, Sathya Sai Baba himself (Glover
2006:10). They constantly measure the distance to Sai Baba through proxemic devices such as gates and signs, which they read as emotion-laden
measuring devices to chart their distance from their spiritual center. The
route to the city of Puttaparthi is laid out to enable a performance of this
calibration, as ornate and repetitive gates and signs with the Sathya Sai
logo are situated throughout the district to inform the traveler of the distance to traverse to arrive at the ashram.

As with Frederyck in the opening vignette, many devotees who were
repeat pilgrims recounted the feelings they had on seeing the district
gate and city gates and realizing that they had arrived in Puttaparthi.
Connie Shaw, author and longterm devotee, writes of her first trip to Puttaparthi and her attendant fears and excitement upon seeing the gates:

> The closer we get to Puttaparthi the more Biblical the people
> seem. . . . *Approaching the ashram property the town gates come into
> view and our hearts race with excitement.* After passing several white
> washed huts with dirt floors and thatched roofs [which have all now
> been removed] we arrive at the edge of Puttaparthi. *I am trembling
> with excitement.* The abode of great peace is indeed a heavenly spot
> like nothing I have ever experienced.   (Shaw 2000:187–189)

Both men and women seem to feel this emotion, though women cry more obviously. Jim confessed to being "all shaky" when he got on line for his first darshan at Prashanti Nilayam and claims that, although he has been back to Puttaparthi ten times since then, he still gets excited and emotional in the ashram. Stephen, a Sai devotee for fifteen years, told me that, as he stood in front of the ashram gates, he felt "a charge, like an electric current of pure energy" course through his system. "It is like recharging your internal batteries, you know . . . like a power source. You get drained of spiritual energy in your everyday life. Here you recharge your batteries. Coming here is coming to the source . . . coming home."[17] So the trip to Puttaparthi is seen as an emotional journey "home" where the "authentic" self is free to emerge and where the distinctions between representation and reality coalesce into one unitary whole (Frow 1991:127–128).

Miracle Ground: The History of the Sacred City

In discussing sacred space, Gerard Van der Leeuw (1986 [1933]) identified four kinds of politics in the construction of any sacred space: a politics of position, every establishment of a sacred place is a positioning; a politics of property, a sacred place is "appropriated, possessed and, owned"; a politics of exclusion, the sanctity of sacred place is preserved by boundaries; and a politics of exile, a form of a modern loss of, or nostalgia for, the sacred. Urban theorist Lilly Kong built upon Van der Leeuw's argument in her examination of Singapore's house churches and their complex relationship to the multiculturalist policy of the Singaporean state in which she suggested these politics must be rethought with reference to emergent transnational sacred spaces (2002). She identified four new politics, a politics of exclusion, a politics of inclusion, a politics of separation, and a politics of hybridization, which she claimed were the basis for understanding religion in a multicultural society. While I am skeptical both of Kong's identification of these trends as clearly defined "politics," as well as what she identifies as the multiculturalist policy of the Singaporean state, she is accurate to suggest that multicultural societies use space to define and codify "insiders" and "outsiders" through processes of inclusion, discrimination, separation, and appropriation. For these scholars, then, sacred space in the multicultural world is all about politics.

But Robert Orsi takes a different view when exploring the world of urban religious processions in New York City. He states that urban religious cartographies are "maps of being" (1999:51), home to "diverse religious ontologies" that link the divine and mundane worlds to "disclose to practitioners particular ways of being in the world, of approaching the invisible beings who along with family members and neighbors make up the practitioner's relevant social worlds and of coordinating an individual's own story with an embracing cultural narrative" (1999:53). Mappings of the city can provide various narratives that aid in the construction of a devotional identity: redemptive, transgressive, exculpatory, or transformational depending upon how the spaces are envisaged, used, and imagined. Orsi argues that "people have acted on and with the spaces of the city to make religious meanings in many different ways," leading to a city space of "diverse religious ontologies" (1999:47–53) in a "multi-vocal serenade."

I build upon these different theories to explore the built world of the sacred city of Puttaparthi and the Sai ashram it enfolds. There are two different strands to this built world: the material (the bricks and mortar buildings), with its architecture, functional spaces, and aesthetics, and the symbolic, with its interpretative and affective components. It is the complex relationship between the double strands—the material world and the symbolic devotional world—and the complementary tension in the equation between the two that I seek to unpack. It is important to note that either end of the equation can be engineered or manipulated to have consequences on the other strand so it is not enough either to speak about the material world or the symbolic world alone (Dillistone 1966). As the material world grows and changes, the concrete place helps to shape the ontological objectives of the Sai devotees, and as the symbolic interpretation shifts, it helps to situate the place and give it significance, recasting the central axis between agency and structure.

Finally, as sociologist Hervieu-Léger notes, the globalization of religiocultural groups is linked to the problem of identity construction as it leads to "novel forms of religious sociability and new configurations of this (modern) tension" (cited in Srinivas 2008:13, 21).[18] The harnessing of the spatial imagination toward increased devotion rests on the Taylorean concept of the social imaginary where large groups of people imagine "how they fit together with others, how things go on between them and their fellows, the expectations that are normally met and the deeper normative notions and images that underlie these expectations"

(Giddens 1991). Palmer suggests that "the experience of ashram life functions in important ways in the lives of all devotees furnishing an important and inspirational example of how humans are to dwell together, ever mindful of being in the presence of god," and that "the peace and Harmony of the ashram provides a beacon of hope, a constant reminder to devotees around the world that if they are willing to 'let go and let Baba' they too will dwell in this peace" (Palmer in Forsthoefel and Humes 2005:114). The key issue for the movement, as S. Srinivas notes in her recent work on Sathya Sai Baba,[19] is one of devotional identity construction for devotees who come from all corners of the world. In his study of colonial Lahore, William Glover skillfully suggests that many South Asian cities have a "distinctive material approach" that fosters moral and social development (2006: xx), and this approach is anchored in the belief that the built world has the power to shape human conduct. Conversely, if one can link the built form to a "way of being," then, by influencing the former, one can presumably govern the latter (2006:xxi). The material world—architecture and urban planning—can, in such circumstances, be used to persuade toward the ontological objective of social and individual transformation. This differs significantly from Foucauldian practices of discipline, because the subject is transformed willingly through constant persuasion by the aspects of the built world around him; a persuasive project rather than a disciplinary one. Thus it appears that Sai devotees are imbued with a sense of agency as they move through the spaces of Puttaparthi because the transformation in identity toward a devotional civic selfhood is believed to be one of choice. The built form of the sacred city and their experience of it is central to the establishment of their devotional identity.

But the sacred city of Puttaparthi seems hardly central to anything at all. It is far from the political and economic centers of power and becomes powerful by virtue of its affiliation with the person of the sacred living being (Eade and Sallnow 1991:7),[20] a strange echo of Frazer's concept of "magic by contagion."[21] As Huang and Weller note in their study of Compassionate Relief—a global Buddhist sect—these emergent sacred cities create new "circuits of devotion" where devotees find their way to the margins (Huang and Weller 2007), reversing traditional understandings of pilgrimage as a movement form the margins to the holy center. Pilgrims to Puttaparthi often stated that Puttaparthi was "off the beaten track," "remote," "difficult to get to," but it was "magical," "special," "worth it" once they got there. Still, the marginality of Puttaparthi enables an understanding of how new postcolonial "ways of seeing" arise from the margins. Edward Soja argues (in discussing the spaces of Los Angeles) that people can consciously choose the margins as spaces of "recentered identity" (1989:96–99). The choosing of marginal spaces such as Puttaparthi as global centers, as Sathya Sai Baba did in 1955, becomes critical to creating a "counterhegemonic identity" (Soja 1989:96), where identity can be reimagined. Devotees reorient spatial "circuits of devotion." They thwart the center/periphery dialogue that haunts globalization (Hannerz 1990) and create new actions, ideologies, identities, and language, building what bell hooks has called "a spatiality of difference" (hooks 1990:145–153) where subjectivities "multiply, connect and combine" (Soja 1989:99). This space frames a new way of seeing where one can view "both center and margin simultaneously" (hooks 1984:ix) and develop a language of power that takes account of the periphery. Puttaparthi as a city is marginal to global spaces of capital, suggesting that it is capable of creating a new language of power that restructures the 1970s representation of difference posed as the problem of the semiosis between cultures.

People from all over the world congregate in Puttaparthi in the hope of meeting Sathya Sai Baba. In 1940, when Sai Baba announced his divinity, Puttaparthi was a village. One had to walk, or travel by bullock cart, and it was cut off from the major highways (Padmanaban 2000:8–10). It was, in fact, like many villages in preindependence India. About a hundred families lived in Puttaparthi at that time (Padmanaban 2000:20–22), and it had one small box shop (Tamil = *potti kadai*), a small school, and was surrounded by fields growing *raagi* (millet) and other dry crops. Sai Baba, unlike other successful gurus, such as Rajneesh who quickly migrated to urban centers and thence to the United States and Europe, announced his intention of remaining in Puttaparthi, which would develop as a "spiritual center," with the naturalist metaphor of a rooted tree to argue for a homegrown spirituality and an authenticity of purpose: "This Tree shall not be transplanted: it will grow where it first rose from the earth" (SSS 1:16). He is believed to have foretold Puttaparthi's growth, "The Sai Pravesh (the advent of Sai) will transform that region into Prasanthi Pradesh (a region of highest peace). There will rise a bhavan (mansion)! Lakhs (hundreds of thousands) of people from all over India, why only India, from all over the world, will come and wait there for Sai darshan (sight of Sai)!"[22] One German Sai devotee exclaimed excitedly on her blog, "It is literally in the middle of nowhere with people from everywhere."[23] The original marginality of Puttaparthi to the global (economic as well as political) enables an understanding of new "ways of seeing" religious space that arise from the margins (Huang and Weller 2007). Edward Soja argues that people consciously choose the margins as spaces of "recentered identity" (1989:96–99), thwarting the center/periphery dialogue that haunts globalization (Hannerz 1990) and building what bell hooks has called "a spatiality of difference" (1990:145-53) where subjectivities "multiply, connect and combine" (Soja 1989:99) in these marginal spaces leading to a multiplicity of voices within the space that Orsi identifies.

As S. Srinivas notes, there was a strong push by the Sathya Sai organization to "sacralize" the city and make it central to the movement through a process of "privileging memorialization" (2008:163–180). The Sathya Sai organization engaged in a massive building program of sacred shrines, museums, and charity-based educational institutions and hospitals, while simultaneously reinventing the mythic in the existing shrines of Puttaparthi to enhance Sathya Sai Baba's increasing charisma through their repatriation, linking them concretely to his life story and his teachings (Leslie-Chaden 1997, Murphet 1971, 1977, Padmanaban 2000).

In the mid 1940s a few of Sai Baba's wealthy and elite devotees raised money to build a small temple (now called the Old Mandir) with accommodations for Sathya Sai Baba in the rear (Padmanaban 2000; Srinivas 2008:54–55). By 1950 the number of devotees outgrew the Old Mandir and Sathya Sai Baba commissioned a new ashram in an area south of the old village, Prasanthi Nilayam, with a huge darshan hall to accommodate devotees. In interviews devotees told me of the issues encountered building the ashram in such a remote village. They recounted them as part of the magic and wonder of Baba. None of them had witnessed these problems firsthand, but had rather heard of them from other devotees: for example, the iron and steel required to hold up the ceiling came from Trichinopoly, over two hundred miles away, and could not cross the Chitravathi River to enter Puttaparthi (Padmanaban 2000). Sai Baba is believed to have materialized a crane and brought workmen from the Tunghabhadra Dam project nearby to raise the iron girders. According to devotee accounts, the ashram compound took two years to build (Padmanaban 2000:25). The material form of Sai Baba's original home in the village changed rapidly under this program. The house where he was born became a Shiva Temple inaugurated in 1973, which spatially traced his divine lineage to the Hindu god Shiva and his female consort Shakti. Several smaller commemorative shrines were erected at various sites in the city that devotees deemed central to the life story of Sai Baba; the tree under which he used to idly sit on hot summer nights near the river when he was a young man, occasionally speaking, singing, and miraculously producing statuettes out of the sandy river bed for his devotee group, became a shrine, and another shrine at the *kalpavriksha* (wish-fulfilling tree) where Sai Baba is believed to have plucked a variety of fruits from one tree. The Venugopalaswamy (Hindu pastoralist cowherd god Krishna playing the flute) temple that Sai Baba's grandfather is believed to have built for the citizenry of Puttaparthi was also refurbished at this time.

The entrance to the ashram was marked in 1975 with the building of the famous Gopuram Gate designed in the South Indian Dravidian style of temple architecture with several stories all decorated with images of playful Hindu gods and goddesses and semidivine beings and capped with the auspicious *gavaksha* (barrel vault) topped with the *amalaka* or divine seeds (Kramrisch 2002 [1946], 2:319). Kramrisch identifies this imagery as a cosmological ordering of the universe where the world of man meets the divine supernal man (*vastuprusha*) (2002 [1946], 1:117).

The Old Mandir gave way to a new building called Prasanthi Nilayam (the core of the current ashram), built to celebrate Sai Baba's twenty-fifth birthday (Srinivas 2008:171). The Prasanthi Nilayam complex held a central prayer room (now the current mandir) and a large darshan hall, several Seva Dal blocks to accommodate volunteers, the Sathya Sai Bookshop, a communications center, and a few "sheds" for visitors to sleep in as well as canteens for food. In 1973 the Poornachandra Auditorium complex was built to seat fifteen thousand people with a suite of rooms above for Sai Baba (where he lived from the 1990s until 2006) and the Prasanthi Nilayam complex was extended with a larger bookshop, bakeries, canteens, more dormitories, gardens, paths and walkways, all painted in muted pastel colors and topped with gold finials, pink lotus capitals, and decorative facades. The main buildings were expanded and pink domes and decorations were added in the twelfth-century "royal style of the southern Vijayanagar empire" (which was known both for its cosmopolitanism and for its aesthetics and praxis of border crossing) and painted in pastel colors (Srinivas 2008: 164–165). In the 1990s the Sai Kulwant Darshan Hall was added to the north of the mandir to accommodate the several thousand devotees who gathered every day.

As time went on more buildings were erected all over the city and the building program within the ashram was enlarged as well. Two museums were added: the Eternal Heritage Museum, built in the North Indian temple style (which collapsed in 1990, killing three devotees), and the Chaitanya Jyothi Museum in 2000. Simultaneously several more shrines and auxiliary religious buildings were added that all enlarged upon the mythic framework of Sathya Sai Baba's life story and cemented (literally his claimed links to other divine and semidivine figures, sometimes through metaphorical subtle allusions and sometimes with direct material connections such as sculptures and artfully decorated frescoes.

A complex of educational buildings—colleges and schools—were built with murals, frescoes, ornate facades, and symbolic sculptures to encourage devotion and the link to the cosmological in opposition to secular (i.e., modern Western education).The Sathya Sai Institute of Higher Learning, a college, has a postmodern facade with a 1950s style clock, a sculpted image of the Hindu goddess of learning, Saraswati, seated on a white swan and surmounted by a pink lotus; the Sri Sathya Sai Higher Secondary School has a shrine to the Hindu god Ganesha in the front; the planetarium or Sathya Sai space theater is capped by a multicolored geodesic dome; and the Music Academy facade is decorated with caryatids of musical instruments including guitars, veenas, and trumpets, which S. Srinivas suggests "symbolizes the harmony of Indian and western music" (2008:179), while the Sathya Sai International Center of Sport has an enormous stadium with a series of thirty-foot-tall sculptures of divine and charismatic religious leaders: the Buddha, the Hindu god of physical prowess Hanuman, Jesus Christ, and Sai Baba himself. Finally, the Sathya Sai Institute for Higher Medical Services (SSSHMS), a teaching hospital with free care for the poor, was built in 1991 to the south of the city and designed by the British architect Sir Keith Critchlow. It is capped by a lotus-crowned dome whose shape apparently symbolizes "a human being with folded arms symbolizing love affection and care."[24]

Throughout the 1980s Puttaparthi developed into a small but serviceable town, as commercial establishments grew and the town expanded to the south and west. Connie Shaw (2000:212) states, that after a "white knuckle drive" down the highway from Bangalore, she noticed that Puttaparthi had changed: "further prosperity in the health, dress and possessions of our people. There is even a new billboard advertising Trot shoes—'like walking on air.' My feelings of 'being home' startle me especially in light of the fact that my initial reaction to India was one of aversion." On October 28, 1985, she recorded in her diary:

The most amazing changes have occurred at Puttaparthi. The main
streets of the town are being paved and there are pretty pastel cottages
and apartments in the place of old thatched shacks and mud huts.
Everyone is better dressed both in the town and in Prasanthi Nilayam
itself. Prasanthi Nilayam is bustling with "sixtieth birthday celebrations" for the upcoming November twenty-third birthday celebrations
and the World Council Meetings the week before.   (2000:212)

Selvaratnam (sixty-seven), of Kuala Lumpur, told me that on his first
trip to Puttaparthi as late as 1980 there were only a few huts in front of the
ashram. The whole of the market and the other cross streets did not exist.
He gestured toward the bustling town, with the rows upon rows of hotels,
lodges, restaurants, photo parlors, money exchange centers, bookstores,
trinket shops, juice bars, and cafés, and said; "None of this was here in
1980. All of it is new." Chitra, who had also been coming to Puttaparthi
since the 1970s, said: "Before, only Prasanthi was there, and not even the
Sai Kulwant Darshan Hall was built. Only Sai Baba's quarters were there,
so we would sit in a circle in front of the Sarve Dharama stambha (a pillar
signifying the unity of all religions at the physical center of the ashram)
for darshan. There was nothing in the town . . . nothing! We had to pack
food for many days when we came." But Puttaparthi grew apace, with the
spreading of Sai Baba's fame and power. As Sai Baba's fame grew and his
power in India rose, Puttaparthi's development reached a new high. But,
as with most urban development in South Asian cities, the remodeling
was accumulated piecemeal over forty years. Other than that for the ashram, no comprehensive development plan influenced the early city building, rather it was built on an ad-hoc arrangement of primary building
blocks based on spatial aggregations of adjacencies and the strategic
gathering of capital through influential patrons.

So the city of Puttaparthi emerged in the twenty-first century from this
systematic material sacralization program in its current form; as a global
sacred cosmopolis, what S. Srinivas terms "an ideal polis" (2008:160) with
worldwide economic- and knowledge-based connections and an infrastructure that emphasized both its local history and its transnational connections. According to S. Srinivas, the rapid growth of Puttaparthi as a sacred center has made urban planners interested in planning its future
growth. Today a comprehensive plan exists for the entire district, with
Puttaparthi as the nerve center for further development. The SSSUDA
(Sri Sathya Sai Urban Development Authority) prepared a draft master

plan in consultation with the SSSO and the ORGINDIA, a New Delhi non-profit agency, in 2005,[25] that is prominently displayed on a concrete bill-board in the bus depot. This push to make Puttaparthi central to subconti-nental and global circuits can already be seen in Puttaparthi's informal infrastructure (Srinivas 2008:165–187). Main Street exhibits connections both with the larger subcontinent and with the world: signs for taxi rental shops advertising fares to Chennai, Mumbai and Bangalore; three Western Union wireless currency transfer shops advertising—on plywood bill-boards on the walkways—currency exchange rates for the U.S. dollar, Brit-ish pound, Nepali rupee, Singaporean dollar, and Japanese yen; medical stores advertising "remedies of all stomach ailments"; restaurants offering "continental meals"; shops for e-mail, the free Internet phone service Skype, cell phone repair services and international phone service; and nu-merous hostelries and hotels with signs for rooms "To Let."

All this points to the fact that the central task of this building program of Puttaparthi as it is understood by devotees and others residing in the city is to help prospective devotees become part of the community of Sai devotion, to adjust to their new reality, to transform them from individuals or nationals to Sai *citoyens sans frontiers*; as such it is a "pedagogic project," as S. Srinivas notes—not one limited to the educational institutions alone, as she suggests (2008), but rather one that encompasses the entire built form of the city. Further, it is not imposed upon the devotee, but subtly persuasive. For, as Margaret Somers and Gloria Gibson observe, while ana-lyzing narratives charting the developmental shift from the episteme of the other to a group identity and the complex relationship to identity poli-tics, culture (and in turn encultured spaces) shapes politics through consti-tutive effects, as morality is shaped, identities are produced and trans-formed, and narratives are constructed and altered (1994:38–39) both for the individual and for the community of devotion. So the central narrative to this building program is transformational of both the landscape as well as the individuals who encounter it and acts as a built narrative toward a powerfully persuasive end that is deemed to be about moral stakeholder-ship (White 2006; Zukin 1995).

Spaces of Entry: Becoming and Being a Sai Devotee

On a material level the first persuasive piece of distinctively Sai architecture— a formal delineation of the sacred Sai territory—that

devotees and prospective devotees encounter, are the numerous gateways on the highway to Puttaparthi that signal one's entry into Sai space.
Architecturally, the gates are an amalgam of styles.

The first gate devotees see is the Sathya Sai Taluk (district) gate near
Pedaballi village on the highway to Puttaparthi, which is in the style of a
Hindu torana gateway (with sculpted garlands) painted pale pink and yel-
low. It carries both the sign of the district and the logo of the Sathya Sai
movement (a lamp with a lotus carrying the emblems of the five "major
world religions" according to the Sai tradition: Islam, Zoroastrianism,
Christianity, Buddhism, and Hinduism). It reads: "Welcome Sri Sathya
Sai Taluk."

When I traveled with devotees to Puttaparthi several of them burst
into tears when we spotted this gateway. Frederyck explained: "a burst of
emotion comes over us when we realize how close we are to Bhagawan."
Mrs. Diaz, a Portugese devotee, said, "I have come from such a distance
(Cordoba and London) that when I see this gate I know I have come near
to Bhagawan." Other devotees echoed her sentiments, saying repeatedly
that the gates "reminded them . . . how close they were to Bhagawan."

A second concrete gateway marks the entry to the Sathya Sai Vidyagiri
complex and the final ornate gateway occurs at the entry to Puttaparthi.
Devotees by this time were hanging out of the bus and car to see the city
and the ashram even though many of them had been there before. The final entryway leading to the ashram is a concrete version of a classic South
Indian Hindu Temple called the Gopuram (windtower) Gate, though it is
not used today, and it was greeted by loud clapping by the devotees I
accompanied.

The series of gates and open spaces creates a feeling of powerful anticipation and energy in the devotee. Shanti told me that she felt "happy"
when she saw the gates thinking "how close" she was "to Bhagawan."
When I accompanied devotees on their travels to Puttaparthi, I saw them
cry, clap, pray, and sing as they suddenly spotted the gateways. At each
gate they would recalculate the distance yet to go and the time it would
take them.

But why is the response so emotional? Many of the Sai devotees come
from very far away and to arrive in Puttaparthi itself is an achievement
for them. But the gates are also emblematic of how they see their lives
when they are "away" from Sathya Sai Baba. Sai devotees argued that Puttaparthi is their true "spiritual home" where they are "at peace" and their
everyday lives, away from Puttaparthi, are "lives of exile."[26] Anna from

FIGURE 2.1. Gate to Sathya Sai Taluk. *Photo courtesy Tulasi Srinivas*

FIGURE 2.2. Gate to Sathya Sai Vidyagiri. *Photo courtesy Tulasi Srinivas*

Turin, a devotee of approximately a decade said: "This is our real home . . . where God is near to us. We think it is Torino or Roma, but that is only the home of our body. Our home of the spirit is here with Swami (the Lord). We always want to come back and back."[27] The gates act as markers of anticipation of a return to this home, close to their spiritual leader/divinity and as separator of the two realms that devotees inhabit—the mundane everyday domain of exile away from Sathya Sai Baba and that of the sacred magical place of Puttaparthi where they are spiritually and emotionally at home.[28]

Thus, symbolically, the gates act two ways: as milestones for devotees to enable them to measure their distance from Sai Baba and as signposts announcing their arrival at the sacred landscape of Puttaparthi. Devotees respond appropriately to the encapsulated competing messages of arrival and distance with mingled cries of thankfulness and pragmatic consideration of judgment of the distance yet to be covered to reach Sai Baba. Devotees measure their own "proxemic desire" for Sathya Sai Baba. Being physically close to the physical form of Sathya Sai Baba is much valued, though all devotees claim, "He is everywhere." The Sathya Sai bio/hagiography encourages the view of closeness to Sai Baba as a "spiritual destination." Kasturi, Sathya Sai Baba's biographer, states: "Sai Baba is not enamoured by tours to see places or admire scenery nor has he the urge to go on pilgrimages since he is the goal of all pilgrimages!" (Kasturi 1968:124). Measurement of distance through devices such as gateways and signs becomes an overwhelming preoccupation for devotees. As Venkat said, "being close to him was the only thing that mattered. We would fight to get a chance to sit at his feet." When asked why, he said, "to be frank, I hadn't thought about it . . . I think it must be because we thought he was God. Who doesn't want to be close to God? Just by being close to Him our lives would change. We would be blessed. Our troubles would just melt away." Joule said, "being close to Bhagawan is what we all live for. Just by being close to him, your life changes." Being in the presence of Sathya Sai Baba implies a blessing, a redemption—where one could change into a better person and have one's trouble dissolve. So the trip to Puttaparthi is seen as a quest or a return to an "authentic" self where the distinctions between representation and reality coalesce (Frow 1991:127–128) into one unitary whole and sighting the gateways on the trip indicates the end not only of the physical journey for devotees, but the beginning of a spiritual journey. The gateways are iconic of a built *narrative of redemption* by return.

According to the devotee Web page, the Gopuram Gate, closest to the ashram, has a special meaning attributable to Sai Baba that echoes the idea of the outer world as one of exile and loss, both physical and moral:

> If you dwell upon the significance of the gopuram, you can realise how holy, how mysterious, how revealing is its purpose. The gopuram beckons to wayfarers who have lost their way and who wander away from truth, "O ye mortals! Blinded by the fog of physical attachments and self-aggrandizing urges, overcome by the miasma of worldly desires, which are fleeting and false, you have forgotten Me, the source and sustenance of you all. Look up to this eternal, ever pure, over-full tower of joy. Come, have faith in the Everlasting Me. Struggle out of the darkness and enter the realm of light, and come to the royal road of Santhi (peace). Come, come, O come!"[29]

So the gates both act as separations between and yet unite these two worlds of the spiritual home and the geography of exile. Furthermore, the gateways—as understood by the devotees in traditional religious terms—are seen as the connection between two realms that are contiguous to devotees—the ordinary and the sacred—in which different dimensions and values occur side by side. The gateways help devotees mark the sometimes conflicting presence of these two worlds. The symbolism of these gateways is not to be underestimated. For devotees, what lies within the gateways is good, valuable, and sacred because of its closeness to Sathya Sai Baba. This does not mean that what lies beyond is automatically profane, but, rather, it is not automatically assumed to be good (Eliade 1987). Thus the gateways act as boundaries between the world of Puttaparthi, where devotees feel the transformative power of Sathya Sai Baba, and "other" spaces, which they suggest must be made sacred, and transformed, through their efforts, through seva (charitable works).

The gates are threshold spaces that site both inside and outside where the differentiation between "inner" and "outer" is not only what is significant but the transformative space in between is as well. The anthropological theorizing about differentiating spaces bears rethinking in light of spaces like the Puttaparthi gateways. These gateways also are reflective of the urban global subject as devotee. As Sanjay Srivastava notes in his analysis of middle-class spiritual devotion and its enspacements, "The contemporary urban subject—ensconced within the various processes we now label "globalisation"—is one located upon threshold

FIGURE 2.3. Gopuram Gate. *Photo courtesy Tulasi Srinivas*

spaces, which are in themselves both the sites and products of these processes."[30] The understanding of a threshold both in terms of space and time, which induces in the subject a feeling of neither here nor there, what Victor Turner has called "inbetwixt and in between," is significant for understandings of mobile transnationalism and for subjects who value mobility but are simultaneously anxious about being rootless.

But not all the gateways are decorative or symbolic alone. To return to the material dimension, as one gets closer to the ashram the gateways become functional and house within them actual gates. They serve a security purpose as they do in traditional Hindu temples to protect the deity and his/her power (and, pragmatically, the wealth of his/her jewelry) from the public. Through the gates at Puttaparthi, accessibility (both visual and physical) is controlled to the sacred center, i.e., the authoritative and charismatic sacred person of Sai Baba (Taylor 1987) and the governance of entry through these gates is enforced by Sai volunteers and security personnel. Like most significant spaces (including Vatican City and the White House), the twinned yet opposing forces of security and transparency have to be accommodated when dealing with Sai Baba. As one gets closer to the sacred center of Sathya Sai Baba, the security imperative increases and only a few core devotees are actually allowed into his personal space within the ashram, very similar to the Hindu temple.[31] The "private sections" of the ashram (as they are known), said to be two large apartments that comprise Sai Baba's home (now situated on either side of the Poornachandra Hall at the center of the ashram, behind Sai Kulwant Darshan Hall), are visually and otherwise inaccessible to the devotees since they have been encompassed by an eight-foot-high gray, unadorned wall on three sides, and the fourth side is protected by the security squad, curtains, and deep balconies. This was the high gray wall that I had spotted when I first visited the ashram.

Devotees told me in whispers that burglar alarms and other forms of invisible security also operated at night "to protect Sai Baba" ever since "the June incident." In June 1993 an assassination attempt was made on Sai Baba[32] in which four young male devotees broke into his chambers and tried to stab him (Brown 2000) They were found when security and the police were called and were killed in the melee that followed the attack. The internal road within the ashram leading to Sai Baba's private apartments above Poornachandra Hall are now constantly under surveillance by closed circuit cameras and armed guards. Individuals with cameras or other recording devices are not allowed near these areas, and few photographs exist. As Sai official photographer Kekie Mistry said, "Nowadays, it is impossible to get photos. The volunteers, you know . . ." implying no one can get close. Only high-ranking members of the Sathya Sai organization are allowed into the walled area around the private apartments. Devotees feel this spatial and visual separation to be right and proper. Shanti said, "You see there are bad people everywhere. What if someone tries to hurt Bhagawan? He Himself will not mind. He will sacrifice himself . . . but why?"

But while personal security is the rationale given for the high walls and burglar alarms, materially the walls also serve as a visual barrier—as a cloak—that symbolically increases the power of the sight of Sai Baba during the open darshan. Since Sai Baba cannot be seen by devotees until he enters the darshan hall, the symbolic value of his presence is made more powerful by his absence at other times. The cloaking of his presence behind walls and gates guards the mysterium tremendum of his presence for devotees. Frederyck said, "It is important that Bhagawan has time to rest and refresh himself. If anyone can go in anytime, then he will have no time for privacy. As it is, he does two darshans and then he does private darshans everyday." Janos (twenty-nine) from Serbia, whom

I met when he was hanging around the gate, said, "I don't mind that I cannot see Him all the time. It makes the times when I can see Him very special. He has said that only when you are ready and when He wills it will you be able to see Him or get blessed. I am willing to wait. . . . I have been here three months and every day I come here. One day He will see me . . . I know that."

The physical separation of gates and walls is reinterpreted as devotional hurdles that signify the spiritual work that a devotee must do in order to merit interaction with Sai Baba.[33] In this logical system a "good" devotee may be permitted into the private quarters, and this reinforces the legitimacy of the high-ranking members who are allowed in to see him. The crossing of these gates is conceived of very differently than that of the marker gates. It is transgressive and therefore wrong and presumably punishable. Former devotees felt differently about this cloaking of Sai Baba's presence. They felt it to be secretive and hidden, linking it intangibly with a lack of trust. To them there is nothing good in this (Brown 2000). David (forty-two) said to me in an e-mail, "If he had nothing to hide or was unafraid of his so-called devotees, why would there be a need for all those gates and all that security?" Venkat (thirty-five) agreed with David: "Ultimately it is not about anything except power. Power over the devotees."

But the symbolism of cloaking Sathya Sai Baba in privacy is only valuable in opposition to his visual accessibility during darshan. Devotees state that in the ritual of seeing and being seen by the divinity of Sathya Sai Baba they experience a moment of ultimate self-transformation, by which they are "captured" spiritually and experience a "complete immersion in Sai Baba's love." The Sai Kulwant Darshan Hall is believed to be the built form of the transformational moment between Sai Baba and devotee. Materially, then, the spatial center of the Sathya Sai ashram is the open-air and transparent Sai Kulwant Darshan Hall where twice-daily ritual darshan of Sathya Sai Baba takes place as a clear statement of the inclusion of all devotees. It is an enormous hall, roofed in green glass and green and gold coffering, that, according to the Sai publicity materials, can seat up to 20,000 people in comfort. I was told that it is paved with a soft white and dark stone and lit by 108 crystal chandeliers. The pillars supporting this edifice have lotus flower capitals where pigeons congregate in large numbers. Kasturi's biography of Sathya Sai Baba, which devotees treat as apostolic literature, recounts the many problems in getting the darshan hall built to enable visual access for all devotees seated there (Kasturi 1968:90–94), including designing a large roof span with no supporting columns so devotees could see Sai Baba with no obstruction. The transparency of the Sai Kulwant Darshan Hall acts in productive tension with the cloaking effect of the high walls around Sathya Sai Baba's personal compound. The dais had an overhanging proscenium decorated in the style of the elaborately carved granite Hindu Hoysala temples of the twelfth century (though this was in molded concrete),[34] with rows upon rows of elephants, horses, and men and women playing musical instruments, painted in the same pastel palette of pinks, blues, yellows, and greens edged with gilt. According to the devotee site describing the mandir, the architecture and aesthetics of the hall follows Glover's theory of architecture as transformative:

> a living testimony to the life and message of Bhagawan Sri Sathya Sai Baba, the mandir speaks eloquently the divine message of the unity of life, universal concord, and harmony through its sculptured angels, humans, and animals, feasting our eyes on the various faces of this aesthetic wonder. The peacocks and snakes, the elephants and lions nestling close to each other on the facade of the mandir in quiet ecstasy speak a meaningful message to those who have eyes to see, ears to hear, and hearts to feel. These sculptured beings on the facade beautifully bring out the drama of transformation and transcendence that can occur if one sincerely strives to sublimate oneself.[35]

Furthermore, all these carved symbols point to a glorious unification of all religions, asserting the umbrellalike, overarching charisma of Sathya Sai Baba. "The central prayer hall is a thing of beauty, joy, and wonder. The five religious symbols descending from top to bottom of the walls on each side of the altar sing silently but sweetly the song of the unity of religions."[36]

The built form of the hall, with its openness and visual accessibility, is key to the feeling of inclusion that devotees feel. One devotee website from Nepal describes the hall as filled with "people from all walks of life and all over the world converging to take a glimpse of Swami."[37] Most of the devotees feel that they are included in the devotional community through their shared pursuit of the adoration of Sathya Sai Baba enabled by the clear sightlines and the aesthetics of the hall: "The kingdoms of plant, bird, beast, and angel have been beautifully featured to substantiate the theme of adoration of the Lord."[38] This view of inclusivity was supported by my interviews with devotees. Shanti said, when discussing the darshan hall before I saw it, "Oh you will be amazed at how beautiful it is. When you sit there waiting for darshan you are both at peace and full of excitement waiting for Swami. Also when you sit there it is like you are one with everyone. Even though we all come from different places we all sit there together waiting." Joule said, "The hall is beautiful. The decorations . . . they all have symbols about Bhagawan and the different types of life that love Him. . . . It is very—how to say it?—very inspiring. And you can see so clearly. Even if Bhagawan is far away you can see Him, no problem."

So if one were to examine the material space of Puttaparthi against the traditional Hindu temples city one would conclude that is not "new" at all, but rather merely a reinvention of the "ideal" cosmological space that is familiar to all Hindus, the typology of the Hindu temple town (Kramrisch 2002 [1946]) with its many encircling courtyards and spaces leading to the guarded sacred center. But because, *unlike* the Hindu temple town, the whole world of devotees gather at Puttaparthi from the four corners of the earth, the city is riven by competing and opposing claims; on the one hand inclusivity of all is an important theme for the city, so *transparency,* which translates as a "welcoming" architecture, while at the same time the person and mystery of Sathya Sai Baba must be kept safe, and so separation, closure, and *secrecy* are also an essential part of the construction of the city.

All in all, the material world of buildings, which are also often considered cosmological and hierophantic, become imbued with greater symbolic powers of persuasion as abstract emblematic and exemplary models of space that in turn create a language of ideal being within that exemplary space. Governing the construction of the sacred Sai city is therefore not inconsequential; it is a strategy of governance of the transformation of the devotional self and of the devotional community.

A Home Away from Home

Devotees recognize that most portions of the world are anxiety creating. Venkat said, "When I was in the Sai school we were never allowed out. Never! Not one day . . . So when I left in 1993 I was quite shocked. It took me many months to get used to going out. To the freedom. I felt as though I did not belong." Not only students but also transnational devotees feel this way while in the "real world," so coming back to Puttaparthi and the ashram is akin to "coming home." Stephen, a devotee from the UK, often mentioned how much he "felt at home" in Puttaparthi, "relaxed" and "alive," and how, when he returned to his "so-called 'home'" in the UK, he often felt "alone," "frightened," and "strange." Moses from South Africa stated, "Africa is the mother ship for all human life. But here it is the spiritual ship, a "home away from home," as you say. I feel safe here. Happy, content." As I said, devotees feel when they are at Puttaparthi that they are "at home"—i.e., in their true spiritual home. Anna (sixty-eight) from Turin, told me, "When I come here I feel I come home. Everyone is welcome . . . nobody is denied. . . . If you are here you can all see Bhagawan all the time." Gianni (thirty-nine), her son, said, "I came here and immediately it was like my home." Shanti, the devotee from Mumbai, India, added, "See how open everything is? It is like Bhagwan's heart. Open for us all to enter and to take our place." The architecture is inclusive according to devotional readings. Anna said: "The buildings are all beautiful here. When I am here I don't miss Turin at all. Why? Because Bhagawan is here . . . this is where I am home because it is His Home and He called me here. This is my new home, close to Bhagawan." According to devotees, the aesthetics and colors of the darshan hall and the ashram is very important in creating this "homelike" harmonious feeling of belonging. For example, the devotee Web site states: "Blue, yellow, and pink are the colors used, communicating the message of the harmony of spirit, intellect, and heart respectively; for blue stands for spirit, yellow for intellect, and pink for heart (love). The rich harmony of the three does result in santhi (peace) and Prasanthi (supreme peace); and that really is the message of the Prasanthi mandir."[39]

Devotees are moved by the pastel vision that Puttaparthi represents. Connie Shaw, the author devotee, says about the architecture of Prasanthi Nilayam: "As we approach the pink, cream and blue gates of Prasanthi Nilayam itself, it occurs to me that the ethereal-looking buildings appear like giant birthday cakes adorned with pastel angels (2000:189).

Joule said when I asked her about the color scheme of the ashram: "It is beautiful, so light so pretty. It makes my heart sing just to see these buildings and the colors. They are calming and peaceful . . . like a refuge. That is what ashram is supposed to be, no?" Stephen said, "Well my home is not decorated like this. But I must say that when I am in Prasanthi I feel relaxed and alert at once. Maybe it is the colors, I don't know. But I feel at ease, at home. A home that is better than my own." To devotees,

FIGURE 2.4. The exterior of Sri Sathya Sai Institute of Higher Medical Sciences in Puttaparthi. *Photo courtesy Tulasi Srinivas*

FIGURE 2.5. The exterior of the Sathya Sai Institute of Higher Learning. *Photo courtesy Tulasi Srinivas*

then, the buildings of Puttaparthi are new, unique, and beautiful. Simultaneously, they assert that the architecture speaks of home and belonging and of a celebratory and welcoming arrival to it after a long period of
exile—not of a home they knew, but a new home of their transformed,
ideal selves.

The City Today: Spiritual Tours, Sacred Sites, and the Construction of Memories

While much of the commercial establishments around the ashram have sprung up unplanned, the planned urban rescaling of the parts
of Puttaparthi owned by the ashram has been seemingly based in the
need to engage the emotion that devotees feel when in the city. S. Srinivas notes quite rightly that the growth and maintenance of the Sai tradition is achieved through a process of memorialization (2008:72–75), but
as Hanna Kim's exemplary work on the Swaminarayan temple in the
Neasden in north-west London demonstrates, using memorialization as
a strategy to establish a nascent tradition is not unique to the Sathya Sai
movement (Kim 2010,; see also Boyer 1977). Emotion is engaged through
the construction and reinvigoration ofdevotees' "memories" of singular
events in Sathya Sai Baba's life story through a tour of emotion-laden
sites in Puttaparthi. Impromptu guides give ad hoc tours of these sites,
both built and natural, as those that "must" be seen to experience devotion completely. Following a tour of these sites, one gets a sense of the
devotional geography of Puttaparthi and the built form of mythopoetic
narratives that create sacred places out of everyday spaces (Srinivas
2008:171, 179).

The architecture of Puttaparthi and of the Prasanthi Nilayam complex
in particular, is a reconfiguring of the landscape that fuses the requirements of devotional temple space, museum, monument, and the aesthetics of a religious theme park in one. The entire town of Puttaparthi is
treated as a museum cum memorial cum temple/*idgah* (mosque) highlighting the life story and syncretic magical divinity of Sathya Sai Baba.
Whereas, in the ashram itself, spectatorship is guided by either sign-
boards or Seva Dal volunteers,[40] in Puttaparthi town it is undertaken by
informal tour guides. For both spaces, the viewing itinerary is constructed in advance, with a particular sequence, and strictly adhered to
by Seva Dal volunteers within the ashram and by tour guides outside of it.

Though seemingly untrained and self-appointed, the tour guides abide by definite routes through the town, focusing on certain sites of memorialization, and they become upset if one suggests overturning the prescribed tour. Therefore, though the tour may appear unstructured to the casual visitor for the potential devotee, there is enhanced meaning in the experience of the tour. Further, for the Sai movement there appears to be a curatorial program in how to understand the city and the ashram as urban fragments of Sai Baba's charismatic divinity.

Also of note is the control of the access to certain sites within the town and particularly within the ashram (such as the mandir, the private quarters of Sathya Sai Baba), both in terms of the visual and spatial access and as well as the constraints on cameras, recorders, notebooks, papers, and pens within the ashram complex. The available publicity materials distributed by the Sathya Sai movement become valuable both pragmatically in order to get a sense of the space of the town and ashram and ideologically in determining how one "sees" the spaces.

The tour on a few occasions that I took it began at the northwest entrance to the town of Puttaparthi where three major temples are visited by Sai devotees, two of which are particularly significant: a temple to the monkey god Hanuman, or Anjanaya as he is popularly known, and a temple to Sathyabhama, consort of Krishna (an avatar of the Hindu god Vishnu) that is believed to have been built by Kondama Raju, Sathya Sai Baba's grandfather. Sai biographer Kasturi notes: "Not only did the Rajus build and endow Gopalaswami Temple,[41] but the devout Sri Ratnakaram Kondama Raju, grandfather of Sathya Sai Baba, dedicated a temple to Sathyabhama, a consort of Lord Krishna; "Kondama Raju used to say in explanation of this unusual tribute to Sathyabhama, that he was inspired to erect the temple because of the events that occurred during a strange dream" (Kasturi 1972:11–16). Close to the Satyabhama temple is a temple to Venugopalaswamy (Krishna playing the flute) where Sai legends claim a prophetic cobra cursed the village to become a ruin of anthills, i.e., "Puttaparthi" (Kasturi 1962:5–8), claimed a savior would be born (Sathya Sai Baba).

Continuing southward into Puttaparthi from the temples, devotees visit the childhood home of Sathya Sai Baba in the old village center. The home was site of many of the childhood miracles of Sai Baba (Kasturi 1972:14–25). It has been converted to a Shiva temple in 1979 and *puja* (worship) is performed there daily. Self-appointed guides in the area, who appeared suddenly every time I visited, indicate the home of Subbamma, the wife of the village *karnam* (accountant), one of the earliest devotees of Sai Baba (Kasturi 1972; Padmanaban 2000). From the Shiva temple, devotees travel southeast to the *kalpavriksha*—a tamarind tree—on a small hill near the Chitravathi River. Devotees told me the story repeatedly of how they had read that from this tree Sai Baba would produce any number of exotic fruits (Kasturi 1962:50,Murphet 1971). The spaces that devotees want to visit because they have heightened value in the life story of Sathya Sai Baba are the high points of the tour.

The memorial tour of the city also visits many naturalistic and animistic sites where Sai Baba is believed to have given his first discourses and performed his first miracles; the Chitravathi River bank in Puttaparthi, where Sai Baba held his first darshan meetings and materialized sweets and images of deities (Kasturi 1968:101) south of the old town, and a banyan tree, which in 1959 Sai Baba identified as being the proper place *for sadhakas* (spiritual aspirants) to meditate and which bears a magical copper plate on which is a cryptogram that he materialized. The tree is believed to have been planted by Sai Baba (Kasturi 1968:88–100), and tour devotees sit below it and meditate. The tour usually includes the Hillview Stadium, the Sathya Sai Educational and Hospital complex, the elephant shed for Sai Gita, Sai Baba's pet elephant, and the *samadhi* (cenotaph) for Sai Baba's parents.

A significant stop on the tour was the Sai mandir within the Prasanthi Nilayam complex, next to the Sarva Dharma Pillar (the pillar with the emblem of the Sathya Sai movement), the axis mundi of the ashram. The symbol encompasses within a lotus of five petals, to which a sixth has recently been added, the *deepa* (lamp) of knowledge, five symbols of world religions—the Islamic crescent, the Christian cross, the Zoroastrian fire, the Buddhist wheel, and the Hindu Om—and a last, sixth, the Jewish star of David. The pillar was seen by devotees as emblematizing the evident and much-admired syncretisim of the Sathya Sai faith. On arrival at the pillar, tour guides closed, with a flourish: "All are welcome here. All religions, all castes, all creeds. Swami has said, 'All castes, all creeds, all religions are one.'" Thus the entire religious world and the nation are all integrated into the body of the sacred city.

While devotees acknowledge the syncretism and internationalism of the tour, they primarily see the spaces as emphasizing their connection with the divinity of Sai Baba through the emotions they feel. Joule, a Dutch devotee, did the tour and stopped at the site of Sai Baba's mother

Easwaramma's samadhi (Kasturi 1968:6–80). She recounted in minute detail the miracle of Sai Baba's birth and, overcome by emotion, began to cry. Stacy (thirty-two), an American devotee, stood on the sandy banks of the Chitravathi River and referenced a well-known story of Sai Baba's miraculous materializations of a silver image of Krishna on the banks of the river: "Can't you just see Swami, with a sweet smile, digging into the sand and producing the silver image? Can you imagine how happy and surprised everyone was?" In telling the story and reexperiencing the mystery and magic of the moment of revelation, she said she felt "spiritually uplifted and rejuvenated."

The rejuvenation is emphasized on one of the highlights of the magical memories tour, the recently built Chaitanya Jyothi (flame of consciousness) Museum, situated on a hilltop in Puttaparthi. Dedicated to Sathya Sai Baba in 2000 as part of his seventy-fifth birthday celebrations (McClean 2005), and built by a Malaysian architect, the museum is a very popular destination for devotees.[42] It reportedly cost $5 million to build,[43] which was raised internationally, and, as of February 2005, can host 1.2 million people.[44] The museum covers approximately 11,000 square feet. The gateway is painted a bright rose pink. Concrete statues of men as *dwarapalika* (gatekeepers) flank the entryway. I was told by a devotee that the museum "is about the mission of Sathya Sai Baba," but it reflects the internationalism of the movement. Built using an architectural language of Moorish domes (made of titanium steel) and Chinese pagodas (with the largest Chinese roof outside mainland China), it is surrounded by koi ponds in which, devotees assured me, "the waters of 108 rivers of India are mixed." As some scholars have suggested, it extends Sai Baba's reach further, as the museum includes images of "Sai Baba straddling the globe, balancing the universe on his finger," and a NASA space photograph that is believed to show Sai Baba's imprint on earth. The publicity materials for the museum stress the miraculous and the magical, even the shattering of the glass doors when Sai Baba first entered is seen as evidence of his positive energy. Although museums are traditionally thought to be didactic, knowledge-producing, and disseminating spaces, Sai devotees suggest that feeling and sentiment are more important in the Chaitanya Jyothi Museum. Col. S. K. Bose, the museum director, emphasizes the experiencing of the museum/memorial as part of its significance, "it is not about *jyana* (knowledge), it is about *bhakti* (devotion)," which has been identified as a key element of guru movements (Srinivas 2008:185).

FIGURE 2.6. The Chaitanya Jyothi Museum. *Photo courtesy Kekie Mistry*

As one enters the museum, one is confronted by a life-size photograph of Sathya Sai Baba. The museum itself has seven different chambers. One passes clockwise through the museum, moving from chamber to chamber, each housing one exhibit devoted to one world religion. The first chamber is dedicated to Hinduism: a tableau of a Hindu marriage and another tableau of a *sannyasin*. Next is Christianity, with the nave of a church and the accoutrements of Catholic ritual as well as other symbols. One moves through Islam, Zoroastrianism, Shintoism, Buddhism, and, finally, to a room with an unspecified form of "Chinese" religion, which I presumed to be Tibetan Buddhism since many representations refer to Tibet. Panels show excerpts from the Koran, the Bible, and Nostradamus prophesying the advent of a seer thought to be Sai Baba, reifying his divine status.

Six rooms on the upper level of the museum are devoted to Sai Baba's life and miracles; links with other divine avatars such as Christ, Rama, Krishna, Buddha, and others are emphasized (See T. Srinivas 2002). The ninety exhibits are audiovisually enhanced with lighting, moving tableaux, and short movies playing on LCD screens with commentary and music. The museum has two large theaters where short documentary movies based on Sai Baba's life or teachings are shown. The ninety exhibits are audiovisually enhanced with lighting, moving tableaux, and short movies played on LCD screens, as well as commentary, music, and other enhancements. Viewers are funneled through the museum at a rapid rate by Sai volunteers at points where they might linger. At the exit of the museum, there is a prayer hall where groups of devotees often hold bhajan sessions before an image of Sai Baba. At the end of the museum's exhibit space is a shop in which devotees crowd to buy trinkets and images of Sai Baba, pens, calendars, and amulets, etc.

The museum is seen by devotees not as a mere recording of Sai Baba's miraculous life but as itself a miracle where education about Sathya Sai Baba and the movement is combined with entertaining televisuals that engage and reinforce the pathways of memory and identification for devotees. The museum enables the Sathya Sai movement to claim a space both at home and in the world in which the plurality of world religions become visually absorbed within the figure of Sathya Sai Baba. Stephen said, upon emerging from the museum, "It reinforced so many things I knew but had forgotten about Swami. . . . Sure, the exhibits can be done better, they are . . . you know . . . but it is the spirit within them that devotees understand. You cannot understand the museum's power unless you are a devotee. It brings back little things you know about Bhagawan and it makes every moment with him more precious." Sylvia (sixty-three) said, "I did not expect anything like this! It leaves an impression on your mind, body, and soul—a place where you come so close to Swami's life through modern technology and other gadgets. He tells us to stay in our own religions . . . that we understand. . . . I ask you, which other religious leader does that? What a wonderful use of technology!" The literature on the Internet focuses on the museum as a teaching tool for devotees and others to learn about Sathya Sai Baba, "the museum takes the visitor through the story of Bhagawan's birth and childhood, the prophecies connected with His Advent, and major milestones in the grand Mission of the Avatar."[45] Devotees are expected to follow a given route through the exhibits and the movies. The governing of viewing of the museum is controlled by the Sai organization through the literature and the museum spaces are controlled through volunteers. However, those who are familiar with the museum's proscribed viewing schedule often rush through the spaces, pushing past slower devotees to get to their "favorite" exhibits or to "good" seats in the front of the theaters, destroying the idea of the space as one of meditative spirituality.

Even though museums are traditionally thought to be didactic, knowledge producing and disseminating spaces, Sai devotees suggest that feeling and sentiment are more important in the Chaitanya Jyothi Museum. As S. Srinivas notes, Col. S. K. Bose, the museum director, emphasizes the experiencing of the museum/memorial as part of its significance, "it is not about Jyana (knowledge), it is about Bhakti (devotion)," which has been identified by the Indian psychologist Sudhir Kakar as a defining emotional element of charismatic guru movements (1991, 2008: 185). The museum underscores the idea that Sai Baba is "an avatar of this age," and the literature states that the museum building is "like a gift-wrapped present from Swami to His devotees." A glossy illustrated book titled *Chaitanya Jyothi, Experiencing the Divine: The Millennium Museum Depicting the Message and Mission of Sri Sathya Sai Avatar* (Prashanti Nilayam: Sri Sathya Sai Seva Organisation) was published in 2001. On the cover is a photograph of an external large sculpture cum fountain at the museum of a hand holding up a globe, and on page 17 the text states that it represents Sathya Sai Baba's hand and arm "holding up the universe."

The ashram literature, as with Sai Kulwant Darshan Hall, focuses upon several valuable points to understand how to view the museum. First discussed are the many problems encountered by the engineers in building "the marvel of the twenty-first century" and how they were all cleared away by Sathya Sai Baba. The stories tell of the making of "authentic" Chinese elements, such as roof tiles in Malaysia, and their international shipping made easy by Sathya Sai Baba, despite governmental hurdles, and the many time constraints in the building of the museum removed miraculously "by a touch of the Divine."[46] The literature also lauds the number of "manhours" taken to build the museum and the miracle of its building in record time.[47] The curatorial program and promotional literature determines that spectatorship in the museum is guided not only by the route one follows to and through the museum but also by determining the emotional interpretation of both the building and the exhibits. I was told by a devotee that the museum "is about the Mission of Sathya Sai Baba" and its "newness and peace,"[48] but it clearly reflects the internationalism of the movement both in the language used ("it leaves an impression on your mind, body and soul—a place where you come so close to Swami's life through modern technology and other gadgets geared to showcase His life")[49] as well as in the imagery of Sai Baba extending into other religious and divine traditions. The promotional literature on the Internet states that the museum "embodies in its very design Swami's teaching on the Unity of Humanity. There are Roman arches; Gothic windows; a Singapore designed fish pool; Moorish domes; Japanese roofing (for the lift shaft); a Greek inclusion on the roof; and Indian religious figures. Japanese flat roofs and the Greek inclusion behind Chinese religious figures with Nandi bull at the rear."[50] For devotees, then, the imagery appears to emphasize the longed-for ideal in which the nation and the world are seen to come together in this building. In fact, as some scholars have suggested, it extends Sai Baba's reach further, as the museum includes images of "Sai Baba straddling the globe, balancing the universe on his finger," and a NASA space photograph believed to show Sai Baba's imprint on Earth, suggesting his divine reach onto the celestial plane. This curatorial program as pedagogy toward transformation is not unique to the Sathya Sai movement, rather, as has been noted in other new religious movements like the Swaminarayan movement, the idea of a temple museum as teaching space is central to the movement and to its successful globalization (Srivastava 2009).

Some of the Internet traffic critical of the Chaitanya Jyothi Museum discuss its exorbitant cost, supposedly $5 million.[51] Explanations cohere around what Srivastava has called "retractable modernity" (2009), where modernity, is, in fact, located in the processes of consumption itself. So, one consumes a wide variety of products of contemporary capitalism—IMAX cinema, the LCD screens, the dioramas, the sculptures and fountains, the city itself—in combination with "spiritual" goods such as religion and internationalism. What devotees hope differentiates the Sai consumption of these goods and images is the devotional discernment that gives them the capacity to take part in these diverse forms of consumption and yet not be drawn into the vortex of unthinking consumption. This, they suggest, is what distinguishes Sai consumption from a more "deracinated" (or "Westernized"), nondevotional form of consumption. Here, as Srivastava comments in his study of the Swaminarayan temple in Delhi, the refashioning of urban space tells us something about idea of different kinds of devotional identity and their perceived relationship to consumption practices and the relationship between space and identity.[52]

Former devotees are skeptical about the museum. Venkat stated, "Tourism is built into this whole experience, and I guess this becomes one more stop for the tourists". Brian Steel referenced his own Web site, where he states;

my amazement at the discovery of the contents of the official Chaitanya Jyoti Museum ("The Flame [or Spirit] of Consciousness"), inaugurated in Puttaparthi in 2000 to commemorate, for posterity, Sathya Sai Baba's Life and Mission, and, above all, his alleged Avatarhood. Everywhere the claims of Divinity are stridently proclaimed but, as the guidebook shows, the quality and nature of much of the assembled evidence and arguments on the subject of Sathya Sai Baba's Divinity and Divine powers is far from convincing.

Further, he states, "most of the simple but gaudily painted statues, exhibits, working models and explanatory posters and labels seem to have been prepared for a mainly juvenile audience" and that the tableaux represented "crude propagandistic excesses."[53] However, despite Steel's aesthetic and other objections to the museum, it seems to have developed as a critical locus in the spatiality of devotion. When I visited there in October 2006, it was packed with curious visitors and devotees. The museum appears to devotees to be a built form of religious "values, rituals, and texts" that can be understood in the "context of the process of moral consumption" (Srivastava 2009:342) whereby the notion of consumption is made to slide to include not only the inherent processes of modernity but also a reverse return to "tradition," making the space of the museum a nostalgic space as wel as a moral space that allows for a future.

But returning to the tour, it appears to create a spatial narrative of a sacred moral geography in and around Puttaparthi that reinforces the sacred power of Sai Baba through emotions that devotees feel, which can appear extemporaneously or be orchestrated to appear by the skillful use of the magical sites. Urban theorist Robert Orsi argues that "people have acted on and with the spaces of the city to make religious meanings in many different ways," leading to a city space of "diverse religious ontologies" (1999:47–53) in a "multi-vocal serenade." This "multi-vocal serenade," an urban symbolic matrix, enables devotees to read various affective and personal meaning into the sacred sites of Puttaparthi.

As devotees inhabit the spaces of Sai Baba's magical youth, they reconsider their own biographies toward a betterment of self more appropriate to bettering the world. For example, Hemlatha, a Sai devotee of twenty-five years from Delhi, commented upon the irony of her life while discussing the tamarind tree believed to be the wishing tree (*kalpavriksha*) of Sai legend: "You know, when I was young I used to have so many wishes. But I was like this tamarind tree. Just like kalpavriksha, without Swami's *siddhi*, can only produce one sour fruit, I too was like that. But with Swami's prema I can do anything I want, but now that I am here, I wish for only one thing . . . peace for my family. I only want peace. See how life is!"[54] Or Stephen, who said, "When I was young I only thought of myself. Not like Bhagawan who thought of the poor and lonely." Or Hui (twenty-three), who said; "We like too much getting more. Not like Bhagawan, who gave away everything when he was a boy." Or like Moses, from Kenya, who said, "I like that Swami brings all people together. Christian, Buddhism, Hindu, Muslim: all together. In the museum I saw that."

Moral Architecture, a Retro-future Aesthetic and Nostalgia

The objective of the material form of Sai city is to "teach" the prospective devotee a Sai devotional "way of being" that is visually and aesthetically "traditional," and therefore easily accepted, but fits their modern and transnational lifestyles, and the governance of devotees to reach this outcome is central to its success. Alexandra Kent, in her study of Sai devotees in Malaysia (2005), suggests that devotees see modernity and tradition as mutually mutable positions. However architects and historians did not see these positions as mutable in the early 1970s, but rather separate and distinct. Robert Venturi, Denise Scott Brown, and Steve Izenour, in their critical volume *Learning from Las Vegas* (1972), created a healthy controversy by calling for architects to be receptive to the tastes and values of "common" people rather than erecting "heroic," self-aggrandizing monuments; a clear criticism of modernist architects like Le Corbusier whose work was considered "inhuman" by many.

In Puttaparthi it would appear that the architecture tells a different story, one based in the need for the building and the city to appear as a transcendent, built cosmology. Urban historian Jyoti Hosagrahar's comprehensive work on the city of Delhi suggests that the contemporary Indian city is neither Indian nor Western but an amalgam of the two; what she terms "an indigenous modernity" (2005). As such, the difference between tradition and modernity is understood in and through the architecture of Puttaparthi to be a symbolic language, parts of which can be combined to signify both a backward-looking and forward-thinking community (Harvey 1989, 2001). Puttaparthi denies the humdrum reality of contemporary devotee's lives by recontextualizing it as part of a mythic perfect sacred landscape of both yesterday and tomorrow in a fabulous peaceful setting that Davis has called "the excavation of the future" (1990). The architectural language of Puttaparthi is multivalent, borrowing metaphors and built forms across time and space, melding historical referents or contexts, which some have called "duplicitous" in relation to other city spaces that do the same such as Las Vegas (Daniels 1989): This spatialized ideology of a retro future is postmodern, and the architectural symbolism requires a language of representation that incorporates a slide from built form to moral ideals, but whose trajectory is "nonetheless contingent upon ongoing processes of [cultural] translation" (Glover 2006:xix).

Connie Shaw, the author devotee, says about the architecture of Puttaparthi town: "We arrive at the edge of Puttaparthi. . . . As we approach the pink cream and blue gates of Prasanthi Nilayam itself it occurs to me that the ethereal looking buildings appear like giant birthday cakes adorned with pastel angels" (Shaw 2000:189). On the highway to Puttaparthi, about seven kilometers from the ashram gate, a series of monumental buildings flank the roadway. The first is the ornate, domed, pink and cream Sathya Sai Super Specialty Hospital, officially called the Sathya Sai Institute of Higher Medical studies, but known locally as "the Hospital." Built by architect to the Prince of Wales Sir Keith Critchlow, the hospital sits facing the highway. With five ornate domes topped with brass finials and long arched arcades, the hospital looks more like an ancient monastery. The hospital offers top-rate, subsidized facilities to the poor of the region by world-renowned doctors and specialists from across the globe.

Further down the highway is the Sathya Sai Vidyagiri (educational) complex comprising a musical college, several schools, a planetarium, a college and a new indoor stadium for the students. Sai Baba founded the Sri Sathya Sai Institute of Higher Learning on November 22, 1981. An autonomous body, it has been recognized by the Ministry of Education, Government of India, and the University Grants Commission (UGC) as a deemed university. Architecturally, it follws the ambivalent modern style of the rest of Puttaparthi. It has a modernist front topped by a statue of the Hindu goddess of learning Saraswati holding a sitar. Part of the educational complex is the Sai Music Academy, a two-story modern building with a roof like an airplane hangar. The caryatids holding up the entryway are a violin and a guitar and the roof profile encloses gilt-edged trumpets. Opposite the music academy is the planetarium that features a multicolored concrete geodesic-domed roof. The planetarium was the source of much pride for devotees because of its modern shape and its message of knowledge. Hemlatha pointed to it and said, "See it is so nice. It is so well designed. All the children go there to learn about the solar system and earth and all that. Swami thinks education is important. I too have sent my children there when they were small. Now they are all engineers in America."

Closer to the town of Puttaparthi, on the left of the highway, is the Hillview Stadium (built in 1984), an open-air stadium of concrete built against a rocky outcrop dominated by the Chaitanya Jyothi Museum. With a seating capacity of thirty thousand, it is the preferred site for sports and "cultural" events as well as Sathya Sai Baba's birthday celebrations. On the hilly outcrop against which the stadium nestles are towering images of "spiritual masters and avatars": Krishna, Shiva, an artificial waterfall symbolizing the river Ganga flowing down from his head, Shirdi Baba (dressed in a faqir's robes), the Buddha, Christ, arms outstretched, and Zarathusthra. At the top is a sixty-five-foot-high statue of the Hindu monkey god Hanuman (giver of strength) (see Alter 1992 b; Lutgendorf 1994, 2003) in a popular pose from the the Ramayana. At the base of the Hanuman statue, but above the other statues, is a giant picture of Sathya Sai Baba, raising his hands in blessing. The aesthetics and coloring of the various sacred figures are familiar to most Indians, as they are drawn from popular calendar art (Jain 2007) in urban India and from the aesthetic local traditions of sculpture in South India. All these sites have a unique architectural form and language associated in the minds of the devotee with Sai Baba and with Puttaparthi. It is clear in viewing the public buildings of Puttaparthi that the language spans sculptural imagery of Hindu cosmology and iconography combined with revelations of modernity.

The architectural vocabulary of Puttaparthi encompasses religious buildings of both North and South India, including domes reminiscent of Mughal mosques and memorials and temple sculptural elements and friezes, drawn from the Pallava (sixth-seventh century CE) and Vijayanagara (fourteenth to fifteenth century CE) dynasties of the south to the Solanki (tenth-thirteenth century CE) and Mauryan (third-first century BCE) dynasties of the north. While the sculptural elements of animals and gods mimic stone carvings of the temples, they are made of concrete and painted. They are given new meaning through innovative readings by Sai devotees by which the architectural language employed substitutes (if read properly) for a language of transformation by Sathya Sai Baba. One

FIGURE 2.7. The Sai Kulwant Darshan Hall. *Photo courtesy Kekie Mistry*

excerpt from Radio Sai publicity material for the mandir that could extend to the entire ashram states:

> It speaks eloquently of the divine message of the unity of life,
> universal concord, and harmony through its sculptured angels, hu-
> mans, and animals . . . The sculptured beings on the facade beauti-
> fully bring out the drama of transformation and transcendence that
> can occur if one sincerely strives to sublimate oneself. The lions,
> elephants, snakes, and peacocks, contemptuously dismissed by us
> as sub-human species, have lifted themselves to a sublime stature
> by practising maitri (friendship), mudita (joy), karuna (compas-
> sion), and upeksha (detachment). The transformation of the human
> into the divine is demonstrated through the sculptures of pamara
> (ignorant one), deva (angel), and hamsa (swan). The pamara, by con-
> stant striving, becomes a devata (angel) and ultimately transforms
> themself into a Paramahamsa (a realised soul). The facade, which
> is the face of the Mandir, expresses the very essence of Bhagavan's
> message.

The postmodern buildings of Puttaparthi take on the look of familiar film sets elaborately built to allude to something else (that is also

familiar) and to some other time (that we recognize in the collective consciousness. The film sets depicted mythical "Hindu" royal and cosmological ancient cities with "recognizable" ancient "Indian" landscapes combined with some futuristic elements such as geodesic domes and giant LCD screens, and it is identifiable by what S. Srinivas calls "multiplicity rather than singularity" (2008:215), where symbols and meanings occur across geographical spaces as well as time spans. The architecture of Puttaparthi creates a three-dimensional, theaterlike experience for the pedestrian, with evocative imagery for role-playing (Cosgrove and Jackson 1987) and consuming the space through singing, dancing, performance, worship, buying, selling, etc. Without irony, the ashram celebrates a global understanding of Indian spirituality by decontextualizing and dehistoricizing the world's historical religious figures and any traditional sacred architecture. Indeed, it offers the verisimilitude of these monuments, such as a Chinese temple in the middle of the Andhra landscape, as compensation for the contemporary loss of historicity. The hybrid architecture is given new meaning, primarily of unity through innovative readings by Sai devotees. An excerpt from Radio Sai publicity material states:

It (the architecture) speaks eloquently of the divine message of the unity of life, universal concord, and harmony through its sculptured angels, humans, and animals. . . . The sculptured beings on the facade beautifully bring out the drama of transformation and transcendence that can occur if one sincerely strives to sublimate oneself. The lions, elephants, snakes, and peacocks, contemptuously dismissed by us as sub-human species, have lifted themselves to a sublime stature by practicing maitri (friendship), mudita (joy), karuna (compassion), and upeksha (detachment). The transformation of the human into the divine is demonstrated through the sculptures of pamara (ignorant one), deva (angel), and hamsa (swan). The pamara, by constant striving, becomes a devata (angel) and ultimately transforms itself into a Paramahamsa (a realised soul). The facade, which is the face of the Mandir, expresses the very essence of Bhagavan's message.[55]

Drawn from the highly colored imagination of Bollywood set designers (Srinivas 2008:180), the artists of the popular mythological *Amar Chitra Katha* religious cartoon books, and images from urban calendar art that are part of a common visual language imagining divinity in urban India

(Kajri 2007), these elements are widespread as accepted Hindu religious architectural iconography.[56]

But while one architectural vocabulary within the city speaks to the glories of the past, it also speaks to a modernist and technologically viable future. Architectural elements in the town of Puttaparthi point to an embracing of modernity (Kent 2005), particularly the Western mastery of science and technology. In the 1970s, when the Sathya Sai college was built, the facade comprised an image of Saraswati topped by a Bauhaus-style clock, which still exists today. The science museum, housed in its futuristic geodesic dome, built in the 1980s, still excites comment. The new titanium-clad domes of the Chaitanya Jyothi Museum house giant LCD screens, computer-based animatronics, and other technological marvels. And I was told repeatedly that the Sai Hospital had the latest "cutting-edge" technology to assist in diagnosis, surgery, and care. Thus the Living Temple for the Living God embodies a spatialized ideology of what I call a retro-futureaesthetic located in a hybrid mix of images of a mythic past and of a technologically based future.

Devotees see this hybrid aesthetic as the ideal architectural language for Sai buildings, regardless of their location, but that is not always an achievable goal, as different countries have various restrictive building codes. In Singapore, the Sai center, Katong, is situated on busy Moulmein Road in the shadow of the Leong Wan Chan Si Chinese temple and a Catholic Church. It began in a small house next-door to the current property and is now housed in a six-story structure. The center, painted a pale gray, has a large two-story glass-arched entryway and would look like any anonymous office building except that the entire building is topped by a dome on which rests a large pink lotus. The gate columns also have pink lotus caps. Whereas in Puttaparthi hybridity expresses itself as retro-future aesthetic in which modernity and Hindu-Islamic elements are balanced, in Singapore it appears that the modern elements are more pronounced, allowing the building to blend into the hypercapitalist landscape of Singapore. On the other hand, the Sai center in Tustin, California, on West First Street, is completely camouflaged in its landscape, except for the large brass lettering identifying it as the Sai center and bookstore and the large picture of Sathya Sai Baba in the entryway.[57] It is built in a Spanish hacienda style with a paved forecourt, white stucco walls, and the red tiled roof common to Spanish churches and missions (such as the famous San Juan Capistrano) in Southern California. The Sai mandir on Effra Road in Wimbledon is a converted red brick church hall (with the steeple removed) and, other than the Sathya Sai emblem on its wall,[58] shows no external sign of hybrid architecture, though the Web site assures devotees that "internal alterations (were) carried out according to the guidelines laid down in our ancient scriptures."[59]

While devotees see the architecture of Puttaparthi as reflective of the divine charisma of Sathya Sai Baba for the nondevotee, the buildings of Puttaparthi take on the look of film sets elaborately built to allude both to something familiar and to some other era, and as such they cross many time periods. "In the city the truth of industrial and commercial society had to be screened in the decent draperies of pre-industrial artistic styles," states Carl Schorske of early twentieth-century Vienna. "Science and law were modern truth but beauty came from history" (Schorske [1981:45], quoted by Nair 2002:1205). Thus historical imagery becomes a resource for defining new ideals of beauty in Puttaparthi, which leads to a new moral vocabulary of public architecture. This moral architecture has a unique symbolic language located in a hybrid retro-future aesthetic that allows for play with readings of history and fantasies of the future.

Following Adorno, Steve Daniels (1989:206) has argued that landscape may be seen as "a dialectical image, an ambiguous synthesis whose redemptive and manipulative aspects cannot be . . . disentangled." The various maneuvers of inclusion, exclusion, memorialization, and multivocality enable an expansion of sacred spaces through a strategic engagement with deliberate ambiguity. During globalization, the plural representations within the spatial imagination simultaneously move across space and time and engage what Ven der Leeuw called the "paradoxical politics of transcendence and permanence," of exclusion and inclusion, of historicity and future to create desired emotional connections among its inhabitants. The spaces of Puttaparthi are dedifferentiated to include a double-coded language—one part modern and another part something else. As Christopher Jencks, the noted architectural critic, states: "This double coding uses ambiguity and contradiction (but unlike postmodernism no irony) to allow us to read the present in the past as much as the past in the present" (1987:340). Cultural and political pluralism are manifested by this eclecticism in real and virtual spaces and in the self-conscious construction of memories and suggested narratives, genres that emphasize ambiguity. Jencks notes, "If a work is resonant enough it continues to inspire unlimited readings" (1987:345), and this resonance is what makes it appealing and accessible to many different people. Such resonance depends on a complex relation to the past, through the displacement of conventions.

Puttaparthi seeks legitimacy by selecting motifs from a range of real and imagined dynastic and cosmological styles, all the while refashioning the language of power in the public realm. The spaces of Puttaparthi are dedifferentiated to include a double-coded language—one part modern and another part something else. The relations between the past and present is a valued subject that often produces a juxtaposition of related and opposed fragments, and this results in diverse and divergent content, appropriate in a pluralistic society. Puttaparthi's pastiche is in tune with the syncreticism of Sai Baba's teachings: it allows for multiple possible interpretations, creating an urban built form of the "matrix of possible meanings," which enables devotees, regardless of their originating culture, to find meaning and comfort in the architectural symbolism. The interaction with the visual, aural, and concrete aesthetics at Puttaparthi is also an integral part of the making of a moral transnational devotional base through a process of moral consumption. This is a context where the active participation in globalization is accompanied by an anxiety about identity and its relationship being a good devotee.

For Sai devotees anything that links them to the sacred space of Puttaparthi and Prasanthi Nilayam is valuable, as it (even momentarily) reduces the feeling of banishment or alienation. Salman Rushdie argues that fantasy helps migrants to relive the place of the imagination (Rushdie 1991:10). Fantasy, based on semitruths, stories, local folklore, is an important narrative structure to assuage the ambivalence of the globalized devotee over the sense of loss of place. In this globalized state of reterritorialization, imagination and fantasy become a necessary alternative for "the real thing" (which is also imagined, as Anderson points out). Marxist geographer David Harvey argues that the positionality of a person in the local—their "cartographic identity"—determines their perceptual field and limits the horizons of their intellectual possibilities (2001:200–203). Such resonance depends on a complex relation to the past and to the semiotics of the present—a tradition reinterpreted—so they have a familiarity of built language with which viewers and users can engage. It is this language that the Sai city of Puttaparthi affords its inhabitants and visitors.

The architecture and aesthetics of Puttaparthi and the ashram speak to the iterative interaction between the Sai enspaced organizational strategies and devotional tactics to enable a whole series of narratives to be

constructed that enable the globalization of the Sathya Sai movement in
the construction of a fluid global devotional identity: first, a narrative of
emotional arrival through the gates that distinguishes the sacred space
within the city, the nonsacred space without, and the in-between space at
the gates, which allows devotees to see the city of Puttaparthi and the Sai
ashram as a spiritual home, a refuge in their everyday lives of spiritual
exile in the rapidly globalizing world; second, a welcoming inclusivity of
all types, religions, races, and ethnicities of devotees seen in the architecture of the open Sai Kulwant Darshan Hall, which leads to a feeling of
tolerance and well-being among devotees; third, a narrative of cloaking of
the sacred figure and the mystery that surrounds his presence in the hidden private quarters, which enables devotees to argue for security and
power while simultaneously articulating a concern for transparency; finally, a narrative of moral consumption of the sites of memory and museums and tours that enables the global subject to see memorialization not
as mere nostalgia but as linking tradition to a bright future through an
educational project. The city of Puttaparthi and the ashram within, at
both the material and symbolic levels, can be seen as an educational, persuasive, and governed project to engage devotees in a transformative and
moral task both in terms of individual identity and the development of a
community.

Virtual Reality and Translocal Devotion

While devotees in Puttaparthi tour sacred sites, devotees in
other parts of the world access the Internet to avail themselves of the
darshan of these sacred spaces. In November 2003, as I sat with Jarkko
and Stephen in a lounge of the International Airport at Heathrow, Stephen had hooked his laptop up to a power source. As he opened it, a
wonderful picture of Sai Baba's head superimposed on clouds above the
pink and gold domes of Puttaparthi floated onto the screen. Jarkko
looked at the screen with unconcealed envy: "I like your wallpaper," he
said.

As I surreptitiously watched the screen, I saw that hundreds of photos
of Sai Baba and personal shots of Stephen in front of the sacred sites of
Puttaparthi kept rotating through in an endless slideshow. Then, automatically, a Sai darshan Web site[60] opened: it was a personal Web site
maintained by technophile devotees in New Jersey that has a visual link

to a "virtual darshan" of Sathya Sai Baba, a visual of the chalkboard at Puttaparthi with Sathya Sai Baba's "thought for the day" updated every twenty-four hours, a "glimpses" link featuring a running slideshow with Sai Baba's sayings alongside, images of him blessing people, pictures of the town, and sacred centers. Below, a banner read: "An email address is not available for Swami. Your prayers to Him in any form reach Him directly."

A Google search for Sathya Sai Baba in 2003 brought up as many as 33,500 sites with many more attachments. Most of these Sai Internet sites are produced and maintained by technophiles outside India and are in video and television formats (Hawkins 1999). Devotees told me they "felt reassured" that, with the click of a mouse, they could, "within minutes," know what was happening in Puttaparthi, how Sai Baba was, and what he had to say to them. The sites provide a continuous living link for devotees scattered around the world (see Feike 2007). The Web site of the SSSO links to local organizations in each chapter within each country and links to the SCT that runs the ashram facilities in India. I found using the Internet sites easy and comfortable and often intuitive. In many Sathya Sai centers the Internet bhajans (devotional songs) are frequently left on for devotees to listen as they gather.

The virtual worlds of Sai devotion are thickening rapidly (Feike 2007),[61] enabling Sai devotees to access darshan and images, maps and photographs of Puttaparthi and the ashram wherever they are. Since many Sai devotees are middle-class professionals and mobile, they rely on the translocality of cybertechnology to keep in touch with Puttaparthi. Sai devotees see both Web pages and religious objects as representations of Sai Baba's divinity and as a portal through which his divinity may shine. For devotees, these spaces are devotional and structured by the divine transcendence of Sai Baba. They allow devotees to be touched by Sai Baba's divinity through e-darshan. As Feike states, the existence of these Web sites forever change the meanings of religion, as they allow in "today's world of sacred globalization, those seeking spiritual fulfillment" to "log on to an information highway that interconnects an international citizenry with the click of the mouse. In the privacy of one's own home, devotees can chant ancient Vedic scriptures, read the divine discourses of Bhagavan Sri Sathya Sai Baba, and maintain a path of devotion said to liberate their souls and enlighten their minds" (Feike 2007:21–22). The Web sites make geography irrelevant in that they "possess the potential to make a unique contribution to global fellowship in the frequently volatile area of inter-religious understanding. Fueling the trend that widespread mobility began, cyberspace diminishes the relevance of location for religious identity. As it widens the social foundation of religious life, cyberspace erodes the basis from which religion contributes to the destructive dynamics of xenophobia. In the process, it lessens potential inter-religious hatred" (Brasher 2001:6, in Feike 2007:23).

So e-darshan is a translocal phenomenon that enables devotees to feel proximity to Sathya Sai Baba, though they may physically be thousands of miles away. But proxemic desire, which is enacted physically in Puttaparthi, is now measured temporally as well. Devotees said they often logged on to get darshan of Sai Baba many times a day. Tejal, a young Indian American woman whom I met in Boston, driving a lime green car with a license plate that read Sai Kid, told me she logs on to the Sai official Web site every day and gets darshan, posts letters, listens to bhajans, and so on, in spite of being "away" at college. She said, emphatically, "It helps me be close to Swami. . . . I feel so happy after I log on and see his face and get darshan. My family goes once in two years to Puttaparthi, but that is not enough. Everyday I feel I must get *darshan*. If I don't, bad things start to happen. I *don't feel* OK."[62] The Sai Web sites enable a feeling of closeness that other images such as photograph, symbols and pictures do not. As S. Srinivas rightly notes in paraphrasing work by Babb and Wadley (1995) on religion and technology in South Asia, "The interface between religion and technology (including electronic and digital forms) creates new publics, new public spheres, and geographies of religion affecting forms of religious mediation" (2008:104). The Web sites are filled with constantly changing images of Sai Baba, photographs of the ashram from various perspectives, and videos of Sathya Sai Baba giving his discourses and virtual darshan. They also permitted interaction with other devotees and provided links to various devotional Web pages so that devotees could skip from one page to another in the search for better images or more appropriate sayings in tune with their current state of mind. Taj said, "I found that the Italian Web site has nice photos of Bhagawan, so, though I don't know Italian, I go there and look for nice darshan pictures." Stephen said, "The videos of *darshan* make me feel I am there," and Jarkko said, "I have bookmarked all these pages that showed pictures of the ashram from where I stayed so I can remember the walk I took every morning to get darshan!" Devotees feel connected emotionally and physically to the ashram and to Sai Baba while they are logged onto the Web sites.

The Web devotional worlds are populated by Sai devotees and, in turn, silently reconstitute the identity of Sai devotees, creating multiple and dispersed identities, social interactions, and transactions of devotion. The virtual portals by which many devotees and potential devotees engage the Sai devotional world collapse private habits of worship and devotion into virtual public domains and in so doing blur the line between private identity and public space.

The cyberworlds of devotion are supported by more traditional media such as television and radio. Liberalization of Indian television and radio Broadcasting shows in the early 1990s with religious content have been ubiquitous, including the famous televisual spectacle of the Mahabharatha (Mankekar 1999). In August 1999 Larson and Toubro, the engineering company, sponsored a show on cable TV titled *The Divine Story of Shirdi Sai and Puttaparthi Sai,* which was very popular because it included clips of real video of Sathya Sai Baba giving darshan to devotees. In the devotees' homes that I visited, nobody did anything for the hour that this show was on. When I happened to be at Shanti's home in Bangalore, there was dead silence during the "TV darshan," as the family insisted on calling it.

Radio Sai Global Harmony is a satellite radio show on WorldSpace Satellite Network and was begun in 2001. It broadcasts Sai Baba's discourses (heavily edited), interviews with prominent devotees, bhajans and songs, sounds of worship, and special musical concerts all day to Africa, parts of Asia, and Europe. Radio programs broadcast news from Puttaparthi and offer insightful commentary on devotional life. From the 1990s on, DVD and CD technologies have enhanced this spread. The Sathya Sai Book and Publications Trust is the legitimate producer of all visual and audio materials relating to Sai Baba, but cassettes and CDs of music by other producers have also been allowed by the SSSO. Videocassettes and DVDs of Sai Baba's many darshans and the festivals of Puttaparthi are produced by the Sathya Sai Book and Publications Trust and are popular sellers.

These new media point to an emergent transnational, devotional, public space that is "multilocational" (Babb and Wadley 1995:75–76) in character, catering to a dispersed devotional population and builds upon traditional devotional space. Moreover, new media such as the Internet are assimilated in a fluid way into a devotional praxis that conforms to the far from standardized and rigid understandings of the status and power of the *murti* (image), which is a fundamental part of Indic religious traditions.

These new media and communication channels enable the spread of Sathya Sai Baba's subtle presence further afield, acquiring new layers of meaning that are reincorporated into the narratives of devotion in a cyclical, dynamic, hermeneutic process.

Devotees treat the Internet, radio, and television as divine portals through which Sathya Sai Baba chooses to present himself to them. Many devotees spoke about their unexpected encounters with Sai Baba's virtual divine presence. Joule described how, when her daughter was undergoing chemotherapy, she was at her computer sending e-mails with tears streaming down her face. Suddenly, "the computer switched off. I was worried that I had lost the e-mail. I was crying, trying to get it back up. Suddenly it came on again and rebooted to the Sai Web page, and I saw a picture of Swami. He was so calm, smiling, like He was telling me, it will be all right. I said, "That is my sign."[63] Shanti told me how she had left her computer on, going to her kitchen, and, when she returned to the screen, Sai Baba's face "was there, and bhajans were playing." She felt that "Baba magically came to (my) side" because to her the Internet is a magical portal to the divine world of Sai Baba; he is able to manipulate its reality as he manipulates the reality of day-to-day life.

Since all space-time can be bent by the divine will, devotees argued that the e-darshan of Sai Baba or that experienced in a vision was the same and as good if not better than darshan, since Sai Baba had sought them out. So his virtual presence is seen as homologous, in that he appears as the answer to prayer and his presence is symbol enough to "change the energy" around a devotee.[64] In fact, devotees believe that sacred healing can occur through the Internet or television since "God is everywhere" and "Bhagwan knows our troubles."

Thus the redemptive experience of e-darshan is very similar to arrival at Puttaparthi. Interface between the new digital forms (Web pages, blogs, virtual video, auditory Web pages, chat rooms) creates new public realms of devotion and new forms of access for devotees to the guru/avatar. It appears that the new spaces of media and communication channels collapse traditional understandings of physical and social space to enable the spread of Sathya Sai Baba's subtle presence further afield and let it acquire new layers of meaning that are reenfolded into the narratives of devotion in a cyclical, dynamic, hermeneutic process.

Toward a Moral Architecture: Emotion, Multivalence, and Diversity

I have chosen ethnographic stories that speak to the way a global devotional identity is forged and expressed in Puttaparthi: from/to (a panorama) the proxemics of desire and its complex links with exile, memorial tours and sites of magic that devotees visit and use as lenses to reinvent and refocus their lives, to the polyvalent architectural language of Puttaparthi that enables various sorts of affiliation through its manipulation of affect. They suggest that a new account of transnational sacred urbanism emerges in which spaces on the limen of global economics and politics such as the Sai city of Puttaparthi create new multivalent spaces of devotional performance that allow for global accessibility. Spaces are thus seen as methods to lead the subject—a thoughtful, creative agent—toward a moral life. The built form of Puttaparthi is an articulation of the SSSO's pedagogy: to mold a person's sentiments and enable suitable emotions that encourage devotion to Sathya Sai Baba. The degree of persuasion varies, but it is never forced. The notion of being able to persuade rests on the "existence of the reflexive subject"(Glover 2006:x) whose capacity for feeling and being can be improved by a transformation of self. And yet, as we have noted, the transformation of self in the Sai case leads seemingly naturally to a transformation of the habitus by which the material form of Puttaparthi is again subject to questioning and improvement—an endless feedback loop.

Puttaparthi and the Sai ashram it encloses create a language of sacred spatiality that points to a new way of being and believing in an era of globalization: *a new moral architecture*. This moral architecture encloses within itself a fundamental ambiguity so that different audiences can read it differently, leading to dynamic outcomes and creating a matrix of possible meaning from which devotees can construct a grammar of devotion that includes the possibility of diversity.

The spaces of Puttaparthi are denotative of a built matrix of narrative voices that are rooted both in the intensity of locality and the extensions of globality. The architectural parable that Puttaparthi presents allows devotees to conceptually "sidestep" the confrontation between the local and the global and engage what Lakshmi Srinivas calls, in her pathbreaking essay on globalization and media, the translocal (2005:319–321) as the space of Puttaparthi becomes—in its familiarity and its distance—a mediating model for these transnational devotees and is simultaneously seen as a place and placeless (Giddens 1991:26), leading one not only to question the empirical value of these categories but also to question the nature of embeddedness and authenticity.

Concordantly, as we see in the architecture of Puttaparthi and the virtual Sai world, the links between proxemics, mobility, and sacred space in the Sai movement suggest that the "practice of pilgrimage and the sacred powers of the shrine are constructed as varied and possibly conflicting representation by the different sectors of the cultic constituency" (Eade and Sallnow 1991:5), thereby linking the traversing space of devotion (the pilgrimage) to the static space of sacredness (the holy city) and to the virtual space of Internet devotion. Sacred space thus needs o be rescaled to encompass the network of the global. Devotees see Sai sacred space as a symbolic narrative matrix into which they can posit their own interpretive meanings, "enact(ing)" and "contest(ing)" (White 2006:52) established affective meanings, to problematize the role of space and scale in constructing, contesting, and legitimizing collective sentiments and values.

The project of Sai devotion both at the individual and community level locates itself in a productive and problematic ambiguity that enables a "human grammar of devotion" (Eck 1988:48), which, in turn, allows for the possibility of pluralism of perspectives combined with empathy. Devotees conceptually "sidestep" the political and emotional confrontation between the "local" and the "global," or in the Sai case the foreign and the indigenous, and engage the translocal (Srinivas 2005:319–321) as the Puttaparthi space becomes—in its familiarity and its distance—a mediating model for these transnational devotees, simultaneously seen as of a place and placeless (Giddens 1991:26), valuable and value free, and ultimately moral and spiritual. Governance of these spaces becomes, in a sense then, the governance of the construction of religious identity during a period of intense globalization. Critical geographer David Harvey has argued that the positionality of a person in the local—their "cartographic identity"—determines their perceptual field and limits the horizons of their intellectual possibilities (2001:200–203), and so the Sai city determines the identity of the devotee. The Sai city leads me not only to question the empirical value of these categories but also to question the nature of embeddedness and authenticity and the consequences of these enspacements for identity.[65]

In sum, the spaces and aesthetics of the sacred city of Puttaparthi are denotative of a built matrix of multivocal and multivalent narratives that allows devotees to have agency in constructing their own new devotional identity (Jacobs 1966), leading us to question our understandings of the public representation of religion. The multivalent sacred spaces of Puttaparthi seem to suggest that the cartographic identities of Sai devotees are limitless as urban global subjects, since they are endlessly reworkable, allowing them a fluidity and agency that is valuable in reallocating meaning and reconstructing identity in a constantly changing world.

Illusion is what you see. Magic is the feeling that accompanies it.
—Criss Angel, magician

Always find a quiet corner after my Darshan where you may enter the stillness and receive the completion of my blessings. . . . Rest assured that when even My Eyes see, you become vitalized and transmuted. Never underestimate what is being accomplished by this act of Darshan. My walking amongst you is a gift yearned by the gods of the highest heaven and here you are receiving the grace. Be grateful.
—Sathya Sai Baba

3   Illusion, Play, and Work in a Moral Community
     Divine Darshan and the Practices
     of Transnational Devotion

Darshan, Devotion, Play, and Healing

Whitefield, Bangalore. February 20, 1998. Harini (forty-two) told me that she had heard (through the devotee's grapevine) that Sathya Sai Baba had moved to Brindavan, his summer ashram some twelve miles outside Bangalore. She said she would accompany me for early-morning darshan. I was excited. This was the first time I would actually get to see Sathya Sai Baba in person. Darshan was between 6 A.M. and 7 A.M., and she said there would be huge crowds (which I did not believe). We left Bangalore at 3 A.M. and we arrived at 3:30 A.M. In spite of the total darkness and the seeming lack of reliable information, several thousand people had already gathered for a glimpse of Sathya Sai Baba. Entering the ashram, we were herded into a "women's only" queue, toward a series of metal detectors, by women Seva Dal volunteers wearing blue neckerchiefs. Following the metal detectors and a brief but thorough full body pat down by the volunteers in charge of security, we were seated on the floor in long rows in an enormous open air *mantap* (pavilion) facing an empty golden throne and a life-size photograph of Sathya Sai Baba. Some "regular" devotees had arrived with their own pillows and shawls, ready for a long wait. Recorded Sai bhajans played softly in the background.

The diversity of the waiting devotees was startling in this small village in South India: Japanese, Singaporeans, Indonesians, Malaysians, Norwegians, Germans, Swiss, Italians, Chileans, Ukrainians, Americans, and British all sat in silence waiting for the darshan of Sai Baba. Most groups had a leader carrying a flag with the name of their home country, so I could pick them out as the sun came up. I was later told by ashram staff that every morning no less than five thousand people from "all over the world" attended darshan, and on festival days the numbers often swelled to twenty thousand people.[1]

The recorded music was replaced at 5 A.M. by a choral group. I was impatient for the darshan to begin, but no one else seemed to share my feelings. Most of the devotees seemed lost in their thoughts, praying, meditating, or occasionally whispering to one another. At 6 A.M. the songs increased in volume and tempo, and Seva Dal volunteers rolled out red carpets, indicating Sathya Sai Baba's route through the mantap. They moved groups of devotees around to make space for the carpet. Harini whispered to me that these "paths" were reconstructed at the last minute, based on Sai Baba's will. Devotees close to the carpeted route sent up a silent prayer of thanks and were silently congratulated by those further away. I noticed one devotee giving a "thumbs up" sign to another who had managed to get into the first row. Everyone edged forward, but they were kept in place by the rope line of volunteers.

Five minutes before the beginning of darshan a hush passed through the crowd, as they all turned to the ornate gateway through which Sathya Sai Baba was expected to appear. With seemingly divine punctuality, Sathya Sai Baba emerged, clad in his orange robe, accompanied by a retinue of devotees all dressed in white. He moved silently, quickly, and surprisingly gracefully, through the aisles, occasionally reaching out to some devotees and gathering the letters that they were holding out to him. Some devotees moved forward and attempted to touch his feet and the hem of his robe.[2] Sai Baba stopped and spoke to several devotees; some burst into tears. As he touched them, they fainted and had to be carried away.

He stopped at the row where I sat, in front of an elderly woman. She spoke quietly to him, crying. I caught the words *no cure*. Suddenly, he whirled his closed fist thrice in the air, producing a cloud of vibhuti, and handed it to her and blessed her. The elderly woman gratefully accepted the vibhuti with bowed head and immediately ate some. In the breeze, some of it fell on me. I absentmindedly started patting it away, all the while trying to pay attention. It was perfumed and delicate. Everyone around me who had received some vibhuti touched it to their eyes and put it in their mouths as *prasadam* (consecrated substance). I felt hands on me taking the vibhuti off of my clothes. I did the same. It melted in my mouth, though the perfume lingered. Sathya Sai Baba continued along the way, gesturing to a group of women who were led away by the volunteers for "private darshan" in the mandir behind the darshan hall.

Wherever Sathya Sai Baba moved in the mantap, the eyes of the entire group followed, but most of the devotees remained sitting, their hands folded in prayer, some swaying as though in an ecstatic trance. The darshan lasted about three quarters of an hour. As suddenly as he appeared, Sai Baba left. After he left, people slowly began to move about and file out of the mantap, discussing their encounter in hushed tones. Everyone was smiling. Harini asked me, solicitously, "Did you get vibhuti?" When I nodded assent, she said, "You are lucky! They say it is all Swami's leela, whether you get good darshan or not."

The Everyday Praxis of Darshan

Every day at dawn and nearing dusk, Sathya Sai Baba engages in the ritual of darshan, with devotees from all over the world gathering in the ornate Sai Kulwant Darshan Hall at his ashram Prasanthi Nilayam in the small town of Puttaparthi in South India. The darshan is a visual spectacle in which the godman and his retinue perambulate through a decorated pavilion filled with crowds of eager devotees, creating a media moment like no other. The carefully orchestrated moment of darshan with thousands of waiting devotees, wafting smells of incense, soft bhajans, and the possibility of the heady experience of nearness to the godman is a memorable spectacle for devotees.

Darshan is thus, as S. Srinivas notes, and as Diana Eck has so comprehensively and evocatively argued, the apotheosis of the devotional experience, a sacred moment for devotees both ritually and experientially (Srinivas 2008; Eck 1988). Devotees state that in the ritual of seeing and being seen by the divinity of Sathya Sai Baba, they experience a moment of ultimate self-transformation by which they are "captured" spiritually and experience a "complete immersion in Sai Baba's love." Lawrence Babb argues that a "personal confrontation" with Sai Baba's miraculous healing ability is a powerful theme in devotees' accounts of their "conversion" to

Sai faith, in which both the seeing of Sai Baba and the accompanying production of magical objects and substances jolts them out of their "amused
skepticism" and into faith in Sai Baba. Babb notes that devotees "see these
experiences as deeply important in their life histories" (1983:118).

Devotees explained to me that darshan was unique: it is the moment of
self-redefinition toward a Sai devotional self for a devotee, where one can
see him (Sanskrit = *darshan*), hear him (*sravan*), touch him (*sparshan*), interact with him (*sambhasan*), and consume magical substances produced
from his body such as ash (*vibhuti*) and ambrosia (*amritham*), in "a visual,
tactile and alimentary intimacy" (Babb 1983:116–124; Srinivas 2008:79).
So devotees see the ritual of darshan as a complete sensory experience:
ocular (they see Sai Baba), tactile (they get touched and blessed), aesthetic
(they experience sitting and waiting), aural (they recite, sing, and pray),
transcendent (they hope for the visual connection between the divinity of
Sai Baba and their own humanity), and healing (they hope for healing
both spiritually and physically), what S. Srinivas describes as "sensorium
of the sacred" (2008:76). The structure of the darshan experience is as
follows.

The darshan itself in Puttaparthi begins after one hour-long set of live
bhajans, which may be preceded by recorded music.[3] As Morton Klass
powerfully demonstrates, in his pioneering work on the Sai movement in
Trinidad, the bhajans and the performance of singing are an essential
part of the service, and the darshan sequence, narratives of constructing
and belonging to a global devotional community, a performative intent
of adoration and worship at the feet of Sai Baba and part of the politics of
a religious revitalization all over the world, creating for diasporic Hindu
communities as well as others an affective link to Hinduism and to India
(1991:129–132). In the darshan hall at Puttaparthi, the locus centralis of
the movement, men and women are seated by Seva Dal volunteers in
separate sections on the floor, cross-legged in the lotus position (except
for the elderly and infirm), barefoot (since footwear is considered pollut-
ing), and in rows, or they are seated at their computers in far-flung places
of the globe (Srinivas 2008:79–91; Feike 2007:58–77). Beginning the
darshan session, Sai Baba arrives from his home ferried to the darshan
hall in a motorcade of several cars, including an all-male retinue and his
security detail. He enters Sai Kulwant Darshan Hall through the northeast gate by the "ladies section" and walks along the red, carpeted aisles
created by the Seva Dal volunteers, passing between seated sections of
devotees. He makes his way through the crowds, collecting letters and

interacting with devotees, but inexorably weaving toward his throne on the dais in front of the mandir. In Puttaparthi, after the perambulatory part of the darshan, Sathya Sai Baba sits on the golden throne, and he may sit there for up to half an hour listening to the choral group sing bhajans and other devotional songs. An *aarathi* (offering of the camphor flame) is made to Sathya Sai Baba, accompanied by the song from the 1970 Bollywood film *Purab aur Paschim* (East and West), as well as to his photograph when he is not present. Sometimes he is decorated or garlanded, depending upon the occasion. Often school children from the Sathya Sai Center for Higher Education will perform. After the bhajan session, Sai Baba regularly retires to the mandir area behind the dais for his own private worship and "private darshan" with some chosen devotees. That may last up to three quarters of an hour, as the choral group continues to sing or recite Vedic hymns. All the devotees wait for his return. When he emerges from the mandir, he and his retinue move through the crowd quickly toward the exit, blessing devotees along the way, collecting yet more letters. He hops into his car, the motorcade wheels away, and he is gone as suddenly as he came. Often many devotees leave after him, but the darshan session is completed with a verse from the *Brihadaranyaka Upanishad* (1, 3, 8): "Lead me from untruth to truth, from darkness to light, from death to immortality," and is followed by the gayatri mantra of invincibility. Songs are sung while the crowd files out, often accompanied by vibhuti (sacred ash) distribution in the Sai centers other than Puttaparthi (Srinivas 2008:91–95).

A central part of the darshan session at Puttaparthi and other Sai centers, from Wimbledon to Tokyo, Delhi, Mumbai, Indianapolis (Bauman 2007:5–6), and Sydney is the performance of devotional music (bhajans and *kirtans*) played and sung by devotees. The Sai choral group is usually seated front and center both in the ashram and in Sai centers.[4] Bauman notes that, in the Indianapolis Sai center, "*bhajan* services themselves represent one popular connection to the Hindu tradition among middle-class Indians and Indian migrant communities. While Sai Baba Center *bhajan* services often include songs from traditions other than Hinduism—'Amazing Grace' is sung at nearly every *bhajan* service in Indianapolis, and Muslim devotional tunes are sometimes incorporated—the great majority of the songs are of Hindu origin." This singing ritual of the service is followed by Sai devotional centers in other countries as well (Klass 1991:132–135). Norris Palmer notes the same sequence in the Sai "world of devotion" he entered at the Sai center in Stockton, California

FIGURE 3.1. Sathya Sai Baba with core devotees before darshan. *Photo courtesy Kekie Mistry*

(Palmer in Forsthoefel and Humes 2005:109–110), as does Alexandra Kent of the Sai center in Malaysia (2005:48–49). In the early days at Puttaparthi, Sai Baba himself led the bhajan singing.[5] He has composed many bhajans himself, as numerous cassette recordings (*Baba Chants the Bhajan*) attest. Individual singing (*kirtan*) is considered by devotees to be a powerful tool of self-actualization, but community singing (*sankirtan*) is believed to be connected to the healing of the world.[6] Devotees evoke the feeling of devotion[7] and enable self-surrender through this singing and recitation.[8] Both these emotions are considered an integral part of the Indic tradition of the poet-saints' devotional music,[9] after that of Dhrupad (encompassing Hindu *bhajans* and the Muslim *quwwali* of Sufi mystics),[10] although increasingly many of the rhythms are gleaned from Bollywood film songs. In the U.S., devotees often listened to recorded bhajans in their cars on the way to work,[11]—"it calms me"—or on road trips—"keeps my 'monkey mind,' as Bhagawan calls it, occupied"—and, of course, during prayer sessions in their homes. A typical bhajan session in most Sai prayer sessions worldwide lasts an hour and begins with the sacred syllable *Om* chanted thrice and followed by recitation of the 108 attributes of Sathya Sai Baba (Sri Sathya Sai Ashtotarashatanamavali); these focus on descriptive nomenclature of the divine, typical of several Hindu sectarian prayers. Even when Sai Baba is not present, devotees sing to his empty chair and to his life-size picture, believing that the vibrations of their worship will reach him (Palmer in Forstheofel and Humes 2005:110). Klass notes that singing bhajans enables a feeling of community among Trinidadian Sai devotees (1991) and Kent suggests that the singing enables Malaysian devotees of Sai Baba to play with the category of modernity to redefine their religious identity within a pluralizing nation-state (Kent 2000, 2005:93–94).

When devotees stay at Prasanthi Nilayam, the entire devotional day is structured around the rhythms of darshan (see Shaw 2000:213–15; Srinivas 2008; and Palmer in Forsthoefel and Humes 2005:109). Devotees begin to assemble in earnest at Sai Kulwant Darshan Hall by 5 A.M., when the ritual cycle culminating in darshan begins with the *Omkara* or the chanting of the sound of the sacred syllable of *Om* twenty-one times in the mandir. Many devotees participate in this chanting as a cleansing early morning ritual before darshan. *Omkara* is followed by the *suprabhatham* (chanting for the waking of the gods) believed to awaken Sathya Sai Baba. The *suprabhatham* is followed by the *sankirtan* and a sacred perambulation around the *nagara* (town), which in this case merely involves a circumambulation of the central areas of the ashram around the private wall of Sathya Sai Baba's sacred apartments, the mandir, the Sai Kulwant Darshan Hall, and the Sarva Dharma Pillar by core devotees. Many devotees often join this procession. The morning darshan usually lasts until 9 A.M., and after some devotees get the much-sought-after "private interview," either in the mandir or in Sai Baba's private apartments.

Afterward, devotees feel they are free until the evening darshan. Most go shopping, make phone calls or e-mail, and so on, within the ashram or outside in Puttaparthi town. Many devotees rush back to the ashram by 2 P.M. in time to join the queue to wait for evening darshan, which takes place between 3:30 and 4 P.M. and usually lasts until 6 P.M. Then it is as though the business of the day was over. Devotees leisurely chat on the lawns and parks of the ashram and return to their rooms by "lights out" at 9 P.M.

Devotees in Sai centers also follow the same routine for their services. Bauman notes that the Indianapolis service

> begins with the incantation of "Om" exactly at 6:15, according to a digital clock located on the altar. For the next forty-five minutes, devotees sing devotional songs, generally beginning with one praising Lord Ganesh. Some of the *bhajans* refer explicitly to Sai, others

only implicitly (since all names and forms are his). After the songs, devotees perform *arati* before the altar and distribute *vibhuti* while singing songs appropriate to both acts. There is then a short meditation, followed by chanting of the *gayatri* mantra, reading from Sai's writings, and announcements. The service concludes when the person making the announcements says "Jai Sai Ram."   (2007:3–4)

Services in the Framingham center, the Singapore temple, and Wimbledon followed the template exactly, only varying in the local language hymns included, which S. Srinivas claims create a "transnational Guru language" where "code-blending and code-switching mechanisms" (drawing from sociolinguistic theory) enable the Sai faith to be "very mobile" (2008:302–307, 314).

As Victor Turner notes in his study of ritual performance among the Ndembu, the well managed, sensual, ritual experience creates and manipulates certain emotions within the performer (Morris 1987). Turner distinguished analytically three (often interwoven) components of ritual performance (Deflem 1991; Turner 1962a and b, 1964, 1967:99–108; Turner and Turner 1982:203–206): 1. communication, where secret knowledge is communicated to the subjects in the form of exhibitions of sacred articles or persons (relics, instruments, sacred ash, images, "what is shown,"), actions (dancing, singing, watching, recitation, gifting, "what is done") and instructions (mythical history, storytelling, parables, discourses, "what is said"); the symbols/persons represent the unity and continuity of the community; and, because of their multivocality, they are often given complex cultural interpretations; 2. ludic deconstruction and recombination of familiar cultural configurations that provoke the ritual subjects to reflect on the basic values of their social and cosmological order; and 3. simplification of the relations of the social structure. As Turner discovered from his study of rites of passage among the Ndembu, these characteristics are particularly applicable during the period of liminality in ritual. Turner's main theoretical advance was to show how rituals are processes, not states, in the social world, which itself is "a world in becoming, not a world in being" (Turner 1974:24).The Sai ritual of darshan creates a community of devotees through the participation of several thousand people in the engagement of the sacred interactional gaze of *seeing* the divinity of Sai Baba and *being seen* by him. Walter Benjamin adds, "the physiognomic aspects of visual worlds in which dwell the smallest things, meaningful yet covert enough to find a hiding place in

FIGURE 3.2. Sathya Sai Baba and devotees at darshan. *Photo courtesy Kekie Mistry*

waking dreams, but which enlarged and capable of formulation, make the difference between technology and magic visible as a thoroughly historical variable" (Taussig 1993:21–29, quoting Benjamin). The "tactile optics" of Sai darshan (to use Taussig's phrase), in which devotees see and are seen by Sai Baba, create these "waking dreams" for devotees where the rational and the magical find a place side by side. The darshan ritual contains the essence of the affective context within which the "intermingling of fantasy and hope" occurs (Taussig 1993), where a "rewiring" of the complete sensual experience is reconstructed as habitual knowledge, necessary for the construction of a Sai devotional identity.

Darshan and Divine Play

For each darshan, devotees gather several hours in advance in long queues that wind around the ashram. The first person in each section is asked to draw lots (on metal tokens) to determine in which order each section gets to be seated in the Sai Kulwant Darshan Hall. Sai devotee Jeannie Alvin, of Escondido, California, describes her experience in the *darshan* queue on December 6, 1999:

The Seva Dals (volunteers) came with the bags of token numbers. Our line got token number 1! We were all so happy! The young Indian girl behind me said, "Get ready to run fast"! We have to go through a checkpoint before entering the hall. There is as much security here as in an airport! One Seva Dal waves an electronic device in front and in back of us, another checks our belongings on one side, and a third checks our purses, which are supposed to be open. I got through the checkpoint and ran! I crossed the aisle where Swami walks, and went to the left. Down went my straw mat, right in the very front row.[12]

The rationale, if one can call it that, of the darshan queue is part of the construction of charisma within the ashram. Devotees told me that the minuscule decisions, apparently made by Seva Dal volunteers and others about seating token numbers and so on, are all in reality Baba's choice and his leela.[13] They believe that by giving in and surrendering they have the best chance of gaining insight into their own motivations. In an interview about the queue system, Magda (also called Meena) said: "When we first came here, we thought in the logical way, I am first in line. I have a right to sit first. But then we learnt about Baba's playful ways and his way of teaching us humility. His leela decide who will see him that day and how close they will get. Nothing is in our hands."

When I said that it seemed to me that the Seva Dal volunteers decided where we should sit, she said, "You are impatient. This is not the Seva Dal, nor is it you, or me. It is all Baba." She elaborated, stating that the lack of control over one's placement in the darshan hall was analogous to the lack of control one actually had over one's own life, and that was Baba's way of demonstrating that his will was larger than any individual. Other devotees echoed Magda's view: Mark from Fiji, Sudipto from London, Selva Raj from Mumbai, Moses from Kenya, Ginny from Singapore, and Danny from Hamburg all confirmed to me that Baba's queue could not be predicted;, and they had all accepted it, though they found it "different at first" (see Shaw 2000:213–25).

So the hand of Sai Baba is seen to invest the choice of seating, and devotees are alert to the calling out of favorable numbers (which are seated closer to where Sathya Sai Baba walks) as a sign of divine favor. Devotees believe that these instances are evidence of Sai Baba's leela, where the divine intent is hidden to mere mortals, to be read as Sai Baba's validation of their devotion. They argue that their chances of being physically close to

him, though seemingly dictated by a series of random chances (what token number they get, how they are seated, where the red carpets are un-
rolled), are really Sai Baba's choices. So, reversing that logic of proximity,
devotees accrue agency, and they believe that the closer they can get to Sai
Baba the more deserving they are. They measure the distance to Sathya
Sai Baba physically. Within the darshan hall, devotees fight to get the seats
closest to where he may walk or sit. They may even push, shove, and rush
to get them.

Devotees constantly talked about their seated distance from Sai Baba
on a given day. Moses, from Kenya, said in despair, "I have tried and tried
to get close for good darshan now for three years, but no matter what token number I get or where I am seated I do not get good darshan. Maybe
I think Swami is telling me something." A year later, he e-mailed me,
ecstatic: "This time I got to sit in the front and Swami asked me to have
private darshan and he gave me a ring!" Aki, a Japanese devotee, was also
in despair: "Always I get bad seat, at the back . . . far, very far." Joule said:
"Today I was so close I could touch Swami! I was in the group that got the
token number 1, and when I got in I ran and sat in the first row!" Venkat,
a biotechnologist and former student at the Sathya Sai Institute for Higher
Education, said to me when I asked him about being seated close to Sai
Baba and the proxemic desire that devotees exhibited, "Definitely! You are
right to call it that. We longed for it. To sit next to him as close as we
could." When I asked him why he felt that way in retrospect, he seemed to
be stumped: "Wow! Actually I never thought about it. It was just one of
those things that I accepted. But if you see it, who would not want to sit
next to God and talk to him? That's why everyone pushes to get close. We
used to feel proud. I was in the music group and played a few instruments
and so during darshan we sat very close to him." Several hundred Seva
Dal volunteers are employed at every point within the ashram to control
this antisocial manifestation of the desire to be close to Sai Baba, and their
tactics in crowd control often lead to conflict and tension between them
and the other devotees.

When I happened to sit close to where Sai Baba walked, and when I
described the incident to Professor S. S. Sivakumar (sixty-three), including the wave of "accidental" vibhuti over me, he said, "Oh! You have so
much Swami *bhava* (grace)." So devotees measure their proximity to Sai
Baba as evidence of their worth: if they are "good" devotees of Baba, they
believe they will get a good darshan, possibly even get a private darshan
with the possibility of a one-on-one conversation with Sathya Sai Baba

(Shaw 2000:257–264). Conversely, a bad darshan, either being ignored by Sai Baba and/or being seated far away, all denote more painful, patient spiritual work to be done. Harini stated: "You see those women sitting near the pillar where He enters? He always talks to them. When I came here with the head of the Sathya Sai Education Trust, she took me with her and we sat there. I could see Him so clearly. I got really good darshan that time." Joule said: "For the first time I came I got seating only at the back. I think I had many, many things to learn. I was very impatient . . . very arrogant. He ignored me that first time. Now I understand that it is His will. It is His *daya* (mercy). I am just thankful to be here!" Proxemic desire is therefore not only a desire to be close to Sai Baba (though that is the major component) but also encases a desire to be acknowledged as a "good" devotee.

Paradoxically, though devotees acknowledge that Sai Baba's leela is important to get a good seat, they structure their entire day around the possibility of a good darshan, spending inordinate amounts of time waiting in queues. Palmer underlines the ritual of devotees waiting for darshan at the "in queues for much of the day in hopes of being chosen to sit closer to the front of the mandir where swami is more likely to make eye contact, distribute vibhuti, accept their letters, listen to their prayers, or possibly provide words of hope or healing" (Palmer in Forsthoefel and Humes 2005:113).This waiting leads to a lot of tension and disputes between devotees, which sometimes flares up and takes on a nationalist flavor, with devotees shouting at each other and often using stereotypes to offend, sometimes even racist language. For example, Stephen said, "I don't complain about other devotees, but last time I came to 'Parthi I was within inches of Swami—within inches. During darshan, He came up to me and was talking to me, asking about me. He knows me because of the work I do in the Wimbledon center, and suddenly this one man, from Holland, next to me fell at His feet and grabbed them, and I could tell He was upset, and He moved away immediately. I felt terrible for Bhagawan . . . all the signs say "do not touch His feet," but no, this man grabs them. Usually the Dutch are so polite. But I did not fight with the guy. I kept quiet." Alistair said, "These American devotees are the worst. They have no sense of what is okay at Prasanthi and they shout if they don't get their way." But Alistair also said, "The Indian devotees, especially the ones from Delhi—they are awful. They push and shove you to get into the row ahead. I have had to shout at one or two who were downright rude." The conflict sometimes turns physical. When I was at the ashram twice I saw a struggle break out between women devotees as they pushed and shoved to get into the hall. In one particularly aggressive instance, one women called another a "stupid cow," but it was clear that the intended victim did not understand the insult.

Leela blamed the Seva Dal volunteers' lack of discernment of "true" devotees and those who mattered for the chaos: "These volunteers cannot distinguish. Luckily, they know me because I have been coming here for so many years, but last week the wife of Brigadier Anand came, and they pushed her away to the back row. I told them, 'Let her sit in front row.' And when Swami came close, He came to bless me and he blessed her also. He gave her vibhuti. She was so happy, she said. 'Leela Ma, it is because of you that Swami blessed me today.' Poor lady, she would not have got good darshan at all." This evidence of Sai Baba's leela in seating continues to influence even the most committed anti-Sai activists; Barry Pittard, the head of the former devotees group JUsT, said of his first interaction with Sai Baba:

> I had been thinking of going to see him for a long time. I said to him silently, "When I come to you please let me surrender. Let me touch your feet." I did not know how this was possible. On my first visit to the ashram I was seated some twenty-five rows back. There was a sea of humanity around me. I thought, "there is no way I can touch him now." He walked through the crowd, and they parted to let him through, and he came and stood in front of me and he said, or rather I think he said, because the mind does strange things, you know, "Barry, you have come." I fell over in surrender and I touched his feet.

But, problems and promises of seating aside, devotees see the performance of darshan, the one-to-one contact, as a silent dialogue between themselves and the divinity of Sai Baba. He is the center of their phenomenological universe. The silent dialogue is modulated by a discourse of faith and devotion that all devotees are privy to. The closer one is to Sathya Sai Baba during the darshan, the better are one's chances of personal interaction. So there is a pragmatic component to proxemic desire: to position oneself to interact with Sai Baba directly in the hope of more one-on-one time with him.

Sai Baba's leela is a key component of darshan and embodied healing for believers whether in situ at the ashram or in the virtual arena (Feike 2007:49–52). Leela is an Indic (largely Hindu) theological concept (sometimes spelled *lila*), which is translated loosely as "divine play" or the "play of gods." "Sai Baba's leela" is an all-encompassing explanation for what is seen by devotees as unfathomable behavior—even seeming favoritism on Sai Baba's part. Harini used this explanation when I witnessed the materialization of vibhuti and as the reason why I "got a good darshan" in spite of not being a devotee. William Sax defines leela as the creation of the world by God into which He enters in the spirit of play/sport (1995:3). A key component of leela is the inability of adult humans to fathom logic within the discursive practice. It is play because it cannot be predicted by human logic, just as child's play is not subject to logic. Sax traces this theological concept of sport to the sacred texts of Hinduism; the Vedas and Upanishads, in which leela is a monistic philosophical concept that describes all reality, including the cosmos, as the outcome of creative play by the divine absolute (Brahman) (1995). Ram Shanker Misra describes leela as the unfathomable play of Brahman the creator: "The world is a mere spontaneous creation of Brahman. It is a *Lila*, or sport, of Brahman. It is created out of Bliss, by Bliss and for Bliss. *Lila* indicates a spontaneous sportive activity of Brahman as distinguished from a self-conscious volitional effort. The concept of *Lila* signifies freedom as distinguished from necessity."[14] Leela also encompasses God's play in coming down to earth as an avatar, often hidden in plain sight from believers and nonbelievers alike. The element of fun, of sport, and of "hide-and-seek," which is a part of play (Huizinga 1971 [1955]; Turner 1982), is an essential element of divine leela. For Hindus, even human suffering is part of the mystery of God's leela (Sax 1995:4–5). In Vaishnavite mythology, leela often refers to the playful activities of the cowherd god Krishna and his devotees, innocent games Krishna played with his cowherd friends, and the erotic games[15] with his lovers, indicating carefree play.[16] Shaivite theology enlarges on the unificatory principle of leela, where it is the play between the cosmic male and female principles of the universe. The logic of leela follows the mythic personal history of Sathya Sai Baba, linking him to Shaivite theology and Vaishnavite mythology as well as Advaita, Dvaita, and Samkhya philosophies (Spurr 2007). Leela is also part and parcel of the mysterious unpredictability of Sathya Sai Baba and, in a circular argument, provides "evidence" of his being a divine avatar. Sai Baba himself has explicitly provided a rationale for the argument that leela is part of the divinity of avatarhood: "avatars seldom give advice directly . . . what they wish to convey they give indirectly" (SSS 23:16). Former devotees such as Robert Priddy have argued that Sai Baba maintains his mystery by "avoiding giving direct answers . . . when he does reply what he says is elliptical and off the point."[17]

But leela, as Sax points out, is more than a theological concept. It is also performative play where human beings perform leelas or dramaturgical acts recreating significant mythological moments in Hinduism, such as the Ram Leela (where the god Rama kills the demon Ravana) performed all over North India. Leela thus encompasses a sacred performance and a representation of sacredness, where sacred and cosmogenic acts are reenacted and represented. As Huizinga argues, the sacred performance creates an "order of things higher than that in which [the performers] customarily live" (1971 [1955]:14–15) and, in that sense, becomes more than drama, a true representation of the sacred event. The function of the sacred performance is not fixed imitation or representation in human terms (mimetic), but is transcendent and methetic (from the Greek *methexis,* meaning a sort of continual readjustment of a wholly interdependent system of descriptive categories, seen as oppositional to mimetic where a copy is fixed): the individual participating in the sacred drama is identified and transported to a level beyond the mundane. Palmer suggests that the idea of Sai Baba's leela is also used in the mundane as a strategy by devotees to defend Sai Baba against accusations of sexual misconduct, and I will examine this idea later (Palmer in Forsthoefel and Humes 2005:117–119). By the same token, devotees assured me that the ritual of darshan was transcendent, not merely representative but a representation of a divine moment of seeing. Stephen said, "Even today, after so many years, when I go for darshan some days I cry like a baby. I feel it is a connection to the divine unlike anything I have felt before." Leela said," it is something special . . . darshan . . . something happens when Bhagawan's eyes meet yours. I cannot explain. You must feel it, only then you know." Shanti noted, "The feeling is different after darshan. You know this earthly realm and what happens here we leave behind when we die and we go to God. But in darshan you can feel that both come together. Through Bhagawan's gaze, through seeing Bhagawan and opening our hearts to his prema we can connect this world and God. This is seva."

The idea of God's play perhaps has been elaborated more widely in Hinduism than in any other religion. God plays with his (or her) devotees, sometimes as a lover, sometimes like a mother with her children, sometimes like an actor in a play. But the key ingredient of leela is the obscurity of divine intent.[18] Gods do what they want, when they want, to whom they want, for the sheer joy of it—the essential prerogatives of leela—acting in the "flow state," about which analysts of sports often write. And humans cannot understand the meanings or nature of true leela because of their own limits in perception and faith. The theoretical lesson is that divine play and playfulness are not rational, not predictable, and not questionable (Sax 1995).

According to Roger Callois, an authority on play and games, play comprises four main patterns: Agon, or games of competition, alea, or games of chance, mimicry, or games of simulation, and ilinx, or games of vertigo (2001 [1961]). In the Sai ritual of darshan, alea is a significant component, as it indicates the favor of destiny, what Sai devotees' term God's will. In all cases, it is a question of surrendering to a kind of "spasm, seizure, or shock which destroys reality with sovereign brusqueness," which occurs when devotes first perceive Sai Baba in darshan. The flow state of play that God engages in leela is made up of equal parts of innovation and the rules of the ludic impulse. In darshan, as in other ritual plays, the task of the devotee is to distinguish which is which.

Therefore, for the devotee, leela is central to what Huizinga (1971) called the connections between playing and knowing. "Contests of knowing," as Huizinga notes, creates philosophies (such as in the Vedas), but knowing through play also constitutes perception at the everyday level. The aesthetics of darshan convert the magic of the divine in the mundane and the mundane into the magical, adding a component of mystery and magic to everyday tasks. In that sense, the play of divinity is made accessible to humans through ritual.

The tactile optics of Sai darshan, in which devotees see and are seen by Sai Baba, are the essence of the affective context wherein the "intermingling of fantasy and hope" occurs, where a "rewiring" of the complete sensual experience is reconstructed as habitual knowledge, necessary for the construction of a Sai devotional identity. Sai devotional identity is domesticated by strategically linking it to the performance in darshan at the Sai ashram in the sacred city of Puttaparthi, embodied behavioral patterns of devotion that subscribe to coded texts including worship, singing, and service work detailed by acceptable grammars of belonging.

But from a nondevotional perspective like my own, darshan appears to be a carefully orchestrated spectacle that manages the various modes of communication of the sacredness of Sai Baba, which Guy Debord defines as the "very heart of social real unreality" (2005 [1995]:8–10). The social practice of darshan is divided between the meaningful reality of

FIGURE 3.3. Sathya Sai Baba and devotees in the private interview room,
1987. *Photo courtesy Fortunecity.com*

the individual interaction that takes place between devotee and divinity
and its representation as the ritual spectacle of seeing, made more complex
by Sai Baba's human divinity and the fact that he can hear and respond,
unlike transcendent divinity. In the darshan that I witnessed, the representation emerged as sovereign social practice in itself. As Debord notes, spec-
tators who take part in the ritual are linked "only by a one-way relationship
to the very center" (2005:22) of the activity: the divinity of Sai Baba.

Work, Self-Transformation, and the Construction of a Devotional Self

But while the gods can play unintelligibly, humans must work to
understand their play and to convert it to personally meaningful action.
The depth of leela is not obligatory or circumscribed, nor is it visible or
understandable to humans. Therefore, devotees feel obliged to "work" to
understand and attempt to predict the meanings of leela, even though
they know that, by definition, they cannot. *So what is play for gods is work
for humans.* In fact ritual (to make sense of God's play) is understood to
be work. In the etymological understanding of the meaning of ritual or
liturgy (*leitourgia*, in the Greek, "public work"), one can find a significant
cultural resource for action surrounding the "limit" experiences of the
emotions that devotees feel and struggle to make sense of (Seligman,
Weller, and Puett 2008). In fact, as Seligman, Weller and Puett observe,
the conventions of ritual allow us to live together in a broken world. Ritual is work—endless work. This understanding of religion as action
builds on Geertz's conception of religion as a symbolic system pointing
to action and Swidler's model of culture as a tool kit.

There are two stages to the work of interpretation of divine play. The first is "detective work": to find the important statement, action, or sign among the many that occur through the devotee's life. The second is "unlocking the riddle": interpreting the sign correctly to find the "right path" for the individual devotee. Devotees work assiduously to ferret out possible clues about the intent of Sai Baba's leela in his discourses, actions, and informal talks. What devotees close to him say about him and report about his actions become authoritative narratives that they mine for hidden meanings. This process is crucial, since it constructs a path or gives direction to the reconstruction of the self into "proper" devotion. Being a "proper," "good" devotee is very important to devotees, though it is difficult to define, being dependent on too many uncontrolled and unknown individual factors such as previous birth karma, the moment of finding Sai Baba, acceding to the constraints of devotional behavior, and the moment of surrender and its meaning and value. Since devotees believe that Sai Baba is omniscient and omnipotent, finding a special hidden clue and interpreting it correctly is important to finding salvation. So while Sai Baba engages illusion and play to draw devotees nearer, they must work to build a devotional self and a moral community.

Devotees argue that the real "work" of self-transformation towards devotion takes place within the body, in the surrender of the mind and the growth of the spirit. According to the devotees, darshan is the first step in removing the spiritual and mental blockages toward shatakshara (surrender) to Sai Baba. Often devotees told me that, during darshan and after, they cried for days and days, releasing all their anger, frustration, and "bad energy." Shanti said: "First time I came and saw Swami, how I cried! For many days, I would cry and cry. My family got fed up! Then I realized after three days of crying that I am ready to undertake His work. He is the one." Joule echoed Shanti's story: "At my first darshan in 1997, I was overtaken by fear and emotion. I cried for all that I had lost, what I had not seen, the people and things I had hurt knowingly, and unknowingly. Weeping is the first step to removing the blockages of the soul. In the heat of your tears, your soul melts, and it is ready for Baba to mold with sadhana (practices) and seva (good works) toward jivan mukti (self-enlightenment)."Often I met devotees who returned from darshan with tears streaming down their faces. Other devotees treated them with gentleness and care. The affective moment of what Moses, in our vignette, termed "divine witnessing" was a powerful one for devotees. Once they had "let go," they felt ready and "open" to start their road to "spiritual recovery." Devotees later identify this moment of intense emotion as one of self-transformation and awareness.

This process of self-transformation often comes as a blinding flash of self-realization to Sai devotees: the emotive moment of darshan appeals across races, classes, nationalities, religions, and cultures. Sai devotees are not exclusive to the Sai religion. Most devotees whom I interviewed emphasized that Baba allowed them to "remain who they were." He did not ask them to convert or change their original faith. Over 70 percent said that they were "Baba devotees first and foremost," but they were simultaneously Catholics, Protestants, Sunnis, Shias, Vaishnavites, Shaivites, Parsis, and so on. Sai Baba himself affirms this view of religion. One of his most popular Web sites opens with his quotation: "I have come not to disturb or destroy any faith, but to confirm each in his own faith—so that the Christian becomes a better Christian, the Muslim a better Muslim, and the Hindu a better Hindu."[19] Devotees appreciate this inclusion of all faiths under one umbrella. They expressed their cynicism about politically engineered religious quarrels, but they said that they find Baba's inclusive distinctions one way of resolving the separation between faiths. Anna said; "Once I saw Bhagawan in darshan I became his follower. He was looking at me so loving. Like Christ, I thought." Afsan said: "What difference does it make, madam? Isa (Jesus), Allah, Krishna, Baba, all are same, no?" For Baba devotees, devotion to Baba was seen as "added onto" an existing faith and often helped the believer discover her original religion once more in a new and creative way.

But there is a larger theoretical takeaway for an anthropology of culture within this "human work to understand divine play" model. In Obeyesekere's theory of the work of culture explicates upon what I see as the overlap between cultural work and divine play in this context. He argues that, in the West, non-Western peoples are often depicted as nonrational in their decision-making processes; in "the assumption of a lack of reflection implicit in the premise of prelogical, mythic or mystical thought," and that members of these societies cannot "improvise" or have "manipulative flexibility" of intellectual capital (Lukes 2000:8). The nub of Obeyesekere's theory is that while these decisions relate to "perceptual and cognitive mechanisms" and are not "culture free" (Lukes 2000:9) culture is not free of them either, where culturally constituted behavior does not preclude the ability to discriminate. Where Obeyesekere is emphatic is that there cannot be a "singular natives' point of view because native voices are multiple and disparate" (Obeyesekere 1992:60, 61, 196). The key takeaway it is important for us to understand is that cultural difference often exists side by side with structural similarities in society, and the two can are often confused by those who seek a cosmopolitan identity and a multicultural society.

Before and After: Finding the Devotional Self

June 21, 2005. Bangalore. Colin Streathern (fifty-eight) an Englishman whom I met at a friend's party. In the UK he works for a prominent drug manufacturer as a scientist and is a part-time novelist. He told me that he comes at least once a year to Puttaparthi, where he has a time-share. He found Sathya Sai Baba after looking for spiritual guidance for many years;

> Before finding Bhagawan, or before He found me, I had done it all ... primal screaming, Freudian analysis ... I even briefly did TM (transcendental meditation). I had been seeking since I was twenty-two ... you know, looking for a guide to teach me about the meaning of life. I had read about Buddhism and Zen practice, about medieval Christianity and Sufi mysticism. But there was no practice, no discipline associated with it. So what do I do with this information? My professors in Cambridge thought I was crazy. I was studying for a dissertation in medieval English history and when I started to talk about searching for spirituality they reacted rather strongly. I remember one day, it was a Thursday (*guruvara*, the day dedicated to the guru in Hinduism)—a strange coincidence? Or maybe it was Bhagawan all along.... I went to have dinner at this small Indian restaurant and I went in and saw this photograph of a man with a head of black hair and I thought ... that is it! Brilliant! It's Him. I sold my car ... it got me £1,000, and tickets to Bangalore via Delhi were about £600, so I bought a ticket to Bangalore and left. That was July 1979. I got to Puttaparthi, and everyone was going for darshan, so I queued up, and that first day Baba asked me in for private darshan. He spoke to me personally and told me that he had been waiting for me to come for a long time! It was magical.

Richard (sixty-seven), Colin's friend, told me, "I've known Colin since we went up together to university. *Before*, he was confused, difficult. He was thought to be very bright, but he was so ... full of himself. He was wealthy and privileged, but he was a git (idiot)! After he came to India, we found he had changed. He was kinder. Now, he regularly works in a center for addicts and alcoholics making lunches during the days off." Colin returned with a glass of water and said, "I found what I needed. A sense of rest, a sense of peace. Bhagawan gifted it me. I had no other way of making this real. Growing up in an upper-class English family that summered in Italy, how could I make sense of this life? That's when it became a carpe diem situation."

Sai devotees refer to the period before meeting Sathya Sai Baba as though it was another life in the distant past: they often say "before" as in "before I came to Puttaparthi . . ."or "before I saw Bhagawan." Angela (thirty-four), a devotee from Mexico City stated, "My family was always very good, you know. They went to church. But I ran away from home with my boyfriend. He was not a good guy. This was before I found Bhagawan. One day He came to me in a dream and told me to come to Puttaparthi. It took me many months to find Him. Now I am so happy." In all the interviews, devotees stressed the changes they saw in their lives after meeting and committing to Sathya Sai Baba. Uniformly, they said that when they met him all their problems seemed to "fade away." Kathy (forty-four), from Iowa, said that her relationship problems disappeared after her trip to Puttaparthi. Her parents were alcoholics and she tended to get into relationships with abusive men, but after meeting Baba she felt so much at peace, having "learned to love herself," that she could pick men who respected her. There were endless stories in the same vein. It was clear that being in Puttaparthi and participating in darshan changed prospective devotee's view of themselves and of their lives, transforming them into devotees. Devotees feel that Sathya Sai Baba had "saved them" from their own lives—that he had made them into "new" human beings with purpose. As Colin said; "I now live life not just for myself. It is not a selfish, hedonistic view of the world as I had before. I live life for others. For my children, for their mother, for my friends, family, for others who I try to help. It makes life so much richer and more meaningful." I was impressed by the belief that devotees exhibited in the telling of their life narratives. It was clear that they believed that Sai Baba had changed their lives for the better.

Working Multiculturalism and Crafting a Devotional Identity

From my interviews and observations it was clear that the devotees come from different religious traditions, different races, ethnicities, and different cultures, and yet they all demonstrate a singular depth of devotion to Sai Baba. Whereas the Sathya Sai movement began with participants from both the rural poor and the elite, his following today is largely middle class and primarily urban, what Swami Aghenanda Bharathi called the "urban alienates" of many different countries and cultures (Bharathi 1962). In fact, Sai Baba's organization recognizes its powerful middle-class devotional base and encourages the affiliation and consolidation of the status of these devotees within their societies.

> Baba's devotees include, most important government ministers, central and state ambassadors, judges, educationists, medical men, psychiatrists, religious leaders of all denominations, social workers and many more eminent personalities in India and abroad. They are rendering very splendid social service to the down-trodden and needy. These eminent men should come forward and find out ways and means to give this single desire of Baba, to put men of character in charge of levels of power, a concrete shape.   (Kulkarni 1990:165)

The uneducated, economically and socially disenfranchised are explicitly excluded in this description of his following but are seen as receivers of charity. Sai devotees have engaged in "good works" for them consistently and fairly effectively. As Hugh Urban has noted, many devotees are anti-Marxist and anti-Communist, which they equate in the Indian context with being atheist (Urban 2003a:86–87), and Weiss speculates that this need to do good might be to fulfill some upper-class guilt (Weiss 2005:10). Devotees, on the other hand, argue that they are building a better world, taking care of their less fortunate brethren, and following Sai Baba's direction. He appeals, in sum, broadly to the pragmatic, flexible technocrats who form a new global middle class: mobile, affluent, and questioning of traditional ritual, religiosity, and values. Devotees are often well-heeled with families, homes, and full and busy professional lives. Many, though not all, of the devotees interviewed were "cosmopolitan" (Hannerz 1990): well traveled and knowledgeable about different cultures. Though a large proportion of his devotees are Hindu and Indian, both within India and among diasporic Indians, he attracts followers from all different religious traditions. Some followers are Muslims deriving from the Sufi tradition in Iran and Afghanistan. A majority of his followers from the West call themselves "seekers" of a "spiritual practice" that conforms to their concepts of modern spirituality, without constraints of traditional religions. They emphasize, when describing the movement, the syncretic, new age facets and its spiritual practice. The Sai devotional base is neither marginal in terms of numbers, nor are the devotees marginal in their societies. Devotees focus on creating a healthy union between body, spirit, and mind for themselves through various forms of healing, psychotherapy, and self-awareness (Heelas and Woodhead 2005:75–79) in keeping with their new age sensibilities.

It is a social science truism that identity at any level (individual, communitarian, tribal, familial, national, and transnational) is constructed through narratives and performances of difference. Therefore identity is never just created *ex situ,* but instead develops through a set of relations with others, in relationship to an alterity, real or imagined. Religion is a key component in the construction of identity both through individual conversion and in collective experiences with fellow believers. Whether the processes of identity formation are considered or unthinking they tend to be innovative, malleable, and promiscuous in that they all use markers of difference to separate or integrate individuals through a process of labeling that is inherently about power.

As Zygmunt Bauman notes, identity is a modern construction that leaves to the wisdom of the individual the many ways in which life lived can "become flesh due to attention on constant principles of orientation" (1998). Contemporary identity is marked by what Paul Heelas and Linda Woodhead term "the turn" in which individuals turn away from worlds and "in which people think of themselves first and foremost as belonging to established and 'given' orders which are transmitted from the past . . . from a life—as to a subjective life . . . which has to do with states of consciousness, states of mind, memories, emotions, feelings, inner conscience and sentiments including moral sentiments like compassion" (2005:3).

Thus for the potential Sai devotee the idea of the good life is not self-indulgence but the pursuit of enriching one's spiritual, emotional, and moral life: to "become who they truly are" and to create a holistic milieu. The anxiety for him is the quest to find oneself and to master the bringing of the sacred to life within their increasingly material and consumer-driven worlds. These are the uncertainties of the unfinished project of identity that haunt modern women and men, rising out of the paradigm of dismantling and reconstruction that modern identity presents and globalization intensifies.

I see a pattern in devotees' establishing faith in Sai Baba: they are beset by serious personal and social issues and, on accepting him as their refuge, they claim that their problems are mitigated or disappear altogether. Generally, potential Sai followers see Baba in India and reconstitute their identities as Sai devotees. Once devotees encounter Baba they often bring family and friends to meet him, and the network generally grows through word of mouth. Sai Baba devotees from all over the world find the immediacy of his presence, and the corresponding lack of abstraction and mystery, both comforting and gratifying. They liked to be able to ask questions and have the instant feedback of "real" answers.

Devotees change themselves through transforming their attitude to their faith. Devotees do not accept the traditional understanding of a religious system that one is born into and has to accept lock, stock, and barrel. Nor do they accept the modernist view of a dualistic choice between religious belief and secular modernity. Devotees chose a modernist approach in which they picked pieces from different faiths. As we have seen in chapter 1, the Sai movement has been proactive in creating a grammar of faith that allows such syncretic devotion. Devotees do not choose one religious system and reject another; they choose parts of different systems, putting them together individually in a pastiche (similar to what Levi Strauss has called bricolage), the way that citizens experience and craft a multiculturalist approach. In a sense then, the Sai devotees "craft" a religious structure and a religious identity for themselves. They self-consciously shape a devotional identity by picking and choosing parts of the Sathya Sai system of belief for which they feel an affinity. "Syncretic devotion" facilitates the creation of a symbolic matrix where individual devotees can create a system of belief that is meaningful to them. Identity is no longer seen as part of the "taken for granted" or the "habitus" (Bourdieu 1977); it becomes a space in which conscious choice occurs not merely between preconstructed identities but also between parts of identities. For Sai devotees, the parts of identities do not meld together to form a hybrid or a "creole" (Hannerz 1990) identity, but remain hard and separate like a mosaic. The mosaic structure enables devotees to call up the required religious identity in the "correct" context. This ability to create a meaningful identity and system of faith out of seemingly disparate parts by picking prices and gluing them together to craft a whole is an essential skill of living in multicultural societies and in the postmodern world. Living in multicultural societies enables one to engage pluralism at the level of crafting one's identity. It gives one a familiarity with the available multicultural palette and grammars available to work. And, strangely enough, the quest for a spiritual identity that is pragmatically viable in the twenty-first century—an eerie echo of Maslow's hierarchy of needs[20]—where self-actualization and self-transcendence appear to be the highest universal quest—dominates media and spawns a whole library of "self-help" literature. From Deepak Chopra to Oprah, the language of this quest, often mistakenly categorized as new age spirituality, is one of unlocking mysteries and seeking hidden treasures of knowledge and self-enlightenment. The quest for self-knowledge is perceived as deep and meaningful and the concepts of the sacred and of personhood often sit center stage in this search for identity.

By gluing together different parts to form an individual religious iden- tity, devotees gain both the power and pleasure of agency (Beyer 1994). In Puttaparthi they are primarily Sai devotees, but back "home," in Amster- dam, Munich, or Houston, they often go to church and attend other faith- based meetings. For example, Joule, from Amsterdam, goes "to church every Sunday and to Sai satsang every Thursday" and seemed comfort- able with the idea. Different religious identities are asserted in different performative contexts. One could argue that Sai devotees engage in both an epistemological and ontological contextuality, which enables the Sai movement to emphasize both the hyperindividuation of the fluid indi- vidual and authenticity and essence at the same time.[21]

In the experience of darshan, the question of choice is located in the construction of religious identity in a globalizing world. With the deterrito- rialization of culture through migration and technological advances com- bined with the softening of the modern nation-state and national identity (Appadurai 1996; Bauman 1998; Castells 2000 [1996]; Ohmae 1988; Rob- ertson, Featherstone, and Lash 1992; Hannerz 1990; Sassen 2006; Brenner 1999a, b), the question of identity and selfhood, as we have noted earlier in this text, is up for grabs. Clifford Geertz's (1983) discussion of Javanese personhood and Dorrine Kondo's analysis of female Japanese factory work- ers argue (like Derrida) that "selves which are coherent, seamless, bounded, and whole are indeed illusions" and "the unitary subject is no longer uni- fied," because it exists only relationally, as a play of differences (Kondo 1990:14, 36). With the softening of the nation-state, we are increasingly faced with redefining the "territorial trap" (Agnew 1994) as a subversion of local collective identity. Forms of socialization become defined in terms other than the territorial or national, such as translocal spaces, diasporic public spheres, exiled community. And spaces become mobile as spatial flows. In the "market for loyalty" (Price, quoted in Appadurai 1996:49), na- tionality has to compete with other possible selfhoods with which it did not have to compete before, such as spiritualist identity, feminist identity, reli- gious fundamentalist identity, ethnic identity, and racial identity; as Appa- durai notes, religious formulations are the most significant in the deterrito- rialized identity constructions that form the basis of translational loyalties

(Berking 2003:254). Everyone is searching for a center "that holds." The construction of a Sai religious self for devotees is merely a piece of the larger puzzle of cultural globalization, which is based on a permanent de- and recontextualization of cultural identities, cultural knowledge, and cultural mores. It is cultural reinvention. That means that cultural knowledge, while it is part of the global circulatory network, is constantly defined and redefined by the addition and incorporation of texts and images from various other cultures. This collection is not aggregative but forms a synthetic fluid matrix of possibilities of choice, which is a subtle process of cultural change. Anthropologists such as Appadurai (1996), Tambih (1997), and others have identified this fluidity as an essential constituent of identity in a globalized world. The Sai movement demonstrates that the concept of fluid devotional identities is central to civil religious devotion in an era of globalization. The concept of "choice" seems to undergo a change, becoming complex and context based. This "syncretic devotion" (Srinivas 2001, 2008) is central to the process by which the Sai Baba movement gathers devotees transnationally.

But this form of self-transformation is only one part of the equation. The radicalization of the ritual of darshan also influences the transformation of the devotees' habitus: the world they live in—as they build a transnational moral community working for the "greater good" at Sathya Sai Baba's express insistence. Devotees argue that as individuals they are transformed by their faith in Sai Baba both physically and spiritually. They link embodied reform to spiritual reform, which leads to the "creation of new hermeneutic and epistemological territories and imaginations." Devotees explained to me that one of the ways to transform the world that Sai Baba encouraged was through service, or seva, for those less fortunate than themselves. Shanti told me that, for her, her call to do seva "came out of" a healing experience she had during darshan with Sai Baba. Joule echoed this idea, as did Carlos (thirty-nine), Timothy, and Stephen. Seva, for devotees, was linked to their experience of healing during the darshan.

Darshan, Healing, and Divine Play

During darshan the receiving of the vibhuti , or any other magical substances, is considered a blessing, part of Sathya Sai Baba's mercy (daya) and kindness (karuna). The consumption of the vibhuti Sathya Sai

Baba materializes and gifts is believed to endow the devotee with happiness, freedom from want, protection from danger, all good things, and healing of the body and mind. Devotees in Malaysia told me how ash appears on Sathya Sai Baba's pictures during their darshan sessions (Kent 2005:4). A Catholic priest who describes the vibhuti in his devotional essay states that it represents the "redeeming Death," a death of the ego (*ahamkara*), the "state of imperishable divinity" (Mazzoleni 1994:88).

While everyone wants to get healing vibhuti from Sai Baba during darshan, the vibhuti also appears in photographs and other places invested with his sacred presence. Sai Baba sometimes gives devotees *akshaya patra* (seemingly divine vessels filled with vibhuti) and photographs of him are occasionally covered in vibhuti. Devotees constantly refer to the Colusa miracle: in 1980 in Colusa, California, in the house of one Dr. Anil Mangru, vibhuti started appearing in quantities. Devotees have congregated at the Mangru home and have made it into a place of Sai pilgrimage within North America. Now devotees consider it a miracle site, and bhajan sessions are held there twice a week, with devotees and onlookers driving in from all over northern California to witness the sacred presence and to partake of the vibhuti.

Sometimes even just the perfume of vibhuti can linger in the air: devotees attribute this to the ineffable presence of Sathya Sai Baba. They mix the vibhuti in water to drink, apply it to their foreheads and eyes, and place it on a part of the body that needs healing. The vibhuti brings home to devotees that Sai Baba is a shamanic, magical healer-physician and that all the many objects and substances that emerge from his body have healing properties. The vibhuti is a sign of his sacred power and healing presence, and devotees see it as a transmutation between the tangible, material world they are aware of and the intangible, spiritual world that he invests. Many devotees told me the lesson learned in witnessing the production of magical vibhuti is that the physical and metaphysical are two sides of the same coin. Devotees believe religious specialists like Sai Baba can straddle them both and transmutate one to another. As Stephen remarked, pithily: "Swami can make the material world immaterial and the immaterial world material. He can heal people and make vibhuti. He is a seer and can see into the future. All this just proves that we are stupid and ignorant in dividing these categories as 'real' and 'unreal.' They are all reality, just different levels of it. And for gods like Sai Baba the line dividing the two is an artificial construction of the closed mind, so they cross it."

Devotees believe that Sai Baba's body is divine and holds a healing power that is transmitted to chosen individuals through his materializations, particularly through the vibhuti. They ingest the materialized vibhuti and rub it all over their bodies, claiming that it cures all illnesses from skin disorders to cancer, following the common Indic/Hindu practice of eating *prasadam* (consecrated food). Prasadam is any substance offered to the gods that takes on the divine properties of the deity through contact and is then distributed to devotees as consecrated material that has magical, often divine properties.[22] The materialized substances and objects work in a realm of the alternate logic of magicality (Kent 2004, 2005:47–48)—of leela where the possibility of a magical cure resides. Devotee Howard Murphet states: "On the subtle plane of being, interpenetrating our physical plane of existence there may be classes of entities for whom our physical space would actually be non existent: our 'here' and 'there' would be all one to them. The ancient wisdom teaches . . . that the physical object can be disintegrated into a subtler substance or 'energy system,' which can be moved by some agency at near light speed, and reintegrated to form the original object" (1971:84).[23]

Almost every devotee has a personal example of a miracle cure. "When I was very sick with heart complaint," Leela related, "Swami gave me some vibhuti and touched me here (on the shoulder) and told me 'take this three times a day, Leela, for twenty-one days and you will be alright.' There was very little when He gave it to me, and I was worried . . . how will there be enough? But as I took it more would be there. I took it and on the twentieth day I was fine." Alistair tells a longer story:

I was diagnosed with colonic cancer in 1997, and the prognosis was not good. I came to 'Parthi and I surrendered to Bhagawan. I was in unbelievable pain. I could not sit up, but I would drag myself to darshan and sit there. Then one day he looked directly at me and gestured for me to go in for private darshan. Behind the curtain he touched my stomach and said; "Very bad. Something bad. It will all be better. Do not worry." He produced a big bagful of vibhuti and gave it to me and told me to take it for three days. I took it immediately, and the next day the pain was better, but I thought I was imagining it. I went back to London two weeks later, feeling much better. When I went to the oncologist for a review, he said, "I don't know what you did, but there is no trace of the tumor."

Gordon (fifty-four) and his wife Hai Jan (thirty-eight) told me of their experience:

> We wanted to have kids but we found we couldn't. Finally we came to India to Pune to adopt a baby, and someone told us about Baba. We came here immediately, and the minute he saw us he took us in for private darshan. There he looked at Hai Jan with such compassion in his eyes and He said: "I know you want to be a mother. Take this." He produced a sticky substance in a cup. "Drink it." Hai Jan was like she was hypnotized. Usually she will ask a hundred questions, but she just took it and drank it. She said it was sweet but smelt spicy. Anyway, to cut a long story short, we went back home and a month later we found out we were pregnant! So now we have two kids; one adopted and one biological. In one year we had two kids! We could not be happier. That's why we have come back .To thank Him. It is all His grace.

Hai Jan's experience is not unique. Sai Baba is often described as having a "hypnotic" effect on his devotees.

Besides producing vibhuti, Sai Baba takes mundane substances and imbues them with healing properties. The combination of the magical substance and prayer is believed to heal the devotee. Mr. Parthasarathy apparently told Murphet that Baba performed a miracle healing on his mother, who was rapidly going blind with a cataract. "Baba placed jasmine petals on the woman's eyes and held them with a bandage. Each day he changed them for fresh ones and at the same time insisted that she go daily for the bhajans. This went on for ten days, and when he took the bandage off for the last time she was able to see clearly" (Murphet 1971:71).

Sai Baba's healing initiatives encompasses within it a critique of Western science. Science is a "cancerous growth" lacking "humanity" and "filling people with emptiness, loneliness, hatred" (Ruhela and Robinson 1976:70–71) This "colossal and all-pervasive" growth has "infected" India, which has "accepted the highly capitalized science of the West as her goal" (Ruhela and Robinson 1976:71). There are many devotees worldwide who have (for various reasons) interacted with the medical and scientific community of the West and found it lacking in humanity and to them this appeal has powerful resonance. Joule, whose mother had been through an unsuccessful round of chemotherapy sessions and who died

(Joule believed) in agony, had suggested to Joule that, when "her time came," she not "go into hospital." "They [hospitals, doctors, and technical staff] don't care," was Joule's comment to me. Shanti, who is very proud that both her sons are engineers in the U.S., told me,

This science, technology and all is a good thing. With cell phones and satellite and Internet and all I can keep in touch with my sons. But what Bhagawan is saying is that when we think science makes us superhuman . . . when we have *ahamkara* (arrogance) and we lose our love for others, then it is a problem. We cannot think we are bigger than God. My sons, they work in Intel and Microsoft, but both of them everyday they get up and do puja to Swami and they go to satsang on Thursdays. I brought them up like that.

Shanti echoes Sai Baba's own thoughts on science. Science and Western thought is only a problem when they rage unchecked (Weiss 2005:13) unaccepting of their limitations. "Bhagavan [Sai Baba as God] has the answer. He has come for this very purpose, to save humanity from the tentacles of unchecked science." Sai Baba "encourages the scientific spirit of inquiry," and he is "fully aware of the benefits that science and technology has showered on mankind" (Ruhela and Robinson 1976:71). It is this spirit that allows scientists and doctors to affiliate with Sai Baba, to work in his colleges and his hospitals. So, as Weiss pertinently notes, the critique does not result in alternate formulations, rather it results in creating alternate institutions. Sai Baba colleges teach "spiritual education" alongside Mathematics and English. His hospitals, where the best of Western-trained doctors and surgeons work, perform biomedical techniques perfected in the West and use Western-invented drugs and technology. There is no Christian Science–style rejection of Western medicine, but rather an additive approach: that Western science must be tempered with spiritual belief and an acceptance of its limitations.

His healing narratives encompass a critique of Western science and an acceptance of their measures all at once. For example, one healing narrative that Weiss quotes (2005:12–14) states:

There was a young girl whose eyesight was hopeless. She could not go out of her house. Because even in the house she could move about only by touching the wall. She had such allergy for sunlight that it would burn her eyes and give her excruciating headaches. She consulted many opthalmic surgeons. But it was not useful to her. So she went to Prasanthi Nilayam [Sai Baba's ashram] and spent her days in prayer to Baba. At long last, one day Baba told her that she could go home as she was completely all right with her eyes and if any trouble were to arise later to apply the drops when she could be freed of the trouble. Baba materialised medicine in a bottle and gave it to her, asking her to apply the drops every day in her eyes which would get complete cure for her. Thus she had regained her eyesight by the Grace of Baba.

(Sarma 1994:86).

The formulation of this story is rather typical and one that is recognizable to devotees. Sai Baba intervenes magically after several scientific endeavors have failed, and he (without human effort) produces a medicine bottle conflating the scientific with divine healing and articulating what devotees see as a powerful critique of the valuelessness of modernity without a spiritual anchor.

In some extreme cases, Sai Baba is believed to inhabit the body of the devotee to effect a cure. Sheela (forty-five), from Kansas City, told me: "Bhagawan's spirit is so great that he pours this into the devotee's body and cures it. Even if someone is dying it can be reversed if Baba's grace is there." Robert (fifty-three), from Boston, said: "In my satsang group there is this woman who had cancer, breast cancer, and she was dying, so she went to Puttaparthi one last time and when she got there Baba looked at her and said: 'I have taken care of everything. This poison is not in your body anymore. It is in mine.' She came back and she has been fine ever since." Murphet also records this transference of illness: "I had read of great yogis taking on themselves the karmic complaints and accidents due to strike their followers" (1971:128). He states that Dr. Kasturi, Sathya Sai Baba's biographer, told him that Baba had taken on himself "mumps, typhoid fever, delivery pains and the scalding burns of his devotees" (128). Yet the divine body only takes on the troubles of the shariram, the human body, in cases of "karmic illnesses." The right situation was required for him to intervene. It does not occur in every case, nor should it.

The most extreme example of Sai healing is the case of a Lazarus-like "raising from the dead." According to Murphet (1971:130–136), Sai Baba revitalized a Mr. V. Radhakrishnan in 1953 in Puttaparthi. Mr. Radhakrishnan went into a coma and "his breathing was that of a dying man." Sai Baba looked at him, and said, "Don't worry. Everything will be alright," and left. The next day Radhakrishanan's son-in-law brought in a nurse who could not find a pulse and an hour later "the patient became very cold," turning blue and stiff. The third day the body was "beginning to smell," and his wife said she wanted to move the body but was told that it could not be done unless Sai Baba ordered it. Sai Baba told her, "have no fear; I am here." He told them all to leave him alone with the corpse. After a few minutes he opened the door, and when they went in they found Mr. Radhakrishnan awake but puzzled by their worry. Sai Baba is recorded as having said to his wife, " I have brought your husband back to you." Murphet states that when he spoke to Mr. Radhakrishnan he had no recollection of his "death" and thought he had simply awoken from his sleep (1971:133). The miracles are problematic, as Spurr notes (2007:41), whether resurrection or materialization of a Swiss watch, because, he argues, they cannot be dismissed as "simple fakes." Spurr (2007:41–43) notes that Haraldsson (1987:222, 339) could find "no direct evidence of fraud," but he also notes that the evidence of Sathya Sai Baba's "purported [miraculous] power is unlikely to be forthcoming" (2007:41). But Sai Baba also sometimes directly addresses the question of his magical powers, suggesting that they are a transaction rooted in love in which he performs his miracles as his "visiting cards," with devotees in turn pledging their love and devotion to him:

All performances of magic . . . are done for the sake of income. These are the tricks of the magician's trade. They constitute a kind of legalized cheating, the transfer of an object form one place to another by the trick of the hand which goes unnoticed. . . . What I do is a different kind of creation. For one thing, I seek no return. For another, I do not cheat people by transferring objects. I create them. For me this is a kind of visiting card to convince people of My love for them and to secure their devotion in return. Since love is formless, I use materializations as evidence of My love.   (Karanjia 1994:28))

Many of you are under the mistaken notion that all My materialisations have worldly significance; it is a gross mistake; don't think like this. These (Materialisations) are ladders that shall enable you to ascend to a bright and ideal future]. . . . Miracles are an innate part of Me. I was with them. They are not acquired after birth through Yogic practices. That is why Swami not only uses these powers freely but extensively over a very wide range for the propagation of the objective for which He has incarnated Himself on Earth. . . . Baba's Miracles show clearly that He is not bound by Time, qualities, and Nature. He is beyond everything. He is everything and everywhere, as the indweller of the Heart. He is the Eternal Witness.[24]

Here Sai Baba denies any form of magical prestidigitation and states that his miracles are in fact divine. But he is also quoted as saying: " [People] . . . exaggerate the role of miracles, which are trivial when compared to My glory and majesty as is a mosquito in size and strength to an elephant upon which it squats" (SSS 1972:38:227). Thus miracles and leela are seen to support his divinity and his religious role, but do not play a major role in his self-definition as divine in order for him to be able to incorporate the nonmagical, or the modern and the scientific, into his rhetoric. It is clear that Sai Baba and his devotees are trying to resist modern definitions of the miracles or place them in a modern context that is deemed acceptable. If we argue, as Roland Robertson does, that globalization leads to a unitary society and culture, we know that religious leaders often do resist the forces of globalization and westernization (1992). As we have noted previously and as Weiss notes (2005), globalization has in reality led to a pluralization of cultures in which cultural contestation occurs as cultural agents "express hegemonic and counterhegemonic ideas" (2005:7). Weiss argues that Sai Baba's miracles are an essential part of his global appeal. In India, as Weiss notes, the oppositions occur between science and Western knowledge and tradition and religion. He states, "I do not view the challenge expressed in Sai Baba's magic as a traditional challenge to modernity, but I rather see it as the contestation of modernity, as the opposition of one notion of modernity by another. Nor do I mean to rigidly juxtapose science and Europe, on the one hand, and belief in the miraculous and India on the other." Rather Weiss argues for a theory that goes beyond an Orientalist discourse of exoticising and infantalizing India and miracles, where Sai Baba's miracles are rhetorical acts that are performative and "that seek to move their audience in particular ways" (2005:7–8).The "particular ways" that devotees are moved are taught and structured by previous devotee accounts in the apologetic literature. They are part of the larger strategy of affiliation through affect that the movement encourages, as can be seen in the devotees' response to Sai architecture in chapter 2.

But this does not mean, as we have noted in the previous pages, that Sai Baba and his devotees do not use science and technology to their benefit. And so Sai Baba "carries on a critique of Western capitalism, materialism and science in his public rhetoric; this rhetoric contains features and traces of the very discourses and processes that it appears to resist so, utilizing many of the symbols and criteria of authority of cultural forms he seems to oppose, Sai Baba demonstrates that the spread of global cultural forms can provide both the challenge to be resisted the same time the very grounds through which this resistance might be effective" (Weiss 2005:8).

But, to return to the problem of devotion and magical healing: as devotees note, the logic of leela's inscrutability to humans is inescapable. Not all devotees can be cured from illness or death. Devotees primarily account for this seeming randomness by talking about leela. Shanti said, "Not everyone can be cured." She told a story of an epileptic who fell ill and died. When his mother met Sai Baba after his death, she was very sad. Bhagawan said to her, "I just saw your boy. Do not feel sad. He is happy. He had only a little karma here on earth which he finished and he was ready to go." They never asked why Baba did not save him. Other devotees have developed logical theories to account for this discrepancy. Sudipto said, "It is all the person's karma. When it is their time to go not even Bhagawan can stop the soul on its journey." Anna said, "When my son falls sick I pray to Swami, but I know sometimes it does not work. He can only help some people, not all. It is destiny, luck." Murphet argues that even Jesus did not cure all those who fell sick: "This sickness is not unto death, but for the glory of God so that the son of god may be glorified thereby" (Murphet 1971:134).

As Comaroff and Comaroff demonstrate in Tshidi Zionist churches, the body is seen as a metaphor for the society, and a healed body is analogous to a healthy society (1992:68–90). Sai devotees see the individual transformation of healing the body as one step on the road to self-betterment, requiring a "healing" of individual character through education and a "healing" of society through service to those less fortunate. Devotees told me that while the leela of physical healing is important as evidence of Sai Baba's divine karuna, it is ultimately merely a symbol for the larger processes of healing that is necessary in society and that each devotee feels compelled to undertake. Devotees work to restore these values through voluntary and charitable work (seva), which they believe enhances their spirituality. Their individual transformations are enacted upon the world, creating a world of moral stakeholders. They see the hermeneutic exercise as a continuation of the healing initiative that begins with the body and ends with their soul. The play of Sai Baba's divine leela is here converted to work, a framework to create "a more perfect world" in a dynamic and unifying quest for social change.

The rhetoric of creating a moral stakeholdership in a new transnational society of equity and betterment is located both in the logic of healing writ large as well as in the logic of the avatar. Since the avatar (Sai Baba) comes down to earth to restore the good, the restoration of a moral community focused upon the common good is part of an avataric program. Sai Baba's discourses echo this logic with a focus on restoring the five basic "human values": *sathya* (truth), *ahimsa* (non-violence), *dharma* (duty), *prema* (love), and *shanti* (peace).[25] This is what my friends and informants meant when they indicated that seva "came out of" healing during darshan. For them the connection was indisputable.

Moral Stakeholding as Institutional Imperative

In June 2005 I spoke to an oncology specialist in Chicago who told me that he spent seven months every two years "serving" at the Sai Hospital in Whitefield very close to where I had witnessed darshan. He said that he spent his own money going to India and treated patients free of charge while he was there. "It is what I have to do as a human being, a doctor, and as a Sai bhakth (devotee). It is my seva for Swami."

Sai Baba's critique of Western medicine and his emphasis on healing and spiritual thought leads naturally to the building of hospitals and colleges. Since he cannot heal everyone, doctors are hired. Since he cannot educate everyone, teachers do it for him. Sai Baba "does not reject Western medical practice as in some way inherently flawed; rather, it is limited in its scope and therefore falls short of the healing efficacy of those institutions which utilize divine supernatural power alongside Western science" (Weiss 2005:13). So the critique of Western hegemonic thought does not locate itself in providing an indigenous alternative that most scholars assume to be the logical culmination of such a epistemic exercise, rather it suggests harnessing Western technology and science toward a higher purpose. Not only does he not demand his devotees renounce the world, but he provides them with the institutions and infrastructure to give them meaningful employment. Weiss suggests that, in so doing, Sai Baba provides a way for his devotees to think about science that includes divinity and the magical. Devotees accept a "revised" view of science in which it is seen as delimiting and not holding universal truths. The takeaway for devotees is that, rather than reject science, science must be made to accommodate the divine. Devotees recognize the value of science and technology, as Shanti did, but at the same time argue that it is limited by what Western thought understands to be knowable. So, as Weiss notes (2005:15), Sai Baba does "not simply insert an exogenous set of modern ideas into a traditional, ancient, local framework," but he reconfigures what is deemed to be traditional itself, updating it to include what he and his devotees feel is the best of Western science and technology while at the same time rejecting a totalizing narrative. So his divinity and his magic become more powerful as they are seen as being able to control the forces of science, which in itself is seen as one of the sources of Western hegemony all over the globe.

Weiss notes that in engaging in a debate about science versus magic Sai Baba's mission itself becomes "universalised and globalised." His magic "confronts, challenges, and eclipses science in the eyes of his followers," and therefore his mission has relevance beyond India. This viewpoint had gained sympathy all over the world, attested to by the viability of this global mission, and the relevance of his critiques of science and Western-style economics, industrialism, and capitalism outside India. And Sai Baba sees this quest of reforming science as one that has worldwide empathy. Ruhela writes:

> Baba's conception of India's future is that India has again to take up its destined role of becoming the Jagat Guru, Teacher of the Whole Mankind, and lead the world with the light of its spiritual knowledge and radiant values. . . . He is building the base for the emergence of the Golden age of humanity now and His global Sai Seva Organization is trying to serve as the instrument to bring about the spiritual and social-economic and cultural changes in the world.   (1991:219)

The Sai Seva Organization, under the umbrella institution of the Sathya Sai Education in Human Values (SSEHV) program for devotees (now officially titled Sathya Sai Educare, though still referred to by this original name in conversation), deals with the "problems of human suffering and pain" through three initiatives: healing, education, and social action. The *healing initiative* is located in the Sri Sathya Sai Institute of Higher Medical Sciences in Puttaparthi (SSSIHMS; 1991) and in Bangalore (2001), the *pedagogical program* in the Sri Sathya Sai Arts and Science College for Women (1968), in Bangalore (1969), for men in Puttaparthi

(1978), a summer course on Indian culture and values (1972), and the Sathya Sai Institute for Higher Learning (1981). Finally, the Seva Service program resides in the Sri Sathya Sai Seva Organization (SSSSO 1965).

The healing initiative is the most well known and least controversial of all three seva armatures. In 1969 the Sathya Sai General Hospital in Bangalore began as a small clinic, run by a Dr. Ganpuley (a nonresident Indian who had returned to India), that was free for the poor farmers and others. Some time in the 1970s, the Ganpuley hospital was donated to the Sathya Sai Health and Education Trust, and in the early 1980s Sai Baba asked a Ghanaian doctor, Dr. Rajeshwari, to move to Bangalore and manage the hospital. By 2001 the hospital had treated 134,000 patients as outpatients and 2,688 as inpatients (Srinivas 2008:115). I was told that it has 306 beds and 12 operating theaters (the missions of Sathya Sai Baba 2005:34–35), and it now sits on 53 manicured acres gifted by the Government of Karnataka. The hospital was built entirely on charitable donations and cost approximately Indian Rs 6,400,000 ($200,000) (Srinivas 2008 113–121)), and it is a veritable city, including a pharmacy, a laundry, a canteen, a cardiac intensive care unit, a neurosurgery unit, an emergency care ward, a blood bank, laboratory facilities, and out- and inpatient facilities. All this care is either heavily subsidized or free for the poor. Between 2001 and 2005 (according to hospital reports), 5,415 cardiac surgeries, 4,790 neurosurgeries, over 15,000 CAT scans, and over 17,000 MRI examinations were conducted at this hospital, and it received uniformly warm reviews and write-ups in the press (Srinivas 2008:115–116).

The SSSO then built a new hospital and medical teaching facility in Puttaparthi. Named the Sri Sathya Sai Institute for Higher Medical Sciences (SSSIHMS), the impressive facility is headquartered in a pink palace-like structure. The 15,000-square-meter teaching hospital was designed by Keith Critchlow, architect to the Prince of Wales. According to the Sathya Sai Organization, it is meant to resemble "a human being with folded arms symbolizing love, affection and care."[26] In the garden is a fountain with an image of Dhanvantri, the divine physician to the gods in Hindu mythology. Dhanvantri is associated with Ayurveda, the indigenous Indic system of medicine.[27] In Hindu myth he is believed to protect the nectar of longevity. The SSSIHMS building has a large golden dome below, the entrance chamber of an elevated prayer hall with a statue of the Hindu god Ganesha, similar to one in the darshan hall, and a garlanded photograph of Sathya Sai Baba.

Sathya Sai Baba announced the initiative to build this free-care hospital on his birthday, November 23, 1990, citing the equality of all in the face of illness:

> Sickness makes no territorial distinctions. Likewise, there will be no differentiation in providing relief. Our intention is to provide relief to all who come, without any charges whatsoever. . . . We decided to set up a hundred-crore hospital near Prashanthi Nilayam. Even as higher education is free here, "higher medicine" also will be free. People spend some lakhs [1 lakh rupees = $35,000] to get heart surgery done in the U.S. What is the plight of the poor? Who looks after them? If they go to the cities, they will not get even basic medicine. Recognizing this fact, we have launched this big hospital project. Whether it is a heart bypass operation, a kidney transplant, a lung operation, brain surgery or eye surgery, everything will be done free. This has been decided upon from the very start of the project. The hospital will be opened on November 22, 1991.
>
> (Sai Baba's birthday discourse, November 23, 1990)

The Sathya Sai hospital in Puttaparthi is larger than the Whitefield operation and includes cardiac and thoracic care centers, uronephrology, ophthalmology, plastic surgery, and intensive care and emergency care units. Between its inception in 1991 and 2005 (according to official sources), it conducted 14,886 cardiac surgeries, 26,483, ophthalmic interventions, and 1,166,546 outpatient evaluations (the Mission of Sathya Sai 2005:23, in Srinivas 2008:115), and, by 2009, according to their Wikipedia Web page, they had performed over 1,700,000 procedures. It has 13 operating theaters, inpatient and outpatient care facilities as well as specialist emergency and intensive care units.[28] There are 55 doctors and 160 nurses in the SSSIHMS and 110 Seva Dal volunteers.

According to devotees, the SSSIHMS is a necessary institution in the infrastructural void of postmodern India. Devotees believe that the hospital restores equity "by providing care for the underprivileged." As Stephen said, "Sai devotees do great things one step at a time. By volunteering time and money, they help with primary health care to a population that would otherwise be forgotten." Joule said, "It is all Bhagawan's prema. Nothing else. His compassion and love for each and every person. He motivates us all." Devotees see the cures effected by the hospital as "miraculous" and enabled by the divinity of Sathya Sai Baba both institutionally and spiritually.

Dr. Shekar Rao, then head of cardiac surgery in SSSIHMS, states: "It is the Divine grace of Bhagawan Baba that is making it possible to do all this work. We performed complex surgical correction on a one-year-old baby with cyanotic congenital heart disease. . . . He developed multiple complications. . . . We gave the child Baba's *vibhuti prasad* and prayed to Him . . . and witnessed that the child made a gradual and complete recovery" (Srinivas 2008:121–122). Devotees often referred to the SSSIHMS as a "temple of healing," bringing together their belief in a holistic approach to global problem solving, incorporating the spiritual component of creating a new transnational moral societal order and the embodied ideal of a cured individual body.[29]

The second institutional imperative was education. I was introduced to the educational infrastructure while visiting the Sathya Sai center in Singapore on a warm summer night. "Brother Jay," a devotee, gave a speech about the institutional emphasis on education:

> Until about fifty years ago, educational establishments everywhere regarded character development and training students to be good citizens as very high priority in their list of priorities. Lately, however, the stress has shifted almost exclusively to imparting worldly skills . . . says Baba, in these troubled times when the whole world is going to pieces, the only way to make the world united is by making each human being a wholesome person . . . Sathya Sai Baba says that education . . . is related to human values. . . . Sathya Sai Baba teaches that human values are innate in every human being and that true education develops the full human potential of every individual. That is what we do in the Education and Human values program at the SSSO.

The Sai education program, also referred to as EHV (Education in Human Values), Educare, or ESSV, is seen as a natural institutional outcome of Sai Baba's role as guru (teacher). Devotees argue that education of youth is necessary to transform the mind and spirit and therefore to establish a new moral order based on the restoration of human values. "Otherwise," as Joule stated (reading from Kasturi's recordings of Sai Baba's words), "irreverence, indiscipline, inefficiency and rootless culturewill prevail" (Kasturi 1980:51).

The education program started with the Bal Vikas program for children in the late 1960s, and in 1981 the current EHV program was begun (Srinivas 2008:146–148). The EHV is spiritual education that is curriculum based for older children, supplementing regular school education (Srinivas 2008:146–148). Today EHV (also confusingly called Educare) is conceived to be a holistic approach that incorporates the five human values and enables self-transformation toward divinity. Brother Anthony says, "That is precisely the difference in Sai EHV and normal worldly education. The latter teaches how to make a good living, whereas the former teaches how to lead a good life." Many devotees including Shanti, Joule, Leela, and Stephen repeatedly recited this Sai saying to me: "If wealth is lost, nothing is lost. If health is lost, something is lost. If character is lost, everything is lost." Stephen elaborated on the quotation: "Character is power. Nothing can be more powerful on earth than character. Riches, scholarship, status, authority are all frail and flimsy before it." Marisa (thirty-eight), from Hong Kong, quoted another, saying, "The end of wisdom is freedom. The end of culture is perfection. The end of knowledge is love. The end of education is character." Devotees explained to me that the only way to create a truly moral community was to educate their children.

The SSSO claims to have schools in thirty-one countries and nineteen Sathya Sai institutes of education for teacher training that have trained fifty thousand teachers. The schools provide free education in which the five Sathya Sai human values weave through the curriculum. The schools are run at the individual Sai center level and incorporate prayers, chanting, singing, and devotional practice. They are based on the national schooling codes in each country, so there is little uniformity across the centers.

Building upon this base of schools, several colleges were begun in India for devotees' children. In July 1968 a college for women was started in Anantapur and in June 1969 one was begun for men in Bangalore. In 1981 all colleges were grouped under the Sathya Sai Institute of Higher Learning. The Institute of Higher Learning hosted 700 male students and 479 female students and approximately 110 faculty at all 3 campuses for the year 2005 and has been given the status of university by the Government of India. The university teaches arts, sciences, commerce, and business education, along with a special diploma in music.

A mandatory component of the educational curriculum is "spiritual education" comprising prayer, meditation, study of religious texts, bhajan singing, yoga, and social work. The goal of "spiritual insight" is stressed as a valuable part of awareness. J. B. Vijaya Simha, an undergraduate student in the sciences in the 1990s, writes, "Swami gives a lot of importance to academic excellence. At the same time He cautions us that we should not get lost in academics, and forget the real purpose for which we have come. *Mere academic advancement, without spiritual insight, is not only useless but positively dangerous.*[30]

Students believe that the right actions and guiding vision of Sathya Sai Baba lead them toward their goals. Dhruva (thirty-four) states: "Swami says all is possible with right speech (*samyak vak*), right vision (*samyak drishti*), and right hearing (*samyak sravanam*). We must always keep good things in mind." Since society is comprised of individuals, "strung like beads on one thread, God"(SSS 1:148), logically it follows for devotees that "service to man is service to God, for He is in every man and in every living being" (SSS 4:251). According to devotees, this emphasis on service antedates the justice-based symbolic language of human rights. As one devotee told me, in an oblique critique of the former devotees' stance on human rights, "Swamis' idea of service is before Western 'human rights' talk, and it means that we are all caring for each other, not just going our own way." The idea of moral stakeholding, and the doctrine of human values on which it is built, is unique to the Sathya Sai movement, though devotees frequently argue that it is similar to other ideas from the subcontinent: those of the Theosophical movement, of Ananda Coomaraswamy, of the principles of the Ramakrishna movement, of Ramana Maharishi's reform, and several other reform movements in Hinduism (Prothero 1999).

The third component of service in society proceeds from the individual through the family to the community and then, upward, to the society (Srinivas 2008:145; Kent 2005:79–83). The individual is the seat of divinity, and each individual is believed to contribute to the seva agenda. It is argued that the family creates the character of the community, which in turn creates the nation-state and the world (SSS 15:160–163). Kent argues that Sai devotees in Malaysia, though they face a resurgent and powerful Islam, repeatedly conflate their work in the Sai mission with that of building a more just and equitable nation (2005:109), and they state that they "show faith in the nation" by creating a better society. Malay Sai devotees, though often of Indian ethnicity, opt to wear the Malay dress of *baju kurung* rather than saris for festive occasions, thereby representing the nation, rather than their faith or ethnic origins (Kent 2005:108), arguing that Malaysia was "all for unity."

Seva takes place primarily at the grassroots level, in the bhajan centers and the samhitis (local organizations). Devotees see themselves as agents of change within these parameters. While they are citizens of various states, with legal and state-based obligations, they see themselves as moral stakeholders in a global society where dynamic change is possible from within. For example, on December 23, 2004, I spoke to an informant, Vijaya (forty-five), who lives in a suburb of Indianapolis, and she told me that she was in a hurry because she was driving sixty miles to help with Christmas dinner at five homeless shelters in the city. "We do it every year," she said cheerfully. "I take Judy, Sheela, I have a regular group. Our Sai samhiti does this every year. A few of us started some ten years ago because we had read that the shelters needed help. We help with the preparation of the vegetables and sometimes we buy what they need. Some of us take our cars, and we drive hot meals out to elderly people who are alone and cannot get out for Christmas." Kathy (sixty-four) said, "I go to an assisted living center every week for two days. I play games and read to people there. I think I help. Any seva is good for them and good for me too. They are short-staffed, and I get some company. Also Swami has said we must all do what we can to make our world a better place. If we don't do it, who will?"These stories are of everyday Sai devotees who take the principles of love and seva very seriously regardless of location, nationality, or ethnicity. Meredith Feike states, in her unpublished dissertation on Sai devotion on the Internet, that Sai devotees were active participants in charitable endeavors in New Orleans during and after the Hurricane Katrina crisis (2007:86), asserting a new humanitarian order:

> One of the last conversations that I had with my consultant prior to my losing contact with him as a result of Hurricane Katrina and its aftermath, focused on how his New Orleans Sai group frequently took lunches to the homeless shelters in the city. He explained that local Sai devotees made dozens of sandwiches for then homeless people who slept around Lee Circle at the edge of the central business district. He also added that several of the devotees volunteered regularly at the Osanam Inn Soup Kitchen on Camp Street.

For devotees Sai Baba is the center of a new moral order in which they are stakeholders. The stakeholdership is largely local and national, but, on occasion, can be international in reach.

Because of the mobility inherent in their professional lives, devotees often acquire an understanding of the world beyond the local. In the Singapore Sai center, in Katong, a young man who went on an exchange program to Edinburgh wrote about the problems of being Singaporean in

Scotland. However, he too helped in the local samhiti and acquired an understanding of Scottish life, albeit through Sai eyes. Thus while seva usually functions within the local context, it is seen as "having global consequences." Devotees repeatedly said, "If we take care of each other, then there will be no pain, no hunger, no disease, no want." They reflect the abiding belief that if "a good program is started, then Swami will provide." Since there is no tithing within the Sai movement, all moneys for seva comes from the samhiti members or from the central SSSO funds. However, seva is not organized by the Sai institution as are education and healing. It is seen as an act of individual gifted devotion to their guru/god. Seva is largely left to the whim of the devotee or the center. As such, centers may give to homeless shelters in their neighborhood, organize blood banks and canned food drives, help at the local temple, gather supplies or toys at Christmas, organize fund-raising activities for care initiatives of local residents, or help with large-scale disaster relief. Kent (2004, 2005) suggests that the Sai movement transforms the materialism of contractual gifts and the accompanying ethos of capitalist self-interestedness into gift giving and disinterested social development. For Sai devotees, Sai Baba's own grace and mercy is the premise and the center of this new moral order for the "greater good" of humankind, building on the principles of social entrepreneurship and charitable engagement through a restoration of valuable human values.

From a Mirror to a Window: Moral Stakeholding and Cosmopolitan Identity

Sai Baba encourages the idea of building a transnational moral community with each devotee as a stakeholder. I asked Joule what she perceived within herself and within the Sai community of devotees. She said, "Before I was looking into a mirror. I only saw myself and my needs. With Swami's help, I now look into a window and I see people and their needs." The self transformation "from mirror to window" that I have focused on in this chapter culminates in the ideal development of a cosmopolitan outlook accompanied by a service mentality on an individual level and the development of a transnational, morally engaged, community on the societal level. According to Sai devotees, what is crucial to sustain both individual development and community vision is strong character and strong values.

The idea of building individuals with inviolable character and strong values is central to the movement's understanding of a transnational moral community and to the focus on education and service. The idea is that character—the development of self through body, mind, and soul—toward a moral engagement with the community is the ideal. The SSSO compares the development of character to the dissoluteness of contemporary culture that pursues Western mores of consumption. The Sai argument is that postmoderns have been enticed by the "success, self aggrandizement, and high living" (SSS 1972:v–vi) to the detriment of their spiritual essence (SSS 1972:189–190), and the Sai avatar "restores" human values through the threefold program of healing, education, and service, transforming the devotee in the process. And, in the process, questioning the hegemony of Western scientific rational thought.

This logic feeds into the basic insecurity that postmoderns have about their hedonistic and material lives: that it is detrimental to the spirit. The Sai religion gives potential devotees the power of agency by allowing them to craft their own religious identities, and they feel empowered to change the world they live in. The devotional self requires work to construct and is aided by the mechanistic structure of syncretism. Syncretic religion (made up as it is of context-based parts stitched together) enables, or rather requires, devotees to make choices (whether these are illusory or real) and so forces the devotee to become an agent in constructing her own devotional selfhood. As Sathya Sai Baba himself says, "It is the actual journey that will reveal the hardships, the delays, the landslips and the potholes, as well as the beauty of the scenery encountered and the magnificence of the final goal. No second hand account can equal the first hand experience" (SSS 1:120).

The value of this unique transformation lies in its ability to create a matrix of ideas from which a variety of understandings of truth and morality that are context based can be contrived by devotees, creating a "template of difference,"[31] which allows devotees to wholeheartedly engage both individualism and moral community. This is not to argue that there is falsehood enacted, but rather to argue that newer spiritual traditions that re-form older traditions create more fluid structures, in keeping with the cultural, social, economic, and other mores of postmodernity. Devotees repeatedly argued that this is possible because all religions spring from a common source and so logically the ritual of darshan could lead to only one outcome for all people of belief: a universal faith consisting of values based in action.

In short, cultural identities and cultural differences are being experienced as socially constructed consciously, and they are accessible to manipulation and change. However this appears to be headed toward a contradiction because when the project of selfhood is made available and malleable, it is very difficult to gather people as a community. This causes a predicament for those who need or want collective actors with consensus and who simultaneously want to guarantee a working space for identity construction. This politics of identity constitutes a form of symbolic mobilization and simultaneous individuation, which consciously and freely breaks the seemingly global understanding of universal equality for a revitalization of the particular.

In describing his comedy and the pathos of the tramp . . . "The mechanics," Chaplin noted, "induced the emotion."

—David Robinson, Chaplin: His Life and Art

Hellenic worlds are replaced here by something different, something subtly androgynous, inverted upon itself. The Orient cannot rejoice in the sweet anarchy of the body—for it has outstripped the body.

—Lawrence Durrell, The Alexandria Quartet

Restrictions, rules, and self controls are the royal road leading to the goal of self-realization. They are not just to bind you, to limit or control you. Do not fret against the rules and regulations that the organization imposes on you; they are laid down for your own good. Regulation is the very essence of creation. The oceans observe their limits and bounds. —Sathya Sai Baba

4   Renegotiating the Body

Muscular Morality, Truancy, and the Satisfaction

of Desire

Sartorial Problems at Puttaparthi: Encountering Perspectives on Asceticism and Desire

November 18, 2001. I visited the Sai ashram in Puttaparthi for the first time. I wore loose *salwar* trousers and a long *kurta*like shirt, similar in style to the *salwar* suits that north Indian women wore. No sooner had I entered the ashram then I was met with annoyed looks from all sides. Undeterred but discomfited, I joined the long queue for darshan with other women devotees. All around me the women devotees were completely covered, either in saris of white or long kaftans and robes with white *duppatas* (scarves). Soon after I sat down in the darshan queue, one of the Seva Dal volunteers came to me and told me that I could not attend darshan since I was "not dressed correctly." The supervisor of the volunteers was summoned, and she looked at me and said, "If Baba calls her, then she will get into the darshan, otherwise she will wait outside." I discovered the problem was that I had not worn a dupatta covering my upper body, and my very loose shirt was not deemed a sufficiently modest covering by the Seva Dal volunteers. As the queue inched forward in the afternoon sun, Seva Dal volunteers repeatedly pointed out my inadequate clothing, but I cleared each checkpoint. I finally reached the entrance to the darshan hall and sat down in a corner. I was perplexed by my sartorial problems. As an Indian Hindu and as someone who had been doing fieldwork in urban Hindu temples in Bangalore, South India, I had frequently worn similar clothing to the temples and had never encountered any opposition. Why was the Sai ashram different, I wondered. Was Bangalore just more cosmopolitan in its dress code, being the global city that it was?

After the darshan, on the way out of the ashram, I counted the thirty or more volunteers who had chastised me on my clothing. I also noticed a big signboard that I had missed on my way in. It stated, in bold red lettering,

> Dress in modest, clean and sober clothing at all times. Your dress reflects your love and respect for Bhagawan. Wearing shorts or sleeveless shirts is strictly prohibited. Women are required to dress down to their ankles and wrap their fronts with a proper shawl. Tight or see-through dresses are not permitted, as also beach or sportswear. Avoid garish clothes. Do not display unorthodox hairstyles, over-matted hair, Tallset hair, etc., or wear large obtrusive hats, especially in the darshan line. Above all, clothe yourself to neither attract nor distract others. —Shri Sathya Sai Baba

As my field entry demonstrates, issues of bodily control and asceticism are central to the experiential world of global Sai devotion, and yet there is a neglect of these issues and their complex implications both at the macro level—for the spread of charismatic religions globally—as well as at the micro level—for documenting the experience of the individual devotee (for the exception, see Csordas 1994a, b). Over the past five years, as contestations over clothing, and the ethnic and national loyalties they are assumed to enfold, have become international newspaper fodder while communities debate (sometimes with increasing violence, as we recently saw in France with the headscarf controversy) the complexity of sartorial choices and their implications for identity affiliations.

Reflecting on it, I came to realize that my innocuous sartorial scuffle at the Sai ashram was actually a complex articulation of a theosomatic space and the cultural meanings and power it engaged—part of a larger taxonomy of practices of discipline that are central to the effective transnationalization of Sai devotion.[1] Indic body understandings are taken by the Sai movement and reworked to engage a global audience, highlighting the problems of translation of knowledge and of the imagination

(Appadurai 1996). As we have seen in previous chapters, Sai devotees accept that becoming a devotee in the Sai movement is an experience where both self and habitus are transformed. Within the movement, the transformation of the body is an essential part of this transformation of self. And so in this chapter I focus on the embodied ascetic practices of Sathya Sai devotees and the embedded problems of cultural translation of this somatic experience. I intend to reflect on the politics of knowledge that shapes conceptions of devotion and desire, through an analysis of the transnational Sai movement's conception of somatic experiences and the varying emotional and moral values inherent in, and assigned to, these conceptions. I argue that the Sai identity of a "public moral and virtuous devotee" is constructed through a reflexive process in which the Sai devotee engages in an elaboration of a public devotional Sai persona based on the concept of individual awareness, tied into a disciplining of the body and its feelings and desires, according to a moral code set down by the Sai organization, which contests the contemporary embedded assumption of therapeutic well-being through a celebration of the body.[2] I argue that new transnational religious movements like the Sai movement appeal to a wider range of devotees not because of their unique articulation of Western exoticized images of eastern religions, but because of a different understanding of the nature of self as it is, and the nature of the self that people would like to become. In this paradoxical, idealistic, and pragmatic, understanding of the self, the Sai movement has tapped into a truly transnational yearning to be a "better" self—a desire that cuts across nationalities and cultures.[3]

Ascetic discipline of the body and globalization have been seen as paradoxical paradigms, since studies of globalization have focused largely on excessive consumption and marketing practices linked to global culture. But Harpham (1987, 1992) argues that asceticism is a "wider cultural phenomenon present in all societies" (Wills 2006:903). Harpham emphasizes that "where there is culture, there is asceticism" (1987:xi). Michel Foucault's postmodern understanding of embodied disciplinary tactics (1997) expands Harpham's argument, suggesting that asceticism is a transformation of the self (Wills 2006:903) through "technologies of the self" (1988, in Wills 2006:903).[4] During large-scale socioeconomic change, such as occurs routinely in globalization, individuals feel decentered (see Heelas 1980), often without social and spiritual anchors to bind them, as they become aware "that views of reality that place the individual at the center of reality are socially constructed." They experience this relativity as alienating and frightening. The transformation of self in any religious movement seeks to overcome this "de-centering" of self (Castelli 2004), arguing that the decentered self, unlike the centered self, is scattered and anomic, not capable of the mastery of the senses that leads to a moral self (Wills 2006:903, quoting Castelli). Consequently, the creation of the moral self requires transformatory practices that re-center the self by silencing the demands of the body through disciplinary tactics. The analysis of this problem turns upon the experiential apprehension of purifying (*sattvic*) embodied asceticism by Sai devotees, and the proscriptions and tactics the Sai movement codifies and dispenses to enable sattvic praxis transnationally.

But, in the logic of Western thought, bodily practices are part of what Nikolas Rose calls "ethnopolitics," a "body of techniques of conduct that relates to ethics that act on the self management of individual and communities of identity" (Rose 2000:1402). The techniques of biopolitics and biopower identified by Foucault shift the discourse toward power—"a new habit of subjectification"—in which, Rose argues, individuals feel compelled to "shape an autonomous identity for themselves through choices in taste, music, goods and habitus," creating a detailed shaping of the daily lives of individuals based on their "pleasures, contentments and fulfillments" (2000:1399) through a "micromanagement of the self-steering practices of its citizens" (2000:1408, 2001:1–5), and citizenship in the Sai community becomes dependent upon conduct (Sassen 2002). As we see, the satisfaction of desire toward happiness is very much a part of this discourse, and, yet, in Foucault's influential work (1980),[5] power and legitimacy expressed through the deployment and engagement of structures of hierarchy and statehood on the body is the sole focus of theorizing (Comaroff and Comaroff 1992),[6] and there is no discussion of the importance of the manufacture, engagement, and location of satisfaction of desire as a strategy of optimization of happiness (Kurasawa 2004). In the literature it appears that embodied control is understood merely in the discourse of oppression, whereas for the Sai devotee the concern is that embodied control is at odds with the life worlds that people inhabit, which are concerned with the shape-shifting, emotive, and overpowering aspects of desire and its satisfaction. But, based on the data in the following pages, it appears that neither the Indic view of the Sai body (Marriott 1989, 1991; Cohen 1989; Srinivas 1952) nor an examination of the body politics (derived from the work of Gramsci and Foucault, seen in the work of Dirks 1992; van der Veer and Lehmann 1999; Guha and Spivak 1988) unpack sufficiently the problem of the reconstruction of selfhood and its emotive embodiment that is part of the devotees' quest, nor do they address the embodied politics of cultural knowledge that leads to this dichotomous juxtaposition, when contrapuntal understandings of desire converge.

By virtue of its global presence, the Sai movement is engaged in the interplay between the codified conception of embodied sattvic disciplinary practice for transnational audiences and its individual expression, often based in global consumption practices (Harvey 2001). The Sai devotee moves between the two ideational poles, living his everyday life in the discourse of capitalistic satisfaction of desires (which is an accepted lifestyle choice), all the while striving toward a therapeutic "self-betterment" program (which is increasingly gaining legitimacy as an alternate "spiritual" lifestyle choice).

As ethnographers move increasingly into studying the areas of mediation that transnational social and religious movements engage, the body becomes a crucible where identity and notions of "self" and "other" are constructed, and reconstructed through learned bodily practices (Giddens 1991; Appadurai 1996; Hannerz 1990; Evans-Pritchard 1951).[7] As such, it is a phenomenological tabula rasa on which the contest of cultures, values, and attitudes is enacted,[8] which is reflective of the conjunctural and situated character of globalization (Bauman 1998).[9]

In South Asia the study of the body has largely focused on the purity/ pollution debate located in the larger local understandings of power and hierarchy (Marriott 1989; M.N. Srinivas 1952, 1962; Redfield 1955, 1956; Gough 1961), though Marriott's (1977, 1991; Cohen 1989) articulation of an indigenous categorization of embodiment (ethnosociology) argued that Hindu bodies were composed of humors (*guna*), emotions (*rasas*), and other constituents, which were in motion as they flowed through the body and self of the individual and through other bodies and selves, linking the self, the cosmological, and the social in a fluid network (Appadurai 1996; Dirks 1992; Raheja 1996; and van der Veer and Lehmann 1999).

The central question in considering notions of embodiment that are culturally specific such as *sattvica* are the problems of travel and translation. How is the circulation of this idea enabled? As it circulates. does it undergo translation? The development of this thesis is, first, built on previous investigations into the role of ethnic identity in forming a postcolonial plural nation and therefore a postmodern self (Asad 1993; Said 1987; Trouillot 2002), pertinent to the questions of the problems of plural interpretations that arise in this chapter, and, second, the examination of studies of South Asian selfhood and representation, primarily through the demonstration, use, and learning of bodily techniques in the service of ritual among marginal groups (Nabokov 2000; Obeyesekere 1970, 1981; Sax 1999; Trawick 1990; Wadley 1975) relevant to the understanding of Sai patterns of embodiments, and the ritualized ways of being of the Sai devotees, and their cultural transmission as coded systems of indigenous knowledge into the global network. I argue that the Sai conceptions of the body can be seen as a differently managed and understood "site for experience"[10] that argues for theorizing an embodied cultural politics of knowledge relevant to transnational religious practice (Hannerz 1990; Appadurai 1996; Beyer 1994).

Desire and the Ascetic Body: Looking Backwards to Look Ahead

In Indic thought, dominated by Hindu philosophy, the body (*shariram*), the soul (*atman*), and mind (*manasa*) are indivisible (Zarilli 1989). So one cannot have a disciplined body with an undisciplined mind or a wayward soul (Alter 1992b:92–98). Hinduism links physical practices of abstention at a deeper level to the salvation of the soul. It is assumed that the play of ascetic bodily techniques allows the mind to engage in emotional states that opens the soul to divinity.

In Hindu philosophy, the dominant philosophical paradigm in the Sai tradition, the understandings of the separateness and opposition between the "this-worldly" (*laukika*) paradigm, comprising the body and its desires, and the "otherworldly" (*alaukika*) world of the soul, and its soteriological quest to find self-knowledge (*atma gyana*) and liberation (*mukti*), is the centerpiece of the human quest. In order to access the esoteric world of self-awareness, the aspirant is believed to need the guidance of a spiritual teacher (*guru*). The human soul (*atman/dehi*), the frail human body (*shariram*) and the accepted goal of self-awareness are epistemologically linked. The body and its spirit are connected, but have different goals and motivations (see Alter 1992a, 1992b; White 2000, 2003); the purpose of the monadic soul that lives within the gross corporeal body is to realize self-knowledge, liberation (*nirvana, moksha*), and truth (*sahtya*) by surrender (*shatakshara*) of the mind (*manasa, chitta*), through the disciplined service and controlled asceticism of the body. The body that is the container for the soul can retard its passage with fleshly desires, since it is gendered, sexualized, and hungry.[11] Cessation of worldly desires in favor of a disembodied liberation of self[12] results in "a highly developed trans-formed and participatory human nature and identity" (Whicher 1998:234–298). External habituated discipline enables the *self* to break free of im-prisonment in the desires of the *body* through a contest of agency. The epistemological understanding lies in the process of self-transformation (Whicher 1998:276) where a mistaken understanding of self located in this-worldliness is corrected and the "real" spiritual identity located in *nirodha* (cessation of this-worldliness) is engaged. Practice of austerities/abstention reorients the self and is expected to bridge the dichotomy of mind and body (Whicher 1998:288). Merit-making actions (*punya karma/seva*), prayer (*puja*), and embodied control (*sattvica* = purity) enable self-transformation.[13] Knowledge and power are united in the self through the process, where "the Knower, the Known and Knowing become one" (Whicher 1998). In this worldview, abandoning the vows of abstention or eating foods that inflame the senses (*rajasic*) are conscious falls from grace that the individual must guard against.[14] Asceticism is habituated through external practice to "transform the self" (Castelli 2004:235) within.[15] The philosophical goal is the indivisibility of body, mind, and self to allow the *self* to seek liberation.

In Sarah Lamb's skillful and poignant work on old age in Bengal, the ravages of the maya of the this-worldly paradigm are documented (2000). The onerous task for Lamb's aging pensioners is to straddle the this-worldliness of their everyday environment, full of the worries, pains, and fears attendant to aging, while preparing themselves mentally and spiritu-ally for the next world, in which all these considerations are mere illusion. This is a task that Sai devotees from all over the world claim to be engaged in as well. The reconstruction of a "better self," however defined, parallels the all-encompassing quest of postmodern identity; as French sociologist Daniel Hervieu-Leger points out,[16] the anxiety of postmodernity is located in the self, and the self becomes an all-encompassing project where both abstention practices and bodily consumption practices (though opposi-tional) form a whole (2001). Thus Sai abstention practices do not allow the "fractured" self of Marriott's theorizing to be unified; rather it remains fractured (Nabokov 2000), but, as it is never seen in abstraction but only in situ, as it were, the problem of it being relational, individual, or fractured is immaterial.

So, in Indic logic, engaging in austerities and physical discipline enables one to emerge stronger not only in bodily terms but "morally, spiritually, socially, physically, and otherwise" (Alter 1992 b). In derived Sai under-standings of embodiment, the ontological and epistemological distinction between the body and the self that resides with it is explained as a house/chariot,[17] and the "real" self is the charioteer, the driver, the active agent, which is echoed throughout Sai Baba's many discourses:

> Use the body as a chariot for reaching liberation through truth. It is your duty to see that on the four wheels of truth, righteousness, peace and love, the chariot moves along the road to the goal. It will move on that road only if it has "less luggage," that is fewer desires, worries and fears. Desires, worries and fears are multiplied when man thinks he is the body with all its appurtenances, rather than understanding he is only the owner of the body.   (SSS 10:127)

Sai Baba compares the corporeal body to "clothes that need to be washed" by a washerman (God) from time to time through prayer. "Resort to washing [the body] from time to time, just as soiled clothes are cleaned by a washerman. . . . God alone—and none else—can cleanse your heart of impurities. Never forget your body is a garment. It is due to ignorance that we see the body as the Self" (Sathya Sai Baba discourses 1990:21–22; also cited in S.Srinivas 2008:124).

The literature of the Sai organization, and the discourses of Sai Baba, underscore the idealized power of abstention as pathway to liberation. Devotees quote Sathya Sai Baba on desire:

> Man's mind is too full of the world. His desires and wants are multi-plying too fast for his capacity to satisfy them; his dreams are far too real for him; they lead him into false victories and absurd adventures. Engrossed in the analysis of the material world, he has lost all sense of sin, sweetness and sublimity; under this new dispensation, truth has become just a word in the dictionary. . . . The only hold that man has in this dreadful darkness is the name of Brahman God. That is the raft which will take him across this stormy sea, darkened by hate and fear, churned by anxiety and terror.   (SSS 6:163)

The body and its desires are seen as weakening the atman within on its quest for liberation (*jivan mukti*). Sai Baba states: "Today man is putting his senses to misuse and as a result his body is becoming weaker day by day. He shortens his life-span by his unsacred vision and by indulgence in sensual pleasures" (Sai Baba discourse Sanathana Sarathi, August

2001:226). In describing embodied desire and the oppositional goal of liberation, Mason and Laing quote Sathya Sai Baba: "We are three people—the one we think we are, the one who others think we are, the one we really are. . . . Until we discover the one we really are I do not think we make much spiritual progress. Pride, ego, self deception bodily appetites are all stumbling blocks" (Mason and Laing 1982:211). Liberation is seen as attainable only through the control of the senses:

> What is *mukti* (liberation)? Liberation is control of the senses. Unless one controls his senses, liberation is not possible. . . . It is only the senses that bring us good or bad. Hence, controlling the senses should be our top priority. . . . In fact, it is only the one who has gained control over the five senses that can comprehend Divinity. Considering God as your sole refuge, dedicate your senses to Him. . . . You often express your inability (to control the senses) thinking "Swami! Is it possible for us?" I am emphatically saying that it is possible.   (Sai Baba, February 23, 2006)[18]

So the Sai body is seen by devotees as a workable site for self-creation,[19] expanding Csordas's embodiment thesis to a greater cultural understanding of the body, suggesting that there are forms of bodily knowledge[20] that are located in the body and are learned through bodily discipline.[21] Sai devotees see abstention tactics as exercises in self-transformation and renegotiation (see Alter 1992b, 1997) of self and divinity and their interaction.

The epistemological opposition between body and soul, agent and site,[22] problematizes the nature of the Sai self as a complex interface that links agency, soul, body, mind, divinity, and desire where all the constructs ironically work both to create the actor and to hold her back from reaching self-actualization. The Sai self is, as Tillich might suggest, a constant critical phenomenological quest incorporating both ontology and episteme to question understandings and evocations of faith (Tillich 2001 [1957]).

Sathya Sai Baba's Divine Body: Perfection, Love and Miracles

As we found in chapter 3, the search for self-transformation begins with the darshan of Sathya Sai Baba. For devotees, interacting with Sathya Sai Baba becomes the point of contact between divinity and humanity. Sathya Sai Baba is recorded as stating; "It is difficult to get a true idea of Me, whom you see. . . ." (SSS 2:103). Devotees repeatedly quoted this passage to underline their inability to understand divinity and their confusion with the fact that what they see in front of them during darshan appears to be a human man. One Web site, titled "Sai Baba—a clear view," states: "God is awesome, horrible, beautiful, magnificent and, most of all, unknowable. Yet we think we can wedge Him into our concepts and judge His actions!"[23] Echoing the idea that devotees cannot comprehend his divinity without a separation of his body from the resident divinity, Sathya Sai Baba alludes to himself as "this body,"[24] referencing the separation between "himself" as the incarnation (*avatar*) versus the human body (*shariram*) that he inhabits: "God can do anything. My Body, like all other bodies, is a temporary habitation; but, My Power is eternal, all-pervasive, ever-dominant."[25] As we noted in chapter 1, Sai Baba conceptually links his human body to his divine self through the *vishwarupa* (all-forms) concept to suggest he is all forms of creation, arguing that the human face people see is just one aspect of his divinity. This argument emerges form the Hindu philosophical understanding of the avatar (as divine descent) and the vishwarupa form of divinity as embedded in the dramatic episode of the Gita where Lord Krishna unveils his "true" vishwarupa (many divinities in one) form to the warrior king Arjuna to demonstrate to him that he was on the side of the good and the pure. This complex formulation of divinity allows for Feuerbach's statement that "God" is an illusory reality that represents to people the qualities they regard as ideal (Hinnells 1984:258).

According to devotees, the Sai body is "beyond human" in its grace, beauty, and ability, and they all react to his body with emotion. Joule from Amsterdam told me; "When I first saw Bhagawan I thought what a kind face, what energetic hair." Mrs. Pal, another informant, said, "I first saw Baba when I went with my mother as a teenager to Puttaparthi, you know, and the first thing I thought was how graceful Baba is. He seems to float above the ground, no?" Swathi, from Kansas City, observed, "Bhagawan has powers, and they are evident in his body. . . . The expression in his eyes says so. It is so kind." The entire body of Sai Baba was described by devotees repeatedly as "love." Devotees told me that when Baba described himself he said, "I am love, love, love." When I asked them what they meant by that, they just repeated it, "Baba is love." The title of the most comprehensive work on his life, published by the Sai Towers Press, is called *Love Is My Form*. Author Padmanaban, in a press release, stated,

"All that Baba does exudes love. At once, either in His physical presence or in remembrance of His enchanting form and personality, one is filled with peace and love." Devotees feel a strong emotional connection to the Sai physical body; the embodiment of this divine love. Phyllis Krystal, one of Baba's ardent devotees, and author, writes about her first encounter with Baba. Krystal records, "As I reached up the high shelf to pull down a book, another book fell down at the same time barely missing my head. I picked it up and was immediately impressed by the picture of the striking looking man on the cover under the title *Baba* by Arnold Schulman. . . . His was not a typically Indian face, though I scarcely noticed the rest of his features as my attention was riveted on his eyes, which seemed to penetrate through to my very core" (1985:1). Other devotees have also mentioned a similar emotional and bodily response to Sai Baba's presence. John Hislop writes of meeting Baba for the first time: "It is difficult and probably impossible to express in words the effect upon myself of that first meeting with Baba. My entire being was profoundly affected and changed. In His presence, at that first meeting the world fell away from me, my entire consciousness was drawn inward, and at a most subtle level of awareness Baba appeared in my heart as love" (1985:15). Shudipto (forty-three) said, "When I first saw Baba in 1990, I was twenty-six years old. I never thought I am emotional type, but when I saw him in Sai Kulwant Darshan Hall, suddenly I found I was crying!" Crying and feelings of emotion were "common" physical reactions to the form of Sai Baba, an expression of his divine love. Devotees also spoke of a "sudden giddiness," "feeling their body as never before," "feeling a healing surge in the body," "feeling unduly energetic as though a battery had powered up," and so on. Connie Shaw states that these emotions are merely symptoms of the body "awakening" to its kundalini powers (2000:328–329) through sadhana or austerity.[26] She claims that this rising *kundalini shakti* (spirit, power) is in fact one of the stages of the subjugation of the ego in the body (*ahankara*) to reach divinity. Shaw's analysis of the kundalini powers will be relevant later in this work.

The embodied divinity of Sathya Sai Baba's body logically retards its human retrograde qualities: because he is divine, his body does not age. Rumors abound among devotees about how his face does not age and his hair has never been gray, in spite of his being in his eighties. A reference on the Internet to Sathya Sai Baba's recent knee or hip surgery and his subsequent confinement to a wheelchair has generated much speculation about whether he needed total knee replacement or hip replacement and subsequently a heated debate as to whether a divine figure should need such surgery. In the debate, devotees claimed that Sathya Sai Baba has all the problems of the human body because he is an avatar—a divine being in a human form—and is aging like any human being to prove his empathy. Former devotees scoff at such "blind" devotion, alleging that Sathya Sai Baba probably dyes his hair on a regular basis and uses hair products to achieve the aureola effect,[27] and he is "merely" an aging human being like any one of them. As Spurr points out (2007:373), the traditional Hindu notion of *swadharma* (individual duty) comes into play here—"all beings it is believed ought to behave in accordance with the *swadharma* appropriate to their birth, and in this case birth in a human form." But Spurr rightly notes that there are theological issues at stake when Sai Baba compresses human and divine. He (2007:353), states, "the avatar is not supposed to act in a non-human way—he takes up human action and uses human methods. . . . If he did not his taking of a human body would have no meaning." Sathya Sai Baba himself presents this understanding in an abstract form when he states, "God assumes a role in the drama of the world in a human form. He has to behave as a human being only . . . this should be clearly understood . . . for every incarnation there are certain rules and regulations" (SSS 38:251), arguing that the role of the human that God assumes is restricting and very real and the two forms intermingle. Thus, when criticized, he stated: "Some ignorant people are commenting on Me saying I have double personality, Daivatham or Divinity most of the time but Manushyatham or Humanity the rest of the time. But have faith in this. . . . God does not change or get transformed" (SSS 1:213). This apparent divinity within Sathya Sai Baba's body and its inherent power extends to visual representations of his body, as is common in Hindu devotion. Devotees create an embodied space for Sathya Sai Baba to dwell in: what S.Srinivas calls "an ethereal body" through the distribution of his image (2008:227). Devotees worship pictures and photographs of Sathya Sai Baba that focus on various parts of the Sai body. This sacred dismemberment, as I call it, is an essential and unique part of the Sai embodiment of divinity, derived from indigenous, folk, Indic medical traditions.[28] Sacred dismemberment defines various body parts and marks them as "extra" sacred. For instance, one popular photograph of Sai Baba focuses upon his feet on a red silk pillow strewn with fresh jasmine flowers as offerings of worship. An American student who was uninitiated into the ways of popular Hinduism looked at the photos of Sai Baba's feet and said pithily, "kinky!" But these pictures of

Sai feet fit into the popular Hindu tradition of touching the feet of a revered elder, saint, or respected person as a sign of submission to their
greater knowledge. Yet another popular picture of Sai Baba focuses upon
his eyes. Underneath the picture is the saying; "In his eyes are mercy."
Devotees believe that Sathya Sai Baba uses his eyes to look into their
deepest thoughts.

Sai Baba provides Sai devotees with constant proof of his embodied suprahuman qualities through his actions, controlled diet, constant kindness, patience, and his devotion to ultimate Brahman. Sai Baba is expected
by devotees to be, and to act, divine. He is expected to eat only sattvic food,
control all bodily urges, and think pure thoughts. The pressure of these
expectations is never discussed, since to do so would be to assume that
Bhagawan was in fact merely human and subject to uncontrollable desires,
like everyone around him. However, in certain interviews, core devotees
made oblique references to this pressure. For example, a core devotee told
me, "Bhagawan has desires like all of us. Only he knows how to control
them. We do not. That is the difference. He knows it is all maya and it will
pass. We do not. He knows that desire leads to downfall. We do not. . . .
Some days are very difficult for Bhagwan. He is restless." Mr. Murthy, an
official at the Sai ashram confirmed that Sai Baba's diet was highly controlled and sattvic to such an extreme that it merely consisted of lightly
cooked unsalted vegetables and fruit,[29] "nothing bad . . . no pickles, no
sweets, nothing! Swami is from Andhra, you know. . . . They like hot food,
but He does not eat." Sai Baba's eating of sattvic food becomes important
in the realm of Sai ontology because devotees point to Sai Baba's own practices as the ideal. Devotees discern, from the way that Sai Baba leads his
life, the constructs of their own ideal contemplative life. Following the Sai
ontology, the body of Sai Baba becomes a central symbolic system through
which they interpret the rest of the world. The emulation of Sai Baba, the
Bhagawan and the guru, motivates Sai devotees above all other concerns.

The Body of Control: Mimesis, Devotion, and the Reshaping of Desire

The body of the devotee and Sai Baba are drawn into a close relationship through darshan and other devotional practices, and the body of
the devotee becomes the site for learning how to construct and establish
a relationship with the divine. Devotees believe that if they are able to

emulate the ideal represented by Baba then they will turn the body away from this world and fix upon the internal world of the atma, through *tapasya*, sadhana, and other forms of control. So the body of the devotee becomes the locus of a contest of agency for the control of desire and the awakening of bhakti. Sai devotion, as previously noted, is the separation of self from desire—ritualized abstention—through separating the self from worldly things, controlling desires and other stimulations, following the path of spiritual knowledge and one's chosen guru. But Sai devotees hasten to add that their desires are not controlled by rituals of abstinence, rather the abstinence reshapes their desires away from food, sex, and worldly goods to self-awareness and spiritual enlightenment. The goal of Sai devotion for devotees is the creation of a "pure" subject through embodied control. Sai Baba encourages and rationalizes this goal for devotees, as Joule referenced:

> You know, we learn all this because Swami shows us the path to become closer to Him. It is easy to get distracted here [in Puttaparthi] as anywhere else. We lose our focus and get caught in day to day . . . But Swami sees and He says [here she reads from a small guidebook]: "You have come to me after much trial and expense, do not waste your time in idle chatter and forming acquaintances. As you have come to this place to lose or get rid of some bad habit that is detrimental, watch your language, be careful, precise, gentle and pure. Stay on your own and practice spiritual exercises. . . . Peace is only derived from an inner-search and is a treasure that is waiting to be discovered in all of you." See, He shows the way. He says that good behavior is important and controlled action is important also.

Sai Baba devotees from different cultural backgrounds are expected to engage in various kinds of austerities, all centered around the dampening of inflamed senses leading to the loss of bodily control. The importance of bodily control (*nāsa*) and meditative control (tapasya) is enacted primarily through avenues that dampen the sensuality and pleasure of life experience, leading to the release of the self from mortal coils of desire (*iccha*). This view is enhanced in legitimacy, supposedly, by Sai Baba himself. He is quoted as giving to R. K. Karanjia, editor of *Blitz*, "a formula" for the relationship between God and man: "Life + Desire = MAN; Life − Desire = GOD" (1976). Furthermore, he warns devotees about the dangerous loss of their selfhood that can occur if and when they give in to their bodily impulses. "Today man is putting his senses to misuse and as a result his body is becoming weaker day by day. He shortens his life-span by his unsacred vision and by indulgence in sensual pleasures. Lakhs of light rays in his eyes are being destroyed because of his unsacred vision. That is the reason that man is developing eye defects."[30] Thus he encourages devotees on a path of discipline and therefore of self-realization.

This reeducation and reorientation of the Sai devotee from the world of capitalist longings to self-control is a reconstruction of the person as well as the social relations she engages in. Shanti stated: "See, I never want for anything. I am at peace. Before I used to quarrel with my mother-in-law over things . . . like jewelry and house and all . . . now no more. I never ask now because I don't need. I don't want new clothes or jewelry . . . anything. I think of Swami and my heart is full. What more I need?"[31] No longer are Sai devotees focused upon their own pleasure, their daily mundane sensations dependent upon this-worldly pleasures, but they are expected to become (and frequently do become) focused with increasing intensity upon spiritual achievement and self-betterment such as helping those less fortunate than themselves through serving at local community shelters, medical camps, libraries, etc.[32] Joule told me, "After being at the ashram many years, I realize how little I need to live. That is real sattvica, when you take from this earth only what you need. You are pure. We all need very little but we have big ego."

Besides this individual relationship with divinity, the devotees are seen by the SSSO and by themselves en masse as a "body" of devotion. They become a metaphorical body in relation to Sathya Sai Baba, as human is in relation to divine. This dyadic relationship is encapsulated in the description of Swami—bhakta (divinity-devotee) and guru-*shishya* (teacher-student). The guru/swami enables the practitioner to convert the negative of sacrifice to the positive of freedom to a higher selfhood; this enables the seamless continuation between theory and praxis.

But austerity is nothing without desire. For austerity to have meaning, desire is a necessary part of the human condition that has to be negated. Several activities are believed to engage the spirit of austerity against the longing of desire: clothing restrictions that enhance modesty, food restrictions that reject sensual and "inflammatory" foods (Srinivas 2008:122–123), restrictions of sexual relations within divinely sanctioned relationships such as marriage, prayer and contemplation both individually and with a community of Sai believers, singing of Sai bhajans praising and adoring Sai Baba, performing some seva for people less fortunate than oneself, and, lastly, reading sacred literature with a Sai devotional group.[33] With regard to the satiation of desire, Shanti, a Sai devotee for twenty years, was paraphrasing Sai Baba when she said:

> Bhagawan has said, the problem is our *iccha* [desires]. We want more of everything; food, clothing, house, car, better job, more money, kids and all that. But that makes you attached. You must be detached. If you are sattvic: no hot foods, no too much of anything, then you become calm, peaceful, happy. The problem is when other people, or your own weakness, make you to eat, enjoy and you cannot resist it. That is the trap. Then you cannot focus on atman or Brahman [ultimate godhead].[34]

The reshaping of iccha away from life's sensual pleasures occurs through repeated bodily self-inscription where a teleological shift is believed to occur in the mind of the Sai devotee that alters not only his perception of the world but also his actions within it. The intention is to please Sai Baba at any cost. Following what they believe Sai Baba to be, devotees mimetically inscribe their bodies, imitating the austerity practiced by Sai Baba. Contrary to the nature of power, agency, and knowledge described by Foucault and others, the devotees embrace the power of the human god over themselves in an intentional relationship.

But it is clear to the Sai movement that devotees come with different perspectives of embodiment based on the cultural lenses through which they view the world. So the questions becomes how can this powerful, embedded, taken-for-granted, culturally specific movement of sattvica— where a particular relationship of the body and spirit is enjoined in discipline toward the end of liberation—be made mobile and relevant to different cultural realms? How is it given wings so that it reaches potential devotees all over the world while still retaining some authenticity? This is the problem that the Sai movement faces in the globalization of its ideals and its practices.

A Ceiling on Desires Program: Institutional Narratives of the Politics of Desire

Sattvic-embodied abstention activities are self-monitored when devotees are in their homes and at local Sai mandirs and centers, but they are severely engaged when at the Sai ashram at Puttaparthi. The global

Sai organization—the SSSO and the SCT—have codified the loose practices of abstention into an ironclad Ceiling on Desires program that is to be practiced by all devotees—an institutionalized narrative of abstention. According to Sai officials, there are four components to the Ceiling on Desires program: curb excessive talk and desires, control expenditures, control the consumption of food, and reduce the waste of energy.[35]

The Sai official Internet page on the code of conduct notes:

> Not only should you curb your desires, and set aside the savings thus gained to serve the poor, all aspirants along the spiritual path should put a rein on growing desires, within an increasingly materialistic, uncaring, wasteful and obsolescence oriented society. . . . Place a "Ceiling on Desires." . . . Do not waste Food . . . do not overindulge in food. Do not waste Energy . . . electricity, water, your own energy (too much talking, anger, jealousy and other negative expressions are equally a waste of Divine energy). Do not waste Time . . . and whatever genuine knowledge you have, use it well. Do not waste Money.

Sai officials repeatedly stated in interviews that Sathya Sai Baba exhorted devotees to adhere to the Ceiling on Desires program. The program is given legitimacy in the eyes of the devotees. Mr. Reddy (seventy-two), an elderly and respected devotee, told me; "Swami has said not only should we practice Ceiling on Desires but we should also teach others. You go look it up." In a talk Sathya Sai Baba gave to the workers of the SSSO in Abbotsbury, Chennai on January 19, 1983, he stated: "You should not only practice yourself but teach others also about this ceiling on desires. You place before God's pictures a lot of food of rich variety as 'naivedhyam (offering). You do this because you know very well that this is coming back to you. So, here too it is swaartham (self-interest) and not thyaagam (sacrifice). The amrithathwa (immortality) or moksha (liberation) will come out of thyaagam." Sai Baba's discourses underline the importance of reshaping desires through abstention and control within the space of the ashram and town of Puttaparthi. Derived from the Ceiling on Desires program were other restrictions on devotees visiting the Puttaparthi ashram. They experience food restrictions (toward a sattvic diet), controls on time and personal energy (toward tapasya), silence, "proper" puja, seva, restrictions against interacting with members of the opposite sex (toward enhanced sexual energy control), and clothing restrictions (toward modesty). Devotees I spoke with constantly complained about the gender segregations and food restrictions.

Gender segregation in the ashram is strictly enforced. The official Sai Web site states, "Men and women are not expected to mix for the sake of passing time either outside or inside the rooms. These distractions pull your being outwardly, promoting duality." Thus, there are queues by gender for the darshan, seating in the Sai Kulwant Darshan Hall and canteen is divided by gender, as it is in bhajan, festivals, and prayer group meetings. Only in the evening, when there is a little free time, are men and women allowed to speak to one another, and usually they are scrutinized by the Seva Dal volunteers.

To generalize, gender segregation is linked in the Sai tradition with embodied modesty, controlled sexual appetites, the importance of purity of the body, and other significant Indic concepts that are widely held in South Asia, although they have become far more stringent with the increasing fears of Westernization (associated with "loose morals") that globalization brings to the fore. Martha Nussbaum has argued that this focus on purity and control is not located in traditional Hinduism but is a relatively recent entrant to the subcontinent imported in the interwar years by Hindutva leaders who wished to emulate fascist dictators in Europe (2008). However, whatever its source, the stringent rules of embodied purity and chastity are enforced at the ashram with rigor and enthusiasm.

The only sexual relations sanctioned by the movement are those within heterosexual marriage. Although, as a realized soul, Sathya Sai Baba is considered to be a *brahmacharya* (celibate), devotees are expected to be monogamous householders. Because of this understanding of sexual relations, accommodations in the ashram are divided by gender; single women and single men sleep in large dormitories and married couples are allowed to apply for "married quarters" to reside together in rooms in the ashram. Problems occur when people do not abide by the established rules of sexual control. The Seva Dal volunteers are very suspicious of Westerners since they feel the practice of "living together" is widespread in the West, is amoral, and cannot be condoned in the ashram. This causes the Seva Dal volunteers in charge of room distribution to act as moral dharma police. Snehalatha (twenty-six), a volunteer from the Badaga tribe in the Nilgiris area of Tamil Nadu, was in charge of distributing rooms one day in August 2005. I watched her as she repeatedly asked people requesting accommodation if they were married. One German couple replied, "No!" so she said, "Then you cannot get married quarters . . . only shed" (dormitory). She refused to talk to them any further and made them sign a register, handing them two keys and directing them to the shed dormitories that were same sex. Then she turned to me and said, "Too much they are! Coming here and asking. . . . Why they cannot get married?" I pointed out that it might be customary in Germany not to get married, and it was just a different social system. She did not agree: "No, no . . . I am Badaga. We are tribal peoples, no? We also had different marriage system, but now marriage is for life until someone dies. Not one day this person, next day another person. Even our birds in India . . . they have only one husband or wife for life. They cry tears when one dies. I myself have seen." When I asked her about her dismissal of the couple, she said, "Otherwise they will try all sorts of tricks. You don't know. Sometime I know they are not married and still they say, yes, we are married; then I give them married quarters. It is their karma if they lie to Swami like that." I asked her if Indians "lied." She replied: "Yes, yes. Now they come with boyfriend, girlfriend, all friend [sic], and they want to stay in married quarters, so I tell them, 'This is not good. If you want to stay like this go outside and stay. There is no problem. Do not pollute the ashram.'"

The different perspectives encountered in a globalizing ideology such as the Sai religion raises the problems of understanding of difference and the conceptions not only of embodiment but of self and its relations within society.

Food on the ashram premises is also strictly controlled—food from outside the ashram is not encouraged, as it does not abide by ashram canons of dietary restrictions. The food cooked at the ashram is vegetarian and follows the norms of the "pure" dietary code that is believed to enable abstention practices (Srinivas 2008:122–123). Deriving from Ayurvedic practice and other indigenous therapeutic ideologies, sattvic foods are believed to coil sexual energies within the body to be redirected through the various energy meridians (*chakras*) to enable self awareness through meditation and regular fasting (Alter 1997).

As devotees check into the ashram, they are given coupons to eat at the Sai canteen on the ashram premises. Until about 1985 the canteen served only South Indian food, but in 1985 the canteen expanded to include North Indian food. For example, Connie Shaw writes of her stay at the ashram on March 19, 1982: "Breakfast in the canteen is an *idli* pancake [steamed rice flour cakes] with a spicy sauce on it, rose milk and a brown vegetarian gravy of some sort" (Shaw 2000:195). In 1990–1995, with a greater non-Indian devotee base, the canteen food underwent a further expansion in its menu. Today, the Sai canteen at Prasanthi Nilayam serves vegetarian pizza,

golden butter puffs, cream cakes, vegetarian burgers, profiteroles, chocolate milk shakes, fruit salad, ice cream, and occasionally some Indian Chinese food in a clean and safe environment.[36] Devotees are actively discour-
aged from eating in the town of Puttaparthi and from bringing "outside,"
i.e., "impure" food into the ashram, for fear it may break the sattvic diet by
appealing to a bodily desire for meat, liquor, spicy foods, and other foods
that inflame the senses.

Sathya Sai Baba has often been recorded discussing the intimate relationship between food, the senses, and self-control. He urges devotees to
follow the sattvic diet of vegetables, fruit, milk, dairy products, and grains
and considers meat eating (including poultry, fish, and eggs) impure, since
it inflames the senses through bloodlust. "Meat eating promotes animal
qualities," he said. "It has been well said that the food one consumes determines one's thoughts. You develop cruelty when you eat the flesh of animals . . . so people who want to be devotees of God must give up eating
meat completely."[37] Sai Baba also urges devotees not to use mind-altering
stimulants, such as liquor and drugs, since this gives an "illusory" view of
the self and allows for cessation of control. He states that "any intoxicant or
stimulant is harmful" (SSS 1:168) and suggests consecrating food before
consumption.[38] For this reason liquor and mind-altering substances are
not allowed on the ashram premises.

However, because of the presence of devotees from all over the world,
the Indic sattvic diet that is based on Ayurvedic (a system of indigenous
South Asian popular medicine where principles are derived from Hindu
religious and social texts , the samhitas) and Unani (system of indigenous
medicine popular in South Asia where principles are derived from Greco-
Arabic medicinal texts systems of medicine, advocated by Sai Baba, has
had to suffer some modifications. As Mr. Murthy explained to me, accommodating diverse devotees' desires in the food department has caused the
sattvic diet to undergo some changes, which he clearly saw as regrettable,
though others did not:

See, originally, we used to all follow the actual sattvic diet of very little oil, spice, and small portions of Indian vegetarian food, with not
much salt. Mainly South Indian only. But nowadays it has changed.
You are asking, How are these cream cakes and pizzas and all sattvic
diet? Yes, I will say you are right to ask. . . . Nowadays we must ad-
just, no? The sattvic diet now only means vegetarian. That is all.
With different peoples coming here, it is not possible to maintain

strict sattvica . . . But we are adamant . . . *no nonveg here!* But some people they do that also. What to do? We try to stop them. That is all we can do. But inside the ashram all peoples they like the food. They say it is so tasty, so good, so healthy.

Devotees like Mr. Murthy believe it is a slippery slope from breaking dietary restrictions to total loss of embodied abstention.

But, as S. Srinivas notes (2008), for devotees a sattvic lifestyle implies more than just food, sexual control, and gender segregation. It encompasses all the "distractions" that the five senses pick up. Sai Baba clarifies his thoughts on the holistic nature of sattvic purity: "*Sattvic* diet does not simply mean the food we take through our mouths: it also means the pure air we breathe through our noses, the pure vision we see through our eyes, and the pure objects we touch with our bodies. All that we take in through the doors of the five sense organs may be described as the *sattvic* diet" (1976b:207). Thus subtleties such as internal purity of thought and motivation are important. Sai Baba's ideas of the sattvic lifestyle go beyond the physical to the social. Devotees are urged to take part in the various activities of the ashram such as the singing of bhajans and the playing of instruments that require long hours of practice (Shaw 2000:199), joining the processions of devotees to enter the mandir for prayer and contemplation on a twice-daily basis, cleaning one's own clothes and utensils, and helping as a volunteer in the ashram in some capacity. All these actions are classified as tapasya. Connie Shaw records: "We are told by an official that we must be patient while waiting in various lines each day for darshan, food, the bank, and the post office. He says the very experience of sitting long hours is part of our learning experience here and that it is good for our spiritual development. It builds character and is called 'tapas' or penance, sacrifice, or spiritual endurance for a higher cause" (197). Shanti related, "The body is like clay. We must take the job to mold it properly—that is all. Bhagawan shows us the way. . . . If we corrupt the body, what is inside will also be corrupt. If we keep it clean, like Bhagawan teaches, then what is inside will be clean also." Alistair, an English devotee I had originally met at Heathrow Airport, echoed Shanti's understanding: "The Seva Dal volunteers are external forces. This only demonstrates the unfinished work of the atman. When the atman is ready, everything falls into place. I don't need people to make sure I keep myself pure. I stick to a sattvic diet and life. I do it for myself . . . to keep myself pure. What you are seeing now in Puttaparthi—the Sai volunteers and their control of people—are in fact an externalization of the anticipated internal controls of the devotee's body."

Joule said, "In the beginning everyone needs help to discipline. That is why in the ashram there are so many volunteers. But for those who obey Swami's rules it is very easy." For Shanti, Alistair, and Joule, the disciplining of the body is an ongoing process where, in time, it is believed that the life of abstention and good works will reconstruct the body. According to the Sai belief, the tools of bodily control that the Sai movement attempts to transfer to devotees define the body both as agent and site (Csordas 1994a:9–10) that employs learned bodily techniques to create specific social acts that, in turn, produce emotional states conducive to liberation.

But, for devotees, power and agency are not controlled externally but are focused upon the conflict between the soul and the world of the *ahamkara* (ego) and the body and its desires. The body of the Sai devotee becomes one that is constantly reinscribed in an effort to get ever closer to the ideal state of egoless disinterested pure action. Contrary to the nature of power, agency, and knowledge described by Foucault and feminist scholars, for Sai devotees, agency resides in an intentionally willed relationship founded on the desire to detach the atman from the body, the "other" of one's own body, and in turn be embodied by the ultimate "other."

In order to encourage devotees toward "proper" abstinence and austerity, the SSSO and the SCT convert the sattvic philosophy into spatialized control of the embodied subject within the ashram. A significant part of the Ceiling on Desires program is the Nine Point Code of Conduct, a codification of appropriate and expected abstentions required for everyone to "easily attain" the "spiritual lifestyle." In the Sai ashram in Puttaparthi, the Nine Point Code takes a literal form including no lights on after "lights out time," no eating of "forbidden foods," no fraternizing between members of the opposite sex, and so on. This codification of "appropriate" behavior is the first step toward the creation of a universal doctrine of the body, to enable people from different cultures with different views on the body to all subscribe to the same values and notions of embodiment. Devotees assert that the Nine Point Code is a code for a "spiritual lifestyle" and that it is central to understanding the meaning of austerity for Sai devotees.

The Nine Point Code is translated literally into several languages and placed on billboards and chalk boards all round the ashram. It is made physically accessible to all members of the Sai movement who visit the ashram through extensive spatialization. The spatialized access becomes international as technophile devotees all over the world who maintain Sai Web sites reembed the Nine Point Code in cyberspace. Devotees are informed of the ashram code before arriving at the ashram through their local Sai groups. The code is also printed in a flyer that is distributed when devotees arrive at the ashram.

This codification of behavior articulates tacit practices rooted within Indic culture into a coherent and simplified code of conduct. The Nine Point Code of Conduct is internationalized as devotees visit the ashram and carry these embodied practices with them to different cultures. The code is reexternalized and respatialized as devotees join various devotional groups in different geographical regions, write books, articles on the Internet, and participate in cyber discussion groups.

The Sai movement takes this particular religiocultural construct—of the concept of the disciplined body as the site of spiritual transformation drawn from embedded Indic practices—that is comprised of both embedded praxis and Sai theology and *makes it mobile*. The Sai movement articulate these embedded practices into a coherent and simplified code. This codification of spiritual discipline toward enlightenment enables a universal access based in easily available rules of praxis rather than esoteric philosophy, which allows for potential devotees from different cultures to engage these seemingly "distant" cultural practices. The codification forms a new process-based language by which many can adopt the practices previously limited to the few. For the cultural translation of a particular cultural form, the originating culture, or cultural movement, must codify the cultural matrix within which the cultural form resides. The taken-for-granted-world has to be made explicit. The codification of the cultural matrix into a series of regulatory principles, or patterns of knowledge, that are transferable is the first step toward cultural translation.

The construction of a new process-based language to describe the different conceptions of faith and emergent spaces of religious sacredness is imperative, on many levels, to the project of globalization.[39] It is necessary to deal with difference, to inform and revitalize studies of religious identity, its links with embodied social practice, and the complex construction of postmodern religious identity. But let us not assume that the first step of codification of these embedded practices somehow removes the anxiety over the translation of this idea of self-imposed austerity for the Sai movement. Sai officials said repeatedly that all Sai devotees may not be able to conform to sattvic ideals because they may not understand them or, more important, may not sympathize with them.

But the Flesh Is Weak: Truancy and the Pursuit of Desire

Whereas the Sai movement attempts to codify and clarify the problems of embodiment, encouraging everyone to engage sattvica, understanding of embodiment is built on a gap that contributes positively to ambiguity and fluidity of interpretation, but, at the same time, acts as a ticking time bomb for interpretation. Sometimes these translations can lead to snowballing problems, as in the few but significant cases of truancy at the ashram.

The Sai principles of abstention and austerity are at odds with the "life politics" (Giddens 1991) of dominant, capitalist consumer culture in which most people live their lives today. Despite the best efforts of the Seva Dal volunteers to keep the devotees on the straight and narrow path to devotion, I found that some devotees failed at the task of self-control. Devotees broke the rules, either sneaking away to eat or meeting their boyfriends and girlfriends after-hours in a café outside the ashram premises. Out of the twenty-three devotees I interviewed who were devotees of three years or less, sixteen confessed to breaking ashram rules in a recent stay. David, a ten-year devotee of Sai Baba and a CEO of a large manufacturing company in Kansas, confessed,

> When I first got to the ashram about eight years ago, I was shocked to see all these rules everywhere. I thought, "You can't do that to me, I'm an adult. I can do what I want." So I used to sneak out regularly to go get some chicken sandwiches in town or to see my girlfriend. I would bring flashlights with extra batteries for sneaking around at night and snacks that I couldn't get at the ashram, and I even brought American cigarettes, like Marlboro, so I could exchange them. Then I got sick real bad and I came back after that, and I said to myself; "Hell, what am I here for? Like what is it I want?" And once I got that far I began to see their point. All this control stuff is only to make you ask yourself, "What is real freedom, right?" and once I got that far I decided it wasn't worth the sneaking around and getting caught. The only person I was cheating on was me! So the next time I came, in 1997, I came clean. No cigarettes, no flashlights, no girlfriend, and I found that I had a great time. . . . It was a learning experience.[40]

Seth (forty-three) a Sai devotee for eight years recalled,

I don't mind the vegetarian food and the going to bed early, but that
first trip when they separated me from my girlfriend I got real upset.
When I tried to see her they said I had to get back to my room. I
fought with those Sai guys. Then the next night I tried to sneak out
after "lights out," you know, like when I was in camp, and I found
some guys sleeping in the corridor outside my room. I thought these
Indian gurus were all about having tantric sex and all that stuff! I
told Stephanie, my girlfriend at the time, "Lets get outta here," so we
caught a bus and we did. But now I realize that was a test for me, and
I failed it.

While devotees play truant, sneaking away from the ashram to engage
in illicit food or sexual intercourse, and there exists, no doubt, the thrill of
"getting away with it " and "not getting caught," but in their reflective discussions there was never a discussion of the thrill of truancy. The discussions
focused solely on the feeling of lingering guilt and of failure, which devotees explained in various ways. Lionel (thirty-four), a British devotee, ratio-
nalized his frequent nightly sojourns into Bangalore: "You know, when I
sneak away and have sex or eat something it makes me a better person. I
have that desire out of me. I need to be a sinner in order to be a saint!"
None of the devotees were proud of their actions of being able to get away
with it. Some of the younger devotees appeared to view their transgres-
sions as minor falls from grace, but falls nonetheless. Harry Chen (twenty-
eight), a Singaporean Chinese youth who was given a severe warning for
buying a pack of cigarettes and smoking them in his ashram room, smiled
and said; "I cheated." When asked what he meant, he elaborated, "You
know, like eating cake on a diet." The eating of cake is a particularly appropriate metaphor since it does not require an audience or participant;
it is about self-control.

While there is an "official" packing list that Sai devotees are given by
their Sai satsang group or temple before they set out for Puttaparthi,
devotees in the Boston satsang told me their "unofficial list" included
flashlights and batteries (for power outages), chocolate, especially Kit Kat
bars and M&Ms, in case the Indian food in the café disagreed with them.
They also packed power bars and packets of hot chocolate for late-night
snacking. Younger devotees told me in whispers that they packed con-
doms, lingerie, and their birth control devices for the quick trips into

Bangalore. Often devotees spent the night in Bangalore and returned to the ashram refreshed and rejuvenated for another round of austerities. Older devotees told me the hardest part was when they did not get "married quarters" and were forced into the gender segregated dormitories. Harry and Dawn, two sixty-something Sai devotees from Tucson, Arizona, told me:

> We bring flashlights (torches) to sneak around at night! We come to Puttaparthi for Baba's birthday every year and sometimes cannot get the married people's accommodation. After "lights out," Dawn has to go to the ladies dormitory and me to the men's dormitory. I'm used to talking to Dawn before bed, so I snuck out and went to her dormitory, but the Sai volunteers found out and they came and took me back. They were very polite about it, but they told me I was breaking the rules and it was not allowed on the ashram premises. Dawn has snuck out too—right, Honey?[41]

Seva Dal volunteers' duties include control of devotee's behavior when it is considered antisocial or goes against the code of conduct enforced at the ashram. The sattvic way is no longer merely an embedded philosophical concept of a conduit to the divine, but is translated into a therapeutic, postmodern, healthful moral ideal. In this worldview the satisfaction of desire leads to self-fulfillment (though momentary) and happiness. Sathya Sai devotees from other cultures come to the understanding of the sattvic with this open-ended spirit, changing the moral value of the original concept.

While the objective of the Nine Point Code of Conduct is to codify embodied behavior, making the sattvic ideal more inclusive and capable of including difference, in some cases it leads to an essentialization of "Eastern" and "Western" cultures as dichotomous. Mr. Sathya and other Seva Dal volunteers who do the job of the dharma police told me they thought that, of the various devotees, Americans and other Westerners are found most frequently breaking the rules of the ashram and are the most difficult to control. Mr. Shiva, who was in charge of the Sai volunteers when I visited the ashram on the night of June 23, 1999, said,

> Usually with Indians very little problem is there. Maybe some smoking, some nonveg (nonvegetarian) food items, but that is all. But, with foreigners, problems are too many. It is very difficult to control

them also. They do not understand when we say it is for your own good. For them no problem with sex, no problem with anything. So it is very difficult to explain to them. Only when Baba says, "this is not good," then only they listen. Before we never had the volunteers. We trusted too much. Also bad people are there in Puttaparthi town who help them in spite of knowing ashram rules.[42]

While we can dismiss devotees' fall from grace as a postmodern or new age phenomenon in which arbitrary legitimacy is accorded to "esoteric Eastern practices" (see Alter paper given on September 8, 2005), the Seva Dal volunteers understand it as a threefold misdemeanor; where the devotee is disobedient to the rules of the ashram, ignores Sai Baba's exhortations, and causes loss of self/soul (atman) that could prevent an individual from attaining spiritual liberation. For Mr. Shiva, as opposed to Harry, smoking a cigarette or drinking a beer was not only prohibited, it also put one's atman back on the road to perdition. When I mentioned to Mr. Shiva that it appeared to me that he thought only Westerners or the Western-educated seemed to break the rules, he said, "What to do, Madam?" followed by, "Saying no to them is very difficult. They are used to just doing what they like." But when I mentioned it to Shanti, she upbraided me for culturally stereotyping people:

No, why do you say that? Sometimes foreigners can be really god fearing. More than us Indians. See in America and all, it is all open. The girl will come home and say, "Mom, here is my boyfriend." Mom will have her own boyfriend, girlfriend *vagera, vagera* (variations). In India, children live with parents until marriage or in hostel. There maybe they learn to hide things and do because they know parents will not approve. I have seen Indians also eat nonveg, drink, and all. Only maybe they do not get caught or scolded so much. People are good and bad everywhere.[43]

This contestation of embodied morality brings to light a cultural translation "gap," where cultural dislocation occurs. Every fall from grace has nuance and meaning, allowing not only for an acceptance of desire but also for the pursuit of happiness as an acceptable and realizable goal. The optimization of desires between salvation and truancy is the problem of choice for devotees that rests on a market ethos and logic of alternate manufacture and satiation of desire.

Reconstructing Translation Through Embodiment

The Sai example suggests that new ways of being and knowing are rapidly entering the global network. But it is clear that in the transfer of the idea of sattvica and tapasya and their codification "subtle shifts in signification" (Alter 2005) occur.[44] The whole question of self realization becomes fraught with contradiction and paradox when the question of truancy rears its ugly head. It raises the analogous and important question of the satisfaction of desire and the value of happiness for the contemporary understanding of self, the optimization of this satisfaction, and, consequently, the problem of finding what is meaningful and legitimate in this world. This brings us back to the important question of the politics of interpretation and the politics of knowledge in this era of cultural globalization.

The politics of interpretation for the globalizing Sai movement is problematic, partly because of its tremendous success: interpretation in this case is built on a gap of understanding that enables ambiguity in the matrix of possible meanings, which in turn enables fresh interpretation. The fresh interpretations allow for the idea/object to have mobility across cultures and for people with different cultural perspectives to engage the idea/object. The gap of understanding acts as an interpretive bridge since it enables various interpretations from differing perspectives, and devotees from different cultures feel a sense of access and agency while making meaning. The mobility of the sattvica concept is built on this unstable bridge.

But the acts of truancy, though seen as reprehensible, illuminate the embodied code itself. It is clear that devotees from various cultures can follow identical behavioral processes with very different interpretations and rationalizations, some superficial and some not. Thus the gap, while it enables ambiguity and mobility, because of this very ambiguity also constructs the resistance. The process is iterative: as one builds meaning upon a gap of understanding, the silences and gaps yawn wider. So, while the concepts travel, they shift and are subsumed across and within contexts. While the Sai movement attempts greater and wider interpretation across cultures, encouraging a shift in the movement, the ideas can become incommensurable.

Discussing issues of embodiment, agency, and selfhood with Professor S. S. Sivakumar (sixty-two), a retired economist from Madras University who teaches economics at the Sathya Sai Institute of Higher Learning, was illuminating in terms of this dichotomous understanding of West and East that some Indian devotees (often themselves Westernized) engaged in. He said, "The point of the discipline is to get to a point of awareness that all this is an illusion . . . maya. The maya is what holds us back from attaining *atma gyana*. That maya—the illusion of power, of status, of all that Veblen talks about—that is the root of these people's problems." Stephen expanded on this idea of Professor Sivakumar': "For bhaktas, the external discipline is contained, controlled, and perhaps repressed; the internal self is truly 'individual' in the manner in which it functions to reach *moksha*. But in the West the illusion is around individuality around which a convincing rhetoric has been built." This understanding of an individual self and agency that Professor Sivakumar and Stephen articulate, I contend, is an expression of the East-West dichotomy, whereby devotees often conflate Westernization and its twin force of contemporary capitalism, focusing upon what they see as its evils, rampant consumerism, lack of self-control, war and violence, overt sexuality, nonvegetarianism, a hunger for economic dominance, and political hegemony (a compilation of the legacy of British colonial encounters in India and other parts of the postcolonial world and more recent encounters with Euro-American television programming), with globalization. Through these strategies of essentialization of East and West, the contemporary Sathya Sai movement is able to transcend its own boundaries. It performs a significant strategic inversion and collapsing maneuver simultaneously: while it is itself a product of globalization, it posits itself as the antidote to many of the problems that globalization and contemporary capitalism bring in their wake.

Because of, or perhaps despite, this inversion, the Sathya Sai movement continued to successfully gather devotees and to engage the concept of sattvica through the Nine Point Code of Conduct until 2003, when allegations of sexual abuse surfaced in the ashram bringing contested understandings of embodiment into sharp focus. To summarize, the Indic assumption of links between bodily control and self-betterment do not always translate effectively to radically different cultures since the goals may be presumed to be different. Embodied control is viewed no longer as a necessary conduit to the divine but as a healthful moral choice. The bodily tapasya of sattvic eating or celibacy, which removes impure desires from the body and calms the passions, in Indic thought, is loosely translated among Western communities and Indian diasporic communities to healthy living, also defined as a choice of postmodern lifestyle, wherein acceptance of the satisfaction of other desires through consumption is considered an equally valuable choice.

Conclusion: Re-envisioning the World of the Self and Remaking the Self in the World

Through shared themes and specific processes that enable cultural translation, the Sai movement attempts the universalization of the concept of the sattvic, derived from popular Hindu understandings of the links between the body (shariram) and the soul (atman). The establishment and spatialization of the Nine Point Code of Conduct combined with tacit understandings of the sattvic lifestyle codes enable an individual understanding of agency and control as well as an individualized relationship to divinity. The codification of the Sai cultural matrix into a series of regulatory principles, or patterns of knowledge, which are transferable, is the first step toward cultural translation. Sai codification and diffusion of these controls attempts to be inclusive of *différence* (Bourdieu 1991: 237), overturning the logic of this difference. Difference after all indicates that there is a symbolic classificatory system in place that enables inclusion of some and exclusion of others; a hierarchy based in dominance that Bourdieu suggests was the "deep structure" of subordination in everyday life. The Sai movement, by codifying sattvic controls, is making them accessible to everyone who wants to follow a sattvic lifestyle, in a sense democratizing the sattvic impulse. The publication of these elaborate embodied codes enables anyone to become a practitioner of a sattvic way of being and therefore a member of the Sai movement. The hope for the Sai organization, and presumably for Sai Baba himself, would be that these codified disciplines would become internalized by the devotees and by the movement to create a habitus of sattvic embodiment. But accompanying these new Sai spatio-embodied codes and devices is the concordant mapping of a moral geography, where discipline is seen as morally good and loss of control is bad, onto globalization.

Focusing on the Sai devotee's body as the site for several encounters and emotions leads devotees to read the body multivocally, as a text both in relation to the physical as well as the transcendent. I suggest that the Sai problematic of embodiment, agency, spirituality, and selfhood attempts to construct a new view of embodiment and asceticism in an era of globalization where assumptions of the "proper" role of desire and happiness are emergent, leading to unexpected contestation and dialogue, as devotees "work through" their culturally embedded assumptions about the body—yet another example of the creation of a matrix of possible meanings leading to a grammar of devotion. In this case the matrix of possible meanings includes some that contest the interpretations fostered by the Sai movement.

Secrecy lies at the very core of power.

—*Elias Canetti*, Crowds and Power

There is only one religion, the religion of love; there is only one language, the language of the heart; there is only one caste, the caste of humanity; there is only one God, who is omnipresent.

—*Sathya Sai Baba*

5   Secrecy, Ambiguity, Truth, and Power

The Global Sai Organization and the
Anti-Sai Network

Death and Scandal in the Sai Ashram

On the night of June 6, 1993, all published accounts are unanimous that four young men were found dead in Sai Baba's personal quarters at the ashram after midnight. The newspaper reports a Mr. Suresh Prabhu (thirty-five), a marine engineer; his elder brother, Vijay Prabhu (forty-five), head of the Sai Vocational Training Center in the ashram; N. Jaganathan (thirty-four), the ashram stationary supplier; and E. K. Suresh Kumar (twenty-three), a recent graduate of the Sathya Sai Institute of Higher Learning, entered Sathya Sai Baba's inner chambers, and attacked four devotees they found there. They were N. Radhakrishna, Sathya Sai Baba's personal secretary; Sai Kumar Mahajan; Anil Paitley (sometimes spelled "Patley"); and Vishnu Bhatt. Venkat (thirty-five), a former student at the Sathya Sai Institute of Higher Studies in Whitefield, told me that students always referred to the deaths as "the June incident." He said that students were woken abruptly that morning and hurried into the hall of the school where they were told by the warden of the hostel that "an attempt has been made on Swami's life by some bad people." According to Venkat, they received no other information for many days and were banned from discussing the incident within the school.

But, according to journalists' reports, the four assailants had apparently concealed knives in their bedding, and at some point in the night they decided to enter Sathya Sai Baba's personal rooms. They stabbed N. Radhakrishna in a nearby room, as well as Sai Kumar Mahajan, and then ran to an inner room and bolted themselves in. Radhakrishna died and Mahajan survived. Sathya Sai Baba, awakened by Mahajan's screams, activated an electronic alarm system. Immediately, floodlights came on, and the ashram was ringed by about one hundred concerned devotees and members of the Seva Dal carrying sticks and other weapons. The police arrived quickly, having been alerted either by Sai Baba's brother and manager, Mr. Janakiramaih, or by the noise, as claimed by Police Inspector K. N. Gangadhara Reddy. They stormed the inner room where the assailants were holed up;[1] in the scuffle that followed, they allegedly shot the assailants dead.[2]

The *Week*, a popular Indian news magazine, was among the first to run a story about the deaths at the ashram and to speculate about the cause.[3] The article, highlighted in a box written by veteran journalist M. D. Riti, was titled "A Plethora of Possibilities," and it evaluated possible reasons for the deaths. It stated that within the SSSO and the SCT the trustees had formed factions: "one faction was led by Baba's younger brother Janakiramaih, and the other was led by Colonel Joga Rao and Mr. Narayan, the Trust Secretary."[4] The *Week* speculated about the causes of the internal fighting, but concluded that all was conjecture, since the ashram was known to be tightlipped. A second allegation made focused on monetary embezzling and lack of accountability; they stated that officials in the Sai organization had been pilfering money from the Vocational Training Center, and N. Radhakrishna had found out about it and threatened to tell Sai Baba. A third allegation, which was never explicitly detailed, suggested that the dead men were attempting to threaten, or perhaps even murder, Sathya Sai Baba, because he had "sexually healed" them when they were students in the educational institution run by the Sai organization. Sai officials ignored all allegations. Indeed, in the weeks following the deaths, no statement came from Sai Baba or the SSSO. But after the shooting, the *Hindu*, a reputable Indian newspaper, reported, "When press persons met Mr. Indulal Shah, chief functionary of the Sri Sathya Sai World Trust, he said, 'the matter is purely internal and we do not wish to have any law enforcement agency investigating into it.'"[5] Despite Mr. Shah's hopes of confidentiality, the Andhra Pradesh state police investigated, but they have never issued a public report about the incident.

The rumors of "sexual healing" that were linked to the deaths lingered and became pervasive. In 1998 former devotees Dave and Faye Bailey released an Internet-based series of accusations, titled "The Findings," in which they claimed to have spoken with several youth, both Indian and non-Indian, who admitted to being sexually healed by Sai Baba. By 1999 the sexual healing issue was inflated through the informal social network of the anti-Sai movement as they made public, online, several instances of supposed sexual healing accompanied by genital oiling, massage, and other sexual acts they claimed Sathya Sai Baba had engaged in with certain disaffected youth. A significant problem (though it was never directly discussed or indeed alluded to in any conversation) was that they were homosexual contacts, and some were allegedly pedophiliac as well. M. D. Riti's scandal-filled report claimed that the deaths occurred because of jealousy among the young men whom Sai Baba favored, with Suresh Kumar angry since Radhakrishnan supplanted him in Sai Baba's affections.[6] These allegations, while serious, have never been proven, but the debate over them between Sai devotees and the anti-Sai network in real and virtual forums is severe, ongoing, and vituperative and involves many characters.

The active anti-Sai network of former devotees that has ballooned surrounding this issue has demanded "the truth" and "justice" for the "victims." They have repeatedly stated that the SSSO and Sathya Sai Baba have been "covering up" and "hiding" the truth. Their activism has resulted in a series of newspaper exposés in the *Telegraph* and *India Today* and a few documentaries by the BBC and other European news organizations. The BBC documentary, titled *The Secret Swami*, called Sathya Sai Baba a pedophile, angering devotees worldwide.[7] It is clear from the many postings on this issue that varied understandings of secrecy and concealment lie at the core of the cultural difference between the SSSO and the anti-Sai network. While I am not interested in the scandal per se, it is useful as an ethnographic moment of crisis to consider the silences, the gaps, and the erasures that occurred as possible keys to unlocking the structure of the Sai global organization and the dialogic understandings and imperatives of transparency and privacy. Studies that focus on power tend to highlight the incommensurability of the functioning of traditional organizations' secrecy and privacy for the globalizing world. Sai devotees and former devotees blur distinctions between truth and concealment to prove transparency counterproductive, and they politicize the condition of transparency, thereby questioning its assumed link with globalization.

Scandal, Empire, and the Problem of Secrecy

Up until this point this book has focused on consensus building through modes of communication—narratives, rhetorics, tactics, and
strategies—to create a community of devotees. But, in examining the Sai
scandal, we unearth a series of new issues that potentially act as roadblocks on the path of cultural translation. According to ethnohistorian
Nicholas Dirks, who studied the British mercantile expansion into India,
scandal is the "crucible in which both imperial and capitalist expansion
was forged" (2006:8). This definition still seems to hold good some four
centuries after the British East India Company came to India. Scandal is a
typical "social drama" in which "a limited area of transparency in the otherwise opaque surface of uneventful social life" emerges (Turner 1967:93,
1962a, 1964). Empires and scandals are linked dialectically as the expansion impulse of empire feeds the secrecy that leads to scandal.

The Sai religious movement can be construed as a global religious
empire. It is brittle at the nodes where intercultural congress occurs, for
the node is where two or more moral systems (often contestatory) meet.
Kathleen Wilson focuses on these nodes, the frontiers of empire. She
states, "Empire . . . (is) in a very real sense the frontier . . . the place where
under the pressure of contact and exchange boundaries . . . were blurred,
dissolved or rendered impossible to uphold" (Wilson, quoted in Dirks
2006:26). These points of contact are the cultural boundaries where several moral perspectives, often in conflict, congregate and create a problematic seam of cultural translation. Applying Michael Herzfeld's significant concept of "cultural intimacy," we can begin to unearth the way
in which Sai subjects negotiate their loyalties at the nexus of conflicting
supranational, national, and local sovereignties and identities. Herzfeld
defines cultural intimacy as "the recognition of those aspects of a cultural identity that are considered a source of external embarrassment but
that nevertheless provide insiders with their assurance of common soci-
ality, the familiarity with the bases of power that may at one moment assure the disenfranchised a degree of creative irreverence and at the next
moment reinforce the effectiveness of intimidation" (1997:3). It seems
that all parties, Sai and anti-Sai alike, were working within frameworks
of cultural intimacy that demanded keeping domestic issues secret.
These conflicting spheres of cultural intimacy were sources of the conflicting demands of loyalties. The challenges brought by the interaction

of the local, national, and transnational cultural sovereignties erupted in this event, creating problems in all three spheres.

I found I was waging an uphill battle when I tried to discuss the scandal and the embedded issue of secrecy. When I raised the issue, I invariably drew a disturbed silence from the devotees.[8] One devotee said: "It is very sad. All this fighting . . . I will be silent." A Sai official from the Kuala Lumpur center asked me brusquely, "Why are you after all this dirt?" Others merely dropped me as a friend. Robert Priddy, an ex-academic, researcher, writer, and very well-known ex-devotee, has written a great deal about the organization, both positively, from his years as a devotee, and then increasingly negatively as he lost faith in Sathya Sai Baba: "it is virtually impossible for outsiders (nonmembers) to study it (the SSSO), and even a well-informed insider is usually restricted to the information allowed to him on a regionally compartmentalized basis." Priddy's quote points to a double difficulty in studying secrets that anthropologists have dealt with repeatedly. One issue is epistemological, and one ethical. How does one access secret knowledge and, if one does, what are the ethics surrounding the secret (Urban 1998)? How can one know an organization that is silent and unseen? And, if one can somehow become an insider, how can one say anything about the organization of which one is a part? Organizations such as the SSSO, comprised of the Sai Central Trust (SCT) and the Sai World Trust (SWT), bring to light problems that are inherent in any attempt to understand another: how does one "know" another?

This problem weaves through any study of globalization and, reflexively, through the anthropological enterprise as well.[9] The problem of secrecy and/or encoded knowledge is one of the everyday problems that people encounter in cross-cultural congress: "the strategies of ellipses, concealment and partial discourse determine ethnographers' relations as much as they do the transmission of stories between generations" (Clifford and Marcus 1986:8). I do not see a way out of this "double bind of secrecy" (Urban 1998:212), but, like Urban, I try to balance both the devotees' and non-devotees' perspectives in my work, at the same time remaining critical of both.

On February 27, 2001, the *Vancouver Sun* reported that the "sex scandal" (as they called it much to the devotees' annoyance) was "rapidly unveiled on various Internet sites. . . . Sai Baba has told his adherents not to sign onto the worldwide web." We are aware that employing methods of silence, of concealment, and of obfuscation have long been considered significant elements of a vigorous political life. F. G. Bailey (1996) and Sissela Bok (1978) have argued that the use of dissembling plays a significant role in the exercise of institutional power and is contingent upon the institutions' understandings of the nature of truth, but neither Bailey nor Bok see their portfolio as necessarily suggesting solutions.

When an organization's institutional life is constructed around the habit of silence as preservation, truth management is not considered deceitful. Rather, as Glenn Petersen points out (1993:334–352) in his study of the politics of concealment among the people of Pohnpei in the Caroline Islands, it turns into "something of a virtue." The habit of concealment becomes a push for status among officials within the organization and serves their interests. When nothing is known with certainty (because of strategies of silence), then it is assumed that everything is ambiguous, and, in the case of a dispute, the possibility of power is retained in a few hands. When I talked about concealment with Mr. Murthy (sixty-eight), an official in the movement, he seemed annoyed:

> You keep saying we are hiding things? Why only us? When global corporations, American companies, hide things, then it is "privacy." They patent everything and protect it and keep so many secrets. Even they do not know what their government does. Like that with Britain also (this was during the beginning of the U.S.-led "war on terror"). When they are told, they look shocked! But, if we don't vomit out everything when they ask us, then we are accused of being secretive. Why? Why should we?

Mr. Iyer (seventy-eight), another official, echoed Mr. Murthy:

> We are being told we must be open, our accounts must be open to audit, our organization must be open to criticism, our belief must be open to change. We have always been open. That is why so many people of different religions come together here to Bhagawan. But now this new culture . . . this Western culture that these MNCs [multinational corporations] bring. They think they are the new *ramrajya* [leadership)] and they lecture to us about values! Did you know that they protect themselves first? . . . what about their intellectual property rights? Engineers who work in India do not get the patent for their hard work. The MNCs get it. This is also secrecy, no? They talk about openness but they practice secrecy . . . only they call it by a

good name, Privacy! So when it is for them, it is privacy, when it is us, then it is secrecy? I tell you, we have all learned to tell lies nicely because of modern business.

Mr. Murthy's and Mr. Iyer's statements point to three significant issues in the globalization of any religious institution with middle-class professional devotees: 1. devotees' awareness of and critique of worldwide structures of power, 2. their awareness of the politicization of transparency, and 3. the importance of accountability within the organization as the basis of public trust. I will discuss the complexities surrounding all three issues in this chapter.

Organizations that operate on a global scale feel the need to present themselves as transparent and accessible; while at the same time, they engage legal and other strategies to protect themselves and their assets. Clearly, the abstract problem is the constructed link between trust and transparency and its understanding as essential to global organizations. I found that devotees politicize this argument by reifying the categories of Indic and Western culture as dialogic so as to lay the foundation for a construction of transparency as an Orientalist and hegemonic project. Many scholars studying the Sai movement tend to err on one side or another. Feike suggests that her discussion of the Sai movement in the United States is premised on the ethnocentric perspective of the dominant society (2007:90), and she parses the words *avatar* and *charlatan* (both used to describe Sai Baba) and details how her family felt that her online study of Sai Baba was "opening herself up to the devil," "evil," and the "demonic"(2007:102–103), leading her to conclude that the Internet is a stage "for the social production of culture" where "cyber-performance" is shaped by the "poetics of sacred globalization" (2007:104).

Secrecy Studies, Globalization, and Transparency

Secrecy has been traditionally understood in three ways. In Marxist terms it is a means of social control (Foucault 1997), in Freudian analysis it is seen as related to sexuality and ritual process (Ottenberg 1984), and semiotically it is a form of communication and narration (Bellman 1984). All three approaches are rooted in the Western post-Enlightenment spirit of inquiry and transparency that renders anything secret untrustworthy. Secrecy is seen in the postmodern era as covering up, something that is unsavory, usually a crime or misdemeanor. This allows Mr. Murthy and Mr. Iyer to bring the valid charges of Western hegemony and Orientalism. For sociologist Georg Simmel, secrecy is a sociological form that stands above its contents.[10] That is, secrecy, as Hugh Urban argues, is not about *what is* secret, but simply the fact that something *is secret*. Simmel's analysis of secrecy exalts mutual non-knowledge where relations are based on concealment: "Relationships being what they are, they presuppose a certain ignorance and a measure of mutual concealment even though this measure varies immensely to be sure" (1950:315). Concealment, for Simmel, was merely a part of, but an important part of, mutual knowledge of the communications between members of society.

But for Simmel the attractiveness of the secret was generated by *the act* of concealment that made secret knowledge desirable. Secrecy, he argued, produced an "enlargement of life" and offered the possibility of a second world alongside the "manifest world" (1950:312, 330). The point of secrecy is that it gives value to what would otherwise be thought of as valueless: information, acts, behaviors. T. M. Luhrmann, whose pathbreaking study of contemporary magic and the secret witchcraft societies in England I draw from heavily, explains that secrecy is about control of the flow of information: "it is about the individual possession of knowledge that others do not have." Secrecy elevates the value of the thing concealed: "That which is hidden grows more powerful and more desirable" (1989:161). Secrets cannot be told easily. In Indic, primarily Hindu, myths, animals, people, demigods, and gods often suffer severe penalties for telling secrets at improper times (Doniger 1986).

The literature on secrecy has focused almost exclusively on its role in esoteric and ritual contexts (Bellman 1984; Urban 1998, 2003b; Ottenberg 1984),[11] focusing on worship and the radicalization of ritual contexts. I will refer to this literature on esotericism later; for now I am interested in the ways that secrecy applies to the nonesoteric crisis of the scandal. Here I draw on Bellman's comprehensive study of secrecy in Poro initiation rites. She argues that secrecy is also endemic in nonesoteric contexts—evidenced through metaphorical speech, talking in a roundabout way, avoidance of topics, and shifting conversational styles—in spite of everyone knowing the "facts" of the case (see also Piot 1993:353)—to constitute new social contexts.[12] I suggest that a strategic institutionalization of secret discourse permeates the Sai movement.

An Empire Without an Army: The Inception and Growth of the International Sathya Sai Seva Organization

The Sathya Sai Seva Organization is a deep, wide, and complex organization with its tentacles in all parts of the Sai ashram and the Sai centers. Through service and spiritual practice, the SSSO aims, in its own words, "to lead people to awareness of their own divinity through the word of Sathya Sai Baba." Potential devotees come in contact with the organization from the moment they step into a Sai temple or satsang group in any part of the world. The SSSO and its various arms organize and control the Sai devotional groups in all countries. Charters and decisions are maintained strictly within the confines of the upper level of the organization. Few pamphlets, leaflets, or memos are available to anyone outside the officers' circle. Therefore access to information about the organization is limited and circumscribed.

Devotees rarely discuss the SSSO except when it intersects with their activities on an everyday level, but they are aware of its presence both at the Sai ashram in Puttaparthi and in the overseas centers. All texts and images used by the Sai movement have at their head the emblem and sayings of the Sathya Sai organization, but many devotees know little about the SSSO, since they have no reason to interact with it except at its very lowest levels. When it began, the SSSO was primarily a grassroots devotional organization consisting of local chapters (*samhiti*; see Srinivas 2008:129–135). The samhiti are local bodies of devotees in villages, small towns, and cities. Any devotee group that has nine regular members can apply to become an official samhiti; any such group with less than nine members is called a *bhajan mandali*.[13] The samhiti are responsible for organizing all of Sathya Sai Baba's charity endeavors, motivate his devotees at the ground level, and keep track of the local financial transactions.

The first samhiti was registered in Bombay (now Mumbai) in 1965. Its original function was to act as a spiritual center where devotees came together for worship and the singing of bhajans, but it grew to undertake seva—educational, charitable, and spiritual services—for the benefit of the community. Mr. Iyer (seventy-eight) said:

Initially you know it all started as bhajan groups and mostly in south only [South India]—Madras, Bangalore, Mysore—some people came from Bombay maybe because of Shirdi. Only after 1960, as I know, that there was any sort of organization. It is all Swami's *daya* [mercy], you know. Then, after 1978 or so, more foreigners started coming, from USA, London, Europe, all that. They came looking for peace. Bhagawan called them. There is no Sathya Sai organization here, there, or anywhere without His will.[14]

As Mr. Iyer indicated, through the 1970s and 1980s, the SSSO grew rapidly to cope with the rapidly increasing devotees, adding extra samhiti as the need arose.

In terms of numbers alone, the growth has been significant. By 1988, 3,864 Sai samhitis were registered; and in 2002 there were approximately 8,447. From 1988 to 2002, across India, an average increase of 306 centers was registered each year.[15] In most states in India there was an increase in growth of bhajan mandalis and samhitis between 1988 and 2002. According to the SSSO, the total number of members in 2002 in India was 461,198, having increased by over 50,000 members since 2000. However, these numbers are all released by the SSSO and are therefore unverifiable.[16]

Still it is clear that the devotional base had expanded enormously. Through word-of-mouth advertising the number of foreign devotees at Puttaparthi increased steadily during the 1960s. Notables included Dr. Sam Sandweiss, a California psychoanalyst, Elsie and Walter Cowan of Tustin, California, who began the Sathya Sai Society and Bookstore, Dr. John Hislop and his wife Victoria, who lived in Mexico, Phyllis Krystal and her husband Sidney, a prominent Los Angeles attorney.,Arnold Schulman, an American playwright, and Dr. Lim and Dr. Yu and other Chinese devotees from Singapore, and others from England and Australia who also made the trek to Puttaparthi. Many later published accounts of these early years, which later became part of the Sai canon,[17] and introduced Sai Baba to many potential followers in the West who were looking for their own spiritual gurus during the counterculture movements of the late 1960s and 1970s. For example, both Arnold Schulman and Howard Murphet were the first "Western" writers to publish books in English about Sai Baba as early as 1971, rapidly followed by John Hislop and Sam Sandweiss. This tradition of educated devotees, who experience a life-transforming moment with Sai Baba and write about it, and these publications in turn being adopted as canonical literature that enables future proselytization, became a hallmark of the Sai movement from this point on.

In 1967 the first overseas Sai center was established in Sri Lanka, followed in 1968 by one in Tustin, California in a bookstore started by the Cowans.[18] Soon the SSSO authorized centers in other parts of the United States (Srinivas 2008:136). Most centers were located in areas with high concentrations of devotees: capital cities or areas of economic importance that had a cosmopolitan culture and a potential or existing Sai devotee base.

The rules for starting a center were identical to those for starting a samhiti in India. They needed at least nine members who had to engage themselves in the three wings of the organization: spiritual, educational, and service. If they had less than nine devotees engaged in all three wings or only engaged in two of the three wings, they called themselves a "group." Alexandra Kent notes that in Malaysia the movement began with Indian devotees who registered the group of committed urban elite Indians and Sinhala Tamils as the Sri Sathya Sai Central Council of Malaysia in 1984 (2005:71).

The Caribbean, with its large diasporic Indian population, soon had a Sai center in Trinidad; another was created in Durban, South Africa. Cen-

FIGURE 5.1. The exterior of the Sathya Sai Center, Singapore. *Photo courtesy Ravi Parthasarathy*

FIGURE 5.2. Meditation Hall, Sathya Sai Center, Singapore; note the photograph of Sai Baba and the awaiting throne. *Photo courtesy Ravi Parthasarathy*

ters were created in Australia, Singapore, and elsewhere in the Far East. Others opened in Italy (1974), the United Kingdom (1969), South Africa (1973), and Australia (1978), as well as in Berlin (1977), Rio de Janeiro (1987), and St. Petersburg (1992).[19] By 1985 there were 420 Sai Baba centers worldwide, including those in India. The United States had over 100 centers and Malaysia had 78. Of the 72 in Europe, the United Kingdom had the most at 45. South Africa had 25, and there were 27 in parts of Africa (Rao 1995:252–255; Srinivas 2008:136–138).

Thus, by 1970, in response to this sudden global swell, the SSSO had formalized its organizational structure into a global template. In what Weber (1968 [1947]) would classify as a move from a charismatic movement to a rational organization, the non-Indian devotees were called overseas devotees. In 1988 the two main devotee groups were categorized as *Indian* and *Global,* terms that have remained part of the organizational nomenclature.

From the beginning, SSSO's activities were divided into three wings—spiritual, service, and educational—and devotee groups and centers all over the world were reconstituted based on this tripartite structure. The Spiritual Wing conducted activities including bhajans (devotional singing), nagarsankirtan (singing while parading through the city), bhajan training, and sadhana (meditation) camps. Those in the Service Wing made hospital visits, set up medical camps, and performed service in homeless shelters and other charitable organizations. And the Educational Wing conducted the nine-year Bal Vikas program for children and implemented the Education in Human Values (known as EHV) program in schools around India.

The growth of the SSSO was marked by a series of conferences and meetings during which reorganization measures were announced.[20] The first all-India conference of the SSSO was held in Madras in 1967. At this meeting, the governing ideology of the movement was instituted in the form of a charter, although surviving devotees disagree about the origin of the charter. While most believe it came as a directive from Sathya Sai Baba himself, some note that Mr. Indulal Shah, a very powerful devotee, drafted much of it. During the 1967 All-India Conference of Sai devotees held at Puttaparthi, the charter governing the organization first made its appearance as a pamphlet, titled *Rules and Regulations*, published by the SSSO. Only one devotee I met had an original copy of this charter.

The original charter designated two arms of the organization: the Sathya Sai Seva Organization (SSSO), to handle the institution and devotee's needs, and the Sathya Sai Trust (SST) to handle finances. The charter stated that the organization was to establish *santana dharma* (eternal righteousness) and did not recognize any separation based on race, religion, color, caste, or creed. It described three major missions. The first was to help the individual become aware of Sai Baba's divinity and to translate into the everyday his love and divine perfection in order to fill the individual's life with harmony, joy, and grace. The second was to help all humanity live by the principles of *sathya* (truth), *dharma* (righteousness), *prema* (love), *shanti* (peace), and *ahimsa* (nonviolence). And the third was to make devotees adhere sincerely to the religions of their forebears, and, therefore, proselytizing was neither possible nor indeed necessary.

Formally speaking, all devotees are supposed to conform to this organizational charter. The Nine Point Code of Conduct that devotees should live by was also tacked onto the charter by Mr. Indulal Shah, said to aid in being a good Sai devotee/citizen. In fact, later versions of the charter elevated the code of conduct to central prominence. They stated that noncompliance with the code of conduct was grounds for dismissal:

Every member of the Organization must undertake *Sadhana* (spiritual discipline) as an integral part of his daily life and abide by the

Code of Conduct. *Non-observance or violation of the Code of Conduct shall disqualify a member from holding any office or from being an active member in the Organization.* The appropriate authority in the Organization may remove any such member from office and declare him disqualified to hold such office or to be an active member of the Organization without assigning any reason.

The SSSO claims that it is still run by the original charter of 1965. According to the official Web site of the SSSO, the contemporary organization is

a service organization with a spiritual core and base, founded under the guidance and inspiration of Bhagawan Sri Sathya Sai Baba, for the benefit of mankind, regardless of differences of religion, race, nationality, caste, creed or sect. The most important objective of the Organization is to awaken in man the Consciousness of the Divinity in him and to encourage him to foster it, so that he could blossom into an earnest seeker. . . . The most significant aspect of the Sai Organization is the voluntary participation of all its members irrespective of caste, color or creed. Nowhere in the history of the world has an Avatar established such an organization in His own lifetime. It is not only established but has taken roots in 137 countries and has acquired global dimensions. It is a unique organization, which has no membership fees and is governed by an unregistered charter for the conduct of its affairs. Collectively, the Sai Organizations represent the largest selfless, totally voluntary Service Corporation ever in the history of human race.

But in 1990 Sai Baba withdrew the old charter, which gave him the sole right to appoint the coordinators in every country, and instituted the current charter, which may be the second or third charter, depending upon whom one asks. In the current charter the hierarchy of Sathya Sai leadership is largely democratic; however, Sathya Sai Baba appoints the highest officials, those he works with most closely, and can also appoint others. Former devotees argue that Sai Baba's handpicking of his closest "ministers" is fundamentally undemocratic.

The existence of the original charter and the introduction of a new one is the source of much rumor and dispute. Many devotees claim that the old charter does not exist and others claim that the new one does not. Some

FIGURE 5.3. The exterior of the Sathya Sai Center, Tustin, California. *Photo courtesy Tulasi Srinivas*

FIGURE 5.4. Meditation Hall, Sathya Sai Center, Tustin, California. *Photo courtesy Tulasi Srinivas*

claim that one overrides the other. The ambiguity regarding the existence and power of the charter adds to the inherent confusion over power sharing within the hierarchy. Regardless of the date and disputed origin of the charter, devotees agree that, after its institution, the SSSO quickly developed its strengths. In 1969 the Seva Dal was instituted along with the Mahila Vibagh (said to be the idea of Sai Baba himself) for women's activities, and Bal Vihar (later Vikas) for children's spiritual education. In 1972 the Sri Sathya Sai Central Trust was instituted to develop and maintain the various Sai properties. In 1975 a World Council of Sri Sathya Sai Organizations was formed in Mumbai.

Contexts and Conflicts: Shifts, Reorganization, and Change in the SSSO

By the early 1990s, significant divergences in opinion between the overseas division and the Indian SSSO officers had arisen. One problem repeatedly mentioned by overseas SSSO officers is that from its inception until 1980, the SSSO appears to have been run as an extended family with expanding circles of trust (Kolenda 1978).[21] Many officials referred to this model as the ideal organizational system: "We are like a *parivar* (family)," "we take care of everyone like one big *khaandan* (family)," "Swami is like a mother and father and we are like his children." This familial system worked well for the organization in India up to a point. But it began to create divisions between the devotees once the movement expanded beyond the diaspora. Non-Indians objected to the family system of management as "archaic and undemocratic," leading to "favoritism and lack of accountability."[22] Devotees wanted a more democratic system and pushed for elected officers rather than those picked by Sathya Sai Baba.

This reorganization led to a great deal of tension between the devotees as some felt the older system was superior and others felt the familial model was merely a way for a few devotees to garner and maintain power. The division was seen by devotees as along Western/non-Western lines (though, in reality, it was split more along generational lines). As we have seen previously, these established cultural fault lines were particularly sensitive for Sai devotees, so any conflict tended to be read as falling along these a priori fault lines. For example, Saianand (forty-eight), an officer from the Mumbai cadre, said, "I ask you why we should have changed? I understand that we should help everyone achieve spirituality, like Swami says. I am also for democracy, but who are they (Western devotees) to ask? And everything we (non-Western devotees) change to accommodate them. But still, see, are they happy? No. Still they ask for more and more."[23] She-fali (thirty-seven) said: "Always we have to accommodate them (Western devotees). If they think it is bad, then we must agree. Why can't they ad-just to our standards for once?" This reification of Western/non-Western, primarily Indian positions often led to furious arguments between friends. Stephen, from London, argued that it was not a question of cultural adjust-ment, but rather of instituting "proper" procedures so that the organiza-tion could function efficiently (by which he seemed to imply that it did not in its current state). Leela, who overheard him, was insulted by what she interpreted to be Stephen's sweeping Orientalist and patronizing state-ment. She responded with a postcolonial critique: "What do you mean? That until *goralog* (white people) came to India nothing was happening here, or what? I don't understand why always they think we have problems that they must solve. They come here looking for our *samskruthi* (culture), our wealth, our wisdom, and then they tell us that we are stupid and we must change. . . . That is so arrogant, no?" The politicized categories were so established as naturally oppositional that devotees and former devotees used them as such and began to seek "evidence" for these "cultural fail-ings" or, alternatively, to use this cultural fault line as "evidence" for insti-tutional problems. Robert Priddy, a notable former devotee and ex-officer in the European SSSO, criticized the SSSO familial model as part of the wider culture of "Indian life":

> The complete disregard of modern "stakeholder" ideas in the SSSO (indeed, the direct opposition to them) involving the abject worship of gurus as infallible is also a pattern set on the basis of prevailing social conditions throughout India. A culture of top-down high-handedness, mismanagement and rich opportunities for control, corruption, and cover-up, *as seen with Western eyes.* Much of the loose ideological back-ing for this "model" is actually found in SSB's predilection for the culture of ancient, feudal India and its forms of social organization, which relied heavily on spiritual purity in teachers and pupils. Even those having much insight or skill are required to do what they are told, though they may have greater experience than their boss.[24]

Around 1996, in response to the criticism of the family model, the SSSO attempted to create a new model of governance based on a global corpo-

rate model, but the Western/non-Western dichotomy had not been resolved analytically and dogged the new infrastructure.

The Indian SSSO stepped in as the unofficial head of the worldwide
organization, and it soon held considerable power over the entire movement. Non-Indian devotees felt marginalized. These reorganizations of
the institutional apparatus achieved the direct opposite of what was intended. Rather than coordinating the various arms of the institution,
resolving culturally based disputes through dialogue, and removing potential cause for misunderstanding, it appears that the upper echelons
of the SSSO emphasized existing divisions and polarized the various subgroups within the organization so they began to act as competing factions
for the favor of Sathya Sai Baba.

The SSSO then further heightened these cultural differences by articulating and reifying the separation of Indian and non-Indian devotees
through their charter. They divided the original charter into two charters;
one for the "Indian" division and one for the "overseas" division. For the
Indian division, the handbook is titled, "Rules and Regulations for Sri
Sathya Sai Seva Organisations, India" and was published soon after the
Sixth World Conference in 1995. The brochure for the overseas division is
titled, "Charter of the Sathya Sai Organization and Rules and Regulations
(for Overseas Countries)." Together, these two handbooks supposedly outline the structure of the contemporary Sai organization, but ideologically
they add to the solidifying of cultural boundaries. Pragmatically, the confusion over which charter or directive was in operation at any given time
was still in evidence in 2006. Devotees always claimed that they knew
which charter or set of rules was in use, but when I brought people together and asked them, they often contradicted one another and quoted
different rule books. Former devotees claimed that a conspiracy existed
to garner all power in certain (primarily Indian) hands, and that the
reorganization of the charters was merely to obfuscate the real (though
informal) lines of control.

Since the scandal in the ashram, there is a strong impulse toward
reorganization, which has found its way down the levels of the organization, with conflicts breaking out over "proper procedure" when participants cannot agree, pointing to a polarization that seemed to accompany
increased globalization. Unfortunately, in several cases (Tokyo and Wimbledon are examples), the contestation has led to irrevocable splits between rival Sai factions, which then set up rival new centers. In talking to
Japanese Sathya Sai devotees, I deduced that just such a split had occurred in the Tokyo Sathya Sai organization, though nobody told me why

the spilt occurred. The original Sathya Sai center in Tokyo is in the sub-urban neighborhood of Higashiyama, in the Meguro-Ku ward of Tokyo. But the new one, I discovered, is in the trendy downtown neighborhood of Roppongi. When I asked devotees of the Roppongi center about the reason for the split, they were more forthcoming than others, yet the reasons were unclear. "We would like all of us Japanese Sai devotees to be one," said Mrs. Suri (forty-six), an Indian expatriate, "but it is not possible. There are too much politics." Mrs. Michiko (thirty-three) said, in a soft voice, "We do not want to fight, but Bhagawan gave us permission for this new center, and so we take it and build this building." The Web site devoted to the Roppongi center states: "We never forget that we need the unity in order to attain the great goal of unifying with the God. . . . We welcome all devotees from India, Europe, Asia and all over the world. We plan to set aside one day of the week . . . for the use of foreign devo-tees when foreign participants reach sufficient number. . . . We sincerely hope that we could recognize the core or the true nature of all these are the same while respecting the differences."[25] The Tokyo spilt and the se-crecy that surrounds it is a forerunner of many divisions within the orga-nization. Splits have occurred repeatedly within the movement, pointing to the existence of subgroups and contestatory factions. Each group uses its closeness to Sai Baba, its esoteric knowledge, and its patrimonial con-nections within the organization to stress its moral dominance, which it sees as justifiable. The ethos of secrecy taken for granted in these groups underlies the dialectic of contestation and consensus between various parts of the organization.

The Contemporary Structure of the SSSO

The contemporary SSSO is a pyramid organization, with Sathya Sai Baba as its titular head. Directly below Sathya Sai Baba is the interna-tional coordinator and below him are the central coordinators (one for each of the five world zones, of which two are the overall authorities in each hemisphere, east and west). Each central coordinator has under him several national coordinators who represent the various nations under his region. The national coordinators, also called national chairmen, in each country oversee the work of centre presidents, group leaders, volun-tary worker members (sometimes called active workers), and aspirant members. They are usually all men.

Uncovering the charters and the various versions of official structuring documents and then unpacking the language of red tape within each one, I understood that every country with ten or more centers has a central council. Those with between three and ten centers have a coordinating committee. Some devotees stated that the central council or the coordinating committee selects the heads of every Sai center within their jurisdiction and they grant future Sai centers and groups affiliation to the SSSO, indicating that Sai Baba's influence reaches down to the centers. Other devotees claimed that all officials up to the national level were elected democratically.

What is clearer is the geographical divisions of devotion. Each center is included within a region, and regions fall into five zones (see appendix). The zones are not based on geography but consist of regions in different locations. For example, zone 1 includes the eastern and western United States (regions 1 and 2), Southern Europe (region 3), Canada (region 4), and the West Indies (region 5). India had 8,447 centers in 2002. Europe followed with 569 centers, Central and South America with 380, Africa with 282, North America with 266, and Austrolasia with 204. Japan has only 20, although the Japanese devotional base, I was told, was growing rapidly. In the Middle East there are 7 centers and groups. In Africa, South Africa leads with 144 centers and groups, and Mauritius follows closely with 127 (corroborated by S.Srinivas 2008:137–138).The largest and most active country in the SSSO is India, and the all-India chairman now appears to be of the same rank as the international chairman. The international chairman is believed by the devotees to act on the directives of Sai Baba himself. How much decision making Sai Baba himself undertakes is debatable.

After the crisis, on April 27, 2003, a new overseeing body called the Prasanthi Council was established. The official announcement published in the Sai newsletter read: "The Council will be responsible for the formulation of plans and agendas, policies, guidelines, and decisions that constitute the governance of the Sai Organization outside of India. In addition to the above, the Council will be a resource for intervention in difficult circumstances where the sanctity of the Divine Name or the welfare of the Sai Organization can be affected."[26] While the Prasanthi Council was convened to prevent future problems, many devotees are still unclear about its function, as it adds to the list of overlapping Sai organizational bodies and charters. Devotees whisper that the Prasanthi Council is the final overseeing body, mandated by Sai Baba to create a plan with policies and decisions for governing the global Sai devotional base. On the other hand, former devotees claim that the Prasanthi Council is simply a publicity arm created to control information about Sathya Sai Baba and the organization.

While the democratic impulse is strong in the lower-order cadres of the Sai movement, it has been dead-ended by a series of reorganizations that gives onlookers the impression that the upper orders of the Sai movement do not appreciate democracy, equality, or openness. Devotees who had been with the organization for some time and seemed to be in charge told me that this impression was incorrect, stating,"we have nothing to hide" and " we are not here to order anyone . . . we are all devotees of Bhagawan," but one core devotee told me emphatically that "loose lips flapping" were "not to be encouraged."

Within the organization each major change was made institutionally and deliberately to add more layers of management of information rather than to strip any away. Therefore the SSSO presents a highly organized face to the world, with a complex and visible political hierarchy that appears accountable. Cross-cutting sets of responsibilities and overlapping titles make for a large degree of flexibility within this seemingly well-organized institution. To the outsider, the SSSO always appears strong, girded as it is with organizational and bureaucratic formalities, but from within it appears nebulous, fluid, and free floating (Petersen 1993:347). I found it was difficult to understand how the organization is run, given its confusing complexity—its many overlapping organizations, its myriad and interlocking lines of control, its lack of structural clarity, its muddied hierarchy, and its lack of articulated directions—but operationally it seems to function seamlessly.

Skepticism and the War Over Truth: Introducing the Global Anti-Sai Network

In 2006 the truth war between devotees and former devotees came to court, as one "victim," of "sexual healing", Alaya Rahm (believed by former devotees to have an ironclad case),[27] filed a lawsuit against the SSSO and Sathya Sai Baba in the California courts.[28] The case was set for trial on April 28, 2006, but in 2007, after many lurid deposition statements detailing his experiences, the court dismissed it when Rahm withdrew the case "with prejudice," meaning he received no compensation.

The Sathya Sai Organization rejoiced, claiming that it had won and that "truth had triumphed" against the evil campaign of mudslinging by the anti-Sai network.

What is known is that the truth war has been driven in large part by the presence of an increasingly influential anti-Sai network. In 1999, during my initial research on the Sai movement in Bangalore, I came across some Web pages on Sai Baba that were negative. Over the next five years, the negative postings on Sai Baba increased, and in 2004, of the 532 Internet sites on Sai Baba, roughly 10 percent were negative. In interviews, members of the anti-Sai network made it clear to me that they do not consider themselves to be "anti-Sai." Their official name is the Just Seekers of Truth (acronym JuST), though they refer to themselves as "former devotees." Many members had been devotees for decades and had written books about their experiences of devotion while they were part of the movement.

JuST is not a significant movement in terms of numbers; I estimate its total strength to be roughly one hundred members, though its unofficial leader, Barry Pittard, confirmed thirty-six members. Still, it is important to take note of this network because it wields considerable influence through activism, using traditional social networking tools and new technologies. Members meet with leaders and politicians, write letters, and get articles published in sympathetic journals and newspapers, on the Internet, and via new media. Recently, in 2006, they were engaged in a virtual mission to prevent the Prince of Wales Organization in the UK and Australia from honoring Sai Baba by sending a group of schoolboy representatives to Sai Baba's birthday celebrations in Puttaparthi.

As the group's development is recent, participatory, and nonlinear, my description must be based on unorthodox "texts" such as remembrances and in-depth interviews with members of the former devotees network and with current devotees. The number of claimants is large, and tracing them complex, so I have limited myself to those who are frequently mentioned and discussed: Glen Meloy, Barry Pittard, Robert Priddy, Tal Brooke, Serguei Badaev, Brian Steel, and Timothy Conway.

Glen Meloy, an retired American business consultant, was a devotee from 1974 to 2000, a member of the First Advisory Board of the Sathya Sai Baba Society, and co-manager of the Official Tustin Book Centre in California. In 1992 he received what he considered a "shocking" letter from a Sai devotee in Puttaparthi who stated that her son had been "sexually abused" by Sathya Sai Baba.[29] Meloy then spoke to several officials of the Sai Movement whom he claimed refused to do anything about the matter. Barry Pittard, an Australian and the current, unofficial leader of JuST (he refuses the titular headship), says that Meloy was told to leave the issue alone by the head of the Sai organization in the U.S., Michael Goldstein. In response in 1998, Meloy began JuST.[30] In recent years the former devotees' movement has grown with the publicity on the sexual abuse allegations—which have not been proven—through Internet exposés and news documentaries. Meloy died in 2001, just as the network had begun to attract many disillusioned former devotees.

In September 2, 2003, a petition began to circulate outlining allegations against Sathya Sai Baba, especially those relating to sexual healing and the deaths at Puttaparthi on June 6, 1993. It called for a properly constituted official enquiry and pressure by governments around the world. By the end the total signatories were 470 in number. Pittard, also a former devotee, was one signatory. As he told me: "I was devoted to Sathya Sai Baba for twenty-five years, I spent a few years around him and for two years taught English literature at all levels in a voluntary capacity (1978–79) at his college in Whitefield, via Bangalore, the first of several large boys' colleges Sathya Sai Baba founded."[31] He was brought into the JuST organization by "a friend"; he says that most former devotees entered the organization the same way. "That is the way 'recruitment' operated," he said; "very much to guard against penetration by any Sai devotees."

Robert Priddy, another signatory of the Sai public petition, was a Sai devotee from 1983 to 2002, a founding member and ex-chairman of the Oslo Center and the coordinator for the country of Norway from 1986–1996. Priddy, born in England in 1936, is the author of *Source of the Dream: My Way to Sathya Sai Baba*. Between 1988 and 1998 he wrote many devotional articles in *Sanathana Sarathi*, the official magazine of the SSSO. An academic, he taught philosophy and sociology at the University of Oslo from 1968 to 1985. In 2000, after resigning as an official in the Sathya Sai Organization, Priddy wrote *End of the Dream: The Sathya Sai Baba Enigma*, in which he was very critical of Sathya Sai Baba. Currently he maintains an influential anti-Sai Web site.

The first person to publish allegations against Sai Baba was the American Tal Brooke, born Robert Taliaferro Brooke, a devotee in 1970 and 1971 and currently the chairperson of the Spiritual Counterfeits Project, a Christian evangelical countercult and apologetics organization.[32] In an extract from his article on the popular Web site exbaba.com he states, "Around 1980 there was uproar in Malaysia: . . . Some members had begun a quiet campaign to discredit Sai Baba after they had conducted personal investigations of his life-style and behavior. This campaign to expose Sai Baba comprises mainly taped revelations by several Malaysian Indian students who claimed that they had been sexually abused by Sai Baba."[33] Brooke has written several books on Indian gurus, new age spirituality, and the occult, and is credited on Wikipedia as being "a worldwide authority on cultic influences." In his spiritual autobiography, *Lord of the Air*,[34] Brooke recounts how he was attracted to the American counterculture of the 1960s with its emphasis on altered states of consciousness, unconventional lifestyles, and exploration of Eastern religions. He wrote a devotee's manifesto, *The Amazing Advent*, which was interrupted by his disillusionment in the late 1970s with Sathya Sai Baba and the movement because, he claimed, of Sai Baba's "sexual acts."[35] Many of his articles in the conservative Christian journal he edits are extremely critical of the culture of India and Hinduism. Former devotees like Pittard say they are "appalled to keep hearing 'Christian plots' against Hinduism, and more such rubbish."[36]

Serguei Badaev was the president of the Sai organization's Moscow Center from 1996 to 2000 and was the deputy national chairman for Russia. He also joined JuST in 2000. He claims he did so in response to the lack of transparency in the organization about the question of sexual healings and other irregularities that he noticed.[37] In our e-mail correspondence, he appeared very knowledgeable about the structure and inner workings of the SSSO, the SCT, and the organizational procedures. In writings on the Web he has been critical of the SSSO and its procedures, providing information in the form of official e-mail correspondence circulated among SSSO administrators that hinted at secret dealings.

Brian Steel is an Australian writer, translator, and Spanish interpreter, teacher, and lexicographer. He was a devotee of Sathya Sai Baba from the early 1980s, although his first visit to Prasanthi Nilayam was in 1988. He occupies a rather different position, though he is formally associated with JuST. In the mid 1990s he was rescued from drowning by two surfers and decided to share his faith. As he puts it:

In 1995, two weeks after being rescued at the last moment from drowning by two teenage surfers after desperately calling out for Sai Baba's help, I had the idea of writing three books about Baba. I then settled down more or less full time to the task of reading as many

more books about Baba as I could find (perhaps 200 in all). In 1997
and 1998 I published two books on Sathya Sai Baba: *The Sathya Sai
Baba Compendium* and *The Powers of Sathya Sai Baba*.[38]

In 1999 he says he came across "several discrepancies" in the Sai literature and in 2000, when the Internet allegations surfaced, he was "profoundly disturbed." I found him honest in his inability to justify his belief in Sai Baba, but he told me he recognized that Sai Baba displayed
certain special powers inexplicable outside the Hindu guru or godman
tradition. He also sees that the SSSO, "whatever its alleged or real internal faults and weaknesses," has carried out much worthwhile charitable
work. He runs several Web sites that catalogue errors, both hermeneutic
and procedural, in Sathya Sai Baba's discourses and in the movement.[39]

Timothy Conway, a former devotee and president of the San Francisco
Sai center between 1981 and 1984, was also willing to discuss his beliefs.
He told me in a personal e-mail that he neither believe(s) that "SSB is
God" nor that he is "the arch-principle of evil." He said Sathya Sai Baba
"has a lot of psychic power and has obviously inspired millions of people,
but it is not clear from where he derives this power. Sathya Sai is himself
a deeply flawed instrument for this power, with major attachments and
aversions complicating and sullying his ministry." For former devotees
like Conway, Sai Baba is a guru with *siddhi* powers (spiritual abilities ob-
tained through penances) who has lost the battle to find divinity.[40]

In a 1994 article a student at the Frei University and a critic of Sai
Baba, Alexandra Nagel,[41] mentioned allegations of "sexual healing" involving oiling of the genitals and describes testimony from several "victims":[42] Jens Sethi, a printmaker from Munich and a devotee from 1988
to 1999; Hans De Kraker, a graphic arts business consultant from Australia, a devotee from 1988 to 1994; Stephen Carthew, a documentary
filmmaker from Australia, a devotee from 1988 to 2000; and Terry Gallagher, an Australian agricultural scientist, a central coordinator of the
SSSO, and a devotee from 1983 to 1993.[43] They all alleged that Sathya Sai
Baba had initiated "sexual healing" and "genital oiling" with them. Many
more incidents have been quoted in an Internet exposé paper titled
"Sathya Sai Baba Exposed: Fraud, Fakery and Molestation" from *Nexus
magazine*.[44]

One of the most famous people to speak out against the sexual healing
was Conny Larsson, a Swedish actor and "spiritual teacher." Like many of
the former devotees, he was a spiritual seeker, first a devotee of Maharishi

Mahesh Yogi as his secretary for a decade, studying transcendental meditation, yoga, and other practices. Larsson followed the Indian spirituality trail all the way to Sri Lanka where he made his fortune selling real estate. He then suffered some kind of breakdown from which he claimed to have been saved by Sai Baba in 1978. He also claims that in 1999 he suddenly realized that he stood "behind a curtain of shame."[45] Larsson angered devotees worldwide by suggesting that there was an essential struggle for the authentic culture (*samskruti*) of India in which the West would protect Indian culture since Indians had failed to do so:

> Culture or not, *we in the West* are happy to announce to you that we will uphold the *Sanatana Dharma* (eternal righteousness) even if your people does not care we will protect the Heritage of Bharat (India). This letter to you is written direct from my hands and could be used as an affidavit if necessary, to any court in the world that will bring the issue up for a trial. I also gladly tell you Baba that I will participate as a first-hand witness whenever I am called to do so. I will not stand behind the "Curtain of shame" any longer and so will not hundreds of other boys all over the world.[46]

Conny Larsson's tinderbox statement about a "clash of cultures" made me look more closely at the composition of JuST in terms of "Western" and "Indian" devotees, and I found that JuST's large activist base is primarily American, European, and Australian. Only two Indian names appear as part of the contemporary structure of JuST: Hari Sampath, an Indian software professional in Chicago,[47] and Sanjay Dadlani, who appears to be a student in the UK. Dadlani has a volatile Internet presence and has been involved since 1997 in several "flame" wars.[48] When I looked into why more secular Indians were not part of JuST, it became apparent to me from postings on former devotees' Web sites that the inference was Indians were "afraid" of the power of Sathya Sai Baba and the SSSO.[49]

However, the anti-Sai network was not always in the Western domain. It was originally Indian in origin, but with a significantly different function and approach. Rather than focusing on the alleged improprieties with young men, the original anti-Sai movement was skeptical about Sai Baba's magical materializations and determined to prove them false. The rationalists versus Sai Baba became the way the local/national anti-Sai group was portrayed in the local media.

In June of 1976 the Indian rationalist, skeptic, and scientist Dr. H. Nara-simaiah, vice chancellor of Bangalore University and a founder of the Bangalore Science Forum, started a "Committee to Investigate Miracles and Other Verifiable Superstitions" and recruited twelve of the best and brightest scientists in India. The Narasimaiah team went to a village close to Bangalore where a young boy, Sai Krishna, was believed to be a protégé of Sathya Sai Baba and claimed to produce vibhuti. On July 15, 1976, the vibhuti miracle was unveiled as fraud.[50] On April 11, 1976, the *Deccan Herald*, a Bangalore newspaper, included a variety of opinions from readers on the problem of divinity in the modern world, underscoring the central fracture between modern skepticism and timeless faith. Mr. J. C. Harvey reminded readers about the miraculous virgin conception of the Mary, mother of Jesus, while Mr. V. T. Rajshekar Shetty took the opportunity to congratulate the team for upholding "a scientific outlook."[51]

The questioning of Sai Baba's powers became a flash point for the rallying of devotees. The debate became organized around the structure of science versus magic, which was seen and recast by Sai devotees as Western thought (modernity) versus Indian thought (tradition), a debate that had a powerfully emotional appeal in a rich culture that was recently released from two hundred years of colonial rule. Devotees were quick to respond to "so-called rationalists" of the scientific community, declaring "that the Nature [*sic*] is everything and there is no conscious being who guides the destiny of this universe" is irrational, while "Baba's miracles, though, have disturbed the scientists. . . . Baba's living example would work out the miracle of weaning away the scientific community from their rigid and irrational stand" (Kulkarni 1990:106–110, in Weiss 2005:12–15). They created an indigenous form of postcolonial critique of Western hegemonic thought that has gained currency in recent years both among Indians who fear the loss of their traditional culture and others, in the West and elsewhere, who fear the power of Western popular culture.

In September of 1976 Sathya Sai Baba invited Mr. Karanjia, editor in chief of a popular journal, the *Blitz*, and a noted skeptic, to interview him. In the interview in response to Karanjia's questioning, Sai Baba said,

> All performances of magic, as you know, are done for the sake of income. They constitute a kind of legalised cheating, the transfer of an object from one place to another by a trick of the hand which goes unnoticed. I do not cheat people by transferring objects, but I create

them. . . . For me this is the kind of visiting card to convince people of my love for them and secure their devotion in return. Since love is formless, I use materializations as evidence of my love. It is merely a symbol.[52]

A month or so after this interview, a physicist on the Narasimaiah team developed a strange skin condition that could not be diagnosed. Soon after, another member of the Narasimaiah team lost twenty years of research in an accident and became mentally unstable as a result.[53] The strange coincidence of problems affecting members of the team set off a storm of speculation and rumor. Journalists at various Bangalore city newspapers likened the Sai investigation to the opening of Tutankhamen's tomb by Howard Carter in 1922 and recounted the wave of bad luck, illness, and death that dogged members of the archaeological team.[54] The circulation of the *Deccan Herald* and other papers that ran the Sai Baba/ Narasimaiah struggle grew in leaps and bounds. Archived newspaper accounts[55] of the struggle between Sathya Sai Baba and Dr. Narasimaiah were quoted in his obituary in January 2006 and brought home to me the shift in priorities from the issue of magical materializations to that of sexual healing.[56]

On his Web site Robert Priddy suggested that by 2000 the SSSO and Sathya Sai Baba were operating in a "bunker mentality," as conspiracies abounded against them. He notes that in the Christmas discourse of 2000 Sathya Sai Baba called his critics Judases and warned devotees not to repeat information they had heard: "If you listen to bad speeches, don't repeat them to anybody. Absolutely never tell it to anybody. Forget to have heard them. Don't tell to your friends, don't disturb their mind."[57] But the secrecy and conspiracy mentality that members of JuST saw in the SSSO and Sai Baba also, I contend, bleeds through to JuST. When I first contacted them in 2004, I was summarily dismissed. I tried yet again in 2006, and they asked for "credentials" to demonstrate my intentions. After I explained my scholarly endeavor and presented what credentials I could, only then was I allowed to correspond with them. Former devotees told me that their "lives were at stake" as are, apparently, the lives of many of the "victims" they represent.[58] It appeared that secrecy was as endemic to JuST as to the SSSO. As Barry Pittard noted in an e-mail to me: "The slightest leak could all too readily result in information falling (not necessarily intentionally) into the hands of the Sathya Sai Org. Yes, secrecy—no doubt of it. And information about it I shall continue to preserve."[59]

These engagements encouraged Sai Baba, his devotees, and the SSSO to develop a sophisticated critique of Western thought that has been aired repeatedly in every confrontation with the press, the West, anti-Sai activists, and secular Indians. In a program for college teachers, Sai Baba urged the return to the values (dharma) found in the Vedas, decrying those who, "enamoured of modern civilisation and bearing the respected designation of social reformers and reconstructors, are trying in manifold deceptive attractive ways to pollute Society itself, by depriving it of Dharma" (Kasturi 1975:23). He conflated Western scientific rational education systems with atheist education and therefore lauded ancient Indian systems of education that were rooted in what he saw as a magical view of the cosmos. This has led to some scholars mistakenly identifying him as a neo-Hindu guru sympathetic to the themes of Hindutva. Sai Baba has repeatedly stated his objection to Hindutva, though that has not prevented him from lauding ancient India as having enjoyed a golden age of thought. "When Westerners became the rulers (British colonial rule), many were lured to the study of their language, for thereby they could secure the 'second' of the four goals of man, namely, riches" (Kasturi 1975:24). According to Sai Baba, "This form of education has shaped the simple innocent students for the villages into votaries of the English language, devoid of the virtues of humility and fidelity, politeness and faith" (Kasturi 1975:25), thus creating one of the few religiously based, indigenous, and embedded postcolonial critiques of the West.

Truth, Talk, and Strategies of Silence

But Isaac Tigrett, a founder of the Hard Rock Café chain and a longtime Sai devotee, did not understand or empathize with the unstated but accepted Sai need for secrecy. He expressed his views on the sexual healing scandal (rather naively) when the BBC cameras were rolling, arguing that even if Sai Baba had "sexually healed" some young men it would not diminish his faith in Sathya Sai Baba. Angered by his comment, members of the anti-Sai network said, "How can it not affect his faith? What does he mean?" Tigrett had unwittingly broken the secrecy cordon the sexual healings had erected in the movement, and his statements became the flash point for discussions about the seemingly contradictory pulls of the sexual healing allegations, inquiry and faith.

But, in the deposition for the case of Alaya Rahm versus the Sathya Sai Society, secrecy was still an issue. One of the lawyers asked about the secrecy surrounding Sai Baba's actions: "Did Alaya Rahm tell you not to tell anybody about the sitting on Sai Baba's lap . . . was it a secret?" The question of concealment became central to the case. Devotees have understood concealment and silence as a central strategy in their everyday behavior as devotees and had specific strategies of silence to combat unwanted behaviors and allegations that dealt with the sexual healing issue. Palmer notes three mechanisms of integration by which devotees dealt with these accusations and integrated them into their worldview: first, that most devotees do not even entertain the possibility Sai Baba could do such a thing, allied with that the idea that the people accusing him are thoughtless and fickle; second, that while critics might have their "facts" correct they do not understand the context of the "sexual encounters" is tantric healing of devotees' sexual energies that have gone awry; third, admitting perhaps some of his materializations to be fraudulent, and the charges of sexual misconduct accurate, but the idea of mere mortals sitting in judgment on God is to "distort the Truth" (see Palmer in Forsthoefel and Humes 2005:117–118). I found that all these strategies of eliding were regularly used by devotees to me as well, and a few more may be added. I parse them into six different types of elisions.

The first strategy of silence I noticed among devotees was to appear to ignore the problem through conversational evasions. When I asked uncomfortable questions about Sai devotees' families, such as whether everyone in the family believed in Sai Baba, they would fix their faces in a polite smile and turn the conversation to matters on sure ground: Sai Baba's miraculous childhood or how they became devotees. Others merely couched their stories in circular engagements during which much tea was drunk and after which we left happily, but nobody answered my question.

For example, when dealing with the problem of magical materializations and the attitude of believers, Gautam (twenty-six) launched into a lecture about British colonialism and how detrimental British rule was to Indian intellectualism and Hindu philosophical thought. He spoke for about twenty minutes on everything ranging from the problem with India's infrastructure [British meanness and lack of forethought], the problem of partition [British political play in the subcontinent], the problem of Pakistan [British spinelessness when faced with threats by a religious minority], Indian intellectual subjugation [British imperialist policies], to the rigidity of the caste system [the British census that solidified the hierarchy]. Last, he said: "The worst of all was the total disregard they [the British] had for our traditions. They made us feel that we were superstitious, and that is what many Indians absorbed. Now they themselves are finding there are many things that their Western science cannot explain. Maybe we should look into our own *samskruthi* [traditions]." To Gautam, as to many devotees, the sexual healing allegations was merely one more instance of a long line of Western injustices against India. Therefore to link the sexual healing with British colonialism seemed to him to be logical. Sometimes these strategies were extended to create a "lesson" for the questioning devotee. For example, Joule said:

> When Swami introduces the Ramayana, he says that the Poet Valmiki called each stanza the Kaanda because it is the name for sugarcane. However crooked a cane may be, whichever section you chew, the sweetness is unaffected and uniform. The stream of Rama's story meanders; nevertheless, the sweetness of Karuna (tenderness, pity, compassion) persists without diminution throughout the narrative. The stream turns and flows through sadness, wonder, ridicule, awe, terror, love, despair and dialogue, but the main undercurrent is the love of Dharma (Righteousness, Morality) and the Karuna (Compassion) it fosters. So it is with us.[60]

The second strategy was to use ambiguous body language to indicate their unwillingness to comment on these contentious issues. When I interviewed them, they waved their hands in a sweeping gesture, to indicate the temporality of such accusations, or moved uncomfortably to indicate the impoliteness of asking these questions on my part. Often I found I did not understand their body language and would be forced into the uncomfortable process of wondering whether it was polite to ask them what they thought. Soon I found there were gestures such as "waving away" that prevented one from asking these questions. When I was nearing an uncomfortable question, devotees would wave their hands to dissuade me. Or they would cross their arms over their chests to, as one devotee said, "say that Sai Baba knows of these silly accusations and we have nothing to say." Devotees engaged "face work" (Goffman 1955) where their faces were carefully controlled when anything controversial about Sai Baba was mentioned.[61] The face work combined with unreadable body gestures allowed for an ambiguity in reading and interpreting

devotee's reactions. This ambiguity is an important tactic for constructing a fluid matrix of meaning in a globalizing religious organization.

The third strategy was to mask the main point and divert attention. In a
rare instance, Mr. Murthy broke the body ambiguity to say, "Swami has
often said that great religious figures are persecuted for showing the path,
and he prophesied that he too will be persecuted like Jesus Christ by many
Judases." Joule said, "Swami is omnipresent and omniscient! He anticipated these problems. He said to us that there would come a time when
people would wantonly accuse Him. All great religious leaders: Jesus, Mo-
hammed, all have been persecuted. Why not Swami? It only shows you as
the book of proverbs says 'pride goeth before destruction and a haughty
spirit before a fall.'" The devotees like Mr. Murthy and Joule who do speak
are very circumspect in their speech, identifying "safe spaces" of circumscribed speech based on metaphors, indirect hedging, circumlocution,
and elliptical stories.[62]

Often devotees used parables from the Sai life story and Sai Baba's sayings and kathas to twist the conversation away from the uncomfortable.
Adam in Singapore said:

> Duty to the guru is paramount. Have you heard the story of devotee
> Adigal? It is in Swami's *Chinna Katha* (1,171). Adigal believed in Saint
> Appar and developed great admiration for him. So he donated lands
> and houses, all in the name of the Saint he had not seen. See how
> faith preceded experience here. There are others who require experi-
> ence before they fix their faith. The first path is more thrilling and
> lasting. One day Appar himself walked into the village, and Adigal
> was delighted and prepared a feast for him. When his eldest son went
> to his garden to cut a few plantain leaves for a dinner, a snake bit him
> and he died on the spot. Adigal, however, was not affected in the
> least; he covered up the corpse, heaping dry leaves upon it and pro-
> ceeded with the feast. The guru Appar, however, said to Adigal, "Go,
> call every one here." Adigal called and the dead son rose. When he
> knew what had happened, Appar said, "Your *bhakti* [devotion] is
> greater than my *shakti* [power]." That is how I feel.[63]

Leela gave me an example from Sai Baba's own life story.

> You remember the story of when Swami was a child and he produced
> all the fruits and sweets for the children of the village? Well at that

time his father thought that he was a *pucca* [real] loafer[good for nothing]and could not do anything. Maybe he also thought he was doing black magic. Anyway, whatever it was, he beat him mercilessly and he thought Swami would stop. But did he stop? No! Then one day he realized his mistake and fell at Swami's feet, and Swami forgave him! Like that, Swami gets many beatings . . . but he always forgives those who beat him because they do it out of ignorance.[64]

So, even when devotees speak, the content need not appear to illuminate the problem at hand to nondevotees.

A fourth strategy would be for devotees to turn the question into a judgment of the interlocutor. When I attempted to discuss the scandal in a direct manner, every devotee I interviewed began the discussion with a rhetorical question, "How can you ask me that?" or, alternatively, "Do *you* think Bhagawan would do something like that?" Aki, a devotee from Japan, smiled in a pained manner when I referred to the allegations and said softly, "Can you believe what people will say about Swami?" looked disappointedly at me and left the room. Part of this strategy was to ask a rhetorical question that placed the onus upon the questioner. Every single devotee I encountered has asked me, "How can this be?" or "Do you believe Baba would do such a thing?" to which the only logical answer from within the system of trust is the negative. Other devotees asked me, with faces of genuine concern, "How can you suggest such a thing after knowing us?" or, "Baba is God . . . would God take advantage of us?"

The final strategy was to make fuzzy any unpleasant details, which included separating oneself from the unbelievers. Devotees never identified either the parties involved or any facts or numbers while speaking. When referring to the allegations of abuse, devotees never articulated the allegations, nor would they identify the accusers, merely calling them "they." Stephen said to me: "They just want to make trouble for Bhagawan. But he himself has prophesied that there will be opposition to Him. He said that long ago. But he also said that He will triumph." Alistair stated: "They are distorters and generalizers because they do not understand. They say all kinds of things because they can no longer feel love."

Devotees recognized my point to them that they were "protecting" Sai Baba, but they denied having any "secret knowledge." For them, the knowledge that one has is seen as inexpressible faith. Rafael (fifty-two), from Rio de Janeiro, said in a moment of honesty and reflexivity, "We keep secrets to protect ourselves from being exploited by small-minded people.

The experience of Baba's love is no secret, no mystery. It is open for every-one to experience. We do not mean that we cannot speak freely because of rules and regulations that bind us. We mean that our experiences of Bhaga-wan cannot be put into words. It is an emotional experience that each per-son must have to understand."[65] As Luhrmann notes, to say that truth can-not be fully grasped except by experience sounds "like a strategic form of impregnability where the belief cannot be rationally challenged" (Luhrmann 1989:148). But, as she also notes, it would be "tendentious to see incommu-nicability as simply a retreat in the face of skepticism" (1989:148) and expe-riential knowledge formulates an environment of trust that is conveyed in symbols, stories and other silent communications.[66]

These discursive strategies of silence allow participants to engage with, and allude to, the subject matter at hand without referring to it directly. Discussion of the subject can be open, while the subject itself remains hid-den and elusive. Further, this allows for the appearance of consensus be-tween conflicting groups, which is necessary for any institution to survive. The scandal conceals certain social realities, and the idea of concealment adds "complex lamination to a social reality in which divergent unsanc-tioned ideas and practices become relegated to the backstage domains of social life" (Murphy 1990:25) and where trust becomes dependent on a set of ritualized behaviors (Cohen 1971) to generate group cohesion (Fine and Holyfield 1996).

Although devotees discuss the allegations when forced to, essentially all the strategies of silence become a voice that emphasizes ambiguity, which appears to be secretive. Ambiguity enables the creation of a matrix of possible meaning that lends itself to fluidity of interpretation.[67] Sai devotees do not assume (except in the case of Sai Baba himself) that there is much correspondence between what is and what is made apparent to them. This helps them in their devotion, but has led to accusations of "blindness" from former devotees. But Sai devotees are silent consciously and strategically in the sense that they are fully aware that some things are hidden and will be revealed in due course. This extends from the metaphysical world to the everyday.

Ambiguity and the Polyvalent Discourse

As we saw in the previous chapter, the concept of a "fall from grace" and the satiation of desire make their way inexorably back through

the network of globalization to Sathya Sai Baba and the institutional narrative. Also, as we have seen in the previous chapter as well as in this one,
former devotees claim that Sathya Sai Baba's embodied control is fictive
and that the genital oil massages he gives young male devotees are sexualized. The issue of the oil massages is contentious and has caused rifts
within the movement and a global Internet-based "search for truth." However, in the process of allegations and counterallegations, the fundamental issue of embodiment that the issue of the oiling massage addresses
has been lost.

In every interview, devotees and officials claimed the allegations of
sexual abuse were a cultural "misunderstanding" of an ancient Indic rite
of control of male sexual energy. A core devotee said:

> People do not understand. Swami is teaching these young men the art
> of controlling their *kundalini shakti* [power].[68] The *kundalini shakti* is
> the source of all energy, whether mental, emotional, psychic, or spiri-
> tual, in man and in the universe; it takes the form of a serpent, coiled
> around the *linga* [genitalia] in the man. Sexual energy is also there,
> but not most important. The aim of *yogic kriya* [exercise to purify] is to
> awaken this cosmic energy through self-purification and concentra-
> tion of mind and to lead it to the higher *chakras* [vortexes of energy in
> the body] and ultimately to *sahasrara* [pure consciousness].[69] Through
> massaging that area [the area between the head of the penis and the
> rectum] the *kundalini* gains power and strength. The energy is power-
> ful. It is not about sex . . . that is a misunderstanding. Because it is
> located there people think it is about sex . . . but no . . .[70]

What the core devotee was referencing was the ancient Hindu yogic *kriya*
(body cleansing technique) in which the practitioner releases libidinous
energy through regular exercises, but retains embodied control to lead to
atma gyana (self-knowledge) through a release of the chakras of energy
within the body. The raising of the kundalini energy through massage is
usually associated with tantric body cleansing, often mistakenly associated purely with sexual gratification, yet in traditional yogic practice it is
thought of primarily as a detoxifying and energy-releasing exercise
(White 2000). Dr. Shankar (sixty-eight), a yogic specialist trained in the
Iyengar and hatha yoga schools in Mysore, clarified:

> Tantra connects you with your body, a way of feeling God. Not feel-
> ing good! The mantra or voice of Tantra comes from above and below

in your body. Our work in yoga is about loosening muscles, releasing locks of fascia, and freeing the body of pain and stiffness. It is common in the West to equate Tantra with sex, but in actuality it is a spiritual science more concerned with individual consciousness and spiritual attainment than this thing. Kundalini Shaktipat is a self-perfecting spiritual practice. In Kundalini Shaktipat the massage is done by pressing the thumb and forefinger in the area between the base of the male organ and the rectum. It is very scientific. That is where Kundalini shakti is.[71]

Stephen, the British devotee from London, subtly supported the claims of Dr. Shankar:

I have had Kundalini massage in Colorado by a registered tantric practitioner. It was interesting. He kept telling me I would be "safe," maybe to avoid being litigated, since he has to grab your bits and pieces . . . and you know for us in the West this can be misconstrued. People can accuse you of rape. . . . But I have had massage in India; even in five-star hotels they don't warn you . . . none of the white towels over the naughty bits, like in England. No, they just go for you, if you know what I mean! It is a different comfort level with personal space and the body. Like it says in the Gita, Indians think of the body like change of clothing and they are cool with it. They forget you are in there.[72]

Stephen continued, stating that, while oiling of the genitals was not part of the program he undertook in Colorado, there was, as he put it "a lot of touching and arousal" as part of the massage and "pleasure and restoration" was part of the process, and the expected goal was "to leave your body behind." He ended by emphatically stating that he did not "condone rape or abuse."

As I was interviewing Harini, she became livid over the allegations of oiling of the genitals. When I brought it up, she refused to let me go further and stopped me in mid-sentence, saying, "See these people can only think of sex! Everything for them is about sex. Thooo! [expression of disgust] Then they blame Swami. How could Swami do such things?" Leela expressed similar disgust when I used the word abuse to describe the feelings of betrayal that former devotees felt when alleging that Sathya Sai Baba sexually preyed on young men and boys: "What rubbish. They do not understand. We have so much samskruti [tradition].Our Hindu understanding of the body is great. They all come here for our traditions, Ayurveda, oil massage, and all, but some they don't understand. So simply they say 'abuse' like that. Because the church in America [the Roman Catholic Church] is like that, they think we are also like that."[73] Ram Das Awle, an American Sathya Sai devotee, agrees on significant points with Leela when he sums up the difference between the Indic and Western esoteric traditions of embodiment and desire:

> Unfortunately, the Western religions seem to thrive on exacerbating the split between the sexual and the Divine, and I believe this makes it especially difficult for Westerners, raised as we were on pristine paintings of the Virgin Mary and cherubs on clouds, to understand Baba's tantric work. In most of the religious traditions in the West, God is up in heaven and sex is a path to hell, and never the twain shall meet. In many of our Scriptures, flat-out repression—along with heavy doses of guilt—seems to be the subtly recommended technique for entrance into heaven. But repression just doesn't work—it ultimately either makes people crazy with desire, or just plain crazy! No wonder so many of our priests and ministers have AIDS, and so many in our culture are either sexually repressed or completely obsessed with sex or totally entangled in guilt about sex![74]

Awle's generalizations about Western religions cogently express many devotees' point of view. Since they have been expressed on Web sites, he is in open conflict with former devotees over the question of sexual correctness. Timothy Conway, a former devotee, posted on the Internet:

> I wrote my M.A. thesis on the cross-cultural phenomenon of *shakti-pat* or "energy empowerment" and I've never seen any document that alleged that the "kundalini" or vital force or subtle energy could or should be awakened in this manner. The question exposing the faulty logic here is that, if the *kundalini* could be raised in this manner, why isn't Sathya Sai Baba providing the same service for less attractive young men, or older men, or any females?[75]

Former devotee Glen Meloy, who was active in opposing Sathya Sai Baba and garnering support among devotee groups to prove that the massages took place, wrote in an open letter, "This reasoning is absurd. . . . Even if the oiling was the only act performed, one could still legitimately question why, if he was really God, does he need to actually touch their genitals? Would not a gesture or a look from the all powerful God of the Universe be enough to effect a healing without touching the individual? . . . We . . . (should) dispel the false notion that *shaktipat* can only be done by touching the genitals or the *muladhara* region."[76] The questions that the oil massage raises are infinite, with varying moral biases and values, but the question that matters here is not whether it is true or untrue, but rather whether the oiling genital massages reveal the logical possibility of a radically different perspective on the body present in the Sai movement. Since devotees argue that there is an avenue of justification, that means that the logics of the body in the movement are different than what I assumed on learning of the genital massage or what Western readers might assume.

Anti-Sai activists argue that the sexual behavior (if it did happen) is criminal behavior, while devotees argue that it is a pathway to spiritual betterment. I suggest that these two versions of truth are both valid to the participants, but they raise issues of validity and valorization in a multicultural society. The potential denouement of Sathya Sai Baba over the issue of sexual healing brings into question the different cultural valorizations and conflicting meanings of a single act. It provides a moment where cultural translation is put to the test and the reach of the global network of the Sai organization is tested. Whose version of the truth should a society accept, and under what terms? Is the allegation of homosexual pedophilia that has been leveled at Sathya Sai Baba a *culturally* viable accusation? We find that in the globalizing world the whole question of self-realization through embodiment becomes fraught with contradiction and paradox, both for the devotees and for the image of Sathya Sai Baba himself. The question we are left with is the problem of incommensurability between traditions when dealing with ideas that are essentially untranslatable.

In the course of my research I came across different readings of the alleged act of sexual healing and genital oiling. According to one interpretation among devotees, the relationship between devotee and Sai Baba is pure and chaste. As Sai Baba has said repeatedly, he stands in lieu of both parents to his devotees. So neither would indulge in any impure activity that threatened this relationship. In complete contrast, some devotees claimed that the genital oiling is a form of tantric intercourse in which the devotee engages at the level of the soul with the guru through the body, and it is not about lust or the body. This dangerous feat is considered impossible by mere humans to replicate and therefore easily misunderstood.

For other devotees, the act is mystical in that it refers to the divine union between divinity and humanity where the human attains nirvana through union with God. In it the Sai bhakta unifies male and female principles of the universe into balance through engagement in this sexual healing. A few devotees say that Sai Baba chose particular devotees to escape the worldly bonds of duality beyond good and evil, here and there, through the *shatakshara* (surrender) of sexual healing. They see it as a gift to these chosen few. Some suggest that varying interpretations are dependent upon one fixity of purpose, and the statement acts as a test to distinguish the devotees' intent of purpose. If, indeed, they accept the claim of sexual molestation, they are not worthy of being Sai Baba's devotees. Finally, one devotee told me that it was a riddle, a test of devotion. If I solved it, I myself would be a "true" Sai bhakta. It is thus a means of finding a true devotional self.

It is no accident that the members of JuST (who are largely from the West) read the sexual healing activity as homosexual assault. While it is true that the English press in India also used the term homosexual for the allegations of abuse in the SSB movement, the combined focus on the gay, bisexual, lesbian, and transgendered rights movement in the West, especially in America, where it is seen to be *the* civil rights movement of the twenty-first century, combined with the shame of the recent unveiling of decades-long sexual assault on minors by priests of the Roman Catholic Church, and the social emphasis on the individual rights and protection of children and of childhood innocence, makes the legal and moral forces underpinning this issue very complex and subject to extreme debate. It also makes the devotees' politicization of the dialogic between Indic and Western culture plausible.

In this political fracture of cultures, the singular act of sexual healing engages what philosopher Paul Ricoeur terms a "conflict of interpretations," an indeterminacy of meaning within a discourse (Ricoeur, quoted in Urban 1998:234). For every utterance and act of Sathya Sai Baba, multiple divergent meanings are articulated and magnified into a constant process of reading and interpreting, rereading and reinterpreting. Hence any given statement is never fixed in meaning, but engages a matrix of possible meanings, a series of possibilities from which devotees act as agents picking and choosing the meaning that best suits their context and problem. As Urban notes, the intended meaning is not only the presumed intention of the author but also the context in which it is received, read, and interpreted.

As Roland Barthes has argued, "the ability of a text to make sense depends less on the willed intention of the author than on the creative activity of the reader."[77] Because of the strategic ambiguity of the text, or act, of a divine being, the basic hermeneutic problem is magnified a thousandfold, as many interpretations are possible. Because the meaning of the text lies in its mystery and its deliberate obfuscation to those who cannot or should not understand, it can be subject to radically different meanings, depending upon the interpreter, the context, and the audience. Only a devotee who is true would be able to decipher the real meaning of the text or act. As such, it is also a riddle and puzzle destined to reveal the "true believer." Even though the ideas circulate through groups, they remain essentially incommensurate because each culture is transforming itself and the idea/object based upon a grammar of previous understandings embedded within the culture. Though cultural translation occurs, it can in certain cases merely affirm cultural differences. So the reenvisioning of the self and the world need not be based on shared understanding, but on differences.

The Spatialization of Silence: Secrecy, Honor, and the Politics of Knowledge

All organizational culture that is political faces a spatial and social separation of the public, what Goffman calls "frontstage" regions separate from those of the hidden "backstage" areas (1959) as part of the social theater.[78] The most common phrase that I heard when discussing silence was, "one does not know what happens behind." The locative *behind* identifies the back regions as hidden in comparison with the transparent, front, public area. It is also accusatory: using the locative *behind* conveys a sense of concealment and moral reprehensibility. Devotees recognize that the *front* and *back* stages of an experience can both be subject to manipulation and so devotees often associate truth "with concealment, secrecy, and intimacy" and untruth with "surfaces and visibility."

Backstage talk is important because it creates a moral value to stakeholdership, defining it in particular and secret ways, where value resides both in propriety and secrecy. These are defined as completely accessible by proper devotees, regardless of status, but unavailable to posturers and false devotees. Thus what is behind, for Sai devotees, is not antithetical to the truth: rather, as Petersen notes, it determines the place of truth and secrecy in Sai devotional culture (1993:343). For Sai devotees, silence is not the opposite of transparency, as it is most widely perceived in contemporary societies, but rather a quality and behavior that emphasizes a restraint to protect the divine honor and ultimate truth of Sathya Sai Baba. To practice this restraint is to comport oneself according to the highest morality of Sai devotees.

Luhrmann suggests that secrecy enables devotion, which in turn enables the control of the uncontrollable. Secrecy handles the unknowable, the uncertain, and the skeptical, which turns the available into the hidden, making it more powerful and more valuable. Secret knowledge protects the knower from the "terrors" of skeptical inquiry, substituting the experience of being close to Sai Baba as the most efficacious form of practice. The transfer of lack of control into control of information performs a naming and framing function, which is later transferred to the everyday. Secrecy becomes the format for trust within the group, and the language of secrecy is the discourse of the everyday among trusted members of the secret group. Thus trust and secrecy become intimately linked in a defensive and therapeutic impulse legitimating devotees' choices to be devotees.

Sai devotees told me that, while they don't "like" secrecy, they practice concealment primarily to retain the honor of Sai Baba. Honor is a precious commodity that devotees claim is in short supply and is enacted through restraint and reserve. They often said that former devotees lacked "honor" or were "not honorable people."[79] Former devotees made the same accusation about devotees and officials. As Julian Pitt-Rivers argues,[80] honor is the "nexus between aspiration and reality, between individual and society" (1974:8), the value of a person in his own eyes and in the eyes of society (1966:22). Sai devotees respect those who protect Sai Baba's honor through strategies of concealment as being honorable themselves. By controlling knowledge about the movement, one gains respect and trust from its members, ensuring the longevity of its organization. Knowing when to be silent is therefore absolutely necessary to preserve one's honor.[81] Strategies of silence are likened to bravery in the face of provocation. For example, Leela and Stephen both related one official's outstanding discretionary ability in the face of what they felt was extreme provocation. Stephen said, admiringly, "He was like Mahatma Gandhi, you know. He kept silent. They asked him questions, and he said, 'That is not for you to ask.'" Leela said, "When journalists came to bother him about these silly things, he said, 'Oh they think they will put Swami on trial. What small-minded people they are. Their *ahamkara* [ego] is so big.' But he did not say anything. He kept quiet. 'Let them find out if they want, I will not tell them anything,' he said. Nobody told them anything, so they left disappointed." This discourse of resistance is considered defensive and in keeping with honorable devotion. Thus devotees are assured of their moral superiority because they do not engage in "petty fights." They "know" the truth. This gives nonbelievers the impression that devotees are very confident in their devotion. An academic at Emerson College in Boston said to me when I gave a talk: "I know Sai devotees in Durban where I am from and I always wondered why they were so calm and superior about their faith. They never defended it, unlike other members of cults and sects. They never proselytized. When I asked one of them, he said, 'You all will realize the truth in time.'"[82]

This model of silence as honorable resistance is powerful. It is allied closely in devotees' minds with the *satyagraha* (nonviolent protest) movement of Mahatma Gandhi, which makes it in their minds a powerful political act of resistance. Yet this restraint is not limited to the political, but is a feature of everyday life (Petersen 1993:335). This analytical process allows devotees to view the allegations as an imperialist and Orientalist face of globalization that needs to be combated. Shanti said,

You see the Western view dominates everything. It is what they like and what they see . . . what they think is right or wrong. We cannot defend ourselves. If they say Bhagawan is corrupt, then we must say he is. If they say He is . . . you know . . . like that (she is too shy to refer directly to the sexual abuse claims), then we must say yes, yes. I don't think that is right. No one is forcing them to come here and become Sai bhaktas . . . are we forcing them? Once they come here they must respect us and our ways, our traditions. Many things they do not understand. They should not judge what they do not understand. That's all I'm saying.[83]

Secrecy is given meaning and value that is seemingly not in accordance with a globalizing imperative that is believed to value transparency. The difference between the rhetoric of globalization and its reality is not lost on Sai devotees.

The net result is that these discursive strategies—restricted access, metaphorical storytelling, and silences—work together to block the flow of information within the organization. In the process, they make secret information inaccessible. And because the secret is indeterminate and ambiguous, its value lies, as Urban notes (1998:239), not in its particular placement or content but rather in the context of transaction. If it is not transacted, it ceases to have value. It must be seen to be exchanged from guru to disciple and from insider to outsider. That which is not transacted ceases to exist and, in an example of circular logic, is not considered to be of divine provenance. In this sense discourse operates as censorship, for what does not come from divinity *should* be silenced. And it offers an alternate kind of distinction and symbolic capital. Hence the dispute over sexual healing unearths contesting moral understandings of silence. It is tempting to place strategies of silence in opposition to truth, but this would be a significant misunderstanding of the SSSO's animating values.

Secrecy as Trust

While there is no consensus on truth within the SSSO, people are able to be autonomous and to simultaneously exert power relations of ordination and subordination. For Sai devotees the challenge is to keep power potent and yet keep secrets concealed—which requires a full epistemology about the movement. The possession of any secret information and its negation through strategies of silence is rewarded by trust within the organization (Luhrmann 1989:146–156). Effective use of strategies of silence acts as currency that devotees can bank to indicate their trustworthiness. Silence leading to trust offers devotees the possibility of rising in the Sai hierarchy by accumulating what Winston Davies has called "upward religious mobility" within the group and the organization. Devotees who can keep information secret are seen as having esoteric expertise that not all can share. For example, devotees were constantly telling me; "So and so knows everything about Baba's younger days. You must talk to her" or "Shanti knows Baba's schedule minute by minute; only she knows his whereabouts" and "Peter knows everything about the history of the Sai movement. He is like a history book." Like all forms of capital, knowledge gives the devotee the right to be an expert, though, in the Sai social world, the experts who truly know are accorded official status.

Access to secret knowledge enables the aspirant to jump over several others and to become part of the inner circle. For example, I tried to speak to the woman who cooks Sai Baba's food. I thought this would be a relatively simple exercise. Yet I still could not speak to her after six years, despite repeated and consistent attempts. Though she had no official position, she was always "busy." When I finally reached her, she told me, "I have not anything for you. Nothing. So, why should we meet?" Guardians of knowledge remain close to Sai Baba through self-censorship.

Devotees rise through the ranks of ordinary devotees into the upper ranks of the "Sairarchy"—hierarchy of Sai officials—by advancing their store of seemingly secret knowledge. As former devotee and Sai official Tim Conway explained to me, devotees rise based upon their ability to keep secret knowledge secret. Another former devotee, who had been an official, told me, "this path enables anyone who is a devotee of Sai Baba and who can close his ears to ascend in the hierarchy. All you have to do is believe what they tell you and not question."

As such, the Sairarchy is an open system of accessibility, one based on esoteric rights and not exoteric ones. The people who can keep secrets— the secret keepers—are trusted and raised high in the Sairarchy. The ability to retain secrets becomes of value, with secret knowledge giving the possessor status within the organization. Conversely, one must have status within the organization to be the possessor of censored knowledge. As Georg Simmel states, "A secret gives one the position of exception" (1950); turning Simmel upside down, it is easy to assert that possessing secrets is a quality of a position of trust and value within an organization. But, in the Sai case, I contend that individual autonomy can exist side by side with hierarchy. The inherent ambiguity in communication in backstage talk makes multiple meanings possible. At the same time, one gains personal autonomy by choosing the meaning appropriate to the context and subject. As contexts change, so do meanings.

Sai officials can constitute a normative order of a situation, penetrate the strategic constructions of the opposition, and also discursively negotiate the construction of a language of secrecy[84] that includes the possibility of alternate interpretations of the scandal (Murphy 1990:27). This knowledge protects the knower from the "terrors" of skeptical inquiry, substituting the experience of being close to Sai Baba as the most efficacious form of practice.[85] The transfer of lack of control into control of information performs a naming and framing function that is later transferred to the everyday. Secrecy becomes the format for trust within the group, and the language of secrecy is the discourse of the everyday among trusted members of the secret group. Thus trust and secrecy become intimately linked in a defensive and therapeutic impulse legitimating devotees' choices to be devotees.

So, while there is no consensus on truth, people are able to be autonomous and to simultaneously exert power relations of ordination and subordination. Some former devotees view this as a tactic of obfuscation, as the "placement of a veneer between flow and perception" (Murphy 1990:241). The truth, therefore, is "behind," concealed away from public view. Sai devotees do not argue for a disentangling of the truth because they believe that the truth thus revealed cannot be true.[86] Rather they produce "acceptable versions of reality embedded in local theories of what constitutes an acceptable account and who is entitled to tell the facts and assess their value and consequence" (Durani 1990:38). To the Taoist principle of "one who knows does not speak and one who speaks does not know" can be added that one who speaks is dishonorable and unsafe. The Sai official who speaks cannot retain credibility (Petersen 1993:339).

The scandal, with its indiscriminate airing of accusations, runs counter to the culture of the Sai institution. Thus secrecy, as Foucault suggests, is a mechanism for maintenance of order and a "shelter for power" (Foucault 1980:101). The hidden domain is considered necessary but not ideal. Within the devotional community there are open spaces and open secrets, which devotees believe it is Sai Baba's right to unveil "when the time comes."

Toward the Matrix of Meaning

When discussing the allegations, devotees repeatedly told me, "we are not ashamed to speak what is on our minds" or "when we choose to speak, then they [the skeptics] will know." Strategies of silence shift the focus from a response to provocation to the proper revelation of information when the time is right—just as Sai Baba's life story allows for the "proper moment" for Sai Baba to reveal his divine self. Sai devotees do not acknowledge discretionary strategies of secrecy and concealment within the organization because it would counter the ideology of restraint and honor to believe that a manipulation of knowledge had occurred.

Thus, while concealment is important, it exists merely as background for the "proper" moment of revelation. After Rahm dismissed his case, the Sathya Sai radio station Heart2Heart sent the following e-mail message, unambiguously titled "Truth Always Triumphs":

Sai Ram Dear Subscriber!

As you are aware, for quite some time now, totally unfounded, despicable, pernicious and absolutely false rumours have been circulating about our Beloved Swami. . . . Over the years, we have received from devotees across the world, many e-mails and letters expressing deep distress and anguish.

We now have some very good news for all devotees, especially for those who for years have been suffering the pain of seeing all these rumours and false allegations being eagerly lapped up by the gullible.

The news is this: The young man who made most of these allegations against Swami and who was the star accuser in the malicious and vicious BBC documentary, filed a case in California in January, 2005. . . . The young man who filed the complaint then dismissed his own lawsuit on April 19th, 2006.The case was then dismissed with prejudice. It means no damages to the plaintiff, and that the case can never be filed again in any court in America or in India.

Yes, dear Subscriber! Truth always triumphs!!

The message that has come out, loud and clear is that TRUTH ALWAYS TRIUMPHS, though it takes its own sweet time to do so. Soon, Radio Sai and H2H will bring to you a special feature giving you all the details of this glorious triumph. Meanwhile rejoice.[87]

Shanti said triumphantly, "in the end there has been no lawsuit because they have no proof." Stephen said, "I always knew this would happen. He said it would. He is God. They [the accusers] are mere humans. He knows everything. What do they know or understand?" Devotees felt pleased, vindicated, and triumphant that Sai Baba's honor was defended. Mr. Iyer told me, "You see, only Baba knows the truth, and he will see that it comes out at the right time. This trial, all this bad talk was for a reason." Core devotees saw Alaya Rahm's decision to withdraw the case as a triumph of Sai Baba's goodness, which he decided to reveal at the "right" time.

Hugh Urban, in his study of the Kartabhajas of Bengal, argues that the contents of secret knowledge are essentially unknowable; he suggests a shift in focus from secret contents to secret strategies, tactics, and metaphors through which "information is simultaneously partially revealed and largely concealed" (1998:212). I have adopted his idea. The strategies and tactics are part of the ongoing production and reproduction of social life that is at the core of this inquiry into institutional structure and longevity. To shift the focus to strategies of secrecy requires discussion of various interpretations and exegesis of the scandal that point to differing moral positions in contact. By gathering insider exegesis and differentiating between them, two levels of analysis can be sustained: the public discourse on the scandal within warring camps and the hidden discourse on the scandal, with *its* warring factions. Together they create a dialectical construction of Geertz's understanding of culture as an "assemblage of texts" (1973:448).[88]

In addition to local exegesis, skeptical commentary from former devotees and others hints at Bakhtin's metaphor of "voices" within the text, where the different voices create further disharmony and contradiction that dislodge the frontstage of manufactured consensus. As Comaroff and Roberts demonstrate among the Tswana, disputants create competing interpretations of events for a variety of reasons, and this conflicting discourse and imagination bleeds into the everyday, giving the hidden significant meaning. As one of my Sai informants told me, in a strange echo of Comaroff's Tswana informant, "Reality is nothing . . . it is all Maya conjured up by Swami" (see Comaroff and Roberts 1981:175).[89] The many-layered discourse encompassing both front- and backstages creates an ambiguity where the real is questionable and the hidden is powerful.

The problem here is to engage this confrontational discourse as a resource to understand the constitution and management of social relations and knowledge. As Urban notes (1998:240), "secrets turn knowledge into property that can be exchanged" and strategies of concealment and obfuscation transform knowledge into a scarce resource. He also notes that secrecy "works effectively to intensify the symbolic value of a given piece of secret information. . . . It maximizes the aura of danger, the sexiness and power that surrounds the particular statement" (Urban 1998:240). I suggest, following Urban, that organizations like the SSSO construe secrecy as a necessity to construct and defend honor. They are alive to the danger inherent in secret information and seek to mitigate it by creating parallel channels of information along which "real" news travels, often uncensored, as opposed to official channels where news is regulated and censored. Hierarchy then becomes a vehicle both to discern what information should be kept secret, and then to control it and keep it hidden, as well as whom to trust.

Notwithstanding the esoteric discourse surrounding the sexual healing, I suggest that the deeper function behind the Sai devotees' silence is to unseat the assumed, modern, Western link between apparent transparency and truth, as leading to trust and an evaluation of integrity. The

SECRECY, AMBIGUITY, TRUTH, AND POWER

Sai devotees make us question the nature of public trust. They offer us an alternate possibility of being in the world, one where the nature of public trust is not expressed in the rhetoric of the "common good," but rather in a concept of goodness and its defense. They shake the dualities of evil and good through defensive postures of honorable silence, thereby excluding the possibility of reality and unreality. To deconstruct and unpack the ordinary ways in which we view our lives and lead toward an understanding of goodness that is based in nonduality would require a different soteriology. Such a state can only be described through metaphor, metonymy, and stories since it lies beyond what is perceived of as "real." Thus devotees employ phrases and acts in which apparent paradox occurs repeatedly (for example, using sexual massage to promote sexual control). The polyvalence of the phrases and the images they conjure up facilitates this ambiguity. The language creates a matrix of possibilities of reference within which devotees operate.

The matrix of possible meaning also functions pragmatically within the devotee base to create a hierarchy founded on the piece of information that is held secret. In the Sai example the boundaries are drawn tightly over what can or cannot be said. The silences, gaps, and erasures in Sai texts and codes of behavior around the massages point to a uniform denial of this activity (if it does exist) and function pragmatically to prevent its transmission. Not only are there different understandings of silence, but also a difference or (mis) reading of the boundaries between the sacred/secular that brings faith and sexuality, and their different contexts, interpretations, organizations, and rituals, into conflict, which is evident also in different political values about service and rights and transparency and organizational accountability.

Cultural Frontiers and Moral Collisions

Between 1993 and 1995, due to the allegations of abuse, Sai Baba's popularity dipped briefly, but then the devotee base remained steady. As one officer of the SSSO told me in confidence, the overall growth of the movement from 1993 to 2003 "exceeded expectations." Between 1990 and 2000 the Sathya Sai devotee base grew from approximately 10 million to 20 million. By 2000 the SSSO had become the ruling body for the Sai movement, and it controlled all access and information. Ex-devotees who were then members of the SSSO, like Robert Priddy, claim that they received written instructions from Mr. Indulal Shah not to refer to the incident at all.[90]

Disentangling conflict presumes that the "truth will out" and that competing versions of the truth will unveil the "real." The phrase implies that the process has an end. But Sai devotees claimed that they desired no end. Since all is ambiguous, the desired end of clarity is unachievable. The only end in sight is loss of honor. The truth cannot be known, and this truth, though it usually refers to events, also extends to metaphysical and esoteric realms. Because devotees cannot agree on one definitive version of events, it is tempting to liken this ambiguity to a lie that is oppositional to truth and sovereignty, but Sai devotees see it differently. Sai devotees understand it to mean that only Sai Baba had access to this ultimate truth, and, until he chose to reveal it, they would continue with the strategies of silence. To JuST, on the other hand, this silence and ambiguity meant that openness and transparency was not valued.

The contest of moral values over the Sai sexual healing allegations points to the fact that this cultural collision has yet to be resolved. As Bauman notes, "the idea of perspective took for granted the decisive role of human perception in the organization of space; the viewer's eye was the starting point of all perspective: it determined the size and mutual distances of all objects falling into a field, and remained the sole reference point for the allocation of objects and space" (1998:31–40). In the moral contest, the observation point of the viewer is somehow privileged, but it is delinked, framed, and separated from its surrounding cultural space to be considered impersonal, what Husserl called a "transcendent subjectivity."[91]

This diversity of moral perspective located in a cultural viewpoint enables the matrix of meaning to be interpreted variously. I do not mean to imply that the crisis and the scandal are situated outside the dominant narratives of secrecy and truth; on the contrary, the matrix of meaning is constructed and enacted precisely on narratives about secrecy and truth. In other words, this scandal provides the conditions for the possibility of agency, despite the narratives of secrecy and truth. In periods of uncertainty, when people search for identity (as we found many potential Sai devotees do), bureaucracies and institutions become increasingly opaque (as we saw with the SSSO) so as to make their strategies invisible to external perspectives and subject to greater manipulation from within.

In using strategies of silence, the Sai devotees and officials work to maintain a complex and constantly mobile political system based on loyalty

to Sai Baba and honor based on this devotional loyalty. The evidence suggests that the SSSO constructs a viable alternate organizational structure
to the accepted worldwide corporate model, one where the management of
secrecy is central to effective globalization. Secrecy and organizational
structure for the Sai movement are two sides of the same coin: they determine how public trust and moral stakeholdership are conceived of and
justified.

*But what becomes of the divinity when it reveals itself in icons, when it is multi-
plied in simulacra? Does it remain the supreme authority, simply incarnated in
images as a visible theology? Or is it volatilized into simulacra which alone deploy
their pomp and power?* —Baudrillard

*Most people desire talismans symbolic of my protection. So I provide them. The
main thing is that these trinkets or talismans, by whatever name you call them,
give people a sense of security and protection they need in time of trouble and create a symbolic link covering the long distances between them and myself.*
—Sathya Sai Baba

6 Out of God's Hands
Reframing Material Worlds

Sacred Objects and Transnational Piety

October 22, 2006. Bethesda, Maryland. The home of Mrs. Susan Ratner (fifty-seven).[1] The entire basement of this four-bedroom home
had been converted into a Sai Baba shrine. In one corner stood an empty
wooden thronelike chair draped with a bright red and gold sari. Behind it
the entire wall (which ran forty feet) was covered in floor to ceiling mirrors, in the center of which a life-size photograph of Sai Baba hung. In
front was a small altar with a bouquet of silk flowers and a bowl of fruit
and an incense burner. The room smelt of the Nag Champa incense,
thought to be Sai Baba's favorite. Walking into the mirrored basement
tricked one into believing that Sai Baba was standing there. Other walls of
the room held garlanded and framed pictures of Sathya Sai Baba at various
stages of his life, giant close-ups of his smiling head, and photos of his feet,
hands, and eyes. In front were a series of small tables on which stood images of Krishna, Rama, the Buddha, Hanuman, Jesus Christ, Shirdi Sai
Baba, and Sathya Sai Baba.

As I recovered from the visual surfeit, I asked Susan where she got
the many pictures, photographs, and sculptures. She waved around the
room, the many Sai rings on her fingers glinting in the lights: "I bought

most of them in Puttaparthi and had them shipped home, except for those (pointing to a number of photographs) . . . those Swami gave me. He also gave me these rings . . ." She explained with pride that her basement shrine was the favorite gathering place for Thursday night bhajans for Sathya Sai devotees in the area; "Some of them drive in from DC."

After we had sat down, Susan put in a video cassette of darshan at Puttaparthi on a small television in the room, and we were transported from the mundane suburbs of Bethesda to the extraordinary environs of Puttaparthi. Sathya Sai Baba was smiling as he circled his hand thrice and dropped a cloud of vibhuti into an adoring devotee's outstretched palm. Susan and the others in the room let out an "Aaaahhhhh!!" of pleasure, which I recognized from familiar devotee interactions as an appropriate voicing of engaged piety.

Commodification is a central practice of globalization, and yet commodities are rarely considered in studies of religious piety. Religious traditions often argue against materialism and this moral bias appears to extend into the study of religious objects as well, except perhaps in the case of Catholicism. Even recent analysis of religious traditions views the individual and collective identity of the consumer as morally bankrupt and in opposition to the role of the moral and engaged stakeholder (Hadsell 2008). But does the devotees' consumption of religious objects play a part in their transformation of self and habitus toward an engaged stakeholderhsip? Is it possible that commodification and mediatization are resources for the politics of knowledge and interpretation? Since globalization shifts the focus from a local frame to a global one, and the rapid spread of these objects across the globe makes this soteriological quest of antimaterialism a transnational one, which is strengthened through the circulation of the gifts across global networks, I argue that an objectification of the spiritual can be understood as a search for a point from which to comprehend life and imbue it with meaning and to reconstruct identity from a lost seeker to an identity as belonging to the movement; in effect, to construct an active piety located in affect (bhaktirasa). Theodor Adorno suggests (1983:233), when referring to Walter Benjamin's writings, that, in the case of tactile aesthetics, "thought presses close to its object as if through touching, smelling, tasting, it wanted to transform itself" (cited in Taussig 1993:19, 145), and we must remind ourselves that, for both Benjamin and Adorno, sensuous materiality, affect, and mimesis were significant as coded language because they formed an integral part of the everyday. Thus materiality and experience are directly linked as the aesthetics of objects and their affectivity and efficacy are closely linked, as an analysis of the interaction between the Sai institution, Sathya Sai devotees, and traders in Sai religious objects—the three prominent fields of the distributive network of globalization—shows.

The Ideal Gift

November 17, 2001. Puttaparthi, Sai ashram. Maria (fifty-one), and Gwen (sixty), two of the women devotees who had been invited to the inner sanctum for private darshan, came out and excitedly showed me the gold rings, pendant, and vibhuti that Sathya Sai Baba had materialized for them. "I am so excited," Gwen said. "In my dreams Bhagawan always gave me a ring, but every time I came to 'Parthi I would leave empty-handed. But I knew! One day I would get my ring! It was a promise Swami had made to me in my dream. Now I have one." She stretched out her hand, and all the women crowded around and admired the ring, which was large and had a ceramic picture of Sathya Sai Baba's head on it. I asked her how she felt. "I am so happy I cannot describe it. I now know that Swami has blessed me personally. I used to worry that I would fall sick again . . . you know, I had cancer . . . but now I know that I am protected by this ring. My cancer will not come back. I know for sure. Swami has blessed me." Leela (sixty-three), one of the Indian women devotees who had not received a "private darshan," said, with a slight acridity in her voice, "It is nice that you got darshan. I used to go home to my puja room and pray because He had not even looked at me for ten years. I felt I must have done something wrong . . . my bhakthi (faith) was not strong . . . that is why Swami did not call me. Many people told me 'sit here, sit there,' when I come for darshan, but . . . He never looked at me! Finally one day, I bought a big picture of Swami and took it home. I told people Swami had given the picture to me. . . . I have not told anyone this until today." She smiled mischievously. "Then one day, it was July 29 last year (2000), the picture was covered with amritam. Since then it has not stopped! Because of Swami's grace, amritam comes pouring from the picture. . . . Now everyone asks to come to my house to see the picture and to get some of the prasadam." The women devotees who had received private darshan clicked their tongues in amazement. Jyothi corroborated Leela's story; "Yes, I have seen the amritam from Leela's picture. Something you cannot believe. Everyday she will wipe it off, everyday more will come. She is really too lucky! Her bhakthi is very strong. . . . Even if we think Swami does not see today or tomorrow, He sees us all the time!"

Sai Baba has sometimes describes the materialization of these objects as leela, or god's play, to indicate its seeming randomness. But among Sai devotees there is a widespread belief that nothing Sai Baba does is random and therefore only pious and worthy devotees get materialized gifts from him. Even today devotees wait with baited breath to see who gets a materialized object. The reception of a materialized object instantly raises one's standing among the community of devotees, as it is read as a sign of divine favor and an index of one's active piety. Among my informants, about one tenth claimed that they had received divine favors from Sathya Sai Baba, although it increased to over half among the officials and upper echelons of devotees. Though devotees do not recognize this class difference, disaffected devotees and skeptics suggested that those in the upper echelons of devotees donate more to the movement, so there is also a "worldly," material relationship embedded in the reception of the gifts. But, regardless of their status position within the movement, devotees, one and all, felt blessed and happy when they received a gift from Sathya Sai Baba, as did Gwen.

The divine gifts that Sai Baba has given to devotees historically during darshan have been recorded in the apologetic literature (Kent 2004:47), and they cover a wide range, each of which they believe is coded to the recipient's needs and all of which have symbolic value to the devotee. For example, author and devotee N. Kasturi writes that "sandalwood images, silver icons, silver sandals, ivory figures, idols in the sacred alloy of the five metals, emblems of Siva in green or blue topaz, and sapphire have all been given. He has also given gem sets and lockets of different varieties as the need and the mood of the moment dictates" (1980:150). I have observed Sathya Sai Baba materialize vibhuti, though he also is said to materialize honey, sweetmeats made of milk, currency notes, his visiting cards, diamond rings, marriage necklaces (in the case of unwed young women), nine-stone rings (which have astrological protective significance for the wearer), talismans, silver and gold rings, gold necklaces with precious stones, pendants and rings with self-portrait inserts, and clothes.

Besides indicating a devotee's piety, gifts are also believed to host multiple narratives based on the modality of the transaction, the intimacy of the interaction with Sathya Sai Baba, the distinguishing characteristics of the gift, and its appropriateness for the devotee. Devotees ascribe power and value to the gift based on the manufacturing and location of these multiple narratives.

The Multiple Narratives of Divine Legitimation

Sathya Sai Baba materializes substances and objects, such as sacred ash (vibhuti), ambrosia (amritam), and sweets or talismans of rings and necklaces with his portrait on them during darshan. Sometimes he calls devotees into his private chamber and materializes specific objects for them, which devotees see as an honorable, blessed event. Devotees record that these miraculous materializations are an important factor "in recruitment to the cult" (Babb 1983:188). Sai Baba himself calls these materializations his "calling cards,"[2] arguing that they are necessary to focus and retain devotees' attention.[3]

Following the work of noted anthropologists, the gifted object can be seen as a sort of ground zero for trade, where a hidden moral economy can be brought to light (Strathern 1997; Yuan 1996) based on tacit codes of obligation, honor and reciprocity (Mauss 2000). According to Alexandra Kent, the divine gifts that Sai Baba gives devotees develop a quasi-contractual relationship between them, where the gift retains some measure of Sai Baba's magic.[4] As she notes, the gifts are all to be "worn on the body," whereby Sai Baba's "imperceptible presence becomes physically contiguous with the recipient" (Kent 2004:48). Sometimes the gifts are given directly either with instructions or with specific articulated future expectations. Gifts also contain an expectation of reciprocity, wherein the receiver becomes indebted to Sai Baba and she repays by participating enthusiastically in the Sai organization's programs. Moreover, the alliances created by these gifts create are asymmetrical and hierarchical: the devotee's behavior and thoughts are controlled (Kent 2004:49) in the guru-bhakta relationship. However, the gifts occasionally appear magically (swayambhu) with no explanation, and devotees assume that the gift is a response to devotional merit or karmic logic.

Most of the objects materialized and gifted by Sathya Sai Baba are, or contain, images of him in his various forms and incarnations. Sathya Sai Baba's claim of Muslim-reincarnated sainthood led to a whole range of materialized religious objects that relate to the Sai Baba Shirdi theme. Sathya Sai Baba has materialized many talismans, particularly between 1955 and 1970 at the height of the Shirdi Sai Baba affiliative period, that show him dressed as a Muslim fakir (saint/holy man) in a *kafni* (white robe) and head cloth, rather than Sathya Sai Baba's usual saffron robe.[5] Rings and pendants of silver and gold feature chiseled images of Sathya Sai Baba dressed and seated in the emblematic pose of Shirdi Sai Baba. Rings with inlaid ceramic portraits often show Sathya Sai Baba with the head cloth of Shirdi Sai Baba hiding his halo of hair. Harini told me that when she once went for private darshan a family from Saudi Arabia was called in as well: "We all went, me and my husband, this Muslim lady and her mother and two kids, and some other people. Swami asked me a few questions about my life and family and he gave me this ring." She showed me a ring with a ceramic portrait of Sathya Sai Baba's face set in gold with cut brilliants all around. "For the Muslim lady, he asked, 'How is your family? Is all OK now with your husband?' She started crying. She said something . . . I don't know what. Then Baba gave her one very nice necklace all of green stone. And in the center was a big pendant with a picture of Shirdi Baba. She was so happy!" Photographs and pictures, with Islamic crescents and stars painted in the colors associated with Muslims—green and white—have all been materialized. When I last visited Puttaparthi, in November 2006, one of the core devotees showed me a three-dimensional crystal lingam, on a gold base, within which was a laser-cut image of Shirdi Sai Baba with Sathya Sai hovering in the foreground; he claimed Sathya Sai Baba manifested the lingam for him in darshan. Materialized images of Sai Baba with Krishna and Rama (the two most powerful incarnations of the Hindu god Vishnu) are also extremely popular. Rings have been materialized that show Sai Baba wearing a headdress of peacock feathers in his hair, drawing from popular folk images of Krishna dressed as Balakrishna (Krishna as a young boy). In some of the ceramic portraits within the rings, Sathya Sai Baba's face is blue, the color that Krishna is believed to be (blue is the color of the infinite in Hindu theology). Pendants are often double sided with images of Krishna or Rama on one side, and Sathya Sai on the other. In one devotee's Mumbai home, in the puja room, in February 2007, I saw a small solid silver statuette of Krishna plying the flute that the devotee claimed Sathya Sai Baba had materialized for her deceased mother.

Sai Baba's proclamation that he was an androgynous divine principle uniting Shiva and Shakti led to another plethora of images, the most popular shows Sai Baba with a crescent moon in his hair seated on a tiger skin (all symbols of the Hindu god Shiva). Sai Baba has materialized chiseled rings with Shiva seated in a typical posture, with the head of Shiva replaced by that of Sathya Sai Baba with his recognizable hair. Other chiseled rings show traditional Hindu iconography of Shiva and bear the words *Om Shri Sai Ram* along the perimeter. Materialized pictures of Sai Baba show him as Shiva or Ganesha (Shiva's elephant-headed son) or in a family portrait with Sathya Sai Baba's head floating above the divine family of Shiva-Shakti and their two sons Skanda and Ganesha. Sathya Sai Baba has also materialized lingam of all different shapes, sizes, and materials during the Mahashivarathri festival and distributed them amongst devotees (Srinivas 2008:94–95). In one instance an important devotee showed me a rosary of *rudraksha* beads (seeds from the tree of the Himalayas worn by Shaivite mystics and priests, symbolic of extreme devotional Shaivism) set in gold that Sathya Sai Baba materialized.[6]

Materialized images in the early 1990s show Sai Baba positioned centrally in a frame with images of Prema Sai and Shirdi Sai in a visual triumvirate echoing the great tradition of the Hindu male triumvirate of Shiva, Vishnu, and Brahma, linking Sai Baba into the larger mythological structure of the "great tradition" of Hinduism. Nearly every devotee account includes some details of Prema Sai (the future incarnation of Sai Baba). Images of Prema Sai on rings and necklaces that have been materialized for "special" devotees are considered very valuable, since they represent a glimpse into the future of the movement, and they are rare.

A doctor I interviewed in Boston has a ring with an image of Prema Sai. The doctor claimed that when he first got the ring in the late 1980s the image was fuzzy and unclear, but it has progressively become clearer and more visible. He told me that he sees the increasing clarity as an ongoing miracle from Sathya Sai Baba, indicating the imminent presence of Prema Sai as approaching: "I will know when I can see His features clearly in this ring that it is the moment for Him to return as Prema Sai."[7]

The most popular Sai Baba poster among Italian Catholic devotees is a holographic image that appears to be of Sathya Sai Baba, but, when tilted slightly, fuses into an image of Jesus Christ in a white and blue robe with his hands outstretched. Yet another image shows Sai Baba's image morphed onto a picture of the shroud of Turin.[8] Samuel Sandweiss, a psychiatrist who has written about his devotional experiences, notes that Sathya Sai Baba created a medallion of Christ which he then morphed into an image of himself: "On April 20, 1972 . . . The devotees said that by a wave of his hand he materialized this small medallion picturing Jesus on its surface. The tiny medallion was passed from person to person . . . for everyone to examine. Taking it back into his hand, Baba blew on it twice transforming the image . . . to that of Lord Shiva."[9] Other images materialized by Sai Baba show Jesus's face in popular iconography with long hair and a benign expression.

All the objects Sathya Sai Baba materializes enable devotees of various religious affiliations to connect to him without feeling the trauma of choice that to them can imply an emotionally difficult shifting of loyalty from one religious figure to another. The plural divine frames depicted in materialized objects pragmatically legitimate Sai Baba's avataric divinity and his charismatic persona as guru and sant.

But theories of sacred transactions are based on the theistic premise that God, man, and object have different value ordinations. However, as Hayley and Das have demonstrated, there is an extreme fluidity between concepts of God and devotee (Samantha 1994:785), and God's submission to humans in Hindu Vedic sacrifice is symptomatic of the devotee's intent and desire (Das 1983:446) as part of the logic of sacrament. In Hindu logic, the deity, man, and object are all plastic substances that change at will, as God can invest all three simultaneously and silently. This fluidity between "substance" and "code" in the Hindu worldview—distinct from Western understanding—extends the field of sacredness (Samantha 1994:786). Thus devotee, divinity, and object are not so easily distinguishable, and the sacredness of Sai Baba is an abstract symbolic concept present in both material and personal representation. It can be experienced as material and spiritual, as immanent and transcendent, as both physical and moral, as an iconic, anthropomorphic, and material representation.

Ironically, having materialized the objects and substances Sathya Sai Baba himself, though presumably present in them, often belittles the *leelas* and gifts, calling them "visiting cards" that enable him to get to the heart of a possible devotee. For example, a popular Web page notes:

Swami often says that miracles are for *'nidarshana'* i.e. establishing divinity and not for *'pradarshana'* i.e. exhibition. He points out the role of a miracle in the overall scheme of his plan: first *chamatkar*, a miracle (literally magic). Then *sanskar*, or refinement. Next comes, *paropakar*, or selfless service, and finally *saakshaatkaar*, or the ultimate vision of the Divine. That is, He attracts us through the miracles, refines our hearts and minds with His teachings, and prods us along the path of selfless service which leads us to self realization.[10]

In yet another parable underscoring the valuelessness of the materialized objects, *Sanathana Sarathi* records a devotee called Mata Betty discussing what Sathya Sai Baba says about the materialized objects:

> Many of you are under the mistaken notion that all My materializations have worldly significance; it is a gross mistake; don't think like this. These [objects] are ladders that shall enable you to ascend to a bright and ideal future. So long as you are in possession of such sacred objects, only pious thoughts will be generated in you. Miracles are an innate part of Me. I was with them. . . . Baba's Miracles show clearly that He is not bound by Time, qualities, and Nature. He is beyond everything. He is the Eternal Witness.[11]

Likewise, Hugh Urban states that "if Sai Baba appears to be a kind of Icon of Materialism and consumerism—the magic and fetishism of the Commodity incarnate—he is also quite strikingly on the other hand one of the greatest critics of Western materialism and consumerism" (2003a:85).

The story of the "valueless" object that captures the fickle human soul because of a craving for material wealth is an oft-repeated lesson in the Sathya Sai devotional literature. In the ultimate story of materialism, Sai Baba materialized the priceless Kohinoor diamond (part of the crown jewels) for MBA students at the Sathya Sai University in Puttaparthi. After passing it around for everyone to look at, he is recorded as saying, "All of you were so engrossed in looking at the diamond. Did any one of you even glance at Me, who created it, as you clamored for a look at that piece of creation? The whole world is like that. It runs after the created, the materialistic desires, and not God, the creator. Money comes and goes. Morality comes and goes. Money and materials are temporary. . . . Then how come these materials will give you lasting joy? Seek the Highest and everything else shall get added on to you." In this understanding, the material object is rejected as "unreal" and a distraction from the truth of divinity, but the objects themselves become a significant signpost indicating the road to self-transformation.

As Weiss noted in chapter 3, Sai Baba's materializations are not simply an opposition to science and rationality but are rhetorical and performative and they stimulate a preferred and learned response from devotees. In terms of the materializations Weiss notes that Sai Baba is believed to materialize one pound of vibhuti per day and this would mean several tons over his lifetime. This quantity of magicality is in itself special and mystical. Furthermore, the public acts of materialization confirm his divinity to his devotees. (Weiss 2005:11) The debate between scientific rationality and magical belief is rendered complex because of Sai Baba's use of magic materializations to formulate a critique of what he sees as the global influence of western society; materialistic, flawed, and arrogant, and this provides a powerful stimulus for devotees both within western societies and outside of them to create resistance the hegemony of Western thought. Thus he conflates science and rationality with the flaws of western society, and this discourse enables him to give new and morally viable to the technology he may use at the ashram. So as Weiss notes, Sai Baba combines a critique of materialistic pursuits with a vision of the reestablishment of a golden age hearkening back to ancient Vedic texts (as seen in the material form of the Puttaparthi ashram). This teaching is not entirely new in South Asia – religious figures as far back as the Buddha and Mahavira have denounced the accumulation of material wealth. Yet the terms in which Sai Baba communicates his message are contemporary, criticizing India's modern economy. As one follower writes: "Materialism . . . has again reared its head. Not only this, but it has received respectability by the backing of the scientific community" (Kulkarni 1990:106–110, in Weiss 2005:12–15).

The antimaterialist philosophy that Sai Baba's rhetoric locates in the objects is a paradox devotees gladly embrace, jaded as they are by their everyday excesses of consumption. Jennifer (thirty-six), a Protestant and Buddhist convert, while shopping for Sai religious objects on Main Street in Puttaparthi, told me: "I come from California, and everyone there has this huge house, and this gigantic gas guzzling car. . . . All the ads on TV tell you to go out and get more stuff! But nobody I know is happy. Swami gives us things and then He says that these things will not make us happy. It is part of the process of moving to the light."[12] Divya (thirty-three), a manager in the export fashion industry and a Hindu from Delhi, corroborated Jennifer's complaint of material excess: "We have become crazy about things. . . . We buy so much. In India before, we had tradition, samskruti . . . we were not so into material things . . . but now everyone wants things. . . . My *dhobi* (washerman) now has a cell phone. . . . Swami tells us things will not give us happiness." The objects therefore, while they are miraculous in being of and by Sai Baba, retain within themselves the negative pull of their materiality (see Babb 1983). Sathya Sai Baba, having created the sacred gift and given it value, emphasizes its valuelessness as a material object per se, claiming that its "real" value lies in its ability to transform the self of the subject devotee, recasting the sacred gift as a signpost along the road of self-transformation, toward abnegation, where material objects fall by the wayside and the "true self" is revealed. In a paradox of affect, this statement of valuelessness increases the value of the object for devotees.

Narratives of Self-Transformation

As we have seen, the gifted objects literally represent Sathya Sai Baba and, for devotees, are a material extension of his miraculous power. In some cases this is indicated either by the frequency of the materializations or by their quantity. For example, the volume of vibhuti materialized,[13] or the number of lingams created and distributed, are factors mentioned by devotees to describe the power of Sathya Sai Baba. Sathya Sai Baba himself sometimes underscores the power of a materialized object by indicating its special symbolic qualities. For example, Al Drucker, a devotee author of many devotional texts, records the materialization of a silver map of India in his book *Love in Action*.[14]

> We all caught our breaths. . . . It had a round black onyx base and on it was a silver map of India. Surrounding the map were 18 jewels that glistened in the dark, from some mysterious inner light. He said that on the map were inscribed 100 Sanskrit verses giving the history of the Avatar from birth to the time when it leaves the body. . . . He said, "I will not reveal the future. Everything will be revealed in due time. Why do you hanker after this object when you have its creator? You have Me and I have you."

As Babb notes, the items and substances materialized are to be conceived as media for their donors' actual presence, and they form an existential link between the donor and the devotee (1983:120).The presence of Sathya Sai Baba in these magical objects appears to be the common denominator in all the objects. What this suggests is that "the power carried and manifested by the substances and objects he gives to others are not simply an impersonal force of some kind, but arises in the context of interactions and relations" between Sathya Sai Baba and the devotee (Babb 1983:120).

Murphet notes that most gifted objects are specific to the receiver; "Taking a green betel leaf he cut a small disc from it which he marked with a symbol. Passing the leaf to me he asked me what the symbol was. . . . I really had no idea. Without enlightening me he took it back and placed it on the youth's palm . . . and when he took his fingers away in the boy's palm lay another disc of about the same size but this one had an enamel front that bore the picture of Vishnu . . . the boys' favorite deity" (Murphet 1977:97). Alistair told me; "About ten years ago Swami asked me in my dream who my favorite god was and I said, 'You Swami!'. When my friend went to Puttaparthi seven years ago, Swami produced a ring with His picture on it and gave it to my friend to give to me. "He said; 'Give this to your friend. The one who loves me!' " I was so excited. My friend gave it to me, and it was a tad small, so I put it on a chain around my neck . . . just to have it on me . . . you know? When I went to Prasanthi the next year, Swami caught sight of it around my neck and said, 'Why are you wearing the ring like that? Swami always makes things correctly. . . . He is a divine jeweler.' He took the ring from me, blew on it and gave it back to me, and it was the right size!" As the devotees' stories demonstrate, the object may be inherently valuable and/or have symbolic value that is believed to denote the value of the devotee's bhakti to Sathya Sai Baba.

The evident power of these objects is integral to their meaning and continuing popularity, suggesting that a great deal lies at stake for the recipient. This affective power is underlined by former devotees' inability to reject the objects of faith. In the BBC documentary movie, *The Secret Swami*, a former disaffected devotee Alaya Rahm (who sued the Sathya Sai organization for sexual abuse and named Sathya Sai Baba in the suit) is followed by the filmmaker to a small shed near his house where he keeps the objects that Sathya Sai Baba materialized for him. Interestingly, the producer of the documentary, Tanya Dutta, did not ask him why he kept so many items of the faith in spite of the betrayal he so obviously felt. Though Rahm is only one such former devotee, this example indicates the affective power of these objects even over those devotees that reject Sathya Sai Baba.

While the materialized objects are transformed through their contact with the sacred being of Sathya Sai Baba from a leaf to a pendant, the objects themselves are believed to carry this magical transformative power within them and be inherently transformative of space and time, capable of transforming people's bodies and minds from sick to well and from skeptical to devotional. For example, Professor Anil Kumar, a teacher in the Sathya Sai educational facilities, suggests that some of the jewels Sathya Sai Baba has produced have come across time, from ancient Hindu mythic figures such as King Rama and his wife Sita (the hero of the epic Ramayana): "Bhagavan crosses all time barriers when He materializes certain things. One year He materialized the ring worn by Lord Rama."[15] Many of the objects, such as the vibhuti and amritam, are believed to be curative and are considered transformational in a biophysical sense; others are talismanic, prophylactics that are metaphysically transformative; and all denote the value of the devotee's bhakti to Sathya Sai Baba. Lawrence Babb has suggested that the most important part of the materializations is not what he materializes but what he does with it: "for almost invariably he gives it to someone, which suggests that what matters most is not the thing itself but the way it connects him with others—in short its significance as a vehicle for a relationship (see also White 1972:874). The practice of this devotional worship and reception of the sacred gift involves transferral of some desirable quality of the donor deity to the recipient who is thereby benefited. In "Sathya Sai Baba's case the ash, *amritham*, sweets and other paraphernalia are *all functional equivalents of this*" (Babb 1983:119; my emphasis).

Furthermore, as Babb notes, in the Indic cultural milieu, personal identity questions are interpreted through the lens of everyday experiences:

> The experience of oneself as an organic being, as an actor and alter in social roles supplies the basis for a conception of self, and this self is in some senses a false self. . . . The aim of soteriological strategies is to "know" the real self that lies hidden under the detritus of normal worldly endeavor and attachment. Such knowledge is not pure intellection remote from experience. Rather it too is grounded in experience, though of an utterly different kind, an experience that is . . . intensely inwards and achieved through arduous cultivation of contemplative insight. Here the real truth about the self is disclosed in direct, unmediated apprehension. Such an experience ideally leaves as its residue the conviction that this more intensely, strikingly and

intuitively experienced identity supersedes the person one previously
thought oneself to be.   (1983:122)

One of the many ways of unearthing this true self is through rejection of
materialism. But, despite this antimaterialist philosophy or because of it,
phenomenologically, for the Sai devotees Sai Baba and the miraculous
objects he produces and gifts are the point of focus in the world, both visual and symbolic.

One of the key problems in discussing materiality with Sai devotees is
their belief that Sathya Sai Baba produces the material objects by transforming energy. Shanti said: "Bhagawan gave me this pendant. When he
got it in his hand it glowed bright like fire. We know when he gives us
these things or he takes lingams from his mouth he is not doing it simply. He is transforming the universal energy to make these things. That
is why they are powerful." And Stephen said, "Actually what He is doing
is not materialization, he is doing transformation. He transforms spiritual energy into objects, or *amrith*, or writing, or healing energy, depending upon what the bhaktha needs. I know in one case he used this energy
to send messages to Nepal where they would be written in turmeric powder. Everyone there called it Sathya Sai Baba's turmeric fax."[16] Sai Baba
himself seems to suggest the creation of the objects is indicative of his
unique power. For example, he told the editor of the Indian Marxist *Blitz*
magazine, Mr. Karanjia, "What I do is a different act of creation. It is neither magic, nor is it *siddhi* power either. For one thing, I seek no return.
For another, I do not cheat people by transferring objects, but I create
them." And: "I totally create. Whatever I will, instantly materialises" (Sandweiss 1986:241). He has extended the power of these objects in his own
life and suggested an evolutionary path to the global awareness of his
spiritual succor in which materializations plays a significant part. As
noted earlier, he has divided his life into four phases in which leelas and
mahimas play a significant part: during the first sixteen years of his life,
he engaged in mischief and playful pranks (*balalilas*); during the second
sixteen years of his life he performed miracles (*mahimas*); in the third
sixteen-year segment of his life he dedicated himself to general teaching
(*upadesha*), while still performing miracles; and from that period (which
would have ended around 1984) forward, Sai dedicated his life to teaching select devotees his spiritual discipline (*sadhana*). Accordingly, devotees have given him the title Maha Mahima Manusha Murthi (the man
of almighty miracles).[17]

Hence the possibility of a hinterland of production of these magical objects cannot be investigated without seeming to question the faith of devotees and the divinity of Sathya Sai Baba. Since those given by Sathya Sai Baba are presumed to be materialized "out of thin air," raising the question of their production is tantamount to declaring oneself a nonbeliever. In some senses devotees are even more sensitive about the materializations than even the charges of sexual healing, because the magicality of their production has been the subject of much debate among the secular press and skeptics in India since the 1970s. When I asked about their production (where they were made), devotees would look at me aghast and say reproachfully, "but Bhagawan gave it to me" implying that he "made" it out of his energy.

For the past thirty years, former devotees have followed Indian skeptics in addressing the whole economy of production as a weak spot in the materializations thesis, and they contend that Sathya Sai Baba is a fraud who merely palms manufactured goods. There has been a whole debate on the Internet about the watches produced by Sathya Sai Baba that are etched with serial production numbers, proving they are of this world and not a transmutation of matter, as contended by the apostolic literature.[18] Skeptics, both Indian and non-Indian, in interviews repeated this "fact." [19] Disaffected devotees often use the fact that the gifts given by Sai Baba are manufactured (sometimes poorly) to argue that Sai Baba has no special powers. In a significant example, in 2002 former devotee Robert Priddy took what he claims Sathya Sai Baba had told him was a diamond ring to a reputable jeweler in Copenhagen where "the 'green diamond' Sathya Sai Baba gave me in 1986 was examined by Mr. Peter Hertz, the Danish Queen Margarethe's jeweler, a top Scandinavian expert on precious stones and diamonds. All was filmed in detail by Øjvind Kyrø's team for Danish TV. The result of the investigation, which took two days, is that the stone is a synthetic green sapphire."[20] Moreover, he claims that "it [the stone] turned out to have a layer of green silver foil behind the stone to enhance the green color and reflect light." Priddy then states that David Bailey, author of the controversial anti-Sai declaration "The Findings" (which detailed the sexual healing allegations), had, in 1999, taken the diamond ring that Sai Baba gave him to a jeweler in Hyderabad who had also discovered foil behind the stone, then claiming that he was the jeweler who supplied Sathya Sai Baba with the rings. Oddly, Bailey neither investigated the jeweler's claim nor recorded the jeweler's name or address. Another former devotee Web site, titled Unmasking Sai Baba, claims that "he apparently has many local jewelers who 'supply' him with these articles." But no local jewelers have stepped forward to claim that they are the original producers of the magical objects.

While former devotees have suggested that objects in the marketplace in Puttaparthi are "the same" as those produced by Sai Baba, and might have the same producer, to the devotee they are markedly different because the objects produced by Sai Baba are magical and those in the stores are most likely manufactured. But, again, no producer has ever stepped forward to take ownership of the Sai objects.[21] In short, the genealogy of materialized objects is obscure, and devotees work hard to ensure the occlusion.

Khushwant Singh, a well-known Indian intellectual and skeptic, has a regular column in the *Hindustan Times*. On March 20, 1999, during a rare visit by Sai Baba to New Delhi, he made the following remarks: "It is not producing *vibhuti* (sacred ash), materializing watches and medallions from the air or regurgitating sivalingas—all such tricks can be performed by magicians and cannot stand the test of scientific scrutiny. The devotees' faith has more solid foundations. They have unquestionable belief that their guru can do no wrong." While Singh's comments can be read as derogatory of the faith that Sai devotees have in Sathya Sai Baba, it is clear that the value of the Sai religious objects lies in this faith, in the community of believers accepting the belief that Sai Baba is a semidivine or divine being who "can do no wrong," and that his representations act as magical portals through which he can project his power (siddhi) and his grace (anugraha) upon them, very similar (in devotional understanding) to medieval European trade in the relics of Christian saints.

The gifting of the materialized objects to the faithful is the key element of transformative interaction between deity and devotee, as it is believed to be the material form of the much hoped for transference of the divinity's grace and power as a blessing to the devotee. The transference of the gift is believed to unearth the *bhaktirasa* of the devotee, transforming him from mere devotee to one that "gives of the heart," where emotion and affect lead the devotee toward true and unrestrained love of God. For example, Harini said, "First time I went for private darshan was in 1968. I went in to Swami's room with my parents and Swami gave me a gold chain with a pendant with Ganesha on one side and Swami's face on the other. Swami knew that I visited a Ganesha temple with my grandmother and He [Ganesha] was my *ishta devatha* [god of choice]!" Farhan (thirty), a Muslim devotee from Bangalore, told me: "When I first went I was due with my first baby. My mother used to pray to Shirdi Sai Baba and to other Babas' [Muslim saints'] *dargahs* [tombs] also. Baba gave me a necklace with Shirdi Baba's picture and he said, 'Your baby will be boy. Give him this necklace.' See Ali wears the necklace now. Nothing Baba does not know!" It was clear from many interviews that while devotees recognized the picking of a divine frame as an act of individual free will, they believed it was actually ordained by the divine will of Sathya Sai Baba himself. As Babb suggests, the devotee chooses a form of divinity that appeals to her, but she cannot really know the parameters that shape the decision. But Sathya Sai Baba does know (Babb 1983:22–123). He knows the "real" devotee, the hidden true self, and the devotees' hopes, fears, and emotions as well as the transformative effect of the divine-human interaction. The individual will of the devotee and the preordained destiny determined by God, which, as Geertz suggests, is the unique characteristic of religious thought (1966:3–4), is known only to Sai Baba. The objects produced, therefore, are both predetermined (by divine will) and undetermined (to the human mind). So, though the gift is transferred, the "real" meaning of the gift is obscure to the devotee. Similar to the tactic of veiling in chapter 1, the divine intent is hidden from the human capacity to know. The obscuration of the devotee's gift implicates both human ignorance and divine omniscience.

Not knowing the true meaning of the gift, devotees are free to see them as objects that create and engage emotion, which enables transcendence. So the gifts become lenses by which devotees are made aware of their moral and noumenal selves (to use Kant's term), which go beyond the everyday, rational secular world. This awareness marks the beginning of the giving of the self to Sai Baba so that it may undergo transformation. It marks the point at which the devotee becomes a person with faith and love (*shraddha*) toward Sathya Sai Baba, not merely a person of belief. As such, it is the movement from being a prospective devotee, or a marginal devotee, to a strong affective connection between devotee and divinity that leads to a devotee's internal transformation. This self-transformation toward faithfulness on the devotee's part is the basis of the social contract between divinity and devotee, a will to transform the habitus of the devotee, which takes the form of service to the less fortunate.

Sathya Sai Baba's constructed metaphysical hierarchy, where the highest status is accorded to antimaterialism and the primacy of the soul, creates a paradox for the devotees that they attempt to bridge through hermeneutic involutions. After underlining the affectivity located in the material gifts and the transformative power it unleashes within them, devotees routinely negate these feelings. This is another form of the focus on abstinence and discipline that we saw in chapter 4.

In interviews devotees often started by saying, "Oh, I was so happy to receive a watch or a pendant . . ." and they would discuss their happiness and sense of self-worth. But, invariably, by the end of the interview, they would reverse what they said. For example, Stephen, who described in happy detail his reception of the Sai gift of a gold watch, an hour later noted, "It is not the watch that made me happy. I could have gotten a watch anywhere. It was the sense of purpose it gave me." Alistair, who received an ill-fitting ring, said, "Having the ring, whether it fit or not, was the beginning of realizing my worth. It was about more than things, you know . . . it was about self-realization and learning my real purpose in life . . . to do seva." Parul (twenty-eight) concurred when discussing a necklace her mother received as a gift; "Yes, my mother got that from Sai Baba, but it is not what He gave her, it is what she is . . . how she helps people. People talk all the time . . . 'Oh he got a gold ring, she got a pendant, she got a diamond *mala* [necklace],' but we know that is not the important thing. We must go beyond the material things to *seva*. That is what Swami teaches." And when I met Gwen, a year after her ring was materialized, she said, looking down at it:

> In the beginning, for six months after I got it, I used to look at it and think, well, I must be worthy that Bhagawan gave this to me . . . but, after six months, I thought, what have I done to deserve this? It is just a ring . . . but I must be clear and pure like the diamond within it . . . like Swami says . . . so I began to serve food at the local homeless shelter and now I am their assistant director. The ring was the path that awoke my real self to helping people. It was Swami's sign. His gentle way of telling me not to be selfish.

In every interview, devotees asserted that the transformative power of the objects moved them from cynical onlookers to devotees and from mere devotees to believers with *shraddha* (a faith or credo),[22] in which the affective ingredient of the "giving of the heart" is an important criteria. Devotees repeatedly reported that the object was merely a talisman to denote their transformative interaction with Sathya Sai Baba, which moved them to prema for him and thence to seva to those less fortunate. A *narrative of affect* where the devotee feels a transformation and connection to Sai Baba is converted to a *narrative of agency* where the devotee begins to actively engage in voluntary work for the community within which he dwells. While devotees experience this as empowering, as a movement from the *passive* state of being affected by divinity to an *active* state of "helping" those less fortunate, the materialized gifts convert devotees into subjects of Sai Baba's agency. Devotees can no longer take a mere aesthetic pleasure in the object (such as a diamond ring), but are subjected to the guilt attendant to owning a powerful material object in the face of Sai Baba's anti-material rhetoric of abstinence, and they move from a sense of selfhood to one of communal duty and invest the object with a power of transformation that in a sense makes it more valuable in their eyes than it would be as a mere decorative or valuable object. Kent notes that the Sai faith promotes "disinterestedness without denying the interestedness that underlies capitalism and modern life," enabling a form of "religiosity generated from Hindu cosmology and philosophy that embraces the reality of "global embourgeoisement" (2005:59). So, while devotees feel they move from affect to agency, they also simultaneously move in the opposite direction, from agency to affect in a transformative maneuver that enables devotees both to retain a spiritual component and yet successfully inhabit a modern and material world.

Trading in Sai Goods

However, over 70 percent of devotees fail to have intimate, private interaction with Sathya Sai Baba or to obtain sacred gifts from him, which has in part led to the emergence of a global distributive network of Sai goods. Today the shops at the intersection of Chitravathi Road and Main Street outside the ashram gates stock an array of Sai objects for sale: visual images and photographs of Sathya Sai Baba, auditory goods in the form of cassettes of bhajan music, recordings of Sai discourses, jewelry, pens, watches, statues, prayer beads, snow globes with pictures of Sathya Sai Baba, crystal lingams, packs of cards with Sathya Sai Baba's images and sayings, pictures of the sacred sites of Puttaparthi, picture postcards of the ashram, calendars, prayer wheels, prayer beads, Tibetan necklaces, incense sticks, amulets, talismans, and other paraphernalia that cater to global spiritual seekers. The shops are packed, from opening to closing

FIGURE 6.1. Main Street, Puttaparthi. *Photo courtesy Tulasi Srinivas*

FIGURE 6.2. Interior of shop selling Sai religious objects on Main Street, Puttaparthi. *Photo courtesy Tulasi Srinivas*

time, with Sai devotees sorting through and buying objects for friends, family, and themselves.

The history of these images for sale in Puttaparthi and beyond parallels the growth of the Sai movement. Kasturi writes of Sai Baba's materialization of his image in November 1950 on the banks of the Chitravathi River: "[Sai Baba] . . . derided all types of pictures now being circulated as incorrect caricatures and, even while talking so, He dug His Fingers into the sands and, lo, there was a fine picture in His Hand, which He showed to everyone present as the authentic portrait representing Sai Baba as He really looked! He gave it to one of the devotees present for Puja."[23] These early sacred objects were fairly modest—a painting or a picture of Sai Baba,or a small silver figurine of him in various avatars. Many of the early Sai images reflected seasonality, such as images of him as the god-king Rama during the Hindu festival of Ramanavami, a popular Hindu god, such as iconography of him as Shiva or Krishna with his face superimposed on popular calendar art images of these gods, the aesthetic of the area, such as him resting on a tiger skin rug or with flowers in his hair and so on. For example, Kasturi states that in 1950, on Shivaratri, Sai Baba produced a series of *sivalingam* (egg-shaped symbols of the phallus associated with the god Shiva) from his mouth for devotees who had gathered at Puttaparthi (1968:108–109).[24]

Long-term devotees reported that, by the mid-1960s, when "foreigners" first started coming to the ashram, they remember traders beginning to sell images of Sai Baba for Euro-American devotees to take back home.[25] So the circulation of the sacred images of Sai Baba images began to be tied up with the global idea of tourist souvenirs to return home with after travel or pilgrimage. According to the father of a shopkeeper on Chitravathi Road, who was himself a vendor of religious objects, the early Western devotees of Sai Baba sought "Orientalized" imagery: "They always asked for picture postcards of Sai Baba on an elephant to send to their friends back home."[26]

In the 1970s the marketplace in Puttaparthi grew to accommodate the influx of devotees demanding religious souvenirs, but it was still not organized. It still consisted of a disaggregation of small traders who operated on the main street, largely ignored by the Sai ashram and the transnational Sai organization. However, by the late 1970s, the sale of the religious objects reached a new high, and Main Street and Chitravathi Road became the commercial district for Puttaparthi, with their primary trade in religious imagery.

At this point the SSSO had already created their own network of retail outlets that sold books, cassettes of Sathya Sai Baba's discourses, and other apostolic literature as well as some images of him. However the SSSO also apparently entered the trade as a regulatory body, sanctioning some objects and declaring others false. How they did this was unclear. Nobody within the ashram wanted to talk about it. They kept directing me to the "official" bookshops and warned me about the traders in the town and their habit of cheating people. Some merchants suggested that the SSSO created a parallel industry of objects that bore the seal of the ashram, which they claimed were the "original" objects, "ashram certified." For example, traders suggested that portraits of Sathya Sai Baba photographed by his "official" photographer, Mr. Padmanaban, were among the certified items and therefore considered authentic. They were difficult if not impossible to obtain. Other images were not certified and easier to obtain and sell. There are questions—whether the SSSO and the ashram only participated in the corporate "branding" of "authentic" objects or whether they also participated in the trade through monetary and other channels—to which I could not find satisfactory answers.

But what was clear in looking at the commercial district of Puttaparthi was that the hierarchy of objects was spatialized. The shops of Chitravathi Road varied: some were large air-conditioned shops with cafés attached (often directly opposite the ashram gates) that stocked original books and cassettes, often claiming to be "certified" by the Sai ashram, and others were smaller shops that stocked all items but did not have certification and were further away from the ashram. This spatialization mirrored the proxemic ideal of the architecture and of devotees' desires, with the most "authentic" shops closer to the ashram and, therefore, to Sai Baba and the less authentic further away.

Moreover, there was commercial sale of images that, as far as the ashram was concerned, was "underground," where the sales were so small the ashram did not bother the vendors. These were box shop vendors (literally, a large box upturned that acted as shop) who either had box shops across drains, and along the smaller lanes, or street vendors who walked on foot carrying a box of goods or pushing small handcarts. An elderly Indian Sai devotee remarked, "In 1972 when I first came to Puttaparthi, it was empty and clean . . . by 1980 it was full of shops selling only pictures, books, and things about Baba. All of them say these things have been blessed by Bhagawan. How is that possible?"[27]

The growth of the nearby city of Bangalore into a worldwide info-tech hub in the late 1980s created a captive market.[28] Direct flights brought Sai devotees by the hundreds to Puttaparthi, and this sudden expansion was met by an equally quick expansion in the commerce of images in Puttaparthi. By the early 1990s this expansion followed the itinerant track of devotees: five star hotels in India began stocking their bookshops discreetly with Sai paraphernalia and airport bookshops in all the urban centers of India carried portraits of Sai Baba, most of them uncertified.[29] By the mid 1990s the Euro-American and South East Asian devotee base increased exponentially, and the trade in Sai objects boomed. Rising devotee numbers and easier access to Puttaparthi coupled with the liberalization of the Indian economy and entry of every kind of currency into the Indian market led traders to set up money changing centers in Puttaparthi sponsored by foreign banks that devotees would recognize, such as HSBC, Swiss Bank, and ING Orange. These currency exchange centers breathed new life into the shops of Chitravathi Road since devotees with easier access to their bank accounts were able to spend their money without fear of being left with no foreign exchange in a strange country. Jeannie Alvin, a young devotee from California, writes of the shops in Puttaparthi in 1999: "[Puttaparthi] is still just a small town, with one barely two lane road with dirt shoulders, and tiny one lane or smaller side streets. If you have been to Tijuana, the shops look like their shops, only there are no radios blaring. And every shop is a Sai Baba shop! Even the Bank of India has an altar to Sai Baba in it, very, very beautiful, with a larger than life-size picture of our darling Sai."

By the turn of the century, the SSSO was the largest religious foreign exchange earner[30] in India, totaling approximately Indian Rs 75 million,[31] and the traders of Chitravathi Road were prosperous. While no reliable figures are available regarding the profit over the sale of Sai images, according to *India Today*,[32] the total investment the SSSO has made in Puttaparthi is Rs 2,000 crore (approximately $400 million), and this includes rental on shops selling images, licensing agreements, real estate holdings, etc.[33]

The Distributive Network of Sai Objects

March 15, 2005. Tustin, California. North America Sathya Sai bookstore in downtown Tustin in Orange County, an area known historically for citrus growing. Driving south along interstate 5 through the various exurbs of the greater Los Angeles area, one comes to shady West First Street in Tustin, with the Santa Ana mountains in the distance, whose center is Pepper Tree Park, dotted with historic pepper trees. On a sunny March afternoon the wooden benches in the park are filled with nannies and prams, and old men dozing in the sun. The Sai center is a Spanish hacienda-style building, with the low white-washed walls and red-tiled roof giving the impression of a spa or retreat, but within is the largest retailer of Sathya Sai objects in North America.[34] One enters the lobby of the center into a light-filled room where three of the walls are covered with books for sale about Sai Baba. On the central wall hangs a gigantic photograph of a smiling Sai Baba in an ornate gold frame. Beneath is a lit glass case holding one of his sacred ochre robes and his *paduka* (slippers). Devotees often prostrate themselves before it. DVDs, photographs, calendars, books, cassettes of Sai Baba's discourses, silk hangings with Sai Baba's sayings printed on them, and other goods fill a back room.[35] I ask Sneha, who works the counter, about the sale of the religious objects: "Yes, yes, we do good sales. Very good. See, many things—books, pictures—are not in stock. We must order from India. Demand is high. After all through Swami's blessings only. Lots of demand."

By the late 1970s some of the devotees within the Sai movement voluntarily started a series of "bookshops" and Sai centers across the world where they held meditation and bhajan sessions and stocked books, cassettes of discourses, other apostolic literature, and some images. The North American bookshop in Tustin, California was started by Elise and Walter Cowan, who donated the property and raised funds to build the center and the bookshop. Similarly, the bookshop and center in Knightsbridge, London was donated by Aime Levy and his wife Sandra. As the Sai movement grew internationally, these distributive channels stocked more images, games, pictures, and other paraphernalia, and they were subsumed into the SSSO. Though still run by volunteers, the bookshops are part of the SSSO. In the early 1990s, the SCT built a large "bookshop" on the ashram premises in Puttaparthi and encouraged devotees to shop within the ashram. Of the overseas bookshops, the Sai bookshop in Toronto became famous in North America for having the "best" objects, with the Sai bookshop in Tustin running a close second. The Sai shop in Toronto often advertises special gifts from Puttaparthi around Christmas time. In November 1998 the Toronto center advertised a new diary with these words: "This handsome leather diary filled with sayings of Shri Sathya Sai Baba and photographs of him is available for purchase. It would be a good present for yourself for Christmas." Sai centers in Brasilia, Wimbledon, Tokyo, and Singapore also sell Sai images and objects. The overseas network of bookshops appear to work rather like individual franchises stocking items that appeal to the Sai devotees of their area, as I found while wandering through Sai bookshops in Toronto, Wimbledon, and Tustin and the Web pages for Singapore, Tokyo, and Moscow, but they are all still staffed by devotee volunteers. To the consumer, the network of bookshops appears to be stand-alone shops managed by the volunteers, but in actuality they are part of the Sai organization.

And the Alaya Rahm legal case in 2005 was served against the American Sathya Sai Organization, with the Sai bookshop in Tustin, called "the bookstore," implicated as the organizational arm of the Sathya Sai Society of America. The expansion of the Sai movement into commercialization has been subjected to demands from the anti-Sai network of former devotees for transparency and accountability. Former devotees claim that the Sai bookshops are *legal cover* behind which the SSSO takes refuge.

Global culture flows in many directions at once (Hannerz 1990; Appadurai 1996; Bestor 2001; T. Srinivas 2002). The economic and political relationship between India and the United States has become more complex in the past couple of years. Cultural goods and accompanying ideologies that move globally from India—sari bedding, henna tattoos, Bollywood music and dance, yoga, Ayurveda—are important components of the increasingly South Asian/Indic-influenced cultural landscape of global life, even though people often do not know their provenance. Globalization and trade treaties serve as the foundation for many UNESCO treaties and conventions on cultural rights and cultural diversity, where often culture becomes synonymous with nationality or the goods and services produced by recognized nation-states. Culture cannot be copyrighted, nor is it static. So cultural industries emerge out of this dynamic between culture and global trade to participate in the global marketplace, and unwittingly culture is transformed by the needs of the global marketplace. At the same time, many components of the global economy have been drawn into India, with liberalization and the offshoring of the service economy. As Bestor suggests, the "global circuits of capital are being rewired" (2001:92), in this case, to include an increasing role for India. Ideational production and economic production link up, and cultural familiarity in one arena—believing in Sai Baba as part of American religious belief—is sustained by familiarity in other realms. This cultural grooming has spread on the heels of the distributive network of the global economy, leading to increased consumption of Sai goods, in the West, and in other countries, such as China and Japan, Korea and Malaysia, that also have new economic and political links with India.

But politics, economics, and international trade make for competition: by the late 1990s the parallel industry and market in Sai objects was as efficient as the ashram, and competition between ashram and the traders of Chitravathi Road led to two interesting outcomes, a fear-based focus on aesthetic perfection and allegations of cheating against the traders.

Alternate Narratives Emergent in Distribution

November 6, 2006. 5 P.M. I went shopping on Chitravathi Road. I spread my purchases over three shops. The first was a rather large air-conditioned shop called Sai Ram Gift shop and houses a café and bookstore. It was crammed with foreign tourists buying incense and wallet sized pictures of Sai Baba. The young clerk who called himself Sai Krishna greeted me with a polite "Sai Ram" and proceeded to show me everything and insisted on switching on all the bright lights in the shop to show me sculpture busts of Sai Baba (which I did not ask for) and repeatedly telling me they were "perfect." I then went further down the road to a small box shop over a drain where an elderly woman whose name was Lakshamma sat amidst a tottering pile of Sai calendars, pictures, sculptures, amulets, necklaces, and lamps. I asked to see a brightly colored statuette of Sai Baba with orange robe and jet black hair, and she took care to say that it had no cracks. While I was there, several devotees came up and examined smaller images with care, taking them into the sunlight and asking her repeatedly if they were damaged in any way before beginning the bargaining process. By the time I visited Khader's cart on Chitravathi Road, closer to the river, which overflowed with colorful Sai calendars, cards, pens, snow globes, and spinning tops, I was very late, and it was dusk. He assured me that all the items were perfect and hurriedly packed what I wanted in the fading evening light. When I returned to my hired car, the Bangalorean chauffeur commented in concern: "You should never buy these things at night. What if they are not all right? We cannot come back. They won't take them. What if there is some problem with the item? 'Mouli idre yenu madodu?'" (What if there is a blemish?).

The degree of perfection of the form of the objects—especially the visual images of Sai Baba—are critically important to the devotees. Because the religious objects are believed to represent the perfect divinity of Sai Baba (*dhruva bera*), they are expected to be perfect themselves. The more perfect in form the image is, the greater its devotional value. Hence Sai Baba and his objectification in these materials becomes self-stylized. Devotees told me that a good image was one that showed the facial features of Sathya Sai Baba so devotees "could see Him properly." The image face was expected to show his compassion (*karuna, daya*) and his grace (*bhava*) through its careful painting and crafting. The slightest chip, blemish, crack, or imperfection (*mouli*) of any kind is taken to be a sign of lack of proper piety and perhaps even of the divinity's anger; this can make the product or indeed the entire lot languish in a backroom unsold. The imperfection of the product is seen as unlucky since it may unconsciously link to imperfections within the devotee-divinity connection. The Hindu belief that images of divinity should not be worshipped if broken or imperfect in any way further contributes to this notion of perfection. The shape of the image, its symbolism, its color, size, and texture: these are the elements that make for either an ideal image or a throwaway.

Every trader on Chithravathi Road told me stories of Sai goods being mishandled and entire consignments being chipped and broken. Raju said: "Navvu yenu stock maduthivi, addu archa yirubeku. Yenu avaraige ishta, ade avarau konkolthare" (in Kannada: What we stock should be perfect. Whatever they like, they buy). In the case of Sai goods, the traders elaborately instruct producers (whom they steadfastly refuse to identify in order to maintain the idea that the objects are magically alive) in the proper techniques for the making of images of Sai Baba for rapid sale and consumers in the packing of the objects for safe transport to locations across the world. Some of the larger shops have separate packing departments, which pack and crate items that devotees have bought for a safe passage to their homeland, and despite the astronomical shipping and packing costs, some devotees ship large images and pictures home for daily worship. Susan Ratner's basement demonstrates this with ample evidence.

However, the typical Sai religious souvenir hunter is swayed by the status appeal and authenticity of the ashram-certified goods. Devotees believe that authentically certified objects have more power (both in imagination and affect), thus more value. The closer the goods are to Sathya

FIGURE 6.3. Close-up of Sai religious objects. *Photo courtesy Tulasi Srinivas*

Sai Baba, the more power they have, and the provenance of this proximity gives them authenticity. Traders who stock certified ashram objects
in certified shops are likely to do better versus the small petty street
traders, because their displays imply that their goods are more authentic. Which brings us to the problem of the recognition and value of
authenticity.

To most people, authenticity resides in the ability to recognize it. Folklorist Regina Bendix argues, "in an increasingly transcultural world . . . the politics of authenticity mingles with the forces of the market," and that declaring that something is "authentic" legitimates it, and by reflection, adds more status and legitimacy to the authenticator as well (1997:10). So while authenticity can be the search for something lost, as we discovered in chapter 2, it is also, paradoxically, the legitimation of something existent either in this world or in the world of affect and imagination. The branding of Sai objects is like the moral architecture of Puttaparthi and the ashram: they are simulacra, self-stylized and self-conscious in many ways.

Devotees often accuse traders of cheating them and having to bargain to get a good price. Jennifer said to me, "All the stores on Main Street cheat you if they think you are new and don't know the ropes. I was told by many people to watch out." Stephen said, in frustration, "Oh, I have had so many fights with them (gesturing to the shops); each day the prices change depending on what they think they can get away with. They look at you and decide what you can afford. I once complained to the police, but that did no good. They are hand in glove with each other. I then complained to the ashram and made someone talk to this one . . . !!! He was charging me 600 rupees a minute for a call to Delhi when I found out the real rate is something like 30 rupees or something ridiculous like that. This was before the standardized phone booths that they have now." In telling stories of their struggle to stock perfect goods, or ashram-certified goods, the devotees and the traders return again and again to the allegations of cheating, which they claim are leveled at them unfairly. By the late 1990s, as the market in Sai objects grew, the SSSO and the Sai ashram began to sound warning notes about this parallel industry in the official welcome booklet given to devotees when they arrived at the ashram:

> Don't pay any attention to those who claim close association with Bhagawan or claim to have inner messages or special blessings of Bhagwan Baba. Don't associate with strangers and encourage them to develop friendship with you by exchanging addresses, etc. You are not required to pay money to anyone anywhere in the ashram except for the services like accommodation, food, etc. Beware of cheats and persons collecting funds. Please note that donations by foreigners for any purpose, either in cash or in kind, either to individuals or to

Organizations (except to specific authorized bodies, such as the Sri Sathya Sai Central Trust, Sri Sathya Sai Medical Trust, Prasanthi Nilayam) are not permitted under the law of the land.

The history of the growth of this global trade underscores the unexpected links in global circuits of capital that draw different cultures together in a web of exchange. A huge source of tension between the Sai ashram and the traders of Chitravathi Road is whether the traders "cheat" the devotees, since the goods sold by the traders are not from Sathya Sai Baba. Of course the question where Sai Baba gets his gifts is never asked since it is presumed that they are magically produced. Some devotees claim that the traders cheat everyone who comes their way, since there is no regulation of them by the Sai ashram. The traders of Chitravathi Road are aggressive dealers often hawking their wares among the devotees. The streets around the ashram can be a challenge. Jeannie Alvin writes of her frustrations in dealing with their persistence:

> I have gone through many phases on how to deal with the noise, clamor, and the constant call of vendors trying to get my attention. At first, I was polite, and said, "No thank you." But it took too much energy. . . . So then I just kept my eyes down and ignored them. I decided that was bad for my karma, because I was not acknowledging the God in everyone. But, the other evening, I was tired, and had just had my fill of the constant "Hello, madam. Just look. Looking is free!" Then, a while later, prayer beads were thrust in my face for the millionth time by a street vendor. I was frustrated. I rolled my eyes, and said "Puh-leese! Go away!" As I walked on, he jumped from one side of me to the other, saying, "Japamala, madam" (prayer beads, madam), over and over, with a teasing but sweet smile on his face. His face was so sweet, I had to laugh. What sweet hearts these people are! My frustration melted away with his charm!

Conversely almost every trader has a horror story of Sai devotees who have complained to the police about them or, infinitely worse in the traders' eyes, have complained to the ashram authorities about them. Though the ashram claims no connections with the traders, traders know that their clientele is based on word of mouth within the ashram and that their clientele is likely to dry up if they have a bad reputation within it. By complaining, traders return repeatedly to the idea that "foreigners" think they are cheats—that foreigners do not understand reassurances of safety or word of mouth guaranteed by the traders and do not trust anyone. The Sai ashram has reacted strongly to the accusations of cheating by devotees, attempting to mandate the nature of interactions between traders and devotees by issuing warnings to the traders and written instructions to devotees in prominent places in the ashram to be wary of traders and touts. The traders argue that the Sai ashram has been very aggressive in trying to control all trade in Sai goods. By claiming that the traders are cheats and that the Sai goods in their stores are not authentic, traders suggest that the Sai ashram has attempted to replace the traders' goods with their own to create a monopoly.

The fear for devotees is that the economic paradigm has subsumed meaningful moral worlds. Hence the effort by the Sai ashram to revert to fundamental moral meaning by emphasizing control over the authentication of the objects. The contestations between ashram and traders are for the control of the interpretation of the objects. Who controls the distribution of the object also controls, to some extent, the meaning of the object. The point of the transaction between the giver and receiver— whether between Sai Baba and his devotees or the traders of Sai Baba goods and buyers of these goods—is the point at which the meaning of the object is imbued.

Reconstructing the Meaning of Sai Objects: Toward a Symbol

While Sai devotees prize the religious objects, they do not consume them uncritically. Devotees rework the affective reception and hermeneutics of devotion of the material object. Lakshmi Srinivas's ethnographic work on Indian film audiences argues that they creatively reconstruct the meaning of the movie text through their "active viewing" practices, which allows them to view the film as they want and make meaning in the viewing.[36] For Srinivas's film audiences, the film is seen as a matrix form that one can view selectively, thus allowing for polysemy through the various selective viewing processes. Following Srinivas's analysis, I argue that Sai devotees appear to reconstruct Sai objects by attaching meanings to them that appear to be their own, informed by their values and worldviews (Carrier 1993),[37] "reshaping the commodities and giving them new meaning"(Munn 1986). With the thickening

FIGURE 6.4. Altar with Sathya Sai images and objects in devotees' home. *Photo courtesy Krishna Chidambi*

FIGURE 6.5. Sathya Sai photograph (late 1970s) at devotee's private altar. *Photo courtesy Tulasi Srinivas*

of material culture at Puttaparthi, I found that Sai devotees divide commodities into a hierarchy based on the nature of their transaction: ephemera (objects that are bought) and sacra (objects that are a sacred gift).[38] For
example, Shanti said: "See Ramesh. He is so close to Swami that he gets
vibhuti and a ring every time he comes here. He wears them all. Next time
look at his hand and you will see he has three rings with Swami's picture.
Tim got a Prema Sai ring last time. He also wears his ring all the time.
He is so lucky!"

The Moral Value of Sai Objects

Tim's enviable gifted ring is part of a group of objects that I call
sacra. They are "special" objects, often with magical curative properties, gifted by Sai Baba to "close" devotees. Sacra are valuable because of
their obvious authenticity. The hierarchy and power of the sacra appear
to be organized by geographic distance to the charismatic center of the
movement, to Sathya Sai Baba himself. Objects closer to Sai Baba, that
were given by him or touched by him, are believed to have greater
power than those acquired from a distance (either through middlemen
or bought at shops), echoing Frazer's concept of magic by contagion
(1995 [1922]:9). Sacra are seen as worth the trouble to obtain. Devotees
see the sacra as multistranded—having them in one's possession demonstrates one's closeness to Baba and one's total dedication to him.
Owning sacra gives the owner power and prestige, but the sacra themselves are powerful in their inherent ability to solve personal problems,
heal illnesses, give material wealth, and protect the devotee and her
family.

When interviewed, devotees stated that photos of Baba taken by
his official photographer, blessed by him, and given to the devotee
personally top the hierarchy of images and were deemed "priceless."
The physical closeness to Baba, the interaction with him—the stating
of the particular problem and the receiving of the gift from him—were
narrated repeatedly, and through the narration the images appeared to
increase in power and value. Second in the hierarchy, but still extremely
desirable, are the sacra that core devotees close to Baba may obtain
for their friends, such as Alistair's ring. Devotees tell stories of how
difficult it was for his "friend" to receive gifts from Sai Baba, conclud-
ing that it was his devotion to Sai Baba that enabled him to obtain
the prized object.

Third in the hierarchy are objects bought in a shop in Puttaparthi but officially "blessed" by Baba, as stated by the merchants. The hierarchy shifts from sacra to what I call ephemera at this point, as the direct inter-action with Sai Baba is lost, though traders attempt to convert some ephemera into sacra by claiming some ephemera are "officially" blessed and "ashram certified" to increase their authenticity. Most images seek legitimacy and desirability by claiming origination in Puttaparthi, if not directly from the hand of Baba. So the ephemera bought at the roadside shops in Puttaparthi are fairly desirable for the average international devotee's point of view. One devotee, Jeannie Alvin, writes of her shop-ping experience in Puttaparthi: "Harry, I got some great little pictures of Krishna, etc. Thinking of you! I just saw a great Ganesh wall hanging for about $6."[39]

With increasing distance from Baba, the ephemera are progres-sively less powerful and desirable (Hawkins 1999). So the ephemera available outside Puttaparthi are lower still in value and power. These ephemera lack the geographic authenticity of being "from Puttaparthi" prized among devotee groups.[40] Jeannie Alvin said she had bought so many pictures of Sai Baba that she had devised a method of keeping the vendors at bay: "I have a new strategy with the vendors. I hold a wallet-sized picture of Sai Baba in one hand. If a beggar or vendor ap-proaches me, I put the picture near my face, and between me and the would-be intruder to my peace. I start saying, 'Sai Baba, you are so beautiful, Sai Baba, Sai Baba.' The vendors and beggars melt away like magic! It is amazing. Thank heavens."[41] Objects acquired at a distance have considerably less power and are less desirable. Finally, the lowest in the hierarchy are the ephemera bought at the Sai centers overseas, since they are neither symbols of the exotic panache of "traveling to India" with which devotees impress their parochial neighbors and friends, nor do they embody the sacredness of the mystical journey to India and to Sai Baba for devotees. These ephemera are seen by the devotees as lacking the power of Puttaparthi ephemera. To overcome this lack of desirability, many of the images are sold with accompany-ing sacred vibhuti sachets. However, certain larger, recognized centers of Sai devotion, such as the Toronto center, do better business in Sai ephemera than others.

Devotees see the possession of authentic ephemera and sacra as part of their evolution as devotees. While one is on the ladder of evolution to true devotion, one is forced to "make do" with the ephemera for sale. The possession of sacra thus indicates not only Baba's favor but also "true" devotion (bhakti with *shraddha*) and self-awareness (atma gyana). Conversely, devotees also believe that when one has attained true self-awareness the objects cease to have any value at all: only the affective connection with Sai Baba is meaningful.

Thorsten Veblen has argued that commodities reflect status onto their owners based on the nature and "value" of the commodity as well as the manner of acquisition. He states: "In order to gain and to hold the esteem of men it is not sufficient merely to possess wealth or power. The wealth or power must be put in evidence, for esteem is awarded only on evidence. And not only does the evidence of wealth serve to impress one's importance" (Veblen 1953 [1899]:35–37). And: "As the population increases in density, and as human relations grow more complex and numerous, all the details of life undergo a process of elaboration and selection; and in this process of elaboration the use of trophies develops into a system of rank, titles, degrees and insignia." The whole world of the sign resolves itself determinately into coding and inscription where the coding represents the full value of the divinity held therein.

But the objects are not mere objects, since they are also magical. So there is an overturning of this rigid hierarchy of religious objects when it comes to "magical" ephemera that emerge ex nihilo (*swayambhu*). These religious objects appear in devotees' lives magically during times of trouble and without immediate contact with Sai Baba. In fact, many devotees, when interviewed, said that at the time the photo or image came into their lives they did not know who the person in the photograph was. Shaw recounts a visit (2000:253) to a small shrine to Baba in Karnataka where pictures of Sai Baba oozed amritam all day long. Leela's picture oozing amritam in the introductory account was echoed by Mridula (sixty-two), a socialite housewife from Delhi, who said,

> I was moving house and I found this photograph of Sai Baba's in a big frame in one of the boxes when I unpacked them. Now I know that I did not pack the photo. But I added it to the puja room pictures because my neighbor said I should not throw it out. By the third month I noticed that there was a trail of ants going to the picture. I kept wiping them off and killing them. Then one day I watched them. They were going to the face of Baba and taking something from the face in their mouths. So I touched the spot and put my

finger in my mouth. It was sweet! Later I realized that Sai Baba had been giving me amritam.[42]

Devotees believe that these intrinsically magical ephemera are evidence of Sai Baba's benevolence as well as his sacredness and divinity. All devotees hope is that the materializations will happen to them and that

FIGURE 6.6. Close-up of Sathya Sai photograph. *Photo courtesy Tulasi Srinivas*

the ephemera act as portal, as it were, to manifestations of Sai Baba's divine power and concrete evidence of his grace upon them. Catherine, whose picture of Sai Baba oozed vibhuti, said; "Every time I have doubts about anything, I think of the miracle of the vibhuti and I know Baba is always there with me, blessing me." Devotees who buy Sai objects in shops or elsewhere always hope that "their" object will be magical; that their picture or statue will blow out clouds of sacred ash. The Sai traders of Chitravathi Road trade in what I call an "economy of hope."

The Object as Simulacra

As I wrote this chapter, I gave portions of it to a devotee, Professor S. S. Sivakumar (sixty-two), a retired professor of economics, Madras University, to comment upon. He said, critically: "I am having a hard time reading this chapter because you call the products of Bhagawan's leelas 'commodities' or 'objects.' They are not 'commodities' or 'objects' to me, or to the hundreds of thousands of devotees. They are *mayavada* (material of divine illusion) . . . you know, Baudrillard understood them as simulacra. To call them commodities, objects, and so on . . . is reductive."[43] Professor Sivakumar points to an important discernment that we have noted: for the devotee, these objects have value above and beyond, located in the metanarrative of transcendence. Sai sacred objects bring to the fore the inadequacy of human reason, and devotees argue that the objects strain the mind to the edges of its conceptuality, enabling it to grapple with the transcendence of Sathya Sai Baba.

Lyotard has argued that in postmodernity all metanarratives, particularly transcendent metanarratives, break down:

> The grand narrative has lost its credibility, regardless of what mode of unification it uses, regardless of whether it is a speculative narrative or a narrative of emancipation). Through postmodernity, we have become alert to difference, diversity, and the incompatibility of our aspirations, beliefs and desires, and for that reason postmodernity is characterized by an abundance of micro-narratives. Simultaneously the breakdown in meta-narrative of transcendence leads to the multiplicity of communities of meaning, the innumerable and incommensurable separate systems in which meanings are produced, contestations of codification, and rules for their

circulation are created is part of our lived experience of postmodernity (1979:37).

Transcendence gets relocated, dispersed over space and time. Devotees, traders, and the Sathya Sai organization—the distributive network
of globalization—become restorative agents as they attempt to reconstruct the narrative of transcendence through their material interactions
and the ensuing interpretations of the objects. The objects are interpreted and reinterpreted, wrapped in layers of meaning to be made plastic, polysemic, and portable, enabling them to recreate some portion of
the metanarrative of transcendence. The reinscription and reordering of
objects is based on the affect located in the transaction, whether in reality
or in the imagination. The global trade in mass-produced sacred objects
runs on an economy of hope.

Professor Sivakumar rightly refers to the sacred objects as simulacra because, by Baudrillard's definition, the simulacra represent no
reality, rather they are self-referential. Baudrillard states: "Abstraction
today is no longer that of the map, the double, the mirror or the concept. Simulation is no longer that of a territory, a referential being or a
substance. It is the generation by models of a real without origin or
reality: a hyperreal" (1994:1). This hyperreality is the transcendent reality of Sathya Sai Baba, which has no referent. But, as Baudrillard
pertinently asks, "What becomes of the divinity when it reveals itself
in icons, when it is multiplied in simulacra? Does it remain the supreme authority, simply incarnated in images as a visible theology? Or
is it volatilized into simulacra where the visible machinery of icons is
substituted for the pure and intelligible idea of God?" (Baudrillard, in
Poster 1998:166–184).

Baudrillard points to the fact that as the object gets deconstructed it
engages new narratives of meaning to give it context and value. In the
Sai Baba case, sacred objects engage "narratives" of morality—of trust,
obligation, reciprocity, and emotion—that create a "moral economy"
(Strathern 1997). Purchase, on the other hand, allows devotees to demonstrate agency and points to the network of global trade—a provisional
economy—that underlies the moral economy. Thus moral economies
such as the Sai exchange of objects are built on top of capitalist networks
and articulate an alternate hierarchy of value (Veblen style) located in
the intangible.

Reframing Material Worlds: From Icon
to Symbol to Simulacra

The social world of commodity exchange among Sai devotees points to what Munn calls a new world of "meaning making" where the icon of Sai Baba acquires the added meaning of being a symbol of status. Gilles Lipovetsky has coined the term *hyperconsumption* where consumption pervades ever more spheres of life, with people consuming more for pleasure and a sense of self than for social status.[44] But I argue that, for Sathya Sai devotees, the acquisition of religious objects is not an abandonment of social status altogether but an alterity in the way that status is being displayed. The reconstructed value of Sai religious commodities vary depending upon the mode of acquisition: through direct gift from Sai Baba, through indirect gift or teleportation, and, last, through purchase, and the concordant "value" held by the commodity is seen as reflective of the value of the devotee.

The examples provided illustrate the concept that space, time, devotees' feelings (affect), and devotees' consumption are all parts of a single material reality. A change in the movement of one dimension of these parameters entails a change or movement in another dimension (Mines 1997:182). The ideal world of gift giving within the Sathya Sai movement locates an entry through fantasy and affect into the consumption of mass-produced religious objects (Baudrillard 1994]). Three embedded perspectival shifts occur, out of which three epistemological maneuvers emerge: the *spatialization* of the objects, as they are made mobile through the myths attributed to them and the images of Sai Baba they carry; *a horologization* of the objects, through the introduction of the temporal by the dealers and traders in Sai objects, analyzing the multiple and often contestatory narratives that are manufactured and located within these epistemological maneuvers; and, finally, an *affectivization* of the objects by the hermeneutic tactics of devotees that imbue them with new meaning and status.

Devotees who are gifted religious objects cherish them and memorialize the interaction with divinity. The memory of this divine memory is imbued with affect. The object becomes a portal for the divinity of Sathya Sai Baba to shine through. The process of getting a gift or buying an object also makes social distinctions where the difference between self and other is discerned. One can either be a pious devotee who gets a gift or a devotee who has to buy one and tolerate his lower status. Following one system of Indic logic—which suggests actions and actors are inexorably linked—the act and actor are not separate, and they are what they are gifted (Marriott 1977:110–111) or they become what they buy (Daniel 1984:84–85). We must therefore conclude that the act of receiving a gift or purchasing an object carries with it different understandings and valorizations about the *devotion* of an actor.

We can conclude that the Sai commodities host all three epistemological maneuvers within them as they are matrices of meanings—plastic forms that are multivalent (based on value acquired in transaction), polyphonic (based on the cultural worlds they traverse), multifocal (based on the position of the speaker), and polytropic (by which they contain and create "tropes" of meaning for devotees)—all of which enable the commodity to go from being locally meaningful to globally accessible. The commodity reveals the multidimensional meaning of the global network as it moves through the global field of Sai devotion aided by trade in religious artifacts.

Further, since Sai divinity cannot be defined as distinctly other to humanity or material worlds, the relationship between human, object, and divinity in the Sai movement is shaded and ambiguous, leading to the object being possibly seen as sublime. The concept of ambiguity emerged first in our discussion of Sai Baba's charismatic appeal and has resurfaced through the chapters of this book variously as paradox, contestation, and abnegation; it is a running theme in cultural translation. Strategic ambiguity enables polysemy and sublimation, and the perception of divinity is not in Aristotelian terms of "either/or," but rather as a position that makes use of both dualistic contrasts and plural variety to validate them all (the spontaneous action of the elements engaged are all part of the divine play). The simultaneous inhabiting of spontaneity and intention shows that divinity is metaphysical, as distinct from, and identifiable with, the object of its creation.

So the object in this context acquires a unique configuration—one that cannot be explained as mere transaction but rather as sublimation of material essences. What is attained in the transaction between two amorphous entities is related to the ambiguity. Whereas the onus lies on the interaction, instead of on the object alone, devotees and traders participate in the transformation of self and habitus located in the promise of the object, enshrining them in a hierarchy of valorization based on their transformative powers (see Mines 1997:173–186).

And what about the larger links between structure and meaning, between network and narrative? Van Loon argues that, for global networks to sustain, these values honor, obligation, reciprocity—that are embedded in the moral exchange of objects are essential (2006). The basis of such moral economies is one of "what is right" in exchange, or befitting in relationality: the "hidden," tacit dimensions of the social and not only the "visible" dimension of modern contract (Strathern 1997:292–300). As we have discussed, the construction of value and meaning and its loss in postmodernity is of vital concern. For Sai devotees, then, value resides not in the dualisms of the modern or the traditional, but in the multistranded ambiguity of the plural and global, in the shift from icon to symbol to simulacra.

Cultures change in ways which some regret and which please others.

—Ulf Hannerz

Let the different faiths exist, let them flourish, and let the glory of God be sung in all the languages and a variety of tunes. That should be the ideal. Respect the differences between the faiths and recognize them as valid as long as they do not extinguish the flame of unity.

—Sathya Sai Baba

In Lieu of a Conclusion

Some Thoughts on Cultural Translation and Engaged Cosmopolitanism

A Global Birthday Celebration

February 15, 2006, Boston, Massachusetts. I was watching, with a group of devotees, a prerecorded video of Sathya Sai Baba's eightieth birthday celebration that I had been sent by a devotee group. It had been recorded by Sathya Sai Baba's videographer. The eightieth birthday celebration promised to be the largest celebration Puttaparthi had ever seen. As usual, the crowd of Sathya Sai devotees from all parts of the world had begun arriving several weeks earlier. National newspapers had estimated that for this Sai birthday five hundred thousand people would be present to receive darshan of Sathya Sai Baba. The date, location, and time flashed on screen, November 23, 2005, Puttaparthi, India, 2 A.M.

The streets of Puttaparthi were lit with lanterns, and the gateways festooned with fading flower garlands and balloons, as a seemingly unending queue of devotees worked their orderly way, past the endless barricades and security, to the Hillview Stadium in the hope of obtaining good seats to watch the celebration. But the previous year had not been good to Sathya Sai Baba. His arthritic knees (or hip, depending upon which devotee you spoke to) had given way and total joint replacement surgery had necessitated the use of a porté car (a golf cart cum wheelchair). But devotees were convinced that this birthday would be a renaissance. Mr. Iyer had said to me immediately after the birthday: "This year, we knew, was going to be the best birthday. Baba is feeling better, and we would all feel his *bhava* (grace)."

As the sun rose in the video and the skeins of mist fell away, we could see that Hillview Stadium was ringed by enormous billboards with inspirational messages: "Let us hope that there will be world wide peace," and "Love all, Serve all." A new giant LCD screen—the largest in India—had been installed at one end. Before dawn, the stadium was packed to capacity, though the skies looked threatening. Mr. K. Anand (sixty-one) said to me, in an aside: "Watch now. Bhagawan will stop the rain. Even that day I was not worried about little rain. Nothing will stop Bhagawan's birthday—*megha* (rain clouds) will become *meghadoota* (rain cloud messenger) bearing good news for the birthday." Though the stadium looked full, more and more devotees arrived and were accommodated.

At 7.45 A.M. the devotees suddenly fell silent. Sathya Sai Baba's pet elephant, the caparisoned Sai Gita, appeared and led the waiting procession of devotees into the stadium. Behind Sai Gita was the birthday procession headed by Sathya Sai Baba in a new silver gray Mercedes Benz convertible coupe. The top of the car was open, and the camera zoomed in on Sai Baba in his special white silk birthday robe. For everyone present, this was a familiar and reassuring sequence of events. He entered the stadium, circled, and ascended the *shanti vedika* (platform of peace) to sit on a gold and silver throne. Seva Dal volunteers, posted at different points, released huge flower rockets, and music blared forth. People of 130 nationalities participated in the procession; the Japanese contingent wore blue kimonos and carried a banner with "Om Shri Sai Ram—Japan" on it. The Greek men devotees wore the traditional white evzone; Turks wore red fez caps; Italian women wore peasant blouses and big red skirts.

A series of speakers including Indulal Shah, formerly world chairman of Sri Sathya Sai Organizations, and Dr. Michael Goldstein, chairman, Prasanthi Council, extolled Sathya Sai Baba's divine virtues. By this time, the sun was high in the sky and the day was warm. Then Sathya Sai Baba gave his annual, long-awaited, birthday discourse, "Realize your Innate Divinity to Achieve Peace." The camera zoomed in for a darshan of his face. Addressing the assembled devotees as "embodiments of love," he touched on familiar themes: first, devotees should believe in him and in themselves as divine: "Easwara sarva bhutanam" (God is the indweller of all beings), a Hindu Advaita philosophy made applicable to a modern quest for identity; the fragility of life and the fixity of desire; "The body is bound to fall someday . . . but the spirit is immortal. The atma [soul] has no end. The body of the senses may be lost with the passage of time, but the spirit lingers on. You think you are the body. But, you are neither the body nor the mind. Mind is nothing but a bundle of desires. One day or the other you have to give up all desires. Give up body consciousness and live in the constant awareness that you are God." Wide sweeps of the audience revealed that many had taken out umbrellas to shield themselves from the sun; others had placed kerchiefs on their heads and faces. Sai Baba reached his final point: the value of moral stewardship in becoming a full and virtuous devotee citizen through seva: "Know that seva is doing for those who are weaker and less fortunate. You should love all and serve all."

After the monumental discourse, Sathya Sai Baba returned to his Mercedes Benz to thunderous applause and rode slowly out of Hillview Stadium. As he left, and the video audience began to talk among themselves, I found myself thinking sadly of Anna, who had started me on this intellectual quest some seven years earlier when she made her joyful way to Puttaparthi for a birthday celebration in honor of Sathya Sai Baba. She had died a few months earlier and was buried in the Piedmont hills. Watching the taped telecast of Sai Baba's birthday celebration without Anna's exuberant commentary, I felt a genuine, though unexpected, sense of loss. I had disliked her for her seeming coercion of me when we first met on the plane to Bangalore, but we had gotten to know and respect each other's points of view as she had acted as one of my unofficial guides through the world of Sai devotion.

In the course of a review of the material that I had gathered on my eight-year journey (from that initial moment of meeting Anna and the ensuing fascination with the movement in Palam Airport in Delhi), it was clear that the Sathya Sai movement had become, and sustained, a global presence. But, in all the illustrations I shared in these chapters, there is a common takeaway for us as students of transnational religious communities and movements: in the process of "going global," the Sathya Sai movement created new or reinvented ways of being and believing— new forms of transnational community, new avenues of sociability, new forms of order, renewed constructions of identity, new forms of devotion, new meanings for ritual, new methods of valorization, new perspectives, new networks, new bases for judging efficacy, reinvigorated categories of

meanings, reinvented cosmogenic myths, a rethinking of ways of understanding the body and its relationship to the soul, new forms of social
interaction, and new ways of categorizing and understanding affect. Despite a few gaps and missteps the Sathya Sai movement has created a way
to become and be a successful global, civil, religious movement that appears to encourage plurality. I do not mean to suggest that the Sai movement is unique, rather I suggest the reverse. Any civil religio-cultural
movement that seeks to go global will probably invent new and reinvent
established forms, ways, methods, categories, strategies, understandings,
and performances in order to take wing.

This vitality, innovation, and expansion of the Sathya Sai movement—
its sheer success at acquiring and engaging "wings" for the Sai faith—has
allowed me to argue that in its conceptualization of multiplicity and alterity the Sathya Sai movement creates a global, modern form of a religious
way of being. Rather than assuming the West is central to the project of
contemporary modernity and identity politics, the Sathya Sai movement
encourages us to question the essentializing tropes of Euro-modernity
and the truth claims vested within. In a sense, then, it allows for a new
postulation of non-Euro-American pluralism and its ideological ally, cosmopolitanism, a cosmopolitanism from the margins of the global network. This movement away from the center lends itself to a questioning of
our understanding of cosmopolitanism and its place as an ideology in a
religiously plural and ethically pluralizing world. I am not arguing that a
cosmopolitanism arising from the margins is necessarily better, merely
different.

As we know from the recent literature, cosmopolitanism is seen as the
cultural condition for the emergence of civil democracy, and it is built
in an environment of multiculturalism, of "difference and variety" (Bauman 1998:46; Nussbaum 2007). Anthony Appiah, a philosopher, es-
pouses cosmopolitanism as the process "to have made it harder to think of
the world as divided between the West and the Rest; between locals and
moderns; between the bloodless ethics of profit and the bloody ethic of
identity; between "us" and "them" (2006:xxi). David Held and colleagues
(1995) have argued that the only real possibility of democratic global governance rests purely in the cosmopolitanist ideal that supports plural societies. Appiah persuasively argues that cosmopolitanism exists and can be
replicated, but where and how is left open for the reader to consider
(2006:xxi). Martha Nussbaum has suggested that the cultivation of a
cosmopolitanist outlook in America might lead to greater tolerance in

the public realm, and she locates the generation of this ideal within a more pluralist curriculum. From the recent literature on the cosmopolitanist imperative, we can understand that cosmopolitanism is critical in negotiating the problems around religion and culture that globalization brings to our lives by edging many societies who are democratic and participate in the free market closer to pluralism.

But it is equally clear from Appiah's and Nussbaum's work that, whereas cosmopolitanism has been highly valued in social thought and in political philosophy, our understanding of it does not come out of nowhere.[1] The modern version grew out of the Enlightenment, where its liberal progressive ideal was linked strongly with imperialist paradigms. So the critical question is: does our current understanding of cosmopolitanism carry this imperialist paradigm? Does it rest awkwardly on a domestication of otherness through the paradigm that Bailey has called the "civility of indifference,"[2] where plurality is merely tolerated by spatial and ideological separation between communities, accompanied by a politics of dominance that roots itself in historical inequalities of race, caste, gender, and class? The philosophical approach to cosmopolitanism births an inevitable question: does our contemporary understanding of pluralism rest on an illusion of civility located in indifference to the other?

Further, while I respect the philosophical and humanist understandings of cosmopolitanism, I find its current theoretical understandings lacking in three areas: 1. articulating the costs (say, in the creation of societal models that emphasize economic hierarchy, as we have seen in the West), 2. giving societies a map on how to induce and encourage cosmopolitan leanings, and 3. appreciating the pluralism enabled by the Sathya Sai movement, underpinned by a matrix of possible meanings and enabled by strategic ambiguity. If we are to move forward we must not only understand the yawning gaps in our articulation of cosmopolitanism as a possible ideology of pluralism but also address what becomes of the other. For, as newspaper headlines demonstrate daily—from the headscarf controversy in France to state-run inquiries into immigrant records in the United Kingdom—we need a common language to be able to discuss the possibility and problems of equity and diversity in multireligious and multicultural societies.

Second, our concept of cosmopolitanism is further muddied by the complications introduced by globalization and the neoliberal marketplace. In the global market, pluralism implies choice, and choice usually implies mutual exclusion. In that sense, the pluralism of the Sathya Sai movement was and is not a matter of choice. It is more a competition for mind space that entails within it the possibility of multiple commitments.[3] The Sathya Sai movement's interpretation of the life worlds of its devotees is about the capacity to attach weighted significance to different desires in life. The competition here is about adding meaning, not about excluding it. For example, the fourfold divinity of Sathya Sai Baba articulated in his life story extends his divinity into the possibility of including gods, demigods, saints, and gurus, all of whom are considered equally valid by the devotee base. So, while devotees might feel a sense of agency in "picking" the form of godhood they feel a kinship to, the underlying principle of plural forms is never diminished by this choice. But teleological pluralism—i.e., what has evolved as a response to the fragmentation of Western Judeo-Christian culture and finds its way into contemporary discourses on cosmopolitanism and pluralism—is about a replacement of a single, lost sacredness. In a sense, then, theorists are struggling to understand the contemporary gestalt, in which people find it possible to hold multiple meanings as they break away from the assumption of a singular commitment. Hence the concept of pluralism itself is political and subject to various meanings based on its derivation.

Given the importance that the ideal of cosmopolitanism plays in the contemporary world, it is not sufficient to have muddied the waters: I want to complicate the perspective further in the hope of achieving some clarity. I suggest we slide our thinking away from the philosophical debate on the nature of cosmopolitanism, and the politics of its meaning that has dominated the academic dialogue, to one of process: how does cosmopolitanism work? For, while the idea of cosmopolitanism has my sympathies, it is, in the end, just another ideology (however right headed) and has all the problems of the politics of implementation that any ideology has. I do not argue for or against cosmopolitanism on any moral grounds, but rather on an evidentiary basis. It appears to me that the Sathya Sai movement speaks to the actuality of how cosmopolitan pluralism works on the ground, what I have called throughout this work, for lack of a better term, engaged cosmopolitanism. Scholars may suggest that engaged cosmopolitanism is just another ideology, and my difference is merely scholarly hairsplitting, but I beg to differ. The origin of engaged cosmopolitanism is not rooted in post-Enlightenment theories of pluralism but the praxis of plural engagements, and as such it is theory derived from process.

I suggest that the data demonstrates that the Sathya Sai movement has an alternate though often unexplored understanding of cosmopolitanism, an engaged cosmopolitanism—one that seems comfortable with the idea of paradox and of oppositions—and I suspect (though there is no time to explore this here) that it is deeply linked to the adjustments Indian society has had to make to structures of caste, class, religion, and ethnic difference over centuries. The vibrant religious and social plurality of South Asia (though undermined in recent times by both Hindu and Islamic fundamentalisms) still holds firm for a populous society with enormous sociocultural difference embedded within it—so deeply embedded in the fabric and ideology of the society that it is often overlooked by indigenes and scholars alike, who focus on the social fractures that exist and that fundamentalisms create and exploit. I am not defending inequalities in Indian society or the recent fundamentalist strikes from both Muslim and Hindu sides, rather I argue that this South Asian understanding of plurality is not rooted in the Greek individualistic idea of being a citizen of the world, but rather an idea of social inclusivity (though not necessarily equality) of various hitherto overlooked groups and their divergent positions. This vibrant understanding of cosmopolitanism and plurality, rife as it is with conflicting opinions and divergent positions, is the ideological and schematic basis for the Sai alternate understanding of cosmopolitanism that accommodates plural understandings, though it is rarely, if ever, recognized by the Sai movement as being so. I do not suggest that this is a *better* form of cosmopolitanism, but merely a *different* one that is rooted in praxis.

Furthermore, I argue that the construction of this engaged cosmopolitanism rests on the building blocks of what I have termed a grammar of diversity toward a true sharing of cultures. The creation of a grammar of diversity rests on the possibility of a matrix of possible meanings in which interpretation constitutes agency. As we have seen, the grammar of diversity and the matrix of possible meanings act strategically to enable the Sai movement to draw in devotees, of various cultures and nationalities, whose lives and stories all enrich the matrix, iteratively. The grammar of diversity, in turn, constructs the rules for an engaged cosmopolitanism that negotiates the complexities of plurality, which enables the movement to cohere in spite of the diversity within it. It is the process of building this matrix and grammar we have explored in the preceding pages.

The matrix of possible meanings is enabled and engaged by a strategic ambiguity that allows devotees the powers of agency both in picking the required ingredients for their personal transformation as well as in reading the material and spiritual world and interpreting it. As in our previously cited example of the multiple forms of Sai divinity, the principle of strategic ambiguity, and its parallel process of extension by affiliation, enabled Sathya Sai Baba, in the early stages of his life, as we saw in chapter1, to extend his divinity to include divine and semidivine figures through a fourfold model of guru-sant-avatar-future and move relatively quickly from an ordinary peasant boy to a global guru with "nomadic charisma." Devotees' agency is focused upon the tactics of unveiling—an interpretive movement enabling devotee agency—to find the authentic divine self they believed Sathya Sai Baba was.

The matrix of possible meanings has included spatial symbols. Potential devotees traveling to the Sai ashram in Puttaparthi were amazed at the "retro-future aesthetics" that governed the hybrid architectural language in the spiritual capital. As we saw in chapter 2, the hybrid architecture allowed for multivalent readings and meanings—the paradoxical concepts of transcendence and permanence were present simultaneously and the categories of local and global were creatively muddled—allowing devotees to feel the anticipation of the future and the new as well as a gentle, pleasurable nostalgia for the traditional. The architecture became an exciting symbol for the idea that the tactics of extension created an economy of faith that drew from the adventure of multiculturalism promised by the global.

It is clear that strategic ambiguity allows for a polysemic symbol and a multiple interpretation of any image or event. Ambiguity allows for "equality cum diversity" where alternate narratives of devotion and new ways of being religious are manufactured and employed, including different ways of seeing connections between evidence and truth. Moreover, the devotees' narratives of travel to Puttaparthi—of prodigality and of redemption—not only predicted their return to their spiritual home but also their mission to remake the world through seva. Seva gave them a moral anchor and certitude as well as a sense of agency in doing good. As they journeyed, they found Sai Baba, but they also found faith, trust, and themselves, both individually and as a moral community. Global virtual networks such as the Internet enabled them to travel to Puttaparthi and feel close to Sai Baba "in their minds' eye." Their home was located in the imagination where they "feel complete" rather than in geographic or national space. Thus the moral architecture enabled a redrawing of traditional boundaries of identity, making faith the primary indicator of citizenship and creating an imagined global community of faith. I suggest that drawing of faith-based networks across the globe encourages multicultural perspectives on a diversity of issues that in turn strengthens the logic of the matrix of possible meanings.

That interpretive matrix provides the rules to negotiate the new plurality of the globalizing world. It helps to triumph over fear and homogenous impulses and provides fertile ground for an engaged cosmopolitanism to flourish. The central problem in encouraging a cosmopolitan mind-set is not philosophical, and it is not freedom, nor even critical thinking, it is the vitality and centrality of complex webs of meanings that exist all around the subject and must be negotiated everyday—an outcome of cultural exchange existing in plural societies.

But I propose that this notion of a spiritual home and exile, in which devotees from varied cultures and nationalities appear to comprehend the valorizing system of closeness to Sathya Sai Baba and become part of it, is an example of the first set of a dyadic pair of cultural translation processes of *cultural awareness* and *cultural disembedding* where cultural forms and ideologies that are rooted within one culture are made portable through a codification process of disembedding. In terms of process, it appears from the data that the first stage of the mobility of any culture is the disembedding of the cultural from its context. Disembedding requires cultural reflexivity to determine both which parts are integral to the phenomenon itself and which can be translated. In the Sai example of the construction of everyday life of the devotee as exile away from the spiritual center, it is what parts of the Hindu notion of exile (as exemplified in the Ramayana), and transformation through exile, can and should be translated and what can be left out, without jeopardizing either the meaning of the idea of exile while still including its affective power for the many hundreds of thousands of prospective devotees who feel themselves to be spiritual exile, though they seem comfortably housed in a hypercapitalist system of consumption. To make these decisions, rendering an embedded cultural form portable, members of the culture must develop a sense of it and what it offers within the larger world: that it feels it has something to offer culturally is very important. In essence, it is a reflexive understanding of being part of the global game with something to offer. Accompanying this position is a sense of power and agency over the process of cultural translation.

For devotees, the Sai movement appears to provide an Indic-derived, yet global alternative to the assumed technocratic, greedy, consumption-based version of contemporary modernity that has dominated post-colonial discourses (Nandy 1987:121–136): a post-Western form (Alter

2004:74–75) of modernity. It engages a transcultural project of self-awareness and reform through which devotees hope to achieve transcendence. Yet the Sathya Sai movement is derived from this exact version of contemporary modernity. The movement contains within it conflicts and paradoxes that we have tried to contend with. For example, darshan, in which all the senses are supposed to be engaged toward salvation of the individual soul. The ritual of darshan is, by its very nature, nondiscursive and repetitive, and this repetition is supposed to give devotees a sense of order. However, the act of darshan is itself quite chaotic, as devotees attempt to get physically close to Sai Baba to fulfill their "proxemic desire" to interact with the godhead.

While devotees had some agency in their seating choice, the question whether one can get good darshan is, as we have seen, mysterious; governed by the whimsical leela of Sai Baba. In praising Sai Baba during darshan through song and prayer, devotees create a "community of sentiment" that interweaves with the other forms of moral community binding devotees from various cultures and nations firmly into one community of faith. But devotees turned their focus to the unveiling of the meaning of leela in the context of their lives and focused simultaneously on the mundanities of life and the transcendence promised by Sai Baba, "working" to make sense of events. They employed a tool kit of options to sort through the matrix of possible meanings offered, engaging them to craft their own devotional identities, through which the conflicts they felt toward other devotees (who are not like them or whose behavior they cannot fathom) were resolved or held in abeyance. The unpacking of the strategic ambiguity of darshan and the work performed by devotees to build meaning and identity enables us to uncover how devotees see the Sai Baba movement as both deriving out of globalization and providing the solutions to its many problems of clashing values and expectations, individual anomie and excessive materialism. The work that devotees do in response to the strategic ambiguity offered by the Sai movement enables a grammar of diversity through individual reconstruction of identity to devotion and community reorganizing toward charitable work. Work, therefore, has two faces—the inner work for the devotee and the outer work for the community—whereby devotees are transformed into morally engaged stakeholders, enabling them to feel empathy with others in a cosmopolitan context. Thus the movement attempts to move beyond the language and the ideas of the modern—beyond simple nationalism, beyond dialogues of multiculturalism, beyond simple capitalist understandings of religion—all the while being rooted within it. The language of the movement seeks to domesticate these ideas and creates practices and performances that engage alterity while mirroring the structure of modernity. For example, the various divine forms of Sathya Sai Baba engage the dominant capitalist discourse but also override it through millennial and transcendent narratives.

In this illustration the Sai movement manages to elide globalization with both problem (since it is a product of modernity and globalization) and solution (in that it supplies answers to many of the problems globalization creates for the individual such as materialist impulses, greed, and so on) in a creative "doubling back" maneuver. I, along with many others, do not want to be confined to Jean Baudrillard's description of postmodern culture as bland, immediate, transparent, superficial, commercial, and without a sense of place. In fact, Sai identity is produced to speak to these very problems. The seeming flexibility of the Sathya Sai movement and its creation of a grammar of diversity that enables an engaged, empathetic cosmopolitanism resting on an acceptance of a pluralism enables it to overcome these imagined hazards of postmodernity.

But this budding empathy does not mean that conflict both within the individual and in society is erased. For example, the body is the locus of conflicting interpretation for the Sathya Sai organization, both in terms of the meaning of asceticism as well as in terms of the purview of human rights. The body is an impediment to salvation, with its desires and hungers, and must be tamed into asceticism to allow the soul to roam free. The Sai antitraditionalist model of transforming this esoteric Hindu philosophy and practice into the Nine Point Code of Conduct enables it to universalize many potential devotees to access its power. I suggest that the codification of the body discipline into the nine-point code is part of a dyadic pair of processes of cultural translation of *codification* and *universalization,* In this second stage embedded systems of meaning are simplified and then codified so that they can be made portable and easily understood. In the Sai codification of sattvica we find a deconstruction and reconstruction of the meaning of the idea of asceticism and how it affects everyday behavior for the devotee. The choice of what is essential to retain both the validity and authenticity of the idea as well as the spiritual health of the practitioner (giving it some cultural and moral heft, as it were) is essential to making the idea worthy of cultural exchange. The codification of the cultural matrix of the originating culture into a series of regulatory principles or patterns of knowledge that is transferable enables the cultural form to become mobile. It enables the cultural form to be disembedded from the cultural matrix. In the second step, the cultural form is disassembled, i.e., the cultural form itself is taken apart and examined. What is extrinsic to the form is discarded, and what is intrinsic for the form to have meaning and power is retained. The intrinsic meaning gives the form its legitimacy and authenticity in the new culture. The cultural form is ready to be made mobile and rides the engines of globalization: migrations of people, new technology, and economic institutions. The codified parts are then made accessible to a larger number of people through various tactics of diffusion such as affiliation or extension. For translation of a particular cultural form, the originating culture must codify the matrix within which the it resides. The taken-for-granted world is made explicit so that the particular cultural form can be contextualized easily.

However, the reality with regard to varying discourses of the body and its disciplining is that cultural translation (regardless of the cultures involved) is neither single nor gradable. Truancy points to variable and valorized understandings of the body and its control. Since the physical body of the devotee and the body of the Sai community are seen as analogous, truancy in asceticism mirrors some issues within the institutional body as well. The conflict over the value of the body in the spiritual encounter and what the spiritual encounter can and should consist of brings out the cracks within translation.

In fact, competing translations occur all the time, though all may not have the same influence or value, and this creates problems of translation, as the various translations are often incompatible or value ridden. But sometimes, as we found in the case of the Japanese Sathya Sai society, the symbolism built on fault lines or gaps can be so strained and weak that it becomes divisive, and unthinking devotees separate themselves into groups or nation, based on the shared meaning they choose to adopt. In this semiotic process, as Baudrillard as noted, the symbols become all-powerful. The embedded question of the semiotic process—i.e., the problematic links and involutions that occur between the real and the representational—weaves though nearly every chapter. The process of cultural translation, as we have seen with the differential understandings of Sathya Sai objects between devotees and the SSSO, is composed of two dynamics that carry on in a temporal parallel formation (though I will unpack them sequentially): the semiotic dynamic and the circulation dynamic.

The first is a semiotic dynamic à la Peirce where there is an iterative attempt to create or appropriate an icon (something of meaning and value) to make it into an index (make it portable) and then into a symbol (revalorize it with new meanings). This cyclical semiotic process is best seen in the Sathya Sai conversion of the sacred gift into commodity and then into a status marker for devotees to demonstrate their proximity to Sathya Sai Baba. The semiotic process can occur along the fault lines between or within culture, leading to several splinter meanings and values that allow for a productive ambiguity.

It is clear from the data of the preceding chapters that cultural translation occurs during the congress between cultures. It is because the Sathya Sai movement is successful in drawing devotees from different nations, religions, ethnicities, classes, castes, and cultures that cultural translation of its ideas is essential.

But devotees from different cultures read the objects differently so as to permit an affective connection, and this allows for a wider devotional base, evidenced in the Sai birthday celebration. The ambiguity allows for a polysemic symbol and a multiple interpretation of any image or event. The Sai material world juxtaposed the matrix of possible meanings that strategic ambiguity (including polysemy and sublimation) enabled against the puzzle of interpretation and meaning construction in which devotees engage. The easily universalizing moral/religious metatext with individually and culturally based mediation is the essence of a successful global religion. I argue that these objects and their interpretive meaning are examples of the third dyadic pair of processes of cultural translation—*latching* and *matching*—in which cultural forms and ideologies are given latching mechanisms that enable them to match up with the interpretive maps of meaning within other cultures. Once the cultural form is made mobile, either by institutions or by the mass migrations of people, it develops latching mechanisms that enable it to match its host cultures. In this process the "original" and seemingly "authentic" meaning of the cultural form undergoes rapid change. Imagine one of the science fiction films of the 1970s where aliens came to Earth in pods. These pods invariably had efficient systems of latching so that the alien spacecraft could easily infiltrate Earth. Cultures that import new forms are cultures that are quick to translate and mold new cultural forms to fit into the dominant culture of reception (which may be hybrid itself). Various cultures, dependent on their familiarity with cultural translation, have efficient and inefficient systems of latching. Cultures that have efficient systems of latching are more mobile in spreading cultural forms and ideologies and in absorbing them as well. The imported cultural forms match certain desires or needs in the host society. When the latching mechanism is efficient, and the match effective, the new cultural form is engaged to the point where it becomes part of the everyday consciousness of people. They forget that it was imported and embedded in the host culture.

Roach has argued in his thoughtful analysis of circum-Atlantic performances of memory through walking in the city, and the links between performance, memory, and substitution, that we use "processes of surrogation," a "universal trans-historical structure" (1996:4) whereby we substitute something with which we are familiar for something that is strange and unknown in order to understand the unknown and render it familiar. He suggests that what he terms a "genealogy of performance" couples kinaesthetic memory of embodied performance with other social forms of memory and that this enables "displaced transmission," "the adaptation of historic practices to changing conditions" where "popular behaviors are transmitted to new locales" (1996:27–28). "Much more happens than transmission of tradition through surrogacy. New traditions may also be invented and others overturned. The paradox of the restoration of behavior resides in the phenomenon of repetition itself: no action or sequence of actions is performed the same way twice; they must be reinvented or re-created at each appearance" (1996:28). This "repetition with revision," which the Sai movement effectively engages in, "illuminates the theoretical and practical possibilities of restored behavior not merely as the recapitulation but as the transformation of experience through the displacement of its cultural forms" (1996:28) when improvisation creeps into these forms and becomes ritualized. Thus the dominant notion that cultural transmission results in a repetition that is static, rigid, conventional, predictable, and uniform is a fallacy. Rather, as we have seen, agency, conflict, and play erupt into the transmission, making it dynamic and variously readable. So, as Rosaldo writes in his analysis of culture (1993 [1989]: 20), culture and cultural transmission nodes are "busy porous intersections" in which "distinct processes crisscross from within and beyond its borders."

So, the multiple possible interpretations of the matrix enable an escape from the stifling dialectics of a unitary understanding of a culture of origination and cultures of reception toward both "ontological complexity" (the inherent complexity of social systems and hybrid cultures) and "semiotic complexity" (our understandings of these complexities and the signs we use to denote them). The dual, intersecting worlds of magical gifted objects and bought ordinary objects highlighted both the mobility of the object, and its value to the devotee, and the object itself revealed the multidimensional meaning of the global network as it moved through the global field of Sai devotion, aided by trade in religious artifacts. But devotees reconstructed the meaning and therefore the value of Sai religious objects based on the mode of acquisition: through direct gift from Sai Baba, through indirect gift or teleportation, and through purchase, and the concordant "value" held by the commodity is seen as reflective of the value of devotee.

In the Sathya Sai movement, symbols, metaphors, and tropes (oral, sensual, textual, and visual) act as accessible, complex, and ambiguous vehicles for meanings, emotions, and experiences that can be infinitely interconnected, leading to different meanings;where the original meaning can be detoured, deflected, or displaced to create a new one. All these meanings are acceptable. In this situation, agency of the devotee is located in the interpretation of knowledge. Individual choice becomes a complex and critical component of the mediation of the matrix. Devotees feel that their contributions become essential for the creation of this overarching matrix, as they transform their selves and habitus into an ideal of devotion performed everyday (Csordas 1994a:68–69). Thus, devotees' thoughts, bodies, lives, and stories all enrich the matrix. For Sai devotees, then, value resides not in the dualisms of the modern or the traditional, but in the multistranded ambiguity of the plural and global, in the shift of the object from icon to symbol to simulacra. Thus the fourth stage of cultural translation processes occurs through the dyad of *contextualization* and *reembedding*, where ideologies and cultural forms are contextualized within the culture of reception of the audience (though the audience may not have been the intended target) and reembedded within this culture, which itself might be a composite hybrid culture. Reembedding is accompanied by contextualization. New cultural forms are given new meanings to make them fit seamlessly into the culture of reception, which is itself evolving. The seeming authenticity and ability to trace the cultural form's lineage and origins become critical for the form to be adopted. It is seen as something external and perhaps exotic that has particular appeal in modern capitalist cultures where inhabitants feel a sense of being "homeless" (Berger, Berger, and Kellner 1973). On the other hand, a cultural form can strike a concordance, in that it can bring up a cultural resonance in the host society where people remember or think they remember the cultural form. An imported cultural form can appeal to this nostalgia and embed itself in the receiving culture. Either way, whether a cultural form appeals to a concordance or a yearning for something strange, for cultural translation to succeed, in-depth knowledge of both the originating culture and the host culture is necessary.

But semiotic processes are generally derived from language, and language, both symbolic and real, has linearity, which allows translation. But, along with culture, we have the whole problem of representation. Representations or signs are all about relationships; what is important about the sign is not itself but its associations (Deleuze and Guattari 1987). Signs make sense because they are part of a network of signs—the network is the signifier—and individual signs are deterritorialized and reterritoralized with regard to different parts of the network. The difference between parts of the network allows for what we called dedifferentiation, which allows for "equality cum diversity," in which alternate narratives of devotion and new ways of being religious are manufactured and employed, including different ways of seeing connections between evidence and truth, as we saw in chapter 5, as devotees, core devotees, and former devotees all understood the "truth" of sexual healing somewhat differently. But in the semiotic process, as Baudrillard as noted (1994), the symbols become all-powerful. Sometimes the symbolism can be so strained and weak that its interpretation becomes divisive, and devotees separate themselves into preordained groups by, say, nation, based on the meaning they choose to adopt. In other cases, the semiotic process leads to a symbol made strong and reified into one static meaning that is authoritarian and against which devotees rebel, as in the case of embodied discipline and asceticism within the ashram to reinterpret the symbol.

Cultural forms and ideologies move across the global web in many directions simultaneously—in a circulation dynamic—and as they do so they morph and shift, acquiring new meanings and reinventing the cultures with which they interact. The network, because of its multidirectionality, constructs a nonlinear flow pattern—a "re-mediation" process (Bolter and Grusin 2000, in Van Loon 2006)—and enables agency in unlikely places via actor access and participation. Through a chronological sequence of themes, motives, and plot lines (such as Sai Baba's life story), usually with a strong moral component that forms the causal structure of a story (such as his vindication at the hands of doubting devotees after his revelations), these modes of communication form a discursive and dynamic matrix of multilayered and polysemic structures of meaning for people to tap into.[4] The matrix of possible meanings is enabled by cultural interaction and interactive reinvention as the process of cultural congress is endlessly repeated. Therefore it articulates different systems of ordering that are not based "a priori on dualisms of subjects and objects"and enables a dissemination of "accumulated intelligence" (Van Loon 2006:309) through the "interconnectedness of a multiplicity of agency that sits quite comfortably along with non-Western belief systems" (309). Networks such as the Sai movement, with their intricate hierarchies and networks of distribution, allow for a complex distribution of knowledge, which, through its many iterations, creates a new politics of knowledge production and sharing.[5]

What flows along these networks are the narratives, strategies, tactics, rhetorics, and other dynamic communicative modes that are central to the transmission of culture. The modes of communication are perforce focused on problems of interpretation and epistemology. They can be in performance form, such as in the praxis of worship and devotion in the Sathya Sai centers, or they can be exculpatory (i.e., giving explanations), as in the case of devotees' narratives of their behavior in the ashram. I suggest that it is at the intersection of the linear rhetoric of modes of communication and the web-diffused network that there is potential for the grammar of diversity to evolve. It is within this intersection that a matrix of social and intellectual contexts exists and possibilities are formed.

But cultural translation can be caught between being too literal, in which case the translation is ineffective since only the original culture can understand the cultural form and its meaning—such as in the embedded Hindu teleological meaning of the poorna avatar, which devotees claim for Sai Baba, or too idiomatic, in which case the cultural form is only meaningful to the translator, as in the subtle shades of divine play and the affect of unveiling divinity in the leela of darshan, which have been insufficiently translated, so *leela* becomes a watered-down concept to many, or too plastic, in which case the authenticity of the cultural form or ideology is at risk. Faulty translation is also in evidence in the transformation of the sattvica ideology to one of bodily health and therapeutic wellness, currently fashionable in the West. We have seen this fine line of translation, whereby these pitfalls are avoided, negotiated by the Sathya Sai movement in this study.

But where the translation becomes truly problematic is when certain untranslatables emerge—where incompatible cultural forms that are unique to each culture, or are guarded as such, erupt into fault lines between cultures as they relate to values or morality—a culture war. For example, as with the example of the Jesus avatar, or most memorably with the problem over sexual healing, consent, and accountability, often there was a historically nuanced incommensurability between the culturally embedded ideas of the Sathya Sai movement and the ideas of devotees from different cultures. When different culturally embedded spatiotemporal understandings come into congress, intercultural communication grinds to a halt and contestations arise. The contestations are symptomatic of where the gaps splay apart and the translation itself becomes hotly contested.

The debate over sexual healing and embodiment, where the value of selfhood and the legal systems attendant to it are based on different cultural understandings of the relationship between self, body, and divinity, is evidence that cultural translation is not merely a one-to-one concordance and that "gaps in translation" sometimes occur, pointing to a clash of perspectives on interpretation: "things look different depending upon where you see them from" (Hannerz 1990:65). At any given time in the global world, people are surrounded by information, managed and raw (called externalizations), and by interacting with these externalizations people begin to construct an identity for themselves through their perspectives on a given problem. As Hannerz notes, the perspective implies "a trained capacity for handling the world in a particular way, and a trained incapacity for handling it another way" (67). Sai devotees demonstrated the value of perspective in every encounter, even during the sacred darshan, as they accepted, negotiated, or contested each other's accepted, "taken for granted" (Berger 1966) worldviews. Development of perspective is evocative of systematic immersion in a continuous iterative round of reinterpretation of cultural and symbolic flows.[6] In a network system the awareness of others' perspectives puts one's own vision and subject position into question. Clifford Geertz's definition of culture as "webs of signification that create meanings and motivations" (1973) seems to foreshadow a congress of different webs of signification through globalization networks.[7]

It is clear that the semiotic process must be interwoven with a process of mobility to enable globalization. Both the symbolic process of making meaning and the process of circulation across space and time need to be parallel processes for globalization to be effective. To reiterate, the complex process of mobility is composed of four dyadic pairs of subprocesses or stages that occur in a linear progression as the cultural form or ideology is made mobile: 1. cultural awareness and disembedding (where the cultural form is taken out of its originating culture or ideology is separated from location), 2. codification and universalization (where the cultural assumptions of the originating culture are codified for transfer), 3. latching and matching (where the cultural form is taken overseas to a new receiving culture and given new meaning, relinking it in new and innovative ways to the originating culture to give it authenticity and value), and, last, 4. contextualization (where the cultural form or ideology is linked to the larger cultural matrix of the receiving culture and made relevant) and reembedding (where the cultural form is embedded into the host culture). These processes of cultural translation are, I argue, key to the practical problem of creating and maintaining any dynamic, successful, transnational, cultural movement.

What this process-based understanding of cultural translation underlines is that connections between cultures are being forged constantly in this era of globalization. The premise of the incommensurability of cultures that was inherited when I started this work, is at best, questionable. Based on the Sathya Sai data, it is clear that the incommensurability of cultures is not a structural condition (as is silently assumed in many works on cultural globalization) but a historical one. If one accepts this, then the historical condition of cultural incommensurability and our understanding of it is changeable. Let me emphasize that we know predicting the future of cultural globalization is a hazardous enterprise, as the "dialectics of flow and closure," according to Birgit Meyer and Peter Geschiere (1999), and networks of globalization are varied, dynamic, and complex. But, if we postulate that another world is possible, the construction of this world rests on the building of a grammar of diversity through these processes of cultural translation toward a true sharing of cultures.

For scholars who may think that I suggest Sai devotees are making a case for total cultural relativism, the discussion of secrecy shows that, for Sai devotees, there is only one truth and that only the divine knows this truth. Therefore the goods, events, disciplines, and services that devotees engage in, they argue, are merely different paths to this truth, and the greater the layering of paths, or of meanings, the better. The processes of the layering of meanings and the plethora of choices (some of which may seem, and sometimes are, contradictory) encased in the idea of the "many leading to the one" is the scaffolding of the grammar of diversity.

If we were to move tentatively from process to argument, we might hesitantly suggest that the grammar of diversity is about inclusion, and it enables us to generate a language, rooted in the many, toward an engaged cosmopolitanism that is a necessary condition for multicultural societies to live in civility. This is the basis of a new pluralism.

Appendix

Global Sathya Sai Centers

Zone	Region	Countries	Centers	Groups
		India		
1	11	United States	192	
	12	West Indies	92	
		Bahamas, Trinidad and Tobago, Surinam, Guyana, Barbados, and other Caribbean Islands		
	13	Canada	33	41
2		Latin America and Puerto Rico	—	
	21	Belize, Costa Rica, Cuba, Dominican Republic, El Salvador, Guatemala, French Guyana, Haiti, Honduras, Mexico, Nicaragua, Panama, Puerto Rico	41	38
	22	Columbia, Ecuador, Peru, Venezuela	—	
	23	Argentina, Bolivia, Brazil, Chile, Paraguay, Uruguay	88	121

(*continued*)

Zone	Region	Countries	Centers	Groups
3		Australia and Papua New Guinea	127	
		New Zealand, Fiji, and Pacific	32	45
		Islands, Philippines, Nepal, Bhutan		
		Sri Lanka	120	
4		Far East (South) Brunei, Indonesia, Malaysia, Singapore, Thailand, Vietnam	113	38
		Far East (Middle) Afghanistan, Bangladesh, Laos, Myanmar (Burma), Pakistan	43	26
5		Far East (North) China PRC, Hong Kong, Japan, Korea, Taiwan ROC	15	19
6		South Europe		
	61	Croatia, France, Italy, Malta, Portugal, Slovenia, Spain, Switzerland	—	
	62	Albania, Bosnia-Herzegovina, Bulgaria, Cyprus, Greece, Macedonia, Montenegro, Romania	—	
7		North Europe	46	103
	71	Austria, Czech Republic, Germany, Hungary, Slovakia	—	
	72	Belgium, Denmark, Greenland, Iceland, Luxembourg, Netherlands, Norway, Sweden	—	
	73	Estonia, Finland, Latvia, Lithuania, Poland	16	21
8		East Europe/Russian speakers Azerbaijan, Armenia, Byelorussia, Georgia, Kazakhstan, Kyrgyzstan, Moldova, Russia, Tagzhikistan, Turkmenistan, Uzbekistan, Ukraine	54	
9		United Kingdom, Republic of Ireland, Africa, Middle East	170	
	91	United Kingdom, Republic of Ireland	6	
	92	Africa South: South Africa, Botswana, Mauritius, Seychelles	96	51

Zone	Region	Countries	Centers	Groups
	93	Central and North Africa and Mauritius Angola, Cameroon, Congo, Ethiopia, Kenya (Nairobi), Ghana, Ivory Coast, Libya, Malawi, Morocco, Nigeria, Rwanda, Senegal, Sierra Leone, Somalia, Swaziland, Tanzania, Uganda, Zambia, Zimbabwe	34	101
	94	Middle East and Gulf (except Israel) Abu Dhabi, Bahrain, Dubai, Iran, Kuwait, Oman, Qatar, Saudi Arabia, Syria, Turkey	21	6

Compiled from Sathya Sai Organization Web site; www.sathyasai.org.

Notes

Introduction

1. "India Shining" was a controversial campaign by the Indian government intended to promote India internationally. It referred to the overall feeling of economic optimism in India after 2003 and the success of the Indian IT boom. The slogan was popularized by the then ruling Bharatiya Janata Party (BJP) for the 2004 Indian general elections. It drew criticism from various political critics of the ruling government for glossing over a variety of social problems including poverty, social inequality, and religious "communal" rioting, and it became a code word for secular scholars to indicate what they believe to be the Hindutva agenda of the BJP.

2. I see multiculturalism as the legalization of equality for all groups within a plural society and their acceptance within the larger society.

3. I realize that some scholars, particularly those studying religion in the subcontinent, might be sensitive to my usage of the term *Indic* since it has been claimed by contemporary Hindu right-wing forces. Let me be clear that I use the term *Indic* to denote a religiocultural entity emergent from the plural Hindu-Islamic religiocultural syncretic matrix of the subcontinent. In so doing I return it to its originary usage as meaning "of the Indian subcontinent." Part of my this study is to reclaim some terms and language from the political and to give them vitality and validity in new arena.

4. The following account draws upon Babb 1986; Bowen 1988; Palmer 2005; Srinivas 2008; and T. Srinivas 2002.

5. Scholarly analysis of the Sathya Sai movement is divided. Within Indian scholarship and elsewhere the movement is sometimes described as neo-Hinduism, that is, part of a long tradition of reform movements within Hinduism stretching back to Swami Vivekenanda and the World Congress of Religion in the late nineteenth century or, more commonly, as a "revitalization" project of South Asian pride in countries with a South Asian diaspora. With regard to the postcolonial project, the Sai movement is often categorized as part of the religious reawakening of the world either categorized as part of a "fundamentalist resurgence" a "nationalist project" where the Sathya Sai faith is seen as a postmodern variant of Hinduism, or a "new age" variation on Hinduism. I myself have been guilty in the past of uneasily describing the Sathya Sai movement as new age or neo-Hindu as I struggled to define it.

6. I will refer to Shri (honorific) Sathya Sai Baba as Sai Baba or Sathya Sai Baba throughout this book because it encompasses both the devotee's point of view and other non-Sai devotees' thoughts and experiences.

7. Sathya Sai Baba, or Sathyanarayana Raju, as he was originally known, was born to a rural, poor, dominant caste, peasant family in the arid village of Puttaparthi in the southern Indian state of Andhra Pradesh on November 23, 1926. At the age of thirteen he is believed to have declared his divinity, stating to his sister-in-law, "I am no longer your Sathya, I am Sai," thereby claiming affiliation with the revered southern Indian saint and Maharashtrian Muslim fakir, Shirdi Sai Baba, who died in 1918. From that time onward legends of his healing, materializations, and spiritual power have grown along with his following.

8. This paragraph borrows from Babb 1986:166.

9. It is very difficult to get an accurate numerical estimate of Sai devotees (see T. Srinivas 2002) for a variety of reasons but estimates state that over 1,000,000 people attended Sai Baba's seventieth birthday celebrations in 1995, and approximately 2 million people from 175 countries attended his eightieth birthday celebrations in 2005.

10. Estimates of the total number of Baba devotees around the world vary between 10 and 70 million, although in a recent article *India Today* puts their strength at 20 million in 137 countries and their net worth at approximately $6 billion.

11. Rigolopoulos reported that there were close to 10 million devotees (1993:377). Today there are 1,200 Sai Baba Centers for promoting the religion in 137 different countries. Another source says that there are over 6,500 Sai Baba Centers in different countries.

12. In Marshall and Van Saanen 2007, an edited volume on faith and development, it is suggested that the Sathya Sai Seva organization has over 8,000 centers. Former devotees suggest that the number is more likely about 1,200.

13. Numbers varied, depending upon whom I spoke to, from 2,000 to 6,000 in 2001. This number of 3,050 is from Padmanaban 2000:viii.

14. See http://www.rediff.com/money/2003/aug/16donations.htm.

15. Today, according to devotees, there are 1,200 Sai Baba Centers for promoting the religion in 137 different countries. In 1993, Rigolopoulos reported that there were close to ten million devotees (377). Another source says that there are over 6,500 Sai Baba Centers in different countries. A few gurus such as Narayana Baba made several trips to Europe and the United States to spread the mission of Sai Baba. Though it did not reach high popularity in the U.S., the gurus were still able to teach many of the religious concepts (Rigolopoulos 1993:375). More recently, in 1967, lectures on Sai Baba were given at the University of California and interest in this group began. During the 1970s, the pace of the movement grew, and Melton reports a growing number of groups in North America, especially the United States. In addition, Sai Baba's group formed a foundation in California and they also publish a Sathya Sai newsletter there (Gordon 1996:868).

16. The Sathya Sai movement had been categorized by social scientists in the Western world as part of the postmodern phenomenon of new age religions or New Religious Movements (NRM). The Sai movement is mentioned as an NRM in Coney 200, 2003; and Lucas and Robbins 2004. It has been studied under the NRM rubric in both Europe and America (Clark 1987; Deutsch 1989; Knott 1987, 1993). Sharma in his work on the Sai Movement in India also refers to it as an NRM (1986). Ackerman and Lee refer to the Sai movement in Malaysia as an NRM (1988) and recently, Arweck and Clarke's bibliography of NRMs in Europe have multiple references to the Sai movement (1997).

17. http://www.sathyasai.org/organize/z1rego1/contents.html.

18. Bharati 1970.

19. "A God Accused," *India Today*, December 4, 2000.

20. Paul Lewis, "The Indian Living God, the Pedophilia Claims, and the Duke of Edinburgh Awards," *Guardian*, November 4, 2006, p. 3.

21. Manu B. S. Rao, "Sai Baba Lashes Out at Detractors," *Times of India*, December 26, 2000.

    "BANGALORE: Sri Sathya Sai Baba on Monday lashed out at his detractors in a rare display of anger while delivering a discourse on the occasion of Christmas at Brindavana, Whitefield ashram here. . . . In an obvious reference to some of what has been written against him in the recent days, Baba said that many have been bought and they speak against him for the money they have received to do so."

22. One of the founders of the Hard Rock chain, Isaac Tigrett, is a Sathya Sai devotee.

23. My inference is that the owners of the Seven Stars Biodynamic yogurt farm, David and Edie Griffiths, are Sathya Sai devotees.

24. *Satya* is an alternative spelling for *Sathya*.

25. A former devotee indicated that Lightstorm was a kind of marijuana. Personal communication with the author, May 5, 2007.

26. Part of series on spiritual and moral leaders that includes Gautama Buddha and civil rights leaders in America.

27. "The problem of Europe," as postcolonial thinkers have called it (Appadurai and Breckenridge 1995; Said 1978; van der Veer and Lehman 1999), is the tendency of social science scholarship to think of Europe as the primary locus of modernity. Thus India's, or, indeed, any other culture's, varied transitions merely become a footnote to the European move toward a fuller modernity.

28. See Hernando de Soto (2000) for a critical analysis of how the West has historically dominated circuits of capital. De Soto's volume reads as a manifesto for developing countries to even the playing field of capital by dissecting what he calls " the mysteries of capital."

29. Derrida argued that Fukuyama's thesis was a disturbing Christian eschatology that spread the idea of Western hegemony as "the new gospel." See Derrida 1994.

30. But this theory of cultural hybridity often is misinterpreted and misapplied leading to the pitfall of "radical particularism" (Kurasawa 2004:8); generating a naive and politicized particularism where locality and alterity are generated as oppositions to globality to encourage "monologues of difference" through the siloization of dialogues.

31. This formulation of the problem has been accepted both by critics and believers alike and has been viewed with some hesitancy, some fear, and some warmth by the various quarters.

32. Doniger 1998:36, 73.

33. Beaulieu 2004.

34. Without the initial help of Dr. V. Vijayalakshmi of ISEC, Bangalore, this work would not have been possible.

35. While I have tried to keep culture and nation separate to avoid essentialist arguments, I found that I sometimes slipped unwarily into conflating the two, since devotees referenced each other's differences through nation and region, they wore sashes indicating their national affiliations, and it was thus an easy point of difference.

36. Joost van Loon, in his paradigmatic essay (2006), describes the global network as a trope that consists of three elements: nodes (where the mesh of the network intersects), links ("basic units of the network"), and mesh ("the shape and pattern of the network, which gives it its functionality"). The network form stresses "fluidity, transformation and ambivalence" (Van Loon 2006:310), leading perforce to plurality (T. Srinivas 2002). The nodes of the network are where cultural congress and cultural translation occur. They are linked to one another sometimes through organizational and organized ties, such as the ordered tiers of executives at the Sathya Sai Seva Organization, or sometimes through fuzzy and unorganized threads, such as a network of Sai devotees of twenty nationalities who happened to be on the same bus that broke down in 1978 on the way to Puttaparthi and who subsequently began ten different Seva centers. The nodes control the cultural reinvention process by locating the patrimony of ideas and goods, making them culturally accessible, and by providing subsidiary information around them that enables "proper" translation. The struggle to control

the nodes is the struggle for power—of both what gets translated as well as how it gets translated, what it means, what its value is, and whom it reaches. So the network 1. works against linearity and chronology by constructing a logic of networking based on relationality and complex connectivity and 2. is ambiguous in its size and shape; where it ends is unclear.

37. Rosenberg 2007.

38. See Spurr 2007:28.

1. Becoming God

1. SSS 2:155–156.

2. All records of his early life have been effectively erased. No records of his birth exist, and the house where he was born has been replaced by a Shiva temple. His mother and his father are long dead. His siblings live in Puttaparthi and are close to him, so they do not speak to anyone outside the movement.

3. Brian Steel, a former devotee, states that there are over six hundred devotee accounts of Sai Baba.

4. At my last count, in 2007, over 157 titles.

5. Padmanaban's magnum opus, *Love Is My Form: The Advent* (2000), was published after seven years of research. Padmanaban, who was Sai Baba's personal photographer from 1985 to 1990, richly illustrates this six-hundred-page volume with many photographs. The book details the first twenty-four years of Sathya Sai Baba's life and draws from every textual source known to Sai devotees as well as two hundred interviews of people who knew Sathya Sai Baba as a boy and young man. This book was supposed to be the first of six or seven volumes to document Sathya Sai Baba's life, but the project was abruptly halted after publication of the first volume.

6. I use *revelation* in the sense of a revelation to the devotees of the true self of Sathya Sai Baba and not in the sense of the Abrahamic concept of revelation as the "Word of God." In Hindu understandings of revelation, divinity that is hidden in plain sight chooses the moment to unmask, revealing the true divinity within (what Rudolf Otto would call the *Numen*) to humans.

7. For example, in a central moment in the fratricidal war of the Mahabharata, a mythic Hindu epic, Krishna the divine descent (avatar) of Vishnu, unveils himself to Arjuna (a king), in His universal form (*vishwarupa*), in the theater of battle.

8. In Thurston's *Caste and Tribes of South India*, the Rajus are described as "The Rajus or Razus; they are known to come from the Godavari basin far north of Puttaparthi in the southern Indian state of Andhra Pradesh. In the Madras census report of 1901 the Rajus are stated to be "perhaps descendants of the military section of the Kapu, Kamma, and Velama castes. At their weddings they worship a sword, which is a ceremony that usually denotes a soldier caste. They say they are Kshatriyas" (Thurston 1909, 6:247.)

9. Nondevotees tend to see this emphasis on his early poverty as affiliating with the "great tradition" of Hinduism through well-known myths of gods and goddesses appearing on earth as powerless and lower-caste individuals.

10. The move from poverty and anonymity to worldwide recognition as a savior is common in many religions. In popular Hinduism, particularly in Vaishnavite myth, there is an understanding that divinity chooses the poorest and most downtrodden to demonstrate his *leela*.

11. Today Eashwaramma is a central figure to the movement, and her ascent began in the mid 1970s. My interviewees often referred to her as "divine Mother," linguistically linking her to "the Mother" of the Aurobindo movement of Pondicherry, India. From the 1970s onward, devotee accounts state that Sathya Sai Baba visited his mother on his birthday, and stories of her divine qualities, including her goodness and love of Sathya Sai Baba, are told. After her death, her *samadhi* (place of death/burial) became a site of significance for devotees; all my interviewees claimed to have visited it and received her blessings. The day of her death, May 6, became a festival, Eashwaramma Day, for all the devotees, especially for the women and girls in the movement. The anti-Sai network has combated the growing influence of Eashwaramma by suggesting that she was in an "incestuous" relationship with her husband, since he was her cousin. However, cross-cousin marriage is established practice in India, and devotees see this claim as a willful misrepresentation of India's marriage mores and a conscious bid to discredit Sathya Sai Baba's mother.

12. The Satyanarayana katha (story) is part of the *Skanda Purana* in *Reva Kund series of the Puranic texts*. It was one of those long-forgotten stories that was revitalized because it claimed to offer material gains. According to the Skanda Purana, the Satyanarayana katha was related by Vishnu to the sage Narada to help humankind achieve their greatest desires.

13. "Years later, when devotees were to ask Sri Sathya Sai Baba whether He was born through *prasava* (ordinary conception) or *pravesha* (immaculate conception), he would point to Eashwaramma, seated nearby, intimating, "Ask her." See Kasturi 1989; http://www.angelfire.com/on/GEAR2000/SaiDiscourse23Nov03.html.

14. Stories involve finding a horse that was lost (Kasturi 1962:7) and "magically" producing sweets for his classmates (Kasturi 1962:17, 31–235); forming a religious-based theater group—the Pandhari Bhajan group (Kasturi 1962:18–23, 27–32; Padmanaban 2000:34–37, 39–42); and composing theologically inspired marketing ballads for use by a local merchant (Kasturi 1962:25–26; Padmanaban 2000:58–60).

15. At this point the hagiography is unclear and divergent. In some accounts he was unconscious for three days, in yet others he recovered twenty-four hours later.

16. While Kasturi suggests that Sai Baba was born in Puttaparthi (1962:8), Padmanaban suggests that in actuality he was born in his mother's village close by (2000:21).

17. S. Srinivas quotes Spurr (2007), who argues that previous scholars have tended to see Sathya Sai Baba's claim as one edging him to Brahminical status, but the *gotra* idea was not confined to Brahmins alone. See Spurr (2007). Thurston and Rangachari further state that the Bharadwaja was the *gotra* of the Bhatraju caste (2001 [1909], 1:223–224). See Srinivas 2008:53.

18. However, according to former devotee and author Brian Steel, this was not strictly true. He asserts that in the biography titled *Love Is My Form*, by Padmanabha, early devotees of Sai Baba and people who lived in Puttaparthi at the time of his revelation claimed that they knew of Shridi Sai Baba. Steel states: "Even in the early hagiographical SSB literature, there is some evidence that what SSB stated was not correct. Prior to the publication of LIMF (Love Is My Form) in 2000, we already had some weak evidence" (1997). Murphet 1971:56: "The name [Shirdi Sai Baba] was only known to a few very old villagers." Also: "known by a few people in the area" (58). Shepherd (1985) writes, "It may be observed that photographs of the Shirdi adept were not difficult to obtain at that time" (n. 77). See http://bdsteel.tripod.com/More/dossistories.htm.

19. However Padmanaban (2000:67–71, 114–116) argues that Sathya Sai Baba already knew of Shirdi Sai Baba and had a picture of him. He also claims that Sathya Sai Baba's uncles were devotees of Shirdi Sai Baba.

20. Interview with Mrs. Shanthi Somayya, December 15, 1998; interview with Mr. Bill Bronson, April 2002; interview with Mr. M. S. Rao, October 8, 1998, interview with Joule De Vrees, July 12, August 18, August 23, 1999.

21. Shirdi Sai Baba was originally from Shirdi, a town in Maharashtra state and at the time of his death had a large following among the Indian middle classes.

22. Mrs. Shanthi Somayya, a Sai devotee of thirteen years standing, told me the story of Sathya Sai Baba (the Sai katha) with great pleasure on many occasions. I thank her.

23. According to Brian Steel, who claims to be neither a devotee nor a former devotee, but whom I met through former devotees and who runs a complex and information-saturated Web site devoted to pointing out errors in Sai Baba's many discourses and texts, the linking of the Sathya Sai persona to the Shirdi Sai persona was a purposefully constructed myth. Steel states: "In addition to making frequent public claims to be the reincarnation of this widely revered saint, SSB made special efforts to describe his affinities with Shirdi: teachings, types of miracles, and sayings, as well as exhibiting pictures of Shirdi in his ashram, which are still prominent to this day. He also made references (including allegedly omniscient ones) to Shirdi's life, especially to older devotees who had worshipped him. All of this played an important part in spreading SSB's fame and in attracting early devotees, including an important number of elderly aristocratic patrons." See http://bdsteel.tripod.com/More/dossistories.htm.—"The Shirdi Sai Baba Stories Under the Spotlight."

24. Sathya Sai Baba's affiliation with the Sufi mystic Shirdi Sai Baba is not viewed with equanimity nor thought of as "a natural succession" by all Sai

devotees. Devotees of Shirdi Sai Baba did and do not necessarily accept Sathya Sai Baba as the inheritor of Shirdi Sai Baba's divine mantle. Kevin Shepherd, a biographer of Shirdi Sai Baba, states; "Hazrat Sai Baba of Shirdi is certainly not to be confused with those gurus who announce themselves as speedily returning reincarnations of him, and who even appropriate his name." See Shepherd 1986:77.

25. In popular Hinduism, Thursday (*guruvara* = Kannada) is the day of the week set aside for the worship of one's chosen guru or preceptor. Thursday is dedicated to the planet guru (Jupiter).

26. Srinivas 2001.

27. The Shirdi Sai myth claims that Shirdi Sai Baba was a Muslim by birth who was adopted by a Hindu upper-caste family. He apparently came first to Shirdi, or was first noticed on the periphery of the village Shirdi, seated under a *neem* (margosa) tree, about the year 1854, and moved into a dilapidated mosque on the outskirts of the village. After moving into the mosque, where the villagers welcomed him, he took to wearing a long shirt—a *kafni*—and tied a cloth around his head. Early accounts claim that he spent his days begging for food and cooking chapatis on a small fire, or *dhuni*. Later accounts state that this fire was sacred and was kept burning for its constant source of sacred ash, or *udhi*, that he distributed and possessed curative powers.

28. Michael Spurr notes in his doctoral dissertation that Sathya Sai Baba's affiliation with Vaishnavism is "long running," especially the Bhagavata Purana and Bhagavad Gita, and that his birth among the "highly regarded bardic caste" may have "contributed to his divine persona" (2007:3).

29. See Brian Steel, "Sathya Sai Baba's Claim to Be the Reincarnation of Shirdi Sai Baba" (updated) unpublished, January 2006, http://bdsteel.tripod.com.

30. Saffron is the color of renunciation in Hinduism, and Sathya Sai Baba always wears a saffron robe. Only on his birthday does he wear a white robe.

31. Mick Brown, journalist at the London *Telegraph* and author of an authoritative exposé of Shri Sathya Sai Baba, claimed that his pictures at this time "looked effeminate," with "his "kohl rimmed eyes, he looked like a woman." Personal communication, September 20, 2006.

32. The next important discourse, discussed both by Padmanaban 2000 and in Vijayalakshmi's memoirs, occurred in 1949 on Vijayadashami Day, the culmination of the nine-day festival of Dussehra (Padmanaban 2000:487), where Baba discussed unselfish love (*nishkama prema*) and compassion.

33. In 1947, devotees groups organized many prayer sessions, including the first *akhanda bhajan* session (singing for bhajans for twenty-four hours) in Bangalore, which later became a regular feature of the movement and which every Sai group hosts from 6 A.M., November 7, to 6 P.M., November 8, all over the world.

34. Parapsychologist Erlendur Haraldsson investigated Sathya Sai Baba's claims of paranormal experiences through observation, films, videotapes, and eye witness accounts to evaluate accusations that Sathya Sai Baba may be engaging in sleight-of-hand magic. Sathya Sai Baba himself, however, never agreed

to participate in the experiments (Haraldsson 1987, 1990; Haraldsson and Osis 1975, 1977).

35. Brian Steel suggests that Sai Baba's claims to divine avatarhood lack credibility, and that many occurred earlier than 1960. He says; "From the very first of his known Discourses (25 or 26 October, 1947—Vijayakumari, pp. 107–109) and from officially recorded Discourses in 1953, Baba makes strong claims to be a living incarnation of God (in Hindu terms, an Avatar, or descent of God on earth). He also makes frequent allusions to the Divine powers of Omnipotence, Omniscience and Omnipresence." See http://bdsteel .tripod.com/More/Claimsnew.htm.

36. Referencing the role of the Hindu *poorna* (full) avatar of Vishnu—Krishna— in his role of charioteer and moral guide during the Mahabharata war, the genesis of Hinduism's Bhagavad Gita.

37. Today the newsletter—available for $11 and INR 50—not only encloses sections of transcripts of Sathya Sai Baba's speeches but essays by devotees about the ashram or their interactions with Sai Baba, activities that have occurred in the ashram, announcements of prospective events at Puttaparthi, and other notes, sayings, and entries.

38. For a detailed explication of the avatar concept and Sathya Sai Baba, see Spurr 2007.

39. One of the seven sages who are the origination point for lineage descent groups among Hindus in India.

40. There has been debate among devotees about when Prema Sai will be born. In interviews some devotees stressed 2026 as the probable year, and others 2016.

41. "What exactly is the meaning of Sai Baba? Sai means Sahasrapadhma (thousand lotuses), Saakshaathkaara (Realisation), etc. Ayi means Mother and Baaba means Father" (SSS 2:6). "I am called Sathya Sai; Saayi (as in Seshashaayi) means reclining. The name is very appropriate, let me assure you" (SSS 2:266).

42. I will refer to Brian Steel as a former devotee because of his extensive and searching criticism of Sathya Sai Baba and the Sai organization and his alignment (though it might be involuntary) with other former devotees. He himself claims not be a devotee or a former devotee.

43. In the Hindu Shaivite tradition, Shiva does not incarnate on earth. So this claim was innovative and peculiar, even in terms of Hindu myth.

44. It is significant to note that there is also a linguistic basis for this. In Hindi the word *kal* means both past and future, as in yesterday and tomorrow. Thus the Indic linguistic imagination leads naturally to a divine form that transcends human time in that past and present are also representations of the future.

45. See http://www.saibaba.ws/teachings/babajesus.htm.

46. Mason and Laing 1982 151–153.

47. See http://www.indiangyan.com/books/otherbooks/sai_baba/sai_baba_and _jesus_of_nazareth.shtml.

48. I am pleased to note that sociologist Smriti Srinivas has engaged similar analytical concepts when discussing Sai Baba's divinity. See Srinivas 2008.

49. Smriti Srinivas identifies two recurring motifs in the representation of Sai Baba: one the reincarnation of the faqir and holy man Shirdi Sai Baba and the other of the avatar a descent of the supreme form of Godhead onto earth. See Srinivas 2008:54–78.

50. The Gita (as it is often called) consists of a dialogue between Lord Krishna and Prince Arjuna on the eve of the great battle of Kurukshetra. Arjuna is overcome with anguish when he sees in the opposing army many of his kinsmen, teachers, and friends, and Krishna persuades him to fight by instructing him in spiritual wisdom and the means of attaining union with God.

51. The poorna avatar descends for the specific purpose of mitigating the anxieties of the pure devotees and protecting the weak from evil. According to popular Vaishnava doctrine, there are two type of avatars, primary avatars and secondary avatars. The most common type of primary avatars are called *svarupavatars,* in which God manifests Himself in His *sat-cid-ananda* (mind-spirit-delight) form. The svarupavatars are subdivided into *amsarupavatars* and poorna avatars. In amsarupavatars Vishnu is fully present in the body but He is manifest in the person only partially.

52. To summarize then, the Upanishads are part of the Vedas and discuss philosophy, meditation, and the nature of God, forming the core spiritual thought of Vedantic Hinduism. They are mystic or spiritual analysis of the Vedas and are known as their end or culmination, Vedānta ("the end—*anta*—of the Vedas"). See Clooney 1991.

53. Vedanta philosophy consists of many different schools of thought such including advaitha vedanta (propounded by Adi Shankara where the world is illusory and there is one supreme godhead Brahman)Vishishtadvaitha (propounded by Ramanuja, where the atman or human soul is part of Brahman and the path to liberation is through bhakti or devotion) and Dvaitha Vedanta (propounded by Madhva where Brahman and the human soul (atman) are separate but again where bhakti is the route to liberation for the soul.

54. The avatar concept was adapted by orientalizing Western occultism, specifically Theosophy and neo-Theosophy. In a series of four lectures delivered at the Theosophical Society at Adyar, Madras, in December 1899, Annie Besant, the president of the society, combined theosophical concepts with classic Vaishnavite ideas. A decade later, her coworker, the apparently clairvoyant Charles Leadbeater, would claim that his young protégé J. Krishnamurti was the avatar of a Cosmic Christ-like being called the Maitreya.

55. The Upanishadic concept of the underlying unity of Brahman, which is revered by many to be the pinnacle of Hindu thought, is relayed to the ordinary Hindu as an expression of the manifestation of the Hindu apotropaic divinity as an aid to humanity in difficult times.

56. Dr. Reinhart Hummel has been director of the Evangelische Zentralstelle fur Weltanschauungsfragen in Stuttgart since 1981. He has been a researcher on guru movements and Eastern religions at Heidelberg University. Dr. Hummel visited the Sai Baba center in Bombay in 1981.

57. "The 'natural' leaders—in times of psychic, physical, economic, ethical, religious, political distress—have been neither officeholders nor incumbents of an 'occupation,'" but "holders of specific gifts of the body and spirit; and these gifts have been believed to be supernatural, not accessible to everybody" (Weber 1968 [1946]:245).

58. According to Weber, the "charismatic community" is based on "an emotional form of communal relationship (Vergemeinschaftung)" (1968:243). The charismatic figure rises up and leads his or her "charismatic community" (Gemeinde)—"an organized group subject to the charismatic authority" (243).

59. Lindholm's emphasis on embodiment is unique, resulting in a collection of ethnographies of South Asian Sufism that examine several aspects of charismatic phenomena including bodily expressions, structure of emotions, and the relation between charisma and modernity (Werbner and Basu 1996). His focal concern is to develop a model of emotions that can adequately explain the universality of charisma and the relationships surrounding it.

60. "Namasmarana is an instrument to realize the Lord. The Name signifies the quality of the Lord, His guna, and so constant contemplation arouses the same guna in the reciter. For Namasmarana, no expense is involved; no materials are needed; there is no special place and time to be provided. No qualification of scholarship or caste or sex has to be proved" (SSS 5:79–81).

61. Shanti interview, August 18, 2003.

62. The most authoritative account, which devotees referred to repeatedly in interviews, was the "official biography" by Narayan Kasturi (1897–1987) who was a close associate and a devotee of Sai Baba for over four decades, from 1948 to the late 1980s. The biography, titled Sathyam, Shivam, Sundaram, comprises four volumes and deals with Sai Baba's life from his birth until the early 1980s. Most subsequent devotees' accounts of Baba rely heavily on Kasturi's account, which is ubiquitous, translated into English and several Indian languages. This "biography" is the central text that devotees discuss repeatedly and use to construct an image of Shri Sathya Sai Baba: "a reflection of the universal, grace bestowing power of the absolute" (Hallstrom 1999:22). Babb 1986 makes the observation that no biography of Sathya Sai Baba can be a mere biography since to write of the private person is an impossibility. The "real" Sai Baba is elusive in these "narratives of devotion." "Thus Sathya Sai Baba cannot be the actual subject of an account if his cult. . . . All that is available are his public surfaces, his self as formally presented as an object of devotional attitudes of his followers. . . . This Sathya Sai Baba is what is known as an avatar, a descent of God to earth. And of this Sathya Sai Baba one can indeed give an account *because his persona is fully*

available in the public domain of religious symbolism" (Babb 1986:161–162; my emphasis). Despite this, a few devotees have tried to write accounts of Sai Baba that are located in biography and philosophy rather than hagiography, but they have often been disputed accounts: former devotees claim them to be worse than regular bio/hagiographies, since they, as one former devotee told me, "give the appearance of being scientific, but are just another myth," and current devotees are mystified and slightly affronted by the attempts of the authors to see Sai Baba somewhat differently (see Gokak 1983:10–24). Former devotees have since been very critical of both the work and the man for not being more critical of what they see as the many faults in the organization and in Sai Baba himself.

63. See Steel's Web page, http://bdsteel.tripod.com/More/.
64. Personal communication with Barry Pittard, convener of JuST (October, November 2006).
65. http://www.marie-lakshmi.com/page25_a.html, a story by Carol Bruce.
66. Some former devotees do not agree, leading to contestation. "Kyra Kitts," a former devotee and blogger, states: "I don't want to attribute to him false powers. I don't see him as an antichrist figure, which if it were true would then certainly make such powers plausible. . . . Myself, I'm not Christian and have been with my root guru Ammachi for the last 10 years. . . . It's simply not a religion/spirituality that I've ever been drawn to, even though I was raised in that faith." See http://home.hetnet.nl/~ex-baba/engels/witnesses/kyra.html#Testimonial. See http://www.sai-fi.net/sathyasaibaba/christians_christianity.html#christian_jeus-is-savior for a list of fundamentalist Christian organizations and individuals who oppose Sathya Sai Baba.
67. Interview with Stephen, May 14, 2003.

2. *Deus Loci*

1. http://www.ramalacentre.com/newsletter03_99_02.htm.
2. See Claire Rasmussen, "Reading the Geography of L.A.," Internet book review. http://www.altx.com/EBR/reviews/rev12/r12ras.htm.
3. I do not mean to imply that Puttaparthi is a theme park.
4. However, let me note that this is not the only way for potential devotees to move toward fuller devotee status. In fact, many who call themselves devotees either make the trip rarely or in some cases have never made the trip to Puttaparthi and may worship Sathya Sai Baba merely in the confines of their home.
5. Former devotee Tal Brooke tested out several possible gurus—living and dead—including Sri Ramakrishna, Ramana Maharshi, Sri Aurobindo, Paramahansa Yogananda, and Maharishi Mahesh Yogi. He then traveled to India in 1969 and, in January 1970, encountered Sathya Sai Baba and became a devotee/disciple, writing several books about the wonders of Sathya

Sai Baba. In response to allegations of sexual abuse, he left the movement and soon thereafter joined an evangelical Christian sect, the Spiritual Counterfeit Project, becoming editor of their in-house newsletter. He contends that Sathya Sai Baba and other gurus are all part of a satanic seduction ring. One could argue that Tal Brooke was a spiritual tourist for the twenty-odd years he was a Sathya Sai devotee.

6. Though in other sects and godmen movements devotees of non-Indian origin frequently were either required to change their names or voluntarily changed their names to correspsonding ones in Hindi or Sanskrit, the Sai movement had no such formalities. Devotees often were known by their given names; only a handful changed them.

7. See http://www.srisathyasaibookcentre.org.uk/ashram-quotes-on-pilgrim age.php.

8. An extract about the pilgrimage to Puttaparthi from a devotee Web page: http://www.katongehv.com/index.html.

9. http://www.srisathyasai.org.in.

10. As an anonymous reviewer noted, Jim's quote is fascinating because the Wizard of Oz is a charlatan, and what empowers the seekers is the journey and their faith.

11. In the early 1970s, when Baba's devotional following began to grow outside India, devotees had to make their own way to Puttaparthi. Often many of them came with an informal guide or someone who had done the trip before, and they would make their way to a hotel in Bangalore for a day or two before renting a car and chauffeur to take them to Puttaparthi if Baba was in residence there. Indira Devi, a yoga teacher and longtime devotee of Baba who lived in California and Mexico, was one such spiritual teacher and tour guide who was responsible for many Americans coming to Puttaparthi in the early years. Devotees often paired up into small groups of four or five interested families and friends in order to make the "frightening" trip to Puttaparthi.

12. Interview with Maria and Anna from Turin, January 22, 2003.

13. Interview with Shashi, July 15, 2005.

14. Interview with Stephen and Bob, June 19, 2001.

15. Interview with Anna, July 20, 1999.

16. Diane Mines has argued compellingly that, in South Asia, specifically Tamil Nadu, the outside, chaotic, and fear-ridden spaces of the *katu* (forest) are opposed to the inside, organized, and civilized spaces of the *uru* (town), in usage, understanding, and feeling. Though Mines's work deals in its entirety with a Tamil embedded understanding of space, devotee's stories point to a similar understanding and usage. Mines 1997.

17. Interview with Stephen, June 19, 2001.

18. Hervieu-Léger's argument (2001) states that modern societies are societies of amnesia, and memories are therefore fragmented. She argues that religious modernity establishes a reinvention and reestablishment of a culture of belief. Hobsbawn and Ranger (1992:3–5) similarly argue that invented

tradition works on the reconstruction of memories through formalization and repetition of ritual elements.

19. No relation to the author of the present work.

20. The "living being as sacred center" model can be an extension of an ancient person-based political patronage model or it can be due to a shift within the religion itself whereby the sacredness moves from one point to another depending upon dogmatic, folk, and other "developments" within the religious theology itself (Eade and Sallnow 1991:9).

21. Frazer 1995 [1922].

22. In "The History of the Mandir: Its Genesis and Growth," http://sathyasai .org/ashrams/prasanthi/history.html.

23. http://girlskirtmission.blogspot.com/.

24. *A Temple of Healing*, p. 8. *A Temple of Healing* is an illustrated brochure distributed by the SSO that publicizes the state-of-the-art Sathya Sai Hospital, discussing its history of medical services with many quotations from Sai Baba's discourses.

25. This plan called for the integration of Puttaparthi and the surrounding villages to boost development in the region. Puttaparthi itself is the centerpiece of the plan. In the draft master plan, the SSSUDA has seen a growth rate of 257 percent in four decades, and Puttaparthi draws 40 percent of the population.

26. Interview, Stephen and Bob, June 19, 2001.

27. Interview, Anna, July 20, 1999.

28. Traditional Hindu temples also have numerous gateways and courtyards that get progressively larger and taller the further away they are from the sacred center. According to Kramrisch, "the central sanctuary surrounded by structures larger than itself, shows the principle of the garbha griha (sanctum sanctorum) extending to the building that holds it. . . . The vision is akin to that of the city of Brahman (Chandogya Upanishad, vol. 8, 1.1) wherein is a small center, a dwelling, in which is a small space" (1976:204).

29. See http://www.saibabaofindia.com/mandir.htm.

30. Srivastava 2009.

31. As Vertovec notes in his study of Hindu temples in London, the Hindu temple "refers to a vast range of institutions" (2000, quoting Fuller 1988:50). But while Hindu temples in India include "a range of Phenomena in terms of architecture, ideological focus and social complexity," in terms of architecture they essentially boil down to courtyards that encircle the central sanctum sanctorum or garbha graha (translated as the womb chamber) and the number and size of the courtyards and temple gateways is denotative of the wealth of the temple (Vertovec 2000:124–125).

32. From "Religion Inc.: Police Action Against the Puttaparthi Godman Is Overdue," *Telegraph Calcutta*, November 21, 2004. http://www.telegraphindia .com/1041121/asp/opinion/story.

33. In a sense, then, the structure of the ashram is very similar to the structure of the Hindu temple, with spaces getting tighter and more controlled as one

approaches the sanctum sanctorum. In the traditional Hindu temple, devotees are expected to circumabulate through several high-walled courtyards
pierced by ornate windtowers in the cardinal directions, which get progres-
sively smaller and darker, until they enter the sanctum lit by oil lamps. The
symbolic value of protecting the mysterium tremendum met the pragma-
tism of protecting the deities, which often had a fortune in gemstones as
decoration. Thus security and protection, combined with visual cloaking,
both symbolic and literal, lies at the heart of Sai sacred architecture.

34. For a complete definition of Hoysala temple style, see Kramrisch 2002
    [1946].
35. http://sathyasai.org/ashrams/prasanthi/history.html.
36. Ibid.
37. http://tradimodern.blogspot.com/2007/05/destination-puttaparthi-and-sai
    -baba.html.
38. Ibid.
39. http://sathyasai.org/ashrams/prasanthi/history.html.
40. Seva Dal volunteers from different Sathya Sai centers all over India work in
    the ashram throughout the year to help pilgrims with questions, to main-
    tain order, and to serve the Sai community.
41. The whole debate about whether Sathya Sai Baba was poor as a child seems
    to be overturned by this fact. However, a point to be noted is that many
    South Asian anthropologists often have found that peasant dominant caste
    families like the Rajus had land but were cash poor. It is presumed that the
    source of the land for the temple was a hereditary gift.
42. The architect Goh say Tong, we are told, worked with the engineers of the
    ECC, the civil engineering division of the global construction company
    Larsen and Toubro, and with the devotees in Singapore and Malaysia to com-
    plete the building in twenty-four months.
43. By an anonymous writer: http://home.no.net/anir/Sai/enigma/wasteful.
44. From Heart2heart, the Radio Sai Listeners Journal: A Monthly e-journal:
    http://media.radiosai.org.
45. http://www.srisathyasai.org.in/Pages/AshramInfo/interested_places.htm.
46. http://media.radiosai.org/Journals/Vol_03/02FEB01/making.htm.
47. For devotees these hours are considered part of their seva to Bhagawan.
48. http://www.2indya.com/2009/02/02/chaitanya-jyoti-museum-visitors
    -place-in-puttaparti-puttaparthi/.
49. Ibid.
50. http://www.indiadivine.org/audarya/ammachi/248082-chaitanya-jyoti
    -testament-living-divinity.html.
51. http://bdsteel.tripod.com/More/pparthivisit08.htm.
52. Srivastava 2009.
53. From http://bdsteel.tripod.com/More/pparthivisit08.htm.
54. Interview with Hemlatha, November 2001.
55. From Heart2heart The Radio Sai Listeners Journal. http://media.radiosai
    .org.

56. One now finds that temple towers all over urban India are repainted in virulently painted oils: the dignified seventh-century Kanchipuram temple in Tamil Nadu, built of soft gray granite with ornate decorations all over its octagonal face, was being repainted with oil paints to conform to urban visual expectations of religious imagery when I visited in 2004.

57. Though the bookstore was registered in 1969 to "disseminate Sathya Sai Baba's teachings in America," the center itself was built on land donated by Walter and Elsie Cowan, longtime devotees of Sathya Sai Baba. Walter Cowan was a cofounder of the Union Oil Company and was believed to be resurrected from the dead by Sathya Sai Baba in 1971. Prior to becoming a Sathya Sai devotee, Cowan was the director of the Kripal Singh Foundation in Anaheim, California. The Sathya Sai Center and Bookstore was started in the Cowan's home in Tustin and later moved to the current building circa 1983. It does $3.1 million in sales annually; see http://www.manta.com/coms2/dnbcompany_dc1izp.

58. Consecrated on January 1, 1981. The disused church and church hall were purchased and donated to the community by a successful Sri Lankan Tamil immigrant, Mr. Ratnasingham, who was a Shaivite and a Sathya Sai devotee, and the complex houses both the Shree Ganapathy Temple of Wimbledon and the Sathya Sai temple. Mr. Ratnasingham apparently started the temple for "Hindu children being brought up in the West," as " he realised how easy it would be to lose our young men and women to the attractions of western ideology, and how much they would lose if they lost the knowledge of our ancient culture and heritage." See http://www.ghanapathytemple.org.uk/history/tribute.htm.

59. http://www.ghanapathytemple.org.uk/history/history.htm.

60. www.eaisai.com.

61. See Feike 2007.

62. Interview, June 12, 2005.

63. Interview, June 23, 2001.

64. Stephen, interview, June 23, 2003.

65. See Srinivas 2005 for a comprehensive and thought-provoking argument on the locally situated and the global.

3. Illusion, Play, and Work in a Moral Community

1. Interview with Sai Seva Dal volunteer, May 18, 1998.

2. This sacred touching, *sparshan*, is a central act in the communication between devotee and deity.

3. Smriti Srinivas notes that a "typical bhajan session lasts for an hour or so. It begins with 'Om' chanted three times, followed by the chanting of the 108 attributes of Sathya Sai Baba and salutations to him (Sri Sathya Sai Ashtotarashatanamavali). . . . Other prayers may be interposed before the main bhajan session. The core of the session begins with the bhajan to Ganesha.

Followed by a bhajan to the guru. For the rest of the session any devotee may sing a bhajan of his/her choice. Many of the bhajans are composed by Baba, or are adaptations of bhajans sung in other parts of India (sometimes through the mere act of the insertion of 'Sai'), part of the repertoire is shared with other gurus or simple recollections of the names of the divine. Many of them have a vocabulary drawn from Sanskrit or Hindustani, terms usually understood by the Indian audience, though regional language bhajans are sung as well. They can be very ecumenical and include references to Jesus, Allah, Buddha, Mahavira and Guru Nanak consistent with Sathya Sai Baba's advice that any name can be used. Several collections of Sai bhajans are available on the market; *Sai Bhajan Mala* (2000) for instance, published by the Sri Sathya Sai Books and Publications Trust, is a collection of 1,008 bhajans dedicated to Sathya Sai Baba, the Guru, Ganesha, Siva, Vishnu, Krishna, Rama the Goddess and Sarva Dharma" (2008:90–91).

4. The bhajan group may include musical instruments such as a harmonium (for tone), cymbals (*manjira*) to keep time, and Indian drums (the *dholak* and the *tabla*) for the beat. In the Framingham center in Massachusetts I found that a guitar was sometimes part of the ensemble and on one occasion in Wimbledon a recorder was included.

5. Bhajans are simple songs consisting of repetitive lines. The lead singer sings the first line and devotees and a choral group follow, rhythmically clapping. The speed, which varies from verse to verse, is set by the lead singer. Most Sai bhajans and kirtans are simple adaptations of traditional Hindu bhajans or kirtans that replace the titular deity with *Sai*, sung in Hindustani, Tamil, or regional languages; the Madrid Sai center sings Spanish bhajans.

6. The kirtans have different notational forms: *leela sankirtan* (description of his many leelas), *guna sankirtan* (the qualities of divinity), and *nama sankirtana* (the names of the divine) (SSS 25:79–80).

7. The bhakti movement was essentially split into those poet-saints who believed in *nirguna* (beyond qualities) and *saguna* (with qualities).While they did not agree on the path to salvation, they did agree that the recitation of the divine name with proper devotional surrender led to devotion to a guru and the company of religious men was essential (Vaudeville 1999). The path of devotion was believed to consist of eight steps: listening to God's glory, singing devotional songs, serving Him, being friends with Him, surrendering to Him, worshipping Him, thinking of him, and saluting Him (de Bary 1957:333).

8. Callewart and Lath (1989:58–64) write of collections of bhajans and the tradition of bhakti singers' lineages and their musical selections from the second half of the sixteenth century.

9. The most famous is the South Indian poet-saint Tyagaraja (1767–1847), in whose compositions music is lauded as spiritual practice. Sai Baba is known to have a fondness for Tyagaraja kirtans, and often bhajan sessions in the ashram begin with his notable and well-loved devotional compositions.

10. The popular selection "Sai Bina Rahe Na Jaaye" (Without Sai there is no life) was sung repeatedly, and is reflective of this Indic Sufi tradition of music.

11. Recorded bhajan collections are available for purchase; *Sai Bhajan Mala* (2000) of the Sathya Sai Book and Publications Trust includes 1,008 bhajans sung to the glory of Sathya Sai Baba.

12. Jeanie Alvins' letter home, December 6, 1999; see http://fweb.inetworld .net/lovesource/pilgrimage_to_india.htm#Preparing

13. The concept of the leela draws from Krishna mythology where Krishna would play tricks on his devotees to drive home a point about the human condition. Often these leelas would involve him taking different forms. The Sathya Sai organization uses the concept of leela fairly freely to describe the queue system and other organizational systems at Puttaparthi.

14. Misra 1998.

15. Martin and Runzo 2000.

16. Haberman 1994.

17. http://home.no.net/anir/Sai/ or http://www.sathyasai.com/baba/Ex-Baba .com/A.Priddy/robert-priddy-deception.html[1.1.2007].

18. In the Tamil *Tiruvilaiyatarpuranam,* Shiva performs sixty-three acts of leela, most, from the human perspective, outrageous. For example, he steals the king's money, produces counterfeit horses that transform at his command into jackals, and humiliates the king. Many of the sixty-three leelas prove that human judgments and perspectives about the divine are limited by human imagination.

19. http://www.eaisai.com/baba/.

20. Maslow 1943.

21. This "contextual identity" is yet another feature of Hinduism and Hindu identity (Marriott 1990).

22. For a thorough description of prasadam see Fuller 1992.

23. See http://groups.yahoo.com/group/saisruthi/message/30.

24. Mata Betty, of New Zealand, " Miracles Are My Visiting Cards," *Sanathana Sarathi,* February 1998, p. 48.

25. Some former devotees argue that one of the key ingredients of moral stakeholding is a commitment to justice, which Sai Baba fails to provide as one of the key elements of human values. They argue that justice and human values are of Western provenance and castigate the whole of Indian society as insensitive to justice. For example, Robert Priddy argues that "the most glaring omission in Sathya Sai Baba's package of 'eternal five values' is one of the keystone values of Western civilization . . . and, interestingly enough, a value which is not much in evidence in the traditional societies of India or the East. Where it has been introduced in the Indian subcontinent, it has very clearly not yet taken very deep root in actual practice. This is the much-prized European value 'justice.' . . . Justice is, in practice, closely related to 'human rights,' both in national laws and European and international conventions. However one looks at it, the idea of human justice is glaringly absent from Sathya Sai Baba's thinking and, moreover, from many of his attitudes and activities. . . . The importance of fairness, social and human rights, suffer and are displaced in his view by 'human duties,' which are determined by 'divine law' and take

no account of individual freedoms or any kind of democratic values. SSB constantly talks about the utopian nature of regimes of ancient India, where divinely-inspired rulers (or even God Kings, like Rama) dealt out justice. Divine law thus supplants human justice based on civilized consensus and individual and social rights. He speaks of 'Divine justice,' which is what he claims to deal out to every one of us sooner or later etc. But not human justice, for he is outspokenly down on human rights, which he does not see as being our right and which he would apparently nihilate in favor of 'human duties' ... duties, note well, as they are or may be prescribed predominantly by him. Accordingly, Sai Baba favors a system of organization with strict top-down rule ... a system that is notoriously insensitive to feedback, unfair to members and furthermore obviously leans towards pedagogical inefficiency and counter-productiveness. Such systems are authoritarian and become totalitarian and cultish when their power is threatened, as is being seen with the SSB movement today. This is anti-democratic ... because legal and social justice—along with human rights—go hand in hand with democratic ideals of organization and government at all levels of society." Priddy states that the five values are fuzzy and often improperly translated. "The five human values are vague and undefined. The simplicity of the 'five values' is deceptive, because each term is so general, imprecise and so conflates many different meanings." See http://home.no.net/anir/Sai/enigma/Human%20Values%20failings.htm.

26. *A Temple of Healing*, pp. 7–8. *A Temple of Healing* is an illustrated brochure distributed by the SSO that publicizes the state-of-the-art Sathya Sai Hospital, discussing its history of medical services with many quotations from Sai Baba's discourses.

27. Fields 2001.

28. *A Temple of Healing*, p. 8.

29. In texts about the hospital, devotees' are organized into four main themes. *Globalization:* means that medical advice and treatments are given to all human beings irrespective of difference; *decommercialization:* means treatment is not linked to the patient's ability to pay; *humanization:* means doctors and health-care workers, all devotees of Sai Baba, adhere to his five values program; finally, *spiritualization* means that every physician recognizes the spirit of their patients (*Mano Hriday* 2004:5). Mano Hriday is a newsletter of the Sri Sathya Sai Institute of Higher Medical Sciences, Bangalore (India).

30. *Trayee Saptamayee*, p. 29 (my emphasis), a commemorative tribute, honoring Sathya Sai Baba's seventieth birthday celebration, published by Sathya Sai Books and Publications Trust.

31. Lakshmi Srinivas, personal conversation, November 22, 2006.

4. Renegotiating the Body

1. I thank my colleagues Paulo Pinto, Keith McNeal, and Michael Hill for their participation in the sessions I organized on the topic of religion, emotion,

and the body at the Society for Psychological Anthropology meetings in 2005 and the American Anthropological Association meetings in 2004. I thank Charles Lindholm, Isabelle Clark-Déces, and Pauline Kolenda for their participation in the sessions and their helpful suggestions with earlier versions of this chapter.

2. So I suggest that the Foucauldian understanding of power and desire are but partial understandings of the phenomenon and that the Sai movement, by adding the ingredient of divinity and codifying austere behavior, changes the structure of the discourse. Foucault's understandings of social power are confined because they assume that the system is closed. Because of the closed system of power and the external repressive controls, "antisocial" behavior is repressed and goes underground.

3. S. Srinivas (2008) refers to this transformation in embodied selfhood as the labor of "biocivic ethics" in which devotees are "healed" and in turn heal the world through what she terms "embodied citizenship" (112–127).

4. Turner suggests that Foucault's understanding of the body, "has no flesh: it is begotten out of a discourse of power (itself an immaterial manalike force), and the desires that comprise its illusory subjectivity are themselves the predicates of external discourses of power rather than the products or metaphorical expressions of any internal life of its own" (Turner, in Csordas 1994a:36).

5. The figure that most accurately captures the structure of the post-eighteenth-century articulation of power is, says Foucault, Jeremy Bentham's Panopti-can. It allows for the invisible surveillance of a large number of people by a relatively small number.

6. In the larger theoretical perspective, there is an emerging struggle over the control of social and cultural theories of the body. On one hand are the Fou-cauldians, theorists for whom the body is representative of isolated individuals who are controlled by repressive outside forces of power wielded by "disembodied institutions" (Turner, in Csordas 1994a:45). And on the other side are the embodiment theorists who view the body phenomenologically as socially connected, relational, the site of experience and learned body techniques for the construction of the power of agency. This body inhabits both subjective and objective states simultaneously, is reflexive, learns new behaviors and bodily ways of "being in this world," and has agency over itself. At times it may even inhabit a subjunctive and hopeful emotional state in relation to the divine.

7. *Harkin* 1994.

8. Skoefeld 1999.

9. There are exceptions to this secular trend such as Coakley 1997; Mellor and Shilling 1997; and, of course, the works of Turner and Csordas.

10. By the early 1980s anthropological studies of the body as it pertained to illness were beginning to surface by they focused primarily upon the effects of trauma and other factors on mental health. The body as "site" for an experience was explored largely in medical anthropology and work on the anthropology of pain. At the same time, exploration in control of the body,

through less extreme phenomena such as dieting, meditation, and image management, were undertaken.

11. Thus the atman's innate spiritual power becomes obscured by the earthly and bodily senses of the five senses (*panchindriyas*) and the five feelings (*panchbhutas*). The *manasa* (mind), and the *shariram* (body) act in synchronicity to create the human being with cognition, intellect, and emotions.

12. From Patanjali's *Yoga Sutra*, circa second to third century CE. See Whicher 1998:273.

13. This is very close to what Durkheim meant by the sacred (2001:36–38, 224, 236–237).

14. Ex-devotees argue that it is Sai Baba's uncontrollable desires for material wealth and sexual gratification that are at the crux of the problem. They suggest that this negation of Sai Baba's desires by the Seva Dal, the Sai Central Trust, the SSSO, and the core devotees is hypocritical. They accuse Sai Baba and the organization of secrecy and deceit. Since the organization stresses the negation of desire for devotees, as well as for Sai Baba, these accusations have been taken very seriously by some devotees who have either turned away from the movement altogether or have sought to defend it by means of extensive Web publishing, books, and other forums for debate.

15. Halliburton 2002.

16. Hervieu-Léger's argument (2001) is that modern societies are amnesiac societies where memory is lost or fragmented and religious innovation is an attempt to reconnect with the chain of belief.

17. In the Kathopanishad, the senses are considered to be horses that are yoked to the chariot of the body and carry it along. The horses need to be controlled by the charioteer, else they will gallop, overturning the chariot and charioteer (SSS 23:87). Control of the body and the senses is therefore imperative to attain mastery of the self.

18. SSS vol. 39, http://www.sssbpt.org/Pages/Pdf/23-02-06.pdf.

19. Haraway argues that location is the core part of "being in a body"—that the body is grounded in its very bodilyness, so to speak, and this includes "a consequence of relatedness, partial grasp of any situation, and imperfect communication" (Haraway 1991:197–198).

20. I draw from recent work of phenomenological sociologists such as Waquant's study of pugilism in Chicago (2004).

21. Waquant calls this theory building based on bodily knowledge a carnal sociology. See Waquant 2004.

22. The study of this separation and its repercussions have been discussed at length in South Asian anthropology. Research on the body and self in South Asia (Marriott 1977, 1990; Cohen 1989) has with some notable exceptions, been set against the larger local understandings of power and hierarchy (Marriott 1977; M.N. Srinivas 1952) as an evocation of the purity/pollution debate. Marriott postulated that in South Asia the body was "fluid and open," which led to a "dividual" selfhood, where the individual was subordinate to the group, unlike the Western self which was "individual." In later

work, bodily narratives were seen as subordinate to the construction of the postcolonial nation (Appadurai 1991, 1996; Dirks 1992; Guha and Spivak 1988), but, subsequently, studies of possession rituals (Nabokov 2000; Obeyesekere 1970, 1981,; Sax 1995; Trawick 1990; Wadley 1975) led to a new construction of selfhood where the body in relation to the self was thought to be subjective and contextual; "the body manipulations and metamorphoses that it enacts have an intensely subjective and existential implications" (Nabokov 2000:15). More recently, South Asian scholars have sought to understand perspectives of pain and loss (Das 1996), of sexuality (Kakar 2008), of old age (Cohen 1989), in which indigenous ethno-histories of the body (Lamb 2000) and ethno-categorizations of bodily types based on indigenous practices of medicine such as Ayurveda and indigenous conceptions of embodied practice such as yoga (Alter 2004) and tantric practice (White 2003) have taken center stage. In these understandings, sensory boundaries, their manipulation, and their affect play a critical part in understanding the nature of postmodern selfhood.

23. See http://www.saibaba-aclearview.com/contents3.html.
24. For example, Sai Baba, in a talk given to students at the Sathya Sai school, alluded to his childhood and, referring to himself, said: "Puttaparthi is a small village. You all know that. This body is one which has not left Puttaparthi and had not seen other places. This body went to a place called Bukkapatnam and there in a school they take a class, which was known as ESLC. And this body was engaged in studying in that class." From "Swamis' School Days," http://www.eaisai.com/baba/.
25. Sai Baba in a Christmas Day discourse, Bombay 1970, Kasturi 1968, 3:136 (U.S. ed.).
26. Other symptoms listed by Connie Shaw include a "fire fountain in the spine," "a feeling of levitation," "deep compassion," and "waves of bliss," "bilocation," "mock pains in the heart as though the body is being reconstructed," strange sensations in the cells as though every atom is being rearranged," "visits by angels," "loss of attachment to family members," "extreme sensitivity to the external world of sound and smell," "painless piercing of the chakras," "seeing a blue dot in the third eye region," "a voracious appetite," "feelings of awe," and so on.
27. As Obeyesekere 1981 demonstrates, the links between charisma healing power and hair extend through many religions.
28. Fields 2001.
29. Interview with Mr. Murthy, June 28, 1998 December 20, 2004.
    In ayurvedic principles there are three types of food and three types of bodies: the sattvic, or renunciate, a food type that tamps down the senses and increases austerity; the rajasic, or the food of kings, which inflames the senses; and the tamasic, or the food of the middle path.
30. Sai Baba discourse of May 7, 2001, *Sanathana Sarathi*, August 2001, p. 226.
31. When discussing jewelry, clothing or other items of luxury, or sometimes even necessity devotees tended to discuss them in terms of desire, especially

needless desire. Devotion, according to devotees, is the separation of self from desire and that occurs through what one Sai devotee told me was made up of four avenues—first, the separation of self from worldly things; second, the control of desires and mental and physical stimulation; third, through following the path of spiritual knowledge; fourth, by following one's chosen guru. Austerity and abstention become bodily knowledge requirements in order to attain the ultimate prize of *atma gyana.*

32. In the West the preparation and distribution of food at homeless shelters and soup kitchens, collection of food at local food banks, raising of money for charitable endeavors, and so on, are popular. I witnessed the cooking and preparation and serving of a Thanksgiving festival meal by Sai devotees at a homeless shelter near Boston. In Singapore devotees often give large donations either to the Sai mandir or to local religious and charitable institutions. In Santiago, Chile Sai devotees organize an annual drive that feeds and clothes thousands of people.

33. Devotees often made time for reading Sai discourses and the magazine of the Sai Baba movement, *Santhana Sarathy,* as well as getting updates of Sai happenings through the official Sai Web site. All these actions are thought to be in devotion to Sai Baba, and, in return, the body gets the benefits of having done such seva to Sai Baba.

34. Interview with Shanti, November 19, 1998.

35. See http://www.saibaba.ws/teachings/ceilingondesires.htm.

36. See http://www.sathyasai.org/ashrams/prasanthi/guidelines.html.

37. *Sathya Sai Newsletter* 19, no. 3 (Spring 1995): 33–35.

38. Sathya Sai Baba's ideas of bodily purity are continuous with those expressed in late nineteenth-century Vedantic Hinduism, developed by the western influenced elite spiritual leaders of India,. See De Michelis 2004.

39. This discourse of purity is linked by the devotees, both through Sai Baba's many speeches and through their own discussions, to an environmentally conscious "clean-living" lifestyle and extrapolated by the SSSO through a global Ceiling on Desires Program as a cleansing effort to remove polluted air, water, and food: "When you sing the Glory of God, the bad germs in the air are destroyed" (*Sanathana Sarathi,* January 1995, pp. 26–27).

40. September 14, 15, 1999, Puttaparthi.

41. September 13, 14, 1999, Puttaparthi.

42. Interview, February 22, 1999.

43. Shanti, phone interview, June 2004.

44. Celibacy is seen no longer as a necessary conduit to the divine but as a healthful moral ideal. In America in the 1960s and 1970s celibacy became something that hippies and counterculture adherents experimented with and was not seen as a commitment. Sathya Sai devotees from the West come to the understanding of Brahmacharya with this open-ended spirit (Alter 2005).

5. Secrecy, Ambiguity, Truth, and Power

1. Riti and Theodore 1993.
2. Two of the assailants, Vijay Shantaram Prabhu and Ravindra Babu, escaped and were caught several months later in Nagpur. When questioned, they were alleged to have stated that there had been a vast conspiracy where five members of the trust had been swallowing Sai Baba's funds. They claimed that they had been framed as making an attempt on Sai Baba's life when they were trying to alert him that a misappropriation of funds was taking place. *Times of India*, October 27, 1993.
3. Riti and Theodore 1993.
4. Other trustees at that time included Mr. Indulal Shah, Mr. Sreenivasan, a prominent devotee from Madras, and Mr. K. R. Prasad of Bangalore. Some documents also list the Rajmata of Bangalore, a member of the Mysore princely family, as one of the trustees.
5. *Hindu*, June 10, 1993.
6. See http://www.saibaba-x.org.uk/8/The_Week-murder_coverage.htm.
7. *The Secret Swami* was broadcast in the UK on Thursday, June 17, 2004, at 21:00 BST on BBC Two.
8. The only passing reference to the anti-Sai movement in S.Srinivas's recent work on the Sathya Sai movement occurs late in her work in the conclusion. She states "Devotees of Sathya Sai Baba are aware of criticisms of their guru. Some think these are disinformation campaigns against their teacher by the religious Right, diatribes by angry ex-devotees who have been disappointed in their (unreasonable) material and spiritual expectations, misunderstandings based on different cultural deployments of the divine-human relationship, or simply, the kind of calumny that accompanies a great soul" (2008:334).
9. I draw from Urban's work (1998).
10. Simmel 1950.
11. Eliade 1976:47; Bolle 1987; Bellman 1984:1; Luhrmann 1989. For major sociological approaches, see Simmel 1950.
12. Bellman 1984. Bellman, in her phenomenological study of secrecy, argues that it constitutes social contexts among the Kpelle.
13. *Rules and Regulations* 2001 (Puttaparthi: SSO), p. 22.
14. Interview, July 30, 1999.
15. Srinivas notes that the growth of the Sai movement within India occurred primarily in the northeastern states, which is puzzling, since, as she states, they were not believers in Shirdi Sai Baba. She writes, "in terms of numbers, states with over 20,000 members included Sikkim (82,650), West Bengal (62,680), Andhra Pradesh (45,950), Kerala (46,500), Tamil Nadu (42,266), Maharashtra (45950), Gujerat (27,848), Madhya Pradesh and Chattisgarh (27,733) and Orissa (20,745)" (2008:132).
16. Srinivas asserts that the growth of the Sai movement was strong in peninsula India where more than five hundred *samhitis* and *bhajan mandalis*

existed in each state, with higher numbers for the states proximate to Andhra Pradesh where Sai Baba's ashram is located (2008:132).

17. See Sandweiss 1975; corroborated by personal communication from former devotee Brian Steel, May 9, 2007.

18. http://www.srisathyasaibaba.org/saiorgan/1.html.

19. *Sathya Sai Seva Organizations Activities-overseas,* 2000 (an internal publication of the SSSO).

20. *Rules and Regulations* 2000 (Puttaparthi: SSSO), annexure 6.

21. Western devotees have a difficult time comprehending and fitting in with this model. Jane, from Santa Barbara, told me, "I hate all this family stuff that they go on about . . . I don't get it."

22. Interview with Jane and Jack, October 23, 2001, Kansas City; Anne, Norway SSSO, June 13, 2001, e-mail to the author.

23. Interview with Mr. Sajanand, October 22, 1998, Bangalore.

24. Robert Priddy, http://home.no.net/anir/Sai/.

25. http://www.saibuilding.org/english/index_e.html.

26. http://groups.yahoo.com/group/saiunity/; accessed June 2002 and removed by October 2009.

27. Two Americans, who were unfamiliar with the Sathya Sai movement, upon hearing about the case commented on the victim's unfortunate name. They pronounced it "A liar I am."

28. Alaya Rahm vs. Sathya Sai Baba Society, filed in the Superior Court of California on January 6, 2005, County of Orange—USA, Case No. 05cc01931. Since then two other young male ex-devotees, Sathya "Satch" Purcell and Ulrich Zimmerman, have alleged that they were sexually abused. See http://home.hetnet.nl/~ex_baba/engels/articles/sathyapurcell06.html for Satch Purcell's written account. Ulrich Zimmerman's account was originally videotaped and put on YouTube in mid-2006, but was removed two months later.

29. Thought to be Sharon Purcell, mother of Sathya "Satch" Purcell, who is believed to have claimed that Sathya Sai Baba was "an astral devil."

30. Barry Pittard, personal communication with author, December 14, 2006.

31. http://home.hetnet.nl/~ex_baba/engels/articles/barryexposeupdate.html.

32. Brooks claimed that Sai Baba had attempted to sexually arouse him in private darshan and anointed his genitalia with oil, claiming that he was raising Brooks's Kundalini in an ancient Hindu rite.

33. In January 1992 the sexual issue began to be discussed among devotees in Holland, when the story of Baba's hugging and genital fondling of Keith Ord (UK), during private interviews in the spring of 1990, came out in a national weekly magazine.

34. Brooke 1976.

35. Brooke 1999.

36. Barry Pittard, e-mail correspondence with author, June 2006 to January 2007.

37. Serguei Badaev, personal communication, June 10, 2006 to December 10, 2007.

38. http://home.hetnet.nl/~ex-baba/engels/witnesses/brian.html.

39. E-mail interviews with Brain Steel, June 2006 to January 2008.

40. Timothy Conway, personal communication, December 9, 2006.

41. Alexandra Nagel spent a few months in the Sathya Sai ashram in 1990. She subsequently published a few critical articles on Sathya Sai Baba drawn from her work as a graduate student/researcher at the Free University of Amsterdam. Nagel 1994. Subsequently Nagel has written several more articles of which one, "A Guru Accused," published on the Internet at http://home.hetnet.nl/~ex-baba/engels/articles/Paper "A Guru Accused".html, August 2001 (accessed April 20, 2004), has been influential.

42. I use the term *victims* within quotations because nothing has been proven against Sathya Sai Baba. It is not meant to demean or diminish their experiences in any way.

43. Nagel 1994:123–153; Vroon 1993.

44. *Nexus Magazine*, vol. 7, no. 5 (August-September 1999); see http://www.nexusmagazine.com/articles/SaiBabaExposed.html.

45. See http://www.saisathyasai.com/baba/Ex-Baba.com/Witnesses/conny-larsson-references.html#ref2.

46. Ibid.

47. http://archive.salon.com/people/feature/2001/07/25/baba/index3.html.

48. Sanjay Dadlani and a devotee called Joe (Gerald) Moreno have also engaged in such vituperative arguments that they have been banned from contributing material to some portions of the Internet.

49. Robert Priddy indicates this on his complex and thorough Web page; see http://home.no.net/anir/Sai/.

50. *Deccan Herald,* July 11, 1976, p. 5.

51. Letters to the editor, *Deccan Herald,* April 11, 1976.

52. *Blitz* interview, July 31–October 2, 1976 in Karanjia 1976, reprinted in Sandweiss 1986:251–253. Web posting, June 1999.

53. Personal letters to author.

54. Reported in the *Guardian*, December 1, 1922.

55. I am grateful to Mr. K. N. Shantha Kumar, managing editor of the *Deccan Herald* group of newspapers in Bangalore, for his help in locating the relevant material in his archives.

56. In the 2004 BBC documentary *The Secret Swami*, Basava Premanand, one of the original skeptics and amateur magician, demonstrated that he could duplicate some of Sai materializations. The BBC documentary reported that even some of Sathya Sai Baba's critics believe he has genuine paranormal powers such as astral flying, mind reading, the ability to heal through touch, and so on. Basava Premanand has been active in the forefront of investigating the deaths at the ashram and the sexual healing allegations and has written an account of the events.

57. From a speech of May 15, 2000, the translation courtesy of Acharya.

58. Barry Pittard, personal e-mail to the author, November 2006.

59. Personal communication, December 14, 2006.

60. Interview, June 14, 2004.
61. Goffman 1967.
62. Kearney 1991:152; see Ricoeur 1978.
63. Interview, November 18, 2005.
64. Interview, April 19, 1999.
65. Interview, November 2003.
66. Seligman 2000.
67. Ibid.
68. The concept of the Kundalini can be thought of as a rich source of psychic or libidinous energy in the body and usually sexual arousal and Kundalini movement are synonymous.
69. There are six scientific yogic techniques, namely, *shat kriyas* or *shat karmas*, which have been developed by the ancient yogis. The *shat kriyas* constitute hatha yoga. The objective of hatha is to maintain a perfect balance between the two pranic flows: solar and lunar. When perfection is established, *prana* (breath/life) flows in *sushumna*, the most important channel of energy situated inside the spinal column.
70. Interview, November 2005.
71. Dr. Shankar said that in Kundalini shakti practice the static formless principle of energy is thought of as Shiva and resides in the male genitalia. The changing principle of fluid consciousness is Shakti, which resides in the female principle. Thus Shiva and Shakti together form consciousness and the universe. This supports Sathya Sai Baba's claim that he is Shiva and Shakti in one. Personal interview, May 14, 2004, Mysore.
72. Interview, January 12, 2006.
73. Interview, January 12, 2006.
74. Excerpt from a Web site titled "Sai Baba and Sex: A Clear View," http://www.saibaba-aclearview.com/contents1.html, which has since been removed.
75. See http://home.no.net/anir/Sai/Oily.htm.
76. Ibid.
77. Barthes 1995:xxiii; see also Barthes 1977.
78. Manning 1991. Manning states that Goffman's use of the metaphor of social life as theater has a significant impact on his thought in three areas: 1. it is central to his changing views about cynicism and trust in everyday life; 2. metaphor in general is a method of sociological inquiry; and 3. metaphor suggests a "limit" that his later work attempts to transcend.
79. Bailey 1991.
80. Pitt-Rivers 1974.
81. See Petersen 1993:343.
82. Author discussion with Emerson faculty, "Deus Loci: A Sacred City, Globalization, Memory and Affect in the Sathya Sai Movement," December 5, 2007.
83. Interview with author, February 20, 2005.
84. Murphy 1990.
85. As Simmel notes, secret societies have a gradual initiation embody hierarchy. He comments, "Secret societies, above all others, carry through the division

of labor and the gradation of their members with great finesse and thorough-
ness" (1950:356–357). Elizabeth Brandt notes that in the Taos pueblo community "knowledge is power in both the spiritual and secular sense and the
use of power must be controlled. . . . Certain kinds of information are declared secret . . . and there is a high degree of concern over the secret"
(1980:126–127).

86. Durani 1990.
87. "Truth Always Triumphs," also titled "The Inevitable Collapse of Calumny,"
transcript of a special broadcast on the Alaya Rahm case by Professor G.
Venkataraman, Heart2heart Radio Sai; see http://media.radiosai.org/
Journals/Vol_04/01JUL06/collapse-of-calumny.htm.
88. Geertz 1973b.
89. Interview with Professor S. S. Sivakumar, July 17, 2006.
90. The incident was apparently discussed as a matter of serious concern among
the core group of devotees, such as Hislop, Sandweiss, and Krystal, in the
U.S. Hislop had apparently written a series of letters to Mr. Shah and other
important members of the SSSO in India about the allegations after receiving letters accusing Baba of sexual molestation.
91. Wilkerson 2000.

6. Out of God's Hands

1. The names of some devotees have been changed at their request.
2. Sathya Sai Baba also materializes real calling cards. The text on the card
reads "Bhagawan, Sri Sathya Sai Baba, Prasanthinilayam, Penukonda ta-
luka, Anantapur (Dist), Andhra Pradesh, India," and it is accompanied by a
photograph of a seated and smiling Sathya Sai Baba.
3. In the seventies and early eighties, heated debate about Sai Baba's powers
took place regularly in local news magazines and newspapers, with prominent scientists, lawyers, politicians, and judges taking both sides. A video
that claims to show Sai Baba performing "tricks" is very popular among
certain groups of Westernized, diasporic Indians.
4. Kent states that Sai Baba gifts retain the spirit of the giver. "Even when it
has been abandoned by the giver . . . still [it] possesses something of him"
(Mauss 1990:12).
5. Saffron is the color of renunciation in Hinduism, and Sathya Sai Baba always wears a saffron robe. Only on his birthday does he wear a white robe.
However, Shirdi Sai Baba always wore a white robe and a head cloth in the
style of Islamic mendicants and fakirs of the late nineteenth century.
6. The seed of the rudraksha tree (*Elaeocarpus granitrus*) holds a very special
place in Hinduism and is credited to possess mystical and divine properties.
In Sanskrit *rudraksha* literally means "the eye of Rudra," or "red-eyed," from
rud, "to cry," and *aksha*, meaning "eye." In one Shaivite story, God himself
(Shiva), on viewing the misfortunes of humanity, shed a tear. This single

tear became the first rudraksha tree and a sign of his compassion. Rudraksha beads are the material from which sacred garlands (108 beads in number) or rosaries are made. In essence, rudraksha is a Saivite rosary.

7. Interview with Dr. Taneja, July 8, 2004, and October 23, 2004.

8. Anonymous reviewers have suggested that the shroud of Turin affiliation is fascinating, as "the shroud has been found to be only a few hundred years old and so has no relationship to Jesus." The question that plagues nondevotees is, of course, the value of Sathya Sai Baba's omniscience, if he materializes objects that have questionable antecedents. However, for many devotees, this does not present a problem, since they argue that the shroud of Turin is real and scientific tests merely have not dated it correctly. Other devotees have chosen to disregard this particular problematic materialization.

9. http://www.saibaba.ws/miracles2/jesusshivamedallion.htm.

10. See http://www.saibaba.ws/miracles2/visitingcards.htm.

11. Mata Betty, New Zealand, *Sanathana Sarathi*, February 1998, p. 48.

12. Interview, November 10, 2005.

13. Howard Murphet states that, on February 18, 1966, he witnessed a vast quantity of vibhuti being materialized. He quotes from his diary entry for that day: "On the stage is a large silver statue of Shirdi Baba in His characteristic sitting posture. Mr Kasturi takes up a small wooden urn about a foot in height, and filled with vibhuti. This he holds above the head of the silver statue, and lets ash pour over the figure until the urn is empty. He shakes it well to make sure that the last grains have fallen out. . . . Now Sai Baba thrusts His arm as far as the elbow into the vessel and makes a churning motion with His arm. . . . Immediately, the ash begins to flow again from the vessel and continues to do so in a copious stream until He takes His arm out. . . . Finally, Shirdi Sai is buried in a great mound of ash—much more than the vessel could possibly have held. Now the urn is placed on the ground; the miraculous, ceremonial ash-bath is over" (Murphet 1971:42–43).

14. A recording of the Proceedings of the Meeting of Sai Organisations of Europe, Hamburg, May 12–15, 1989.

15. See http://www.saibaba.ws/miracles/ramatime.htm. From an interview with Professor Anil Kumar. http://www.radiosai.org/Journals/Vol_02/04Feb15/05_Moments_Memories/memories.htm. *Radio Sai E-Magazine*, February 15, 2004, Radio Sai Web site.

16. Stephen is referencing a story in which Sai Baba sent instructions astrally, and they appeared on a plate of turmeric powder in the devotee's home in Nepal. See http://sss.vn.ua/india/karnataka/bangalore/dsc06962.jpg.

17. "Man of Mighty Miracles," by Sri Ghandikota V. Subba Rao, from *Sri Sathya Sai Eternal Charioteer*, November 23, 1990.

18. The apostolic literature retells a story told previously by Dr. Bhagavantham (Sathya Sai Baba's translator from the 1970s to the late 1980s). He stated that Sai Baba gifted the prototype of a Seiko watch to the CEO of the Seiko company, a watch that the manufacturer had kept in a safe in Japan before traveling to India. According to the literature, the CEO, when this miracle

occurred, became an "ardent" devotee. Since Dr. Bhagavantam's story was not strong on details, Dr. Kovoor, a skeptic, was purported to have made inquiries with Shoji Hattori, president of the Seiko watch company in Tokyo to verify the facts. According to Mr. Kavoor, Mr. Hattori wrote back, "I am in no way able to further your knowledge as regards the man mentioned in your letter, Mr. Sai Baba. Neither I, nor any members of my staff, have ever made the acquaintance of this individual. I am sure that these reports are completely unfounded." See http://www.saiguru.net/english/articles/15seiko .htm; accessed August 15, 2009. But this story about materialization and the dispute over it was recounted to me by Sai devotees to show the disrespect of skeptics as well as by former devotees to argue that Sai Baba was merely a traditional illusionist.

19. I am not defending the inherent magic of these objects, but merely stating that I never encountered such a found object in my work.

20. See http://home.no.net/anir/Sai/enigma/RingExposed.htm.

21. Former devotees claim that the producers are silent out of fear of retribution by the powerful officials of the Sathya Sai movement. Even a former devotee who started a successful import-export business of "spiritual statues" (JBL enterprises) did not name his producers.

22. *Shraddha* is a difficult term to translate. It implies both faith and belief (bhakti), both mental pursuits with an added component of affect where love (prema) is an important component of the faith. See Smith 1998 [1979]:233, n. 51. Cantwell Smith argues that Sankara's exegesis of the term *shraddha* is *sraddhayà àstikyabuddhayà* (217, n. 22), which he translates as "awakening to transcendence" (59).

23. See Kasturi 1962, 1:27, chapter 1.

24. Shivaratri (night of Shiva worship) is sacred to Shaivites all over India. The festival usually falls on the thirteenth, or fourteenth, day of the dark half of Phalgun (February-March). Devotees spend the day fasting and the night singing songs of praise for Shiva and his consort Parvati. The Shiva linga is in the form of a rounded stone and is the symbol of Shiva and the creative force of the Universe.

    Lingam (also linga: Sanskrit, meaning "gender" in general and also "phallus," in particular, according to some etymologists) is used as a symbol for the worship of the Hindu god Shiva.

25. Interview with Kalyani, June 20, 2000; interview with Shanti, January 2001.

26. Interview with Atmaram, June 2004.

27. Interview with Mr. Selvaraj, December 24, 2004.

28. In the late 1980s Bangalore became one of the "hot zones" (Friedman 1997; Heitzman 2004) of technology in the country, attracting the new software companies and their employees. Today Bangalore is a center for all those interested in engineering, software technology, chip building, information technology, and related fields. Engineers and other professionals have poured into the city, and the population has grown from 3.4 million in 1985

to 5.5 million in 2000 and is projected to reach 7 million in 2011 (Heitzman:2004, quoting Bangalore Development Authority 2000 statistics).

29. See Shaw 2000.

30. Rediff.com news agency reported, August 16, 2003, "The largest recipient of foreign contribution was Sri Sathya Sai Central Trust, Rs 88.18 crore (Rs 881.8 million)." See http://www.rediff.com/money/2003/aug/16donations.htm.

31. It is very difficult to estimate the direct financial assets of the Sai organization since the organization does not reveal its internal accounting. According to detractors, "The *Economist* had a front page notice about the 'Sai Baba Empire' in early 1990, where they estimated his assets at over US$2 billion. They also reckoned him to be the No. 1 foreign exchange earner in India at that time. Conservative calculations put the current total figure much higher than two billion. Isaac Tigrett contributed US $39 million to the Puttaparthi Hospital. The Canadian metal dealer, James Sinclair, alone contributed US $600 million in 1990 as announced by Indulal Shah at the 70th birthday celebrations." See http://www.saibabaexpose.com/Prem1b.htm. But Sai Baba stated in a discourse that a donation of 100 crores was received anonymously from New York (see SSS 27:82).

32. "Seventy-five Years of Sai Baba: Faith and Controversy," *India Today*, December 4, 2000.

33. In comparison, the information technology industry, which is the largest foreign exchange earner for India, is projected to have an annual revenue in 2008 of $87 billion, according to a NASSCOM-McKinsey report.

34. The official wholesale and retail distributor of Sathya Sai Baba literature in the United States, as authorized by Sathya Sai Baba in 1969; the land was donated and the center built by a longtime devotee of Satya Sai Baba's, Mrs. Elsie Cowan, a member of the core group of Sai devotees in America. The book center operates within the jurisdiction of the Sathya Sai Baba Society, a nonprofit corporation registered in the State of California.

35. One of the newest items received by the Sai center was a game called Spiritual Play. "Rather like Monopoly," said Ratna Priya, one of the assistants at the center, "it teaches us about spirituality"; interview, April 22, 2006.

36. See T. Srinivas 2002; and Srinivas 1998.

37. http://www.saibabalinks.org/articles.htm.

38. This is my appellation for them. Devotees make the distinction, but it is not named.

39. Sunday, September 26, 1999, 10:33 P.M. Jeannie Alvin writing to her family and friends about her trip to Puttaparthi to see Sathya Sai Baba. Excerpted from a Web page: http://fweb.inetworld.net/lovesource/pilgrimage_to_india.htm#Preparing.

40. http://groups.msn.com/SriSathyaSaiBabaVirtualCommunity/general.msnw.

41. Jeannie Alvin, writing to her family and friends, http://fweb.inetworld.net/lovesource/pilgrimage_to_india.htm#Preparing.

42. Interview with Mridula, January 25, 1999, and June 28, 2003.
43. Interview, January 20, 2006.
44. Lipovetsky 1994. I use the term in a value neutral sense, not in the pejorative sense.

In Lieu of a Conclusion

1. Contemporary understandings of cosmopolitanism have a very specific provenance and do not derive "from nowhere." Peter Van der Veer suggests that the view from a cosmopolitanist perspective is an eighteenth-century European Enlightenment one, a "colonial cosmopolitanism" that is secular. Van der Veer suggests that the alternative to this colonial cosmopolitanism is found in the discourse that surrounds the idea of "spirituality." See van der Veer 2003.
2. Bailey 1996.
3. This pluralism, i.e., what seems to mark the Indic religious traditions, is more about multiple meanings and attachments. Ram Prasad Chakravarthi, in evolving a theory that demonstrates it is metaphysically possible to take the world as consisting in a multiplicity of potentially incompatible realities, calls this originary pluralism *multiplism,* and he suggests it is embedded in an extremely complicated interpretation of Indic religious logic (personal communication).
4. Fisher 1984.
5. For Castells (1996), networks are also the basic "grid" of contemporary social structure.
6. As Bauman notes: "It (the idea of perspective) took for granted the decisive role of human perception in the organization of space: the viewer's eye was the starting point of all perspective: it determined the size and mutual distances of all objects falling into a field, and remained the sole reference point for the allocation of objects and space" (1998:31–40). The human eye became the vantage point from which to view the world. And the observation point of the viewer was privileged. The observation point is somehow delinked from the cultural space around—framed and separated—so that it is considered impersonal, what Husserl called "transcendent subjectivity."
7. Clifford Geertz's famous definition of culture, in which he argues for a concept of culture that is semiotic: "Believing, with Max Weber, that man is an animal suspended in webs of significance he himself has spun, I take culture to be those webs, and the analysis of it to be therefore not an experimental science in search of law but an interpretative one in search of meaning. It is explication I am after, construing social expression on their surface enigmatical" (Geertz 1973:4–5). The definition that argues for a semiotic interpretation sets the stage for the various understandings of culture that occur in the global era of late modernity. It calls for a context-based understanding in which "explication" and the interpretive search for meaning is

privileged. It seems almost as though Geertz were anticipating the mobility both in space and across time that the concept of culture is now subject to, as we see in the examples of the Sai movement. Calling for interpretive understandings argues that while "social expressions" may look alike, or be "enigmatical," they can be read variously, indicating a politics of power of the interpretative reading that lies underneath its surface, which must be unearthed for the interpretation to be valid.

References

Abu-Lughod, Lila. 1991. "Writing Against Culture." In Richard Fox, ed., *Recapturing Anthropology: Working in the Present*, pp. 137–162. Santa Fe: School of American Research.

——— 1997. "The *Interpretation of Culture*(s) After Television." *Representations* 59:109–134.

Ackerman, S. E., and R. L. M. Lee 1988. *Heaven in Transition: Non-Muslim Religious Movements and Ethnic Identity in Malaysia*. Honolulu: University of Hawai'i Press.

Aditya, Sudha. 1992. *Sathya Sai's Amrita Varshini*. 2d ed. Prasanthi Nilayam: Sai Towers.

Adorno, Theodor. 1983. "A Portrait of Walter Benjamin." In *Prisms*. Trans. Samuel Weber and Sherry Weber. Cambridge: MIT Press.

Agnew, John. 1994. *Mastering Space: Hegemony, Territory, and International Political Economy*. New York: Routledge.

Aitken, Bill. 2004. *Sri Sathya Sai Baba: A Life*. New Delhi: Viking.

Alter, Joseph S. 1992a. "The 'Sannyasi' and the Indian Wrestler: The Anatomy of a Relationship," *American Ethnologist* 19:317–336.

———1992b. *The Wrestler's Body: Identity and Ideology in North India*. Berkeley: University of California Press.

——— 1994. "Celibacy, Sexuality, and the Transformation of Gender into Nationalism in North India." *Journal of Asian Studies* 53:45–66.

——— 1997. "Seminal Truth: A Modern Science of Male Celibacy in North India." *Medical Anthropology Quarterly* 11:275–298.

———— 2004. *Yoga in Modern India: The Body Between Science and Philosophy.* Princeton: Princeton University Press.

———— 2005. "Yoga Today: Reflections on Sexuality and the Politics of Knowledge." Paper presented at the Annual Conference on South Asia, Madison Wisconsin, September 8.

Amit, V., ed. 2000. *Constructing the Field: Ethnographic Fieldwork in the Contemporary World.* London: Routledge.

Ammerman, Nancy T, ed. 2006. *Everyday Religion: Observing Modern Religious Lives.* New York: Oxford University Press.

Ansell-Pearson, Keith. 2005. "The Reality of the Virtual: Bergson and Deleuze." *Comparative Literature* 120:1112–1127.

Anthias, Floya. 2001. "New Hybridities, Old Concepts: The Limits of 'Culture.'" *Ethnic and Racial Studies* 24:619–641.

Appadurai, Arjun. 1988. *The Social Life of Things.* Cambridge: Cambridge University Press.

———— 1991. "Global Ethnoscapes: Notes and Queries for a Transnational Anthropology." In Richard G. Fox, ed., *Recapturing Anthropology: Working in the Present,* pp. 191–238. Santa Fe: School of American Research Press.

———— 1996. *Modernity at Large: The Cultural Dimensions of Globalization.* Minneapolis: University of Minnesota Press.

Appadurai, Arjun, and Carol Breckenridge. 1995. "Public Modernity in India." In Carol Breckenridge, ed., *Consuming Modernity: Public Culture in a South Asian World,* pp. 1–20. Minneapolis: University of Minnesota.

Appiah, Kwame-Anthony. 2006. *Cosmopolitanism: Ethics in a World of Strangers.* New York: Norton.

Ardener, E. 1985. "Social Anthropology and the Decline of Modernism." In J. Overing, ed., *Reason and Morality,* pp. 47–70. London: Tavistock.

———— 1989. "Social Anthropology and the Decline of Modernism." In M. Chapman, ed., *Edwin Ardener: The Voice of Prophecy and Other Essays,* pp. 191–210. Oxford: Blackwell.

Arweck, Elisabeth, and Peter B. Clarke. 1997. *New Religious Movements in Western Europe: An Annotated Bibliography.* Westport: Greenwood.

Asad, Talal. 1986. "The Concept of Cultural Translation in British Social Anthropology." In James Clifford and George Marcus, eds., *Writing Culture: The Poetics and Politics of Ethnography,* pp. 141–164. Berkeley: University of California Press.

———— 1993. *Genealogies of Religion: Discipline and Reasons of Power in Christianity and Islam.* Baltimore: Johns Hopkins University Press.

————, ed. 1983. *Anthropology and the Colonial Encounter.* London: Ithaca.

Babb, Lawrence A. 1983. "Sathya Sai Baba's Magic." *Anthropological Quarterly* 56:116–123.

———— 1986. *Redemptive Encounters: Three Modern Styles in the Hindu Tradition.* Berkeley: University of California.

———— 1987. "Sathya Sai Baba's Saintly Play." In Hawley John, ed., *Saints and Virtues,* pp. 168–186. Berkeley: University of California Press.

————1993. "Sathya Sai Baba's Miracles." In T. N. Madan, ed., *Religion in India*, pp. 277–292. New York: Oxford University Press.

Babb, Lawrence A., and Susan S. Wadley, eds. 1995. *Media and the Transformation of Religion in South Asia*. Philadelphia: University of Pennsylvania Press.

Bailey, F. G. 1991. *The Prevalence of Deceit*. Ithaca: Cornell University Press.

————1993. *The Witch-Hunt, or, The Triumph of Morality*. Ithaca: Cornell University Press.

————1996. *The Civility of Indifference: On Domesticating Ethnicity*. Ithaca: Cornell University Press.

Bakhtin, Mikhail. 1981. *The Dialogic Imagination*. Ed. Michael Holquist. Trans. Caryl Emerson and Michael Holquist. Austin: University of Texas Press.

Balagangadhara, S. N. 2005.'The Heathen in His Blindness . . .': Asia, the West, and the Dynamic of Religion. New Delhi: Manohar.

Balu, Shakuntala. 1981. *Sai Baba. Living Divinity*. London: Sawbridge.

Banham, Reyner. 1971. *Los Angeles: The Architecture of Five Ecologies*. London: Penguin.

Barber, Benjamin R. 1995. *Jihad Versus McWorld: How Globalism and Tribalism Are Reshaping the World*. New York: Ballantine.

Barth, Fredrik, ed. 1969. *Ethnic Groups and Boundaries: The Social Organization of Culture Difference*. London: George Allen and Unwin.

Barthes, Roland. 1977. *Writing Degree Zero*. New York: Hill and Wang.

————1995. *The Barthes Reader*. Ed. Susan Sontag. New York: Hill and Wang.

Bass, B. M. 1988. "Evolving Perspectives on Charismatic Leadership." In J. A. Conger and R. N. Kanungo, eds., *Charismatic Leadership: The Elusive Factor in Organizational Effectiveness*, pp. 40–77. San Francisco: Jossey-Bass.

Basch, Linda, Nina Glick Schiller, and Cristina Szanton Blanc. 1994. *Nations Unbound: Transnational Projects, Postcolonial Predicaments, and Deterritorialized Nation States*, Pennsylvania: Gordon and Breach.

Baskin, Diana. 1990. *Divine Memories of Sathya Sai Baba*. Prasanthi Nilayam: Sri Sathya Sai Books and Publications Trust.

BBC. 2004. *Secret Swami*. Television documentary.

Baudrillard, Jean. 1975. *Mirror of Production*. St. Louis: Telos.

————1994. *Simulacra and Simulations*. Trans. Sheila Faria Glaser. Ann Arbor: University of Michigan Press.

————1998. "Simulacra and Simulations." In Mark Poster, ed., *Selected Writings*. Stanford: Stanford University Press, 1998.

Bauman, Chad. 2007. "Educating the God Man's Children: The Sai Baba Center of Indianapolis." American Academy of Religion presentation, unpublished paper.

Bauman, Zygmunt. 1998. *Globalization: The Human Consequences*. New York: Columbia University Press.

Beaulieu, Anne. 2004. "Mediating Ethnography: Objectivity and the Making of Ethnographies of the Internet." *Social Epistemology* 18, nos. 2, 3 (April 2004): 139–163.

Beckford, James A., ed. 1986. *New Religious Movements an Rapid Social Change*. London:Unesco/Sage.

Bellah, Robert N. 1970a. "Civil Religion in America." In *Beyond Belief: Essays on Religion in a Post-Traditionalist World*, pp. 168–189. Berkeley: University of California Press.

——1970b. "Between Religion and Social Science." In *Beyond Belief: Essays on Religion in a Post-Traditionalist World*, pp. 237–259. New York: Harper and Row.

——1976. "New Religious Consciousness and the Crisis of Modernity." Berkeley: University of California Press.

Bellman, Beryl. 1984. *The Language of Secrecy: Symbols and Metaphors in Poro Ritual*. New Brunswick, NJ: Rutgers University Press.

Bendix, Regina. 1997. *In Search of Authenticity*. Madison: University of Wisconsin Press.

Benhabib, Seyla. 1996. *Democracy and Difference*. Princeton: Princeton University Press.

——2006. *Another Cosmopolitanism*. New York: Oxford University Press.

Benthall, Jonathan. 1992. "The Great Anteater's Attractions." *Anthropology Today* 8:1–2.

Berger, Peter L. 1977. *Facing Up to Modernity*, New York: Basic Books.

——1979. *The Heretical Imperative*. New York: Doubleday.

——1997. "Four Faces of Global Culture." *National Interest* 49:23–30.

Berger, Peter L., Brigitte Berger, and Hansfried Kellner. 1973. *The Homeless Mind: Modernization and Consciousness*. New York: Irvington.

Berger, Peter L., and Samuel P. Huntington. 2002. *Many Globalizations*. New York: Oxford University Press.

Berger, Peter L., and Thomas Luckmann. 1966. *The Social Construction of Reality: A Treatise in the Sociology of Knowledge*. Garden City, NY: Doubleday.

Berking, Helmuth. 2003. "'Ethnicity Is Everywhere': On Globalization and the Transformation of Cultural Identity." *Current Sociology* 51:248–264.

Berman, Marshall. 1988 [1981]. *All That Is Solid Melts into Air: The Experience of Modernity*. New York: Simon and Schuster.

Bernard, H. R. 1995. *Research Methods in Cultural Anthropology*. Newbury Park, CA: Sage.

Bestor, Theodore. 2001. "Supply Side Sushi: Commodity, Market and the Global City." *American Anthropologist*. 103:76–95.

Beyer, Peter. 1994. *Religion and Globalization*. Thousand Oaks, CA: Sage.

Bhabha, Homi. 2004 [1994]. *The Location of Culture*. New York: Routledge.

Bhagavantham, S. 1976. "Lord of Miracles." In Satya Pal Ruhela and Duane Robinson, eds., *Sai Baba and His Message: A Challenge to Behavioural Sciences*, pp. 228–235. Delhi: Vikas.

Bhagwati, Jagdish. 2004. *In Defense of Globalization*. New York: Oxford University Press.

Bharathi, Agehananda. 1962. *The Ochre Robe*. Seattle: University of Washington Press.

——— 1970. "The Hindu Renaissance and Its Apologetic Patterns." *Journal of Asian Studies* 29:267–287.

Biju, Matthew, and Vijay Prasad. 2000. "The Protean Forms of Yankee Hindutva." *Ethnos* 23:516–535.

Bivins, Jason. 2007."Beautiful Women Who Dig Graves: Richard Baker-Roshi, Imported Buddhism, and the Transmission of Ethics at the San Francisco Zen Center." *Religion and American Culture* 17:C1–C4.

Bloch, Maurice. 1975. "Introduction." *Political Language and Oratory in Traditional Society.* New York: Academic.

Bok, Sissela. 1978. *Lying.* New York: Vintage.

Bolle, Keese, ed. 1987. *Secrecy in Religion.* New York: Brill.

Bolter, Jay, David Grusin, and Richard Grusin. 2000. *Remediation: Understanding New Media.* Cambridge: MIT Press.

Boot, Ken, and Tim Dunne, eds. 2002. *Worlds in Collision: Terror and the Future of Global Order.* New York: Palgrave Macmillan.

Borawoy, Michael, ed. 2000. *Global Ethnography: Forces, Connections and Imaginations in the Postmodern World.* San Francisco: University of California Press.

Bose, Sugata, and Ayesha Jalal. 1998. *Modern South Asia: History Culture, Political Economy.* New York: Routledge.

Bourdieu, Pierre. 1977. *Outline of a Theory of Practice.* New York: Cambridge University Press.

——— 1990. *In Other Words: Essays Towards a Reflexive Sociology.* Trans. Matthew Adamson. Stanford: Stanford University Press.

——— 1991. *Language and Symbolic Power.* Cambridge: Polity.

Bourdieu, Pierre, and L. J. D. Waquant. 1992. *Invitation to a Reflexive Sociology.* Chicago: University of Chicago Press.

Bourdillon, Michael, and Meyer Fortes, eds. 1980. *Sacrifice.* New York: Academic.

Bowen, David. 1988. *The Sathya Sai Baba Community in Bradford: Its Origins and Development, Religious Beliefs and Practices.* Leeds: University of Leeds Press.

Boyer, M. Christine. 1977. *The City of Collective Memory: Its Historical Imagery and Architectural Entertainments.* Cambridge: MIT Press.

Brandt, Elizabeth. 1980. "On Secrecy and the Control of Knowledge: Taos Pueblo." In S. T. Tefft, ed., *Secrecy: A Cross-Cultural Perspective,* pp. 123–146. New York: Human Sciences.

Brasher, Brenda. 2001. *Give Me That Online Religion.* San Francisco: Jossey-Bass.

Brenner, Neil. 1999a. "Beyond State Centrism? Space, Territoriality, and Geographical Scale in Globalization Studies." *Theory and Society* 28:39–78.

——— 1999b. "Globalization as Reterritorialization: The Re-scaling of Urban Governance in the European Union." *Urban Studies* 36:431–451.

——— 2003. " 'Globalization' as a State Spatial Strategy: Urban Entrepreneurialism and the New Politics of Uneven Development in Western Europe." In Jamie Peck and Henry Yeung, eds., *Remaking the Global Economy: Economic-Geographical Perspectives,* pp. 197–215. Thousand Oaks, CA: Sage.

Brooke, Tal. 1976. *Lord of the Air.* Berhamstead: Lion.

——— 1999. *Avatar of Night.* Berkeley: End Run.

Brosuis, C., and M. Butcher, eds. 1993. *Image Journeys: Audio Visual Media and Cultural Change in India*. New Delhi: Sage.

Brown, M. F. 1997. *The Channeling Zone: American Spirituality in an Anxious Age*. Cambridge: Harvard University Press.

Brown, Mick. 1998. *A Spiritual Tourist: A Personal Odyssey Through the Outer Reaches of Belief*. New York: Bloomsbury.

——2000. "Divine Downfall." *Daily Telegraph*, August 28, 2000.

Bruner, Edward. 1986. "Experience and Its Expressions." In Victor Tuner and Edward Bruner, eds., *The Anthropology of Experience*, pp. 3–30. Urbana: University of Illinois Press.

Bruner, Edward. 1986. *Experience and Its Expressions*. Nilayam: Sri Sathya Sai Books and Publications Trust.

Bucar, Elizabeth. 2007. "Creative Conformity: The Feminist Politics of Catholic and Shia Women," Ph.D. diss., University of Chicago.

Bukatman, Scott. 1999. "There's Always Tomorrowland: Disney and the Hypercinematic Experience." *October* 57:55–78.

Burghart, Richard, ed. 1987. *Hinduism in Great Britain: The Perpetuation of Religion in an Alien Cultural Milieu*. London: Tavistock.

Burke, Timothy. 1996. *Lifebuoy Men, Lux Women: Commodification, Consumption, and Cleanliness in Modern Zimbabwe*. Durham: Duke University Press.

Cabezón, José Ignacio. 2006. "The Discipline and Its Other: The Dialectic of Alterity in the Study of Religion." *Journal of the American Academy of Religion* 74:21–38.

Callewart, Winand M., and Mukund Lath. 1989. *Hindi Padavali of Namdev*. Delhi: Motilal Benarsidass.

Callois, Roger. 2001 [1961]. *Man, Play, and Games*. New York: Free Press.

Carr, David. 2006. The Reality of History. In Jorn Rüsen, ed. *Meaning and Representation in History*, pp. 123–136. New York: Berghahn.

Carrier, James G. 1990. "The Symbolism of Possession in Commodity Advertising." *Man* 25:693–706.

Casanova, J. 1994. *Public Religions in the Modern World*. Chicago: University of Chicago Press.

Castelli, Elizabeth A. 2004. *Martyrdom and Memory: Early Christian Culture Making*. New York: Columbia University Press.

Castells, Manuel. 2000 [1996]. 2d ed. The Rise of the *Network Society*, vol. 1: *The Information Age: Economy, Society and Culture*. Cambridge: Blackwell.

Chapman, M. Edwin, ed. 1989. *Ardener: The Voice of Prophecy and Other Essays*. Cambridge: Blackwell.

Chattopadhyay, Swati. 2005. *Representing Calcutta: Modernity, Nationalism, and the Colonial Uncanny*. London: Routledge.

Chodorow, N. 1997. *The Power of Feelings; Personal Meaning in Psychoanalysis, Gender, and Culture*. New Haven: Yale University Press.

Clifford, James. 1988. *The Predicament of Culture*. Cambridge: Harvard University Press.

Clifford, James, and G. E. Marcus, eds. 1986. *Writing Culture: The Poetics and Politics of Ethnography*. Berkeley: University of California Press.

Clooney, Francis X. 1991. "Binding the Text: Vedanta as Philosophy and Commentary." In Jeffrey R. Timm, ed., *Texts in Context: Traditional Hermeneutics in South Asia*, pp. 46–59. Albany: SUNY Press.

Coakley, Sarah. 1997. *Religion and the Body*. New York: Oxford University Press.

Cohen, Abner. 1969. *Customs and Politics in Urban Africa*. Berkeley: University of California Press.

——1971. "The Politics of Ritual Secrecy." *Man* 6:427–448.

Cohen, Lawrence. 1989. *No Aging in India: Alzheimer's, the Bad Family, and Other Modern Things*. Berkeley: University of California Press.

Coleman, Simon, and Peter Collins. 2004. *Religion, Identity, and Change: Perspectives on Global Transformations*. London: Ashgate.

Comaroff Jean. 1985. *Body of Power, Spirit of Resistance: The Culture and History of a South African People*. Chicago: University of Chicago Press.

Comaroff, Jean, and John Comaroff. 1991. *Revelation and Revolution: Christianity and Colonialism in Africa*. 2 vols. Chicago: University of Chicago Press.

——1992. *Ethnography and the Historical Imagination*. Boulder: Westview.

——1993. *Modernity and Its Malcontents: Ritual and Power in Africa*. Chicago: University of Chicago Press.

Comaroff, John L., and S. A. Roberts. 1981. *Rules and Processes: The Cultural Logic of Dispute in an African Context*. Chicago: University of Chicago Press.

Conger, J. A., and R. N. Kanungo, eds. 1988. *Charismatic Leadership: The Elusive Factor in Organizational Effectiveness*. San Francisco: Jossey-Bass.

Conlon, Frank. 1982. "A Nineteenth-Century Indian Guru." In Michael A. Williams, ed., *Charisma and Sacred Biography*, pp. 127–148. Atlanta: Scholars.

Cooney, Gabriel. 1994. "Sacred and Secular Neolithic Landscapes in Ireland." In David L. Carmichael, Jane Hubert, Brian Reeves, and Audhilde Schanche, eds., *Sacred Sites, Sacred Places*, pp. 32–44. London: Routledge.

Cort, John E. 2001. *Jains in the World: Religious Values and Ideology in India*. New York: Oxford University Press.

——2002. Singing the Glory of Asceticism: Devotion of Asceticism in Jainism. *Journal of the American Academy of Religion* 70:719–742.

Cosgrove, D., and P. Jackson. 1987. "New Directions in Cultural Geography." *Area* 19:95–101.

Cowan, Elsie. 1976. "Sai Baba and the Resurrection of Water Cowan." In Satya Pal Ruhela and Duane Robinson, eds., *Sai Baba and His Message: A Challenge to Behavioural Sciences*, pp. 237–245. Delhi: Vikas.

Csordas, Thomas. 1988. "Stirling Award Essay: Embodiment as a Paradigm for Anthropology." *Ethos* 18:5–47.

——, ed. 1994a. *Embodiment and Experience*. Cambridge: Cambridge University Press.

——1994b. *The Sacred Self: A Cultural Phenomenology of Charismatic Healing*. Berkeley: University of California Press.

————1997. *Language Charisma Creativity: Ritual Life in the Charismatic Catholic Renewal*. Berkeley: University of California Press.

————2004. "Asymptote of the Ineffable: Embodiment, Alterity, and Theory of Religion." *Current Anthropology* 45:163–185.

Cvetkovich, Ann, and Douglas Kellner, eds. 1997. *Articulating the Global and the Local: Globalization and Cultural Studies*. Boulder: Westview.

Daniel, Valentine E. *1984. Fluid Signs: Being a Person the Tamil Way*. Berkeley: University of California Press.

————1994. "The Individual in Terror." In Thomas Csordas, ed., *Embodiment and Experience*, pp. 229–247. Cambridge: Cambridge University Press, 1994.

Daniélou, Alain. 1964. *Hindu Polytheism*. London: Routeledge and Kegan Paul.

Daniels, S. 1989. "Marxism, Culture, and the Duplicity of Landscape." In R. Peet and N. Thrift, eds., *New Models in Geography*, 2:196–220. London: Unwin Hyman.

Das, Gurcharan. 2001. *India Unbound*. New York: Knopf.

———— 2002. *The Elephant Paradigm: India Wrestles with Change*. New Delhi: Penguin.

Das, Veena. 1983. "Language of Sacrifice." *Man* 18:45–62 (n.s.).

———— 1996. "Language and the Body: Transactions in the Construction of Pain." *Daedalus* 125:67–91.

Davis, Mike. 1990. *The City of Quartz: Excavating the Future in Los Angeles*. New York: Vintage.

Dawson, Lorne L. 2006. *Comprehending Cults*. Oxford: Oxford University Press.

De Bary, Theodore. 1957. *Sources of Indian Tradition*. Princeton: Princeton University Press.

Debord, Guy. 2005 [1995]. *The Society of the Spectacle*. Trans. Ken Knabb. Rebel.

De Certeau, Michel. 1984. *The Practice of Everyday Life*. Trans. Steven Rendall. Berkeley: University of California Press.

Deflem, Mathieu. 1991. "Ritual, Anti-Structure, and Religion: A Discussion of Victor Turner's Processual Symbolic Analysis." *Journal for the Scientific Study of Religion* 30:1–25.

Deleuze, Gilles, and Felix Guattari. 1987. *A Thousand Plateaus*. Trans. Brian Massumi. Minneapolis: University of Minnesota Press.

Delvecchio-Good, Mary-Jo. 1992. *Pain as Human Experience: An Anthropological Perspective*. Berkeley: University of California Press.

De Michelis, Elizabeth. 2004. *The History of Modern Yoga: Patanjali and Western Esotericism*. New York: Continuum.

Derrida, Jacques. 1994. *Specters of Marx: The State of the Debt, the Work of Mourning, and the New International*. New York, Routledge.

Desjarlais, Robert. 1999. "The Makings of Personhood in a Shelter for People Considered Homeless and Mentally Ill," *Ethos* 27:466–489.

De Soto, Hernando. 2000. *The Mystery of Capital: Why Capitalism Triumphs in the West and Fails Everywhere Else*. New York: Basic Books.

Devi, Indira. 1975. *Sai Baba and Sai Yoga*. New Delhi: Macmillan.

Dillistone, F. W. 1966. "The Function of Symbols in Religious Experience." In F. W. Dillistone, ed., *Myth and Symbol*, pp. 1–14. London: S.P.C.K.

Dirks, Nicholas B. 1992. "Castes of Mind." *Representations* 37:56–78.

——— 2006. *The Scandal of Empire: India and the Creation of Imperial Britain.* Cambridge: Harvard University Press.

Doniger, Wendy. 1981. *Siva: The Erotic Ascetic.* Oxford: Oxford University Press.

———1982. *Women, Androgynes, and Other Mythical Beasts.* Chicago: University of Chicago Press.

———1986. *Dreams, Illusions, and Other Realities.* Chicago: University of Chicago Press.

———1998. *The Implied Spider.* New York: Columbia University Press.

——— 2005. *The Bedtrick: Tales of Sex and Masquerade.* Chicago: University of Chicago Press.

Douglas, Mary. 1982 [1970]. *Natural Symbols: Explorations in Cosmology.* New York: Pantheon.

———1989 [1966]. *Purity and Danger.* New York: Ark.

———1996. *The World of Goods: Towards an Anthropology of Consumption.* New York: Routledge.

Douglas, Mary, and Stephen Ney, eds. 1998. *Missing Persons: A Critique of the Personhood in the Social Sciences.* Berkeley: University of California Press.

Drucker, Al, ed. 1988. *Bhagawan Sri Sathya Sai Baba: Discourses on the Gita.* Prasanthi Nilayam: Sri Sathya Sai Book and Publications Trust.

Dubuisson, Daniel. 2003. *The Western Construction of Religion: Myths, Knowledge, and Ideology.* Baltimore: Johns Hopkins University Press.

Durani, Alessandro. 1990. "Intentionality and Truth: Some Preliminary Remarks" Unpublished MS.

Durkheim, Emile. 2001. *The Elementary Forms of Religious Life.* New York: Oxford University Press.

Eade, John, and Michael J. Sallnow, eds. 1991. *Contesting the Sacred: The Anthropology of Christian Pilgrimage.* London: Routledge.

Eck, Diana. *Darshan.* 1988. New York: Columbia University Press.

——— 2006. *A New Religious America: How a "Christian Country" Has Become the World's Most Religiously Diverse Nation.* San Francisco: Harper.

Edensor, Tim. 2000. "Walking in the British Countryside: Reflexivity, Embodied Practices, and Ways to Escape." *Body and Society* 6:81–106.

Eisenstadt, S. N. 2002. *Multiple Modernities.*Edison, NJ: Transaction.

Eliade, Mircea. 1976. *Occultism, Witchcraft, and Cultural Fashions.* Chicago: University of Chicago Press.

———1987. *The Sacred and the Profane: The Nature of Religion.* New York: Harcourt Brace.

Elias, Norbert. 1978 [1969]. *The Civilizing Process,* vol. 1: *The History of Manners.* Oxford: Blackwell.

——— 1982. *The Civilizing Process,* vol. 2: *State Formation and Civilization.* Oxford: Blackwell.

———1994. *The Civilizing Process: Sociogenetic and Psychogenetic Investigations.* Rev. ed. Oxford: Blackwell.

———2000 [1939]. *Über den Proze;sz der Zivilisation. Soziogenetische und psycho-genetische Untersuchungen,* vol. 1: *Wandlungen des Verhaltens in den weltlichen Oberschichten des Abendlandes;* vol. 2: *Wandlungen der Gesellschaft. Entwurf einer Theorie der Zivilisation.* Basel: Verlag Haus zum Falken.

Ernst, Carl W. 2005. "Situating Sufism and Yoga." *Journal of the Royal Asiatic Society* 15:15–43.

Erskine, Toni. 2002. "'Citizen of Nowhere' or 'the Point Where Circles Intersect'? Impartialist and Embedded Cosmopolitanisms." *Review of International Studies* 28:457–478.

Evans-Pritchard, E. E. 1951. *Kinship and Marriage Among the Nuer.* New York: Oxford University Press.

Ewing, Katherine. 1990. "The Illusion of Wholeness: Culture, Self, and the Experience of Inconsistency." *Ethos* 18:251–278.

Fabian, Johannes. 1983. *Time and the Other: How Anthropology Makes Its Object.* New York: Columbia University Press.

Feike, Meredith. 2007. "Logging on to Sai Baba." Ph.D. diss., Louisiana State University.

Fields, Gregory P. 2001. *Religious Therapeutics: Body and Health in Yoga, Ayurveda, and Tantra.* Albany: SUNY Press.

Fine, Gary Alan, and Lori Holyfield. 1996. "Secrecy, Trust and Dangerous Leisure: Generating Group Cohesion in Voluntary Organizations." *Social Psychology* 59, no. 1 (March 1996): 22–38.

Fischer, Michael. M. J. 2004. *Emergent Forms of Life and the Anthropological Voice.* Durham: Duke University Press.

Fisher, Walter R. 1984. "Narration as Human Communication Paradigm: The Case of Public Moral Argument." *Communication Monographs* 51:1–22.

Fitzgerald, Timothy. 2003. *The Ideology of Religious Studies.* New York: Oxford University Press.

———2007. *Discourse on Civility and Barbarity: A Critical History of Religion and Related Categories.* New York: Oxford University Press.

Forsthoefel, Thomas, and Cynthia Humes, eds. 2005. *Gurus in America.* Albany: SUNY Press.

Foucault, Michel. 1980. *Power/Knowledge.* Ed. Colin Gordon. New York: Pantheon.

———1988. *"The Technologies of the Self."* In Paul Rabinow, ed., *Essential Works of Foucault, 1954–1984,* vol. 1: *Ethics: Subjectivity, and Truth.* pp. 223–251. New York: New York Press.

Fox, Richard G. 1991. *Recapturing Anthropology: Working in the Present.* Santa Fe: School of American Research Press.

Fox, Richard G., and Barbara J. King. 2002. *Anthropology Beyond Culture.* Oxford: Berg.

Frazer, James George. 1995 [1922]. *The Golden Bough.* New York: Touchstone.

Friedman, Thomas. 2000. *The Lexus and the Olive Tree: Understanding Globalization.* New York: Farrar, Straus and Giroux.

————2007. *The World Is Flat: A Brief History of the Twenty-First Century*. New York: Picador.

Friedman, J. 1992. "Narcissism, Roots, and Postmodernity: The Constitution of Selfhood in the Global Crisis." In Scott Lash and Jonathan Friedman, eds., *Modernity and Identity*, pp. 331–366. Oxford: Blackwell's.

Frow, John. 1991. "Tourism and the Semantics of Nostalgia." *October* 57:23–51.

Fukuyama, Francis. 1992. *End of History and the Last Man*. New York: Free Press.

————1995. *Trust: The Social Virtues and the Creation of Prosperity*. New York: Free Press.

Fuller, C. J. 1992. *The Camphor Flame: Popular Hinduism and Society in India*. Princeton: Princeton University Press.

Ganapati, Ra. 1981. *Baba: Satya Sai*. Part 2. Chennai: Satya Jyoti.

————1985. *Baba: Satya Sai*. Part 1. Chennai: Sai Raj.

Geertz, Clifford. 1966. "Religion as a Cultural System." In M. Banton, ed., *Anthropological Approaches to the Study of Religion*. New York: Praeger.

———— 1973a. *The Interpretation of Culture: Selected Essays*. New York: Basic Books.

————1973b. "Thick Description: Toward an Interpretive Theory of Culture." In *The Interpretation of Culture: Selected Essays*, pp. 3–30. New York: Basic Books.

———— 1983. "Centers, Kings, and Charisma: Reflections on the Symbolics of Power." *Local Knowledge*. New York: Basic Books.

————1986. "Making Experience, Authoring Selves." In Victor Turner and Edward Bruner, eds., *The Anthropology of Experience*, pp. 373–380. Urbana: University of Illinois Press.

Gellner, D. N., and E. Hirsch. 2001. "Introduction: Ethnography of Organizations and Organizations of Ethnography." In D. N. Gellner and E. Hirsch, eds., *Inside Organizations: Anthropologists at Work*, pp. 121–146. Oxford: Berg.

Gerson, Greg. 1997. "A Heuristic Explanation of the Teachings of Sri Sathya Sai Baba." MA thesis, California Institute of Integral Studies.

Ghooi, Chiranjit. 1996. *Bhakthi and Health*. Delhi: B.R.

Giddens, Anthony. 1991. *Modernity and Self-Identity: Self and Society in the Late Modern Age*. Stanford: Stanford University Press.

————2003. *Runaway World*. New York: Routledge.

Glover, William J. 2006. *Making Lahore Modern: Constructing and Imagining a Colonial City*. Minneapolis: University of Minnesota Press.

Glucklich, Ariel. 2001. *Sacred Pain: Hurting the Body for the Sake of the Soul*. New York: Oxford University Press.

Godelier, Maurice. 1999. *The Enigma of the Gift*. Trans. Nora Scott. Chicago: University of Chicago Press.

Goffman, Erving. 1955. "On Face-work: An Analysis of Ritual Elements in Social Interaction." *Psychiatry* 18, no. 3 (August): 213–31.

———— 1959. *The Presentation of Self in Everyday Life*. Garden City, NY: Doubleday-Anchor.

————1967. *Interaction Ritual: Essays on Face-to-Face Behavior*. Garden City, NY: Anchor.

———1974. *Frame Analysis: An Essay on the Organization of Experience.* Cambridge: Harvard University Press.

Gokak, V. K. 1980. *Golden Age.* Prasanthi Nilayam: Sri Sathya Sai Books and Publications Trust.

———1983. *Bhagwan Sri Sathya Sai Baba: An Interpretation.* New Delhi: Vikas.

Gold, Daniel. 1987. *The Lord as Guru: Hindu Sants in the North Indian Tradition.* New York: Oxford University Press.

———2005. "Epilogue: Elevated Gurus, Concrete Traditions, and the Problems of Western Devotees." In Thomas Forsthoefel and Cynthia Humes, eds., *Gurus in America,* pp. 219–226. Albany: SUNY Press.

Goldberg, Ellen. 2002. *The Lord Who Is Half Woman: The Ardanarisvara in Indian and Feminist Perspective.* Albany: SUNY Press.

Goody, Jack. 1996. *The East in the West.* Cambridge: Cambridge University Press.

Gordon, Melton J. 1996. *Encyclopedia of American Religions.* Detroit: Gale.

Gough, Kathleen. 1961. *Nayar; Central Kerala.* Berkeley: University of California Press.

Graeber, David. 1996. "Beads and Money: Notes Towards a Theory of Wealth and Power." *American Ethnologist* 23:4–24.

Greenfeld, Liah. 1985. "Reflections on the Two Charismas." *British Journal of Sociology* 36:17–32.

Gregory, C. A. 1995. *Gifts and Commodities.* London: Academic.

———1997. *Savage Money: The Anthropology and Politics of Commodity Exchange.* Amsterdam: Harwood Academic.

Grimshaw, Michael. 2001. "Tourist, Traveler, or Exile: Redefining the Theological Endeavor." *Journal of Religion* 81:249–270.

Gross, Rita. 2004. "Religious Identity, Scholarship and Teaching Religion." In José Ignacio Cabezón and Sheila Greeve Devaney, eds., *Identity and Politics of Scholarship in the Study of Religion,* pp. 113–133. New York: Routledge.

Guha, Ranajit, and Gayatri Chakravorty Spivak, eds. 1988. *Selected Subaltern Studies.* Vols. 1–4. New York: Oxford University Press.

Gupta, Akhil, and James Ferguson, eds. 1996. *Anthropological Locations: Boundaries and Grounds of a Field Science.* Berkeley: University of California Press.

———1997. *Culture, Power, Place: Explorations in Critical Anthropology.* Durham: Duke University Press.

Haberman, David. 1994. *Journey Through the Twelve Forests.* Oxford: Oxford University Press.

Hadsell, Heidi. 2008. "From Citizens to Ambassadors: Pondering Community in a Global Age." *Reflections: The Bulletin of the Yale School of Divinity* 94:16–20.

Halbfass, Wilhelm. 1988. *India and Europe: An Essay in Understanding.* Albany: SUNY Press.

——— 1991. *Tradition and Reflection: Explorations in Indian Thought.* Albany: SUNY Press.

Halbwachs, Maurice, and Lewis Coser. *On Collective Memory.* Chicago: University of Chicago Press, 1992.

Halliburton, Murphy. 2002. "Rethinking Anthropological Studies of the Body: Manas and Bōdham in Kerala." *American Anthropologist* 104:1123–1134.

Hallstrom, Lisa Lasell. 1999. *Mother of Bliss: Anandamayi Ma (1896–1982)*. New York: Oxford University Press.

Hannerz, Ulf. 1990. *Cultural Complexity: Studies in the Social Organization of Meaning*. New York: Columbia University Press.

——— 2002. *Transnational Connections*. New York: Taylor and Francis.

Hanson, Karen Tranberg, and Carter A. Roeber, eds. 1999. "Rationale, Romance, and Third World Cities." *City and Society* 11:1–2 (special issue).

Haraldsson, Erlendur. 1987. *"Miracles Are My Visiting Cards": An Investigative Report on the Psychic Phenomena Associated with Sri Sathya Sai Baba*. London: Century.

——— 1990. The Miraculous and the Sai Baba Movement. *Religion Today* 6:6-9.

Haraldsson, Erlendur, and K. Osis. 1977. "The Appearance and Disappearance of Objects in the Presence of Sri Sathya Sai Baba." *Journal of the American Society for Psychical Research* 71:33–43.

——— 1975. "Nothing Up His Sleeve: The Materializations of Sri Sathya Sai Baba." *Theta* 16 (Fall): 3–5.

Haraway, Donna. 1991. "A Cyborg Manifesto: Science, Technology, and Socialist-Feminism in the Late Twentieth Century." In *Simians, Cyborgs, and Women: The Reinvention of Nature*. New York: Routledge, 1991. http://www.stanford.edu/dept/HPS/Haraway/CyborgManifesto.html.

Harkin, Michael E. 1994. *"Contested Bodies: Affliction and Power* in Heiltsuk *History* and *Culture. American Ethnologist* 20:586–605.

Harpham, G. G. 1987. *The Ascetic Imperative in Culture and Criticism*. Chicago: University of Chicago Press.

——— 1992. "Old Water in New Bottles: The Contemporary Prospects for the Study of Asceticism." *Semeia* 58:134–148.

Harvey, David. 1989. *The Condition of Postmodernity: An Enquiry Into the Origins of Cultural Change*. Oxford: Blackwell.

——— 2001. *Spaces of Capital: Towards a Cultural Geography*. New York: Routledge.

Hawkins, Sophie B. 1999. "Bordering Realism: The Aesthetics of Sai Baba's Mediated Universe." In C. Brosuis and M. Butcher, eds., *Image Journeys: Audio Visual Media and Cultural Change in India*, pp. 142–156. New Delhi: Sage.

Hawley, J. S. 1987. "Morality Beyond Morality in the Lives of Three Hindu Saints." In J. S. Hawley, ed., *Saints and Virtue*, pp. 52–73 . Berkeley: University of California Press.

Hayden, Dolores. 1997. *The Power of Place: Urban Landscapes as Public History*. Cambridge: MIT Press.

Hayley, Audrey. 1980. "A Commensal Relationship with God: The Nature of Offering in Assamese Vaishnavism." In Michael F. C. Bourdillon and Meyer Fortes, eds., *Sacrifice*, pp. 107–112. New York: Academic.

Heelas, Paul. 1980. *Religion, Modernity, and Postmodernity*. Malden, MA: Blackwell.

Heelas, Paul, and Linda Woodhead. 2000. *Religion in Modern Times: An Interpretive Anthology*. Malden, MA: Wiley Blackwell.

———2005. *The Spiritual Revolution: Why Religion Is Giving Way to Spirituality*. Malden, MA: Blackwell.

Heesterman, J. C. 1985. *The Inner Conflict of Tradition: Essays in Indian Ritual, Kingship, and Society*. Chicago: University of Chicago Press.

Hefner, Robert W. 1998. "Multiple Modernities: Christianity, Islam, and Hinduism in a Globalizing Age." *Annual Review of Anthropology* 27:83–104.

Held, David, and Anthony McGrew. 2007. *Globalization Theory: Approaches and Controversies*. London: Polity.

Held, David, Anthony McGrew, David Goldblatt, and Jonathan Perraton. 1999. *Global Transformations: Politics, Economics and Culture*. Stanford: Stanford University Press.

Herbert, Jane. 1994. "Sacred Beliefs and Beliefs of Sacredness." In David L. Carmichael, Jane Hubert, Brian Reeves, and Audhilde Schanche, eds., *Sacred Sites, Sacred Places*, pp. 9–19. London: Routledge.

Hervieu-Léger, Danièle. 2001. *Religion as a Chain of Memory*. New Brunswick, NJ: Rutgers University Press.

Herzfeld, Michael. 1990. "Pride and Perjury: Time and Oath in the Mountainous Villages of Crete." *Man* 25:305–322 (n.s.).

——— 1997. *Cultural Intimacy: Social Poetics in the Nation-State*. New York: Routledge.

Hinnells, John, R. 1984. "Secular Alternatives to Religion." In John R. Hinnells, ed., *The Penguin Dictionary of Religions*. London: Penguin.

Hislop, John S. 1978. *Conversations with Sathya Sai Baba*. San Diego: Birth Day.

———1985. *My Baba and I*. San Diego: Birth Day.

———N.d. *Conversations with Bhagavan Sri Sathya Sai Baba*. Rev. ed. Prasanthi Nilayam: Sri Sathya Sai Books and Publications Trust.

Hobsbawm, Eric, and Terence Ranger, eds. 1992. *The Invention of Tradition*. Cambridge: Cambridge University Press.

Hochschild, Arlie R. 1983. *The Management Heart: Commercialization of Human Feeling*. Berkeley: University of California Press.

Hoffer, Eric. 1951. *The True Believer: Thoughts on the Nature of Mass Movements*. New York: Harper and Row.

Hooks, bell. 1984. *Feminist Theory from Margin to Center*. Boston: South End.

———1990. *Yearning: Race, Gender, and Cultural Politics*. Boston: South End.

Hosagrahar, Jyoti. 2005. *Indigenous Modernities: Negotiating Architecture and Urbanism*, London: Routledge.

Hoskins, Janet. 1998. *Biographical Objects: How Things Tell the Stories of People's Lives*. New York: Routledge.

Howe, Leo. 2001. *Hinduism and Hierarchy in Bali*. Sante Fe: School of American Research.

Howes, David, ed. 1996. *Cross Cultural Consumption*. New York: Routledge.

Huang, Julia C., and Robert P. Weller. 2007. "Charisma in Motion: The Compassion Relief Movement in Taiwan, Japan, Malaysia, and the United States." In Sherman Cochran, David Strand, and Wen-hsin Yeh, eds., *Cities in Motion: Coast and Diaspora in Modern China*, pp. 272–295. Berkeley: Institute of East Asian Studies.

Huntington, Samuel P. 1996. *The Clash of Civilizations and the Remaking of the World Order*. New York: Simon and Schuster.

Huizinga, Johan. 1971 [1955]. *Homo Ludens*. Boston: Beacon.

Hutchinson, Brian. 1992. "The Divine-Human Figure in the Transmission of Religious Tradition." In Raymond Brady Williams, ed., *A Sacred Thread: Modern Transmission of Hindu Traditions in India and Abroad*, pp. 92–124. Chambersburg: Anima.

Inda, Jonathan Xavier, and Renato Rosaldo, eds. 2001. *The Anthropology of Globalization: A Reader*. Malden, MA: Blackwell.

Inden, Ronald. 1988. *Imagining India*. Malden, MA: Blackwell.

Irani, Dara. 1982. *The First Pilgrimage to Sathya Sai Baba*. Tustin, CA: Sathya Sai Book Center of America.

Ivakhiv, A. J. 2001. *Claiming Sacred Ground: Pilgrims and Politics at Glastonbury and Sedona*. Bloomington: Indiana University Press.

Jackson, Peter, and Jan Penrose, eds. 1994. *Constructions of Race, Place, and Nation*. Minneapolis: University of Minnesota Press.

Jacobs, Jane M. 1996. *Edge of Empire: Postcolonialism and the City*. New York: Routledge.

Jagadeesan, J. 1977. *Journey to God: The Malayasian Experience*. Kuala Lumpur.

Jain, Kajri. 2007. *Gods in the Bazaar: The Economies of Indian Calendar Art*. Durham: Duke University Press.

Jameson, Fredric. 1991. *Postmodernism; or, The Cultural Logic of Late Capitalism*. Durham: Duke University Press.

Jencks, Charles. 1978. *The Language of Postmodern Architecture*. New York: Rizzoli.

——— 1987. *Post-modernism: The New Classicism in Art and Architecture*. New York: Rizzoli.

Jurgensmeyer, Mark. 1987. "The Radhaoswami Revival of the Sant Tradition." In Karine Schomer and W. H. Mcleod, eds., *The Sants: Studies of a Devotional Tradition of India*, pp. 329–355. Delhi: Motilal Benarsidass.

——— 1991. *Radhaoswami Reality: The Logic of a Modern Faith*. Princeton: Princeton University Press.

——— 1996. "A New International Religion: Radhaoswami." In Raymond Brady Williams, ed., *A Sacred Thread: Modern Transmission of a Hindu Tradition*, pp. 278–299. New York: Columbia University Press.

Kakar, Sudhir. 1982. *Shamans, Mystics, and Doctors: A Psychological Inquiry Into India and Its Healing Traditions*. New York: Knopf.

——— 1991. *The Analyst and the Mystic: Psychoanalytic Reflections on Religion and Mysticism*. Chicago: University of Chicago Press.

——— 2008. *Culture and Psyche: Selected Essays by Sudhir Kakar*. New York: Oxford University Press.

Kamaraju, Anil Kumar. 2007. *Satyaopanisad*. http://www.saiwisdom.com/ anilkebook/. Accessed July 3, 2007.

Kapferer, Bruce. 1972. *Strategy and Transaction in an African Factory*. Manchester: Manchester University Press.

———, ed. 1977. *Transaction and Meaning: Directions in the Anthropology of Exchange and Symbolic Behavior*. Philadelphia: Institute for the Study of Human Issues.

———2003. *Beyond Rationalism: Rethinking Magic, Witchcraft, and Sorcery*. New York: Berghahn.

Karanjia. R. K. 1976. "Bhagawan Sri Sathya Sai Baba's First Interview Given to a Journalist." *Blitz*, September.

———1994. *God Lives in India*. Puttaparthi: Saindra.

Kasturi, Narayan. 1960–1980. *Sathyam Sivam Sundaram: The Life of Bhagavan Sri Sathya Sai Baba*. 4 vols. Prasanthi Nilayam: Sri Sathya Sai Books and Publications.

——— 1962. *Sathyam Sivam Sundaram: The Life of Bhagavan Sri Sathya Sai Baba*. Mangalore: Sanathana Sarathi.

——— 1968. *Sathyam Sivam Sundaram: The Life of Bhagavan Sri Sathya Sai Baba*. Prasanthi Nilayam: Sanathana Sarathi.

——— 1969. *Sathyam Sivam Sundaram: The Life of Bhagavan Sri Sathya Sai Baba*. 4 vols. Rpt. Tustin, CA: Sathya Sai Book Center of America. http://vahini.org/sss/sss.html. Accessed March 20, 2007.

———1972. *Sathyam Sivam Sundaram: The Life of Bhagavan Sri Sathya Sai Baba*. Bombay: Sri Sathya Sai Educational Foundation.

———1975. *Sathya Sai Speaks*, vol. 1 .Tustin, CA: Sri Sathya Sai Baba Book Center of America.

——— 1980. *Sathyam Sivam Sundaram: The Life of Bhagavan Sri Sathya Sai Baba*. Prasanthi Nilayam: Sri Sathya Sai books and Publications Trust.

———1989. Eashwaramma: *The Chosen Mother*. Prasanthi Nilayam: Sri Sathya Sai Book and Publications Trust.

Kearney, M. 1995. "The Local and the Global: The Anthropology of Globalization and Transnationalism." *Annual Review of Anthropology* 24:547–565.

Kearney, Richard. 1991. *Poetics of Imagining: From Husserl to Lyotard*, pp. 152. London: Harper Collins.

Kent, Alexandra. 2000. "Ambiguity and the Modern Order: The Sathya Sai Movement in Malaysia." Ph.D. diss., University of Goteborg.

———2004. "Divinity, Miracles, and Charity in the Sathya Sai Baba Movement of Malaysia." *Ethnos* 69:43–62.

———2005. *Divinity and Diversity: A Hindu Revitalization Movement in Malaysia*. Honolulu: University of Hawai'i Press.

Kessing, Felix M. 1987. *The Menomini Indians of Wisconsin: A Study of Three Centuries of Cultural Contact and Change*. Madison: University of Wisconsin Press.

Khilnani, Sunil. 1999. *The Idea of India*. New York: Farrar, Straus and Giroux.

Kim, Hanna. 2001. "Being Swaminarayan: The Ontology and Significance of Belief in the Construction of a Gujarati Diaspora." Ph.D. diss., Columbia University.

———— 2007. "'Edifice Complex': Swaminarayan Bodies and Buildings in the Diaspora." In A. Mukadam and S. Mawani, eds., *Gujaratis in the West: Evolving Identities in Contemporary Society*, pp. 59–78. Newcastle: Cambridge Scholars.

————2008. "Managing Deterritorialisation, Sustaining Belief: The Bochasanwasi Shree Akshar Purushottam Swaminarayan Sanstha as Ethnographic Case Study and Theoretical Foil." In A. Geertz, M. Warburg, D. Christensen, eds., *New Religions and Globalization: Empirical, Theoretical and Methodological Perspectives*, pp. 225–242. Aarhus: Aarhus University Press.

———— 2010. "Public Engagement and Private Desires: BAPS Swaminarayan Temples and Their Contributions to the Discourses on Religion." *International Journal of Hindu Studies*.

King, Richard. 1999. *Orientalism and Religion: Postcolonial Theory, India, and "the Mystic East."* London: Routledge.

Klass, Morton. 1991. *Singing with Sai Baba: The Politics of Revitalization in Trinidad.* Boulder: Westview.

Kleinman, Sheryl, and Martha A. Copp. 1992. *Emotions and Fieldwork.* Thousand Oaks, CA: Sage.

Knott, K. 2005. *The Location of Religion: A Spatial Analysis.* London: Equinox.

Kolenda, Pauline. 1978. *Caste in Contemporary India.* Menlo Park, CA: Cummings.

Kondo, Dorinne. 1990. *Crafting Selves: Power, Gender, and Discourses of Identity in a Japanese Workplace.* Chicago: University of Chicago Press.

Kong, Lilly. 2001. "Mapping 'New' Geographies of Religion: Politics and Poetics in Modernity." *Progress in Human Geography* 25:211–233.

———— 2002. "In Search of Permanent Homes: Singapore's House Churches and the Politics of Space." *Urban Studies* 39:1573–1586.

Kramrisch, Stella. 2002 [1946]. *The Hindu Temple.* Vols. 1 and 2. Delhi: South Asia.

Krishnamani, M. N. 2001. *Divine Incarnation: A Mystery.* New Delhi: Rajan.

Krystal, Phyllis. 1985. *Sai Baba: The Ultimate Experience.* Los Angeles: Aura.

————1990. *Sathya Sai: The Yugavatara,* Bombay: Bhishma.

————1992. *Cutting the Ties That Bind: Growing Up and Moving On.* Newburyport, MA: Weiser.

Kulkarni, S. D. 1990. *Sri Sathya Sai: The Yugavatara (A Scientific Analysis of the Baba Phenomenon).* Bombay: Shri Bhagavana Vedavyasa Samshodhan Mandira.

Kuppinger, Petra. 1998. "The Giza Pyramids: Accommodating Tourism, Leisure, and Consumption." *City and Society Annual Review*, pp. 105–119.

———— 2006. "Pyramids and Alleys: Global Dynamics and Local Strategies in Giza." In Diane Singerman and Paul Amar, eds., *Cairo Cosmopolitan: Politics, Culture, and Urban Space in the New Middle East*, pp. 313–345. Cairo: American University of Cairo Press.

Kurasawa, Fuyuki. 2004. *The Ethnological Imagination: A Cross-Cultural Critique of Modernity.* Minneapolis: University of Minnesota Press.

Lamb, Sarah. 2000. *White Saris and Sweet Mangoes: Aging, Gender, and Body in North India.* Berkeley: University of California Press.

Langford, Jean. 1995. "Ayurvedic Interiors: Person, Space, and Episteme in Three Medical Practices." *Colonial Anthropology* 10:330–366.

Lash, S., and J. Friedman. 1992. *Modernity and Identity.* Oxford: Blackwell's.

Leavitt, J. 1996. "Meaning and Feeling in the Anthropology of Emotions." *American Ethnologist* 23:514–539.

Lee, Carolyn. 1998. *The Promised God Man Is Here: The Extraordinary Life-Story, the "Crazy" Teaching Work, and the Divinely "Emerging" World-Blessing Work of the Divine World-Teacher of the "Late-Time," Ruchira Avatar Adi Da Samraj.* Middletown, CA: Dawn Horse.

Lee, Raymond L. M. 1982. "Sai Baba, Salvation, and Syncretism: Religious Change in a Hindu Movement in Urban Malaysia." *Contributions to Indian Sociology* 16:125–140 (n.s.).

Leela, M. I. 1995. *Lokanatha Sai.* Guindy: Sri Sathya Sai Mandali.

Leslie-Chaden, Charlene. 1997. *A Compendium of the Teachings of Sathya Sai Baba.* Prasanthi Nilayam: Sai Towers.

Levitt, Peggy. 1999. *Transnational Villagers.* Berkeley: University of California Press.

——— 2007. *God Needs No Passport: Immigrants and the Changing American Religious Landscape.* New York: New Press.

Levy, R. I. 1984. "Emotion, Knowing, and Culture." In R. A. Shweder and R. A. LeVine, eds., *Essays on Mind, Self, and Emotion*, pp. 214–237. Cambridge: Cambridge University Press.

Lindholm, Charles. 1993. *Charisma.* Cambridge: Blackwell.

——— 1998. "Prophets and Pirs: Charismatic Islam in the Middle East and South Asia." In Pnina Werbner and Helene Basu, eds., *Embodying Charisma: Modernity, Locality, and the Performance of Emotion in Sufi Cults*, pp. 209–234. New York: Routledge.

Lipovetsky, Gilles. 1994. *The Empire of Fashion.* Trans. Catherine Porter. Princeton: Princeton University Press.

Low, Setha M., and Denise Lawrence-Zúñiga, eds. 2003. *Anthropology of Space and Place: Locating Culture.* Malden, MA: Blackwell.

Luhrmann, T. M. 1989. "The Magic of Secrecy." *Ethos* 17:131–165.

——— 1996. *The Good Parsi: The Fate of a Colonial Elite in a Postcolonial Society.* Cambridge: Harvard University Press.

Lukes, Steven. 2000. "Different Cultures, Different Rationalities?" *History of Human Sciences* 13:3–18.

Lutgendorf, Phillip. 1994. "My Hanuman Is Bigger Than Yours." *History of Religions* 33:211–245.

——— 2003. "Evolving a Monkey: Hanuman, Poster Art, and Postcolonial Anxiety." In Sumathi Ramaswamy, ed., *Beyond Appearance? Visual Practices and Ideologies in Modern India*, pp. 71-112. New Delhi: Sage.

Lutz, Catherine A., and Geoffrey M. White. 1986. "The Anthropology of Emotions." *Annual Review of Anthropology* 15:405–436.

Lutz, Catherine A., and L. Abu-Lughod. 1990. *Language and the Politics of Emotion*. Cambridge: Cambridge University Press.

Lynch, Owen M. 1990. *Divine Passions*. Berkeley: University of California Press.

Lyotard, Jean-Francois. 1979. *The Postmodern Condition: A Report on Knowledge*. Minneapolis: University of Minnesota Press.

Maclean, Mark. 2005. "Chaitanya Jyothi: The Sai Baba Museum." *Material Religion: The Journal of Objects, Art and Belief* 1:300–301.

McCutcheon, Russell T. 1997. *Manufacturing Religion: The Discourse on Sui Generis Religion and the Politics of Nostalgia*. New York: Oxford University Press.

McKean, Lisa. 1996. *Divine Enterprise: Gurus and the Hindu Nationalist Movement*. Chicago: University of Chicago Press.

McMartin, Grace. 1982. *A Recapitulation of Baba's Divine Teachings*. 2d ed. Hyderabad: Avon.

Madan, T. N., ed. 1991. *Religion in India*. New York: Oxford University Press.

Mandaville, Peter. 2007. "Globalization and the Politics of Religious Knowledge: Pluralizing Authority in the Muslim World." *Theory, Culture, and Society* 24:101–115.

Mankekar, Purnima. 1999. *Screening Culture, Viewing Politics: An Ethnography of Television, Womanhood, and Nation in Postcolonial India*. Durham: Duke University Press.

Manning, Phil. 1991. 'Drama as Life: The Significance of Goffman's Changing Use of the Theatrical Metaphor." *Sociological Theory* 9:70–86.

Mano Hriday: Newsletter of the Sri Sathya Sai Institute of Higher Medical Sciences. 2004. Vol. 2, no. 1.

Marcus, George E. 1998. *Ethnography Through Thick and Thin*. Princeton: Princeton University Press.

Marling, Karal Ann. 1991. "Disneyland 1955: Just Take the Santa Ana Freeway to the American Dream." *American Art* 5:168–207.

Marriott, McKim. 1977. "Hindu Transactions: Diversity Without Dualism." In Bruce Kapferer, ed., Transaction and Meaning: Directions in the Anthropology of Exchange and Symbolic Behavior. Philadelphia: Institute for the Study of Human Issues.

——1989. *India Through Hindu Categories*. Delhi: Sage.

——ed. 1990. *India Through Hindu Categories*. New York: Sage.

——1991. "On Constructing an Indian Ethnosociology." *Contributions to Indian Sociology* 25, no. 2 (n.s.).

Marshall, Katherine, and Marisa Van Saanen, eds. 2007. *Development and Faith: When Mind, Heart, and Soul Work Together*. Washington, DC: World Bank.

Martin, Nancy, and Joseph Runzo. 2000. "Krishna and the Gender of Longing." In *Love, Sex, Gender in the World Religions*, pp. 238–256. Boston: Oneworld.

Marx, Karl. 1977. "On James Mill." In David McLellan, ed., *Karl Marx, Selected Writings*. pp. 14–123. Oxford: Oxford University Press.

Maslow, A. H. 1943. "A Theory of Human Motivation." *Psychological Review* 50:370–396.

Mason, Peggy, and Ron Laing. 1982. *Sathya Sai Baba: Embodiment of Love*. London: Sawbridge.

Masuzawa, Tomoko. 2005. *The Invention of World Religions, or, How European universalism Was Preserved in the Language of Pluralism*. Chicago: University of Chicago Press.

Mauss, Marcel. 1990. Trans. W. D. Halls. *The Gift: The Form and Reason of Exchange in Archaic Societies*. London: Routledge.

Mazzoleni, Don Mario. 1994. *A Catholic Priest Meets Sai Baba*. Faber, VA: Leela.

Mellor, Phillip A and Chris Shilling. 1997. *Reforming the Body: Religion, Community Modernity*. London: Sage.

Melton, Gordon. 1993. "Another Look at New Religions." *Annals of the American Academy of Political and Social Science* 527:97–112.

Meyer, Birgit, and Peter Geschiere, eds. 1999. *Globalization and Identity: The Dialectics of Flow and Closure*. Boston: Blackwell.

Middleton, John. 1973. "Secrecy in Lugbara Religion." *History of Religion* 2:299–316.

Miller, Daniel. 1994. *Modernity: An Ethnographic Approach*. Oxford: Berg.

——— 1995. "Anthropology, Modernity and Consumption." In Daniel Miller, ed., *Worlds Apart: Modernity Through the Prism of the Local*, pp. 1–22. London: Routledge.

Mines, Diane P. 1997. "Making the Past Past: Objects and the Spatialization of Time in Tamilnadu," *Anthropological Quarterly* 74:173–186.

Mintz, Sydney. 1985. *Sweetness and Power: The Place of Sugar in Modern History*. New York: Viking.

Misra, Ram Shanker. 1998. *The Integral Advaitism of Sri Aurobindo*. Delhi: Motilal Banarsidass.

Moore, Sally Falk. 1987. "Explaining the Present: Theoretical Dilemmas in Processual Ethnography." *American Ethnologist* 14:727–736.

Morinis, Alan E. 1984. *Pilgrimage in the Hindu Tradition. A Case Study of West Bengal*. New York: Oxford University Press.

Morris, Brian. 1987. *Anthropological Studies of Religion: An Introductory Text*. New York: Cambridge University Press.

Munn, Nancy. 1986. *The Fame of Gawa: A Symbolic Study of Value Transformation in a Massim (Papua New Guinea) Society*. Cambridge: Cambridge University Press.

Murphet, Howard. 1971. *Sai Baba: Man of Miracles*. London.

——— 1977. *Sai Baba Avatar: A New Journey into Power and Glory*. San Diego: Birth Day.

——— 1980. "The Finger of God." *Golden Age*.

——— 1982. *Sai Baba: Invitation to Glory*. Delhi: McMillan.

——— 1983. *Walking the Path with Sai Baba*. York Beach: Weiser.

Murphy, William P. 1990. "Creating the Appearance of Consensus in Mende Political Discourse." *American Anthropologist* 92, no. 1 (March 1990): 24–41 (n.s.).

Myers, Fred R., ed. 2001. *The Empire of Things: Regimes of Value and Material Culture.* Santa Fe: School of American Research Press.

Nabokov, Isabelle. 2000. *Religion Against the Self: An Ethnography of Tamil Ritual.* New York: Oxford University Press.

Nagel, Alexandra. 1994. *De Sai Paradox: Tegenstrijdigheden van en rondom Sathya Sai Baba.* Amsterdam: Free University.

Nair, Janaki. 2002. "Past Perfect: Architecture and Public Life in Bangalore." *Journal of Asian Studies* 61:1205–1236.

Nandy, Ashis. 1983. *The Intimate Enemy: Loss and Recovery of Self Under Colonialism.* New Delhi: Oxford University Press.

——1987. *Traditions, Tyranny, and Utopias: Essays in the Politics of Awareness.* New Delhi: Oxford University Press.

——1995. *The Savage Freud and Other Essays on Possible and Retrievable Selves.* Princeton: Princeton University Press.

——2003. *The Romance of the State and the Fate of Dissent in the Tropics.* New York: Oxford University Press.

Narayan, Kirin. 1989. *Storytellers, Saints, and Scoundrels: Folk Narrative in Hindu Religious Teaching.* Philadelphia: University of Pennsylvania Press.

——1997. *Mondays on the Dark Night of the Moon: Himalayan Foothill Folktales.* With Urmila Devi Sood. New York: Oxford University Press.

Narayan R. K. 1958. *The Guide: A Novel.* New York:Viking.

Nederveen-Pieterse, Jan. 2003. *Globalization and Culture: Global Melange.* New York: Rowan and Littlefield.

Nussbaum, Martha. 2007. *The Clash Within: Democracy, Religious Violence, and India's Future.* Cambridge: Belknap.

Nyomarkay, Joseph. 1967. *Charisma and Factionalism in the Nazi Party.* Minneapolis: University of Minnesota Press.

Obeyesekere, Gananath. 1981. *Medusa's Hair: An Essay on Personal Symbols and Religious Experience.* Chicago: University of Chicago Press.

——1988. *The Work of Culture: Symbolic Transformation in Psychoanalysis and Anthropology.* Chicago: University of Chicago Press.

——1992. *The Apotheosis of Captain Cook: European Mythmaking in the Pacific.* Princeton: Princeton University Press.Ogunkolati, D. N. *Africa for Sai Baba.* Prasanthi Nilayam: Sri Sathya Sai Books and Publications Trust.

Ohmae, Kenichi. 1988. *The Borderless World: Power and Strategy in the Interlinked Economy.* New York: Ballinger.

Orsi, Robert. 1999. *The Gods of the City.* Bloomington: Indiana University Press.

Ortner, Sherry. 1984. "Theory in Anthropology Since the Sixties." *Comparative Studies in Society and History* 26:126–166.

——2005a. *Anthropology and Social Theory: Culture, Power, and the Acting Subject.* Durham: Duke University Press.

——2005b. "Subjectivity and Cultural Critique." *Anthropological Theory* 5:31–52.

Osbourne, Arthur. 1957. *The Incredible Sai Baba: The Life and Miracles of a Modern-Day Saint.* Mumbai: Orient Longman.

Ottenberg, Simon. 1984. *Boyhood Rituals in an African Society: An Interpretation.* Seattle: University of Washington Press.

Owens, Bruce. 2000. "Envisioning Identity: Deity, Person and Practice in the Katmandu Valley." *American Ethnologist* 27:702–735.

Overing, J. 1985. *Reason and Morality.* London: Tavistock.

Padmanaban, R. 1992. *Prasanthi Guide.* Puttaparthi: Sri Sathya Sai Towers.

———2000. *Love Is My Form: The Advent, 1926–1950.* Puttaparthi: Sri Sathya Sai Towers.

Palmer, Norris. 2005. "Baba's World: A Global Guru and His Movement." in Thomas Forsthoefel and Cynthia Humes, eds., *Gurus in America,* pp. 97–122. Albany: SUNY Press.

Parry, Jonathan and Maurice Bloch, eds. 1989. *Money and the Morality of Exchange.* Cambridge: Cambridge University Press.

Peck, Jamie, and Henry Yeung. 2003. *Remaking the Global Economy: Economic-Geographical Perspectives.* Thousand Oaks, CA: Sage.

Petersen, Glenn. 1993. "Kannegamah and the Pohnpei's Politics of Concealment." *American Anthropologist* 95:334–352.

Phipps, Peter. 1996. *Sathya Sai Baba and Jesus Christ: A Gospel for the Golden Age.* 3d ed. Auckland: Sathya Sai Publications New Zealand.

Piot, Charles D. 1993. "Secrecy, Ambiguity, and the Everyday in Kabre Culture." *American Anthropologist* 95, no. 2 (June): 353–370.

Pitt-Rivers, Julian. 1966. "Honor and Social Status." In J. G. Peristiany, ed., *Honour and Shame: The Values of a Mediterranean Society.* Chicago: University of Chicago Press.

——— 1974. *Mana: An Inaugural Lecture.* London: London School of Economics.

Prothero, Stephen. 1999. *Asian Religions in America: A Documentary History.* New York: Oxford University Press.

Punzo-Waghorne, Joanne. 2004. *The Diaspora of the Gods: Modern Hindu Temples in an Urban Middle-Class World.* New York: Oxford University Press.

Putnam, Robert. D. 1995. "Bowling Alone: America's Declining Social Capital." *Journal of Democracy* 6:65–78.

Rabinow, Paul. 1977. *Reflections on Fieldwork in Morocco.* Berkeley: University of California Press.

Raheja, Gloria Goodwin, and Ann Grodzins Gold. 1992. *Listen to the Heron's Words: Reimagining Gender and Kinship in North India.* Berkeley: University of California Press.

Ralli, Lucas. 1993. *Sai Messages for You and Me.* 4 vols. Prasanthi Nilayam: Sri Sathya Baba Books and Publications Trust.

Ramanujan, A. K. 1989. "Where Mirrors and Windows: Towards an Anthropology of Reflections." *History of Religion* 28:187–216.

Rao, K. L. 1966. "The Concept of Sraddha." Ph.D. diss., Harvard University.

Rao, M. N. 1995. *You Are God.* Puttaparthi: Sai Towers.

Rappaport, Nigel, and Joanna Overing. 2000. *Social and Cultural Anthropology: The Key Concepts.* New York: Routledge.

Rasmussen, Claire. 2001. "Reading the Geography of L.A." http://www.altx .com/EBR/reviews/rev12/r12ras.htm.

Rasmussen, Susan J. 1995. *Spirit Possession and Personhood Among the Kel Ewey Tuareg*. Cambridge: Cambridge University Press.

Reddy, W. 1997. "Against Constructionism: The Historical Ethnography of Emotions." *Current Anthropology* 38:327–351.

Redfield, Robert. 1955. "The Social Organization of Tradition." *Far Eastern Quarterly* 15:13–21.

——1956. *Peasant Society and Culture: An Anthropological Approach to Civilization*. Chicago: University of Chicago Press.

Reisebrodt, M. 1999. "Charisma in Max Weber's Sociology of Religion." *Religion* 29:1–14.

Ricoeur, Paul. 1970. *Freud and Philosophy: An Essay on Interpretation*. New Haven: Yale University Press.

——1978. "The Metaphorical Process as Cognition, Imagination, and Feeling." In Sheldon Sacks, ed., *On Metaphor*, pp. 141–159. Chicago: University of Chicago Press.

——1991a. *Ricoeur Reader: Reflection and Imagination*. Ed. M. Valdes. Toronto: University of Toronto Press.

——1991b. *From Text to Action: Essays in Hermeneutics II*. Trans. K. Blamey and J. Thompson. London: Athlone.

Rigolopoulos, Antonio. 1993. *The Life and Teachings of Sai Baba of Shirdi*. New Delhi: Sri Satguru.

Riti, M. D., and Stanley Theodore. 1993. "High Intrigue—Deadly Power Struggle at Puttaparthi." *Week*, June 20, pp. 28–30.

Ritzer, George. 1993. *The McDonaldization of Society*. Los Angeles: Pine Forge.

Roach, Joseph R. 1996. *Cities of the Dead: Circum-Atlantic Performance*. New York: Columbia University Press.

Robertson, Roland. 1992. *Globalization: Social Theory and Global Culture*. London: Sage.

Robertson, Roland, W. Featherstone, and S. Lash, eds. 1992. *Global Modernities*. London: Sage.

Roof, Jonathan. 1994. *Pathways to God: A Study Guide to the Teachings of Sai Baba*.

Rosaldo, M. Z. 1984. "Toward an Anthropology of Self and Feeling." In R. A. Shweder and R. A. LeVine, eds., *Culture Theory: Essays on Mind, Self, and Emotion*, pp. 137–157. Cambridge: Cambridge University Press.

Rosaldo, Renato. 1993 [1989]. *Culture and Truth: Remaking Social Analysis*. Boston: Beacon.

Rose, Nikolas. 2000. "Community, Citizenship and the Third Way." *American Behavioral Scientist* 43:1395–1411.

——2001. "The Politics of Life Itself." *Theory, Culture and Society* 18:1–30.

Rosenau, James N. 2003. *Distant Proximities: Dynamics Beyond Globalization*, Princeton: Princeton University Press.

Rosenau, James N., and James Der Derian, eds. 1992. *Global Voices: Dialogues in International Relations*. Boulder: Westview.

Rosenberg, Scott. 2007. "Anything You Can Do, I Can Do Meta." *Technology Review* (February), pp. 36–37.

Rubel, Paula G., and Abraham Rosman, eds. 2003. *Translating Cultures: Perspectives on Translation and Anthropology.* Oxford: Berg.

Ruhela, S. P. 1991. *In Search of the Divine: A Comprehensive Research Review of Writings and Researches on Sri Sathya Sai Baba Avatar.* New Delhi: M.D.

———1996. *Sri Sathya Sai Baba and the Press (1972–1996),* New Delhi: M.D.

———2000 [1994]. *The Sai Trinity: Shirdi Sai, Sathya Sai, and Prema Sai Incarnations.* New Delhi: Vikas.

Ruhela, S. P., and Duane Robinson. 1976. *Sai Baba and His Message: A Challenge to Behavioural Sciences.* Delhi: Vikas.

Rushdie, Salman. 1991. *Imaginary Homelands: Essays and Criticism.* London: Granta.

Said, Edward W. 1978. *Orientalism.* New York: Pantheon.

———1987. "Representing the Colonized: Anthropology's Interlocutors." *Critical Inquiry* 14:205–225.

Samantha, Suchitra. 1994. "The 'Self Animal' and Divine Digestion: Goat Sacrifice to the Goddess Kali in Bengal." *Journal of Asian Studies* 53:779–803.

Sandweiss, Samuel. 1975. *Sai Baba: The Holy Man and the Psychiatrist.* San Diego: Birth Day.

———1986. *Spirit and Mind.* San Diego: Birth Day.

Sarma, A. B. 1994. *Baba: The Super Human.* Madras: Sarma.

Sassen, Saskia. 2006. *Global Networks, Linked Cities.* New York: Routledge.

———2007. *A Sociology of Globalization.* New York: Norton.

Sathya Sai Baba. 1953–2004. *Sathya Sai Speaks.* Vols. 1–33. Puttaparthi: Sri Sathya Sai Books and Publications Trust. http://ssbpt.info.

———1972. *Sai Discourses in "Sathya Sai Speaks."* Puttaparthi: Sri Sathya Sai Books and Publications Trust.

———1976a. "Why I Incarnate." In S. P. Ruhela and Duane Robinson, eds., *Sai Baba and His Message,* pp. 23–29. New Delhi: Vikas.

———1976b. *Sadhana: The Inward Path.* Prasanthi Nilayam: Sri Sathya Sai Books and Publications Trust.

———1976–1992. *Summer Showers in Brindavan.* Series 1–13. Dharmakshetra. Bombay: Sri Sathya Sai Educational Foundation.

———1999a. *Sree Gurucharanam: A Compilation of Divine Discourses of Bhagavan Sri Sathya Sai Baba During Guru Poornima (1956–1998).* Puttaparthi: Sri Sathya Sai Books and Publications Trust.

———1999b. *Swami's Discourses to the Overseas Devotees.* Tustin, CA: Sathya Sai Book Center of America.

———2001. *Sai Baba Discourse: "Sanathana Sarathi," August 2001,* p. 226. Puttaparthi: Sri Sathya Sai Books and Publications Trust.

———2002. *Guidelines to Active Workers of the Sri Sathya Sai Seva Organizations.* Puttaparthi: Sri Sathya Sai Books and Publications Trust.

———2003. *Senses for Selfless Service.* Puttaparthi: Sri Sathya Sai Books and Publications Trust.

Sax, William S. 1995. *The Gods at Play: Lila in South Asia.* Oxford: Oxford University Press.

———1999. *Dancing the Self: Personhood and Performance in the Pandav Lila of Garhwal.* Oxford: Oxford University Press.

Schomer, Karine. 1987. "Introduction." In Karine Schomer and W. H. McLeod, eds., *The Sants: Studies in a Devotional Tradition in India,* pp. 1-17. Delhi: Motilal Benarsidass.

Schomer, Karine, and W. H. McLeod, eds. 1987. *The Sants: Studies in a Devotional Tradition in India.* Delhi: Motilal Benarsidass.

Seligman, Adam B. 2000. *Modernity's Wager: Authority, the Self, and Transcendence.* Princeton: Princeton University Press.

Seligman, Adam B., Robert P. Weller, and Michael J. Puett. 2008. *Ritual and Its Consequences: An Essay on the Limits of Sincerity.* NewYork: Oxford University Press.

Sen, Amartya. 2005. *The Argumentative Indian: Writings on Indian History, Culture, and Identity.* New York: Picador.

———2006. *Identity and Violence: The Issues of our Times.* New York: Norton.

Seshadri, Hiramalini, and Seshadri Harihar, eds. 2002. *The "Science" of Medicine: Where Modern Science Meets Spirituality.* Chennai: Giggles Book Shop.

Shah, Indulal H. 1979. *Sixteen Spiritual Summers.* Prasanthi Nilayam: Sri Sathya Sai Books and Publications Trust.

———N.d. *I, We and He.* Bombay: Jehnaz.

Sharma, Arvind. 1991. "New Hindu Religious Movements in India." In James A. Beckford, ed., *New Religious Movements and Rapid Social Change,* pp. 220–239. London, Delhi and Thousand Oaks, CA: Unesco/Sage.

Shaw, Connie. 2000. *Wake Up Laughing: My Miraculous Life with Sai Baba.* Johnstown, CO: Om.

Shepherd, Kevin R. D. 1985. *Gurus Rediscovered: Biographies of Sai Baba of Shirdi and Upasni Maharaj of Sakori.* Cambridge: Anthropographia.

Shils, Edward. 1965. "Charisma, Order, and Status." *American Sociological Review* 30:199–213.

Shukla, Sandhya. 2008. Keynote speech. "Cross-Cultures of Modern Harlem". Alana Conference on Ethnicity, University of Vermont.

Simmel, George. 1906. "The Sociology of Secrecy and Secret Societies." *American Journal of Sociology* 11:441–498.

———1950. "The Secret Society." In Kurt Wolff, eds., *The Sociology of George Simmel,* pp. 345–376. New York: Free Press.

Sinclair-Brull, Wendy. 1997. *Female Ascetics: Hierarchy and Purity in Indian Religious Movements.* Honolulu: University of Hawai'i Press.

Singh, Khushwant. 1973. "Godmen and Their Disciples." *Illustrated Weekly of India.* Bombay, March 18.

Skard, H., J. Palard, and J. M. Woerling, eds. 2008. *Gods in the City: Intercultural and Inter-religious Dialogue at Local Level.* Local and Regional Action. Council of Europe Online Publishing.

Skoefeld, Martin. 1999. "Debating Self, Identity, and Culture in Anthropology." *Current Anthropology* 40:417–431.

Smith, Michael Peter. 2005 "Power in Place/Places of Power: Contextualizing Transnational Research." *City and Society* 17:5–34.

Smith, William Cantwell. 1998 [1979]. *Faith and Belief: The Difference Between Them*. Oxford: Oneworld.

Soja, Edward W. 1989. *Postmodern Geographies*. London: Verso.

———1996. *Thirdspace: Journeys to Los Angeles and Other Real and Imagined Places*. Malden, MA: Blackwell.

Somers, Margaret R., and Gloria D. Gibson. 1994. "Reclaiming the Epistemological 'Other':Narrative and the Social Construction of Identity." In Craig Calhoun, ed., *Social Theory and the Politics of Identity*. Boston: Wiley-Blackwell.

Sperber, D. 1985. "Interpretive Ethnography and Theoretical Anthropology." In *On Anthropological Knowledge: Three Essays*. Cambridge: Cambridge University Press.

Spurr, Michael J. 2007. "Sathya Sai Baba as Avatar: 'His Story' and the History of an Idea." Ph.D. diss., University of Canterbury.

Spyer, Patricia, ed. 1998. *Border Fetishisms: Material Objects in Unstable Spaces*. New York: Routledge.

Srinivas, Lakshmi. 1998. "Active Viewing: An Ethnography of the Indian Film Audience." *Visual Anthropology* 1:323–353.

———2002. "The Active Audience: Spectatorship, Social Relations, and the Experience of Cinema in India." *Media, Culture, and Society* 24:155–173.

———2005. "Communicating Globalization in Bombay Cinema: Everyday Life, Imagination and the Persistence of the Local." *Comparative American Studies* 3:319–344.

Srinivas, M. N. 1952. *Religion and Society Among the Coorgs of South India*. Oxford: Clarendon.

———1962. *Caste in Modern India and Other Essays*. Delhi: Asia.

Srinivas, Smriti. 1999. "Sai Baba: The Double Utilization of Written and Oral Traditions in a Modern South Asian Religious Movement." *Diogenes* 47:114–129.

———2001. "The Advent of the Avatar: The Urban Following of Sathya Sai Baba and the Construction of Tradition." In Vasudha Dalmia, Angelika Malinar, and Martin Christof, eds., *Charisma and Canon. Essays on the Religious History of the Indian Subcontinent*, pp. 293–309. Delhi: Oxford University Press.

———2008. *In the Presence of Sai Baba: Body, City, and Memory*. Boston: Brill.

Srinivas, Tulasi. 2002. "A Tryst with Destiny: The Indian Case of Cultural Globalization." In Peter L. Berger and Samuel P. Huntington, eds., *Many Globalizations*, pp. 89–116. New York: Oxford University Press.

———2010. "Building Faith: Religious Pluralism, Pedagogy and Governance in Sathya Sai Sacred Spaces." *International Journal of Hinduism Studies* (special issue).

Srivastava, Sanjay. 2009. "Urban Spaces, Disney-Divinity and Moral Middle Classes in Delhi." *Economic and Political Weekly* 54, nos. 26, 27 (June 27, 2009): 345.

Stallybrass, Peter. 1998. "Marx's Coat." In Patricia Spyer, ed., *Border Festishisms: Material Objects in Unstable Spaces*, pp. 183–208. New York: Routledge.

Starett, Gregory. 1995/1996. "The Political Economy of Religious Commodities in Cairo." *American Anthropologist* 97:51–68.

Stark, Rodney, and William Sims Bainbridge. 1987. *A Theory of Religion*. New York: Lang.

Steel, Brian, ed. 1997. *The Sathya Sai Compendium: A Guide to the First Seventy Years*. York Beach: Weiser.

Steele, Meili. 1996. "Democratic Interpretation and the Politics of Difference." *Comparative Literature* 48:336–342.

Stiglitz, Joseph E. 1999. *Globalization and Its Discontents*. New York: Norton, 1999.

——2006. *Making Globalization Work*. New York: Norton.

Straight, Belinda. 2002. "From Samburu Heirloom to New Age Artifact: The Cross Cultural Consumption of Mporo Marriage Beads." *American Anthropologist* 104:7–21.

Strathern, Marilyn. 1997. "Partners and Consumers: Making Relations Visible." In A. D. Schrift, ed., *The Logic of the Gift*, pp. 292–311. London: Routledge.

Swallow, D. A. 1982. "Ashes and Powers: Myth, Rite, and Miracle in an Indian Godman's Cult." *Modern Asian Studies* 16:123–158.

Synott, Anthony. 1993. *Body Social: Symbolism, Self, and Society*. New York: Routledge.

Tambiah, Stanley. J. 1990. *Magic, Science and Religion and the Scope of Rationality*. Cambridge:Cambridge University Press.

——1997. *Leveling Crowds: Ethnonationalist Conflicts and Collective Violence in South Asia*. Berkeley: University of California Press.

Taussig, Michael. 1980. *The Devil and Commodity Fetishism in South America*. Chapel Hill: University of North Carolina Press.

——1993. *Mimesis and Alterity: A Particular History of the Senses*. New York: Routledge.

Taylor, Donald. 1984. "The Sai Baba Movement and Multi-Ethnic Education in Britain." *Religion Today* 1:13–14.

——1987. "Charismatic Authority in the Sathya Sai Baba Movement." In Richard Burghart, ed., *Hinduism in Great Britain: The Perpetuation of Religion in an Alien Cultural Milieu*, pp. 119–133. New York: Tavistock.

Thrift, Nigel. 2004. "Intensities of Feeling: Towards a Spatial Politics of Affect." *Geografiska Annaler* 86B:57–78.

Thurston, Edgar, and K. Rangachari. 2001 [1909]. *Castes and Tribes of Southern India*. 7 vols. New Delhi: Asian Educational Services.

Tillich, Paul. 2001 [1957]. *Dynamics of Faith*. Canada: Harper Collins.

Tilly, Charles. 2005. *Identities, Boundaries, and Social Ties*. New York: Paradigm.

——2007. *Democracy*. Cambridge: Cambridge University Press.

Timm, Jeffrey R. 1992. "Scriptural Realism in Pure Nondualistic Vedanta." In Jeffrey R. Timm, ed., *Texts in Context: Traditional Hermeneutics in South Asia*, pp. 127–146. Albany: SUNY Press.

Tomlinson, John. 1999. *Globalization and Culture*. Chicago: University of Chicago Press.

Trawick, Margaret. 1990. *Notes on Love in a Tamil Family*. Berkeley: University of California.

Trouillot, Michel-Rolph. 2002. *Anthropology Beyond Culture*. Ed. Richard G. Fox and Barbara J. King. Oxford: Berg.

———2003. *Global Transformations: Anthropology and the Modern World*. New York: Palgrave Macmillan.

Turner, Victor W. 1962a. *Chihamba, the White Spirit: A Ritual Drama of the Ndembu*. Rhodes-Livingstone paper no. 33. Manchester: Manchester University Press.

———1962b. "Themes in the Symbolism of Ndembu Hunting Ritual. *Anthropological Quarterly* 35:37–57.

———1964. "Betwixt and Between: The Liminal Period in Rites de Passage. In J. Helm, ed., *Symposium on New Approaches to the Study of Religion: Proceedings of the 1964 Annual Spring Meeting of the American Ethnological Society*, pp. 4–20. Seattle: American Ethnological Society.

———1966. "Color Classification in Ndembu Ritual: A Problem in Primitive Classification." In M. Banton, ed., *Anthropological Approaches to the Study of Religion*, pp. 47–84. A.S.A. Monograph no. 3. London: Tavistock.

———1967. *The Forest of Symbols: Aspects of Ndembu Ritual*. Ithaca: Cornell University Press.

———1974. *Dramas, Fields, and Metaphors: Symbolic Action in Human Society*. Ithaca: Cornell University Press.

———1995 [1969]. *The Ritual Process*. Chicago: Aldine.

Turner, Victor W., and Edith Turner. 1995 [1978]. *Image and Pilgrimage in Christian Culture*. New York: Columbia University Press.

Urban, Hugh B. 1998. "The Torment of Secrecy: Ethical and Epistemological Problems in the Study of Esoteric Traditions." *History of Religions* 37:209–248.

———2003a. "Avatar for Our Age: Sathya Sai Baba and the Cultural Contradictions of Late Capitalism." *Religion* 33:73–93.

———2003b. *Tantra: Sex, Secrecy, Politics, and Power in the Study of Religion*. Berkeley: University of California Press.

Vaudeville, Charlotte. 1999. *Myths, Saints, and Legends in Medieval India*. New Delhi: Oxford University Press.

Vanaik, Achin, Praful Bidwai, and Harbans Mukhia, eds. 1996. *Religion, Religiosity, Communalism*, New Delhi: South Asia.

Van der Leeuw, Gerard. 1986 [1933]. *Religion in Essence and Manifestation*. Princeton: Princeton University Press.

Van der Veer, Peter. 1994. *Religious Nationalism: Hindus and Muslims in India*. Berkeley: University of California Press.

——— 2001. Imperial Encounters: *Religious Modernity in India and Britain*, Princeton: Princeton University Press.

———2003. "Colonial Cosmopolitanism." In Steven Vertovec and Robin Cohen, eds., *Conceiving Cosmopolitanism: Theory, Context, and Practice*, pp. 165–180. Oxford: Oxford University Press.

Van der Veer, Peter, and Hartmut Lehmann, eds. 1999. *Nation and Religion: Perspectives on Europe and Asia.* Princeton: Princeton University Press.

Van Gennep, Arnold. 1960 [1909]. *Rites of Passage.* Chicago: University of Chicago Press.

Van Loon, Joost. 2006. "Network." *Theory, Culture, and Society* 23:307–314.

Van Mannen, John. 1988. *Tales of the Field: On Writing Ethnography.* Chicago: University of Chicago Press.

Veblen, Thorsten. 1953 [1899]. *Theory of the Leisure Class: An Economic Study of Institutions.* New York: Signet.

Venturi, Robert, Denise Scott-Brown, and Steve Izenour. 1972. *Learning from Las Vegas.* Cambridge: MIT Press.

Vertovec, Steven. 1999. "Three Meanings of Diaspora Exemplified in South Asian Religions." *Diaspora* 6:277–299. http://www.transcomm.ox.ac.uk/working %20papers/diaspora.pdf.

——2000. *The Hindu Diaspora: Comparative Patterns.* London: Routledge.

Virilio, Paul. 1997. *Open Sky.* Trans. Julie Rose. London: Verso.

Vroon, Piet. 1993. "Santa Claus in India." *Indian Skeptic* 6:8–16.

Wadley, Susan S. 1975. *Shakthi: Power in the Conceptual Structure of Karimpur Religion.* Delhi: Munshiram Manoharlal.

Wallerstein, Immanuel. 1974. *The Modern World-System,* vol. 1: *Capitalist Agriculture and the Origins of the European World-Economy in the Sixteenth Century.* New York: Academic.

——1984. *The Politics of the World-Economy: The States, the Movements, and the Civilizations.* Cambridge: Cambridge University Press.

—— 1991. *Geopolitics and Geoculture: Essays on the Changing World-System.* Cambridge: Cambridge University Press.

Walsh, William. 1983. *R. K. Narayan: A Critical Appreciation.* Chicago: University of Chicago Press.

Waquant, Loic. 2004. *Body and Soul: Notebooks of an Apprentice Boxer.* Oxford: Oxford University Press.

Warrier, Maya. 2005. *Hindu Selves in a Modern World.* London: Routledge.

Waters, Malcolm. 1995. *Globalization.* New York: Routledge.

Watson, James L. 1997. *Golden Arches East: McDonalds in East Asia.* Stanford: Stanford University Press.

Weber, Max. 1958 [1946]. *From Max Weber.* New York: Oxford University Press.

——1968 [1947]. *On Charisma.* Chicago: University of Chicago Press.

——1978. *Economy and Society.* Berkeley: University of California Press.

Weeks, John R. 2003. *Unpopular Culture: The Ritual of Complaint in a British Bank.* Chicago: University of Chicago Press.

Weiner, Annette. B. 1992. *Inalienable Possessions: The Paradox of Keeping While Giving.* Berkeley: University of California Press.

Weiss, Bard. 1996. *The Making and Unmaking of Haya Lived World: Consumption, Commoditization and Everyday Practice.* Durham: Duke University Press.

Weiss, Richard. 2005. "The Global Guru: Sai Baba and the Miracle of the Modern." *New Zealand Journal of Asian Studies* 7, no. 2 (December 2005): 5–19.

Weller, Robert P. 1999. *Alternate Civilities: Democracy and Culture in China and Taiwan*. Boulder: Westview.

Wendt, Alexander. 1999. *Social Theory of International Politics*. Cambridge: Cambridge University Press.

Werbner, Pnina. 1996. "Stamping the Earth with the Name of Allah: Zikr and the Sacralizing of Space Among British Muslims." *Cultural Anthropology* 11:309–338.

———1998. "Langer: Pilgrimage, Sacred Exchange, and Perpetual Sacrifice in a Sufi Saint's Lodge." In Pnina Werbner and Helene Basu, eds., *Embodying Charisma: Modernity, Locality, and the Performance of Emotion in Sufi Cults*, pp. 95–116. New York: Routledge.

———1999. "Global Pathways. Working-Class Cosmopolitans and the Creation of Transnational Ethnic Worlds." *Social Anthropology* 7:17–35.

Werbner, Pnina, and Helene Basu, eds. 1998. *Embodying Charisma: Modernity, Locality, and the Performance of Emotion in Sufi Cults*. New York: Routledge.

Whicher, Ian. 1998. "Yoga and Freedom: A Reconsideration of Patanjali's Classical Yoga." *Philosophy East and West* 48:272–322.

White, Charles S. J. 1972. "The Sai Baba Movement: Approaches to the Study of Indian Saints." *Journal of Asian Studies* 31:863–878.

White, David Gordon. 1998. *The Alchemical Body: Siddha Traditions in Medieval India*. Chicago: University of Chicago Press.

———2000. *Tantra in Practice*. Princeton: Princeton University Press.

———2003. *The Kiss of the Yogini: Tantric Sex in South Asian Contexts*. Chicago: University of Chicago Press.

White, Geoffrey. 2006. "Landscapes of Power: National Memorials and the Domestication of Affect." *City and Society* 18:56–61.

Wikan, U. 1992. "Beyond the Words: The Power of Resonance." *American Ethnologist* 19:460–482.

Wilkerson, William S. 2000. "Objectivity from Subjectivity: A Review of Jan Patocka's Introduction to Husserl's Phenomenology." *Human Studies* 23:91–97.

Williams, Raymond Brady. 1988. *Religions of Immigrants from India and Pakistan: New Threads in the American Tapestry*. Cambridge: Cambridge University Press.

———, ed. 1992. *A Sacred Thread: Modern Transmission of Hindu Traditions in India and Abroad*. Chambersburg: Anima.

Willner, Ann Ruth. 1984. *The Spellbinders: Charismatic Political Leadership*. New Haven: Yale University Press.

Wills, Lawrence M. 2006. "Ascetic Theology Before Asceticism? Jewish Narratives and the Decentering of Self." *Journal of the American Academy of Religion* 74:902–926.

Wilson, Elizabeth. 1991. *The Sphinx and the City: Urban Life, the Control of Disorder, and Women*. Berkeley: University of California Press.

Wimbush, Vincent L., and Richard Valantasis, eds. 1993. *Asceticism*. Oxford: Oxford University Press.

Wolf, Martin. 2004. *Why Globalization Works*. New Haven: Yale University Press.

Worthington, Valmai. 1995. *Journey to Puttaparthi: A Visitor's Guide*. Faber, VA: Leela.

Yuan, Yunxiang. 1996. *The Flow of Gifts: Reciprocity and Social Networks in a Chinese Village*. Stanford: Stanford University Press.

Yoga Sutra. 1982. 3d ed. New Delhi: Oriental.

Zarilli, Phillip. 1989. "Three Bodies of Practice in Traditional South Indian Martial Art, Social Sciences, and Medicine." *Social Science and Medicine* 28:1289–1309.

Zukin, Sharon. 1995. *The Cultures of Cities*. Oxford: Blackwell.

Index

Aarathi (offering of camphor flame), 160

Abode of supreme peace (Prasanthi Nilayam), 10, 13, 15, 61, 94, 108, 111, 115, 116, 118, 125–29, 137, 143, 148, 164–65, 211, 219, 255, 311, 332; architecture of, 131–32; darshan everyday at, 158; deaths at, 232–34

Abstention, 206–7, 214, 216–23, 224

Accessibility, narratives of, 97

Accountability, 233

Adharma (evil), 63, 71

Adigal, 263

Adi Shankara, 356n53

Adorno, Theodor, 283

Advaita tradition, 63

Affectivity, 37, 300, 320

Agency, 85, 113, 199, 329; narrative of, 300; transforming, 90–92

Age of modern evil, 63, 71

Age of modern evil (Kali Yuga), 63, 71

Aghenanda Bharathi (Swami), 177

Agon, 171

Ahamkara (arrogance), 185

Ahimsa (nonviolence), 16, 190

Akhanda bhajans, 354n33

Alaya Rahm v. Sathya Sai Baba Society, 371n28

Alea, 171

The Alexandria Quartet (Durrell), 201

Algier, Horatio, 89

Allah, 68, 174, 363n3

All-India Conference (1967), 244

Alterity, 44

Alvin, Jeannie, 164, 304, 311, 315, 377n39, 377n41

Amar Chitra Katha religious cartoon books, 144

The Amazing Advent (Brooke), 254

Amazing Grace hymn, 160

Ambiguity, 265–71; in body language, 262–63

Ambiguity, strategic, 271

Ambrosia, 284, 286, 294, 316–17

Ambrosia (amritam), 284, 286, 294, 316–17

Ammachi, 358n66

Amnesiac societies, 367n16

Amritam (ambrosia), 284, 286, 294, 316–17

Anand, K., 324

Androgyny, 66

Angel, Criss, 156

Anjanaya; *see* Hanuman

Anti-Sai activism, 16–17, 41, 47, 269; Baba's leela in seating influence, 168; bookshops and, 306; on gifts, 296; on museum, 138–39

Anti-Sai network, 234, 235, 252–60, 352*n*11

Anti-Sai petition, 254

Anubhava (divine grace), 13

Anuraga-bhava (love for lover), 80

Apasthamba Suthra (Brahma Sutras), 56

Apologetic literature, 58

Appadurai, 180

Appar, 263

Appiah, Anthony, 326, 327

Architecture: hybrid, 330; moral, 140–48, 153–55; of Prasanthi Nilayam, 131–32; of Puttaparthi, 131–32, 140–48

Arjuna, 80, 84, 210

Arrogance (ahamkara), 185

Art of Living Foundation, 99

Asceticism: bodily practices and, 202; body, desire and, 206–9; desire and, 201–6; globalization and, 203–4

Ashram, 61, 116; certified goods, 303, 308–10, 315; Hindu, 360–61*n*33; important function of, 113; private sector of, 125; restrictions, 128–29; *see also* Puttaparthi

Atma gyana (self-knowledge), 106, 180, 206, 266, 369*n*31

Atman (soul/self), 72, 206

Austerity, 224; desire and, 215

Authenticity, of goods, 303, 308–10, 315

Autohagiographical, 55

Avatars (incarnation), 10, 62, 71, 72, 85, 91, 356*n*51, 356*n*54; of ages, 88; Sathya Sai Baba as, 68–70, 91

Awle, Ram Das, 268

Ayurveda, 192, 219, 268

Baba (father), 65; *see also* Sathya Sai Baba

Baba (Schulman), 211

Baba Chants the Bhajan, 161

Babb, Lawrence, 13, 47, 53, 158, 292, 294, 298

Babu, Ravindra, 370*n*2

Backstage talk, 271–72

Badaev, Serguei, 253, 255

Bad darshan, 167

Bailey, David, 234, 296

Bailey, Edward, 76

Bailey, F. G., 237

Bailey, Faye, 234

Balakrishna, 287

Balalilas (playful pranks), 295

Bal Vihar; *see* Bal Vikas program

Bal Vikas program, 194–95, 244, 247

Bangalore Science Forum, 258

Bangalore University, 258

Banham, Rayner, 97

Barthes, Roland, 271

Baudrillard, Jean, 8, 319, 333, 334, 338

Bauman, Zygmunt, 178

BBC, 234, 277

Bellah, Robert, 90

Benjamin, Walter, 163, 283

Bentham, Jeremy, 366*n*5

Berger, Peter, 33–34

Besant, Annie, 356*n*54

Betty, Mata, 290

Bhagavad Gita, 63, 71, 356*n*50

Bhagavantham, 375*n*18

Bhagawan (God), 10, 61, 79

Bhajans (devotional music), 3, 9, 18–19, 38, 60, 93, 99, 100, 103, 107, 136, 149, 150, 151, 156, 158–62, 182, 184, 195, 196, 218, 221, 240–41, 243, 283, 300, 305, 354*n*33, 362–63*nn*3–5, 363*n*7, 364*n*11; *see also* Chanting

Bhajans Mandali, 240

Bhaktas; *see* Devotees

Bhakti (devotional), 58

Bhakti movement, 363*n*7

Bhaktirasa, 297

Bharadwaja, 65

Bharadwaja gothra, 56

Bharati, 9

Bharatiya Janata Party (BJP), 347*n*1

Bhat Raju caste, 54

Bhatt, Vishnu, 232

Bhava (grace), 324

Biopolitics, 204

Biopower, 204

BJP; *see* Bharatiya Janata Party

Birth, 55

Bliss, 169

Blitz magazine, 214, 258, 295

Blue Thirst (Durrell), 93

Bodily control (nasa), 214

Bodily practices: asceticism and, 202; Hindu, 205–6; identity and, 204–5; Sai movement and, 202–3

Body, 367n17, 367n19, 367n22; ascetic discipline of, 203–4; cultural theories of, 366n6; desire and ascetic, 206–9; devotion of, 215; divine, 183, 209–13; as impediment to salvation, 333–34; language, 262–63; as metaphor for society, 189; socially informed, 19

Bok, Sissela, 237

Bollywood, 144, 160

Bookshops, 305–6; anti-Sai activism and, 306; see also specific bookshop

Bose, S. K., 134, 137

Brahma, 288

Brahman (supreme godhead), 72, 169, 356n55

Brahmanas, 63

Brahma Sutras, 56

Brandt, Elizabeth, 374n85

Brihadaranyaka Upanishad, 160

Brindavan, Whitefield ashram, 50, 61

British East India Company, 235

Bronson, Bill, 353n20

Brooke, Tal, 253, 254–55, 358n5

Brother (manoj), 99

Brown, Denise Scott, 140

Brown, Mick, 354n31

Buddha, 59, 117, 142, 282, 291

Bunker mentality, 259

Butler, Judith, 35

Calling cards, 187, 286, 289, 374n2

Callois, Roger, 171

Camphor flame offering (aarathi), 160

Canetti, Elias, 232

Capital, 350n28

Carter, Howard, 259

Carthew, Stephen, 256

Cartographic identity, 146

Caste ambiguity, 54

Castes and Tribes of South India (Thurston), 351n8

Ceiling on Desires program, 216–23, 369n39

Celibacy, 369n344

Central coordinators, 250

Certified objects, 303

Chaitanya Jyothi, Experiencing the Divine: The Millennium Museum Depicting the Message and Mission of Sri Sathya Sai Avatar, 137

Chaitanya Jyothi Museum, 12, 134, 135, 136–39, 142, 145

Chakravarthi, Ram Prasad, 378n3

Chanting, 80, 162, 362n3; namasmarana, 18, 51, 79–81, 357n60

Chaplin: His Life and Art (Robinson), 201

Character, 195; building, 198–200

Charisma, 86, 330; belief and, 88–90; constructed, 75–78; darshan queue, 164–66; nomadic, 10, 90–92, 330

Charismatic Christian community, 89

Charismatic community, 357n58

Charitable endeavors, 15, 189, 369n32; see also Seva

"Charter of the Sathya Sai Organization and Rules and Regulations (for Overseas Countries)" (SSSO), 249

Chen, Harry, 225

Chieftain (raja), 60

Children, education of, 194–95

Chincholi, 60

Chinna Katha (Sathya Sai Baba), 263

Chitravathi River, 133, 134

Chitravathi Road trade, 302–4, 307, 311, 318

Choice, 337

Chopra, Deepak, 99, 179

Christian eschatology, 350n29

Christianity, 9, 87, 99; see also Jesus Christ

Christian Sai miracle, 86

Christmas Discourse, 69

Chronotrope, of divinity, 54

Clash, of civilizations, 26–27

Cloth, 59

Cloth (lungi), 59

Clothing, for darshan, 201–2

Cobra, 55

Codification, 223, 228–30, 333–34

Colusa miracle, 182

Committee to Investigate Miracles and Other Verifiable Superstitions, 258

Commodification, 283

Compassionate Relief, 113

Complete incarnations (poorna avatar), 62, 71, 85

Complexity, 36

Confrontational discourse, 278
Consecrated substance (prasadam), 158, 183
Constructed charisma, 75–78
Consumption, 320–22, 331; see also Sacred
   objects; Sai objects
Contemporary identity, 178
Contextualization, 337–38, 341
Conversational evasions, 261–62
Conway, Timothy, 253, 256, 268, 275
Coomaraswamy, Ananda, 196
Corporate model, 248–49
Cosmopolitanism, 6, 326–31, 378n1;
   of devotees, 177; moral stakeholding
   and, 198–200; see also Engaged
   cosmopolitanism
Counterhegemonic identity, 114
Cowan, Elsie, 241, 305, 362n57, 377n34
Cowan, Walter, 241, 305, 362n57
Creator/creation, 290
Credibility, 47
Critchlow, Keith, 117, 141, 192
Critical thinking, 43
Criticism, 39
Cross-cultural comparisons, 35–37
Crowds and Power (Canetti), 232
Crying, 173
Cultural awareness, 331
Cultural disembedding, 331
Cultural form, 333–34
Cultural globalization, 22–35, 228; analysis
   metric, 36; method of study development,
   37–46; unintended consequences of, 23
Cultural hybridization, 31, 350n30
Cultural intimacy, 235
Cultural matrix, 223
Cultural translation, 223, 235, 323–42;
   awareness and disembedding, 331, 341;
   codification and universalization, 333, 341;
   contextualization, 337–38, 341; latching
   and matching, 335–36, 341
Culture(s), 24–25, 333–37, 378n7; of
   complaint, 37–46; differences existing
   with similarities, 174–75; itinerant, 32;
   latching, 335–36, 341; nation and,
   306–7, 350n35; pluralization of, 188;
   religion and, 3–4; transmission of, 339; of
   travel, 93–97; war, 340
Cyberworlds, of devotion, 148–52
Cyclical semiotic process, 335

Dadlani, Sanjay, 257, 372n48
Daniels, Steve, 146
Dargahs (tombs), 298
Darshan, 13–14, 54, 59, 60, 114, 213, 332;
   bad, 167; clothing for, 201–2; devotees
   before, 161; divine, 156–58; divine play
   and, 164–72; everyday praxis of, 158–72;
   healing, divine play, and, 181–90; from
   Internet, 149–52; magic of, 171; morning,
   162; from nondevotional perspective,
   171–72; religious identity and, 179–81;
   for removing blockages, 173; Sathya Sai
   Baba and devotees at, 164; sensory
   experience of, 159; structure of
   experience of, 159–64; transcendent
   ritual of, 170; for universal faith of values
   based in action, 199
Das, Gurcharan, 31
Dasya-bhava (servant-master fealty), 80
Davies, Winston, 274
Debord, Guy, 171–72
Deccan Herald (newspaper), 258, 259
Decommercialization, 365n29
Dedifferentiation, 99, 338
Deepavali (festival of lights), 60
De Kraker, Hans, 256
de Saint-Exupéry, Antoine, 50
Desire, 208, 217; ascetic body and, 206–9;
   asceticism and, 201–6; austerity and, 215;
   cessation of, 206–7; pursuit of, 224–27;
   reshaping, 213–16; Sathya Sai Baba on,
   208; satiation of, 216, 228; see also
   Ceiling on Desires program
Deterritorialization, of culture, 32
Deus Loci, 93–155
Devi, Indira, 11
Devotees, 12–13, 57, 58, 172, 215, 348nn9–11,
   358n4, 359n11; attitude to faith of, 179; on
   avatarhood, 85; becoming, 119–28; being
   good, 173; cherishing gifts, 320–21;
   complaining of, 39–46; cosmopolitanism
   of, 177; daily rituals of, 18–19; at darshan,
   164; before darshan, 161; Internet
   connecting, 148–50; link to sacred space,
   146; middle-class, 177; packing list, 225;
   potential, 46; power over, 126; sacred
   space influencing, 153–55; on Sai Baba's
   leela, 173; spaces of entry, 119–28; stories,
   53–54; storytelling of, 83; transformative

power of gifts, 292–300; truth of, 338; type of, 13; Western medicine and, 190–91; work for spirituality, 189; worth of, related to seating, 166–67; *see also* Devotion; Pilgrims; Prospective pilgrim; Seva

Devotion, 12, 38, 369n31; body of, 215; Chaitanya Jyothi Museum about, 134; cyberworlds of, 148–52; grammar of, 106; healing and, 189; hermeneutics of, 78–88; human grammar of, 154; literal translation of words related to, 84; personal, 77; religion related to, 99; reshaping desire and, 213–16; sacra and, 315–16; syncretic, 179; translocal, 148–52; transnational, 156–58, 202–3; travel and, 93–97; *see also* Bhajans

Devotional (bhakti), 58

Devotional identity, 171; space and, 112; working multiculturalism and crafting, 176–81

Devotional music (bhajans), 3, 9, 18–19, 38, 60, 93, 99, 100, 103, 107, 136, 149, 150, 151, 156, 158–62, 182, 184, 195, 196, 218, 221, 240–41, 243, 283, 300, 305, 354n33, 362–63nn3–5, 363n7, 364n11

Devotional politics, 20–21

Devotional self: finding, 175–76; work, self-transformation and construction of, 172–76

De Vrees, Joule, 353n20

Dhanvantri, 192

Dharma (right conduct/duty), 13, 16, 71, 190, 211

Dhrupad, 161

Dhruva bera, 308

Diaz (Mr.), 120

Dirks, Nicholas, 235

Disembedding, 331

Disembodied institutions, 366n6

Dislocation, 106

Disneyland, 97

Displaced transmission, 336

Distribution, 42

Diversity, 7, 153–55, 329, 341–42; *see also* Grammar of diversity

Divine androgyny, 66

Divine body, 183, 209–13

Divine gifts, 284–85; *see also* Materializations; Vibhuti

Divine grace, 13

Divine grace (anubhava), 13

Divine incarnation, 86–87

Divine legitimation, 286–92

Divine play or miracle (leela), 14, 56, 164–69, 285, 332, 364n13, 364n18; darshan and, 164–72; Ram, 170; seating arrangement and, 164–69; as watered-down concept, 339; work and, 172–74

Divine story (purana), 52

The Divine Story of Shirdi Sai and Puttaparthi Sai (TV show), 151

Divine vessels, filled with vibhuti, 182

Doniger, Wendy, 35

Dow, Thomas, 77

Dreams, waking, 163–64

Drucker, Al, 292

Durrell, Lawrence, 93, 201

Dussehra (nine nights of victory), 60

Dutta, Tanya, 293

Duty (dharma), 13, 16, 71, 190, 211

Dvaita tradition, 63

Dynamic ethnography, 45–46

Eashwaramma, 55, 134, 352n11

Eck, Diana, 158

Economies, of faith, 93–97

E-darshan, 149–52

Educare; *see* Sathya Sai Educare

Education, 16, 141–42, 194–96, 199

Education in Human Values (EHV), 194–95, 244

EHV; *see* Education in Human Values

Embodied citizenship, 366n3

Embodiment, 228–30

Emerson College, 273

Emotion, 77, 80–81; construction and, 131; of darshan, 173; *see also* Namasmarana chanting

Empire, 235–38

The Encyclopedia of Religion and Society (Bailey), 76

End of the Dream: The Sathya Sai Baba Enigma (Priddy), 254

Energy transformation, 295

Engaged cosmopolitanism, 6–7, 323–42

Ephemera, 315–16

ESSV, 194

Eternal Heritage Museum, 117

Ethics, secrecy and, 236
Ethnopolitics, 204
Europe, as locus of modernity, 350n27
Evangelische Zentralstelle fur
    Weltanschauungsfragen, 357n56
Evening darshan, 162
Evil (adharma), 63, 71
Exclusion, 146; politics of, 111
Exile, narratives of, 97, 109–10

Faith, 106, 179, 298; economies of, 93–97
faith, and love (shraddha), 298, 299, 376n22
Family model, 247–48
Fantasy, 146, 171; darshan related to, 164
Father (baba), 65
Feike, Meredith, 197
Festival honoring Guru (Gurupoornima
    Day), 65
Festival of lights (Deepavali), 60
Film, 143–44, 146, 312
Focault, Michel, 203–4, 276
Food restrictions, 217, 219–21
Former devotees; see Anti-Sai activism
Foucault, Michel, 204, 216, 222, 276, 366nn2,
    4–5
Fourfold complexity of divine personhood,
    of sathya Sai Baba, 70–76, 328, 330
Fragmagration, 32
Freedom, 169
Free will, 76
Frei University, 256
Freudian analysis, 175
Friedman, Thomas L., 27, 30
Fundamentalism, 27

Gallagher, Terry, 256
Games, 171, 377n35
Gandhi, Mahatma, 272, 273
Ganesha, 117, 192, 288, 297
Ganpuley (Dr.), 192
Gates, 120–25, 121, 124; as devotional hurdles,
    126
Gautam, 261–62
Gautama Buddha, 349n26
Geertz, Clifford, 90, 172, 180, 298, 340, 378n7
Gender segregation, 217–19, 221
Genealogy of performance, 336
Geschiere, Peter, 341
Gibson, Gloria, 119

Giddens, Anthony, 31, 33
Gifts, 284–300; anti-Sai activism and, 296;
    cherishing, 320–21; divine, 284–85;
    self-realization from, 299; transcendence
    from, 298, 319; transformative power of,
    292–300
Giving, of heart, 299
Global guruhood, constructed charisma and,
    76–78
Globalization, 1–6, 7, 40, 123–24, 146,
    333, 365n29; ascetic discipline of body
    and, 203–4; characteristics of, 25;
    commodification central practice of, 283;
    cultural, 228; decentering from, 203–4;
    forces of, 188; interpretation and, 228;
    misunderstanding of, 29; morality and,
    218; of religio-cultural groups, 112; sacred
    spaces during, 146; secrecy and, 236,
    238–39; spacial imagination and, 96–97;
    transparency and, 234; see also Cultural
    globalization
Global localization, 31
Global network, 350n36
Global Sathya Sai Centers, 343–45
Glocalization, 32
Glover, William, 113, 127
God (bhagawan), 10, 61, 79
God-man, 57
Goh say Tong, 361n42
Goldstein, Michael, 254, 324
Gopalaswami Temple, 132
Gopuram Gate, 120, 123, 124
Grace (bhava), 324
Grammar of diversity, 6, 329, 332, 333, 341–42
Griffiths, David, 349n23
Griffiths, Edie, 349n23
Gross, Rita M., 47–48
The Guide (Narayan, R. K.), 89
Guru, 70–71; Americans in search of, 11;
    searching for, 98
Guru-avatar, 62
Guru-bhakta relationship, 286
Gurupoornima Day (festival honoring
    Guru), 65
Guru-sant-avatar-future model, 74
Guru-sant-avatar model, 73, 75

Habit of concealment, 17–18
Hagiography, 55

Halo, 57
Hannerz, Ulf, 323
Hanuman, 80, 132, 142, 282
Haraldsson, Erlendur, 354n34
Hard Rock chain, 19, 260, 349n22
Harvey, David, 31, 146, 154
Harvey, J. C., 258
Hattori, 376n18
Healing, 14, 87, 158, 159, 191, 199; darshan
    and, 181–90; of people, 9, 54, 60, 61;
    of Sathya Sai Baba, 59–61, 183–86, 311;
    see also Magical cures; Sexual healing
    allegations
Hearing, 196
Heart2Heart, 20, 276–77
Heelas, Paul, 8, 178
Held, David, 25, 326
Hertz, Peter, 296
Hervieu-Leger, Daniel, 112, 207
Herzfeld, Michael, 235
Hillview Stadium, 133, 142, 324, 325
Hindu (newspaper), 233
Hindu ashram, 360–61n33
Hinduism, 9, 66–67, 348n5; ashrams of,
    360–61n33; bodily practices in, 205–6;
    cycle of creation in, 72; God's play in,
    170–71; images of divinity in, 308;
    Prasadam, 183; saffron color of
    renunciation in, 354n30; sects within,
    4; Shaivite tradition in, 65, 355n43; temples
    of, 128; on Thursday's, 354n25; Vishnavite,
    62; see also Leela
Hindustan Times, 297
Hindu temples, 128, 360n28, 360n31
Hindutva, 218, 260
Hindu Vaishnavite tradition, 62
Hislop, John, 53, 54, 56, 67, 74, 86, 88, 211,
    241, 374n90
Hislop, Victoria, 241
Honor, 271–74, 278
Hope, 171; darshan related to, 164
Horologization, of objects, 320
HSBC, 304
Humanization, 365n29
Hummel, Reinhart, 357n56
Huntington, Samuel, 26–27
Hurricane Katrina humanitarian work, 197
Hybridization, 31, 111
Hyperconsumption, 320

Iccha, 214, 216
Icon, 335
Ideal gift, 284–300
Identity, 33–34, 178, 200; bodily practices
    and, 204–5; cartographic, 146;
    contemporary, 178; cosmopolitan,
    198–200; counterhegemonic, 114; crisis,
    56; darshan and religious, 179–81;
    devotional, 112, 171, 176–81; pilgrimage
    and, 94–95; recentered, 114; religion and,
    31; of Sathya Sai movement, 203; space
    and, 138
Ilinx, 171
Illusion, 57
Illusion (maya), 57, 229
Imagery, urban space and mythical, 12
Imagination, 146; spatial, 96–97
Imperfection (mouli), 308
Incarnations (avatars), 10, 57, 72, 356n51,
    356n54; complete, 62, 71, 85; divine,
    86–87; Sathya Sai Baba as Shiva-Shakti,
    65–66
Incest, 352n11
Inclusion, 111, 146
Inclusivity, 95, 127–28
Indebtedness, 286
Index, 335
India, 101, 102, 370nn15–16; divisions in, 61;
    inequalities in society, 329; Ministry of
    Education, 141; US economic relationship
    with, 306; Westernization of, 28–31;
    see also Hinduism
India Shining, 347n1
India Today (newspaper), 12, 234, 304, 348n10
Indic, term usage, term, 347n3
Indira Devi, 359n11
Individual duty (swadharma), 211
Individual singing (kirtans), 161
ING Orange, 304
Institute of Social and Economic Change, 38
Interaction, 42
International coordinator, 250
International Sai Organization (ISO), 15–16
Internet, darshan from, 149–52
Interpretation, 43, 224; politics of, 228
Islamic sufi sainthood, 66
ISO; see International Sai Organization
Iyer (Mr.), 99, 237, 238, 239, 240, 241, 277, 324
Izenour, Steve, 140

Jaganathan, N., 232
Jain laity, 59
Janakiramaih (Mr.), 233
Jencks, Christopher, 146
Jesus Christ, 10, 68–69, 86–88, 142, 174, 282, 288–89
Jivan mukti (self-enlightenment), 173
June incident, 232–34
Just Seekers of Truth (JuST), 168, 253–55, 257, 259, 270, 280

Kabir, 58, 80
Kadiri, 56
Kafni (robe), 58
Kaikeyi (Queen), 109
Kakar, Sudhir, 137
Kali Yuga (age of modern evil), 63, 71
Kalki, 71
Karanjia, R. K., 214, 258, 295
Karma, 189
Karmic illnesses, 186
Karur, Karnataka, 60
Kasturi, Narayan, 51, 53, 57, 62, 63, 81–82, 110, 122, 126–27, 132, 186, 194, 285, 302, 357n62, 375n13; on Raju family, 54
Katha (story), 52
Kavoor (Mr.), 376n18
Kent, Alexandra, 8, 13, 38, 63, 67, 87, 140, 161, 162, 242, 286
Klass, Morton, 159, 160, 162
Kim, Hanna, 131
Kirtans (individual singing), 161, 363n9, 363nn6–7
Kitts, Kyra, 358n66
Klass, Morton, 159
Kodaikanal, 61
Kondo, Dorrine, 180
Kong, Lilly, 111
Kovalam beach, 63
Kripal Singh Foundation, 362n57
Krishna, 11, 58, 62–63, 72, 132, 134, 142, 169, 174, 210, 282, 287, 302
Krishnamurti, J., 356n54
Krystal, Phyllis, 211, 241, 374n90
Krystal, Sidney, 241
Kuala Lumpur, Malaysia, 67
Kumar, Anil, 82, 294
Kumar, E. K. Suresh, 232, 234

Kundalini shaktipat, 211, 266–67, 268, 373n68, 373n71
Kyrø, Øjvind, 296

Laing, Ron, 69, 209
Lamb, Sarah, 207
Larsson, Conny, 256–57
Latching, 335–36, 341
Leadbeater, Charles, 356n54
Learning for Las Vegas (Izenour), 140
Leela (divine play or miracle), 14, 56, 164–69, 285, 332, 364n13, 364n18; Ram, 170; seating arrangement and, 164–69; as watered-down concept, 339; work and, 172–74
Lefebvre, Henri, 95
Leong Wan Chan Si Chinese temple, 145
Levy, Aime, 305
Levy, Sandra, 305
Liberation, 206–9, 216
Life, as pilgrimage, 101
Life is a Game, Play It (game), 20
Lightstorm, 20, 349n25
Lila; see Leela
Lim (Mrs.), 94
Lindholm, Charles, 77, 357n59
Lingam (sphere representing sexual/powerful form of Shiva), 60, 302; see also Sivalingam
Links, of network, 350n36
Lipovetsky, Gilles, 320
Liturgy, 172
Living Temple for the Living God, 145
London Telegraph, 354n31
Lord, 61; in human form, 57
Lord of the Air (Brooke), 254
Lotus flower, 15, 133
Love, 62, 298; between friends, 80; for lover, 80; between mother and child, 80; universal, 16, 62, 81, 190
Love in Action (Drucker), 292
Love Is My Form: The Advent (Padmanaban), 210, 351n5, 353n18
Loyalty, market for, 180
Luhrmann, T. M., 239, 272
Luxury items, 368n231

Ma Amritanandayamayi, 99
McDonaldization, 2, 3, 27, 31
Madhura-bhava (sweet love for divine), 80

Magic, 182; *see also* Vibhuti

Magical cures, 183–87, 189, 314; science v., 191

Magical objects, 159, 292, 296, 297, 316–18; meaning of, 337

Magical reincarnation, 57

Magical thinking, 14

Mahabharata, 11, 71, 151, 351n7, 355n36

Mahajan, Sai Kumar, 232–33

Maha Mahima Manusha Murthi (man of almighty miracles), 295

Maharashtra, 57

Maharashtrian Muslim faqir, 57

Maharishi Mahesh Yogi, 256–57, 358n5

Mahashivarathri (night of Shiva worship), 60, 288

Mahavira, 291

Mahila Vibagh, 247

Mahimas (miracles), 9, 10, 14, 56, 86, 133, 158, 164–69, 172–74, 187, 193, 285, 295, 364n13, 364n18; of birth, 55; Christian Sai, 86; Colusa, 182; Committee to Investigate, and Other Verifiable Superstitions, 258; Man of almighty, 295; *see also* Leela; Materializations

Maison, Peggy, 69

Mangru, Anil, 182

Man of almighty miracles (Maha Mahima Manusha Murthi), 295

Manoj (brother), 99

Margarethe (Queen), 296

Marijuana, 349n25

Marriage, 218–19

Maslow's hierarchy of needs, 179

Masquerade, 83

Masulipatam, 63

Matching, 335

Material, of divine illusion, 318

Materialism, 290–95

Materiality, 283–84

Materializations, 16, 61, 115, 182, 187, 261, 284–300, 374n2

Material of divine illusion (mayavada), 318

Material worlds, reframing, 320–22

Matrix, of meaning, 276–79

Mauryan dynasty, 142

Maya (illusion), 57, 229

Mayavada (material of divine illusion), 318

Media, 148–52

Mediatization, 283

Meditative control (tapasya), 214, 217, 221, 228, 229

Megha (rain clouds), 324

Meghadoota (rain cloud messenger), 324

Meloy, Glen, 253–54, 268

Memorialization, 131, 132

Memorial repetition, 79

Memory, 336

Mesh, of network, 350n36

Meyer, Birgit, 341

Michiko (Mrs.), 250

Middle-class devotees, 177

Mines, Diane, 359n16

Ministry of Education, India, 141

Miracles (mahimas), 9, 10, 14, 56, 86, 133, 158, 164–69, 172–74, 187, 193, 285, 295, 364n13, 364n18; of birth, 55; Christian Sai, 86; Colusa, 182; Committee to Investigate, and Other Verifiable Superstitions, 258; Man of almighty, 295; *see also* Leela; Materializations

Misra, Ram Shanker, 169

Mistry, Kekie, 125

Mobile description, 45

Mobility, 341

Moral architecture, 140–48; emotion, multivalence, and diversity, 153–55

Moral community, 156–200

Moral economies, of Sai objects exchange, 318–19

Morality, 290; collisions of, 279–81; globalization and, 218; perspective and, 280

Moral stakeholding, 190, 196, 332, 364n25; cosmopolitan identity and, 198–200; as institutional imperative, 190–98

Moral superiority, 273

Moreno, Joe (Gerald), 372n48

Morning darshan, 162

Mother (sai), 65

Mouli (imperfection), 308

Movement, term defined, 4–5

Muktananda Paramahamsa, 98

Multiculturalism, 7, 326, 347n2

Multilocational devotion, 151–52

Multiplism, 378n3

Multi-sited ethnographies, 44

Multi-vocal serenade, 139

Murphet, Howard, 74, 82, 87, 183, 184, 186–87, 189, 241, 293, 375n13

Murthy (Mr.), 213, 220, 221, 237, 238, 239, 263

Music Academy, 117

Music spanning the city (nagarasankeertana), 79–80

Muslim seer (Faqir), 10, 56, 57, 287

Mysore, 60

Nagarasankeertana (music spanning the city), 79–80

Nag Champa incense, 20, 282

Nagel, Alexandra, 256, 372n41

Namasmarana chanting, 18, 51, 79–81, 357n60

Name changes, 359n6

Naming, 79, 85

Nanapanthi order, 58

Nandy, Ashish, 31

Narasimaiah, H., 258–59

Narayaba Baba, 349n15

Narayan, Kirim, 81, 233

Narayan, R. K., 89

Nasa (bodily control), 214

National coordinators, 250

Nationalism, 27

Nehru, Jawaharlal, 6

Neutrality, 47

New Religious Movements (NRM), 349n16

New York City, 112

Nexus magazine, 256

Nilekani, Nandan, 30

Nine nights of victory (Dussehra), 60

Nine Point Code of Conduct, 222–23, 226, 229, 230, 244–45, 333

Nodes, of network, 350n36

Nomadic charisma, 10, 90–92, 330

Nonviolence (ahimsa), 16, 190

NRM; see New Religious Movements

Numen (sacred being), 76, 351n6

Nussbaum, Martha, 26, 27, 218, 326.327

Objectivity, 47

Official Tustin Book Centre, 253

Old Mandir (temple), 60

Omkara, 162

Omnipotence, 53

Omnipresence, 53

Oprah, 179

Oral story-telling, 81

ORGINDIA, 119

Orsi, Robert, 112, 115, 139

Otherworldly paradigm, 206

Otto, Rudolf, 351n6

Oxford University, 200

Packing list, 225

Padmanaban (Mr.), 53, 210, 303, 351n5, 353nn18–19

Pain and loss, 368n22

Pairley, Anil, 232

Pallava dynasty, 142

Palmer, Norris, 53, 57, 66, 67, 72, 160, 170

Pandhari Bhajan group, 352n14

Paradoxical politics, of transcendence and permanence, 146

Paramahansa Yogananda, 358n5

Parthasarathy (Mr.), 184

Particularism, radical, 350n30

Peace, 16, 190; abode of supreme, 10, 13, 15, 61, 94, 108, 111, 115, 116, 118, 125–29, 131–32, 137, 143, 148, 158, 164–65, 211, 219, 232–34, 255, 311, 332; platform of, 324

Pedagogical program, 191

Perspective, 340, 378n6

Petersen, Glenn, 237, 271

Pilgrimage, 98–100; identities and, 94–95; Sathya Sai Baba as goal of all, 110

Pilgrims, 99–107

Pithas (seats of Vishnavite Hinduism), 62

Pittard, Barry, 253, 254, 255, 259, 358n64

Pitt-Rivers, Julian, 272

Planetarium, 141–42

Platform of peace (shanti vedika), 324

Play; see Leela

Playful pranks (balalilas), 295

"A Plethora of Possibilities" (Riti), 233

Pluralism, 7, 8, 33, 146, 179, 188, 326–29, 341–42, 378n3

Politics, sacred space relating to, 111–12

Polyvalent discourse, 265–71

Poorna avatar (complete incarnations), 62, 71, 85, 356n51

Poornachandra Auditorium, 116, 125

Potential devotees, 46

Poverty, 54–55

Power, 366nn3–4; bodily practices and, 204; hierarchy and, 205

The Powers of Sathya Sai Baba (Steel), 256

Prabhu, Suresh, 232
Prabhu, Vijay, 232, 370n2
Practices (sadhana), 173, 295
Prasad, K. R., 370n4
Prasadam (consecrated substance), 158, 183
Prasanthi Council, 251–52
Prasanthi Nilayam (abode of supreme peace),
    10, 13, 15, 61, 94, 108, 111, 115, 116, 118, 125–29,
    137, 143, 148, 164–65, 211, 219, 255, 311, 332;
    architecture of, 131–32; darshan everyday
    at, 158; deaths at, 232–34
Prema (universal love), 16, 62, 81, 190
Premanand, Basava, 372n56
Prema Sai, 65, 66, 68, 73, 85, 288, 355n40
Prema Sai Baba, 67
Priddy, Robert, 169–70, 236, 248, 253, 254,
    259, 279, 296, 364n25
Primal screaming, 175
Prince of Wales Organization, 253
Princess (rani), 60
Private darshan, 125, 158, 160, 166–67, 175,
    183, 184, 284, 287, 297, 371n32
Privileging memorialization, 115
Priya, Ratna, 377n35
Prodigality: antinarratives of, 97; narrative
    of, 108–9, 110
Prospective pilgrim, 99–107; building
    relationships, 105; India and, 101–2;
    transformations of, 104–6
Pugilism, 367n20
Purab aur Paschim (film), 160
Purana (divine story), 52
Purcell, Sathya "Satch," 371n28, 371n29
Purcell, Sharon, 371n29
Purity, 369nn38–39; pollution debate, 205
Puttaparthi, 10, 11, 12, 54, 56, 58–61, 70,
    94–97, 201, 217, 221–27, 240, 283,
    291, 301, 330, 348n7, 352n16, 360n25;
    architecture of, 131–32, 140–48; ashram
    entrance, 116; building world of, 112–13;
    double-coded language of space, 146; gates
    of, 120–25, 121, 124; as home away from
    home, 128–29, 131; as ideal polis, 118;
    marketplace, 300, 301, 302–4; modernity
    in, 144–45; moral architecture of, 153–55;
    narratives of exile and prodigality, 107–11;
    postmodern buildings of, 143–46;
    returning from, 108; Sanskrit studies
    academy in, 62; Shaw's experience
    of, 110; spiritual tours, sacred sites,
    memories, 131–40; SSSO building up,
    115–19; tourism and, 107; transformation
    of, 114–15; see also Chitravathi Road trade;
    Prasanthi Nilayam

Queue system, 164–67

Radhakrishna (Mr.), 82
Radhakrishnan, V., 186–87
Radhakrisna, N., 232–33, 234
Radical particularism, 350n30
Radio Sai, 52, 143, 144, 277
Radio Sai Global Harmony show, 151
Rahm, Alaya, 252, 261, 276–77, 292, 371n28,
    374n87
Rain cloud messenger (meghadoota), 324
Rain clouds (megha), 324
Raising from dead, 186
Raja (chieftain), 60
Rajeshwari (Dr.), 192
Rajmata, of Bangalore, 370n4
Rajneesh, 98, 114
Raju, Kondama, 132
Raju, Ratnakaram Kondama, 54, 132
Raju, Sathyanarayana, 54; see also Sathya
    Sai Baba
Rajus, 351n8
Rama, 62–63, 72, 80, 109, 262, 282, 287,
    294, 302
Ramakrishna movement, 196
Ramana Maharishi, 196, 358n5
Ramanuja, 356n53
Ramayana, 71, 80, 262, 331
Ram Leela, 170
Rani (princess), 60
Rao, Joga, 233
Rao, M. S., 353n20
Rao, Shekar, 194
Rao, Thirumal, 60
Rasmussen, Claire, 96
Rationalists, 257–58
Ratnasingham (Mr.), 362n58
Ratner, Susan, 282
Ravana, 170
Ravi Shankar, 99
Recentered identity, 114, 115
Reconstruction, 57–58
Reddy (Mr.), 217

Reddy, K. N. Gangadhara, 233

Redemption: lack of comfort part of, 103; narratives of, 97, 100, 122

Reembedding, 337

Reincarnation, 58, 73; Shiva-Shakti, 54; *see also* Incarnations

Rejuvenation, of tour, 134

Relationality, 36–37

Religiocultural movement, 5

Religion, 61; alterity linked with, 44; Chaitanya Jyothi Museum chambers dedicated to, 135; culture and, 3–4; devotion related to, 99; identity and, 31; materialism argued against by, 283; movement and, 5; in postmodern world, 21; of Sathya Sai Baba, 66–67; Satya Sai movement drawing from several, 9; as symbolic system, 172; technology and, 149–52

Religious images, 58

Religious movements study, 46–49

Renouncer, 56

Repetition, 80; memorial, 79; with revision, 336

Representations, 338

Reterritorialization, of culture, 32, 146

Revelations, 351n6; moments of, 53–54; of true self, 56–57

Ricoeur, Paul, 270

Right conduct (dharma), 13, 16, 71, 190, 211

Rishikesh, 62

Riti, M. D., 233, 234

Ritual performance, 163, 172

Robe (kafni), 58

Robertson, Roland, 188

Robinson, David, 201

Roman Catholic Church, 268, 270

Rose, Nikolas, 204

Roshi, Baker, 32

Rudraksha, 288, 374n6

Ruhela, S. P., 67

Rules and Regulations (SSSO), 244

"Rules and Regulations for Sri Sathya Sai Seva Organisations, India" (SSSO), 249

Rushdie, Salman, 146

Sachs, Jeffrey, 45

Sacra, 314–16

Sacred, 367n13

Sacred ash (vibhuti), 9, 181–83, 194, 258, 285, 286, 294, 297, 375n13

Sacred being (numen), 76, 351n6

Sacred city, history of, 111–19

Sacred divinity, 72

Sacred journey; *see* Pilgrimage

Sacred objects, 20–21; mass production of, 318–19; transnational piety and, 282–84

Sacred performance, 170; *see also* Leela

Sacred personhood, 73, 75, 76, 86; transforming, 90–92

Sacred space, 111, 153–55; devotees influenced by, 153–55; devotees link to, 146; during globalization, 146; politics relating to, 111–12; *see also* Sacred city

Sacred spectating, 14

Sacred touching, 362n2

Sacred transactions, 289

Sacrifice, 84

Sadhana (practices), 173, 295

Saffron, 354n30, 374n5

Sai (mother), 65

Saianand, 247

Sai Baba: Man of Miracles (Murphet), 82

Sai Baba Centers, 348nn11–12, 349n13

Sai Baba for Beginners (comic book), 20

Sai Central Trust; *see* Shri Sathya Sai Central Trust

Sai education program, 194–96

Sai Gita, 324

Sai Global Harmony, 20

Sai goods: distributive network of, 304–7; trading in, 300, 302–12

Sai Hospital, 145, 190

Sai katha, 55, 61, 88

Sai Krishna, 258

Sai Kulwant Darshan Hall, Prasanthi Nilayam, 13, 116, 118, 125, 126, 127, 137, 143, 148, 211; seating arrangement in, 164–65, 332

Sai Music Academy, 141

Sai objects: distribution of, 307–12; moral value of, 314–18; as simulacra, 318–19; symbolism of, 312, 314–19

Sai Ram Gift shop, 307

Sairarchy, 275

Sai religious objects, 301, 309, 313

Sai sacred objects, 20–21

Sai satsang, 180

Sai Seva Organization, 191

Sai Towers Press, 210

The Sai Trinity (Ruhela), 67

Sai Vocational Training Center, 232, 233

Sakamma (Mrs.), 60

Sakhya-bhava (love between friends), 80

Samhiti, 240–41

Samkhya tradition, 63

Sampath, Hari, 257

Sanathana Sarathi (way of charioteer)
     newsletter, 11, 62, 68, 70, 254, 290, 355*n*37

Sandweiss, Sam, 82, 241, 288, 374*n*90

Santana dharma, 244

Santhana Sarathy, 369*n*33

Sant tradition, 71

Saraswati, 117, 141, 145

Sarva Dharma image, 15

Sarva Dharma Pillar, 133, 162

Satchitananda (Swami), 61

Satguru (true spiritual teacher), 58

Sathya (Mr.), 226

Sathya (truth), 8, 16, 71, 190, 206

Sathyabhama, 54, 132

Sathyam, Shivam, Sundaram (Kasturi), 51, 62,
     357*n*62

Sathyanarayana Raju; *see* Sathya Sai Baba

Sathya Sai Baba, 4, 50–52, 57, 75, 156, *164,*
     172, 201, 232, 263, 282, 323, 348*n*6;
     abstinence encouraged by, 214;
     antimaterialist philosophy of, 290–92;
     apologetic literature of, 58; articulation of,
     9; astral instructions of, 375*n*16; as avatar,
     68–70, 91; becoming devotee, 119–28;
     bhajan composition of, 161; birthday
     celebration of, 60, 323–25, 335; birth
     records of, 351*n*2, 352*n*13, 352*n*16; on body,
     208; Brooke on, 358*nn*5–6; "bunker
     mentality" of, 259; calling cards of, 187,
     286, 289, 374*n*2; on ceiling on desires,
     217; Chaitanya Jyothi Museum devoted to
     life and miracles of, 135–36; childhood of,
     82, 361*n*41, 368*n*24; Chitravathi River
     miracles of, 133; clothing guidelines by,
     202; Colusa miracle, 182; cover-up
     accusations against, 234; on desire, 208;
     divine body, 183, 209–13; domestication of
     emotions encouraged by, 80; feeling saved
     by, 176; first public discourse of, 60; on

food and self-control, 220; fourfold
     complexity of divine personhood of, 70–76,
     328, 330; as fraud, 296; as God incarnate,
     86; healing power of, 59–61, 183–86, 311;
     hypnotic influence of, 184; image of, 19–20;
     inaccessibility of, 53; inhabiting bodies, 186;
     Kerala tour of, 63; Krishna affiliation of, 58;
     language of, 84; lashing out of, 349*n*21;
     lawsuit against, 252–53, 261; leela and
     seating arrangement, 164–69; on
     liberation, 209; life story, 52–70; lingam
     materialization of, 60; from local guru to
     national spiritual leader, 59–63, 65;
     magical and healing powers of, 59–60,
     183–86, 311; magic denied by, 188; as Maha
     Mahima Manusha Murthi, 295; in
     Masulipatam, 63; materializations and, 16,
     61, 115, 182, 187, 261, 284–300, 374*n*2;
     miracles, 61, 289–90; moral stakeholding
     and, 198–200, 332, 364*n*25; Murphet and
     true self of, 74; mystery of, 170; name
     meaning, 355*n*41; from national guru to
     international divinity, 65–70; paralysis of,
     65; paranormal experiences of, 354*n*34;
     from peasant boy to local guru, 54–59;
     personal interaction decreasing, 60;
     persona of, 90–91; pet elephant of, 133, 143,
     324; photographs of, 59, 63, *64,* 302, 307–8,
     313, 317, 351*n*5, 354*n*31; pilgrimages to,
     94–95; as poorna avatar, 85; questioning
     powers of, 257–59; real devotee known
     by, 298; religious images of, 58;
     Sathyanarayana story, 352*n*12; saving
     humanity from Western science, 184–85;
     scorpion sting story, 50–51, 55–56; in
     search of, 98–107; security to protect, 125;
     sexual abuse allegations, 229, 233–34, 236,
     253–55, 266–68, 293, 359*n*5, 367*n*14,
     371*n*29, 371*nn*32–33, 372*n*42, 372*n*56,
     374*n*90; sexual misconduct of, 16, 18, 170;
     as Shirdi Sai Baba reincarnation, 58;
     Shirdi Sai persona myth, 353*nn*23–24; as
     Shiva-Shakti incarnation, 65–66; shrine
     for, 60; spaces of entry to, 119–28; spiritual
     destination relating to, 110; Spurr on,
     354*n*28; SSSO leadership and, 251; Steel on
     avatarhood of, 355*n*35; stories of, 81–82;
     "thought for the day," 149; transformation

Sathya Sai Baba (*continued*)
  of, 348*n*7; transformative katha, 91;
  unmasking Web site, 296–97; unselfish
  love discourse of, 354*n*32; Western
  medicine critique of, 190–91; Western
  thought criticized by, 260; worldwide
  followers of, 12; as yagavatara, 88; as young
  man, 59; *see also* Anti-Sai activism;
  Darshan; Devotees; Miracles; Prasanthi
  Nilayam; Puttaparthi
Sathya Sai Baba Central Council of America,
  16
The Sathya Sai Baba Compendium (Steel), 256
"Sathya Sai Baba Exposed: Fraud, Fakery, and
  Molestation" (*Nexus magazine*), 256
Sathya Sai Baba leela, 14
Sathya Sai Baba Society, 253, 371*n*28
Sathya Sai Book and Publications Trust, 151
Sathya Sai Bookshop, 116
Sathya Sai Center (Singapore), *242, 243*
Sathya Sai Center (Tustin, California), *246*
Sathya Sai Center and Bookstore, 362*n*57
Sathya Sai Center for Higher Education, 160
Sathya Sai College, 109, 145
Sathya Sai Educare, 16, 191, 194
Sathya Sai Educational and Hospital complex,
  133
Sathya Sai Education in Human Values
  (SSEHV), 191; *see also* Sathya Sai Educare
Sathya Sai Education Trust, 167
Sathya Sai General Hospital, 192
Sathya Sai Health and Education Trust, 192
Sathya Sai hospital, 192–93
Sathya Sai Institute for Higher Education, 166
Sathya Sai Institute for Higher Learning,
  192, 195
Sathya Sai Institute for Higher Medical
  Services (SSSHMS), 117
Sathya Sai Institute for Higher Medical
  studies, 141
Sathya Sai Institute of Higher Learning, 117,
  130, 229, 232
Sathya Sai Institute of Higher Studies, 96
Sathya Sai International Center of Sport, 117
Sathya Sai movement, 63, 325–26, 349*n*16;
  about devotees of, 12–13; altar locations, 12;
  alternative to modernity, 331–32; bodily
  practices and, 202–3; boundaries
  transcended by, 229; charitable work

of, 15; codification of discipline in, 223,
  228–30; cosmopolitanism of, 327–29;
  factions in, 233; finances of, 377*n*31; as
  Hindu revitalization movement, 5; India
  growth of, 370*nn*15–16; introduction, 8–22;
  lotus flower as emblem of, 15; ministry
  expansion, 60–62; mission of, 13; moral
  code of, 203; museum reflecting
  internationalism of, 137–38; pluralism
  of, 327–28; public identity of, 203; as
  religious movement, 5; scholarly analysis
  of, 348*n*5; science and technology use,
  188–89; secrecy in, 235–39; sexual healing
  allegations, 16; struggles of, 17; virtual
  world of, 148–50
Sathya Sai Seva Organization (SSSO), 16,
  52–53, 119, 199, 215, 217, 222, 304, 350*n*36,
  367*n*14; central coordinators of, 250;
  charter of, 244–45; compartmentalization
  in, 236; contemporary structure of,
  250–52; corporate model for, 248–49;
  cover-up accusations against, 234; credo
  of, 67; democracy in, 245, 247–48, 252;
  difficulty in studying, 236; education
  wing of, 244; factions in, 233, 249–50;
  family model for, 247–48; inception/
  growth of, 240–45, 247; international
  coordinator of, 250; lawsuit against,
  252–53, 261; national coordinators of, 250;
  reorganization of, 247–50; retail outlets
  of, 303; service wing of, 243–44; spiritual
  wing of, 243; truth in, 274; Western
  thought criticized by, 260
Sathya Sai Society and Bookstore, 241
Sathya Sai Society of America, 306
Sathya Sai Speaks collection, 79, 93
Sathya Sai Super Specialty Hospital; *see*
  Sathya Sai Institute for Higher Medical
  studies
Sathya Sai Taluk gate, 120, *121*
Sathya Sai Vidyagiri complex, 141
Sathya Sai Vidyagiri gate, 120, *121*
Sattvica, 205, 207, 215, 216, 221, 224, 228,
  229, 333, 339
Satya (truth); *see* Sathya
Satyagraha, 273
Satyanarayana pujas, 55
Satya Sai Nag Champa incense, 20
Sax, William, 169

Scandal, 235–38

Schmitz, Kenneth L., 76

Schooling, 55–56

Schorske, Carl, 146

Schulman, Arnold, 211, 241

Scorpion sting story, 50–51, 55–56

SCT; see Shri Sathya Sai Central Trust

Seats of Vishnavite Hinduism (pithas), 62

Secrecy, 17, 18, 128, 260, 278, 373n85; Anti-Sai
network, 235; criticism and, 259; faction
splits and, 249–50; globalization and,
238–39; intra-organizational, 273–74; as
protection from skepticism, 272; scandal
and, 235–38; spatialization of, 271–74;
strategies of, 261–65, 272–74, 276, 277;
theories of, 238–39; as trust, 274–76;
truth and, 341

Secret knowledge: desirability of, 239;
organizational power from, 274–75; as
protection, 272

The Secret Swami (documentary), 234, 293,
372n56

Secularization modernity theory, 30

Seeking, 177; spiritual travel and, 98–100

Seiko watch gift, 187, 375–76n18

Self (atman), 72, 206

Self-actualization, 179

Self-censorship, 275

Self-control, 62, 225; food and, 219–21

Self-enlightenment (jivan mukti), 173

Self-inscription, 216

Self-knowledge (atma gyana), 106, 180, 206,
266, 369n31

Self-realization, 58–59, 174, 215; from gifts,
299

Self-transcendence, 179

Self-transformation, 52, 181, 290, 292–300;
darshan and, 158; work of, 173–74

Semiotic dynamic, 334–38

Sen, Amartya, 26

Senses, 367n17, 368n22

Separation, politics of, 111

Servant-master fealty (dasya-bhava), 80

Service, 196–99; see also Seva

Sesha, 63

Sethi, Jens, 256

Seva (work for less fortunate), 62, 173, 189,
330; on global level, 197–98; on individual
level, 196–97

Seva Dal, 131, 164–66, 201, 218, 233, 247,
361n40; control by, 221, 224, 226; on
truancy, 227

Seva Service program, 192

Seven Stars Biodynamic yogurt farm, 19,
349n23

Sexual abuse allegations, 229, 233–34, 236,
253–55, 266–68, 293, 359n5, 367n14,
371n29, 371nn32–33, 372n42, 372n56,
374n90

Sexual control, 218, 225

Sexual healing allegations, 16, 18, 233–34,
252, 254, 256–57, 260–62, 269, 280, 296,
338, 340

Sexual misconduct, of Sathya Sai Baba, 16,
18, 170

Sexual relations, 218–19

Shah, Indulal, 233, 244, 280, 324, 370n4

Shaivite tradition, of Hinduism, 65, 355n43

Shakti, 9, 65, 66, 287–88

Shaktipat, 268–69

Shankar (Dr.), 266–67

Shanti (peace), 16, 190

Shanti vedika (platform of peace), 324

Sharing, 104

Shatakshara (surrender), 173

Shaw, Connie, 110, 117–18, 129, 141, 211, 219,
221, 368n26

Shepherd, Kevin, 354n24

Shetty, V. T. Rajshekar, 258

Shirdi (town), 58, 353n21

Shirdi Sai Baba, 9, 51, 54–57, 65–66, 85, 142,
282, 286, 288, 298, 353n19; myth of,
354n27; Sathya Sai Baba reincarnated
from, 9, 58; Sathya Sai Baba worshipping
image of, 60

Shirdi Sai groups, Sathya Sai group tension
with, 58

Shirdi Sai Partha Sai Divyakatha teleserial, 58

Shiva, 9, 65, 142, 287–88, 302

Shiva (Mr.), 226, 227

Shiva lingam; see Sivalingam

Shivaratri, 302, 376n24

Shiva-Shakti (male-female), 54

Shraddha (faith and love), 298, 299, 376n22

Shrine, 60

Shri Sai World Trust (SWT), 233, 236

Shri Sathya Sai Central Trust (SCT), 15, 99,
217, 222, 236, 247; factions in, 233

Shroud of Turin, 288, 375n8
Shukla, Sandhya, 6
Siddhi (self-control), 62
Signs, 338
Simha, J. B. Vijaya, 195
Simmel, Georg, 239, 275
Simonyi, Charles, 43
Simple fakes, 187
Simulacra, 318–19
Sinclair, James, 377n31
Singapore temple, 145
Singh, Khushwant, 297
Singing: individual, 161; see also Chanting;
    Devotional music
Sinha, Shashi, 107
Sita, 294
Sivakumar, S. S., 166, 228–29, 318, 319
Sivalingam, 302, 376n24
Sivananda (Swami), 61
Skanda, 288
Skanda Purana, 352n12
Skepticism, 272
Social imaginary, 112
Socialization, 180
Social life, as theatre metaphor, 373n78
Socially informed body, 19
Social power, 366n2
Soja, Edward, 32, 114, 115
Solanki dynasty, 142
Somatic embodied regime, 19
Somatic experience, 203
Somayya, Shanthi (Mrs.), 353n20, 353n22
Somers, Margaret, 119
Soul (atman), 72, 206
Source of the Dream: My Way to Sathya Sai
    Baba (Priddy), 254
Souvenirs, 302
Space, 93–97; of entry, 119–28; of recentered
    identity, 114; see also Moral architecture
Sparshan (sacred touching), 362n2
Spatiality of difference, 114, 115
Spatialization: of objects, 320; of silence,
    271–74
Speech, 196
Spiritual Counterfeits Project, 254
Spiritual destination, 122
Spiritual education, 195–96
Spiritualization, 365n29
Spiritual Play (game), 377n35

Spiritual searching, 98–100
Spiritual teacher, true, 58
Spiritual travel, 97; seeking and, 98–100;
    see also Puttaparthi
Spurr, Michael, 53, 55, 56, 63, 65, 211, 354n28
Sreenivasan (Mr.), 370n4
Sri Aurobindo, 358n5
Srinivas, Lakshmi, 37, 153, 312
Srinivas, Smriti, 5, 12, 13, 19, 58, 70, 113, 115,
    118, 119, 131, 137, 144, 150, 158, 159, 163, 211,
    221, 353n17, 356nn48–49, 362n3
Sri Ramakrishna, 358n5
Sri Sathya Medical Trust, 311
Sri Sathya Sai Arts and Science College for
    Women, 191
Sri Sathya Sai Ashtotarashatanamavali, 161
Sri Sathya Sai Central Council of Malaysia,
    242
Sri Sathya Sai Central Trust, 311
Sri Sathya Sai Higher Secondary School, 117
Sri Sathya Sai Institute of Higher Learning,
    141
Sri Sathya Sai Institute of Higher Medical
    Sciences (SSSIHMS), 130, 191, 192–94
Sri Sathya Sai Seva Organization (SSSSO), 192
Sri Sathya Sai Urban Development Authority
    (SSSUDA), 118–19
Srivastava, Sanjay, 123, 138
SSB movement, 270
SSEHV; see Sathya Sai Education in Human
    Values
SSSHMS; see Sathya Sai Institute for Higher
    Medical Services
SSSIHMS; see Sri Sathya Sai Institute of
    Higher Medical Sciences
SSSO; see Sathya Sai Seva Organization
SSSSO; see Sri Sathya Sai Seva Organization
SSSUDA; see Sri Sathya Sai Urban
    Development Authority
Steel, Brian, 65, 69, 138–39, 253, 255–56,
    351n3, 353n18, 353n23, 355n35, 355n42
Steele, Meili, 34
Stephen, 248, 264, 267, 272
Story (katha), 52
Strategic ambiguity, 271
Streathern, Colin, 175–76
Study circle, 78
Subamma, 57
Sufism, 9, 357n59

Suprabhatham, 162
Suprahuman, 53
Supreme godhead (Brahman), 72
Suresh (Mr.), 232
Suri (Mrs.), 250
Surrender (shatakshara), 173
Surrogation, processes of, 336
Swadharma (individual duty), 211
Swallow, 56
Swaminarayan movement, 138
Swayambhu (magically), 286
Sweet love, for divine (madhura-bhava), 80
Swiss Bank, 304
SWT; see Shri Sai World Trust
Symbols, 335, 338; interpretation of, 34; power of, 334
Syncretic devotion, 179

Tactile optics, of Sai darshan, 164, 171
Tantra, 266–69
Tantric literature, 66
Tapasya (meditative control), 214, 217, 221, 228, 229
Technology, 149–52, 377n33
Telegraph (newspaper), 234
Teleological pluralism, 328
Teleportation, 61
Temple of Healing brochure, 360n24, 365n26
Temples, 60, 145, 362n56; Gopalaswami, 132; Hindu, 128, 360n28, 360n31; Leong Wan Chan Si Chinese, 145; Singapore, 145
Thakur, Sheela, 67
Theory of masquerade, 83
Theosophical movement, 73, 196, 356n54
Theotókos, 55
Third space, 32
This-worldly paradigm, 206–7
"Thought for the day," 149
Three-in-one phenomenon, 68
Thursday, 175, 354n25
Thurston, Edgar, 351n8
Tigrett, Isaac, 260, 349n22, 377n31
Tiruvilaiyatarpuranam, 364n18
TM; see transcendental meditation
Tombs (dargahs), 298
Tomlinson, John, 23, 28, 46
Torture specialist, 56
Tourist souvenirs, 302
Traders: cheating, 310; horror stories of, 311–12

Traditions, 336
Train metaphor, 22
Transcendence, 76, 170, 175, 275; from gifts, 298, 319; paradoxical politics of, 146; self-, 179
Transcendental meditation (TM), 175, 275
Transformation, 51–52, 199; narratives of, 97
Translation: failures, 86–88, 339–40; problems of, 334; of stories, 52
Translocal devotion, 148–52
Transmission, 335–36; of culture, 339
Transnational devotion, 156–58, 202–3
Transparency, 17, 234, 238–39, 273, 280
Travel, cultures of, 93–97
Trayee Saptamayee, 365n30
Triadic typology, 73
Truancy, 224–28, 334
True spiritual teacher (satguru), 58
Trust, secrecy as, 274–76
Truth (sathya), 8, 16, 71, 190, 206; management, 237; perception and, 18; secrecy and, 341
"Truth Always Triumphs" (Heart2Heart), 276–77
Tshidi Zionist churches, 189
Tswana, 278
Turmeric powder, 295
Turner, Victor, 124, 163
Tustin, California center, 100, 145, 241, 242, 246, 304–6
TV darshan, 151
Tyagaraja, 363n9

UGC; see University Grants Commission
UNESCO, 306
Union Oil Company, 362n57
United States (US), 306
Universalization, 333
Universal love (prema), 16, 62, 81, 190
University Grants Commission (UGC), 141
Unknown, understanding of, 336
Unmasking, of Sai Baba website, 296–97
Unveiling, 68, 72, 83, 85, 210, 298, 330
Upanishads, 63, 356n52
Uravakonda, 50, 55
Urban, Hugh, 177, 239, 270, 274, 277, 290
Urban alienates, 177
Ursus, 60
US; see United States

Valmiki, 262

Valorization, 37

Valueless object, 290

Vancouver Sun (newspaper), 236

Van der Leeuw, Gerard, 111, 146

Van der Veer, Peter, 378n1

van Loon, Joost, 350n36

Vatsalya-bhava (love between mother and child), 80

Veblen, Thorsten, 316

Vedanta philosophy, 356n53

Vedic literature, 66

Veiling, 68, 72, 83, 85, 210, 298

Venkatagiri, 60

Venkavadhootha, 54

Venturi, Robert, 140

Venugopalaswamy, 116, 132

Vibhuti (sacred ash), 9, 181–83, 194, 258, 285, 286, 294, 297, 375n13

Vijayalakshmi, V., 350n34

Virgin birth, 55

Virilio, Paul, 37

Virtual reality, 148–52

Vishnavite Hinduism, 62

Vishnu, 132, 287, 288, 293

Vishwanathan (Mr.), 109

Vision, 196

Visiting cards; *see* Calling cards

Vivekenanda, 348n5

Waking dreams, 163–64

Walsh, William, 89

Web devotional worlds, 148–52

Weber, Max, 357n59, 378n7

Week (magazine), 233

Weeping, to remove blockages, 173

Westernization, 218, 229

Western science and medicine, 184–85, 190–91

White, Charles, 4

Williams, Raymond, 71

Willner, Ruth, 77

Wilson, Kathleen, 235

Wimbledon center, 145–46

Wishing tree, of Sai legend, 139–40

Woodhead, Linda, 8, 178

Work: charitable, 15; of devotional self, 172–76; humanitarian, 197; leela and, 172–74; in moral community, 156–200; of self-transformation, 173–74; for spirituality, 189; *see also* Seva

World Conference of Sai Organizations, 69

World Congress of Religion, 348n5

World Council of Sri Sathya Sai Organizations, 247

The World is Flat (Friedman), 30

Worship sequence, at Shirdi, 58

Wright, Thomas, 77

Yin and yang, 66

Yoga, 63, 373n69

Yugavatara (avatar of the ages), 88

Zarathusthra, 142

Zimmerman, Ulrich, 371n28

GPSR Authorized Representative: Easy Access System Europe, Mustamäe tee
50, 10621 Tallinn, Estonia, gpsr.requests@easproject.com